Microsoft
Office 4.2
Survival Guide
for Macintosh

Microsoft Office 4.2 Survival Guide for Macintosh

by
Charles Seiter

Tonya Engst

Barrie Sosinksy

Hayden
Books

Microsoft Office 4.2 Survival Guide for Macintosh

©1995 Hayden Books, a division of Macmillan Computer Publishing

Library of Congress Catalog Number: 94-73415
ISBN: 1-56830-173-1

97   96   95   4   3   2   1

Interpretation of the printing code: the rightmost double-digit number is the year of the book's printing; the rightmost single-digit number is the number of the book's printing. For example, a printing code of 95-1 shows that the first printing of the book occurred in 1995.

To Our Readers

Dear Friend,

Thank you on behalf of everyone at Hayden Books for choosing *Microsoft Office 4.2 Survival Guide for Macintosh* to enable you to learn about the exciting new features of the Office suite on the Macintosh. Each Office application has received its own treatment by an author who is an expert in that field. By the end of this book, you should feel comfortable with writing documents in Word, creating spreadsheets in Excel, and designing presentations in PowerPoint. We hope that you find the tips, suggestions, and examples throughout the book helpful in your everyday Macintosh world.

What you think of this book is important to our ability to serve you better in the future. If you have any comments, no matter how great or small, we'd appreciate your taking the time to send us email or a note by snail mail. Of course, we'd love to hear your book ideas, too.

Sincerely yours,

David Rogelberg
Publisher, Hayden Books and Adobe Press

You can reach Hayden Books at the following:

Hayden Books
201 West 103rd Street
Indianapolis, IN 46290
(800) 428-5331 voice
(800) 448-3804 fax

email addresses:

America Online:	Hayden Bks
AppleLink:	hayden.books
CompuServe:	76350,3014
Internet:	hayden@hayden.com

The Hayden
Books Team

Publisher
David Rogelberg

Managing Editor
Patrick J. Gibbons

Acquisitions Editor
Karen Whitehouse

Development Editors
Barbara L. Potter
Marta J. Partington

Copy/Production Editor
Barbara L. Potter

Technical Reviewer
Michael J. Partington

Publishing Coordinator
Rosemary Lewis

Interior Designer
Fred Bower

Cover Designer
Karen Ruggles

Production
Gary Adair, Angela Calvert, Dan Caparo, Laurie Casey, Kim Cofer, Dave Eason, Jennifer Eberhardt, Rob Falco, David Garratt, Aleata Howard, Shawn MacDonald, Joe Millay, Erika Millen, Beth Rago, Gina Rexrode, Erich J. Richter, Christine Tyner, Karen Walsh, Robert Wolf

Indexer
Chris Cleveland

Composed in
Stone and MCP Digital

About the Authors

Charles Seiter

Charles Seiter, Ph. D, is the author of Hayden Books' *Excel 5 Starter Kit* and 15 other computer books. He has been a contributing editor of *Macworld* for 11 years, and he specializes in scientific and technical software, spreadsheets, databases, and programming languages. When Charles is not working on computer books, he designs biochemical instrumentation for biotechnology firms in the San Francisco Bay area. Charles can usually be reached at chseiter@aol.com and welcomes suggestions or tips about Microsoft Office.

Tonya Joy Engst

Tonya Engst works on the editorial staff of *TidBITS*, a free electronic newsletter about the Macintosh, that is distributed weekly on the world-wide computer networks. Tonya has also written books about using Microsoft Word and maintains a Web site about word processing on the Macintosh.

Tonya grew up in Ithaca, a small town in the New York state Finger Lakes region. She graduated from Cornell University with a major in communications and a minor in the history and philosophy of science and technology. After graduating, she worked in a variety of technical positions for Cornell's Information Technologies department. In 1991, Tonya set her sights westward and took a job with the Macintosh Word support group at Microsoft. Besides answering many questions via phone and electronic mail, Tonya helped maintain Microsoft's internal knowledge base of questions and answers and acted as a mentor to less experienced support engineers. After almost three years, Tonya left Microsoft to pursue writing more seriously. She finished *The Word Book for Macintosh Users* in 1994, and in 1995, she followed up with *The Word 6 Starter Kit*.

Find out more about Tonya via the World-Wide Web at

http://king.tidbits.com/tonya/tonya.html

Barrie Sosinsky

Barrie Sosinsky, a longtime Macintosh devotee, started by buying one of the first Macintosh II computers that Apple produced. That computer still delights his two year old and just keeps right on ticking.

Barrie is the author or coauthor of 18 computer books that range on such topics as desktop database systems, integrated software, desktop publishing, and system software. He has also written over 70 articles on Macintosh- and PC-related topics. His recent books include *Develop Your First Visual FoxPro Application in 14 Days, The Acrobat Quick Tour, The Warp Book, ClarisWorks Companion,* and *Using FileMaker Pro.* Occasionally during his writing, he gets to sleep.

In 1994, Barrie established Killer Apps, Inc., a consulting and database vertical market software development house in Newton, Massachusetts. His company does workgroup database systems for specialized markets, develops online help systems, and creates electronic publications. Among the products that his company specializes in are Visual FoxPro, FileMaker Pro, Adobe Acrobat, and others. Barrie can be reached at the following online addresses: Internet, `basman@killerapps.com`; CompuServe, `72020,2311`, `AOL`; and AppleLink, `KillerApps`.

Barrie wishes to acknowledge the work of Elisabeth Parker, an associate at Killer Apps, who coauthored the material in the PowerPoint section of this book. This is Elisabeth's first contribution in the area of computer books, but she also coauthored *The Acrobat Quick Tour.* Prior to working at Killer Apps, Elisabeth Parker published *The Fine Print,* an independent monthly magazine that focused on Boston's arts community, and she worked as a computer graphics consultant.

Contents
at a Glance

Table of Contents

XIX

Introduction

Nearly a decade ago, the people who ran Microsoft made a momentous decision about software design, a radical departure from any earlier software design philosophies: the bigger the better. Microsoft Office 4.2 for the Macintosh is a direct product of this Microsoft philosophy—which has produced many good results and a few that aren't so good. This book is called a *Survival Guide* because it's going to tell you how to get all the goodies Microsoft has loaded into its software without enduring the trials and drawbacks of the program. Let me explain.

What Goes into Software?

In the old days, programmers would try to see how many features they could cram into a limited space. For example, the original IBM PC spreadsheet, Lotus 1-2-3, was designed to fit comfortably in 256KB of RAM. The reason for this design choice was that most IBM PC users had only this much memory, and memory was expensive. The idea of asking software users to buy new hardware to accommodate a software product was considered not to be shrewd marketing at all. As a result, the features that finally ended up in 1-2-3 were a compromise—some possible features were left out because the designers couldn't fit them into 256KB.

But memory prices started to fall throughout the 1980s; microprocessor speed started doubling every few years; and disk drives kept getting bigger. Looking at these trends, Microsoft's software design teams concluded that there were two simple principles for designing successful software in this new environment: find out what features people want and give 'em the features.

The idea was to load up the programs with everything the users requested. If this meant that the software was huge and somewhat slow . . . well, faster computers with lots of RAM and bigger hard drives would make these problems go away—eventually.

In retrospect, this plan certainly worked. This method of software design pretty much conquered the universe and left most of Microsoft's competitors gasping in its wake, struggling to keep in the swim. The programs in Microsoft Office have a huge market share in both the Macintosh and Windows market (Excel, alone, has over 90 percent of the spreadsheet business).

A Nice Big Office

No one would dispute that Microsoft has provided all the features that users could ever want in Microsoft Office 4.2. In fact, Microsoft has provided many features that you probably never thought of and even more features that you will probably never use. Each of the three big pieces of Office—Word 6, Excel 5, and PowerPoint 4—is the biggest program of its kind the world has ever seen.

To install the complete version of Microsoft Office on a Power Mac, for example, you need to have 100MB of free space on your hard drive. After installation, the program reduces itself to a mere 76MB, but this size is still pretty formidable, especially if you are trying to use a Duo or PowerBook. That's why this *Survival Guide* will have lots of installation tips that indicate which parts of Office you can throw overboard (to install only when you specifically need them).

Sometimes you win

One of the great strengths of Office is that it makes up its own substantial world, providing a software solution for nearly every problem that you encounter in business (hey, that's why it's called *Office*). Besides this benefit, the individual parts work very nicely together, too. You can make a table in Excel, for example, and link it into a Word document or a PowerPoint slide. And the link is "live" so that when your Excel numbers change, they will automatically change in the corresponding Word and PowerPoint documents. Another great strength is that most commands do exactly what you would expect, whether you're using Word, Excel, PowerPoint, or Microsoft Mail, for that matter.

Sometimes you lose

There is, however, a big problem with big software. In the Macintosh graphical interface, every time you make a mouse-click, a program has to scroll through its list of all possible actions to find out which one you have selected. What this means, roughly, is that when a program doubles in size, it slows down by nearly a factor of 2—unless someone does some clever optimization. It also means that strange bugs and system problems are about twice as likely.

That's why this book not only has lots of speed tips (to help Office get its giant bulk out of its own way), but it also has all sorts of advice on keeping Office from unpleasant interactions—crashes, in fact—under Macintosh System 7.5. These crashes have bothered lots of pioneer users of Office 4.2. Microsoft's official policy, however, is to deny that crashes can be happening. Well, they happen a lot, and this book provides the information that you need to prevent this problem in the first place. At Hayden Books, we take survival seriously.

Getting Going in the First Place

If you are the gloomy type who likes to peruse the online help bulletin boards from software vendors, you are likely to find—from America Online to CompuServe and everywhere in between—a section called "Office Problems."

The two most important categories of problems are crashes during installation (where you never actually get the software running) and mystery crashes during operation (where you are tearing your hair out on a regular basis).

In this book, installation advice is found in the Appendix so that the installation section could be as long as necessary without disrupting the page numbering of the rest of the book. Believe me, the Appendix continued to grow rapidly during the whole preparation time of this book. As more users got more experience with Office, funny new crash-inducing wrinkles kept appearing.

So you may want to read this book from back to front because the Appendix may be the first place you need to look for installation tips. Even if you think you have installed Office correctly, if you are experiencing mystery crashes or freezes, you may want to re-install by following the hard-won advice in this book.

There are two chapters dealing with System 7.5, and, once again, if you need troubleshooting help, you may want to look at the second of these as your introduction to this book. If you have been using Microsoft software for some time, you can probably get a Word document written and printed by yourself. But it's unlikely that anything in the past has prepared you for some of the amazing glitches that can affect Word 6 under System 7.5. It just shows what can happen when two software giants, in this case Microsoft and Apple, work with near-total lack of cooperation.

"Surviving" Microsoft Office

Surviving Office is sort of like surviving Manhattan. It's big; it's tough to find the best way to get around; it makes tons of demands; and to get the most out of it, you need lots of special information. But after you learn your way around and find out where the good stuff is, it's got the greatest collection of services in the world. Think of this book as your Michelin Guide to the facilities in Microsoft Office.

This *Survival Guide* covers the following features:

◆ The best features of Word

◆ The best features of Excel

◆ The best features of PowerPoint

◆ The best features of Microsoft Mail

- ◆ Using the applications together
- ◆ Exchanging data
- ◆ Modifying your installation for size efficiency
- ◆ Fine-tuning Office for speed
- ◆ Staying out of trouble with Office and System 7.5

If you are using Microsoft Office, you have already made a big investment in money. If you are using it every day, you are also making a huge investment in time. This book will pay for itself the first week you use it, even if you are making minimum wage. Just getting Microsoft Word to load in one minute instead of six minutes every day will make everything delightful, and if you use the tips and tricks in this book, you will save yourself hours of time over the course of a year.

Part I

System 7.5

by **Charles Seiter**

The people who design software, both at Apple and at Microsoft, have decided in recent years that the voice of the people must be heard. System 7.5 and Microsoft Office incorporate not only dozens of user-suggested features but also bits of clean-up shareware and utility programs licensed from third-party developers.

The result of giving the people what they want is that both System 7.5 and Microsoft Office are very large programs, often duplicating each other's features and occasionally, via extension conflicts, getting in each other's way. Part I of the strategic plan for surviving Microsoft Office focuses on the most useful new features of System 7.5 and then on the best techniques for avoiding subtle conflicts that lead to mystery crashes when System 7.5 and Office collide.

Chapter 1

Exploring the New
Features in System 7.5

At any time of day or night, you can drive by Apple's main parking lot in Cupertino, CA, and see hundreds of cars. Each one corresponds to one or two Apple employees toiling away. And what are they doing? Well, a rather large number of them are thinking up cool things to throw into the next version of the Macintosh System software. Every time there's a new revision of the system, there's a long list of goodies in it for you. In this chapter, you're going to find out how System 7.5 can make your Mac workday more fun and productive by reading about these points:

- ◆ The new Find File utility
- ◆ Internet access through MacTCP
- ◆ Stickies, the new onscreen notes
- ◆ Extensions Manager
- ◆ Window Shades to reduce desktop clutter
- ◆ File and application locking
- ◆ PC Exchange and Macintosh Easy Open
- ◆ Memory Manager

Find File

The computer you are using these days is very likely to have at least 200MB of hard drive space. Think about what this means for a minute. The text in a 300-page computer book takes up a bit less than a megabyte. So you could have the equivalent of 200 books on your hard drive, broken up into chapters and so forth. That's a lot of information, and that's a lot of files to wade through to find the one you want at any given time.

Knowing about this potential file-finding nightmare, Apple has provided a slick new utility for finding information on your hard drive. If you did an Easy Install of System 7.5 (see the Appendix)—disregarding all the well-meaning advice you'll find in this book—you will see an item called Find File under the Apple menu. If you took our advice, however, and performed a minimum installation (also in the Appendix), you will see Find File under the Apple menu because you put it there yourself.

But at least it's there, one way or another. After you select Find File from the Apple Menu, you see the dialog box shown in Figure 1.1.

Figure 1.1   The basic Find File dialog box—just the beginning.

You might be excused for interjecting at this point, "So what?" After all, this dialog box looks more or less like the Find dialog box from System 6. The fun begins, however, when you click the More Choices button. You can then add some specific items to the File characteristics so that Finder can get the information you need—and rapidly, too.

At each click on More Choices, another bit of search criterion appears (see Figure 1.2). In practice, some of this information is likely to be more useful than others for finding files. If, for example, you can remember a range of possible dates for the file that you want to find, that information cuts down enormously on the number of files that the Find utility has to check to get to the one you want. If you have two years' worth of files on your drive, and you can narrow down your search to one week by using the options in the Date Created scrolling list, then your Mac has to search through only one percent of the files on your hard drive. Trust me, narrowing down the search is impressively faster than looking through the whole drive.

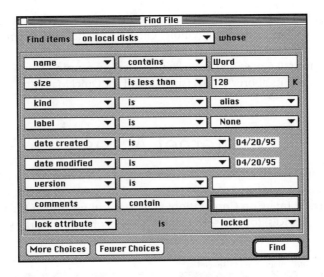

Figure 1.2   Plenty of Find File choices.

When the file search is over, the amazing all-new Find File utility gives you all the files at once in a convenient Items Found dialog box (see Figure 1.3). What makes this dialog box special is that the items are as live as they are on the desktop. If your search has found an application, you just double-click it to open it. The same is true for files—just double-click the file as you would with a desktop file.

Besides this active list of files, the dialog box contains the location of the selected file in the lower half of the split dialog box. Simply select a file to see the file's location.

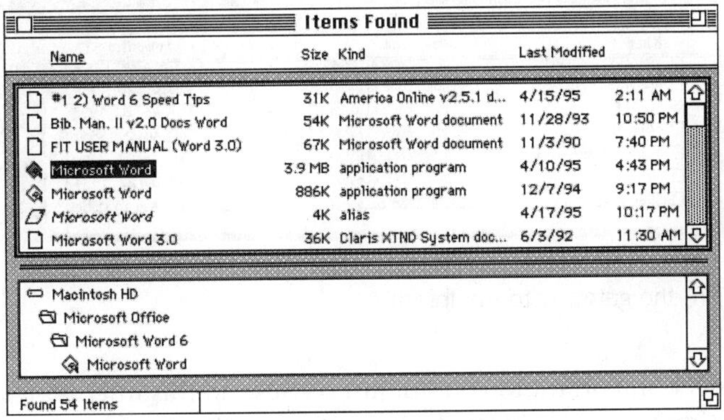

Figure 1.3   The Items Found dialog box—it lists both files and locations.

One use for Find File in connection with Microsoft Office is the removal of old files from applications that you are not using anymore. Often an application, when installed, diligently stuffs information all over the place in the System folder. You can track down leftover parts of applications in the Preferences and Extensions folders by running Find File and by using the application name and its abbreviations (such as QM for QuickMail) and approximate dates as your search criteria.

Internet Access

In System 7.5, Apple has finally added a control panel called MacTCP (see Figure 1.4), which is necessary to run most Internet-access software. Used in connection with the program InterSLIP and provided free by InterCon Corporation, your Mac can use any of the software for ftp (file transfer protocol) services, for access to Gopher servers, or to the World-Wide Web.

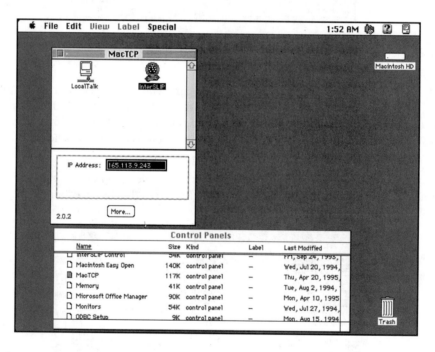

Figure 1.4   MacTCP, the gateway to the Internet.

This control panel is important to you not just because all this Internet-related stuff is the latest computing craze but also because Microsoft and other large companies are increasingly moving to Internet-based customer support as a replacement for phone-based customer support. For example, most of the files of tips, updates, and installation hints that Microsoft provides can be found at the following ftp site:

```
ftp.microsoft.com
```

And a more visual organization of information can also be found at the following World-Wide Web site:

```
http://www.microsoft.com/
```

You should know a few things about access to this information bonanza. First, setting up the access is difficult. The setup of MacTCP alone is too complicated for this book (see Figure 1.5). Second, besides the setup of MacTCP, you need to puzzle out the details of InterSLIP setup (see Figure 1.6) or MacPPP setup, another Internet communications protocol application. Fortunately, you can consult the *Internet Starter Kit,* another best-selling book published by Hayden Books, by Adam Engst (Tonya Engst did the Word part of this book) for advice on getting hooked up through MacTCP. Although System 7.5's Internet connection through MacTCP is too complex to cover in detail here, at least you don't have to turn to strangers for advice!

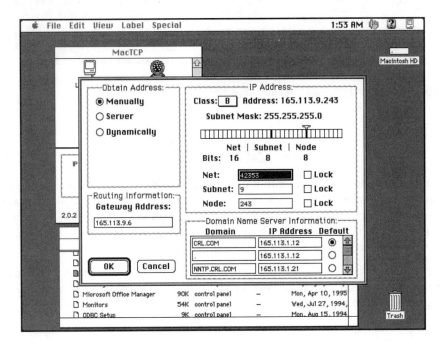

Figure 1.5 MacTCP setup, not a simple business.

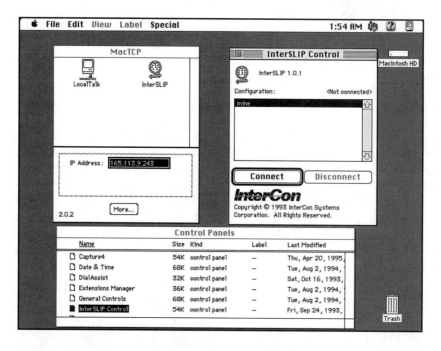

Figure 1.6   MacTCP and InterSLIP, working together.

Stickies!

If you did an Easy Install or a minimum installation, you will find Stickies as an option under the Apple menu. Because this is the second time I have mentioned installation, I want to make this point here: you should consider doing the installation in the way this Office book recommends in the Appendix. Believe me, I've gone through the pain of finding out which parts of the Apple system are 100 percent compatible with Microsoft Office!

Anyway, a Sticky is just a little floating note that appears on the desktop. It's the exact electronic equivalent of the ubiquitous Post-it note. A typical use of a Sticky is as a reminder of meetings or as a short to-do list.

To activate Stickies, choose the Stickies command from the Apple menu. You then see a screen like the one in Figure 1.7—here you can see one new note on the desktop. You can do all sorts of things with Stickies, just as if they were files. Stickies even have their own menus. Under the File menu, you can take text out of a Sticky and save it to another file, or you can import a note that you wrote (probably in a word processor). Were you so inclined, you could actually use Stickies as a primitive text database—one Sticky for phone numbers, another for business memos, and so forth—although you will probably prefer big-time applications, such as Microsoft Word and Excel, for more serious chores. At any rate, Apple never leaves things in their simplest form, so it has also endowed Stickies with the font and style capabilities of a small word processor. Simply choose the Text Style command from the Note menu (or press ⌘-T) to get the dialog box that you see in Figure 1.8. From here, you can format your Stickies to your heart's content.

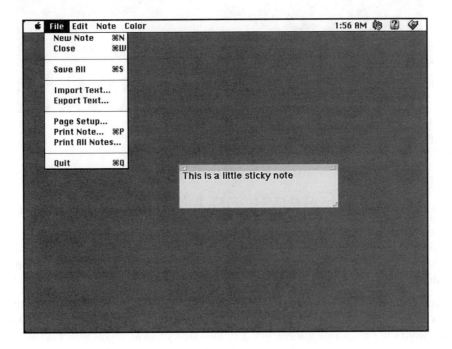

Figure 1.7 Stickies—little desktop notes to yourself.

13

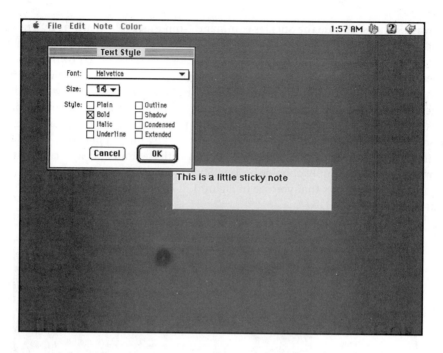

Figure 1.8 Stickies with style.

Extensions Manager

The reason that the control panel called Extensions Manager is included with System 7.5 is that 7.5 itself includes an absolute explosion of extensions. The Easy Install option leaves you with more than 40 extensions, and most of the software that you use will add in more extensions.

For starters, you don't need most of these extensions. For example, Apple has provided you with extensions for managing nearly every printer that Apple has ever manufactured. You can remove from the Extensions folder the extensions that you know you won't be using, or you can use Extensions Manager to turn them off. Simply select Extensions Manager from the Apple menu and click off the extensions that you don't need in day-to-day practice (see Figure 1.9). Click a checked item to turn it off—click an unchecked item to turn it on.

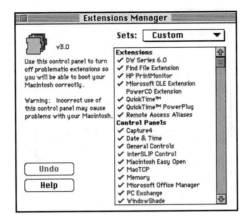

Figure 1.9   Extensions Manager in action.

Extensions Manager turns out to be your easy way out of a dilemma. Microsoft Office simply does not agree with certain third-party (not Apple, not Microsoft) extensions (more on this issue in Chapter 2). When you find out which extensions cause problems, you can then define a custom extensions set by turning off the offending extensions, pulling down the Sets menu (see Figure 1.10), and giving your set a name with the Save Set command (see Figure 1.11).

Similarly, you can select a set of extensions and control panels for use with only certain printers or certain communications software and then give the items in the set their own names in Extensions Manager. From the time it takes your Mac to start up, you will want a minimal working set of extensions most of the time because it takes time to load the extensions on startup.

Figure 1.10   Picking out a custom extensions set.

Figure 1.11 Naming a special set for Office use.

Window Shades

The Window Shade control panel solves a problem that has been bothering Mac users for ten years: what do you do when the desktop becomes so cluttered with open windows that you can't find *anything*? Window Shade lets you hide everything except the title of a window, thus drastically reducing the amount of desktop real estate devoted to any single window.

The Window Shade controls (see Figure 1.12) are simplicity itself. Unless you are fascinated by needless complication (or insist on concocting a keystroke combination), you can just select the option for double-clicking on the title bar of the window. This option means that when you double-click the right-hand side of the title bar, the window rolls up, leaving only the title part of the window onscreen.

When you use Window Shade judiciously, you can reduce an unreadable mess like the one in Figure 1.13 to the harmony, bliss, and clarity of the screen in Figure 1.14. All you have to do is perform the Window Shade double-click maneuver on the windows on the desktop until they are rolled into title bars. In using Office, you may want to keep special sets of Word files, for example, in a rolled-up Word Files window for ready reference. I've checked out Window Shade under lots of circumstances and haven't hit any conflicts with Office, so use this feature to your heart's content.

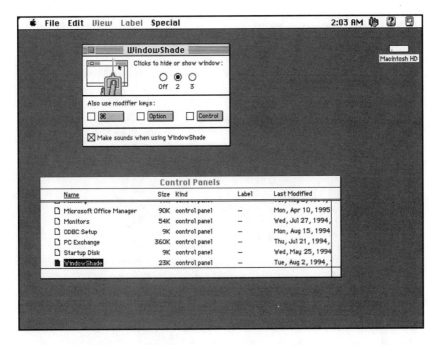

Figure 1.12   Window Shade—the ultimate desktop clean-up device.

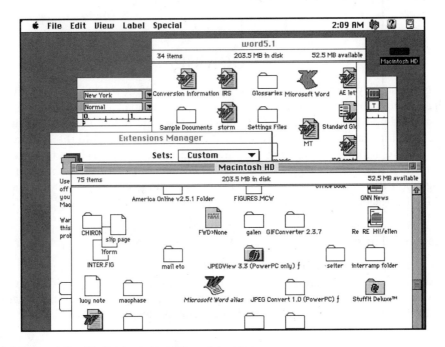

Figure 1.13   Look familiar? A typically cluttered desktop.

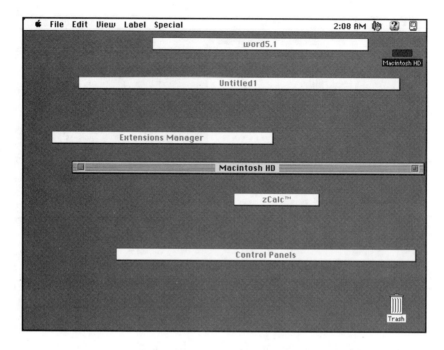

Figure 1.14   A cleaner desktop with Window Shade.

Locking

There is one slightly negative aspect of the new Window-Shade oriented desktop: it makes it much easier to throw things into the Trash by accident. An inadvertent single click in the title bar of a rolled-up window can select the whole window. And then if you are dragging something else to the Trash, you could find yourself dragging the window to the Trash along with it. You need some protection against this sort of event, and Apple has built the protection into the Get Info dialog box (see Figure 1.15) under the Finder File menu. The option of physically locking whole floppy disks has always been available, but applications and folders are now individually lockable by clicking the Locked check box in this dialog box.

Figure 1.15 shows Microsoft Word's Get Info dialog box. To lock another application, open the application and press ⌘-I on your keyboard.

Now if you drag a locked application to the Trash and are about to empty the Trash, you not only get the warning in Figure 1.16, but the System actually refuses to get rid of the application. When you consider the time invested in installing the Office suite, it makes sense to lock Word, Excel, and PowerPoint as convenient insurance against accidental disaster.

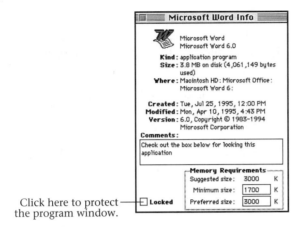

Figure 1.15   The Locking option in a Get Info dialog box.

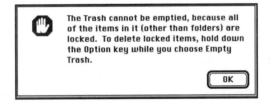

Figure 1.16   Oops! System 7.5 doesn't let you trash a locked application.

PC Exchange

If you are using Microsoft Office at work, there's an excellent chance that you are working with people who are generating files under the Windows version of Office. And happy people they are, too, because Office is fast, compact, and pretty much trouble free on a Windows-based PC. (As a curiosity, most of the problems in Office for the Macintosh arise from Microsoft's insistence on using Windows programs that have been relaundered through a translator to produce the Mac Office programs rather than writing them as real Mac applications using Mac development tools.) At some point, you will probably have to use Word or Excel files from the PC side of the fence.

There are two convenient features in System 7.5 to help you with converting files. The first is a control panel called PC Exchange (see Figure 1.17), which was first introduced in System 7 and lets Macintosh computers read PC disks in the standard SuperDrive. By clicking the Add button in the PC Exchange dialog box, you can pick file types from the DOS/Windows world and the applications that can open them in the Mac world. To help you in navigating Office, you should know that .MCW at the end of a filename identifies it as a Microsoft Word file from Windows, and .XLS similarly indicates an Excel file. By looking at the extensions, you then can pick Word or Excel as the Mac application that translates and opens these files.

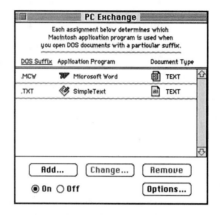

Figure 1.17   PC Exchange opens DOS disks and reads their files.

Macintosh Easy Open (Figure 1.18) is an extension in System 7.5 that essentially automates PC Exchange. When Easy Open is installed, a control panel for setup shows the basic Easy Open fact: after you activate Automatic document translation, all your problems are solved. Now you can double-click a file on a PC disk in your Mac or a PC file on a network server, and the System scurries around in the background finding the appropriate translator, ultimately opening the file in the correct application. If you are interested in the mechanics of these operations, Don Crabb's *Guide to Macintosh System 7.5*, also by Hayden Books, is the best available reference.

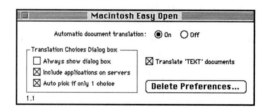

Figure 1.18   Macintosh Easy Open solves many translation problems.

Memory Manager

There are many serious issues involving memory management, System 7.5, and Microsoft Office. Figure 1.19 shows the Memory control panel, part of every System installation, and a number of its options.

One choice you should make while running Office is to set Cache Size in the Disk Cache option to 96K. It would be nice to have a cogent explanation for this setting, but the fact is that the 96K setting is straight from the recommendations of Microsoft's customer support and, in fact, does seem to speed things up a bit.

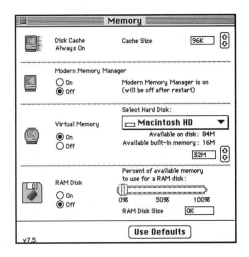

Figure 1.19 Memory—some critical choices.

Another bit of advice from Microsoft support technicians is to set the Modern Memory Manager to Off. When the setting is On, it means that the System expects to be dealing with applications that have been designed for a proper Macintosh 32-bit computing environment. Apparently on a few key points, this isn't quite what happens with software prepared by Microsoft's Windows-to-Mac conversion machinery.

The last memory issue concerns virtual memory, which is the use of hard drive space to substitute for RAM. If you are obliged, for example, to run Excel on a Power Mac with a mere 16MB of RAM, you need to turn on the Virtual Memory option because 16MB isn't enough, and you will get strange error messages if you try to start Excel. The reason this setting requires some attention is that you are unlikely to succeed in installing Microsoft Office with the Virtual Memory option on, so you have to switch it off during installation. If you didn't know that you should turn it on again to run the actual applications, you may easily think that the installation failed.

This chapter has covered some special System 7.5 goodies that you will need to make Office perform properly. In the next section, you will find out how to keep these large and complex software objects—System 7.5 and Microsoft Office—from getting in each other's way. This is not a trivial issue and is one of the reasons that *survival* is part of this book's title.

Chapter 2

Making Office and

System 7.5 Work Together

When you use Microsoft Office and System 7.5 together, you may get the impression that the designers of these two pieces of software were completely unaware of each other's efforts. As it happens, this is pretty much the case. Therefore, System 7.5 abounds in features that can make Office crash, and Office can easily cause the System to hang in the course of the day. In this chapter, you're going to find a way to get through a whole week at the office without a crash by reading about these points:

- ◆ Understanding what causes crashes in the first place
- ◆ Handling System extensions
- ◆ Identifying the crash-prone utilities
- ◆ Making a safe System 7.5 installation
- ◆ Making a safe Office installation
- ◆ Using a two-hard-drive setup
- ◆ Managing Office in 7.5 with virtual memory

Why Crashes Occur

The crude explanation for the crashes is that System 7.5 and Office duplicate many of each other's features, and they make assumptions about what bits of memory may be available for these features. The Open Doc architecture, for example, and Publish and Subscribe are Apple's ways to make "live" links between documents. In Microsoft-land, OLE2 does the same thing. Because these programs deal with communication between applications, they sometimes compete for the same memory. And when applications compete, *you're* the one who loses. If two applications want the same space in RAM, it's likely that your Mac will simply crash.

Let's assume that you have installed Office—apparently successfully—but that every now and then the whole thing freezes your Mac. This situation is especially true on Power Macintoshes. If you are lucky, you can get out of the freeze by using the ⌘-Shift-Esc keystroke combination and get a chance to do a proper restart. In fact, it's a good idea to keep ⌘-Shift-Esc in mind at all times, not just for Office applications, because it gives you a chance at a graceful exit from *any* crashed application.

If you're not lucky, the only way out is to turn off your Mac, which produces the scolding dialog box that tells you that you should always proceed through the Shut Down command under the Special menu in the Finder. You already know the proper procedure, and it's pretty aggravating to see that message several times a day.

Actually, it's beyond aggravating—it's lethal. Every time you do a plain turn-it-off instead of a restart, you risk introducing little glitches into the System software. If you have to do several turn-it-offs a day (say, four times or so), it's a near certainty that you will see at least a question mark icon on startup or even the dreaded Sad Mac, which calls for major repair action. If your Mac can't do a proper closing of files and applications, those files and applications can accumulate little bits of damage that eventually make big problems on the hard drive's directory. And when the directory has problems, sometimes your Mac simply pretends that your hard drive is not there at all. Uh-oh.

Preventing crashes is a big reason why you want to get a stable, noncrashing System 7.5/Office installation. Besides the inconvenience of a crash, if it happens enough, you may have to send your Mac out for service. Maybe you have good local service, but prices range up to $80 an hour with a one-hour minimum in most big cities.

Extension conflicts

If you have ever called Microsoft Customer Support with a complaint about System crashes, the first thing the support technician probably told you is that you have an extension conflict—and probably a System 7.5 extension conflict, at that.

That may be true, but it's not very helpful. *Extensions,* you may recall, are the little "system helpers" that add functions beyond the System core function set. Because many of them are optional (extensions for different printers or extensions for communications software), they haven't been built into the basic core set because you may not need them. One type of familiar extension is the screen saver, and another less familiar but very important type is the extension (such as Microsoft Office Manager) that controls communications between applications.

There used to be only a handful of these extensions, but over the years, the extensions have expanded their role in the Mac operating system. In System 7.5, there are dozens of new extensions, and these extensions have required Apple to build in the Extensions Manager, a special System 7.5 control panel that can turn individual extensions on or off.

Now as the System gets loaded with extensions, the probability that they will all play nicely with each other starts to shrink. The probability that one of Apple's 60 or so extensions in the standard installation of System 7.5 will *not* have a conflict with any third-party extension is close to zero. And then the probability that Microsoft extensions won't conflict with anyone else's extensions is very small indeed. When you hear the term *extension conflict,* it doesn't mean a simple error message onscreen, either. It means that your Mac doesn't start up at all or that it starts up and then crashes or that it crashes while you're in the middle of doing some valuable work. A *conflict* is the polite way of saying that the mouse cursor is no longer moving, the Mac no longer responds to your commands, and the only way to get going again is to shut the thing off and try to reboot.

So you have to figure out which extensions are causing a conflict if you are experiencing mystery crashes while running Microsoft Office. In principle, you can use the 7.5 Extensions Manager to turn off extensions one at a time in the hope of debugging the conflict with Office, but this approach has its drawbacks. First, you will probably crash so many times before you figure out which extensions to turn off that your hard drive will lose its mind and need serious repair. Second, you will waste endless hours performing this investigation. These hours could have been spent doing other things for your business (typing a letter, making up a budget, or creating a presentation).

Another approach is to do the opposite. Simply hold down the Shift key while restarting your Mac. This action turns off all extensions after the restart. Then, if you are still interested, you can use Extensions Manager to turn on your extensions one at a time until you find a conflict. The bad news is that you'll find plenty of conflicts. Many of your favorite extensions are going to run afoul of Office. So hang in there and read through this entire chapter: I'll show you how to duck the whole ugly issue.

Special conflicts

At this point, the next piece of advice may come too late for you because it concerns a conflict so drastic that you probably couldn't get Office installed if you haven't sidestepped it some-how. Most screen savers not only cause the Office Setup program to bomb during installation, but they also cause various Office applications to crash (a lesson the authors learned from bitter experience in preparing this book). Most of these same screen savers worked perfectly well with System 7.1 and the previous versions of Microsoft Office—but under System 7.5 and Office 4.2, you use them at your own risk.

Basically, the problem is that the Setup program for Microsoft Word needs the uninterrupted attention of your Mac, and it simply freezes on most screen savers at the point when the screen saver tries to take over the screen. Because the setup installation disks take at least 15 minutes for a minimal installation, your standard screen saver setting will likely cause an interruption in the installation sequence that will be unrecoverable.

It's Okay to Trash Your Screen Saver

Here is some good news for you, however. You may be using a screen saver under the mistaken impression that it's an absolute necessity to have one to avoid screen burn-in. This was true in the old days of monochrome Macs, but today, it is almost impossible to burn the Apple menu into a color monitor because there's enough wobble in the convergence of the red, blue, and green guns in a color monitor to make burn-in a rarity. So get rid of your screen savers if you want to cut down on the number of crashes that you experience with Office.

Similarly, some communications programs check in from time to time to see whether you have any mail. Some mail programs are death itself to Office Setup and viral pneumonia to Office applications. (I have no idea what you have to do to get CE Software's QuickMail to work with Office, for example, because I gave up trying after three weeks of chatting with customer support at CE Software and Microsoft.) The problem apparently is that QuickMail checks the clock every now and then to see if it's time to look for new mail, and when it checks the clock, it causes a conflict (it's checking the System clock that makes for screen saver problems).

The online customer support boards of major vendors are full of reports of conflicts between different email systems and Microsoft Office. I wish that there was an obvious trick or work-around to make third-party communications work, but for now, you can read the chapter on Microsoft Mail and call your communications software vendor and ask about Office compatibility.

Fixing Everything: Drastic Measures

If you have persistent Office crash problems, the least time-consuming way to get things up and running is to bite the bullet and go for a System 7.5 re-install. Find your Macintosh System disks, insert Install Disk 1 in the floppy drive, and get ready for a short but merry ride (see Figure 2.1). Just keep clicking Continue until you get the screen in which you make the System choices.

Figure 2.1   A new System installation is your best bet for Office happiness.

When you originally installed System 7.5 for the first time (assuming that you didn't buy a new computer with the System already installed), you probably picked Easy Install (see Figure 2.2) because it was the first choice presented to you when you clicked the Continue button in the Install screens. If you are going to use well-behaved but limited software, such as Claris Works, Easy Install is the best choice. But this installation option makes for a big, fat, rich System with lots of possibilities for conflict with Office. It installs loads of extensions with potential conflicts with Office's own extensions, and a System with lots of extensions also loads much slower on startup than a leaner System. Therefore, especially when you are working with a giant package like Office, a smaller System installation makes more sense.

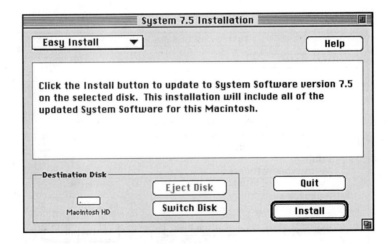

Figure 2.2   Don't choose Easy Install if you plan on using Office.

You can see some of this fatness and richness by peeking into the Custom Install option (see
Figure 2.3), which appears under Easy Install in the scrolling list. You'll be back at this choice
later because you need to add some components after you do the Minimal installation (see
Figure 2.4), which seems to work best with Office. Instead of using Easy Install, which puts
virtually everything into your System (including possible Office conflicts), you can do a
Minimal installation first and then install a few extras later by using Custom installation.
Minimal installation gives you a smaller System and a better understanding of just what got
loaded.

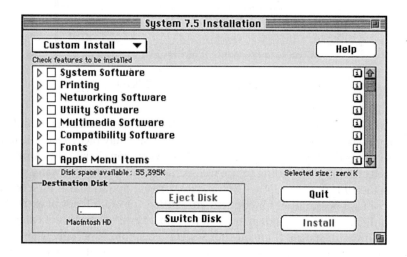

Figure 2.3   Custom installation, for adding System components later.

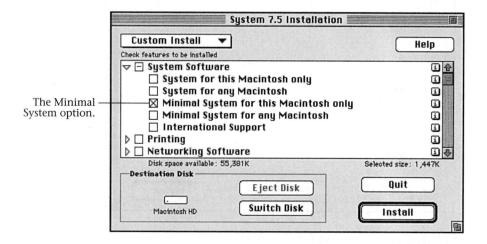

Figure 2.4   Minimal installation: the place to start for Office.

The problem with a standard System installation is that it often overwrites a few components, but it's usually smart enough to check which components are already installed, and in most cases, it doesn't touch them. The standard installation means that you can be writing a few new components into your System while leaving possible conflicts lurking on your hard drive. You need something better than this kind of installation for smooth sailing with Office.

Thus when you are looking at the dialog box in Figure 2.4, you want to use the ⌘-Shift-K keystroke combination. Of course, this keystroke combination is mentioned nowhere in the standard Apple documentation, but it's the key to making the new installation solve your old problems. Use the combination when you see Minimal Install as an option.

This keystroke combination forces what is known as a "clean install." A clean install puts your entire old System into a folder named Previous System, which means that the new System has only new components and no potentially damaging "leftovers." When you press the keystroke combination, you see the choices in Figure 2.5. Click the button for Install New System Folder and then click the OK button.

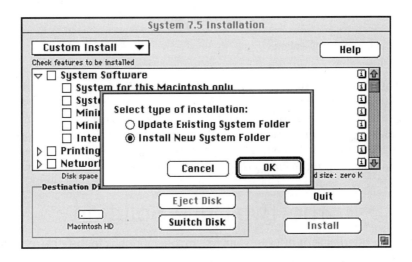

Figure 2.5   Choose the Install New System Folder option.

After you click OK, you are returned to the Installation dialog box, but this time there's a difference: the Install button has been changed to one that says Clean Install (see Figure 2.6). This change in the dialog box means that you're on the right track. Click the Clean Install button and then shuffle disks as required into the floppy drive.

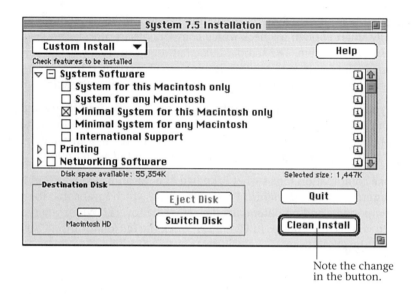

Note the change
in the button.

Figure 2.6   The Clean Install option.

This installation is indeed minimal, but never fear. All your old extensions and control panels have been stashed in the Previous System folder, and you can try adding back the most essential items later. You may find, actually, that you like working with the Minimal System because it makes performance truly snappy. You can add back the standard Apple control panels and Apple menu items and so forth either by dragging them into the new System folder or by fetching them from the Previous System folder created by the Clean Install.

The Two-Drive Solution

If you have an external SCSI drive in your system, one option is to install Microsoft Office and Minimal System 7.5 on one drive and a full-blown System 7.5 with all your gooey, Office-conflicting extensions on the other. You can use the control panel called Startup Disk to pick which System to use. When you are going to have a session with Office, you pick the Office drive as the startup drive, and if you are using non-Office software, you pick the other drive as the startup drive. This technique is actually easier than it sounds and was used as the solution to get parts of this book written!

To use the two-drive solution, do the following:

1. Perform the Clean Install of the Minimal System on your internal drive, preferably with the external drive either detached or turned off.

2. Start your Mac with the external SCSI drive attached and turned on. You should see both your internal and external drives represented on the desktop.

3. Start with Install Disk 1 and click Continue until you get to the Easy Install option, but perform the Easy Install on the *external* drive.

4. Drag the Startup Disk control panel from the Control Panels folder of the System folder onto your internal disk.

Now every time you turn on your Mac, you have the option, before shutting down, of selecting the startup drive with the Startup Disk control panel. If you will be working in Office in your next session, select the internal drive as the startup choice. If you want to use all your old Mac software with loads of extensions and everything else (screen savers and so forth), go to the Startup control and pick the external drive as the Startup Disk for the next session. Look at it this way: at this point, a pretty good hard drive is actually cheap compared to Office itself, and this is one of the best general problem-solving work-arounds available.

Cleaning Up the Office

The version of System 7.5 that you have installed by the procedure in the preceding section is pretty much guaranteed not to be a source of conflicts. To save you even more time, you should also consider performing a minimum installation of Office itself and then adding elements later (see the Appendix) for the following reasons:

◆ The Office suite takes 29 floppies.

◆ If you try for a full installation at one sitting, and it crashes several times on disk 21 or 23, you'll find yourself downright grumpy by the end of the day.

◆ If you try a minimum installation, your chances of success are greatly improved, and you can go back to the installation set later and add features a few at a time.

Get out Install Disk 1 for Office (see Figure 2.7), and while you're at it, please *read* the Readme Before Installation file (it has some tips for the disk set that you have, which may contain newer versions of Word or other applications) and slavishly do anything it tells you—the advice changes a bit every few months. Just by clicking the Continue buttons, you get to the screen where you can select the Minimum installation (see Figure 2.8), which is just what you want to do.

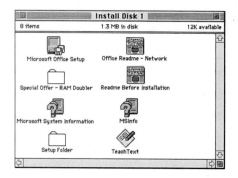

Figure 2.7 Disk 1 out of 29 in the Office setup.

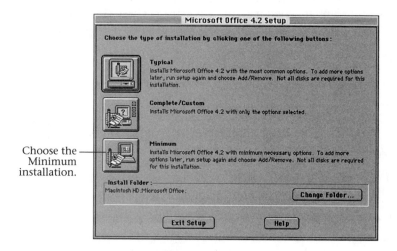

Choose the
Minimum
installation.

Figure 2.8 Minimum, the right place to start an installation.

One argument in favor of the Minimum installation is based on size alone. The full installation is an amazing chunk of code. For example, Microsoft Word is 22MB alone—if someone had written about a word processing program in a computer magazine a few years ago, the article would have been taken as an April Fool's joke (see Figure 2.9, taken from the Custom Installation dialog box). Nonetheless, here it is: Word 6, Excel 5, and PowerPoint 4 are even bigger. But the minimum installation for the whole three-item Office suite altogether takes only 20MB or so, even on a Power Mac.

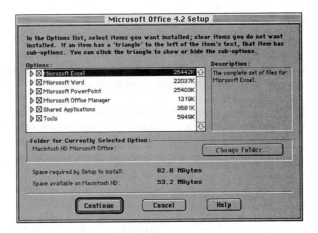

Figure 2.9 Bigger installations make for more potential conflicts.

If you've had lots of problems, the procedure is to track down the elements of your previous Office installation and delete them. You need to get rid of the folder called Microsoft Office and the folder called Microsoft. After these folders are gone, you would normally have to look in the System folder under Extensions, Control Panels, and Preferences, but because you have installed a Minimal System 7.5, all that other stuff has been swept away into the Previous System folder, to be deleted later at your leisure.

Anyway, this Minimum installation—it would be nice if software vendors could pick one, *Minimal* or *Minimum*, and stick with it as a convention—of Office is guaranteed to run with no conflicts under Minimal System 7.5. You have to install Chooser and your printer driver from the Previous System folder to get printed output from the Office applications. And you have to add, selectively, the components to get your Mac running again on a network. But at least you will know, following this procedure, which software element is causing trouble if you start crashing again. It will, by definition, be the *last* element you added (you want to add the elements one at a time so that you can keep track of them).

A Word About Virtual Memory

There's a funny bit of business about virtual memory and Office. Please recall that virtual memory enables space on your disk drive to substitute for actual RAM, and that it has been overhauled in System 7.5 to deal with Power Macs. Virtual memory is particularly critical on Power Macs because Power Mac applications tend to be 40–80 percent bigger than their 680x0 counterparts.

The funny business is that Microsoft Office requires virtual memory to be turned off (in most cases) to install properly. Then Office requires virtual memory to be turned on (see Figure 2.10) if you want to run several applications at once and you don't have mountains of RAM. Oddly, one of the ways you find out that you need to turn on virtual memory is that Excel 5 gives you an error message, such as `Can't Find MicrosoftDialogLib`.

Excel can find it all right, but it doesn't have enough RAM to load it. If your installation was successful and you get one of these error messages, you need to allocate more memory by following these steps:

1. Perform the Minimal installation of System 7.5.

2. Start the installation again, select Custom, select Control Panels, and check the box for Memory.

3. You can also drag the Memory Control Panel to the System folder from the Previous System folder that you created with a Clean Install.

4. Restart your Mac. If you had trouble installing Office, go to the Memory control panel and click the Off button for Virtual Memory. Reinstall Office.

5. Now go back to the Memory control panel and turn on virtual memory so that you can actually run Office.

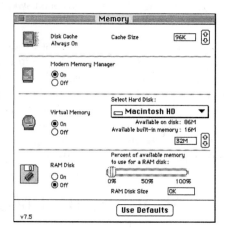

Figure 2.10   Virtual memory: Off to install Office; On to run it.

A little experimentation will convince you that despite Microsoft's claims to the contrary, your System takes a big performance hit when you resort to virtual memory. More's the pity because a combination of demand and yen versus dollar problems has meant that memory prices have not fallen but have risen slightly over the last few years. The 24MB of RAM that would make Office really happy now costs much more than the software itself!

The aim of Part I of this book is to explain some nice and useful features of System 7.5 and then to explain how to make System 7.5 live with Microsoft Office 4.2. To a certain extent, Apple and Microsoft started digging a tunnel at each other from opposite sides of a mountain. They met in the middle, but the tunnels didn't match up perfectly. I strongly recommend that you use the minimum versions of both pieces of software so that you have a clear path through the middle of the tunnel. Don't let the terms *minimum* or *minimal* fool you: System 7.5 and Office make up one of the most feature-filled combinations you have ever seen—even in their minimal forms.

Part II
Word 6

by **Tonya Engst**

Microsoft Word is the biggest word processor ever developed, at least until now. It includes scores of new features—some great, some merely helpful, and some outright puzzling. As is the case with all really large programs, the first version was not completely debugged, and some peculiar wrinkles have survived in version 6.0.1, too (although 6.0.1 is a definite improvement on its immediate predecessor).

To compensate for the grief of the occasional Word crash, Part II presents ways to use Word 6's new features most effectively so that you will come out well ahead of the time spent on your tasks. Everything you ever wanted in a word processor—and many things that you haven't even thought about—can be found in Word 6. You will learn how to set up, edit, format, and print your documents. You will also learn how to add pizzazz to your words with tables, borders, and graphics. And on top of all this, you'll learn how to do these tasks quickly, too. Think of this part of the book as a very long Tip Wizard on paper!

Chapter 3
Getting Started with Word

In many a Microsoft Word book for Macintosh, every third paragraph or so would warn you that failure to follow the instructions in the book would result in spinal injury. Fortunately, Word doesn't *really* cause you spinal injury (unless you use it while driving or skiing), but Word can cause all sorts of Macintosh-related plagues and problems if you don't learn the basics of how to use it.

Before you can build a house, you must know how to use hammers, screwdrivers, paint brushes, and so on. Similarly, you must know about toolbars, dialog boxes, and other important tools before you can create the best documents you can with Word. After you read this chapter, you'll be able to check the following items off your need-to-know checklist:

- ◆ Starting and quitting Word
- ◆ Creating, opening, and closing a document
- ◆ Using Backup Copy and Automatic Save to avoid accidents
- ◆ Locking a document with a password
- ◆ Converting documents to and from Word 6 format
- ◆ Learning about the status bar, toolbars, menus, and rulers
- ◆ Viewing documents in different ways
- ◆ Using keyboard shortcuts
- ◆ Feeling comfortable in dialog boxes
- ◆ Understanding Word's underlying psychological state (how Word thinks about the structure of a document, including character and paragraph formats, sections, templates, and fields)

First Things First: Starting Word

Think of starting Word in the same way that you think of switching on an appliance, such as a food processor. If you don't turn on the food processor, you can't process food; similarly, if you don't turn on Word, you can't process words. Technically speaking, starting a program is known as *launching,* and there are several ways to launch Word. Two common methods require you to double-click an *icon,* a picture representing a file or folder stored on disk (see Figure 3.1). Table 3.1 has the details.

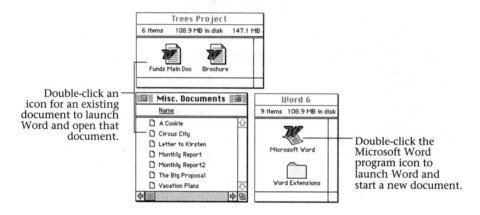

Figure 3.1   Double-click to launch Word.

You can change the way icons appear by clicking on a window that has icons and then choosing a different option from the View menu.

Table 3.1

How to Start Word

Goal	Method	Tip
To launch Word and make a new document.	Double-click the Microsoft Word program icon (note that double-clicking a folder called Microsoft Word opens only the folder; it does not launch Word).	In most cases, the icon is loose in the main hard drive window, or it is in the Microsoft Word folder.

Goal	Method	Tip
To launch Word and open an existing document.	Double-click the icon representing that document.	The document can be anywhere. If you can't find it, try using the Find command in the File menu.

If the Microsoft Word program icon looks dim and fuzzy, you've already launched Word; the icon is reminding you that you can't launch Word twice. When Word finishes launching, you may see a dialog box called Tip of the Day. Click the OK button to exit the dialog box.

After Word finishes launching, a number of items appear onscreen, including a document window. A document window is an open space where you can start a new creation—a financial report, love letter, party invitation, or whatever you like. Figure 3.2 shows a document window.

The document window that comes up when you launch Word takes on settings that most people want to use for most documents. For example, the top margin gets set for one inch so that if you print the document, the body text begins one inch from the top of the page. Word doesn't randomly invent settings; instead, Word finds them in a special file called Normal.

Normal is a *template,* a file that stores text and formats on which other documents are based. As you read this book, you will find that you can change most anything about Normal. The Normal template lives in the Templates folder. If you throw away the Normal template (or put it in a location where Word can't find it), the next time you launch Word, Word makes a new Normal template. The formats in the new template are predetermined by Microsoft.

Launching Word causes important changes to occur in the Applications menu, which is represented by an icon in the upper right-hand corner of the screen. Specifically, note the following:

◆ The Applications menu icon is now Word's icon—a *W.*

◆ In the Applications menu, Microsoft Word has a check mark next to it, indicating that Word is the *active* application.

◆ The Finder is also listed in the menu (the Finder is the application in which you double-clicked an icon in order to launch Word). The Finder does not have a check mark because it is not the active program.

◆ To switch into the Finder temporarily, choose Finder from the Applications menu. You can also switch by clicking in part of the screen that goes with the Finder, such as a Finder window or the *desktop,* the area behind all the open windows on a Macintosh screen (see Figure 3.2). If you switch into the Finder, you can switch back into Word by choosing Microsoft Word from the Applications menu or by clicking in a Word document window (if you can see a document window).

◆ To switch into the Finder and hide all Word windows, press Option while you switch. When you later switch back to Word, the Word windows reappear.

41

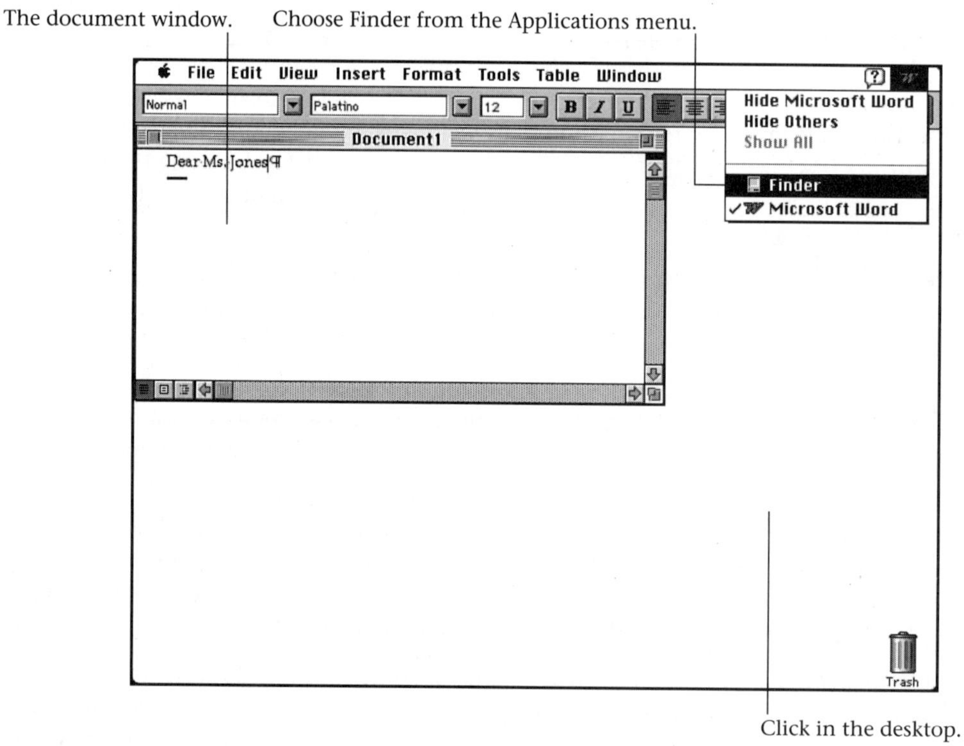

The document window.   Choose Finder from the Applications menu.

Click in the desktop.

Figure 3.2   To switch into the Finder temporarily, click in it or choose it from the Applications menu.

Starting a New Document After Launching Word

After you have launched Word, you can use the new document window that came up, but if you need to start a second file, you certainly may do so. Most likely, you'll want to base the new file on the Normal template. If you are new to computers, note that computer people often use the terms *document* and *file* interchangeably. You'll notice that I use them interchangeably throughout this book.

To create a file based on the Normal template, click the New button (the leftmost button) on the Standard toolbar or press ⌘-N.

Templates

To open a new document that is based on a template other than the Normal template, follow these steps:

1. Go to the File menu and choose New. The New dialog box appears and displays a list of templates and *wizards*, built-in help that simplifies the task of creating a complex document (see Figure 3.3). The wizards all have the word *Wizard* in their names. Templates do not have *Wizard* in their names.

2. From the Template list, select the template on which you want to base the document.

3. In the New area at the right, select Document.

4. Click the OK button.

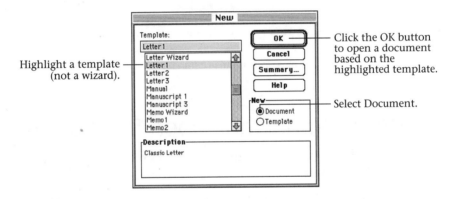

Figure 3.3   Use the New dialog box to open a document based on a template.

Wizards

Technically speaking, wizards are extremely complicated templates. You can make your own wizards, but first you must become a WordBasic expert. (In other words, it takes a wizard to make a wizard.)

Microsoft invented wizards to help people who need to create complicated documents but who don't have the time or knowledge to create them from scratch. For example, the Newsletter Wizard asks questions about how it should set up a newsletter, and it sets up a document based on your answers. To try out a wizard, follow the steps for opening a template (look back a paragraph or two) but open one of the items that has *Wizard* in its name.

For example, if you open the Calendar Wizard, Word offers friendly dialog boxes that ask for input on what you want a calendar to look like (see Figure 3.4). Based on your input, Word creates a calendar.

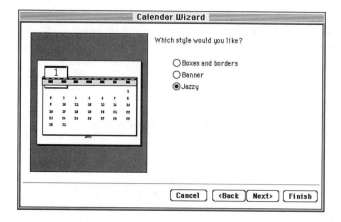

Figure 3.4   The Calendar Wizard helps you create a calendar.

The All-Important Open Dialog Box

The Open dialog box helps you open existing files, but it's not always the easiest way to open them. Before you worry about using the dialog box, consider these alternatives:

◆ Switch into the Finder (read back a few paragraphs to find out how) and then double-click the icon for the file that you want to open. If the Mac beeps or does not permit you to switch back to the Finder, you may have a dialog box open. Click the OK or Cancel button to close the dialog box.

◆ To reopen a file that you opened recently, choose it from the File menu. If nothing shows, turn on Recently Used File List in the General card of the Options dialog box from the Tools menu. After you turn it on, files that you have opened begin to show in the menu.

If you want to try a more sophisticated opening technique, or if you need to open a file that came from a different program, use the Open dialog box. Here are the steps:

1. If the document is on a floppy disk, put the floppy disk in the disk drive. Similarly, if the file is on a network volume (such as a file server), connect to that volume (use the Chooser in the Apple menu).

2. Go to the File menu and choose Open (you can also click the Open button on the Standard toolbar or press ⌘-O). The Open dialog box appears (see Figure 3.5).

3. The name of a disk appears in the upper right-hand corner of the Open dialog box. If the name is not correct for the file that you want to open, click the Desktop button to show available disks in the list at the left. Double-click the name of the correct disk. The disk name should appear at the upper right and in the location pop-up menu.

Caution: If you eject a floppy disk by using the Eject button in the Open dialog box, keep the disk around until you restart or shut down because the Mac may want the disk back before it can continue with what you are doing. To eject a disk properly, drag its icon to the Trash or click the disk's icon and then choose Put Away (⌘-Y) from the File menu.

4. After choosing the correct disk, work your way to the correct location on the disk. The goal is to make the location show in the location pop-up menu. To move down into a folder, double-click the folder name. To move up out of a folder, use the location menu to select a location higher in the hierarchy.

5. When the correct location shows in the pop-up menu, you should see the file that you want to open listed below the location. If you don't see the file, you may have to scroll down in the list. To open the file, double-click the filename.

To move quickly to an item in the list, type the first letter in the item's name. The Macintosh automatically selects the first file or folder whose name starts with that letter.

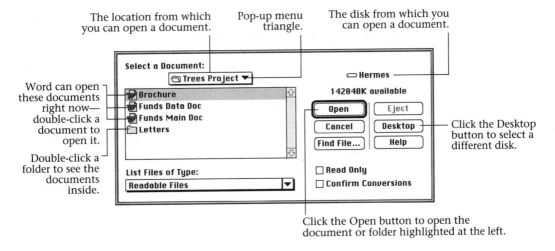

Figure 3.5 Use the Open dialog box to open documents.

Saving a Document

Saving is of paramount importance. Not saving your documents makes as much sense as leaving ice cream in the sun, leaving wine in the freezer, or chalking a mural on the sidewalk during a rain storm.

When you type in Word or change settings (such as margins) and formats (such as italics), all your edits and changes get stored in random-access memory, also known as RAM. RAM is powered by electricity, and if for any reason the steady flow of electricity to your Mac is interrupted, you lose the information in RAM. The flow could stop due to something as mundane as a power outage, as unexpected as a space alien invasion, or as unfortunate as a frozen Mac.

To keep documents around permanently, you must save them to a disk, usually your hard disk. To save a document for the first time or to save a document and change its name or location, follow these steps:

1. With the document window active, go to the File menu and choose Save As. Word responds by displaying the Save dialog box (see Figure 3.6).

2. The Save dialog box works in much the same way as the Open dialog box, so look back a few paragraphs if you need more detailed information. The file saves to the disk showing in the upper right-hand corner, and it saves to the location showing in the location pop-up menu.

3. Type a name for the file in the Save Current Document As box.

4. If you are saving the file as a regular Word document, leave the Save File as Type option set at Word Document. If you want to save the file in a different format so that a different program, such as WordPerfect, can use it, choose the format from the Save File as Type menu.

5. Click the Save button. As Word saves, it shows a progress indicator below the Word window.

To save all open documents, as well as new macros and AutoText entries, drop down the File menu and choose Save All. To save the document in a folder that doesn't exist, click the New button to make a new folder. After you have saved a file once, you don't have to use the Save As command to save it again. You can simply use the Save command. Either press ⌘-S or click the Save button on the Standard toolbar.

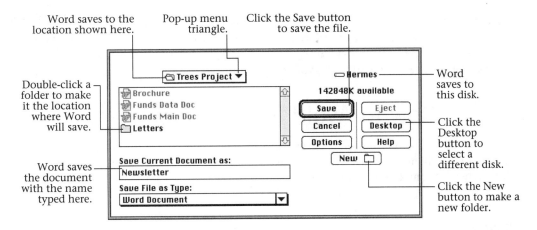

Figure 3.6   In the Save dialog box, select the correct disk and location for your document.

Caution: If your work is important, don't leave it saved on just one disk. At the end of each day or week (depending on the importance of what you do), copy each important document to another disk. That way, if one disk goes bad, you have another copy on another disk. You can also purchase a backup program.

Word's maximum file size is about 32,000 kilobytes. Even so, if you have a file larger than 100 kilobytes, it's large enough. The only exception is if your document is artificially large due to a number of graphic images. At around 100,000 characters of text, you'll be happier if you break the file into a series of smaller documents. Smaller documents are faster to work with and less prone to problems. Use the Copy and Paste commands to break the document up—if you don't know about Copy and Paste, you can find out about them in Chapter 4.

To give you an idea of how file size and character count translate to real life, this chapter (without the graphics) is about 50,000 characters, and the Word file for this chapter takes up a little more than 50 kilobytes of disk space. To find out how many characters are in a document, go to the Tools menu and choose Word Count.

After you save a document once, Word may do a *fast save*, if you save it again. A fast save goes faster because Word doesn't save the entire document again; instead, Word saves just your changes. If Word is set to do fast saves, every tenth time that you save, Word saves the document with a *full save*. The full save completely rewrites the document. Fast saves tend to create complex documents from Word's point of view because Word must keep track of the changes. If you make a lot of changes, you create a lot of information for Word to track. Full saves simplify the document and give Word a fresh start.

How to Avoid Losing Documents

The Backup Copy and Automatic Save (also known as *autosave*) features team together to decrease the chance of disaster if a document becomes damaged or your Mac's power gets cut off. Table 3.2 compares the two options.

Table 3.2

Differences Between Automatic Save and Backup Copy

Feature	How it works	Cautionary tip
Backup Copy	Immediately after saving a document, Word normally deletes the preceding version. With Backup Copy on, the preceding version sticks around.	Backup Copy keeps only the most recently saved copy. It does not keep copies of the document from each time you save and cannot be customized in this respect.
Automatic Save	Saves after a time interval that you specify and stores files in a temporary holding spot on disk (an invisible folder). If you crash, the next time you start Word, the files automatically open (most of the time).	You still must manually save documents because Word deletes automatically saved documents when you quit Word.

To turn on Automatic Save or Backup Copy, open the Options dialog box from the Tools menu and select the Save card. You should see check boxes for Always Create Backup Copy and Automatic Save Every. If you turn on Automatic Save, you must enter how often you want to autosave in the Minutes box (see Figure 3.7). To access the Save card while you are in the Save dialog box, click the Options button.

This check box controls whether Word keeps a backup copy.

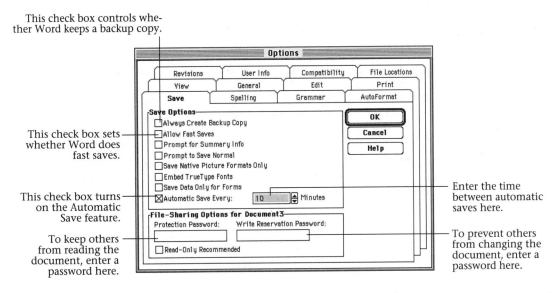

This check box sets
whether Word does
fast saves.

This check box turns
on the Automatic
Save feature.

To keep others
from reading the
document, enter a
password here.

Enter the time
between automatic
saves here.

To prevent others
from changing the
document, enter a
password here.

Figure 3.7   Use the Save card to turn on and off features related to saving.

Preventing People from Changing
a Document

A document that you can open and view, but not change, is known as a *read-only* document. If you can view and change a document, then you have *read-write access* to the document.

Word offers a feature called Write Reservation Password, which sets things up so that a document can be opened and viewed but cannot be changed unless you type the password. If you do lock a document, the next time someone tries to open it, that person will see a dialog box much like the one in Figure 3.8.

Figure 3.8   A Write Reservation Password requires you to know the password in order to change a particular document.

Turning on the Write Reservation Password

To turn on the password for the active document, follow these steps:

1. Go to the Options dialog box from the Tools menu and select the User Info card.

2. At the top of the User Info card in the Name text box, enter the name that you want to appear when Word asks for the password (see Figure 3.8).

3. Click the tab for the Save card.

4. At the bottom of the Save card, type a password in the Write Reservation Password text box. As you type, bullets appear. Each bullet represents a character in the password. The password can be as short as one character, as long as 15 characters, or anywhere in between.

Caution: Passwords are case-sensitive; that is, Word considers the password *SECRET* to be completely different from the password *secret*.

5. Click the OK button. The Confirm Password dialog box appears.

6. Type the same password that you entered in the Save card and click the OK button.

Turning off the Write Reservation Password

To remove the password, you must know the password so that you can open the document with read-write access. After you open the document with read-write access, go into the Save card and delete the bullets from the Write Reservation Password text box.

Keeping People Out of a Document

If you want to prevent people from accessing a document, you can password protect it. Passwords keep snoopy co-workers out of your résumé as you search for a better job, housemates out of your spicy love letters, and ill-meaning no-goods out of your files.

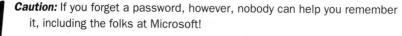

Caution: If you forget a password, however, nobody can help you remember it, including the folks at Microsoft!

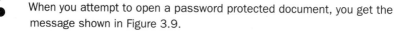

When you attempt to open a password protected document, you get the message shown in Figure 3.9.

Figure 3.9   You must know the password in order to open a password protected document.

Adding a Protection Password works much like adding a Write Reservation Password (see "Turning on the Write Reservation Password," a few sections back).

Closing a Document

Closing a document makes sense if you want to get it out of the way. To close a document, click the close box at the upper left-hand corner of the document window (see Figure 3.10). If a document is not completely saved when you close it, Word asks whether you want to save the changes. Be sure to click the Yes button if you do want to save them.

To close all open documents, press Shift while dropping down the File menu. When the Shift key is down, the Close command changes to Close All. Choose Close All.

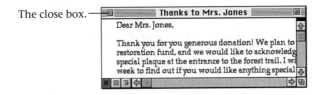

Figure 3.10   Click the close box to close a document's window.

Quitting Word

After you finish using Word, go ahead and *quit*. To quit, go to the File menu and choose Quit (or press ⌘-Q). As Word quits, it closes any open document windows. If a document is not completely saved, Word asks whether you want to save it. It's a good idea to quit Word before you restart or shut down.

When you quit, Word saves changes made to templates and changes made to the Word Settings (6) file. To save those changes at any time before you quit, choose Save All from the File menu.

When you quit, Word releases the RAM that it was using, giving you more space in RAM to launch other programs. Notice that after you quit, the Applications menu no longer lists Microsoft Word.

Converting Your Files

Do you need help opening documents that came from other word processors or from someone who doesn't use Word 6 for the Macintosh? In either case, keep reading for general pointers and a few specific tips. If you are looking for information about importing graphics, see Chapter 8.

Opening a document that is not a Word 6 document

To open a document that is not in Word 6 for the Macintosh format, follow these steps:

1. Launch Word.

2. From the File menu, choose Open. Word displays the Open dialog box.

3. From the List Files of Type pop-up menu, select the converter that most closely matches the format of the file you want to open.

4. Use the controls in the Open dialog box to look at the location where the document is stored.

5. Select the document and click the Open button.

Word opens the file. After the file opens, if you save it with the Word Document file type, the file can convert into a regular Word 6 document.

> **Caution:** To move a file to or from a DOS/Windows disk, you must set up your Macintosh to read the DOS/Windows disk. Any Macintosh new enough to run Word 6 came with software that enables you to read and format such a disk. Newer Macintoshes come with an extension called PC Exchange (put it in your Extensions folder, reboot, and your Mac can automatically read and format DOS/Windows disks); older Macintoshes came with a program called Apple File Exchange (double-click the Apple File Exchange icon to use the program).

Saving a document in a different format

To save a document in a format other than Macintosh Word 6, try these steps:

1. With the file open in the active window, choose Save As from the File menu. The Save As dialog box opens.

2. In the Save As dialog box, type a different name for the document. If the document will end up on a DOS or Windows computer, use 11 characters or fewer to name the document.

3. From the Save File as Type pop-up menu, select the file format closest to the format that you want. (If you are converting between Microsoft Word or MicrosoftWorks—any version, any computer—and there is not a specific converter, try using the Rich Text Format converter. The Rich Text Format converter also works for converting files into WriteNow.)

4. Make sure that you are set up to save the file where you can conveniently find it again and click the Save button.

Word saves the file in the format that you specified.

Using the Rich Text Format (RTF) in emergencies

Rich Text Format—usually called RTF for short and also known as the Interchange Format—has helped more Word documents out of bad situations than virtually any other fix-it procedure known. "RTFing" a corrupted document sometimes removes the corruption, resulting in a normal, healthy document. A corrupted document is one that doesn't work right—perhaps the styles don't apply to certain paragraphs or random text shows up in the headers.

If you think you have a corrupted document, test it by trying to make the same problem appear in another Word document. If you can't and you are sure you understand how to use Word correctly with respect to the problem, you probably have a corrupted document on your hands.

To see if RTF can fix the corruption, try these steps:

1. Go to the File menu and choose Save As.

2. In the Save As dialog box, type a different name for the file. It's important to type a different name!

3. Select a location for the file (be sure to save it where you can find it again).

4. From the Save File as Type menu, choose Rich Text Format.

5. Click the Save button. Word saves a copy of the document in RTF.

6. From the File menu, choose Close. Word closes the potentially corrupted document.

7. From the File menu, choose Open.

8. Use the Open dialog box to locate and open the copy of the file that you saved in RTF. Word converts the copy back into Word format and opens it as a new document. If you want to sound highly technical, you can now tell people that you "RTFed" the document.

If saving the file as an RTF file has fixed the corruption in the document, the problem won't exist in the new document, which you can save and use preferentially.

Sharing files with Macintosh Word 5 users

As a Word 6 user, you live on easy street when it comes to sharing documents with people who use Word 5 (5.0, 5.0a, 5.1, and 5.1a). To open any Word 5 document, you simply double-click its icon. Saving a Word 6 document in Word 5 format is also easy. From the File menu, choose Save As. In the Save Document as Type pop-up menu in the Save As dialog box, choose either Word 5.0 or Word 5.1 for the Macintosh (choose Word 5.0 if you aren't sure). After the document is in Word 5 format, anyone who uses Word 5 can double-click the document's icon and open the document in Word 5.

Caution: If you have Word 5 and Word 6 installed on the same Macintosh, double-clicking a Word 5 file may cause the file to open in Word 6. To open a Word 5 file in Word 5, use the Word 5 Open dialog box.

Choosing the Correct Word 5 Converter

Word 5 users beware: the version of the converter that you use can make a big difference. If you want to share a Word 5 document with someone who has Word 6, you have no problem because Word 6 can open any Word 5 document.

However, if you try to open a Word 6 file, you must first have the correct converter in the correct folder. (To avoid this problem, tell your Word 6 friend to save the file as a Word 5 document!) The correct folder is called Word Commands, and the correct converter is called Word 6 for Macintosh&Windows. For a while, Microsoft shipped a converter called Word 6 for Macintosh/Windows, but this converter had many failings—it usually didn't work at all. (Note that the good converter has an & in its name.)

Word 5 users can acquire the good converter by contacting Microsoft, downloading it from an online service, or copying it from the Microsoft folder that comes with Office. It is legal for a Word 5 user to get a copy of the converter from the Word 6 Microsoft folder. Word 5 users can download the converter from the Internet at the following URL address:

```
ftp://ftp.microsoft.com/Softlib/MSLFILES/MSWRD6.HQX
```

Finding additional converters

If a converter you need is not available via the Save and Open dialog boxes, check to see whether the converter comes with Word but is not currently installed. To find out which converters come with Word, follow these steps:

1. From the Help menu, choose the Search For Help On command. The online help appears.

2. Type **converters** in the upper-left text box.

3. Select converters from the list of options and press Return.

You can also find the converter information on (or near) page 593 in the *User's Guide* that came from Microsoft.

If you don't have a converter installed, you can install it by running Microsoft Office Setup again. (It doesn't take nearly as long to install just a converter!) After you reach the dialog box where you select exactly what gets installed, look for converters under Microsoft Word in the Converters and Filters section or under Tools in the Shared Converters section.

In the past, Microsoft has released new converters at a regular rate, and I expect it will continue to do so. Microsoft also has a history of improving the features in existing converters, so if a converter doesn't work or appears to be missing, it's worth asking around to see if anything has changed.

If Microsoft cannot provide the correct converter, the program that you want to convert to or from may have one. If neither program has a useful converter, try using an intermediate format to perform the conversion. For example, if you can't export into WordPerfect 4.2 format but you can export into WordPerfect 5.1 format, find someone who has 5.1 and use it to save into 4.2 format. As another example, you can use Rich Text Format as an intermediary between Word and WriteNow—Word and WriteNow can both open and save into the Rich Text Format.

To convert Word into HTML format as part of setting up a World-Wide Web site (a popular method for providing information to the Internet), you can use an RTF to HTML converter. Several of them float around online, and at least one of them is posted on the TidBITS FTP site in the Word Book directory. The URL address is

```
ftp://ftp.tidbits.com/pub/tidbits/thewordbook
```

You should also check out World of Words, a Web site that has an area devoted to Microsoft Word. If Microsoft ever comes through with a Macintosh version of its Word Assistant program (which helps you create HTML documents in Word), World of Words will have information about it at the following URL address:

```
http:/king.tidbits.com/tonya/WOW/
```

Finally, consider purchasing a third-party conversion program. Before you buy the program, make sure that it does the conversion that you need. If you are truly desperate and have an obscure format to convert, try a service bureau.

Customizing a Conversion

Because different word processors have different ways of handling similar document elements, it is virtually impossible for programmers to create a converter with a perfect conversion. Most translators do a good job, but if you expect perfection, you will be disappointed.

To find a wealth of excellent and detailed information about what to expect from a particular conversion, how to customize the way a conversion works, and how to do batch conversions, double-click the Word Read Me Help file (it should be in the folder where Word is installed). In the contents of the Help file, click File Conversion and read as much of the help as needed (click the underlined text to see more information).

Toolbar Tips and Trivia

Now that you understand how to convert, open, save, and close documents, you are ready to move on to learning about Word's tools. In each document window, you see a wide array of buttons and controls (see Figure 3.11) unless you have changed the defaults. Few people memorize every button and option offered, so don't panic about knowing every little detail.

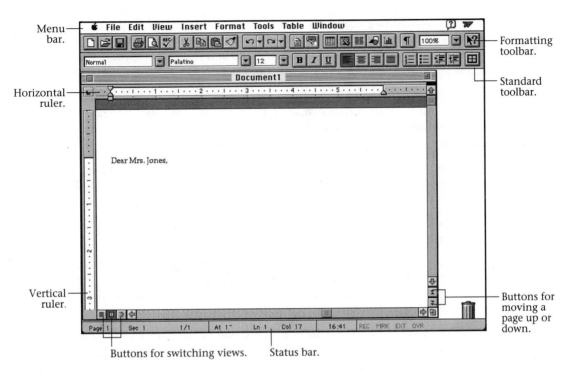

Menu bar.

Formatting toolbar.

Standard toolbar.

Horizontal ruler.

Vertical ruler.

Buttons for moving a page up or down.

Buttons for switching views.   Status bar.

Figure 3.11   Word offers a cornucopia of controls.

Word has numerous toolbars customized for your convenience so that you can quickly access tools for a particular task, such as bordering paragraphs or drawing pictures. By default, the Standard and Formatting toolbars appear when you launch Word (see Figure 3.12); other toolbars may appear as needed.

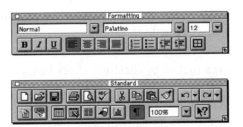

Figure 3.12   The Formatting and Standard toolbars.

57

The toolbars contain buttons grouped together for a particular purpose. If you move the pointer slowly over a button, a name tag, called a ToolTip, pops down from the button. To turn the ToolTip display on or off, go to the View menu and choose Toolbars. In the Toolbars dialog box, the Show ToolTips check box at the lower right controls the display of ToolTips.

To issue the command represented by a button, click the button. A few commands, such as the Zoom Control on the Standard toolbar, are pop-up menus, and you can either click the triangle and choose an option from the menu or type your own option in the menu box and then press Return.

To enlarge toolbar buttons, choose Toolbars from the View menu. Turn on the Large Buttons check box and click the OK button. To further customize toolbar buttons, go to the Tools menu and use the Toolbars card in the Customize dialog box (see Chapter 9).

You can adjust toolbars in many different ways. If you adjust a toolbar, the adjustment becomes the default until you change it again.

◆ You can "dock" toolbars on any edge of the screen by dragging them to a different edge, but if you dock them on one of the sides, pop-up menus (such as the Font menu) turn into less convenient buttons. To drag a docked toolbar, drag on the gray area behind the buttons.

◆ Rearrange docked toolbars (the ones at the edge of the screen) by dragging them around in the region at the edge of the screen. People with larger monitors will have a larger region in which to drag.

◆ If you drag a toolbar below the top of the document window, it converts into a floating toolbar.

◆ "Float" a toolbar by double-clicking in the gray area surrounding its buttons.

◆ Move a floating toolbar by dragging its title bar or the gray area behind the buttons.

◆ Change a floating toolbar's shape by dragging its resize box.

◆ Close a floating toolbar by clicking its close box or convert it into an anchored toolbar by double-clicking in the gray area surrounding the buttons (see Figure 3.13).

◆ To hide or show a toolbar by clicking a check box, choose Toolbars from the View menu.

◆ To show or hide a toolbar rapidly, use a shortcut menu. To see the menu, press Control and click any part of any toolbar.

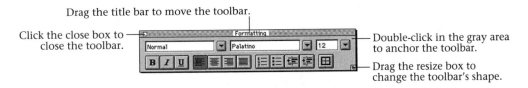

Drag the title bar to move the toolbar.

Click the close box to
close the toolbar.

Double-click in the gray area
to anchor the toolbar.

Drag the resize box to
change the toolbar's shape.

Figure 3.13   The trick to controlling a floating toolbar is knowing where to click.

The Marks on the Status Bar

The status bar gives information about the location of the insertion point, the time, and the mode (see Figure 3.14). You can hide or show the status bar in the View card of the Options dialog box from the Tools menu. If you have trouble understanding the cryptic text on the status bar, here's an explanation:

◆ Page and Sec tell the page and section that your insertion point is in. If you have inserted page numbers, Page refers to the number that will print and not necessarily to the order of the pages in the document. Double-click Page to bring up the Go To dialog box and go to a different part of the document.

◆ To the right of the section number, the status bar shows how many pages are in the document, up to and including the page holding the insertion point. The bar also shows the total number of pages in the document. For example, 4/8 means the insertion point is on the fourth page of an eight-page document.

◆ At refers to how far the text will be from the top of the page if you type at the insertion point.

◆ Ln indicates how many lines the insertion point is from the top of the page. It does not include text in the header.

◆ Col tells how many characters the insertion point is from the left edge of the column. Col is a throwback from old-style word processors that could use only monospaced fonts, where each character has exactly the same width as the others.

◆ The time tells what time it is. You cannot remove the time from the status bar. To set the time, use the Date & Time control panel (start by choosing Control Panels from the Apple menu).

◆ REC is short for *record* and comes into play if you record macros (see Chapter 9).

◆ MRK stands for *mark* and changes from gray to black while you revise a document via the Revision command.

♦ If EXT is black, the Extend Selection option is active (see Chapter 4).

♦ If OVR is black, you are in Overstrike mode, in which what you type replaces text to its right (see Chapter 4).

♦ On a PowerBook, the rightmost item is a battery life indicator, which attempts to let you know how much charge is left in your battery.

♦ Double-click REC, MRK, EXT, or OVR to toggle in and out of the modes they represent.

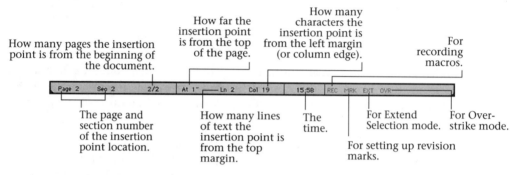

Figure 3.14 The status bar.

The status bar also shows tips. As you point to an option on a toolbar or menu, watch the status bar to remind yourself of what the command does.

How to Rule the Rulers

The marks on a ruler give information about the layout of the currently selected paragraph, or if you have nothing selected, they give information about the paragraph holding the insertion point. If you have more than one paragraph selected, the marks refer to the first paragraph in the selection. To hide or show the ruler, choose Ruler from the View menu. In Page Layout View, a vertical ruler shows in addition to the horizontal ruler.

The most common use of the horizontal ruler is to change the indents, which control where the text falls in relation to the side margins. You can also set tab stops, column widths, and margins.

Generally speaking, when you make an adjustment in the ruler, it affects selected paragraphs. Or if you don't have any text selected, it affects the paragraph holding the insertion point. The gray part of the ruler indicates the margin; the white part starts at zero and indicates the space between the margins (see Figure 3.15).

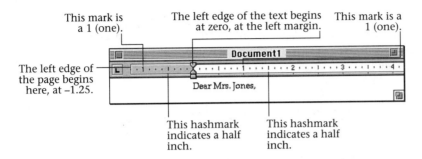

Figure 3.15   The gray area extends from –1.25 to 0, indicating that the left margin is at 1.25 inches.

Switching the View

Word has different views for doing different things. The buttons on the left side of the horizontal scroll bar enable you to switch views, and because these buttons spend their entire lives waiting to be clicked, you may as well stroke their egos by clicking them now and again (see Figure 3.16). You can also switch views by choosing them from the View menu.

If you switch views frequently, consider memorizing keyboard shortcuts for switching: ⌘-Option-N puts you in Normal View; ⌘-Option-P switches you into Page Layout View; ⌘-Option-O puts you in Outline View; and ⌘-Option-I takes you to Print Preview.

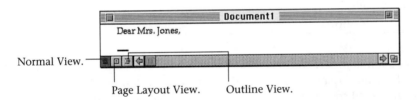

Figure 3.16   Click a button to switch the view.

Use Normal View for working with text, without concerning yourself with layout details, such as snaking columns, correctly positioned graphics, and headers or footers. Page Layout View works much like Normal View but offers the advantage of showing the layout as it will print. Page Layout View also has a vertical ruler.

Outline View is probably the most ignored view, and it's a real shame because it enables you to organize and reorganize information, create traditional outlines, and automatically apply built-in heading styles (see Chapter 5).

Master Document View extends Outline View so that you can work with more than one document at once (see Chapter 5).

61

Print Preview enables you to see Word's best guess as to how your document will print. Word 6 offers a new Print Preview feature called Shrink to Fit, which eliminates the last page in a document if the text runs over to that page by a small amount. Chapter 10 explains Print Preview more thoroughly.

Using Keyboard Shortcuts

Keyboard shortcuts help you get things done quickly. Predefined keyboard shortcuts appear in the menus, to the right of their commands. For example, if you look on the File menu, you'll notice that the Save command is followed by the symbol ⌘-S. The symbol means that you don't have to choose Save from the menu in order to use the Save command; instead, you can use the keyboard. In this case, you'd press the ⌘ key and the S key at the same time. Table 3.3 matches common symbols that appear in Word with keys on the keyboard.

Table 3.3

Keyboard Shortcuts

Symbol	Keyboard key
⌘	Command (sometimes the key shows an apple, too)
⌥	Option
⇧	Shift
⌃	Control

The menus show a few keyboard shortcuts, but you can find even more by choosing Customize from the Tools menu. After the Customize dialog box comes up, select the Keyboard card. A list of menu names and special options appears at the far left, and if you select an item from the list, the commands that go with that option appear in the Commands list. If you select a command that has a keyboard shortcut associated with it, the shortcut shows in the Current Keys box (see Figure 3.17). Click the Close button when you finish looking.

Select a command from the Commands list.

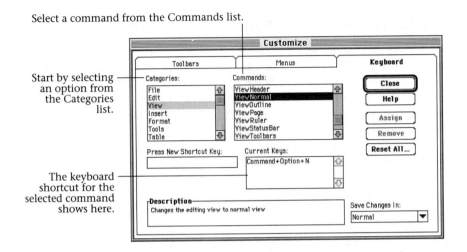

Start by selecting an option from the Categories list.

The keyboard shortcut for the selected command shows here.

Figure 3.17   It's easy to discover keyboard shortcuts.

Menus for Novices and Keyboard Enthusiasts

Most of the time, Word's menus work like the menus in any other program. The *drop-down* menus come down from the menu bar, and a small black triangle symbolizes the presence of a *pop-up menu*. For example, in the Note Options dialog box, you can customize the behavior of footnotes or endnotes. The dialog box has two small black triangles—one for the Place At menu and one for the Number Format menu (see Figure 3.18). To open the Note Options dialog box, go to the Insert menu, choose Footnote, and click the Options button in the Footnote and Endnote dialog box.

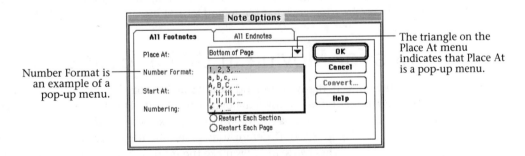

Number Format is an example of a pop-up menu.

The triangle on the Place At menu indicates that Place At is a pop-up menu.

Figure 3.18   The Note Options dialog box has two pop-up menus.

Using the keyboard with the drop-down menus

Normally, you use the pointer to choose menu commands, but if you activate the menu bar, you can choose menu commands by pressing keys on the keyboard. The official keyboard shortcuts for activating the menu bar are ⌘-Tab and F10. Either one works, in theory, but you may run into problems. If you have Microsoft Office Manager installed, pressing ⌘-Tab will switch you between launched applications. If you don't have an extended keyboard, you won't have an F10 key. So, if you use Microsoft Office Manager or have a standard keyboard, use the Customize dialog box to assign a different keyboard shortcut. Menu Mode is the official command name that you will need to customize.

For the sake of the rest of these directions, this book tells you to press ⌘-Tab to activate the menu bar. I decided to stick with ⌘-Tab for historical reasons—Word 5 also uses ⌘-Tab to activate the menu bar.

In any event, to get started with using the keyboard to activate the menu bar and drop down the menus, press ⌘-Tab and then note that each menu name has a small underline beneath one of its characters. Press that character to drop down the menu or to choose a menu item. (For example, press T to drop down the Tools menu and then press R to start a mail merge.) You can also use the Left- and Right Arrow keys to move to menus and the Up- and Down Arrow keys to move within menus.

Press ⌘-Period to deactivate the menu bar and not choose any menu options.

Using the shortcut menus

Shortcut menus offer quick access to commands that relate to a particular item. To display a shortcut menu, press Control and click an item of interest. For example, if you Control-click a field, Word reacts by displaying a menu that helps you control the field.

To see a list of all the shortcut menus, open the Menus card in the Customize dialog box from the Tools menu. Pop up the Change What Menu and look at menus that end with (Shortcut).

Tips for Moving in Dialog Boxes

As you have probably noticed, many commands lead to dialog boxes, where you can select or type various options (think of it as having a dialogue with Word). Due to the large number of options built into Word, Microsoft organized most dialog boxes with *cards,* which you select by clicking their *tabs* (see Figure 3.19). Different sources use slightly different terminology for the dialog boxes, but I think that *cards* and *tabs* make the most sense, so I used these terms in this book.

Click a tab (such as the User
Info tab) to switch to its card.

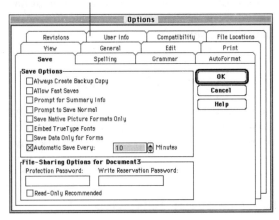

Figure 3.19   The Options dialog box has many cards.

To see cards and tabs in action, check out the Options dialog box, which you access by
choosing Options from the Tools menu. The dialog box has many different cards that are
analogous to index cards in an index file (perhaps the most common use of index cards and
files is for storing recipes). To move to a different card, such as the General card, click the tab
at the top of the card. Press Control-Tab to switch which card shows at the front of the dialog
box.

On most monitors, you can view the dialog boxes in two different ways. By default, Word
displays dialog boxes in much the same way that they appear in Word for Windows. To get a
compromise between Macintosh- and Windows-like dialog boxes, turn off the check box for
3D Dialog and Display Effects. The check box is in the General card of the Options dialog box.
Most dialog boxes shown in this book sport the non-3D look.

Many dialog boxes offer tiny triangles that you can click to increase or decrease the number in
their associated boxes. To see several examples of these triangles, choose Paragraph from the
Format menu and look at the Indents and Spacing card. If you don't want to click the triangles, you can also type a number in the box or, with the insertion point in the box, press
the Up- or Down Arrow keys to increase or decrease the number.

In any dialog box, press the ⌘ key to see keyboard shortcuts that you can issue in the dialog
box. For example, if you press ⌘ while in the Font card of the Font dialog box, the *i* in *Hidden*
gets an underline. If you press ⌘-I, Word turns on or off the Hidden format.

A few dialog boxes offer check boxes. In all cases, a clear check box means the option is off,
and a checked check box means the option is on (by checked, I mean filled with an X). In

some dialog boxes, such as the Font dialog box, a check box may be filled with gray. The gray color means that only some of the text selected in the document has that check box option applied. In a few uncommon circumstances, the gray coloring means that circumstances prohibit you from changing the option.

How Word Thinks

If you know how someone thinks, you can often anticipate what that person is going to do next. Word isn't nearly as complex as a real-life person, but if you have an idea of what's going on from Word's virtual point of view, you have a much better chance of steering Word where you want it to go.

Characters and character formats

Just as atoms are in many ways the fundamental building blocks of the universe, characters (such as *w*, *%*, and *8*) are the fundamental building blocks of a Word document. A number of the formatting options offered in Word are applied by character, and these formats are aptly named *character formats*. For example, Bold is a character format, and you can emphasize any letter that you want in a word by making it bold. See what happens when you add Bold character formatting to the word **zebra**? The word visually takes on the striped quality of the animal!

Paragraphs and paragraph formats

To extend the atom analogy, if characters are like atoms, then paragraphs are like molecules. In Word's opinion, a paragraph ends every time you press Return. If you have nonprinting characters showing, you'll see a paragraph mark representing the place where you pressed Return. Nonprinting characters can show onscreen but never on a printout. Some formats (such as custom tabs, indents, and centering) apply by paragraph. For example, you can center an entire paragraph by clicking the Center button on the Formatting toolbar, but you cannot center just a few characters in the middle of the paragraph.

When you turn on centering, type a paragraph that takes on the centering format, and then press Return, Word ends the paragraph and starts a new paragraph. The new paragraph will also be centered, unless you turn off centering. To turn off centering, you must first have the insertion point in the new paragraph or highlight something in the new paragraph. Then you click the Center button on the Formatting toolbar.

Sections and section formats

Some formatting (such as page numbering) doesn't make sense to apply by character or by paragraph. For example, you may want the first few pages of a document to have Roman numeral page numbers and the rest of the pages to have regular Arabic numerals. As another example, you may want most of a document to print in the usual portrait orientation, but then you want a few pages to print sideways in the landscape orientation. Orientation refers to how text flows from left to right on a printed page.

When you start a document, it consists of one section (under most circumstances), and all the paragraphs share the same section-based formatting. If you decide that you don't want the same formats to apply to the entire document, you can insert section breaks to divide the document into separate sections.

The status bar shows the number of the section containing the insertion point. For example, Sec 3 means that the insertion point is in section three.

Inserting and formatting section breaks

To insert a section break, click where you want the break, go to the Insert menu, and choose Break (or press ⌘-Enter). The Break dialog box appears. In the Section Breaks area, select Next Page to make the section break also be a page break. If you don't want the section break to be a page break, too, select Continuous. Click the OK button to finish inserting the section break. If you have trouble seeing section breaks, switch to Normal View.

To change whether a section break is continuous or acts like a page break, follow these steps:

1. Click in the section directly below the section break that you want to change.

2. From the File menu, choose Document Layout.

3. When the Document Layout dialog box appears, select the Layout card.

4. Use the Section Start pop-up menu to change the way the section begins and then click the OK button.

Applying section formats

To apply a section-based format in the traditional method, first click in the section (so that the insertion point is in the section) or highlight at least a portion of the section. Then apply the format from the appropriate dialog box, toolbar button, or keyboard shortcut.

In previous versions of Word, many people forgot to click or highlight before applying formatting. Word 6 helps you avoid this problem in the dialog boxes where you apply section-based formats. The dialog boxes offer an Apply To menu where you indicate where Word should apply the formatting.

To see an Apply To menu, go to the File menu and choose Document Layout. Look at the lower left of the Margins card. Depending on what you select in the Apply To menu, Word may insert section breaks for you, thus dividing the document while applying the section-based formatting to the appropriate section only.

Deleting section breaks

To delete a section break, click directly beneath the section break and then press Delete. After you press Delete, the text that was above the section break takes on the section formatting of the text that was below the break. (If you have trouble seeing a section break, switch to Normal View.)

Templates

Every document you create is based on a template. The template tells Word how you want to start—what margins to use, which font, and so on. Most people, most of the time, don't need to think much about templates. If you start a Word document and don't specifically select a template for it, the document uses a template called Normal.

To base a new document on a template other than Normal, go to the File menu and choose New. In the resulting dialog box, select the template that you want to use.

If you want to or need to know more about templates, keep reading. Otherwise, skip the rest of this section and devote your brain cells to some other task, such as locating a snack.

A template has three main parts—examples, styles, and commands:

- ◆ Examples are text or graphics that appear in all documents based on the template. For example, a student can create a template for reports that contains the cover page with text that he always uses, along with the correct margin, font, and page number formats.

- ◆ Styles are the styles that you want available in all documents based on the template. For example, in creating a report template, you can customize the built-in heading styles so that you like the way your document looks after you set it up in Outline View.

- ◆ Commands are AutoText entries, macros, toolbars, drop-down menus, and keyboard shortcuts. For example, a hard-core Word user can add special keyboard shortcuts, customized menus, AutoText entries, and a custom toolbar to a template.

Caution: If you think your Normal template is damaged in some way and causing problems, you can test your theory by launching Word while pressing the Shift key. By pressing the Shift key, you tell Word to ignore the Normal template and use the built-in factory defaults, instead. The next time you launch Word, if you don't press the Shift key, Word will use the Normal template.

Creating a new template

To create a new template, open a new document and then go to the File menu and choose Save As. Along with giving the document a name, assign it the Document Template type (from the Save File as Type menu), and save it in Word's Templates folder. Now that the document is saved as a template, add examples, styles, and commands as needed.

◆ Add the text, graphics, and so on that you want to appear in all documents based on the template.

◆ Change or create styles so that the styles in the template match the way you want the styles to work.

◆ If you customize the toolbars, menus, or keyboard shortcuts in the Customize dialog box, be sure to choose the name of the template from the Save Changes In pop-up menu at the lower right. Similarly, when you create AutoText entries in the AutoText dialog box, choose the template from the Make AutoText Entry Available To pop-up menu. And, finally, if you create macros, be sure to store them in the template.

To start a file based on your template, go to the File menu and choose New. If you saved the template in the Templates folder, you should see it in the list of templates. Select the template and click the OK button.

If you find yourself frequently using and setting up templates, be sure to check out the Organizer dialog box, which you open by choosing Templates from the File menu and then clicking the Organizer button. With the Organizer dialog box, you can move macros, styles, AutoText entries, and toolbars from template to template, between documents and templates, and from document to document.

Attaching a template to an existing document (commands and styles)

If you already have a document started and realize that you want to access the styles and commands in a different template, you can attach the template. Go to the File menu and choose Templates. In the resulting Templates and Add-ins dialog box, click the Attach button and then open the template. If you turn on the Automatically Update Document Styles check box, the styles from the template come in and override styles currently in the document. For example, the Normal style in the template overrides the Normal style in the document.

Attaching a template globally (commands only)

If you are working in Word and want the commands from a template available, you can attach a template as a global template. To accomplish this, go to the File menu and choose Templates and Add-ins. If a template that you want to use as a global template does not show in the list of global templates, click the Add button and use the resulting Open dialog box to open the template.

To activate a global template, turn on its check box. After you finish activating global templates, click OK. The commands available in the template remain active until you quit Word.

Fields

Word loves *fields*. Fields are little blanks that Word gets to fill in. For example, when you insert a page number, you insert a field, called PAGE. If the *result* of the PAGE field shows, you see a page number, but if the *code* shows, you see something like {PAGE}. When you show the result of a field, Word fills in the field with what Word thinks is the correct information. Sometimes, though, Word is wrong about the correct way to fill in a field, and you must update the field either by Control-clicking the field to display a shortcut menu or by using the commands shown in Table 3.4.

To make sure that all fields update before they print, go to the Options dialog box and use the Print card to turn on the Update Fields check box.

Use the View card in the Options dialog box to control the way that default fields appear onscreen. To see results, clear the Field Codes check box. To see codes, check the Field Codes check box. You can also change the selection in the Field Shading menu to control when fields show with shading.

To lock a field so that it never updates again (unless you unlock it), select the field and then press ⌘-3. To unlock a field, select it and press ⌘-4.

If you use fields frequently, you may want to memorize or customize the commands shown in Table 3.4. Chapter 9 explains how to make your own keyboard shortcuts and add commands to menus and toolbars.

Table 3.4

Field Commands for People Who Use Fields Frequently

Action	Command name	Default keyboard shortcut
Update selected field(s)	UpdateFields (in the All Commands category)	F9 or ⌘-Option-Shift-U
Switch between showing a selected field's code and result	ToggleFieldDisplay (in the All Commands category)	Shift-F9
Switch between showing all codes and results	ViewFieldCodes (in the View category)	Option-F9

Now that you have had a chance to get yourself accustomed to the general workings of Word 6 and its tools, you should have visions of section breaks, shortcut menus, and status bars dancing in your head. Unless you are feeling too dizzy to continue, flip ahead to Chapter 4, which explains how to get something done in Word, with a strong focus on how to type and how to edit.

Chapter 4

Typing and Editing in a Document

Whether you are new to computers, fairly comfortable with them, or a true computer wizard, read this chapter to learn how to use many of Word's special typing and editing features. For example, in addition to text, you can add numbers, bullets, and special characters to your documents. After you write the text, you then can make all sorts of changes to it. You'll find out how to do many things in this chapter, including the following points:

◆ Typing text, numbers, special characters, page breaks, and so on

◆ Using and moving the insertion point

◆ Selecting and deleting text

◆ Using the Undo feature

◆ Moving text around

◆ Using the Find and Replace commands

◆ Taking advantage of AutoCorrect and AutoText

◆ Inserting dates

◆ Viewing statistics about a document

◆ Using the Thesaurus and the Spelling and Grammar Checkers

Adding Text

If you've used a word processor before, you know that to add text, you start typing. Text that you type appears just left of the insertion point, a little vertical line. Text wraps when it reaches the end of a line, meaning that you don't have to press Return to start a new line; Word starts a new line for you. When you reach the end of a paragraph, press Return to start a new paragraph.

> **Caution:** Don't use spaces to line up things. Find out about using tabs or tables instead (see Chapters 6 and 7, respectively).

Numbers

Typing numbers from the row of numbers at the top of the keyboard works any time, but you may have to turn on Num Lock before you can use the numeric keypad. To turn on Num Lock, press Shift-Clear—the Clear key is on the numeric keypad, just above the 7, and it's not always clearly labeled. To turn off Num Lock, press Shift-Clear again.

Bullets

Bullets are those dots that people use to emphasize points in a list. Bullets usually look like •, although you can get fancy and use special characters, such as diamonds, arrows, or hearts. To type a bullet, press Option-8.

If you use numbers or bullets to begin entries in a list, make Word do the numbering or bullets automatically (see Chapter 6).

Quotation marks

The world of typography offers two main types of quotation marks—curly (also called smart) quotes and primes (also called straight quotes or hash marks). Curly quotes look curved or curled and are used to quote conversation and special terms. Primes look completely straight or close to straight and are used to express units of measurement (see Figure 4.1).

> Sue said, "I want the the blue fabric." The shop kept the blue fabric on the second level, about 13' off the ground.

Figure 4.1 This quotation uses curly quotes to quote speech and primes to indicate a unit of measurement.

To type a curly quote, use the Prime/Quote key to the right of the Colon/Semicolon key. By default, Word is set up to type curly quotes, even though a prime appears on the key. To turn off the default, follow these steps:

1. From the Tools menu, choose AutoCorrect. The AutoCorrect dialog box appears.

2. Turn off the check box for Change 'Straight Quotes' to 'Smart Quotes.'

3. Click the OK button. With the Smart Quotes AutoCorrect feature off, you can type a prime by pressing the Prime key.

If you find yourself turning smart quotes on and off, note that Word comes with a command that switches smart quotes on and off. You can make the command accessible through the Customize dialog box. To find the command in the Customize dialog box, select the All Commands category and look for a command called ToolsAutoCorrectSmartQuotes.

If smart quotes are on and you use the Replace command to search for primes and replace with smart quotes, regardless of what the quotes look like in the Replace dialog box, you get smart quotes out of the Replace operation.

Hyphens and dashes

Hyphens and dashes all look about the same, but from a typographic perspective, each type of dash and hyphen looks slightly different and serves a different purpose. Table 4.1 summarizes different dashes and hyphens and shows how to create them.

Table 4.1

Hyphens and Dashes

Character	Purpose	Examples	Shortcut
Hyphen	For compound words (such as *fresh-baked*) or splitting a word over a line break	fresh-baked action-ready high-resolution	Hyphen
Optional hyphen	Splits a word over a line break but shows only if the word happens to fall at the end of a line and split	Use for a long word (such as *information* or *concentration*), where you want to control how the word hy- phenates if it splits over a line break	⌘-Hyphen

continues

75

Table 4.1 Continued

Character	Purpose	Examples	Shortcut
Nonbreaking hyphen	For a compound word so that the word never splits over a line break	Use for a long word that you always want on the same line, such as a phone number	⌘-~ (Tilde)
En dash	For ranges of numbers or dates used in place of a hyphen when half the compound word is a proper name	June 22–28 8:30–12:30 Monday–Friday	Option-Hyphen
Em dash	For abrupt breaks in thought	Driving takes too long—let's take a plane instead.	Shift-Option-Hyphen

Hyphens balance the appearance of text on a page. If the text is set *ragged right* so that the exact end of each line of text varies slightly, the right edge of the text tends to have an uneven appearance. By hyphenating the text, you allow some words to split between lines, resulting in a more even appearance. In the case of *justified text*, where the right edge of each line ends in exactly the same place, you may end up with awkward globs of white space between words or, worse yet, with rivers of connected white globs pouring down the page. Hyphenating allows more words to fit on a line, reduces globs of white space, and dries out those unattractive rivers.

When it comes to making hyphens, you can type them yourself or ask Word for hyphenation assistance.

If you habitually type two hyphens for an em dash, use AutoCorrect to set up two hyphens as a "mistake" and an em dash as the fix. Flip ahead a few pages to find out about AutoCorrect.

Automatic hyphenation

To make Word insert optional hyphens at awkward line breaks, follow these steps:

1. Go to the Tools menu and choose Hyphenation. The Hyphenation dialog box opens (see Figure 4.2).

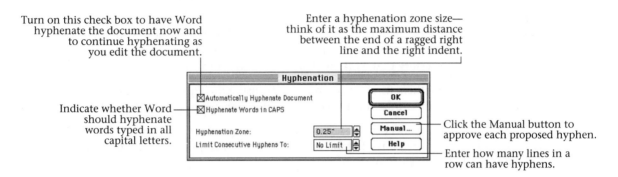

Turn on this check box to have Word hyphenate the document now and to continue hyphenating as you edit the document.

Enter a hyphenation zone size—think of it as the maximum distance between the end of a ragged right line and the right indent.

Indicate whether Word should hyphenate words typed in all capital letters.

Click the Manual button to approve each proposed hyphen.

Enter how many lines in a row can have hyphens.

Figure 4.2   Set up how you want to hyphenate.

2. Turn on the Automatically Hyphenate Document check box.

3. Indicate whether you want to hyphenate words spelled with capital letters.

4. Enter a size for the hyphenation zone. For ragged right-aligned text, a smaller zone translates to less ragged text and more hyphens. For justified text, a smaller zone gives fewer unsightly white blotches between the words.

5. Enter a limit for how many consecutive lines can end with hyphens.

6. Click the OK button.

Word inserts optional hyphens so that some words split from one line to the next. Word also continues to insert and remove hyphens as you edit the document.

To remove hyphens from a paragraph or to exclude a paragraph from being hyphenated, highlight the paragraph and turn on the Don't Hyphenate check box in the Text Flow card of the Paragraph dialog box.

If you want more control over the hyphens, you can click the Manual button in the Hyphenation dialog box to indicate exactly where each word should break.

Miscellaneous special characters

Lots of people get stuck when it comes to typing a character that doesn't appear on the keyboard. After you know what keyboard shortcuts to use, you can type lots of uncommon characters, such as copyright symbols, accented characters, and mathematical symbols. For example, the keyboard shortcut for the copyright symbol (©) is Option-G.

Each font offers slightly different characters, and which characters you can type depends on which fonts you have installed on your Macintosh. To find out more about your fonts and learn the keyboard shortcuts for special characters, you can use Word's Symbol command or the Key Caps desk accessory that works with any Macintosh program.

If you are making a mathematical equation, consider using the Equation Editor that comes with Word. Go to the Insert menu, choose Object, and then select Microsoft Equation 2.0.

The Symbol command works best for viewing characters in the font that you are currently typing in or in a specialized font that doesn't contain normal alphabetic characters. To use the command, follow these steps.

1. Drop down the Insert menu, choose Symbol, and select the Symbols card (see Figure 4.3). For a quick reference to common special characters and keyboard shortcuts, look on the Special Characters card in the Symbol dialog box.

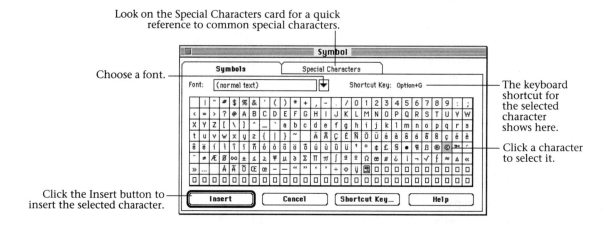

Figure 4.3   The Symbols card helps with inserting uncommon characters.

2. Make sure that your font of choice shows in the Font menu. You can look at a specialized font, such as Symbol, or you can look at an option called (normal text). The (normal text) option shows the characters in the font and point size of the characters currently surrounding the insertion point in your document. For example, if the insertion point is in a paragraph formatted in Times 14-point, (normal text) shows the characters available in Times 14-point.

3. Click a particular character. The character enlarges so that you can see it easily; the status bar displays the ASCII character value; and the keyboard shortcut that you press to type the character shows at the upper right of the card. If you memorize the keyboard shortcut, you can use it later to quickly type the character without opening the Symbol dialog box.

4. If you want to insert the selected character, click the Insert button.

5. Click the Close button to exit the Symbol dialog box.

In the Symbol dialog box, if you choose anything except for (normal text) from the Font menu and then insert a character from that font, you'll find that you can't change the character to a different font. Microsoft added this feature so that the character stays correct, even if you change the font of the text surrounding it.

Using Key Caps

Key Caps is a desk accessory from Apple that lives in the Apple menu on most Macs. By glancing at the keyboard displayed in Key Caps, you can view the characters available in any installed font. To switch fonts, choose a different font from the Key Caps menu (it's up on the menu bar). To find out how to type less common characters, watch the Key Caps display while pressing Shift, Option, or Shift-Option (occasionally pressing the Control key also reveals a special character or two). With Palatino chosen from the Key Caps menu, for example, I learned that pressing Shift-Option-K results in an apple character.

When you click on characters shown in the Key Caps window or type on the keyboard, the characters display in the text box rectangle at the top of the window. After the characters show in that window, you can copy and paste to move them into your document, or you can memorize the keyboard shortcut and use it later.

In Key Caps, when you press the Option key, some keys display with thick edges. A thick edge indicates that you can use the key in conjunction with the Option key to place a special mark above a character, such as the tilde (~) that goes above the *n* in many Spanish words. For example, to create an ñ, follow these steps:

1. Press Option-N and release both keys. Nothing happens.

2. Type **n**. The *n* appears with a tilde over it, *ñ*.

Similarly, to create an *á* character, try these steps:

1. Press Option-E and release both keys.

2. Type **a**. The *á* appears with an accent above it.

Typically, these shortcuts work only to put special characters over vowels. The ñ is an exception, not the usual case.

Nonprinting characters

If you press a key that doesn't insert characters but does move the insertion point (such as the Return key), you may see a nonprinting character. Most nonprinting characters affect where text appears, but they do not print. For example, if you press the Return key to move the insertion point to the next line, you may see a paragraph mark, which indicates the end of the paragraph.

Sometimes people confuse the Enter and Return keys. When I tell you to press Enter, it means (as you might expect) that you press the key labeled Enter. Most keyboards have the Enter key at the far right (on the numeric keypad). If you don't have a numeric keypad, hunt around for the key. The Enter key on my PowerBook Duo 230 is just right of the Spacebar.

Table 4.2 shows common nonprinting characters.

Table 4.2
Nonprinting Characters

Symbol	Character name	What it does	Shortcut
¶	Paragraph mark	Ends a paragraph	Return or Enter
¶	Space mark	Acts as a space	Spacebar
→	Tab mark	Creates blank space in a line of text	Tab
↵	Soft return mark	Moves text to the next line without ending a paragraph	Shift-Return
¤	End-of-cell or end-of-row mark	The last character in a table cell or a mark to the right of a table row	No shortcut

Nonprinting characters never print, and you control whether they show onscreen through the View card in the Options dialog box from the Tools menu (see Figure 4.4). To switch on all nonprinting characters, use the Show/Hide button in the Standard toolbar. You can also assign the switch to a keyboard shortcut; look for Show All under the All Commands category in the Customize dialog box from the Tools menu.

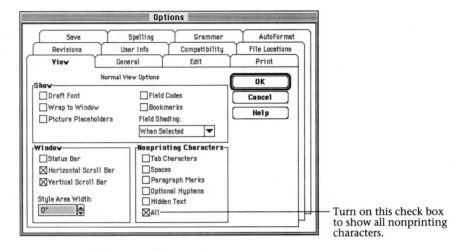

Turn on this check box
to show all nonprinting
characters.

Figure 4.4   Use the View card to control how you see nonprinting characters onscreen.

Page breaks

When you fill a printed page worth of text, Word automatically inserts a soft page break. In
Normal View the page break looks like a dotted line. Page Layout View displays a document as
though it consists of white sheets of paper on a gray desk, so you see about one-quarter inch of
gray "desk" in place of a page break. To insert your own page break (also called a hard page
break), press Shift-Enter. A hard break looks like a dotted line, punctuated in the middle with
the label Page Break.

To delete a hard page break, highlight the page break (it's easier to find the page break in
Normal View). With the page break highlighted, press Delete. To delete an automatic page
break, you must figure out why Word thinks the page break should be there and then change
your setup so that Word doesn't think the page break should belong.

Moving the Insertion Point in Text

The insertion point is a small vertical line, and text that you type always appears just left of
the insertion point. The most straightforward way of moving the insertion point is to click
where you want it to go (you may need to scroll to the right place), but if you have a long
document, try one of these techniques to move around faster:

◆ To move up, down, right, or left, press the appropriate arrow key.

◆ To move to the next word, press ⌘–Right Arrow; to move back in a similar manner,
press ⌘–Left Arrow.

◆ To move to the end of a paragraph, press ⌘–Down Arrow; to move to the start of a
paragraph, press ⌘–Up Arrow.

◆ Choose Go To from the Edit menu. The Go To dialog box appears, and you can
   enter a page number for where you want to go. If you want to get fancier with the
   dialog box, select an element from the list at the left. Follow the directions at the
   right to move efficiently around, based on that element. To open the Go To dialog
   box, press ⌘-G, or double-click Page on the status bar (at the lower left).

Word has plenty more keyboard shortcuts for moving around, and to find them, you can hunt
around in the Keyboard card on the Customize dialog box from the Tools menu. In the All
Commands category, look for commands that start with *Word, GoTo, Page, Para,* and *Char.*

After you know a keyboard shortcut for moving the insertion point, you can combine that
shortcut with the Shift key to select text. For example, ⌘–Right Arrow *moves* the insertion
point right one word, so Shift-⌘–Right Arrow *selects* right one word.

Selecting Text

Word, like most Macintosh programs, usually wants you to select things before you change
them or do more with them. For example, to make some text bold, select the text and then
issue the Bold command (by clicking the Bold button, pressing ⌘-B, or via the Font card in
the Font dialog box).

In most Macintosh programs, you drag the pointer over the text to select it, and the text
selects character by character as you drag. The text highlights as you drag over it, indicating
that you have selected it (see Figure 4.5).

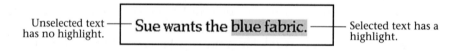

Unselected text ——— **Sue wants the blue fabric.** ——— Selected text has a
has no highlight.   highlight.

Figure 4.5   Selected text has highlighting behind it.

By default, Word is set up so that you select text character by character within one word, but
if you try to select more than one word, the selection goes word by word. If this feature gets
in your way, use the Edit card in the Options dialog box from the Tools menu to turn off
Automatic Word Selection.

Because selecting text by dragging over it is tedious for long selections, you can use a variety of
tricks to select text. Here are a few popular ones:

◆ To select a word, double-click the word.

◆ To select a sentence, ⌘-click it.

- To select a paragraph, triple-click the paragraph.
- To select a line, slide the pointer left of the line so that the pointer becomes an upper-right pointing arrow. Click once.
- To select forward, press Shift–Right Arrow repeatedly.
- To select backward, press Shift–Left Arrow repeatedly.
- To select a large block of text, click where you want the selection to begin. Scroll up or down so that you can see where you want the selection to end. Shift-click where you want the selection to end.
- To select an entire document, press ⌘-A.
- Turn on Extend mode by double-clicking EXT on the right side of the status bar. Press an arrow key to extend a selection in that direction. Keep pressing the key to continue extending the selection. Turn off Extend mode by double-clicking EXT again.
- To remove a selection, click an unselected spot in the document window.

Deleting Text

To delete text in any Macintosh program, including Word, follow the three basic rules of Macintosh deleting:

- Rule 1: Clicking to the right of text and then pressing the Delete key deletes the text, character by character.
- Rule 2: To delete larger amounts of text quickly, select the text and then press the Delete key.
- Rule 3: If you select text and then start typing, whatever you type replaces the previously selected text.

Word takes advantage of a key on the extended keyboard called the Forward Delete key. An extended keyboard has function keys (such as F2 and F9) as well as a bunch of keys that are grouped together that include Help, End, and PageUp. The Forward Delete key is usually directly under the Help key. It has a "Del" label on it, and it also has an X in an arrow-like object pointing to the right. To forward delete, click to the left of what you want to delete and then press the Forward Delete key.

Word extends these basic rules with two features of its own—Typing Replaces Selection and Overtype Mode—which you turn on and off in the Edit card of the Options dialog box from the Tools menu.

If you turn off Typing Replaces Selection, then Rules 2 and 3 of "Deleting Text" don't apply. If you are unsteady with the mouse and new to the Macintosh, you might consider turning off Typing Replaces Selection to avoid unpleasant deletion accidents. Just remember to turn it back on after you come up to speed!

With Overtype Mode on, text that you type replaces text to its right. You can quickly turn on or off Overtype Mode by double-clicking OVR on the status bar.

Undo Typing or Formatting

Word enables you to remove changes that you've made to a document. To take back the most recent change, press ⌘-Z or use the Undo command on the Edit menu. If you need a more complicated fix, use the Undo and Redo controls on the Standard toolbar (see Figure 4.6).

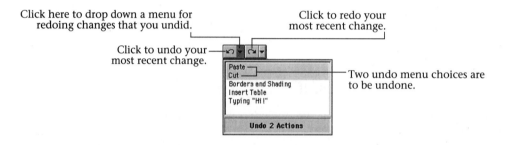

Figure 4.6   The Undo menu box lets you choose exactly what you want to undo.

You can click the Undo and Redo buttons just once or repeatedly to take back or put back one or many changes. To undo one or more changes, click the down-pointing triangle between the Undo and Redo buttons. A menu pops down listing changes, and you can drag down over recent changes to choose exactly how many you want to undo. If you undo more than you intended, use the Redo button to fix things up.

Moving Text

Moving text can be as simple as dragging it about onscreen, or it can involve the slightly more involved Cut, Copy, and Paste commands. If you need to collect and move noncontiguous bits of text, use the spike. Keep reading to find out about each method.

Drag and drop

To move text by dragging it, follow these steps (to copy text instead, press Option while you drag):

1. Select the text.

2. Position the pointer over the text. The pointer should look like an arrow.

3. Press the mouse button and wait a moment. The pointer should have a little picture coming out of its tail, which looks like a dog-eared sheet of paper. If you don't see a picture coming out of the pointer, turn on Drag-and-Drop Text Editing in the Edit card of the Options dialog box from the Tools menu.

4. Keep the mouse button down and drag the pointer about onscreen. You see a faint dotted line coming from the point of the arrow. The line is where the text goes after you release the mouse button. You can drag text within a document or across the edge of the window into another Word document window.

5. When you have the pointer and its line in the right spot, release the mouse button.

Moving Your Formatting

If you drop or paste text into a second document, formatting may not move as you expect. If the style applied to the dropped or pasted text exists in the second document, the text formatting may change. For example, if the Normal style is Times 14-point in one document, and you drop or paste Normal-styled text from that document into a second document where the Normal style is Palatino 10-point, the text takes on the second document's Normal style and ends up in Palatino 10-point.

On the other hand, if the dropped or pasted text has a style that doesn't exist in the second document, the style copies into the second document and the formatting of the dropped or pasted text does not change.

Cut, Copy, and Paste

The Cut, Copy, and Paste commands work for moving almost anything in a document, including text. You can also use Cut, Copy, and Paste to transfer items between different programs. Cut moves a selection; Copy duplicates a selection.

To issue a Cut, Copy, or Paste command, choose it from the Edit menu or click its buttons on the Standard toolbar (the Cut button has a scissors on it, and the Copy and Paste buttons appear to its right). If you use Cut, Copy, and Paste frequently, you'll probably want to memorize their keyboard shortcuts, which show in the Edit menu. In any event, here are the steps for Cut, Copy, and Paste:

1. Select the text or item you want to copy or move.

2. Issue a Copy or Cut command (Copy copies things; Cut moves them). The copied or cut selection transfers to the Clipboard, which temporarily holds the selection so that you can paste it someplace else. To see the contents of the Clipboard, go to the Window menu and choose Clipboard.

3. You can paste into the same document, into another Word document, or into a document from some other program. Open the document that you want to paste into.

4. Position the insertion point where you want the selection to move and then issue the Paste command.

Caution: The Clipboard holds only one selection at a time. For example, if you copy a graphic of a banana, the banana graphic goes on the Clipboard. If you then copy a paragraph of text, the banana disappears from the Clipboard and gets replaced by the paragraph of text. Also, note that the content of the Clipboard exists only in RAM, so if you turn off or restart the Macintosh, the Clipboard content disappears.

Spiking

Spiking enables you to cut more than one selection from a document (or documents) and keep the selections together in a location called a *spike*. At any time, you can insert the entire collection of spiked selections into a document. The selections come off the spike in the order that you added them; that is, the first selection on the spike comes off first. For example, you may have a list of office supplies that your office manager distributes as a Word 6 document (see Figure 4.7).

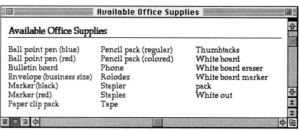

Figure 4.7   If you want to move only some list entries to a second document...

To insert the contents and empty the spike, position the insertion point, don't type anything, and press ⌘-Shift-F3. If you don't have an F3 key, use the Customize dialog box to set up an alternative shortcut for the InsertSpike command. You'll find InsertSpike in the All Commands category.

For another way to collect multiple selections in one holding spot, check out the Scrapbook, a utility that usually lives in the Apple menu.

Deleting the spike

To delete the spike, go to the Edit menu and choose AutoText. When the AutoText dialog box appears, select Spike from the list of AutoText entries. With Spike selected, click the Delete button. Word regenerates the spike if you insert another selection on it.

Finding Text

To find text in a document, use the Find command, which looks for text based on spelling, formatting, or a combination. Here are the steps:

1. From the Edit menu, choose Find. The Find dialog box appears (see Figure 4.10).

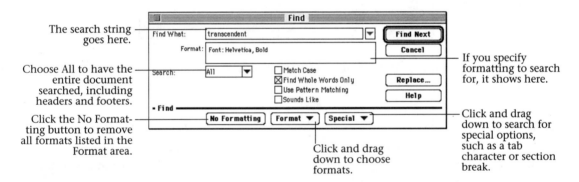

Figure 4.10   In the Find dialog box, indicate the text and/or formatting that you want to find.

2. In the Find What box, type the text that you want to find. The text in the Find What box is called a *search string*. To find something that you can't type, try one of these techniques:

    ◆ To find formatting, drop down the Format button menu and open the appropriate dialog box for the format that you want to search for. Figure 4.10 shows the Find dialog box set up to find every instance of *transcendent* in Helvetica bold. If you want to find only formatting, regardless of which text has the formatting, leave the Find What box blank.

◆ To find a nonprinting character (such as a tab, page break, or paragraph mark), choose it from the Special button menu. The character appears in the Find What box as a code.

◆ To find a space, press the Spacebar. You don't get a code indicating space, but if you watch closely, you'll see the insertion point move a tiny bit.

◆ You can specify a character based on its ASCII value. For example, if you are fixing up a file that came from a different word processor and now has many little squares in it, you can search for the square. To find the ASCII value of the square, switch out of the dialog box and select the square. With the square selected, go to the Insert menu and choose Symbol. When the Symbol dialog box comes up, look at the left side of the status bar—you should see a character number. Memorize that number and then type it into the Find What text box with a caret. So if the character number is 10, type ^10.

◆ You can also paste text into the Find What box.

3. Set the Search menu. If you set it for Up or Down, Word searches up or down from the insertion point but does not search in the header or footer. To search the complete document, set the Search menu to All.

4. Set the various check boxes appropriately:

◆ Match Case finds text in which the capitalization exactly matches what you typed in the Find What box.

◆ Find Whole Word Only sets up the find so that you don't find the search string in longer words. For example, to prevent Word from finding *strawberry* when you search for *berry,* turn on Find Whole Words Only.

◆ Use Pattern Matching is for a more complex search. Pattern Matching is beyond the scope of this book.

◆ Sounds Like means Word tries to find text that sounds like the search string.

5. To find any version of your search string, regardless of the formatting, make certain that no formats show beneath your string. If formats show and you don't want them, click the No Formatting button.

6. After going through all this preparation, click the Find Next button. You can continue clicking the Find Next button as Word continues finding your search string in the document. Click the Cancel button when you finish.

To change the capitalization of a lot of text, use the Change Case command (in the Format menu).

Replacing Found Text

The Replace command helps you quickly change text and formatting in a document. To use the Replace command, follow these steps:

1. To replace only a portion of a document, select that portion. To replace an item throughout the entire document, don't select anything.

2. From the Edit menu, choose Replace. The Replace dialog box opens, offering you areas for entering what you want to find and what you want to replace (see Figure 4.11).

3. To find text or replace with text, type the text in the appropriate box. (To find out about finding or replacing based on things you can't type, see step 2 in the "Finding Text" section earlier in this chapter.) To access a recent find or replace string, pop up the menu at the far right of the Find What or Replace With text area (click the little triangle).

4. To use the Special and Format button menus to set up special characters or formatting, first place the insertion point in the Find What or Replace With box and then choose an option from the button menu. To clear formatting from an area, click in the text box for that area and click the No Formatting button.

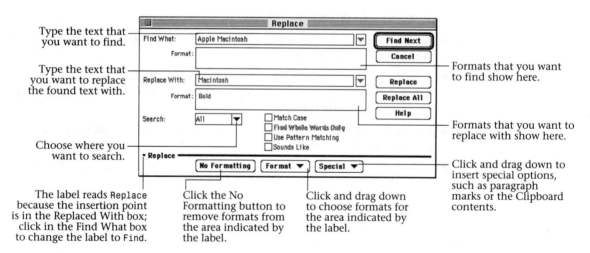

The label reads Replace because the insertion point is in the Replaced With box; click in the Find What box to change the label to Find.

Click the No Formatting button to remove formats from the area indicated by the label.

Click and drag down to choose formats for the area indicated by the label.

Figure 4.11   Set up the Replace dialog box to search for one thing and replace it with another.

5. Choose a search direction from the Search menu. Choose All to search the entire document, including headers and footers. If you choose Up or Down, the search moves forward or back from the insertion point, but it does not look in headers or footers.

6. Set the check boxes to match what you want to do:

  ◆ With Match Case on, Word finds and replaces based on the exact capitalization in the Find What and Replace With boxes. If you turn off Match Case, Word finds text that matches the text in the Find What box, regardless of capitalization, and Word replaces it so that the text retains its original capitalization.

  ◆ Turn on Find Whole Words Only to prevent Word from finding words that contain the search string.

  ◆ Turn on Use Pattern Matching to replace based on a pattern. Pattern Matching is beyond the scope of this book.

  ◆ Turn on Sounds Like to make Word try to find words that sound like the search string.

7. To approve each replacement, click the Find Next button. Word finds the first instance of the text and formatting specified in the Find What area. You can respond in three ways:

  ◆ To replace the found instance, click the Replace button.

  ◆ If you don't want to replace the found instance, but you do want to move on to the next instance, click the Find Next button.

  ◆ To replace the found instance and all other instances in the document, click the Replace All button.

8. If you want each replacement made automatically, click the Replace All button.

Correcting Your Mistakes

While you type, a feature called AutoCorrect waits for you to make mistakes. If you make a mistake that AutoCorrect knows about, AutoCorrect automatically fixes it. For example, if you start a new sentence with two capital letters instead of one, AutoCorrect makes the second letter lowercase. As another example, if you type *recieve*, Word substitutes the correctly spelled *receive*. When you type a word that has a mistake, AutoCorrect corrects it after you finish typing the complete word and any punctuation (or a Return or Tab).

To find out exactly which mistakes AutoCorrect corrects and to customize AutoCorrect, go to the Tools menu and choose AutoCorrect. The AutoCorrect dialog box appears (see Figure 4.12).

! *Caution:* Word stores AutoCorrect entries in the Normal template. Be sure to back up the template if you spend a lot of time customizing AutoCorrect.

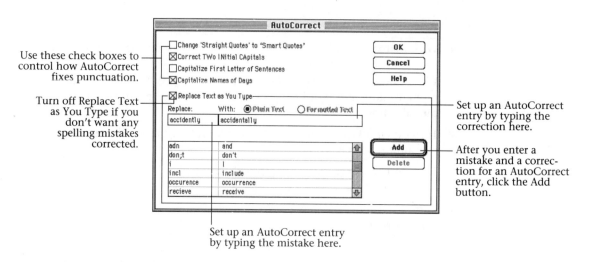

Use these check boxes to control how AutoCorrect fixes punctuation.

Turn off Replace Text as You Type if you don't want any spelling mistakes corrected.

Set up an AutoCorrect entry by typing the correction here.

After you enter a mistake and a correction for an AutoCorrect entry, click the Add button.

Set up an AutoCorrect entry by typing the mistake here.

Figure 4.12 AutoCorrect automatically fixes common typing mistakes.

Making an AutoCorrect entry

If you commonly make a particular spelling mistake, use the AutoCorrect dialog box to set up an AutoCorrect entry. Here are the steps:

1. In the Replace text box, type the mistake. The mistake must be 31 characters or less.

2. In the With text box, type the correction, which can be 255 characters or less. If you highlight the correct text before opening the AutoCorrect dialog box, that text automatically appears in the With text box.

3. Click the Add button.

4. Make sure that the Replace Text as You Type check box is on.

5. Click the OK button.

If you want the correction formatted in a particular way, or if you want the correction to be a graphic, follow these steps:

1. In your document, select the correctly formatted text or graphic. The graphic must be in the text layer (see Chapter 8).

2. Open the AutoCorrect dialog box by choosing AutoCorrect from the Tools menu.

3. The selection should appear in the With text box, but don't worry if it doesn't all appear. Select the Formatted Text radio button.

4. Type a "mistake" in the Replace text box.

5. Click the Add button.

You can use AutoCorrect to insert commonly used phrases (such as *I look forward to your reply*). Make the phrase a fix and set up a short "mistake" to go with the phrase. If you set AutoCorrect up in this way, you are using AutoCorrect much like AutoText or its Word 5 equivalent, the Glossary. Table 4.3 later in this chapter compares AutoCorrect to AutoText.

Deleting an AutoCorrect entry

To delete an entry, select it from the list of entries and click the Delete button.

Turning off AutoCorrect

To turn off AutoCorrect, open the AutoCorrect dialog box. The first group of four check boxes controls punctuation; turn off these check boxes to disable them. Turn off the Replace Text as You Type check box to disable AutoCorrect's spelling features. `

Using AutoText

AutoText stores longish chunks of text that you don't want to type repeatedly. For example, if you always begin a business letter with one of three introductory paragraphs and end with one of three possible closing paragraphs, you can make AutoText entries for them all and insert them when needed.

When to use AutoText

If you have a good working knowledge of Word, you may wonder about the point of AutoText because many features store bits of text. Historically speaking, AutoText is the Glossary that's been around since Word 4 or probably even earlier. In earlier versions of Word, the Glossary held dates and times. To insert dates and times now, use the Date and Time command on the Insert menu.

New features—including templates, macros, and AutoCorrect—are squeezing AutoText out, and in many cases, AutoText is not as useful as one of the newer features. Table 4.3 compares the features.

Table 4.3

Comparing Templates, Macros, AutoText, and AutoCorrect

Feature	Pro	Con
Template	Templates store pretyped text and formatting for an entire document. A template works well for a letter you always start and finish in exactly the same way.	If you need to mix and match bits of standardized text, templates aren't flexible enough to save you any time.
AutoText	You can assign pretyped text to a button or menu.	An AutoText entry can be quite long. If you don't assign an entry to a button or menu, it takes extra effort to insert it.
AutoCorrect	AutoCorrect makes it easy to insert pretyped text, making it an especially easy feature for beginners.	AutoCorrect entries are limited to 255 characters. You can't assign an entry to a button or a menu. Because you must memorize the "mistake" that triggers Auto-Correct, it doesn't make sense to use it for entries that you rarely use.
Macro	Macros offer tremendous versatility. A macro can open a template, insert pretyped text of most any length, and can be assigned to a button, menu, or keyboard shortcut.	Macros are not a great feature for beginners due to the complex nature of creating, naming, and storing a macro. Macros may be overkill for the simple action of typing a paragraph or two.

Making an AutoText entry

To make an AutoText entry, follow these steps:

1. Type, format, and highlight whatever it is that you want to put in the entry.

2. Click the Insert AutoText button on the Standard toolbar or choose AutoText from the Edit menu. The AutoText dialog box appears (see Figure 4.13).

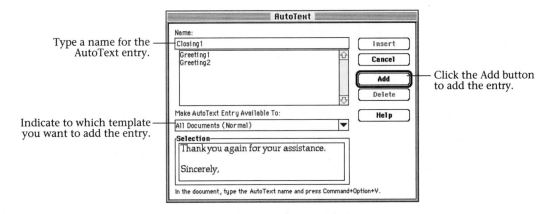

Type a name for the AutoText entry.

Indicate to which template you want to add the entry.

Click the Add button to add the entry.

Figure 4.13 To create an AutoText entry, enter a name and choose a template.

3. In the Name box, type a name for the entry.

4. From the Make AutoText Entry Available To menu, select the template to which you want to add the entry. If you choose All Documents (Normal), the entry adds to the Normal template and you can access it at any time.

5. Click the Add button. Word creates an AutoText entry and closes the AutoText dialog box.

Inserting an AutoText entry

To retrieve an AutoText entry, you can use several different techniques. Pick the technique that makes sense for you.

You have memorized the entry name

Type the name of the entry and then click the AutoText button or press ⌘-Option-V. Word inserts the entry in place of its name.

You can't recall the entry name

If you can't remember the name of the entry, follow these steps to insert it:

1. Place the insertion point in the location where you want to insert the entry.

2. From the Edit menu, choose AutoText. The AutoText dialog box appears onscreen.

3. In the AutoText dialog box, select the name of the entry that you want to insert.

4. Select whether you want the entry inserted with formatting. (In theory, Formatted Text gives you formatting; Plain Text does not.)

5. Click the Insert button. Word inserts the entry.

A better way over the long term

Use the Customize dialog box from the Tools menu to assign entries to keyboard shortcuts, menus, or buttons. In the Customize dialog box, look in the AutoText category (toward the bottom of the list) to find your entries.

You can even create a toolbar consisting completely of AutoText entries. Chapter 9 explains how to create a new toolbar. Figure 4.14 shows a toolbar, configured by using the Customize dialog box to have buttons for a few AutoText entries.

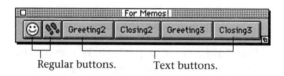

Regular buttons.   Text buttons.

Figure 4.14   If you use AutoText a lot and have screen real estate to spare, you can set up a toolbar of AutoText entries.

You can also make a new menu to hold your entries, and you can assign keyboard shortcuts to entries. A menu and keyboard shortcut combo enables you to use the keyboard shortcuts normally, but if you forget them, you can use the menu as a reminder. Find out more about setting up menus in Chapter 9.

Automatically Updating Dates

To insert the date and have the date constantly update as the days roll by, try these steps:

1. Go to the Insert menu and choose Date and Time. Accordingly, the Date and Time dialog box opens (see Figure 4.15).

2. Select a date style.

3. Turn on the Insert as Field check box.

4. Click the OK button.

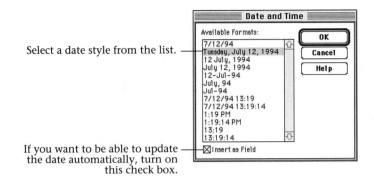

Select a date style from the list.

If you want to be able to update the date automatically, turn on this check box.

Figure 4.15 You can insert dates as updating fields or as static text.

The date inserts as a field, so that after you insert the date, it may appear as the correct date, or it may appear looking something like {TIME \@"MMMM d,yyyy"}, which means that you have field codes showing. Whenever you update the field, the date automatically adjusts to the current date. To toggle a field between its code and result, Control-click the field and choose Toggle Field Codes from the resulting shortcut menu.

Making Word Type Information About Your Document

Using a few of the fields that come with Word, you can make Word type information about a document, including the document title, size, number of characters, and more. Here are the steps:

1. Position the insertion point where you want the information to end up. To position the insertion point in the header or footer, Choose Header and Footer from the View menu. If necessary, click the Switch Between Header and Footer button to see the footer.

2. Go to the Insert menu and choose Field. The Field dialog box appears, as shown in Figure 4.16.

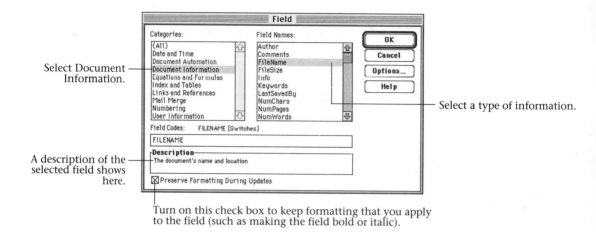

Select Document Information.

Select a type of information.

A description of the selected field shows here.

Turn on this check box to keep formatting that you apply to the field (such as making the field bold or italic).

Figure 4.16   Use the Document Information category to insert updating information about a document.

3. From the Categories list at the left, select Document Information. Word responds by showing Document Information fields in the Field Names list to the right.

4. Select a type of information from the Field Names list and click the OK button.

The information inserts as a field, so if you see something like {FILENAME /* MERGEFORMAT}, you have the field code showing.

Finding Information About a Document

To find out the length of text in terms of characters, words, lines, and so on, follow these steps:

1. Highlight the part of a document that you want to know about, or to find out about the entire document, don't highlight anything.

2. From the Tools menu, choose Word Count.

The Word Count dialog box appears and displays various counts. If you have a long document, the counts look fuzzy until Word finishes counting everything; the progress shows in the status bar. Word Count never counts text in a header or footer.

To find out all sorts of specialized information about a document, use the Customize dialog box from the Tools menu to get at a command called Document Statistics. You can find Document Statistics in the File category, and you can add it to a button, menu, or keyboard shortcut. If you issue the Document Statistics command, you discover the amount of time you've spent editing the document, the date you last printed, and so on.

The Thesaurus

Use the Thesaurus as an online reference for identifying synonyms (words with similar meanings) and antonyms (words with opposite or somewhat opposite meanings).

To open the Thesaurus, go to the Tools menu and choose Thesaurus. The Thesaurus dialog box appears (see Figure 4.17). If you selected text before opening the dialog box, the text appears at the upper right.

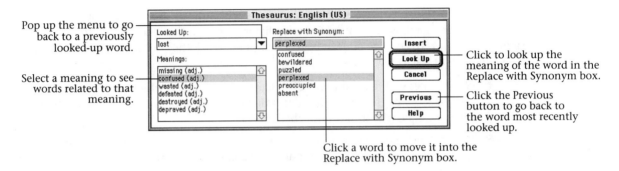

Pop up the menu to go back to a previously looked-up word.

Select a meaning to see words related to that meaning.

Click to look up the meaning of the word in the Replace with Synonym box.

Click the Previous button to go back to the word most recently looked up.

Click a word to move it into the Replace with Synonym box.

Figure 4.17 Use the Thesaurus to find synonyms and antonyms.

Click the Look Up button to find out more about the word in the box at the upper right. After you click the Look Up button, the Thesaurus moves the word into the Looked Up menu and shows possible meanings for the word. If you select a meaning, the Thesaurus shows words related to that meaning. The Thesaurus may also offer Antonyms or Related Words; if it does, click those options to see their entries.

Double-click a word in the right-hand list to put it in the box at the upper right and then look up meanings for it.

Click the Previous button to go back to the preceding word that you looked up, and use the Looked Up menu to go back to any word you already looked up.

Proofing with the Spelling and Grammar Checkers

Use the Spelling and Grammar Checkers to double-check the spelling and grammar in your document. This section explains how to use the Spelling Checker but touches only lightly on the Grammar Checker. The Grammar Checker consumes a tremendous amount of disk space (1.5 megabytes) and on the whole is far less useful than spending even a small amount of time with a book about grammar, such as Strunk and White's *The Elements of Style*.

Setting up the Spelling Checker

To get the most out of the Spelling Checker, take a few minutes to set it up. Typically, the Spelling Checker compares all the words in the document to words listed in its main dictionary. If a word in the document doesn't match a word in the main dictionary, the checker alerts you to the problem.

Custom dictionaries

A custom dictionary supplements the main dictionary with unusual words that you use frequently. Use the Spelling card in the Options dialog box from the Tools menus to set up custom dictionaries. To activate or deactivate a dictionary, click the check box to its left. You can do any or all of the following:

◆ Word comes with a dictionary called Custom Dictionary, which may show in the list of custom dictionaries. To use this dictionary to store uncommon words that you use frequently, turn on the check box to its left.

◆ To start a new custom dictionary, click the New button. The Save dialog box appears. In the Save dialog box, name the dictionary, select a location, and click the Save button.

◆ To make Word aware of a custom dictionary that doesn't show in the list (such as a custom dictionary from Word 5 or a user dictionary from Word 4), click the Add button to display the Open dialog box. Locate the dictionary and click the Open button.

◆ To take a dictionary off the list (so that Word is no longer aware of it), highlight the dictionary and click the Remove button.

Word lists a dictionary with its path (how to get to it from the main level of your hard drive). The length of the path may make it impossible to see a dictionary's name. To see the name, try highlighting a dictionary and then clicking the Edit button. After clicking the Edit button, close the Options dialog box and then look at the name of the active window. The name of the window is the name of the dictionary. Close the active window.

Miscellaneous preferences

The Spelling card in the Options dialog box also offers a few check boxes that customize how the Spelling Checker operates.

In the Suggest area, you may turn on Always Suggest to make Word offer alternatives to misspelled words. Turn on From Main Dictionary Only if you want those alternatives to come only from the main dictionary. If you don't want the Spelling Checker to flag words in uppercase or words that include numbers, turn on the appropriate check box in the Ignore area.

Checking a second language

If you work with more than one language, consider purchasing a foreign language dictionary that plugs into Word (of course, this works only for a language that has a Word 6 dictionary). Unfortunately, foreign language dictionaries from earlier versions of Word do not work with Word 6. To purchase a dictionary that contains words from a different language or from a special profession, contact Alki Software at (206) 286-2600. Alki is the official distributor of foreign language dictionaries.

If you have a foreign language dictionary, you can apply the corresponding language format to text that you want to proof with that dictionary. To format text in a particular language, select the text and choose Language from the Tools menu. In the Language dialog box, highlight a different language and click the OK button (see Figure 4.18).

In the Options dialog box, you can assign a second language to a custom dictionary. Use the Language menu at the bottom of the Spelling card.

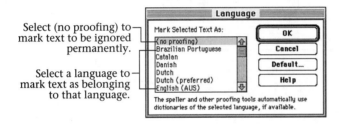

Figure 4.18   Use the Language dialog box to set how the Spelling Checker will check text.

Setting up text to be ignored permanently

If you type text in a document and want the Spelling Checker always to ignore it, no matter what, apply the (no proofing) format. To apply the format, select the text, go to the Tools menu, and choose Language. In the Language dialog box, scroll to the top and select (no proofing). Finally, click the OK button (see Figure 4.18).

If you apply (no proofing) frequently, consider setting it up as a character style (see Chapter 5).

Using the Spelling Checker

To use the Spelling Checker, try these steps:

1. To check a portion of a document, highlight that portion. Otherwise, don't highlight anything.

2. Click the Spelling button on the Standard toolbar or choose Spelling from the Tools menu. The spelling check begins, and when the checker finds an error, the Spelling dialog box appears onscreen. At the upper left of the dialog box, you should see an error message, which is usually Not in Dictionary. The word that brought on the error shows next to the error message (see Figure 4.19).

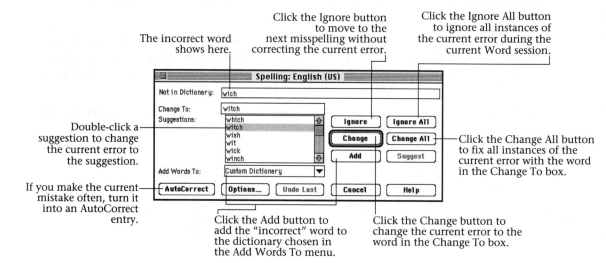

Figure 4.19   The Spelling dialog box offers assistance with spelling errors.

3. You can react to the error with a variety of responses:

   ◆ To find the next error without changing anything, click the Ignore button.

   ◆ To skip this error and any others just like it, click the Ignore All button. Ignore All continues to ignore the error until you quit Word. If you quit and then launch Word again, Word forgets about ignoring the error.

   ◆ To add the "error" to a custom dictionary, choose the dictionary from the Add Words To menu and then click the Add button.

   ◆ To fix the error yourself, type a correction in the Change To box and click the Change button. You can also click the Change All button to fix this and all instances of the error at once.

   ◆ If you commonly make the error, turn it into an AutoCorrect entry. First, type or select the correction. Second, click the AutoCorrect button. (Flip back several pages to find out more about AutoCorrect.)

   ◆ To fix the error with one of the listed suggestions, double-click the suggestion. (If Word doesn't automatically list suggestions, click the Suggest button.)

4. When you finish with the Spelling Checker, exit the dialog box by clicking the Cancel button or the close box. You can also press ⌘-W or ⌘-Period.

Setting up the Grammar Checker

Before running the Grammar Checker, it makes sense to personalize the Grammar Checker so that it checks for problems that you want to fix. Use the Grammar card in the Options dialog box from the Tools menu to personalize the Grammar Checker.

Using the Grammar Checker

The controls in the Grammar dialog box work much like those in the Spelling dialog box (albeit more slowly). Here are the steps for using the Grammar Checker:

1. To check only a portion of a document, select that portion; to check an entire document, don't select anything.

2. From the Tools menu, choose Grammar. The Grammar dialog box appears onscreen (see Figure 4.20).

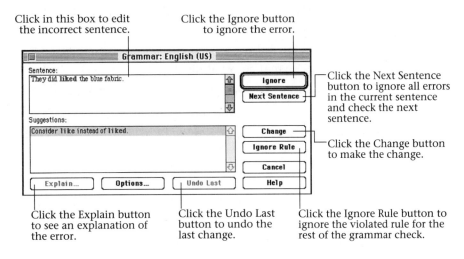

Click in this box to edit the incorrect sentence.

Click the Ignore button to ignore the error.

Click the Next Sentence button to ignore all errors in the current sentence and check the next sentence.

Click the Change button to make the change.

Click the Explain button to see an explanation of the error.

Click the Undo Last button to undo the last change.

Click the Ignore Rule button to ignore the violated rule for the rest of the grammar check.

Figure 4.20   Use the Grammar dialog box to find out what Word thinks of your grammar.

3. The Grammar Checker works through the document and identifies possible problems. If the Grammar Checker finds a problem, you can respond in one of the following ways:

103

◆ To ignore the problem but look for other problems in the same sentence, click the Ignore button.

◆ To ignore the problem and skip to the next sentence, click the Next Sentence button.

◆ To fix the problem, edit the text in the Sentence area and then click the Change button. The insertion point must be in the Sentence area when you click the button.

Caution: You cannot type a curly quote in the Sentence area.

◆ If you like one of the suggested solutions, select the suggestion and then click the Change button to fix the problem. (If the Change button is dim, you must make the change yourself in the Sentence area.)

◆ If Word uses a grammatical rule that you don't want to follow, click Ignore Rule. Word ignores the rule for the rest of the grammar checking session.

◆ If the Explain button is available, click it to see an explanation of the problem.

◆ To undo the last change, click Undo Last.

◆ If you get tired of using the Grammar Checker, click the Close button.

4. When Word finishes proofing the document, a Readability Statistics window appears. To find out what the statistics mean, click the Help button.

5. To complete the grammar check, click the OK button.

Now that you know something about using Word for writing and editing, you are ready for the next chapter, which explains how to set up documents.

Chapter 5

Setting Up a Document

In this chapter, I write about working behind the scenes in a document to set up everything correctly. Don't try to learn all this stuff at once—you'll overload your brain and find yourself wallowing in self-doubt. Refer to this information when you need help or when you want to expand your Word know-how. If you do learn everything here, you can check the following items off your list:

◆ Setting margins

◆ Figuring out orientation

◆ Changing the vertical alignment

◆ Creating headers and footers

◆ Making page numbers

◆ Saving time with styles

◆ Making your life easier with Outline View

◆ Working with super-long documents in Master Document View

◆ Setting up chapter numbering

Setting Up a Page

The information here explains how to set up the look of document pages in a general way. You won't find much about text, fonts, or paragraphs. Instead, you'll find help with setting up margins, headers, page numbers, and so on —formats that affect the overall look of a page.

If you plan to make a simple document (where each page is set up the same way as all the other pages), just skip ahead and read about whatever it is that you want to do.

On the other hand, if you think you'll want to set up different pages in different ways, be aware that most of these formats apply by section. You may recall reading about sections at the end of Chapter 3, but to be sure that you know enough about sections to understand what's going on, here is a quick review:

◆ To insert a section break, press ⌘-Enter or choose Break from the Insert menu. A section break separates parts of a document so that you can apply different formats (such as margins) to the different sections.

◆ To apply a format to only one section, click in that section and then apply the format.

◆ To apply a format to more than one section, highlight at least part of each section and then apply the format (to highlight an entire document, press ⌘-A).

◆ If you use section formatting frequently, you'll become accustomed to the Apply To pop-up menus in many of the dialog boxes. You can also use the Apply To menus to specify where the formatting applies. Depending on what you choose in an Apply To menu, Word may even insert section breaks for you.

◆ Toward the left side of the status bar, Word gives information about what section the insertion point is in.

Margins

A margin makes more sense when you print a document than when you look at it onscreen. On the printed page, the margin is the distance between the text and the edge of the page. You can set the margin numerically or visually, whichever way works best for you.

To set different side margins for a small portion of text, consider changing the indents for that text instead of changing the margin. To find out more, see Chapter 6.

Setting margins numerically

To enter numbers for the height and width of your margins, follow these steps:

1. Click in the section or select the sections that you want to format.

2. From the File menu, choose Document Layout and make sure that the Margins card shows at the front (see Figure 5.1). To switch quickly into the Document Layout dialog box, double-click the gray part of a ruler.

Under most circumstances, set the top and bottom margins for At Least.

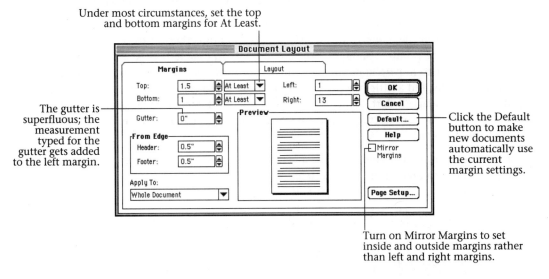

The gutter is superfluous; the measurement typed for the gutter gets added to the left margin.

Click the Default button to make new documents automatically use the current margin settings.

Turn on Mirror Margins to set inside and outside margins rather than left and right margins.

Figure 5.1   You can set margins numerically in the Margins card of the Document Layout dialog box.

3. Enter the margin measurements in the appropriate boxes. As you think about what measurements to enter, consider the following:

   ◆ If you plan to print the document double-sided and then bind it, turn on Mirror Margins and give the inside margin extra room for binding. The inside margin falls on the left of odd-numbered pages and on the right of even-numbered pages.

   ◆ If you plan to print single-sided and to bind the document along the left edge of each page, increase the left margin to accommodate the binding. Or set a gutter measurement; Word adds the gutter to the left margin.

4. Make sure that the Apply To menu setting matches where you want to apply the margins.

5. After you finish setting up the margins, click the OK button.

Setting margins visually

To see the text move as you set the margins, you must be in Print Preview from the File menu or Page Layout View from the View menu with the rulers showing. To show the rulers, choose Ruler from the View menu or click the View Ruler button on the Print Preview toolbar.

Each ruler consists of a gray region representing the margin and a white region representing the area between the margins. If you place the pointer directly over the boundary between the two regions, the pointer changes shape and looks like a double-headed arrow (see Figure 5.2). You may have to move the pointer carefully within the boundary area to make it change shape properly, but a little practice goes a long way. With the double-headed arrow pointer, drag the boundary. A dotted line extends from the pointer to help you see what you are doing. To better see the various dimensions involved in setting the margixn, press Option while you click the boundary.

Earlier versions of Word did not have a vertical ruler and, as a result, you could not change the top and bottom margins by using a ruler.

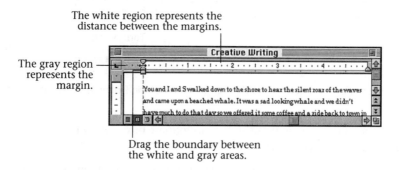

Figure 5.2 Drag the edge of the gray area to change the margins.

Orientation

Orientation controls how text shows up on the printout. Most of the time, people print in the Portrait orientation, with the text flowing across the narrow portion of the paper. Occasionally, it make sense to rotate the text 90 degrees and print it in Landscape orientation across the wide portion of the paper.

If you have trouble keeping track of Portrait and Landscape orientations, think about art. Typically, portraits of people are tall and skinny because people tend to be much taller than they are wide; therefore, Portrait orientation produces a page that is tall and skinny. On the other hand, landscape paintings tend to be short and wide in order to fit in lots of scenery; therefore, Landscape orientation produces a page that is short and wide to make more room for extra long lines of type.

To change the orientation, follow these steps:

1. Click in the section or select the sections that you want to change. (In previous versions of Word, you could not change the orientation for only a portion of the document.)

2. From the File menu, choose Page Setup to bring up the Page Setup dialog box for your printer (each printer has a slightly different Page Setup dialog box). The Page Setup dialog box appears onscreen (see Figure 5.3).

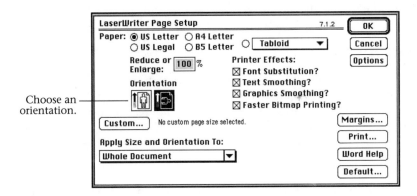

Figure 5.3   Set up the orientation in the Page Setup dialog box.

3. In the Page Setup dialog box, select an orientation.

4. Click the OK button.

Caution: If you have problems with Landscape pages switching to Portrait when printed, turn on the Each Orientation in the Document check box in the Print dialog box.

Vertical alignment

By default, text aligns to the top of a page, but you can also center text on a page or justify it. If you center text, the spaces between the lines and paragraphs don't change, but the text jumps to the center of the page. When you justify text, you increase the space between paragraphs so that the paragraphs spread apart and take up a full page.

To change the vertical alignment, follow these steps:

1. Click in a section or select the sections in which you want to apply the alignment.

2. Go to the File menu and choose Document Layout. When the Document Layout dialog box appears, select the Layout card.

3. In the Layout card, choose an alignment from the Vertical Alignment menu.

4. Click the OK button.

To see a justified or bottom alignment, switch to Page Layout View from the View menu or Print Preview from the File menu.

Headers and footers

Headers sit in the top margin and hold repeating text; *footers* sit in the bottom margin and hold repeating text. Each header and footer throughout a document can be exactly the same, or you can divide the document into sections and have a different header and footer in each section. If you want to delve a little deeper, you can vary which header or footer prints on each page to an even greater degree.

Here are the basic steps for making a header or footer:

1. To add the header or footer to a particular section only, click in that section. To add the header or footer to more than one section, highlight the sections where you want to add the header or footer. To highlight the entire document, press ⌘-A.

2. From the View menu, choose Header and Footer. In response, the Header and Footer toolbar appears, the document text grays out, and a header box appears at the top of the page (see Figure 5.4). If the document has more than one section or type of header, Word labels the header. To view headers and footers quickly while you are in Page Layout View, double-click in the gray area that acts as a page break.

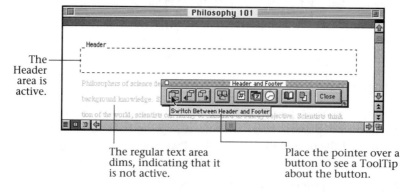

The Header area is active.

The regular text area dims, indicating that it is not active.

Place the pointer over a button to see a ToolTip about the button.

Figure 5.4   A number of changes occur after you choose Header and Footer from the View menu.

3. If you want to see the footer, switch to the footer by clicking the Switch Between Header and Footer button. You can switch back to the header by clicking the button again.

4. If you want a page number, date, or time in the header or footer, click the appropriate button on the Header and Footer toolbar. Note that the page number, date, and time are fields. If you don't want a date or time to update, you can lock it, thus preventing it from even thinking of updating. To lock a field, select it and press ⌘-3. To unlock a field, select it and press ⌘-4.

5. Type the text that you want in the header or footer. To center- or right-align text, use the default tab stops at 3 and 6 inches. If you press Tab once, the insertion point aligns under the 3, and text that you type centers under the 3. If you press Tab again, the insertion point moves under the 6, and text that you type right-aligns from the 6 (see Figure 5.5).

6. After you finish, click the Close button on the Header and Footer toolbar to return to the main part of the document.

The center tab stop centers text.

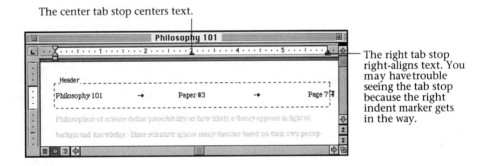

The right tab stop right-aligns text. You may have trouble seeing the tab stop because the right indent marker gets in the way.

Figure 5.5   Use the header's default tab stops to center- and right-align text.

Normally, headers and footers are only a few lines long, and they sit happily in the margins with no special problems. If you type more than a few lines in a header or footer, however, it will begin to impinge on your document text. You can handle this situation in several ways:

◆ To move document text down and make room for a header (or up to make room for a footer), go to the File menu, choose Document Layout, and select the Margins card. Using the Margins card, choose At Least for the margin in question. (At Least is the default.)

◆ To make document text overlap the header or footer text, use the Margins card to set the relevant margin to Exactly. However, if you set the top margin to Exactly, you can place a graphic or box in the header so that the graphic overlaps the text or the box borders each page (see Chapter 8).

◆ Consider moving the header or footer closer to the edge of the page, as explained in the next set of steps.

Changing the location of a header or footer

To move a header or footer up or down, try these steps:

1. Click in the section holding the header or footer that you want to move or—if the header or footer spans more than one section—highlight at least a portion of each section.

2. Go to the File menu, choose Document Layout, and bring up the Margins card.

3. In the From Edge area, change the distance of the header from the top of the page or the footer from the bottom of the page.

4. Click the OK button.

> **Caution:** Many printers cannot print closer to the edge of a page than about .5 inches. When printing a legal-size document, many printers can't get closer than about .9 inches. Don't put your headers and footers so close to the edge that they can't print! See Chapter 10 for more information.

To move text in the header or footer left or right, indent the text. You can find out about indents in Chapter 6.

Different header and footer on the first page

If you don't want the same header or footer on the first page of a document (or section), turn on a first-page header and footer. A common use of a first-page header is to keep it blank so that the first page appears to have no header. Here are the steps:

1. If your document has more than one section, click in the section where you want a first-page header and footer.

2. Go to the File menu, choose Document Layout, and select the Layout card.

3. In the Layout card, turn on the Different First Page check box and click the OK button.

To put text into the first-page header or footer (or if you just want to look at it), choose Header and Footer from the View menu. This time, the header shows up with a First Page Header label (see Figure 5.6). If you don't see the label you expected, click the Show Previous or Show Next button on the Header and Footer toolbar.

If you have a first-page header, Word labels the header as a First Page Header.

If you have more than one section, Word labels the header to which section the header applies.

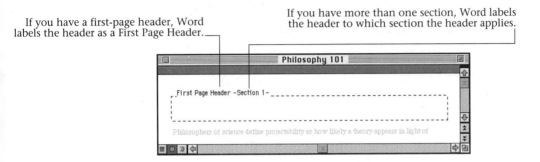

Figure 5.6 Word labels first-page headers.

Page numbers

If you read earlier parts of this chapter, it should come as no surprise that page numbers go by section, so if you insert a section break or two, you can switch the numbers on and off by section or change what they look like by section. For example, a popular page numbering approach is to use lowercase Roman numerals for the introductory section of a document and then switch to regular Arabic numerals for the main part of the document. As long as you remember to slap in a section break after the introduction, you shouldn't have any problem switching the numbering.

Inserting page numbers

To insert page numbers, follow these steps:

1. If the document has more than one section, click in the section where you want the page numbers to go. To put page numbers in more than one section, highlight at least a portion of each section where you want the numbers.

2. From the Insert menu, choose Page Numbers. The Page Numbers dialog box appears, and the Preview area shows where Word plans to insert the page numbers (see Figure 5.7).

3. Select a position. Notice that Word puts the number in the header or footer.

4. Choose an alignment.

Choose a page number position.

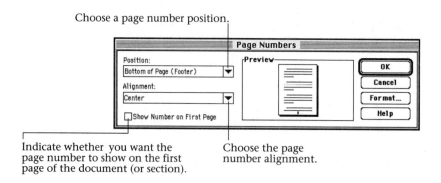

Indicate whether you want the
page number to show on the first
page of the document (or section).

Choose the page
number alignment.

Figure 5.7   The Page Numbers dialog box assists you in inserting page numbers.

5. To print a page number on the first page of the document (or section) turn on
   Show Number on First Page.

6. Click the OK button.

Word inserts a page number in the header or footer. The page number is a field, called Page. If the number looks like {PAGE}, you have field codes showing (see Figure 5.8). Word frames the Page field so that you can drag the frame about if you want to move it slightly, although to change the alignment, it's better to go back into the Page Numbers dialog box.

To change the character formatting of a page number inserted through the Page Numbers dialog box, change the Page Number style. (See "How Styles Save Time and Hassle" later in this chapter.)

The page number's field is framed. With field codes
showing, the page number's field does not look like a
number.

Figure 5.8   A page number inserted through the Page Numbers dialog box is a framed field, and with field codes showing, it looks like this.

Deleting a page number

To delete a page number, first open the header or footer by choosing Header and Footer from the View menu. If the page number is in the footer, click the Switch Between Header and Footer button at the left side of the Header and Footer toolbar. To delete the number, select it and press Delete. If the page number is framed, click the framed edge to select the frame and then press Delete.

You may have to delete the number from more than one header or footer if you set up different headers and footers for different sections or if you have a first page header or footer. Use the Show Next and Show Previous buttons on the Header and Footer toolbar to move around.

Changing the starting page number

The starting page number is the actual number that appears on the first page of a document or section. Most of the time, you want the starting number to be 1, but you can change it to a different number. Here are the steps:

1. If you are changing the number for a section, click in that section. If you are changing the number for multiple sections, select at least a portion of each section.

2. Go to the Insert menu and choose Page Numbers. The Page Numbers dialog box appears.

3. Click the Format button. The Page Number Format dialog box is displayed (see Figure 5.9).

4. Type the starting page number in the Start At text box and click the OK button. Read step 5 before clicking anything else.

5. Be sure to click the Close button to close the Page Numbers dialog box.

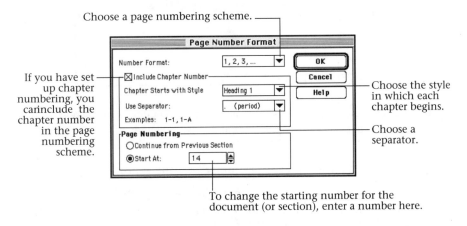

Figure 5.9   Use the Page Number Format dialog box to change the starting page number and the type of page number.

Changing the numbering scheme

The numbering scheme goes by section, and the steps for changing the scheme are much like the steps for changing the starting number. In the Page Number Format dialog box, select a format from the Number Format menu.

To include the chapter number in the page numbering scheme, you must set up chapter numbers, as explained toward the end of this chapter. With the chapter numbers set up, you can turn on the Include Chapter Number check box. You must choose the heading style that corresponds to your chapter titles, and you can also choose a separator. In Figure 5.9, the pages are set up to number as 1.1, 1.2, 1.3, and so on.

If you enter an Arabic numeral in the Start At box and then change the Number Format to Roman numerals, Word changes the Arabic numeral to its Roman numeral equivalent.

When you finish setting up the numbering scheme, click the OK button. Click the Close button to exit the Page Numbers dialog box.

Eliminating the page number from the first page

The technique for removing the page number from the first page of a document (or section) depends on how you originally inserted the page number. To find out how you inserted the number, highlight it in the header or footer. If a frame appears (a thick-edged box with hatch-marks on the edge), then you put the page number in through the Page Numbers dialog box. If a frame fails to appear, you put the page number in via the Header and Footer toolbar (see Figure 5.10).

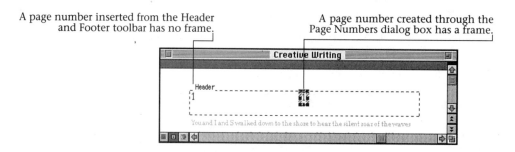

Figure 5.10   Although few people will want to insert two page numbers in one header, this figure shows both types of page numbers in the same header.

After you know how you inserted the page number, try the appropriate option:

◆ If you used the Header and Footer toolbar to insert the page number, set up a first-page header and footer and don't put a page number in the header and footer on the first page. (Refer to the "Different header and footer on the first page" section a few pages back.)

◆ If you used the Page Numbers dialog box to insert the page number, click in the section with the first page that should not have a page number. To eliminate the page number, go to the Insert menu and choose Page Numbers. In the Page Numbers dialog box, turn off Show Number on First Page and click the OK button.

Inserting the total number of pages

To use a numbering scheme where you indicate both the page number and the total number of pages (so that your footer reads, for example, page 22 of 45) use the NumPages field. To insert the field, follow these steps:

1. Click where you want the total number of pages to show. If you inserted the page number by using a button on the Header and Footer toolbar, click to the right of the number. If you used the Page Number dialog box, you can't click to the right of the number. The number consists of a framed field, and you need to look at the field's code. If you can't see the code, Control-click the page number to bring up the shortcut menu and choose Toggle Field Codes. Click directly after the } and inside the frame border, as shown in Figure 5.11.

Click here.

Figure 5.11   Position the insertion point by clicking just after the field but before the frame border.

2. Type a space (with the Spacebar), the word **of**, and then type another space. It may take Word several seconds to respond to your typing.

3. From the Insert menu, choose Field. The Field dialog box appears.

4. Under Categories, select Document Information and then under Field Names, select NumPages.

5. Click the OK button.

6. A NumPages field appears (see Figure 5.12). As needed, highlight any page number fields, Control-click to bring up the shortcut menu, and choose Toggle Field Codes to show the field results.

Figure 5.12   After you insert the NumPages field, the page numbering setup should look like this (turn off field codes to see the result).

How Styles Save Time and Hassle

A style holds a collection of formats that you can apply to text all at once. For example, in a résumé, you can format all your topic headings (such as Education, Experience, Special Skills, and so on) with a style that comes with Word called Heading 1. You can set up Heading 1 to include bold, Times 14-point, and a bottom border (see Figure 5.13).

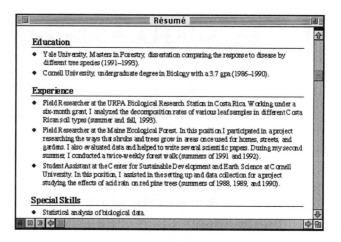

Figure 5.13   Each topic heading is formatted with Heading 1; in this example, Heading 1 includes bold, Times 14-point, and a bottom border.

After setting up the topic headings with Heading 1, you can easily change the formatting of the topic headings by simply changing the style. Changing a style takes much less time than changing each topic heading individually. For example, you can experiment by changing the font or the border (see Figure 5.14).

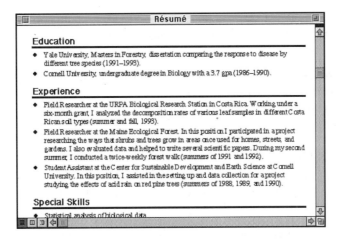

Figure 5.14   To see what the résumé would look like with topic headings formatted with Helvetica 14-point and a thicker border, change the Heading 1 style.

In a longer document, it pays to use the built-in heading styles for topic headings and sub-headings. The heading styles tie into Outline View to make reorganizing the document super-easy (flip ahead a few pages to find out how), and they tie into the Table of Contents command so that you can make a table of contents with almost no effort whatsoever. You can also set up cross-references to topics formatted with heading styles (see Chapter 7).

Another use for a style would be to format text with an invisible style that tells the Spelling and Grammar Checkers to ignore the text permanently. For example, you may want the Checkers to ignore email addresses (such as tonya@tidbits.com). Because email addresses are often formatted with a special font to make them stand out, the style would include the No Proofing character format and the special font formatting. You may run into a similar situation with regular street addresses.

Styles may be saved in templates, so if you get fairly involved with styles, you can set up different templates with different style sets. In this way, if you set up styles for the perfect cover letter, you can make a cover letter template that contains those styles, and whenever you open a document based on that template, the styles will be instantly available. But wait, there's more! If you then decide to change the cover letter template, you can retroactively change cover letters that you have already made so that they take on the changes in the template.

How Word thinks about styles

Styles come in two basic categories—character and paragraph. As the names suggest, *character styles* can apply to just one character or many characters. *Paragraph styles* can apply to just one paragraph or to gobs and gobs of paragraphs.

As far as Word is concerned, every character always has two styles applied: a paragraph style and a character style. Most of the time, if you don't do anything special, the paragraph style is Normal and the character style is Default Paragraph Font.

If you change formatting directly by clicking a toolbar button (such as Bold) or choosing a format via the Format menu (such as Font or Paragraph), Word considers that formatting direct formatting. Almost always, direct formatting overrides style formatting.

How to tell which style is applied

To find out which paragraph style is applied, click in the paragraph of interest and look in the Style box at the left side of the Formatting toolbar. Paragraph styles appear in bold; character styles in plain text.

To print a list of styles in a document, go to the File menu and choose Print. In the Print dialog box, choose Styles from the Print menu. Finally, click the Print button.

For a spiffy way of finding out more about the formatting, click the Help button on the Standard toolbar and then click a character. A cartoon-style bubble appears that discusses the character's formatting (see Figure 5.15). Press ⌘-Period to stop looking at the bubble.

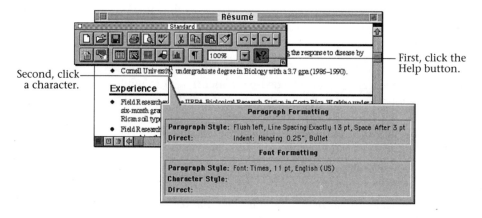

Figure 5.15 The formatting bubble tells all about formatting applied to a character.

For a constant reminder regarding paragraph styles, show the styles onscreen in the left margin. To set this up, use the View card in the Options dialog box to increase the Style Area Width to about one-half inch. Change the width to zero if you don't want to see styles any more.

How Word applies styles for you

If you just sit back and give Word its head, Word does a lot of styling work for you. Word uses built-in styles to format documents as you create them. For example, if you insert a page number, the page number automatically gets the Page Number character style. To see how this works, look at Figure 5.16 and consult Table 5.1.

Built-in styles are based on Normal, so if you modify Normal, you get a cascading effect through your document of similarly modified styles.

Table 5.1
Common Built-In Styles

Style	What it does
Caption	A paragraph style for labels and caption text that you create with the Caption feature.
Default Paragraph Font	By default, applies to characters that have no other character style.
Footer	Formats text typed in the footer (text at the bottom of the page in the special footer area).
Footnote Reference	A character style for footnote reference numbers and marks.
Footnote Text	A character style for footnote text.
Header	Formats text typed in the header (text at the top of the page in the special header area).
Heading 1, Heading 2, ... Heading 9	Applies automatically to levels in Outline View. Useful for formatting topic headings in any document.
Normal	By default, applies to paragraphs that have no other paragraph format.
Page Number	Applies to page numbers that are the result of a Page field, such as page numbers inserted through the Page Numbers dialog box or the Page Numbers button on the Header and Footer toolbar.
TOC 1, TOC 2, ...TOC 9	Paragraph styles for levels in a table of contents.

You can make a copy of the list and then move office supplies that you need from the copy to the spike (see Figure 4.8).

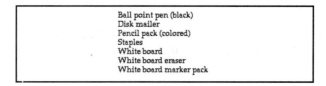

Figure 4.8   ...add the list entries that you want to move to the spike...

After adding all the entries to the spike, you can then insert the spike into a memo where you request those supplies (see Figure 4.9).

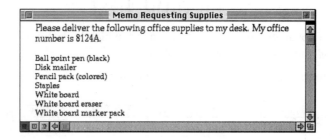

Figure 4.9   ...and then insert the spike in the second document.

Adding to the spike

To add a selection to the spike, press ⌘-F3. If you don't have an F3 key, use the Keyboard card in the Customize dialog box to make a suitable keyboard shortcut. The command to customize is under the All Commands category, and it is called Spike.

Inserting the spike

To insert the contents of the spike, follow these steps:

1. Position the insertion point where you want the contents to end up.

2. Type **spike**.

3. Press ⌘-Option-V.

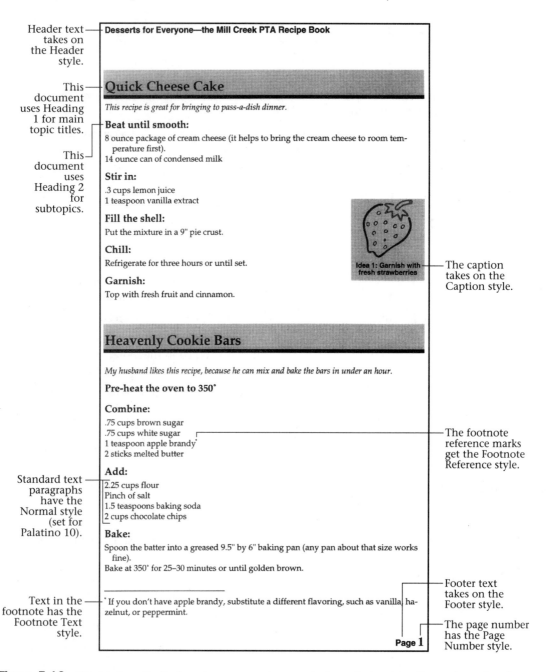

Header text takes on the Header style.

Desserts for Everyone—the Mill Creek PTA Recipe Book

This document uses Heading 1 for main topic titles.

Quick Cheese Cake

This recipe is great for bringing to pass-a-dish dinner.

Beat until smooth:

8 ounce package of cream cheese (it helps to bring the cream cheese to room temperature first).
14 ounce can of condensed milk

This document uses Heading 2 for subtopics.

Stir in:

.3 cups lemon juice
1 teaspoon vanilla extract

Fill the shell:

Put the mixture in a 9" pie crust.

Chill:

Refrigerate for three hours or until set.

Garnish:

Top with fresh fruit and cinnamon.

Idea 1: Garnish with fresh strawberries

The caption takes on the Caption style.

Heavenly Cookie Bars

My husband likes this recipe, because he can mix and bake the bars in under an hour.

Pre-heat the oven to 350°

Combine:

.75 cups brown sugar
.75 cups white sugar
1 teaspoon apple brandy[*]
2 sticks melted butter

The footnote reference marks get the Footnote Reference style.

Add:

Standard text paragraphs have the Normal style (set for Palatino 10).

2.25 cups flour
Pinch of salt
1.5 teaspoons baking soda
2 cups chocolate chips

Bake:

Spoon the batter into a greased 9.5" by 6" baking pan (any pan about that size works fine).
Bake at 350° for 25–30 minutes or until golden brown.

Footer text takes on the Footer style.

Text in the footnote has the Footnote Text style.

[*] If you don't have apple brandy, substitute a different flavoring, such as vanilla, hazelnut, or peppermint.

The page number has the Page Number style.

Page 1

Figure 5.16 Word automatically formats common document elements (such as those shown here) with built-in styles. Except for the page number and footnote reference mark, this document has no character styles, so text uses the Default Paragraph Font style.

How to apply styles yourself

To apply a paragraph style, either click in the paragraph or highlight any portion of it. To apply a style to more than one paragraph at once, you must highlight at least a portion of each paragraph. To apply a character style, highlight each character to which you want to apply the style. In either case, after you click or highlight, you must indicate which style you want. Here are a few techniques:

◆ Select the style from the Style menu on the Formatting toolbar. To see additional styles, press Shift while you drop the menu.

◆ Go to the Format menu and choose Style. From the Styles list on the left side of the Style dialog box, select a style and then click the Apply button. (Use the List menu at the lower left to change what styles you can see.)

◆ Use the Customize dialog box from the Tools menu to assign a style to a keyboard shortcut, menu item, or button. (In the Categories list, scroll down to find Styles.)

◆ You can automatically apply built-in heading styles by setting up your document in Outline View (flip ahead a few pages to find out how).

Caution: Character and paragraph styles can have odd interactions when applied to the same text. The problem occurs if both styles include a character format that toggles, such as bold. For example, if the character style calls for bold, but the paragraph style does not, you get bold. But if the character style and the paragraph style both call for bold, the bold toggles off. In the case of nontoggling formats, such as a font or color, the character style overrides the paragraph style.

How to modify styles

You can change a paragraph style quickly, or you can go through an involved routine that involves tunneling through several dialog boxes. The quick method lets you change a style only for the current document; the involved method lets you change the style for the current document and for the document's template. The involved method also lets you see exactly what you are doing and exert more control over the style.

The quick way to modify a style

To change a style quickly, follow these steps:

1. To change a paragraph style, highlight a paragraph that has the style you want to change; to change a character style, highlight just one character that has that style.

The style that you want to change should show in the Style menu on the Formatting toolbar.

2. Change the formats of the highlighted text so that they match how you want the style to be set up.

3. Click once on the Style menu. The box highlights.

4. Press Return. The Reapply Style dialog box appears (see Figure 5.17).

5. Turn on the Redefine the Style Using the Selection as an Example radio button and click the OK button.

The first option changes the style.

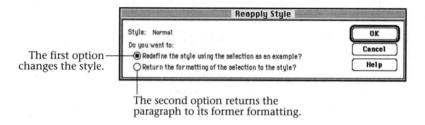

The second option returns the paragraph to its former formatting.

Figure 5.17   Select the first option to change the style to match the text selected in the document.

The slow way to modify a style

The slow method of changing the formats in a style involves the Style dialog box. Here are the steps to try:

1. From the Format menu, choose Style. The Style dialog box appears.

2. Select the style that you want to change from the list of styles at the left and click the Modify button. The Modify Style dialog box appears (see Figure 5.18).

3. Select a Based On style. The Based On style supplies formats that you don't specify. For example, if you don't specify the font for a character style, the character style uses the font in the style that it is based on.

4. Indicate the style that follows a paragraph in the style undergoing changes. For example, after typing a topic heading in the Heading 1 style, if you press Return to start a new paragraph, you probably want the new paragraph to have the Normal style.

The Style for Following Paragraph formats a new
paragraph in the style undergoing changes.

The style undergoing changes.

The Based On style fills in formats that are not specified for the style undergoing changes.

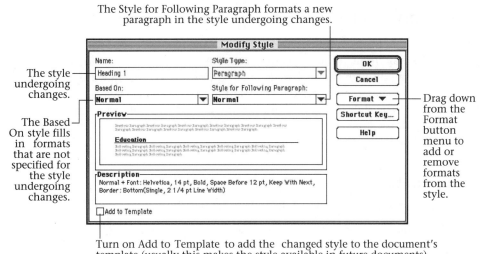

Drag down from the Format button menu to add or remove formats from the style.

Turn on Add to Template to add the changed style to the document's template (usually this makes the style available in future documents).

Figure 5.18   Use the Modify Style dialog box as the control center for changing a style's formats.

5. Drag down the Format button menu to access dialog boxes for additional formats. If you modify a character style, a number of the options in the Format button menu appear grayed out. The grayed out options are for paragraph styles only. If you go into a dialog box and make changes that you want to add to the style, click the OK button to exit that dialog box.

Use Language to format text for a specific language or to format text so that the spelling and grammar checker ignore it (No Proofing sets text up to be ignored).

6. Turn on the Add to Template check box to add style modification to the template on which the document is based. Style changes apply to the active document and to new documents based on the template.

To make an old document retroactively take on the changes, open the old document. With the old document active, go to the File menu and choose Templates. Turn on the check box labeled Automatically Update Document Styles and click the OK button.

7. To exit the Modify Style dialog box and keep the changes that you made to the style, click the OK button.

8. Back in the Style dialog box, click the Close button.

How to create a new style

Making a new style works in much the same way as modifying a style. You can make a new style the quick way through the Style box on the Formatting toolbar, or you can make a new style the slow way through the Style dialog box. Unfortunately, the quick Style box method does not work for character styles, so if you want to make a character style, you must use the Style dialog box. The Style dialog box also lets you add a new style to a template and gives you access to some of the more esoteric styling options (although Microsoft didn't manage to add the styling gel and color treatment options).

The quick way to create a new style

To create a paragraph style quickly, follow these steps:

1. Format some of the text in your document with the formats that you want in the paragraph style.

2. Highlight some of the formatted text or place the insertion point within the formatted text.

3. Click once on the Style menu. The box highlights.

4. Type a name for the new style and press Return.

Word automatically creates a new paragraph style with the name that you typed in the Style box.

The slow way to create a new style

The slow method works almost exactly like the slow method for modifying a style, and you can find detailed steps if you flip back a page or two. In brief, to create a new style, you open the Style dialog box and click the New button. Word responds by opening a New Style dialog box, and your mission is to enter a name for the new style (in the Name text box) and choose the formats for the new style.

How to delete and move styles

To delete a style from a document, go to the Format menu and choose Style. In the Style dialog box, select the style that you want to delete and then click the Delete button. The style disappears from your document, and you never see it again unless the style is also saved in a template.

To delete a style from a template, use the Styles card in the Organizer dialog box. Open the Organizer dialog box by opening the Styles dialog box and then clicking the Organizer button.

After you delete a style from a template, the style no longer shows up in new documents based on the template. To delete a lot of styles, just select a bunch of them at once. To select a noncontiguous list of styles, press ⌘ while you click them.

You can also use the Organizer dialog box to move styles from one document to another document, between a document and a template, or from one template to another template.

Making an Outline

Outlining offers a powerful and helpful way to set up documents. Here are just a few of the tasks it helps with:

 ◆ Organizing topics in a document

 ◆ Creating a formal outline

 ◆ Automatically applying built-in heading styles to the topic headings as you set them up—which helps with a number of tasks, such as generating a table of contents

To switch into Outline View, choose Outline from the View menu, press ⌘-Option-O, or click the Outline button (one of the buttons on the left side of the horizontal scroll bar). Outline View has a special toolbar (see Figure 5.19).

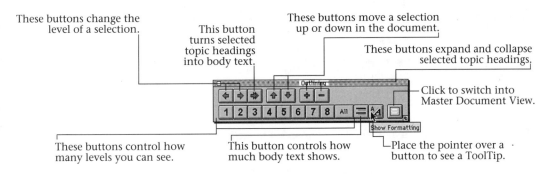

Figure 5.19   The Outlining toolbar appears when you switch into Outline View.

How Outline View corresponds to other views

Outline View revolves around levels of importance, with up to nine levels of importance for people having intricate ideas. Outline View indents levels of lesser importance so that you can easily see the relationships. Figure 5.20 shows a document-in-progress that uses three levels of heads and has body text.

"Quick and Easy Desserts" is a level one topic.

"Quick Cheese Cake" and "Heavenly Cookie Bars" are level two topics.

"Combine" is a level three topic.

Figure 5.20   This outline has three levels.

Topic headings in each level automatically end up in a built-in heading style. Word conveniently has nine built-in heading styles so that each heading style maps to a topic heading level. For example, a level two heading takes on the style called Heading 2. If you don't like the looks of the heading styles, go ahead and change them. Flip back a few pages to find out how.

If you don't work much in Outline View, but you format your headings with the heading styles, when you switch into Outline View, paragraphs formatted with a heading style become topic headings in the outline. For example, if you write a report with eight main topics and assign each topic heading the style called Heading 1, Outline View shows each topic heading as a level one heading. Figure 5.21 shows the text from the preceding figure in Normal View.

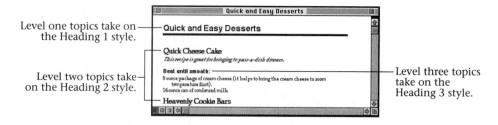

Level one topics take on the Heading 1 style.

Level two topics take on the Heading 2 style.

Level three topics take on the Heading 3 style.

Figure 5.21   The heading levels in the outline correspond to the heading styles in the document.

If you need to make a table of contents based on topics formatted with heading styles, Outline View becomes even more useful. In just a few clicks, you can generate a table of contents based on text formatted in heading styles. Figure 5.22 shows the headings from the preceding figure, fleshed out a bit and transformed into a table of contents. You can also make cross-references to paragraphs formatted with heading styles (see Chapter 7).

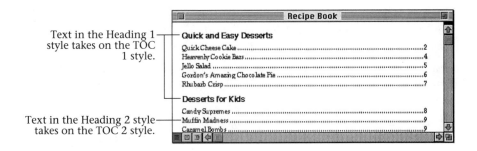

Text in the Heading 1 style takes on the TOC 1 style.

Text in the Heading 2 style takes on the TOC 2 style.

Figure 5.22 The table of contents was made after the document was more complete, and it includes two levels—paragraphs formatted with Heading 1 or Heading 2.

How to set up headings and body text

When you first enter text in Outline View, Word assigns it to a level one heading. If you want the text to be a lower-level heading, click in it and then click the Demote button. To make a heading into body text (text that is not a heading), click the Demote to Body Text button. To promote a heading or body text to a higher level, place the insertion point within its text and click the Promote button.

You can easily identify topic headings because they always have a plus or minus sign at their left. A plus sign means the heading has subheadings or body text that goes with it. A minus sign means the heading has no subheadings or body text. Body text has a box instead of a plus or minus sign.

If a heading has related subheadings or body text, you can select them all by clicking the plus sign. With the entire topic selected, you can promote and demote the heading, and the entire selection changes levels accordingly.

How to move headings around

Editing techniques that work in other views also work in Outline View, so you can use Cut, Copy, and Paste as well as Drag and Drop. To move a heading to a different location, select the heading and drag it to a different spot. To move a heading along with its subheads and body text, select the heading by clicking its plus sign.

How to view the outline selectively

To make text temporarily disappear and then reappear, try these techniques:

◆ To see one less level than you see now, click the Collapse button. Click the Expand button to see one more level than you see now.

129

◆ To see headings of a certain level and higher, click the corresponding Show Heading button (the buttons labeled 1 through 8). After clicking the button, you won't be able to see body text. Click the All button to see all levels and body text.

◆ To shrink a particular heading down so that you can't see its body text or subheadings, double-click its plus sign. Double-click its plus sign again to show the subheadings and body text again.

◆ To show only the first line of all body text paragraphs, click the Show First Line Only button. Click it again to show all body text paragraphs completely.

A gray line indicates that you have hidden some of the text that goes with that topic.

How to control outline formatting

The idea behind Outline View is that you are mostly interested in the text and how topics relate to each other. To help you achieve this state, Outline View ignores paragraph formatting assigned to the text. In addition, you can personally control whether character formatting (such as bold or underline) shows by clicking the Show Formatting button.

Levels in Outline View indent to the default tab stops; if the default tab stop is set for one inch, each level indents one inch farther than the preceding level. To change the default tab stop so that the levels indent to a different amount, follow these steps:

1. Switch to Normal or Page Layout View.

2. Press ⌘-A to select the entire document.

3. Go to the Format menu and choose Tabs. The Tabs dialog box appears onscreen.

4. Enter a measurement in the Default Tab Stops box.

5. Click the OK button.

How to number an outline

To number headings, use the Heading Numbering feature, a complete no-brainer if everything goes right and you don't need anything complicated. Here are the steps:

1. From the Format menu, choose Heading Numbering.

2. Double-click the button (those big boxes are buttons) that shows the numbering that you want. Word numbers your outline and continues numbering it appropriately as you edit the outline.

To change the numbering style, go back to the Heading Numbering dialog box and double-click a different button. You can also click the Remove button in the dialog box to remove all the numbers.

To find out how to include chapter numbers in the numbering scheme, see "Setting Up Chapter Numbering" later in this chapter.

How to print an outline

To print from Outline View, go to the File menu and choose Print, just as you would to print from any other view. When Word prints from Outline View, it matches the onscreen outline in a few important ways:

◆ Word prints with a 6-inch wide expanse for text (regardless of how you set the margins).

◆ Word prints only the headings and body text currently showing so that you can expand the entire outline and print it all, or you can selectively expand and collapse it so that only certain parts print.

◆ The plus, minus, and box signs in the left margin don't print.

Using a Master Document

Use a *master document* to join documents together in order to work with them as a group. Each document that you bring into a master document is called a *subdocument*. Subdocuments exist as independent files on your hard disk, but you edit them within the context of the master document, either in the master document's window or in their own windows.

By combining subdocuments into a master document, you can make a table of contents or index for the entire group. You can create cross-references between different documents in the group, use the Find and Replace commands across all documents at once, and so on. For example, a book author can put each chapter in a separate file and then join the files in a master document.

You can create and edit a master document just as you would any other document, except that if you look at the master document in Master Document View, you can add, organize, and remove subdocuments.

Caution: To avoid problems, never move or rename subdocuments unless you do so through the master document. Remember to make frequent and complete backups because the master document enables you to make sweeping changes very quickly.

Starting a master document

Before you can successfully start a master document, you must be comfortable with Outline View and the built-in heading styles; these directions assume that you understand how to use them.

To start a master document, go to the View menu and choose Master Document. Word switches to Outline View and displays the Master Document toolbar (see Figure 5.23).

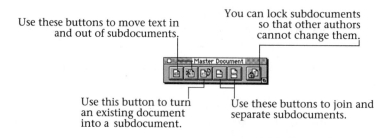

Use these buttons to move text in and out of subdocuments.

You can lock subdocuments so that other authors cannot change them.

Use this button to turn an existing document into a subdocument.

Use these buttons to join and separate subdocuments.

Figure 5.23   Use the Master Document toolbar to set up a master document.

Each subdocument must begin with text formatted in the same heading style. You can create subdocuments from scratch or by adding an existing document (see Figure 5.24):

◆ To convert text typed in the master document into a subdocument, select the text and click the Create Subdocument button. When you save the master document, Word automatically names any new subdocuments and saves them in the location holding the master document.

◆ To turn an existing document into a subdocument, first make sure that the document uses heading styles to organize its topics and that it begins with a paragraph formatted in the appropriate heading style. Second, in the master document, create a blank paragraph and position the insertion point in that paragraph. Click the Insert Subdocument button. Word displays an Open dialog box, where you can locate and open the existing document.

After you set up a master document with subdocuments, you can rearrange the master document in Outline View without paying any attention to which text goes in which subdocument. You can also switch into any of the other views and work with the document just as you would work with any other document. If you want to edit a subdocument in a separate window, double-click the subdocument's icon in Master Document View.

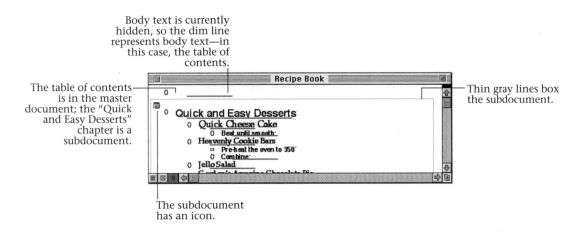

Body text is currently hidden, so the dim line represents body text—in this case, the table of contents.

The table of contents is in the master document; the "Quick and Easy Desserts" chapter is a subdocument.

Thin gray lines box the subdocument.

The subdocument has an icon.

Figure 5.24   To use a master document to manage the book about desserts shown in Figures 5.20–5.22, you can set up different subdocuments for each chapter.

Caution: Whenever you make any sort of change that you want to affect the entire master document and its subdocuments, be sure to work in the master document's window.

Organizing subdocuments

After you have set up a master document, you can rearrange the subdocuments in a variety of ways:

◆ To move a copy of the text of a subdocument into the master document, click the subdocument's icon in Master Document View and then click the Remove Subdocument button.

◆ To free a subdocument from the master document, click the subdocument's icon and press Delete. The document now exists only as an independent file.

◆ To split a subdocument into two subdocuments, select the paragraph that you want the split to be above. Click the Split Subdocument button.

◆ To change the name or disk location of a subdocument, double-click the document's icon to open the document in a separate window. With the separate window active, go to the File menu and choose Save As. In the Save As dialog box, you can save the file with a different name and location.

Caution: When working with master documents, watch out for three limitations: you cannot have more than 80 subdocuments; the size of the master document subdocuments cannot exceed 32 megabytes; and you must have enough extra disk space to back up the master document and subdocuments regularly. You need to be able to revert to any of the last-saved versions, just in case something goes wrong.

Setting Up Chapter Numbering

If you set up chapter numbering, you can include the chapter number in page numbers, list numbering schemes, and caption numbers. Word can also automatically number chapter titles and chapter subheads.

Chapter numbering works with the built-in heading styles, so you must format each chapter title with a specific heading style, such as Heading 1 or Heading 2. If you want to number subheads, you must also format them with appropriate heading styles.

To turn on chapter numbering, follow these steps:

1. From the Format menu, choose Heading Numbering. The Heading Numbering dialog box appears.

2. The Heading Numbering dialog box offers six possible numbering options. For example, the upper-left option numbers each Heading 1 paragraph with an uppercase Roman numeral, each Heading 2 paragraph with an uppercase letter, and each Heading 3 paragraph with an Arabic numeral. In contrast, the lower-left option adds "Chapter One" to the beginning of all Heading 1 paragraphs. If one of the six numbering options looks like what you want, select the option, click the OK button, and skip the rest of these steps. If none of the options looks right, click the Modify button.

3. The Modify Heading Numbering dialog box enables you to customize how Word numbers each level (see Figure 5.25). To customize a level, first display the level in the scrolling list at the right. After displaying the level, consider the following:

   ◆ Use the Number Format options to set exactly how Word numbers a level. Figure 5.25 shows level one entries set up to begin with the text "Chapter One," "Chapter Two," "Chapter Three," and so on.

   ◆ Click the Font button to select character formatting for the number as well as the text before and after.

   ◆ If you don't want a level's numbering to begin at 1, enter a different number in the Start At box. Note that you can set the numbering for each section back to the Start At number by turning on the Restart Numbering at Each New Section check box.

◆ Change the alignment of the number with respect to each other.

◆ To create a hanging indent, turn on the Hanging Indent check box. A *hanging indent* occurs when the first line in a paragraph begins left of the rest of the paragraph.

4. Click the OK button after you finish customizing the heading numbering.

Don't worry if the Preview at the lower right of the dialog box doesn't reflect reality. It's not something that you did—it's a problem with Word.

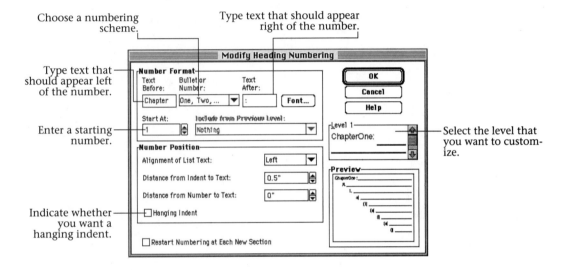

Figure 5.25 Customize chapter numbering by selecting a level and then selecting options for the level.

If you mastered all the information in this chapter, consider yourself an official Word wizard. If you just browsed in this chapter to find useful tips and tricks, consider yourself a normal Word user. Either way, get ready for the next chapter, which discusses how to make some interesting changes in the look of the words in your document.

Chapter 6

Formatting Your
Words and Paragraphs

Word documents are filled with words and paragraphs, and if you don't format them in a creative way, your documents may look dull, drab, and downright unattractive. To liven up a document, consider applying an interesting format or two. The information in this chapter explains how to apply basic character and paragraph formats and how to create special effects. Here's what's covered:

- Tips and tricks for applying basic character formats
- Changing the capitalization
- Setting up hidden text
- Applying character spacing and kerning
- Creating a drop cap
- Making white type on a black background
- Using WordArt to create unusual special effects
- Indenting and aligning text
- Creating a drop cap
- Adjusting the amount of space between paragraphs and lines of text
- Becoming an expert at using tabs
- Adding bullets or numbers to list entries
- Setting up a multilevel list
- Sorting list entries

Character Formatting Basics

Character formats (such as bold and blue) can apply to one character at a time or to many characters at once. Here is a list of tips and techniques to add to your personal formatting repertoire:

◆ To format text, highlight the text and use a toolbar button, keyboard shortcut, or the Font dialog box to apply the format.

◆ If you apply a format with nothing highlighted and then type without moving the insertion point, the text that you type has the applied format.

◆ To copy formatting from one area to another, highlight text that has the formatting. With the text highlighted, click the Format Painter button on the Standard toolbar. Highlight the text to which you want to copy the formatting and watch the formats from the first selection "paint" onto the second selection. (To paint the copied format more than once, double-click the Format Painter button. You can then paint formatting over and over again. Click the button again to turn off format painting.)

◆ Click the Help button on the Standard toolbar and then click a character to see a formatting bubble, which tells exactly what formats are applied. Press ⌘-Period to dismiss the bubble.

◆ If you consistently apply the same formatting, consider setting up a character style (see Chapter 5).

Removing formatting

Remove formatting by turning it off. For example, if you made text bold by clicking the Bold button on the Formatting toolbar, you can remove the formatting by selecting the text and clicking the Bold button again. You can also press ⌘-B to toggle Bold off, or you can go to the Format menu, choose Font, and (on the Font card) select a different font style.

To remove all directly applied character formatting (not applied through a character style), highlight the text and press ⌘-Spacebar to issue the ResetChar command.

The Formatting toolbar

The Formatting toolbar has buttons for bold, italic, and underline. Clicking the buttons turns the formats on and off. The toolbar also has pop-up menus for style, font, and point size. To choose an option from a toolbar menu, click once in the menu box to highlight the box. Then type the option that you want to use and press Return. This technique works especially well for changing the font size, and you can type in sizes that don't show in the menu.

You can make a toolbar button for any character format. Use the Toolbars card in the Customize dialog box from the Tools menu.

The Font pop-up menu has two lists. The top list shows recently used fonts (they are at the top so that you can choose them quickly). The bottom list shows an alphabetical list of all fonts installed (see Figure 6.1).

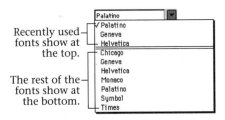

Recently used fonts show at the top.

The rest of the fonts show at the bottom.

Figure 6.1   The Font menu on the Formatting toolbar has two lists.

The Style pop-up menu does not show all available styles. To see them all, press Shift as you pop up the menu. Character styles show in plain text; paragraph styles show in bold.

Keyboard shortcuts

Many formats come with predefined keyboard shortcuts, and Table 6.1 shows the most common shortcuts. You can also use the Keyboard card in the Customize dialog box from the Tools menu to reassign a keyboard shortcut.

Table 6.1

Character Formatting Keyboard Shortcuts

Command	Shortcut
Bold on/off	⌘-B
Hidden Text on/off	⌘-Shift-H
Italic on/off	⌘-I
Point Size down one point	⌘-[
Point Size up one point	⌘-]
Remove all character formats	⌘-Spacebar
Small Caps on/off	⌘-Shift-K

continues

Table 6.1 Continued

Command	Shortcut
Subscript on/off	⌘-=
Superscript on/off	⌘-Shift-=
Switch to Symbol font for the next typed character	⌘-Shift-Q
Underline on/off	⌘-U

Font dialog box

The Font dialog box offers one-stop shopping for character formats, with a complete selection in only two cards. To open the dialog box, go to the Format menu and choose Font.

Each card in the Font dialog box has a Default button, and clicking this button makes the formatting setup on that card a default for the current template. In most cases, the active template is the Normal template. If the active template is the Normal template, the change will automatically show up in new documents.

To make the change affect an old document (as long as the old document is based on the Normal template), open the old document, go to the File menu, and choose Templates. In the Templates dialog box, turn on Automatically Update Document Styles and click the OK button. This technique works for any template—if you change the style in a template called My Monthly Reports, for example, you can open an old report and retroactively import style changes in the template.

So if Normal is the active template and you want to make Times 14-point the default for text that you type in the current document and in new documents, select Times 14-point and then click the Default button (see Figure 6.2). After you click the Default button, Word tells you what the active template is and asks whether you want to save the change.

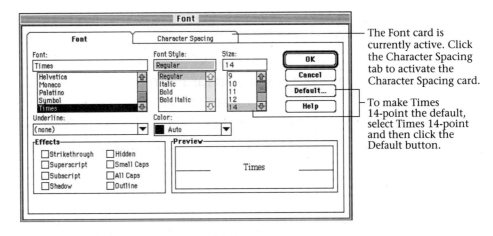

The Font card is currently active. Click the Character Spacing tab to activate the Character Spacing card.

To make Times 14-point the default, select Times 14-point and then click the Default button.

Figure 6.2   You can set up default font formatting in the Font dialog box.

How to Change Case

The Change Case command switches text between upper- and lowercase. Change Case doesn't format text; instead, it changes the characters. To use the Change Case command, select the text that you want to change, go to the Format menu, and choose Change Case. Word displays the Change Case dialog box (see Figure 6.3). In the Change Case dialog box, select an option and click the OK button.

> **!** **Caution:** Title Case capitalizes the first letter in every word, so if you want a proper title, make sure that you go back and lowercase the first letter in such words as *in*, *the*, and *at*.

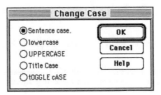

Figure 6.3   Select a case option.

In contrast to the Change Case command, the Font card (in the Font dialog box) offers check boxes for All Caps and Small Caps. All Caps and Small Caps do not change the case of characters but, instead, change the appearance of the characters. All Caps makes letters look like uppercase letters; Small Caps makes letters look capitalized and increases the size of the letters that are truly uppercase (see Figure 6.4).

Figure 6.4 All Caps and Small Caps change the appearance of text.

Special Effects

If you want to format type in a special way, you may need special know-how about how a feature works or about how to combine several seemingly unrelated features.

Hidden text

You should format text as hidden if you want the text to be in the document only occasionally. For example, if you prepare a handout for a presentation, you can add speaking notes to the handout but format the notes in hidden text. When you print the handouts for the audience, you can print with hidden text not showing, but when you print your own copy, you can print with hidden text showing so that the speaking notes are interspersed throughout the handout.

If hidden text appears in a document, it appears with a dotted line beneath it (see Figure 6.5), but if hidden text prints, it prints normally without the dotted line.

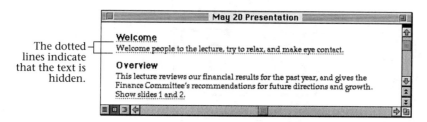

Figure 6.5 Hidden text appears onscreen with a dotted line beneath it.

To format a selection as hidden text, either press ⌘-Shift-H or turn on the Hidden check box on the Font card (in the Font dialog box). To remove the Hidden format, reverse the process by selecting the text and then pressing ⌘-Shift-H, or by turning off the Hidden check box.

To control whether you see hidden text onscreen, use the View card in the Options dialog box from the Tools menu. The Nonprinting Characters area has a check box for hidden text. You can also use the Options dialog box to control whether hidden text prints, but the check box is on the Print card. Of course, if you show hidden text onscreen but do not print hidden text, page breaks that show onscreen in Normal and Page Layout View may not be in the same place in Print Preview or when you print.

> **Caution:** If you use the hidden format, pay attention to hard page breaks that you insert. It's easy to format them accidentally as hidden text.

Character spacing and kerning

If you want to move characters horizontally so that they end up closer together or farther apart, use either the Character Spacing card in the Font dialog box or the Tracking option in WordArt (flip ahead a few pages to find out about WordArt). For example, in the word *Word,* if you use a large type size, the *W* and the *o* may have an ungainly amount of space between them. *Word* would look better with the *o* slightly closer to the *W.*

Character spacing works for any font, and it adjusts the spacing in a uniform way.

Kerning works for *proportional fonts,* fonts where some letters (such as an *i*) are skinnier than others (such as a *w*). Use kerning to make a consistent amount of white space between characters, particularly between characters in large point sizes. Why bother? Because uneven blobs of white space between characters create an unbalanced feeling and distract people from reading your message.

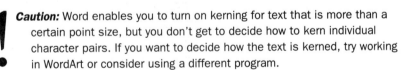

> **Caution:** Word enables you to turn on kerning for text that is more than a certain point size, but you don't get to decide how to kern individual character pairs. If you want to decide how the text is kerned, try working in WordArt or consider using a different program.

Drop cap

A drop cap can introduce a new topic and add visual interest to an otherwise boring stretch of text.

To insert a drop cap, follow these steps:

1. Click the paragraph in which you want the drop cap.

2. From the Format menu, choose Drop Cap. The Drop Cap dialog box appears (see Figure 6.6).

3. Select a position for the drop cap.

4. Choose a font for the drop cap.

5. Indicate the drop cap height in the Lines to Drop box.

6. Enter the distance that the drop cap should be from the text.

7. Finally, click the OK button. Word uses a frame to position the character as a drop cap.

8. To further adjust the distance of the drop cap from the text, select the cap, go to the Format menu, and choose Frame. In the Horizontal area of the Frame dialog box, adjust the Distance from Text and then click the OK button.

To remove drop cap formatting, select the drop cap, go to the Format menu, and choose Drop Cap. When the Drop Cap dialog box appears, select None (at the upper left) and click the OK button.

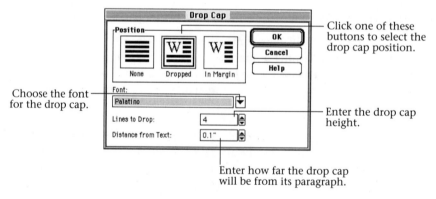

Figure 6.6   Use the Drop Cap dialog box to set up a drop cap.

White type on a black background

You can create a paragraph of white text on a black background by formatting the type with the color white and then applying black paragraph shading. Here are the steps:

1. Highlight the paragraph that you want to change.

2. From the Format menu, choose Font. After Word displays the Font dialog box, select the Font card (see Figure 6.7).

3. In the Font card, choose White from the Color menu.

4. To make the white text easier to see on a black background, select Bold from the Font Style menu.

5. Click the OK button. The Font dialog box closes, and the text disappears behind its highlighting (you can't see the text because it is white).

6. Go to the Format menu and choose Borders and Shading. Select the Shading card (see Figure 6.8).

7. Select Solid (100%) shading.

8. Click the OK button to return to the document.

9. To see the white text on the black background, click elsewhere in the document to remove the highlighting.

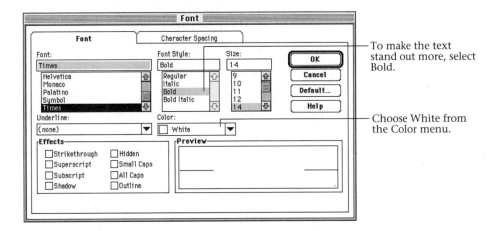

Figure 6.7   Make the characters white and bold.

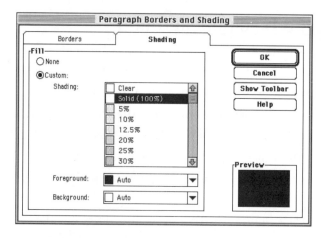

Figure 6.8 Select Solid (100%) for the shading.

Rotating, twisting, bending—WordArt

WordArt can twist text in all sorts of ways to create all sorts of unusual formats. Use WordArt to create headlines and highly stylized bits of text. When you use WordArt, you create objects (think of them as little pictures) that insert into the text layer. More technically speaking, the objects "embed" into the text layer. To move a WordArt object into a drawing layer, cut the object and paste it into a text box, as explained in Chapter 8.

In any event, to call up WordArt and make an object, follow these steps:

1. Go to the Insert menu and choose Object.

2. When the Object dialog box appears, select Microsoft WordArt and click the OK button. A WordArt window appears (see Figure 6.9).

3. Type some text in the Enter Your Text Here box and then click the Update Preview button. The text should appear in the Preview window at the lower right.

4. Turn on the Resize Frame check box if you want the edge of the WordArt object to expand or shrink automatically in order to be just large enough to hold the text in the Preview. The Resize Frame check box applies to the framelike box that surrounds all WordArt objects, and it also applies if you decide to frame the WordArt object.

5. Experiment with the available formats to apply all sorts of weird and wonderful effects. Click the Apply button to see what the WordArt object looks like in the document or click the OK button to close WordArt and return to the document.

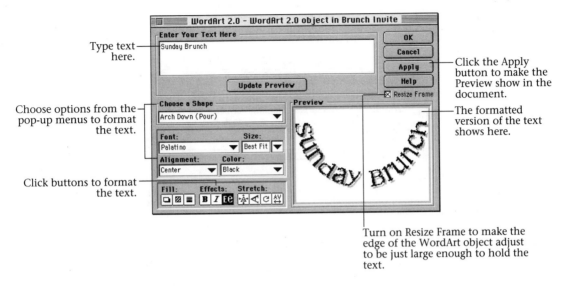

Type text here.

Click the Apply button to make the Preview show in the document.

Choose options from the pop-up menus to format the text.

The formatted version of the text shows here.

Click buttons to format the text.

Turn on Resize Frame to make the edge of the WordArt object adjust to be just large enough to hold the text.

Figure 6.9   The WordArt dialog box is the control center for twisting and styling text.

Indenting a Paragraph from the Margin

Now that you know all about character formatting and how to create special typographical effects, you can add visual interest (or even excitement) to documents with special paragraph formatting.

To move a paragraph left or right, or make it wider or skinnier, you should adjust the paragraph indents. Word has three indents that work together to control where each line in a paragraph begins and ends (see Figure 6.10).

◆ The left indent controls where every line in a paragraph starts, except for the first line. If you set a left indent at zero, the lines begin at the left margin.

◆ The first-line indent controls where the first line in a paragraph starts.

◆ The right indent controls the end of each line in a paragraph. If you set a right indent at zero, each line ends at the right margin.

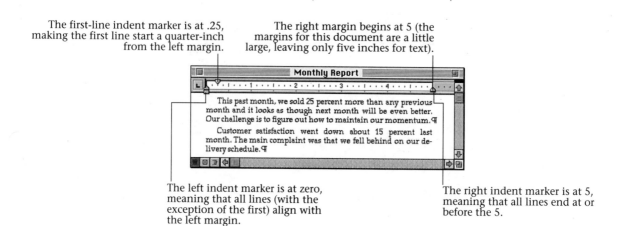

The first-line indent marker is at .25, making the first line start a quarter-inch from the left margin.

The right margin begins at 5 (the margins for this document are a little large, leaving only five inches for text).

The left indent marker is at zero, meaning that all lines (with the exception of the first) align with the left margin.

The right indent marker is at 5, meaning that all lines end at or before the 5.

Figure 6.10   Each paragraph has three indents: first-line, left, and right.

To adjust a paragraph's indents visually, click in the paragraph and then move the appropriate indent marker on the ruler. If you drag the little box below the left indent marker, the first-line and left indent markers move together.

If you have the Formatting toolbar showing, use the Decrease and Increase Indent buttons to change the indent.

To numerically adjust indents, click in the paragraph that you want to adjust, go to the Format menu, choose Paragraph, and bring up the Indents and Spacing card. The card has boxes for entering the left and right indents, but to change the first-line indent, use the Special area. Here's how it works:

◆ None makes the first-line indent line up with the left indent.

◆ First Line makes the first line of the paragraph start to the right of the rest of the paragraph. Use First Line instead of typing blank spaces or a tab at the start of a paragraph (over time, you'll save hundreds of keystrokes).

◆ Hanging sets up a *hanging indent,* where the first line starts left of the rest of the paragraph. To make a hanging indent for a numbered or bulleted list, let Word do the indenting, numbering, and bulleting for you (see "Formatting a List" later in this chapter).

When you set a hanging indent, you can let text flow smoothly along the first line, or you can type a small amount of text at the upper left and then press Tab to insert a tab character. After you press Tab, the insertion point jumps in the first line to the left indent (see Figure 6.11).

If Word does not move the insertion point to the left indent, open the Options dialog box from the Tools menu, select the Compatibility card, choose Microsoft Word 6 from the Recommended Options For menu, and then turn off the Don't Add Automatic Tab Stop for Hanging Indent check box.

The first-line indent makes the
first line of each paragraph
begin at zero.

The left indent lines
up text under the 1-
inch mark.

The tab character
moves the first line
of text forward to
the left indent.

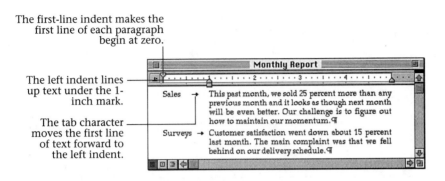

Figure 6.11 Use a tab character with a hanging indent to make text line up in a particular way.

Aligning a Paragraph

You can align a paragraph in relation to the indents, and you get three choices for how the text aligns (see Figure 6.12):

◆ Align Left makes a paragraph flush left, meaning that it lines up with the first-line and left indents. Most paragraphs in conventional reading material are set flush left.

◆ Center centers each line of text in a paragraph between the left and right indents, with the exception of the first line in a paragraph, which centers between the first-line and right indents. If you center text, consider breaking the lines unevenly. An uneven break adds visual interest and makes it crystal clear that you intended to center the text.

◆ Align Right makes a paragraph flush right, meaning that it lines up evenly at the right indent.

◆ Justify makes each line in a paragraph line up evenly with the left (and first-line) indent and with the right indent. Consider hyphenating justified text to reduce unsightly white gaps between words (see Chapter 4). The last line in a paragraph does not justify, and under most circumstances, you wouldn't want it to. If you want the last line in a paragraph to justify, end the last line with a soft return character (press Shift-Return).

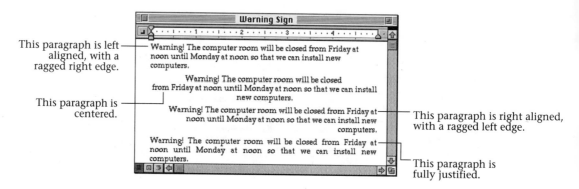

Figure 6.12 You can horizontally align paragraphs in four different ways.

If you have the Formatting toolbar showing, use the Alignment buttons to apply different alignments. You can also change alignment by clicking in the paragraph, choosing Paragraph from the Format menu, selecting the Indents and Spacing card, and choosing an alignment from the menu at the lower right.

Adjusting White Space Between Paragraphs

White space between paragraphs helps to separate them visually. You can put different amounts of space between paragraphs to help readers understand the flow of your ideas. For example, you can put more space before a main topic heading than before a regular body text paragraph.

You can always press Return a few extra times to make blank lines, but in the long run, it's easier to have the paragraphs do the spacing on their own. If you edit the document and the page breaks shift, blank lines may end up awkwardly placed at the top or bottom of a page. To change paragraph spacing, follow these steps:

1. Click in the paragraph.

2. From the Format menu, choose Paragraph, or double-click in the white area of the ruler. In the Paragraph dialog box, select the Indents and Spacing Card.

3. Enter amounts for the spacing before and after. Word expects the amounts to be in points (there are 72 points in one inch).

4. Click the OK button.

Paragraph Spacing

In a few special cases, Word ignores paragraph spacing. If you add spacing before a paragraph, you don't get the spacing if the paragraph is the first paragraph in a document or if a hard page break immediately precedes it. Also, if you add spacing after a paragraph and the paragraph falls at the bottom of a page, the extra space disappears into the bottom margin.

The way paragraph spacing happens near a page break can change, depending on how the Compatibility Options are set. If you have problems with paragraph spacing and page breaks, experiment with two check boxes: Suppress Extra Line Spacing at Top of Page and Suppress Extra Line Spacing at Top of Page Like Mac Word 5.x. To access these options, go to the Compatibility card in the Options dialog box. Look in the list of options for Microsoft Word 6.0.

Changing White Space Between Lines

The white space between the lines has a profound effect on the readability and flow of a document. Word automatically looks at the size of the largest character on a line and sets the spacing a little bit larger than the size of that character. To override the way Word sizes lines of type, follow these steps:

1. Click in the paragraph that you want to change, or highlight a group of paragraphs.

2. From the Format menu, choose Paragraph and select the Indents and Spacing card (see Figure 6.13).

3. In the Indents and Spacing card, choose a line spacing option. For line spacing, Word uses points as its default measurement unit. There are 72 points in one inch. To enter a measurement using inches, type **in** after the number. For example, to enter one-half inch, type **.5 in**. The best option depends on what you want to accomplish:

    ◆ Single spacing sets each line a tiny bit larger than the size of the largest character on that line.

    ◆ 1.5 Lines spacing and Double spacing increase single spacing by 150 and 200 percent, respectively.

    ◆ At Least spacing sets each line at least as large as the measurement you enter. If a line contains a big character or graphic, the line expands to be "at least" big enough to accommodate it.

♦ Exactly spacing sets each line to the exact height you specify. A big graphic or character will be cut off if it doesn't fit.

♦ Multiple spacing sets each line to the normal Single setting, multiplied by the number in the At box. For example, to increase the spacing to 110 percent of Single, enter **1.1** in the At box.

4. After setting up the line spacing, click the OK button.

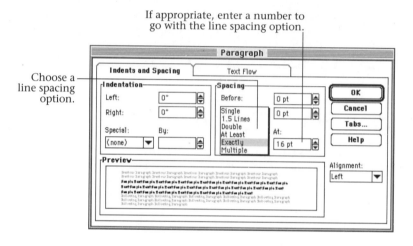

Figure 6.13   Adjust line spacing in the Paragraph dialog box.

Creating White Space with Tabs

If you need to adjust type horizontally within a line, a tab may be just the ticket. Keep in mind, however, that tabs are somewhat outdated. Often, setting up a table or snaking columns makes more sense than setting up tabs (see Chapter 7).

Tabs have two important parts (it takes two to tango):

♦ The tab stop in the ruler

♦ The tab character typed in the line of text

The tab stop tells text (typed after the tab character) where to start. Word comes with default left tab stops set at every half inch. If you have keen eyesight, you can see them as subtle marks at the bottom of the ruler. If you press Tab while typing, a tab character inserts in the text, and the insertion point jumps ahead to the next tab stop. Text that you type after the tab character continues from the tab stop (see Figure 6.14). If the tab stop is a default stop or a left tab stop, the left edge of the continuing text lines up under the stop.

Tab characters may show onscreen, but they never print. You can control whether tab characters show onscreen in the View card of the Options dialog box from the Tools menu.

To insert a tab character within an existing table cell, press Option-Tab.

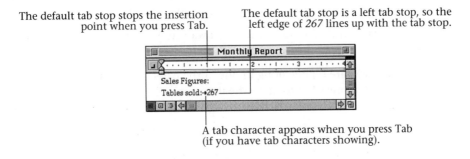

The default tab stop stops the insertion point when you press Tab.

The default tab stop is a left tab stop, so the left edge of *267* lines up with the tab stop.

A tab character appears when you press Tab (if you have tab characters showing).

Figure 6.14   A default tab stop lines up text based on the left edge of the text.

Adjusting default tab stops

You can move the default tab stops for any paragraph, so if you prefer stops once every inch for some paragraphs and every two inches for others, Word can arrange that. You can also change the default tab stop for an entire document. To change the default, try these steps:

1. Click in the paragraph that you want to change or highlight all the paragraphs you want to change.

2. Go to the Format menu and choose Tabs. The Tabs dialog box appears.

3. In the Default Tab Stops text box, enter the distance that you want.

4. Click the OK button.

Creating a custom tab stop

A custom tab stop deletes all default tab stops to its left. For example, if you have default tab stops every half inch and you put a custom tab stop at 1.1 inches, the half-inch and one-inch tab stops disappear. If you remove the custom tab stop at 1.1 inches, the default tab stops come back.

153

To make a custom tab stop, follow these steps:

1. Click the paragraph in which you want the stop to apply. You can also highlight a group of paragraphs and thus apply the stop to the entire group.

2. If the ruler is not showing, go to the View menu and choose Ruler.

3. Select a stop by clicking the Tab Alignment button (on the left side of the ruler). Each time you click you get a different stop until you cycle back to the beginning. Table 6.2 explains what each stop looks like and what it does.

4. Click the ruler in the location where you want the tab stop located. For example, if you want the stop 1.5 inches in from the left margin, click at 1.5 on the ruler.

5. That's it! If you are typing along in one of the paragraphs that you highlighted in step 1, you can press Tab to make the insertion point jump to the 1.5-inch mark (see Figure 6.15).

Decimal tab stop.

Tab character.

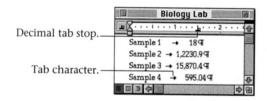

Figure 6.15 A decimal tab stop at the 1.5-inch mark causes text after the tab character to line up based on the decimal point or where the decimal point would be if you did type it.

Table 6.2

Tab Stop Symbols and Alignments

Symbol	Name	What it does
L	Left	Lines up the left edge of text with the tab stop
⊥	Center	Centers text under the tab stop
⊥	Decimal	Aligns the decimal point (usually a period) under the tab
⌐	Right	Lines up the right edge of text with the tab stop

Moving a custom tab stop

To move a tab stop, click in the paragraph that the stop goes with (or highlight a bunch of paragraphs that the stop goes with) and then drag the stop to a new position on the ruler. Press Option while you click and drag a tab stop to see precise measurements.

Changing a tab stop's alignment

To change the way text lines up beneath a custom tab stop, highlight the paragraphs that you want to change and then choose Tabs from the Format menu. In the Tabs dialog box, select the tab stop that you want to change from the Tab Stop Position list, select a new alignment, and click the OK button (see Figure 6.16).

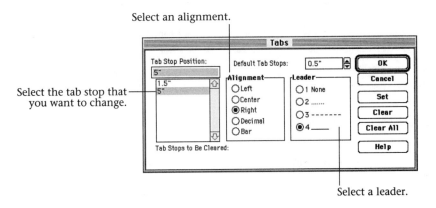

Figure 6.16   Use the Tabs dialog box to customize tab stops.

Adding a tab leader

Most of the time, you want the space taken up by the tab character to be blank. But you can put little dots or a solid underline in that spot, if you want, by adding a leader to the tab stop. To add a leader, open the Tabs dialog box and select the stop that you want to change. Select a leader from the Leader area and click the OK button (see Figure 6.16).

Removing custom tab stops

To remove just one tab stop, click in the paragraph that it goes with or select all the paragraphs that it goes with. Then drag the stop about an inch down from the ruler. The stop disappears, and text re-aligns based on the default tab stop. To completely remove the tab, delete the tab character in the text.

You can also clear tabs for selected text while you are in the Tabs dialog box. If you want to remove all custom tab stops from a document, press ⌘-A to highlight the document, open the Tabs dialog box, click the Clear All button, and then click the OK button.

Formatting a List

A list typically consists of a string of short, related paragraphs, such as addresses, suggestions, events, and so forth (see Figure 6.17). If your list is more of a tabular arrangement with rows of related information, see Chapter 7 for more information about tables.

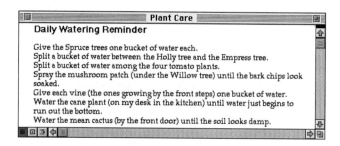

Figure 6.17   A basic list without any special formatting...

To make a list easier to read, you can apply various formats (see Figure 6.18).

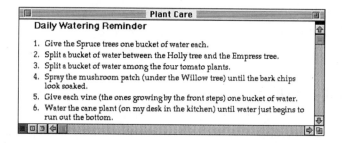

Figure 6.18   ...can be dramatically improved by adding extra space after each entry, as well as by adding numbers and a hanging indent.

You can even display the list in snaking columns (see Figure 6.19). For more information about snaking columns, see Chapter 7.

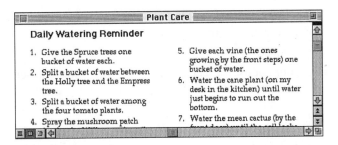

Figure 6.19   The list, from the preceding two figures, shown in snaking columns.

Special formatting with bullets and numbers

To make a list more readable, consider beginning each entry with a number, bullet, or any special character. Although you can type bullets and numbers by hand, you can speed up the process by using the Bullets and Numbering paragraph formats. To get the most out of using bullets and numbering, keep two points in mind:

◆ You can make bullets or numbering part of a style.

◆ As you type a list formatted with bullets or numbers, each new paragraph automatically starts with a bullet or with the next number in the sequence.

To apply bullets, highlight the list entries and click the Bullets button on the Formatting toolbar. Numbering works in a similar manner—first highlight the entries and then click the Numbering button.

You can also apply Bullets and Numbering formats by selecting list entries and choosing Bullets and Numbering from the Format menu. In the Bullets and Numbering dialog box, switch to the appropriate card (Bulleted for bullets; Numbered for numbers). In the card, click one of the big example buttons for a style of numbers or bullets and then click the OK button.

Removing and skipping bullets and numbers

To remove bullets, highlight the formatted entries and click the Bullets button. Similarly, to remove numbering, highlight the entries and click the Numbering button. The Bulleted and Numbered cards also offer Remove buttons; click them to remove bullets or numbering from selected list entries.

If the insertion point is in an entry that should not have a bullet or number, you can temporarily turn off the formatting by issuing the Skip Numbering command on the shortcut menu. Simply control-click the bullet or number in the text to bring up the shortcut menu. If you issue Skip Numbering, the numbering (or bullets) should continue in the next paragraph. (The Skip Numbering command skips both numbers and bullets.)

To stop the bullets or numbering for good, either click the Numbering (or Bullets) button on the Formatting toolbar or choose Stop Numbering from the shortcut menu (Control-click the bullet or number where you want to stop). The Stop Numbering command stops both numbers and bullets.

If you use the Customize dialog box from the Tools menu to assign keyboard shortcuts to the bullets and numbering options, note that the command for turning bullets on and off is called FormatBulletDefault. Similarly, the command for turning numbers on and off is FormatNumberDefault.

Customizing the appearance of bullets

To change a bullet's size, color, or character, follow these steps:

1. Select the bulleted entries that you want to change.

2. From the Format menu, choose Bullets and Numbering. Select the Bulleted card.

3. In the Bulleted card, if one of the six big buttons shows the bullet that you want, click the button, click the OK button, and skip the rest of these steps. Otherwise, click the Modify button. Word displays the Modify Bulleted List dialog box (see Figure 6.20).

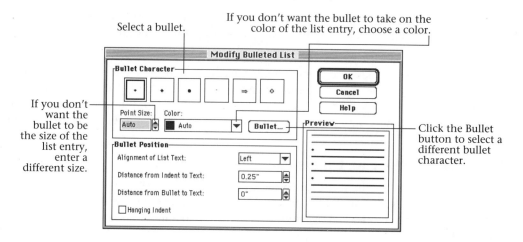

Figure 6.20   Use the Modify Bulleted List dialog box to set up special bullet formats.

4. To change the bullet size, enter the size. If you leave the point size at Auto, the bullet will be the same size as the text, or more technically speaking, the bullet takes on the point size applied to the paragraph mark at the end of the list entry.

5. To make the bullet a different color, choose a color. Leave the color set to Auto to make the bullet the same color as the text (actually the paragraph mark at the end of the entry).

6. To change the bullet character, click the Bullet button. The Symbol dialog box opens. In the Symbol dialog box, select the character that you prefer to use. You can switch between a few of your installed fonts by choosing a font from the Symbols From menu. Click the OK button after selecting a character.

7. After you finish modifying the bullet, click the OK button.

Customizing number formatting

To change the numbering scheme in a wide variety of ways, try these steps:

1. Select the numbered entries that you want to change.

2. Select the Numbered card in the Bullets and Numbering dialog box.

3. In the Numbered card, click the Modify button. Word displays the Modify Numbered List dialog box (see Figure 6.21).

4. You can customize the numbering in many ways:

    ◆ Choose a numbering scheme from the Number menu.

    ◆ Use the Start At box to indicate with which number the list should begin.

    ◆ To put text before the numbers, type the text in the Text Before box. In most cases, type a space after the text so that the text doesn't run right into the number. For example, you can type **Action Item** or **Query** (note the extra space after the words). You can also customize text that appears after a number, such as a colon or a right parenthesis.

    ◆ To change the character format of the number and the text that goes before and after the number, click the Font button.

5. After you finish customizing the numbering, click the OK button.

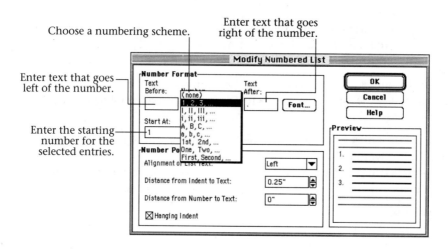

Figure 6.21 Set up the formatting for list numbers.

Special formatting for list entries longer than one line

If your list entries take up more than one line of text, you can make the list look more attractive by setting up a special indent, adding extra space between entries, and making sure that list entries don't separate awkwardly over page or column breaks.

Setting up space before and after

If your list entries take up more than one line, add a little more space between entries to help readers see the entries as separate elements. To change the space between entries, you can change the space after a paragraph or the space before (you can also change both options). Here are the steps:

1. Highlight entries that you want to format.

2. Go to the Format menu and choose Paragraph. Select the Indents and Spacing card.

3. Enter measurements in the Before and After boxes. The default unit of measurement is the point, so you should try a number between 4 and 24 points first and then work from there.

4. Click the OK button.

Making a special indent

If you applied Bullets or Numbering formatting to your list, don't set up the indent by using these directions; instead, turn on the Hanging Indent check box in the Modify Bulleted List or Modify Numbered List dialog box. If you aren't using Bullets or Numbering formatting, however, set up a special indent by following these steps:

1. Highlight the entries that you want to indent.

2. From the Format menu, choose Paragraph and select the Indents and Spacing card.

3. From the Special pop-up menu, choose an indent:

    ◆ A hanging indent makes the first line of an entry start left of the rest of the lines.

    ◆ A first-line indent makes the first line of an entry start right of the rest of the lines.

4. Figure out how far left or right you want the first line to begin in relation to the rest of the lines and enter the distance in the By box. (If the Preview in the Indents and Spacing card is sufficiently clear, use it to fine-tune the distance.)

5. Click the OK button.

Preventing awkward page (or column) breaks

Use the Keep Lines Together paragraph format to keep all the lines in each entry together on the same page or column. If you apply Keep Lines together and an entry doesn't fit completely on one page or column, the entire entry jumps to the top of the next page or column. Here are the steps for applying the Keep Lines Together format:

1. Highlight the entries.

2. Go to the Format menu and choose Paragraph. Word displays the Paragraph dialog box. Select the Text Flow card.

3. Turn on the Keep Lines Together check box.

4. Click the OK button.

Formatting multilevel lists

A multilevel list uses indents to indicate the importance of entries in the list. The entries in each level can have separate numbering schemes, and as such, you can create a standard-looking outline or set up a wide variety of bullets and numbering schemes (see Figure 6.22).

The first level uses Roman
numerals followed by periods.

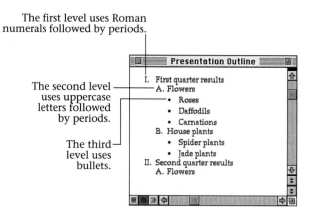

The second level
uses uppercase
letters followed
by periods.

The third
level uses
bullets.

Figure 6.22   This multilevel list has three levels, and each level uses a different bullets or numbering
scheme.

> *Caution:* You cannot use text formatted with built-in heading styles in a
> multilevel list. To number text formatted with Heading styles, use the
> Heading Numbering command on the Format menu.

To set up multilevel list formatting, follow these steps:

1. Select the entry or entries that you want to format. (If you haven't started the list
    yet, just place the insertion point where you want the list to begin.)

2. Go to the Format menu, choose Bullets and Numbering, and select the Multilevel
    card.

3. Click one of the six list-numbering options. If you don't want to customize the
    option, click the OK button and skip the rest of these steps. If you do want to
    customize the option, click the Modify button to open the Modify Multilevel List
    dialog box.

4. Each level in the list can have its own formatting, so to format a particular level,
    select it from the scrolling list at the right.

5. After selecting a level, you can apply formats to it.

6. After you finish formatting the entries, click the OK button.

Now that you have set up the list, you can move entries from level to level by clicking the
Decrease or Increase Indent button on the Formatting toolbar. You can also use the keyboard:
press Option-Shift–Left Arrow or Option-Shift–Right Arrow. As you move an entry, it takes on
the bullets or numbering for its level.

Caution: If you format an existing list, Word figures that everything with a left indent of less than .5 inches from the left margin is of level one importance. Everything between .5 inches and 1 inch is of level two importance, and so on, with the level of importance changing every half inch.

Sorting a List

Word can sort paragraphs into alphanumeric, numeric, or temporal order, based on the first letter, number, time, or date in the paragraph. Alphanumeric order means that numbers sort first in numeric order and then characters sort in alphabetic order. When sorting, Word ignores bullets or numbers attached to a paragraph through the Bullets and Numbering commands. (To find out how to sort a table, see Chapter 7.)

Basic sorting

To sort a list, such as the list in Figure 6.23, follow these steps:

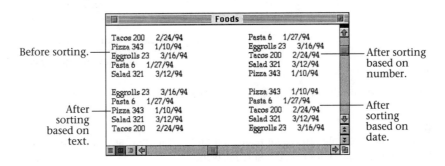

Figure 6.23   You can sort a list in several different ways.

1. Select the list.

2. Choose Sort Text from the Table menu. The Sort Text dialog box appears (see Figure 6.24).

3. Select Paragraphs in the Sort By menu.

4. From the Type menu, select what you want to sort by.

5. If you selected Text in the preceding step, click the Options button and use the Case Sensitive check box to control whether upper- and lowercase versions of the

same character always sort together. Turn on the check box to make them sort together; turn it off if you don't care whether they sort together or intermingle. Click the OK button.

6. Indicate whether you want to sort in ascending or descending order.

7. Click the OK button.

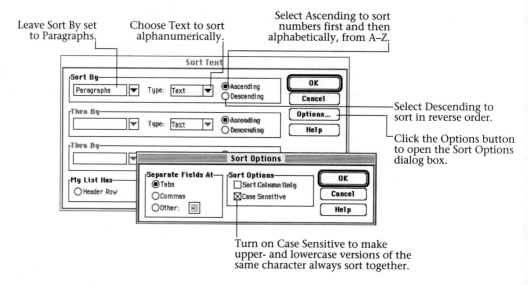

Figure 6.24   Use the Sort dialog boxes to set up sorting a simple list.

Caution: If you plan to create a long list and sort it later, set up a sample list first to make sure that the sort will work.

Now that you know how to format words and paragraphs to make a more interesting document, look for detailed instructions in the next chapter about adding even more interesting elements, such as tables, footnotes, TOCs, and so on.

Chapter 7

Adding Different Elements to Your Document

In this chapter, I discuss stuff that most people don't do every day. Even people who use Word for hours and hours a day don't use all these features. Even so, if you need one of these features, it wouldn't do to leave you up the figurative creek with no instructions. The instructions here help you figure out the following:

◆ Creating a table

◆ Setting up snaking columns

◆ Making text wrap around graphics by using the Frame command

◆ Making things overlap

◆ Creating a table of contents

◆ Inserting footnotes and endnotes

◆ Numbering and captioning figures, tables, charts, and so on

◆ Making cross-references

◆ Setting up hypertext links

◆ Creating an index

Starting and Formatting a Table

A table, one of Word's best features, provides a grid for lining things up in columns and rows. Tables work wonders for organizing numbers, comparing ideas, writing scripts, and so on. You can even do simple math inside a table.

> **Caution:** Use section-based, snaking columns when you want to type all the way down a page in one column and then start typing in the next column. Flip ahead a few pages to find out how.

Word offers three main ways to start a table, and I recommend using the way that looks most convenient to you.

- If you like using dialog boxes, start a table by choosing Insert Table from the Table menu.

- If you like using wizards, go to the Table menu, choose Insert Table, and then click the Wizard button.

- If you have the Standard toolbar showing, figure out how many rows and columns you want to begin with and then drag them down from the Insert Table button on the Standard toolbar (see Figure 7.1).

4 x 3 Table

Figure 7.1   To start a table, drag it out from the Insert Table button.

A table's row-and-column structure forms a grid, where each box is called a *cell*. If you have nonprinting characters showing, you'll see an end-of-cell mark in each cell and an end-of-row mark at the end of each row. Typically, a table shows onscreen with gridlines around each cell. If you can't see gridlines in your table, choose Gridlines from the bottom of the Table menu.

Each cell works like its own little page, with the sides of the cell acting like margins. If you type more than one line into a cell, the text wraps down to the next line and the entire row gets taller to make room for the second line of text (see Figure 7.2). In earlier versions of Word, an enormous number of people ran head-on into a problem where a table row couldn't get taller than a page. Microsoft finally fixed this problem in Word 6.

If you type more than one line of text in a cell, the text wraps to make another line.

An end-of-cell mark appears after the last character typed in each cell.

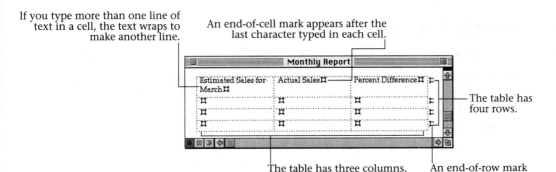

The table has four rows.

The table has three columns.

An end-of-row mark ends each row.

Figure 7.2   A table has columns and rows.

Caution: Gridlines don't print, but if you apply borders, the borders will print. To apply borders quickly, click inside the table and choose Table AutoFormat from the Table menu. Or to make your own borders, see Chapter 8.

If you click in a cell and then look at the ruler, you see that the cell has its own set of indent markers. You can drag the indent markers to adjust how text wraps within the cell. (See Chapter 6 to learn more about indents.) A table automatically has a little space between columns so that text in different columns stays separate. That space shows on the ruler, and in that space sit column markers, which you drag to adjust the column widths (see Figure 7.3).

Drag an indent marker (such as this first indent marker) to adjust how text wraps within a cell.

Drag a column marker to move the edge of a column.

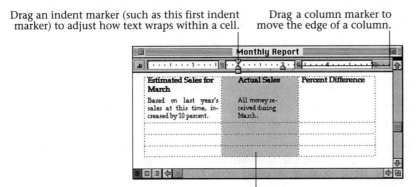

In this column, the indents are adjusted so that the text indents from the column sides.

Figure 7.3   The ruler for a table shows indent and column markers.

Selecting inside a table

To change the appearance of a table, you must know how to select cells, rows, and columns.

◆ To select a cell, place the pointer over the middle of the cell (don't click, just place). The pointer should look like an I-beam. Slide the pointer toward the left edge of the cell and stop sliding when the pointer changes into a single arrow. With the pointer looking like a single arrow, click once.

◆ To select a row, place the pointer over the middle of a cell in the row (don't click). The pointer should look like an I-beam. Slide the pointer toward the left edge of the cell and stop sliding when the pointer changes into a single arrow. Double-click. (To select more than one row, keep the button down on the downstroke of the second click and drag up or down to select additional rows.)

◆ To select a column, press Option and click once in the column. (To select multiple columns, press Option and click down. Before releasing the button, drag over the columns that you want to select.)

◆ To select the entire table, press Option and double-click the table.

Adjusting column and cell widths

Word offers two methods for changing the width of a column—dragging the column edge or dragging a column marker in the ruler. In either case, as the width changes, columns to the right resize proportionately so that the table stays the same width.

If you don't highlight anything when you change the width of a column, you change the width throughout the table. If you only want to adjust widths in part of the table, highlight that part of the table and then drag a column edge or column marker.

Here are a few tricks for changing cell and column widths in special ways:

◆ To change the width of the two columns bounded by the edge that you drag and to keep the table the same size, press Shift while dragging.

◆ To change the width of the column left of the edge that you drag and change the size of the table, press ⌘-Shift while dragging.

◆ Even out the widths of columns by pressing ⌘ and dragging the edge of a column. Word evens out all columns to the right of the edge that you drag.

Controlling row height

Rows automatically expand to accommodate any text and graphics inside. To make a row taller than its automatic size or to impose a minimum or maximum height, follow these steps:

1. Highlight the row or rows that you want to format.

2. Go to the Table menu and choose Cell Height and Width (or double-click a column marker). When the dialog box opens, select the Row card.

3. In the Row card, use the Height of Rows menu to set the row height (see Figure 7.4).

   ◆ To make the row an exact height, select Exactly and enter the height in the At box. By default, Word measures row height in points (there are 72 points in one inch).

   ◆ To make a row a certain height and allow it to expand further if it over-flows, select At Least and enter a height in the At box.

   ◆ To make the row high enough to hold the contents of the row, select Auto.

4. Click the OK button.

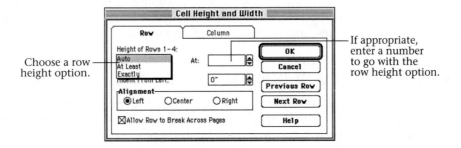

Figure 7.4   You can set the height of a row in three main ways: Auto, At Least, or Exactly.

Adding and removing columns and rows

If a table has the wrong number of columns or rows, Word offers several methods for remedying the situation.

Deleting columns and rows

To delete columns or rows, highlight the columns or rows in question and choose Delete Rows (or Delete Columns) from the Table menu.

Adding rows

Adding a row takes two steps. First, click in the row beneath the spot where you would like to place the new row. Second, choose Insert Rows from the Table menu. To add several rows at once, highlight several rows below where you want the new rows to go and then choose Insert Rows. Word inserts the number of rows that you selected. To add a row at the bottom of a table, click in the lower-right cell and press Tab.

Adding columns

The steps for adding columns work much like the steps for adding rows. Begin by highlighting the column to the right of where you want to add the column. Finish by choosing Insert Columns from the Table menu.

To add several columns at once, highlight several columns (to the right of where you want the new columns) and choose Insert Columns. Word adds the number of columns that you selected.

To add a column to the far right of the table, press Option and click once just to the right of the table. A thin column to the right of the table should be highlighted. With the thin column highlighted, choose Insert Columns from the Table menu.

You can click the Insert Table button (on the Standard toolbar) instead of choosing Insert Rows (or Columns) from the Table menu. Because you have a row or column selected, the button's ToolTip calls it the Insert Rows (or Columns) button.

Moving the insertion point inside a table

If you use tables a lot, it's worth your time to use keyboard shortcuts for moving the insertion point in a table. Table 7.1 lists commands and keyboard shortcuts. For the shortcuts that require an extended keyboard, use the Customize dialog box from the Tools menu to customize them (if you don't have an extended keyboard).

Table 7.1

Commands and Keyboard Shortcuts for Moving Around in a Table

Where you can move	Command name	Default keyboard shortcut
Ahead one column	NextCell	Tab
Back one column	PrevCell	Shift-Tab
Last cell in a row	EndOfRow	Option-End
First cell of a row	StartOfRow	Option-Home
Bottom of a column	EndofColumn	Option–Page Down
Top of a column	StartofColumn	Option–Page Up

Doing math inside a table

If you want to do serious math, you definitely need to use Excel. If you want just a little math, you can place a special formula field inside a table and instruct that field to do calculations based on the contents of the table. To insert such a field, follow these steps:

1. Go to the Table menu and choose Formula. The Formula dialog box appears (see Figure 7.5).

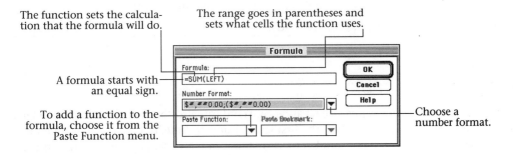

The function sets the calculation that the formula will do.

The range goes in parentheses and sets what cells the function uses.

A formula starts with an equal sign.

To add a function to the formula, choose it from the Paste Function menu.

Choose a number format.

Figure 7.5   Use the Formula dialog box to do calculations on numbers entered in a table.

2. Enter a formula. Word may guess a formula, and if Word guesses, you can use the guess or enter your own formula. A basic formula has two parts: a function and a range. The *function* sets the type of calculation and the *range* sets what cells to do the calculation on. Table 7.2 shows samples of how ranges work in formulas. To see the available functions, look in the Paste Function list. If you choose a function from the list, it adds to the formula.

3. Choose a number format.

4. Click the OK button.

The field appears in the document.

Table 7.2

Examples of Ranges in Formula Fields

Formula	What it does
=SUM(ABOVE)	Adds the numbers in all cells directly above the cell holding the formula until it gets to the top of the table, a blank cell, or a cell that contains text. You can also use the ranges (BELOW), (LEFT), and (RIGHT).

continues

171

Table 7.2 Continued

Formula	What it does
=SUM(A1:B2)	Adds the numbers in a box defined by cell A1 (the upper-left cell) and B2 (second column, second cell). Notice that a letter indicates the column, and a number indicates the row.
=AVERAGE(2:2)	Averages all numbers in the second row.
=AVERAGE(C:C)	Averages all numbers in the third column from the left.
=PRODUCT(A1, C3)	Multiplies cells A1 and C3.

Sorting text in a table

In addition to sorting paragraphs (see Chapter 6), Word can also sort tables into alphanumeric, numeric, or temporal order, based on the first letter, number, time, or date in the paragraph. (Alphanumeric order means that numbers sort first in numeric order and then characters sort in alphabetic order.) In a table, you can sort based on the contents of one (or more) columns (see Figure 7.6).

! **Caution:** If you plan to create a long list and sort it later, set up a sample list and make sure that the sort will work.

Word first sorted the table by the Assignment column.

Word then sorted the table by the First Name column.

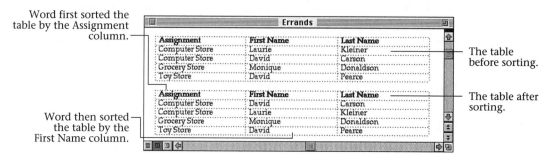

The table before sorting.

The table after sorting.

Figure 7.6   You can sort a table based on the contents of more than one column.

If you are sorting in a table, you click in or select the table, choose Sort from the Table menu, and use the Sort dialog box to set up the sort.

◆ If the first table row has generic headings that you don't want sorted, select the Header Row radio button at the bottom of the dialog box; if you want the first row included in the sort, select the No Header Row radio button.

◆ Set up the Sort By and Then By areas, as needed. If you want to sort based on one column only, you need to set up only the Sort By area.

◆ Note that Column 1 means the leftmost column, Column 2 the second from left column, and so on.

The sort from Figure 7.6 was set up in the Sort dialog box, as shown in Figure 7.7.

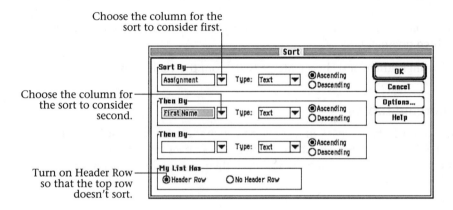

Figure 7.7   Use the Sort By and Then By areas to set up a two-column sort.

Table tips and tricks

When setting up a table, you can run into an assortment of special problems and less common situations.

Special considerations for tall cells

If you type a lot of text in one cell, the cell may interact awkwardly with a page break. To change whether a page break can occur within a row, highlight the row and bring up the Cell Height and Width dialog box (double-click a column marker in the ruler or go to the Table menu and choose Cell Height and Width). Look in the Row card.

A check box called Allow Row to Break Across Pages controls whether page breaks occur in the middle of cells or whether a cell pops to the next page if it doesn't fit completely on its original page.

Moving the table down from the top of the document

If you have a table stuck at the top of the document, click with the I-beam pointer in the upper left of the upper-left cell. The insertion point should appear at the upper left of the table. (If you have trouble keeping the pointer looking like an I-beam, click near the top left of the cell and then use the arrow keys to move the insertion point to the upper left.) With the insertion point at the upper left, press Return. Word inserts a blank paragraph above the table.

Splitting and merging cells

You can split and join cells that are in the same row. Highlight the cells and choose Split Cells from the Table menu. In the Split Cells dialog box, enter the number of columns into which you want each highlighted cell to split. For example, if you select two cells and then enter **2** for the number of columns that you want, you end up with four cells: two cells for each cell that you highlighted originally.

To merge cells, highlight them and choose Merge Cells from the Table menu.

Splitting and merging tables

To split one table into two tables, click in the first row that you want in the second table and then choose Split Table from the Table menu. To merge two tables into one, remove all the text between them. If only a paragraph mark separates them, highlight the paragraph mark and cut it out.

Page breaks

If you insert a page break within a table, the table splits into two. To create a page break without splitting the table, follow these steps:

1. Click at the top of the row below where you want the break.

2. From the Format menu, choose Paragraph. In the Paragraph dialog box, bring forward the Text Flow card.

3. In the Text Flow card, turn on the Page Break Before check box and then click the OK button.

Tab characters

To type a tab character, press Option-Tab. If you use a decimal tab stop, you don't have to type a tab character into a cell; Word automatically inserts an invisible tab character.

Setting up a table row at the top of each page

If the first row in a table contains column headings and the table extends through more than one page, you can make the column headings repeat at the top of each page. Before you do this, make sure that you have at least two rows in the table—the top row that has headings and at least one other row, which does not have headings.

Highlight the row holding the headings and choose Headings from the Table menu. After you set up table headings, if you change anything in the heading row, the changes show on all pages (in Page Layout View and Print Preview).

> **Caution:** Headings repeat only after a soft page break. They do not repeat after a hard page break.

Changing the space between columns

By default, Word inserts .15 inches of blank space between columns, adding .075 inches of blank space to each side of each column. To adjust the space between columns, follow these steps:

1. To adjust the entire table, click anywhere in the table. To adjust only a few rows in a table, specifically select those rows.

2. From the Table menu, choose Cell Height and Width (or double-click a column marker on the ruler) and then choose the Column card.

3. In the Column card, enter a measurement in the Space Between Columns box and then click the OK button.

Positioning the left edge of a row or table

You can position the left edge by dragging the appropriate column marker in the ruler, but the Cell Height and Width dialog box offers better control. To use the dialog box, follow these steps:

1. Highlight the row or rows that you want to adjust.

2. From the Table menu, choose Cell Height and Width (or double-click a column marker). When the dialog box opens, select the Row card.

3. In the Row card, select an Alignment radio button or enter a measurement in the Indent From Left box. For example, to move the selection one-half inch into the left margin, enter -.5.

4. Click the OK button.

Copying or cutting text from a cell

Be careful when you copy or cut text and then paste it in another cell. If you include the end-of-cell mark with the copied or cut text and then paste the text into a different cell, the pasted-in text replaces anything that was in the cell before. This problem also occurs with Drag and Drop.

To prevent this problem from happening, do not include the end-of-cell mark with the text that you copy or cut. Then when you paste the text into another cell, the cell will contain its preceding contents and the pasted contents.

Setting Up Snaking Columns

Because snaking columns go by section, you can also call them section-based columns. A *snaking column* usually consists of text that reads all the way down one column on a page and then continues at the top of the next column on the page.

If you feel a little fuzzy about how to work with sections, look for information about sections toward the end of Chapter 1. Otherwise, here are the steps for setting up snaking columns:

1. Select or click in the appropriate spot.

2. From the Format menu, choose Columns. The Columns dialog box appears (see Figure 7.8).

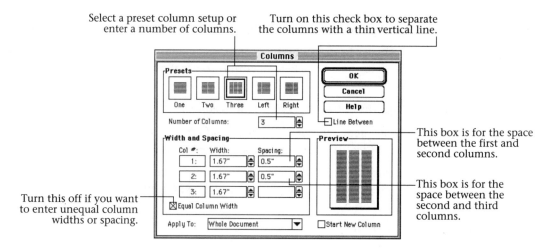

Figure 7.8   The Columns dialog box helps with setting up columns.

3. Set how many columns you want. Enter a number or select a Presets option. Instead of opening the Columns dialog box, you can drag out the number of columns that you want from the Columns button on the Standard toolbar.

4. If you want to customize a column width or the space between two columns, note that you must turn off Equal Column Width first. If you type numbers, the Preview doesn't update; to see the update, press the arrow keys on the keyboard or click the little up- and down triangles in the dialog box.

5. To place a vertical line between each column, turn on Line Between.

6. If Start New Column is on, turn it off.

7. Click the OK button.

Word formats your document and gives you columns. Now that you have columns, here are a few tips for making them do what you expect them to do:

◆ In Normal View, you see only one column at the left side of the page. Switch to Page Layout View or Print Preview to see the column layout.

◆ To line up columns evenly at the bottom, make sure that they have a section break after them and format the break with the Continuous option. (If they still don't line up evenly, open the Options dialog box, select the Compatibility card, look at the options for Microsoft Word 6, and turn off the Don't Balance Columns for Continuous Section Starts check box. You can make this a default by clicking the Default button.)

◆ If columns begin at the top of a new page and you don't want them to do so, format the section break before the columns as Continuous.

◆ On the ruler, notice that each column has its own white area. If you click in a particular column, you get indent markers for that column. You can change column widths by dragging the boundaries between the gray and white areas.

◆ To change anything about the column layout, go back to the Columns dialog box (with the appropriate text selected) and make the change. To open the Columns dialog box, double-click on the ruler in the gray area between two columns.

Making Text Wrap Around a Paragraph or Graphic

To separate a bit of text (or a graphic) so that the rest of the text flows around it, use a paragraph format called framing. *Framing* takes place in the text layer. For example, you may want to center a statement in the middle of a page to make it stand out more.

Here are the steps for setting up a frame:

1. Make sure that whatever you want to frame is in a separate paragraph from anything else. Framing is a paragraph format, so it's important to work with paragraphs.

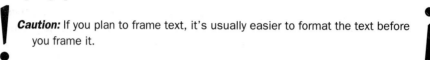

> **Caution:** If you plan to frame text, it's usually easier to format the text before you frame it.

2. Make sure that you are in Page Layout View and then select what you want to frame.

3. Choose Frame from the Insert menu. Word responds, as shown in Figure 7.9, by placing a frame around the selection, bordering the selection, inserting an extra paragraph mark, and anchoring the frame to that extra paragraph mark. Use the Zoom menu on the Standard toolbar or choose Zoom from the View menu to zoom to a size that shows how a frame looks on the page.

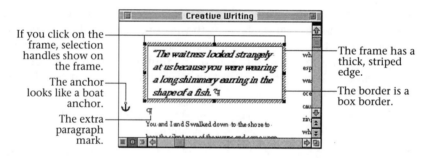

Figure 7.9 Word adds a frame, border, anchor, and paragraph mark after you frame something.

4. The next step depends on what you want to do with your frame. Here are a few possibilities:

   ◆ If you leave the frame alone, it remains aligned with the left margin, and the text wraps around it with a small gap between the frame and the text. If you add or delete text above the frame, the frame moves up or down correspondingly in the document.

   ◆ To change the frame's size, select the frame, click the frame itself, and drag a selection handle in the appropriate direction (see Figure 7.9). Text inside a frame behaves as though the edges of the frame are its margin. If you change the width of the frame, the text moves accordingly.

   ◆ If you like the idea of the frame moving up or down as you add or delete text, but you want the frame to start in a different spot, select the frame and position the pointer over the frame so that a four-way arrow sticks out of the bottom of the pointer. With the four-way arrow pointer, drag the frame to a different location.

◆ Adjust the indents for text within a frame to move the text closer to or farther from the edge of the frame.

5. If the possibilities in step 4 aren't enough, use the Frame dialog box to further manipulate your frame (see Figure 7.10). To access the dialog box, select the frame (after selecting the frame, you should see selection handles), go to the Format menu, and choose Frame. Or for a shortcut, double-click a frame (right on the edge) to open the Frame dialog box. I won't pretend that complex framing is easy to do—be prepared to experiment with different settings.

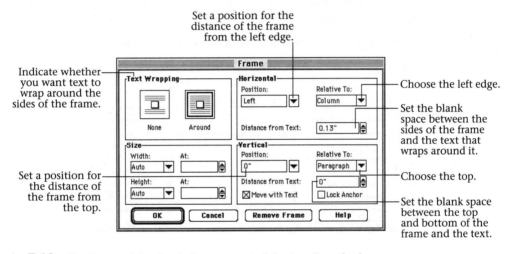

Figure 7.10   The Frame dialog box helps you control the location of a frame.

If you know that you eventually want to put a graphic in your document but you just want to insert a placeholder for now, you can insert an empty frame and use the frame as a place-holder. To insert an empty frame, click in an empty paragraph and then choose Frame from the Insert menu. The pointer turns into a crosshair. Use the crosshair pointer to drag out the shape of the frame.

Making Things Overlap

To make items overlap, take advantage of Word's three layers. The layer that text usually goes in is aptly named the text layer. Anything in the front drawing layer overlaps the text layer, and the text layer overlaps anything in the back drawing layer.

Any item created by using the Drawing toolbar goes into the front drawing layer (and can easily be moved into the back layer). So one way to make an item overlap the text layer is to make it by using the Drawing toolbar (see Chapter 8). For example, you can create a special effect by making a big gray oval and then move the oval into the back drawing layer so that the text overlaps the oval.

If you have an item in the text layer (text, graphics, OLE objects, and so on), you can move the item into either drawing layer and have it overlap other text. Here are the steps:

1. Select what you want to put in the drawing layer.

2. Cut or copy the selection.

3. Bring up the Drawing toolbar either by clicking the Picture button on the Standard toolbar or by using the Toolbars command in the View menu.

4. Click the Text Box button (on the Drawing toolbar). If you are not in Page Layout View, Word reminds you to switch. The pointer should look like a crosshair.

5. With the crosshair pointer, drag out a text box. Make the box a good size for holding the selection from step 1 (see Figure 7.11).

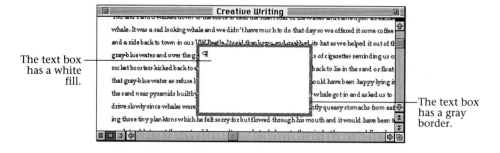

Figure 7.11   Create a text box in a drawing layer so that text or graphics can overlap the text layer.

6. Paste the selection into the text box.

7. You may need to adjust the text box before everything overlaps in the way you want it to (see Chapter 8).

Creating a Table of Contents

To make a table of contents, you first mark text in your document, and then you generate the table of contents. The table of contents is based on the text that you mark in the document. You can mark text for inclusion in the table of contents by applying a particular style or by inserting a special field, called the TC field.

Word automatically applies special styles to entries in a table of contents, and the styles are called TOC 1, TOC 2, TOC 3, and so on. The TOC styles correspond to levels of importance. For example, the table of contents in Figure 7.12 shows two chapter titles, and those titles are of level one importance. Because they are of level one importance, they are formatted with TOC 1. Figure 7.12 also shows items of level two importance that are formatted with TOC 2. A table of contents needs only one level of importance, and if that's all you have, don't worry too much about levels.

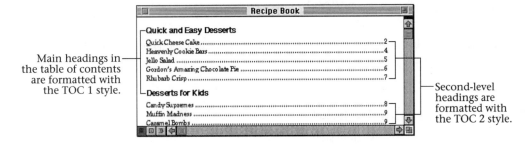

Main headings in the table of contents are formatted with the TOC 1 style.

Second-level headings are formatted with the TOC 2 style.

Figure 7.12   A table of contents can have levels, and Word uses a TOC style to format each level.

Marking entries

Word understands three different techniques for marking text for a table of contents. You can mix and match methods, or you can use the same technique for the entire document. The easiest technique is to use the heading styles built into Word, but you can also use your own paragraph styles or insert a TC field. If you use styles, you end up putting complete paragraphs (usually topic headings) into the table of contents, so if you need to mark less than a paragraph, use a TC field.

Marking entries with styles

To mark an entry by using a style, click in the paragraph that you want to mark as an entry and then apply the style. Use the same style for all entries that go with the same level of importance. In general, use the built-in heading styles—format level one text with Heading 1, level two text with Heading 2, and so on (see Figure 7.13). If a style (such as Heading 1) isn't available from the Style menu on the Formatting toolbar, press Shift while popping up the menu.

Main headings in the document are
formatted with Heading 1; they map to
TOC 1-formatted table of contents entries.

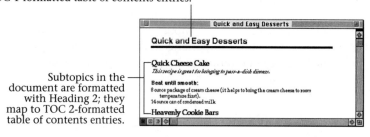

Subtopics in the
document are formatted
with Heading 2; they
map to TOC 2-formatted
table of contents entries.

Figure 7.13   The table of contents in Figure 7.12 came from text formatted with built-in heading
styles.

Marking entries with TC fields

To set up a TC field, follow these steps.

1. Highlight the text that you want to mark.

2. Press ⌘-Shift-Option-O (that's an "oh," not a zero). The Mark Table of Contents
   Entry dialog box appears (see Figure 7.14).

In most cases,
leave the
identifier set at C.

Enter a level
for the entry.

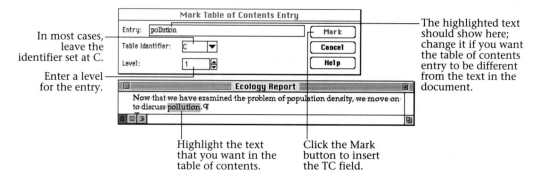

The highlighted text
should show here;
change it if you want
the table of contents
entry to be different
from the text in the
document.

Highlight the text
that you want in the
table of contents.

Click the Mark
button to insert
the TC field.

Figure 7.14   To make a table of contents entry without using a paragraph style, use the Mark Table
of Contents Entry dialog box.

3. If necessary, change the entry level.

4. In most cases, leave the identifier set at C. (*C* stands for "contents" in table of
   contents.)

5. Click the Mark button. The dialog box remains open and a TC field appears in the
   document (see Figure 7.15).

6. If you want to insert more TC fields, leave the dialog box open and continue selecting text and marking it.

7. After you finish, click the Close button.

The result of a TC field may display as nothing at all. If you want to see the TC field as a code, note that the code displays in hidden text.

The field
name is TC.

\l "1" means the entry
goes with level one.

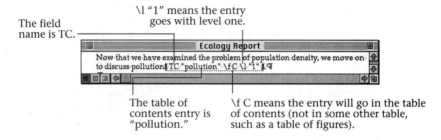

The table of
contents entry is
"pollution."

\f C means the entry will go in the table
of contents (not in some other table,
such as a table of figures).

Figure 7.15   The result of a TC field shows coded information about the field.

Generating a table of contents

You can generate a table of contents at any time, so feel free to try an experimental table of contents after marking only a few entries. Here are the steps:

1. Position the insertion point where you want the table of contents to appear.

2. From the Insert menu, choose Index and Tables and then select the Table of Contents card.

3. If you used the built-in heading styles to mark all the table of contents entries, skip ahead to step 7. Otherwise, click the Options button to open the Table of Contents Options dialog box (see Figure 7.16).

Fill in the TOC Level
for styles used to
mark entries.

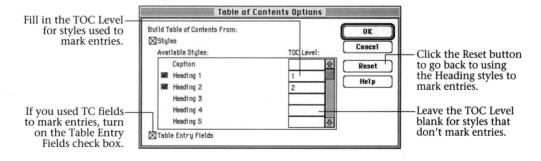

Click the Reset button
to go back to using
the Heading styles to
mark entries.

If you used TC fields
to mark entries, turn
on the Table Entry
Fields check box.

Leave the TOC Level
blank for styles that
don't mark entries.

Figure 7.16   Indicate how Word should look for table of contents entries.

4. If you used styles to mark table of contents entries, turn on the Styles check box and use the scroll bar to find the styles that you used. For each style that you used, type a number to indicate the level it should map to.

5. If you used any TC fields to mark entries, turn on the Table Entry Fields check box.

6. Click the OK button to return to the Table of Contents card (see Figure 7.17).

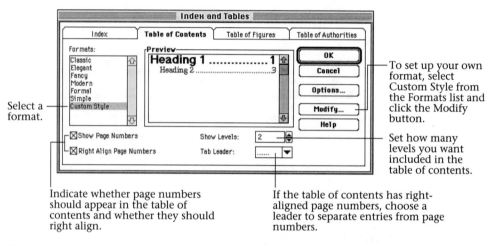

Select a format. — To set up your own format, select Custom Style from the Formats list and click the Modify button.

Set how many levels you want included in the table of contents.

Indicate whether page numbers should appear in the table of contents and whether they should right align.

If the table of contents has right-aligned page numbers, choose a leader to separate entries from page numbers.

Figure 7.17   Use the Table of Contents card to format and preview a table of contents.

7. To make page numbers appear in the table of contents, turn on the Show Page Numbers check box. To right align the page numbers, turn on Right Align Page Numbers. Finally, choose a tab leader.

8. Indicate how many levels you want in the table of contents. For example, if you used Heading styles 1–5 for your document, but you want only the first two levels to appear in the table of contents, enter **2** in the Show Levels box.

9. Pick a format. If you don't like the suggested formats, select Custom Style and then click the Modify button. If you click the Modify button, Word switches you into a special version of the Style dialog box, where you can modify any of the TOC styles (see Chapter 5).

10. Click the OK button.

Word churns through the document, finds the marked entries, and creates a TOC field. If you have the result showing for the field, you see a table of contents.

Updating a table of contents

To update the table of contents, update the TOC field. Updating the TOC field works much like updating any field—you click in the field and then press F9 (or Control-click to use the shortcut menu). Most fields update without asking you any questions, but the TOC field puts up a dialog box asking what exactly it should update (see Figure 7.18). Just update the page numbers if you haven't added or removed any entries.

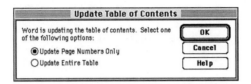

Figure 7.18   A dialog box appears when you update the TOC field.

Making Footnotes and Endnotes

Word takes a lot of the pain out of making footnotes and endnotes by handling the numbering and positioning for you. Word thinks of footnotes and endnotes as separate entities. Footnotes appear on the page you reference them on, but endnotes appear at the end of the document or at the end of each section. You can use only footnotes, only endnotes, or both.

Inserting a footnote or endnote

To create a footnote or an endnote, follow these steps:

1. Position the insertion point where you want the reference mark to appear in the text. If you know that the options in the Footnote and Endnote dialog box are correct, you can insert a footnote by pressing ⌘-Option-F. To insert an endnote, press ⌘-Option-E.

2. From the Insert menu, choose Footnote. The Footnote and Endnote dialog box appears (see Figure 7.19).

3. Indicate whether you want to insert a footnote or endnote.

4. The position in which the note will insert shows on the right side of the Insert area. To change the position, click the Options button to open the Note Options dialog box and select a card (All Footnotes for footnotes; All Endnotes for endnotes). In the card, choose a position from the Place At menu and click the OK button (see Figure 7.20).

Word shows where the footnote
or endnote will be placed.

Select the type of note.

Word shows the
numbering
scheme the note
will use.

To have Word number
the note for you, select
AutoNumber.

To use a custom mark, select
Custom Mark and enter the mark.

To change the note
positions or to change the
AutoNumber numbering
scheme, click the Options
button.

If you have trouble typing
the custom mark, click the
Symbol button and select a
mark.

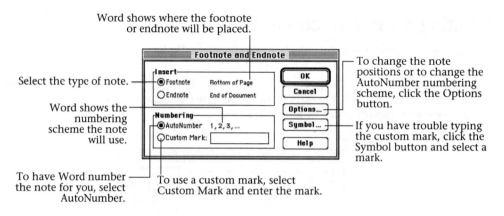

Figure 7.19   The Footnote and Endnote dialog box shows how a footnote or endnote will appear
after you insert it.

Click the tab to view the
All Endnotes card.

Choose a location
for the notes.

Enter a starting
number for the
notes.

Select Continu-
ous to make the
numbering run
straight through
the document.

Choose a
numbering
format.

Select Restart Each Section or Restart Each
Page to make the numbering reset to 1 at the
start of each section or page.

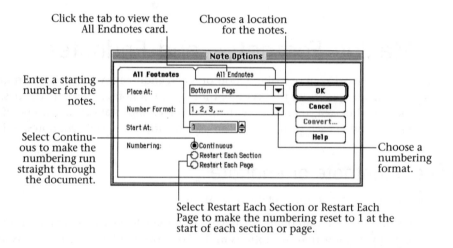

Figure 7.20   Use the Note Options dialog box to customize footnotes and endnotes.

5. Select how you want the footnote or endnote to be numbered:

    ◆ If you want Word to handle the numbering and renumbering, select
       AutoNumber. You can customize the way AutoNumber works by clicking
       the Options button, which brings up the Note Options dialog box (see
       Figure 7.20).

    ◆ If you select Custom Mark, you must handle the numbering yourself, so
       select Custom Mark at your own risk. The AutoNumber choices include
       alphabetic characters and special marks, such as the asterisk, dagger, double-
       dagger, and so on. If you select Custom Mark, enter the mark you want to

use. If you have trouble typing the mark, click the Symbol button to jump into the Symbol dialog box. In the Symbol dialog box, double-click the character that you want to use.

6. Click the OK button. Word shows a split window with two panes. In the lower pane, you should see the insertion point flashing directly after a new reference mark (see Figure 7.21). (If Word does not show a split screen, it's okay. You aren't seeing a split because you are in Page Layout View.) In the split window view of the notes, use the menu at the top of the note pane to switch between viewing footnotes and endnotes.

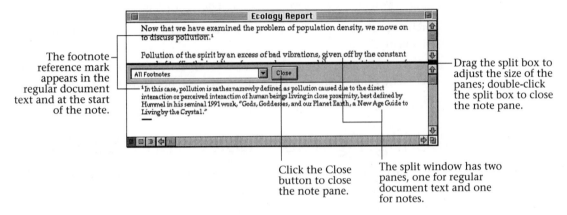

The footnote reference mark appears in the regular document text and at the start of the note.

Drag the split box to adjust the size of the panes; double-click the split box to close the note pane.

Click the Close button to close the note pane.

The split window has two panes, one for regular document text and one for notes.

Figure 7.21   Enter the text of a note in the note pane.

7. Type the note text.

8. If you have a Close button, click it. (If you are in Page Layout View, you won't have a Close button; instead, just scroll up or down to continue working on the document.)

To make two reference marks in the main text of the document correspond to one reference note, set up one reference mark and note normally and then use the Cross-reference command to set up the second mark (flip ahead a few pages to find out how).

Deleting a note

To delete a note, highlight the reference mark as it appears in the regular document text and cut the mark. After you cut the mark, the entire note disappears.

Formatting reference marks and notes

You can format reference marks and text just like any other bits of text, but to globally change them, modify the appropriate character style—Endnote Reference or Footnote Reference. Similarly, note text has the following character styles—Endnote Text or Footnote Text. See Chapter 5 for help with styles.

Editing an existing note

In Page Layout View, you can edit notes directly on the page. The notes don't show in Normal View, but you can split the window and show the notes at the bottom by choosing Footnotes from the View menu. If you become involved in editing notes, try these tips:

◆ To switch to the text of a note, double-click the reference mark in the main part of the document.

◆ To move the insertion point to the spot after a reference mark in the main part of the document, double-click the corresponding reference mark in the note area.

Numbering Figures, Tables, and So On

Word comes with a captioning feature that helps you number a series of items (such as tables, drawings, or equations) throughout a document (see Figure 7.22).

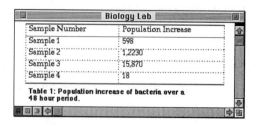

Figure 7.22   Word makes captions for special document elements, such as tables.

Word helps with making captions in three main ways:

◆ Word keeps track of caption numbering so that you do not need to go back and redo numbers by hand, even if you insert items nonsequentially.

◆ The AutoCaption feature can automatically insert captions.

◆ Word can number more than one series of items in a document. For example, you can number tables as one series and figures as a separate series. Different labels (such as *Table* and *Figure*) distinguish each series.

Inserting a caption by hand

To insert a caption, follow these steps:

1. Select the item that you want to caption.

2. From the Insert menu, choose Caption. The Caption dialog box appears (see Figure 7.23) and shows a proposed caption at the upper left. The proposed caption has a label and a number.

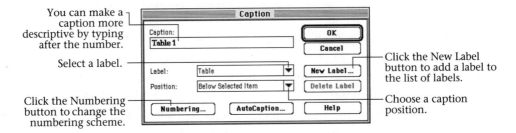

You can make a caption more descriptive by typing after the number.

Select a label.

Click the Numbering button to change the numbering scheme.

Click the New Label button to add a label to the list of labels.

Choose a caption position.

Figure 7.23   Use the Caption dialog box to set up a label and numbering scheme for a series of captions.

3. To change the proposed label, select a label or create your own label by clicking the New Label button.

4. To change the numbering, click the Numbering button. In the Caption Numbering dialog box, select a scheme from the Format menu. If you decide to include the chapter number, you must have the chapter number set up with the Heading Numbering command (see Chapter 5 for more information). When you finish the numbering setup, click the OK button.

5. In the Caption dialog box, click the OK button to insert the caption.

The caption should appear. If you have field codes showing, the caption appears as an SEQ field.

Making Word automatically insert captions

To make Word do more of the captioning work, use AutoCaption. AutoCaption doesn't retroactively put captions in a document, but it does add captions as you insert new items. Here are the steps for setting it up:

1. From the Insert menu, choose Caption. The Caption dialog box appears.

2. Click the AutoCaption button to bring up the AutoCaption dialog box (see Figure 7.24).

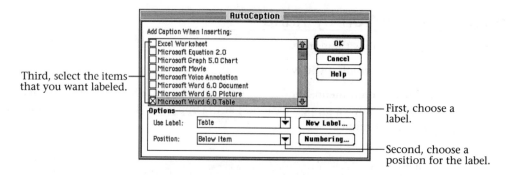

Third, select the items that you want labeled.

First, choose a label.

Second, choose a position for the label.

Figure 7.24   Use the AutoCaption dialog box to set up Word to insert captions automatically.

3. Select a label and a position for the caption. For example, to caption each table in a document, you can select Table as the label and Above Item as the position.

4. Select the item (or items) that go with the label and position. For example, to number tables, select the Microsoft Word 6.0 Table check box.

5. Click the OK button. In the future, after you insert an item that you selected in step 4, Word inserts a caption with the correct label and number.

Word formats all captions in the Caption paragraph style. If you don't like the formats in the style, change them. Chapter 5 explains how.

Changing a used caption label

What if a document has a whole series of captions, but the label or the numbering scheme (or both) is wrong? If a set of captions all have the same label, you can change all the captions by changing just one. Here are the steps:

1. In the document, highlight one of the captions that you need to change.

2. Go to the Insert menu and choose Caption. The Caption dialog box appears.

3. Correct the problem. It's okay to change the label and the numbering scheme.

4. Click the OK button. Word fixes all the captions that have the same label as the caption you clicked in step 1.

Making Cross-References

Word has a handy cross-referencing feature that makes it easy to refer to topic headings, captions, footnotes, and more. After you set up a cross-reference, Word helps keep the cross-reference up-to-date. Here are the steps:

1. Position the insertion point where you want the cross-reference to begin.

2. From the Insert menu, choose Cross-reference. The Cross-reference dialog box opens (see Figure 7.25).

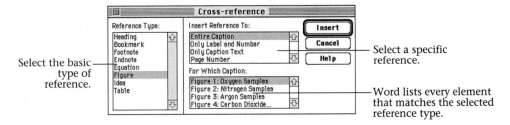

Figure 7.25   Use the Cross-reference dialog box to set up cross-references.

3. Select a reference type. Table 7.3 explains more about each reference type.

4. After you select a reference type, Word looks through the document for all instances of the chosen reference type and lists them at the lower right. Choose the instance to which you want to make a cross-reference.

5. From the Insert Reference To list, select the information that you want to reference. (You can come back right away and insert another piece of information, so don't worry if you want to insert more than one piece.)

6. Click the Insert button. The cross-reference appears in the document, but the dialog box stays open (in case you want to adjust the position of the insertion point and then insert another cross-reference).

7. Click the Close button after you finish using the dialog box.

Be aware that cross-references are actually fields. If the fields cross-reference incorrectly or look extremely strange, use techniques for working with fields to make them behave. Keep in mind that cross-references update when you switch into Print Preview or when you print.

Table 7.3

Items That You Can Cross-Reference

Item in the Reference Type list	Information
Heading	A heading is any paragraph formatted with one of the built-in heading styles.
Bookmark	A bookmark refers to a chunk of text that you have marked and given a name.
Footnote and Endnote	Footnotes and endnotes are references set up through the Footnote command on the Insert menu.
Equation, Figure, Table	These items refer to labels used in captions. You can find out more about them a little earlier in this chapter.
Other	Anything else listed in the Reference Type list is a custom label that you set up in the Caption dialog box.

Setting Up Hypertext Links

Hypertext links may sound like they are from the moon (or perhaps an ivory tower), but you can set up links within documents that make it easy to jump from one location to another. For example, if people will be reading your Word document online, you may want to put in a few links that let readers jump directly from the table of contents to the main topic headings.

Recently, hypertext links have received a lot of press—they are the way people move around on the World-Wide Web, an extremely popular way to use the Internet. If you are reading this section because you want to know how Word can help you make documents for displaying on the Web (such as a home page), flip to the section on conversions in Chapter 1.

Hypertext links can use two different fields:

◆ The GoToButton field lets you jump to any bookmark, a mark that helps you move quickly to a desired location.

◆ The MacroButton field lets you run any macro. You can set up macros to jump to many different document elements.

The GoToButton is easier to set up if you aren't particularly comfortable with macros, but the MacroButton gives you more power and flexibility, and the macro isn't particularly difficult to record.

Setting up a GoToButton field

To create a GoToButton field, follow these steps:

1. Insert a bookmark for the destination. To create a bookmark, select the text, go to the Edit menu, and choose Bookmark. In the Bookmark dialog box, type a name for the bookmark and then click the Add button.

2. Position the insertion point where you want the hypertext link.

3. Go to the Insert menu and choose Field.

4. In the Field dialog box, select the Document Automation category and then select the GoToButton field name.

5. Click the Options button. The Field Options dialog box opens (see Figure 7.26).

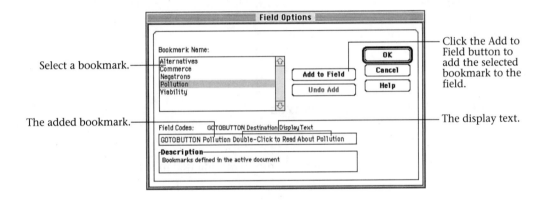

Figure 7.26   Add a bookmark and type the display text.

6. From the Bookmark Name list, select the bookmark to which you want to link.

7. Click the Add to Field button. The bookmark name appears in the text box toward the bottom of the dialog box.

8. After the bookmark name, type the name that you want to appear on the button. The name, called the "display text," will be the text that shows in the document.

9. Click the OK button to return to the Field dialog box and then click the OK button to return to the document.

When the GoToButton field displays its results, all you will see is the display text. Double-click the display text to move to the bookmark.

You can format the display text much as you would format any other text in the document. For example, if the field is in a paragraph by itself, you can make it look more like a button by putting a paragraph border around it (see Chapter 8 to find out about borders).

Setting up a MacroButton field

The steps for making a MacroButton field are virtually identical to those for making a GoToButton field. In the Fields dialog box, select MacroButton. In the Field Options dialog box, you may have to do a bit of scrolling to find your macro.

Making an Index

To create an index, you must complete two main steps—first, marking the entries; and second, generating the index. The entries get marked with a field called XE, and the index is a field called INDEX. Table 7.4 shows the main possibilities for what entries can look like in the actual index.

Table 7.4

Common Index Entries Used in Indexes

Entry	Comments
Apple, 4, 255	A basic entry in a run-in or indented index
Page Setup, **308**	A basic entry with a bold page number
PowerBooks, 42–56	A basic index entry using a bookmark to set a page range
Dogcow. *See* Page Setup	A basic index entry with a cross-reference
Apple, 1-4, 5-255	A basic index entry that includes the chapter number and the page number
Apple PowerBooks Duo 230, 44	A three-level entry in an indented index
Apple: PowerBooks; Duo 230, 44	A three-level entry in a run-in index

Marking index entries

Entries tell Word which information and page numbers are put in the index. You can set them up one at a time with no automation; one at a time but with a little automation; or via a concordance table, which lists all the information that you want Word to use.

Marking entries one at a time

To mark an entry, follow these steps:

1. Click on the page to which the entry corresponds or select the actual text that will make up the entry.

2. From the Insert menu, choose Index and Tables. In the resulting dialog box, click the Mark Entry button or press ⌘-Shift-Option-X to open the Mark Index Entry dialog box (see Figure 7.27).

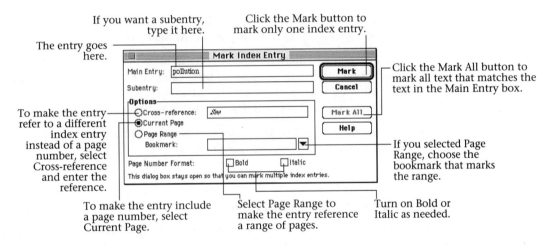

Figure 7.27 Mark text for inclusion in the index and indicate exactly what the index entry should look like.

3. If you selected text in step 1, it shows in the Main Entry box. You can edit the main entry text or type additional text.

4. To make a two-level entry, enter the second level in the subentry box. In the unlikely circumstance that you need a third-level entry, type a colon after the second-level entry and then type the third level.

195

5. Select a reference option:

 ◆ Cross-reference gives you a reference as shown in the fourth example in Table 7.4 (the Dogcow). Type the text for the cross-reference in the Cross-reference box.

 ◆ Current Page gives you a page number. The index uses the same numbering scheme as the page numbers. (Chapter 5 explains how to change the page numbering scheme.)

 ◆ Page Range gives you a range of pages, such as the range shown in the fifth example in Table 7.4. To indicate the correct page range, set up a bookmark that spans the correct range. To create a bookmark, select the text, go to the Edit menu, and choose Bookmark. In the Bookmark dialog box, type a name for the bookmark and then click the Add button. After you have the book-mark set up, you can choose it from the Bookmark menu in the Mark Index Entry dialog box.

6. If you want the page number (or page range) to be in bold or italic, turn on the corresponding check box at the bottom of the dialog box.

7. You are now ready to mark the entry. You can mark only one entry (at the location of the selection or the insertion point) by clicking the Mark button, or you can mark all identical entries by clicking the Mark All button. If you choose to mark all identical entries, Word marks the first identical entry in each paragraph.

8. The dialog box does not close (in case you want to mark more entries). After you finish marking entries, click the Close button.

Marking entries with a concordance file

If you have a lot of entries to mark, and if you want them to appear in the index with plain text page numbers, you can type all the words in one document (called a *concordance file*) and then use the AutoMark feature to mark all the entries.

To set up the concordance file, follow these steps:

1. Press ⌘-N to start a new document based on the Normal template.

2. In the first line of the document, type the first word or phrase that you want to index. Word matches this word or phrase exactly to the text in the documents that you mark, so be extra careful with spelling and punctuation.

3. Under normal circumstances, when Word processes the concordance file you are creating, Word takes the text that you typed in step 2, marks it in the document, and includes it in the index. If you don't want the exact same text to end up in the

index, press Tab, and then type the text that you want in the index. For example, you may want *chocolate* and *Chocolate* to be indexed as *Chocolate.*

4. Press Return.

5. Continue steps 2 through 4 until you have entered all the text. You don't need to press Return after entering the last line of text.

6. Save the file just as you would save any other file.

To use the concordance file for marking text, follow these steps:

1. In the document that you want to index, go to the Insert menu, choose Index and Tables, and then select the Index card.

2. On the right side of the Index card, click the AutoMark button. The Open dialog box appears.

3. Locate and open the concordance file. Word searches the document for text that matches the entries in the concordance file and marks the text that it finds as index entries. If the same entry occurs more than once in the same paragraph, Word marks only the first entry.

Viewing index entries

An index entry is actually an XE field, and it has two peculiarities:

◆ Its code is the same as its result, so showing or hiding a code doesn't change its appearance.

◆ Word formats an XE field as hidden text, so you can't see it if you have the check box for viewing hidden text turned off. (The check box is located in the View card of the Options dialog box from the Tools menu.) The light gray underline beneath the XE field is your clue that the field is formatted as hidden text.

Generating an index

If you have a few index entries marked, you can make an index. Here are the steps:

1. Position the insertion point at the spot where you want the index to begin.

2. Go to the Insert menu, choose Index and Tables, and select the Index card (see Figure 7.28).

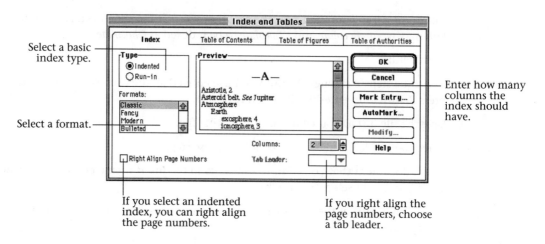

Select a basic index type.

Select a format.

Enter how many columns the index should have.

If you select an indented index, you can right align the page numbers.

If you right align the page numbers, choose a tab leader.

Figure 7.28   Set up the basic formatting for the index.

3. Select an index type. For an indented index, you can right align the page numbers, and if you right align the numbers, you can choose a tab leader for the page numbers. Note that as you select different options, the Preview area shows what they will look like in the index.

4. Select an index format. If you don't like any of the formats, select Custom Style from the Formats list and click the Modify button. If you click the Modify button, Word switches into the Style dialog box and lists the nine index styles. Index 1 corresponds to index entries that have no subentry. If you have subentries, and you make an indented index, Index 1 corresponds to main entries, Index 2 to second-level subentries, Index 3 to third level subentries, and so on.

5. Select the number of columns that you want the index to have. If the index is supposed to have more than one column, you must be in Page Layout View or Print Preview to see the multiple columns.

6. Click the OK button. Word churns through the document, looking for index entries and incorporating them into the index.

The index appears as an INDEX field, and if you have the field result showing, you'll see an index. To update the index, click in the index and then press F9 (or Control-click the index and choose Update Field from the shortcut menu).

You should now have a good understanding of how to insert special document elements such as regular tables, tables of contents, cross-references, and captions. The next chapter explains how to import and create graphics.

Chapter 8

Using Graphics and Borders

This chapter fills you in on how to work with graphics and how to make borders. By *graphics,* I mean pictures that you bring into Word or create with the Drawing toolbar; by *borders,* I mean straight lines that run along the edges of paragraphs. These two elements can really add to the overall visual impact of your documents. Look for these topics to be covered in this chapter:

- ◆ Understanding basic background information about handling graphics in Word
- ◆ Pasting graphics into Word
- ◆ Converting graphics into Word
- ◆ Creating new graphics
- ◆ Moving graphics and text between layers
- ◆ Moving graphics around within a layer
- ◆ Creating borders

How Word Thinks About Graphics

How Word treats a graphic depends on which layer the graphic is in. Word has three layers: a front drawing layer, a text layer, and a back drawing layer. Think of the layers as three sheets of clear plastic:

◆ Items on the front drawing layer block items on the other layers.

◆ Items on the text layer (such as text that you type) block items on the back layer.

◆ Items on the back drawing layer fall behind items on the other layers.

For a graphic to overlap (or underlap) text, the graphic must be on one of the drawing layers (see Figure 8.1). For text to flow around the graphic, the graphic must be on the text layer, where you can frame it.

Headers and Footers also have layers, so you can create a *watermark*—a light-colored picture that sits beneath the text of a document—by placing a graphic or a stylized bit of text in the back drawing layer of the header or footer.

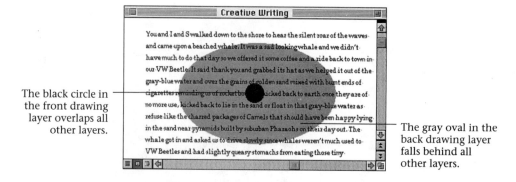

The black circle in the front drawing layer overlaps all other layers.

The gray oval in the back drawing layer falls behind all other layers.

Figure 8.1 Word has three layers—the front drawing layer, the text layer, and the back drawing layer.

The drawing layers

If you create a graphic by using Word's drawing tools, the graphic appears in the front drawing layer, but you can move it to the text layer or to the back drawing layer. In Normal View, shapes from the drawing layers don't appear. Switch to Page Layout View to see the shapes. If you temporarily don't want to see the shapes in Page Layout View, turn off the Drawings check box on the View card in the Options dialog box from the Tools menu.

The text layer

Everything you create in Word falls on the text layer, except for graphics that you make by using the Drawing toolbar. If you import a graphic, it imports into the text layer. You can leave it in the text layer or switch it into a drawing layer.

The text layer treats graphics like big characters. For example, a 3-inch high graphic sits in the regular text stream of a document just as a *W* would if you formatted it to be 3 inches tall.

Whether you import graphics or create your own, you'll find them easier to work with if you know a few basic techniques for handling graphics in the text layer:

◆ If a graphic cuts off at the top, you may have line spacing set too low. To change the line spacing for a paragraph, select the paragraph and then choose Paragraph from the Format menu. In the Paragraph dialog box, select the Indents and Spacing card and choose Auto from the Line Spacing menu.

◆ If a graphic appears as an empty box, you have Picture Placeholders turned on in the View card of the Options dialog box. With Picture Placeholders on, imported graphics and graphics in the text layer show as boxes. When graphics show as boxes, scrolling past them should go faster.

◆ To resize a graphic in the text layer, click an edge of the graphic. Clicking an edge selects the graphic, and you should see selection handles on the edges of the graphic. To change the size of the graphic, drag one of the selection handles (see Figure 8.2). To crop the graphic, Shift-drag a handle. To undo any cropping and scaling, ⌘-double-click on the graphic.

◆ To more precisely crop or scale a graphic, select the graphic, go to the Format menu, and choose Picture.

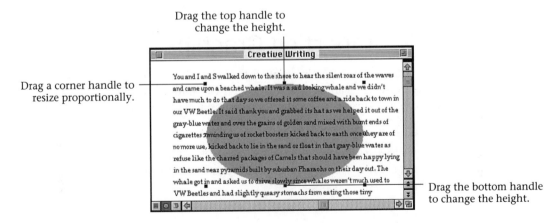

Figure 8.2   Use the selection handles to resize a graphic in the text layer.

◆ To position a graphic in a specific location in the text layer, set up a table or a frame. If you set up a table, you can put the graphic in one cell and then place related text in a different cell.

◆ To edit a graphic in the text layer, you must double-click the graphic. A Picture window opens, and the graphic appears with a boundary line around it (see Figure 8.3). Use the Drawing toolbar to edit the graphic (look ahead a few pages to learn more about the Drawing toolbar). When you are ready to return to the text layer, click the Reset Picture Boundary button and then the Close Picture button (both buttons are on the Picture toolbar).

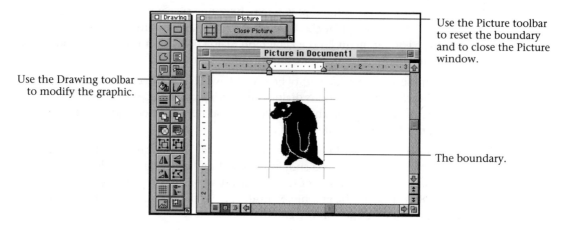

Use the Picture toolbar to reset the boundary and to close the Picture window.

Use the Drawing toolbar to modify the graphic.

The boundary.

Figure 8.3   If you double-click a graphic in the text layer, a Picture window opens for editing the graphic.

Importing Graphics

Word has two techniques for bringing in graphics made in other programs—pasting and converting. If you convert, you can completely convert the graphic, or you can link to it so that the graphic exists as a separate file and does not substantially increase the size of the Word document.

! **Caution:** Use linking with care until you are certain that it works well on your Macintosh because linking requires a good deal of cooperation among programs.

Pasting

Because virtually every Macintosh graphics program supports the Cut, Copy, and Paste commands, the traditional method of moving graphics around is to cut, copy, and paste them. In transferring the graphic through the Clipboard (which you must do in order to paste), the graphic may lose a substantial portion of its quality. However, if you paste graphics from PostScript-oriented programs (such as FreeHand or Illustrator), you can use a special trick to preserve the quality. Here are the steps for pasting a graphic into Word:

1. Open the graphics file in an appropriate program (such as MacDraw, SuperPaint, Illustrator, or Freehand).

2. Select the graphic.

3. From the Edit menu, choose Copy (or press ⌘-C). If you are in a PostScript-based program and want to include the underlying PostScript code with the screen picture (so that you don't lose any quality in bringing the picture into Word), press ⌘-Option-C to copy the graphic.

4. Open the Word document in which you want to paste the graphic and position the insertion point where you want the graphic to go.

5. From the Edit menu, choose Paste. You can also press ⌘-V or click the Paste button on the Standard toolbar.

The graphic appears in the text layer.

Converting

Word comes with graphics that you can import for your own use. The clip art is in the folder, called ClipArt, in which you installed Word. Word also comes with translators that can convert EPS, TIFF, PICT, WPG, and PAINT files into the text layer of a Word document. To convert a file, follow these steps:

1. Place the insertion point in the location where you want the graphic to appear.

2. From the Insert menu, choose Picture. A special Open dialog box appears (see Figure 8.4).

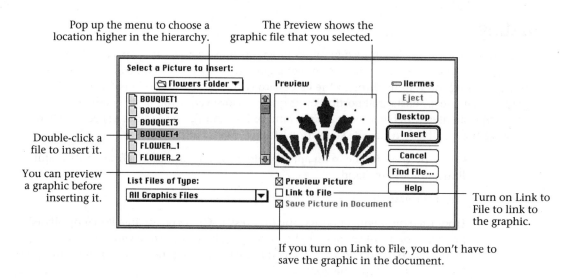

Pop up the menu to choose a
location higher in the hierarchy.

The Preview shows the
graphic file that you selected.

Double-click a
file to insert it.

You can preview
a graphic before
inserting it.

Turn on Link to
File to link to
the graphic.

If you turn on Link to File, you don't have to
save the graphic in the document.

Figure 8.4   The dialog box for converting a picture has a few special options.

3. To link to the graphic so that when the original copy of the graphic changes, the copy in the Word document changes as well, turn on the Link to File check box. Otherwise, turn off the check box.

4. If you link to the graphic, you don't have to store a copy of the graphic in the Word document. By not storing the copy, you keep the file size of the document more reasonable, but you slow things down because Word must access the original file to show the graphic. (If Word can't find the graphic file, it shows the last known version of the graphic, and the graphic may not look that great when it prints.)

5. Locate and open the graphic.

Word will take a few moments (or even minutes) to convert the graphic.

To bring a PostScript text file into Word, open it just as you would open any text file. After you open the file and view the PostScript commands, if you want to send the commands to a PostScript printer and have the printer interpret them, you must put the commands in a Print field (see Chapter 10).

Creating Your Own Graphics

To create graphics in Word, use the buttons on the Drawing toolbar (see Figure 8.5). The buttons enable you to create shapes, and the shapes get placed in the front drawing layer, unless you are working in the Picture window.

Word offers many methods for displaying the Drawing toolbar, so feel free to use whichever method is easiest for you. Here are a few possibilities:

◆ Click the Drawing button on the Standard toolbar (it looks like a collection of shapes).

◆ Control-click a toolbar to bring up the Toolbar shortcut menu and choose Drawing.

◆ From the View menu, choose Toolbars. Turn on the Drawing check box and click the OK button.

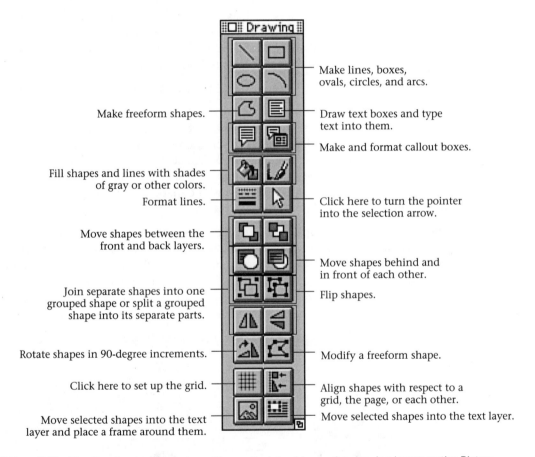

Make lines, boxes, ovals, circles, and arcs.

Make freeform shapes.

Draw text boxes and type text into them.

Make and format callout boxes.

Fill shapes and lines with shades of gray or other colors.

Format lines.

Click here to turn the pointer into the selection arrow.

Move shapes between the front and back layers.

Move shapes behind and in front of each other.

Join separate shapes into one grouped shape or split a grouped shape into its separate parts.

Flip shapes.

Rotate shapes in 90-degree increments.

Modify a freeform shape.

Click here to set up the grid.

Align shapes with respect to a grid, the page, or each other.

Move selected shapes into the text layer and place a frame around them.

Move selected shapes into the text layer.

Figure 8.5   The Drawing toolbar helps with creating graphics in the drawing layers or the Picture window.

The Drawing toolbar offers tools for making basic shapes, which you can color and combine to create images. You can type text by creating a text box or a callout box and then typing inside the box.

To create a shape, click the corresponding button. Click where you want the shape to begin and then drag out the shape. To make a regular shape, press Shift while you drag out the shape. For example, to draw a circle, click the Ellipse button and then press Shift while dragging.

If you double-click a shape button, you can draw more than one instance of the shape without clicking the button again.

If you select the Freeform button and then start dragging, you can draw any shape. Dragging works much like drawing with a pencil. When you finish drawing the shape, double-click. To make a freeform shape with straight edges (such as a star), click where you want one edge to start and then click where you want the edge to end. Continue clicking until you have drawn all the edges. Double-click to stop drawing the shape. You can also make a freeform shape (such as an ice cream cone shape) with some edges straight and some drawn by hand.

After making a shape, you can change its appearance by selecting the shape and then doing something to it.

Use the selection pointer to select a shape. The pointer looks like an arrow when it isn't over a shape or a toolbar. To make sure that you have a selection pointer, click the Select Drawing Object button. With the selection pointer, click on the shape. If you have trouble selecting a shape, click on the edge of the shape. To select multiple shapes at once, press Shift while you click on the shapes or drag out a selection box around the shapes. The selection box has a dashed outline, sometimes referred to as "marching ants."

To format the edge or color of a shape, select the shape, go to the Format menu, and choose Drawing Object. To open the Drawing Object dialog box, Control-click on a shape and choose Format Drawing Object from the resulting shortcut menu. The Fill and Line cards offer many options for formatting shapes (see Figure 8.6). If you open the Drawing Object dialog box without selecting anything, any changes that you make become defaults for new shapes.

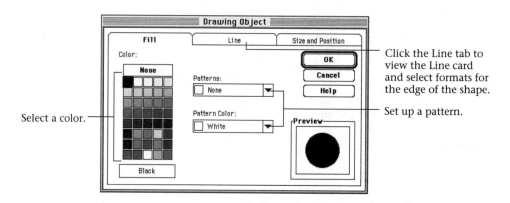

Figure 8.6 You can change the appearance of a shape in the Drawing Object dialog box.

Moving Text Between Layers

To move text from the text layer into one of the drawing layers, first highlight and cut the text. Second, using the Drawing toolbar, insert a text box or a callout box. The box automatically goes into the front drawing layer. Finally, paste the text into the box.

To move text from a drawing layer into the text layer, highlight the text within its box, cut the text, place the insertion point where you want the text to go, and then paste the text in place.

Moving Graphics Between Layers

To move a graphic (such as an imported graphic, a chart, or a WordArt object) into a drawing layer, try these steps:

1. In the text layer, select and cut the graphic.

2. On the Drawing toolbar, click the Text Box button.

3. Drag out a text box. The insertion point should be inside the text box at the upper left.

4. Paste the graphic into the text box. If necessary, resize the box to make the graphic fit nicely (drag a selection handle).

5. The text box (and hence the graphic) is in the front layer. If you want it in the back layer, select the text box and click the Send Behind Text button.

To move a graphic from a drawing layer into the text layer, select the graphic and click the Create Picture button on the Drawing toolbar.

Aligning Shapes

To make the edges or centers of a few shapes line up (see Figure 8.7), use the Align Drawing Objects button. Select the shapes and then click the button. In the resulting Align dialog box, select the appropriate options and click the OK button.

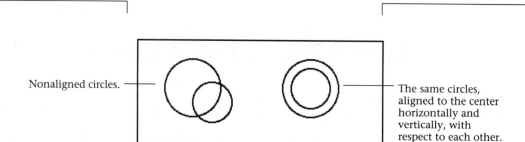

Nonaligned circles.

The same circles, aligned to the center horizontally and vertically, with respect to each other.

Figure 8.7   Use the Align dialog box to set up concentric circles.

How Word Moves Shapes for You

If you select a shape and have nonprinting characters showing, you should see an anchor. The anchor does not mean that the shape has nautical yearnings; instead, it indicates that the shape is attached to a particular paragraph (see Figure 8.8). If you move the paragraph in the course of editing the document, the shape moves along, as well.

The anchor.

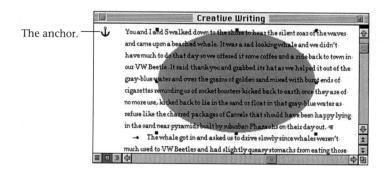

Figure 8.8   Each shape has an anchor.

Moving Shapes Within the Drawing Layer

You can move shapes visually by dragging them, or you can move them numerically by entering measurements in the appropriate dialog box.

Moving shapes by dragging

To move a shape, place the selection pointer (click the Select Drawing Objects button to get a selection pointer) over the edge of the shape (but not over a selection handle) and then drag the shape. Press Shift while moving a shape to move it only horizontally or vertically. If the shape has a color or pattern filling it, you can also place the pointer over the shape's interior.

As you move shapes, the grid may affect the movement. The *grid* is an invisible cross-hatching of lines (much like a window screen), which you can modify by clicking the Snap to Grid button. In the Snap to Grid dialog box, you can set the spacing between the gridlines, and you can activate the Snap to Grid option (see Figure 8.9).

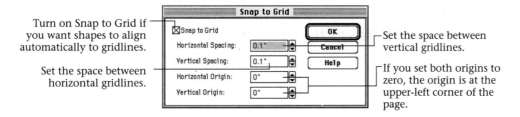

Turn on Snap to Grid if you want shapes to align automatically to gridlines.

Set the space between horizontal gridlines.

Set the space between vertical gridlines.

If you set both origins to zero, the origin is at the upper-left corner of the page.

Figure 8.9   You can adjust how the grid works in the Snap to Grid dialog box.

With Snap to Grid on, shapes automatically line up with the gridlines. If you set the gridlines farther apart than the default (.1 inch) and move shapes with Snap to Grid on, you feel the invisible gridlines attracting the shapes. To toggle Snap to Grid off or on while you move a shape, press ⌘ while dragging the shape.

To "nudge" a shape over a small amount (approximately one point), press Option–arrow key. The arrow key that you press determines the direction of the nudge. Or to move an object to the next gridline in a particular direction, select the object and then press one of the arrow keys.

Moving shapes numerically

To move a shape numerically, select the shape, go to the Format menu, and choose Drawing Object. In the Drawing Object dialog box, select the Size and Position card. To quickly bring up the Size and Position card, double-click the shape's anchor. Even though the shape is on the drawing layer, you can position the shape with respect to items in the text layer. If you enter a measurement for the horizontal or vertical position, Word measures over from the top or left edge of the item in the text layer that you choose in the From menu.

Each shape has an anchor, and if you turn on the Lock Anchor check box, the shape locks to its paragraph and always stays on the same page as the paragraph.

Creating Borders

The Drawing toolbar enables you to create boxes around paragraphs and to place lines on a page. You can even use the Size and Position card in the Drawing Object dialog box to position a box or line with respect to a paragraph and to lock the box or line in place.

Word comes with a Borders and Shading dialog box and a Borders toolbar, which enable you to make boxes and lines, called borders. Borders apply as a paragraph format, and can be added to styles. Table 8.1 points out the key differences between using the Drawing toolbar and using a border or some other method for creating boxes and lines.

Table 8.1

Borders and Shading Versus the Drawing Toolbar

What you can do	Borders	Drawing toolbar
Box a word within a longer paragraph.	Not possible.	Use a text box with a custom line. If you want the word in the text layer, turn the word into a picture.
Box a paragraph.	Easy to do, easy to control.	Easy to do, not as easy to control as you edit the document.
Box pages.	You can box all the paragraphs on a page, but if you edit the page so that the page breaks move, you have to redo the boxing.	Put a big box in one of the drawing layers in the header. Because the box is in the header, it repeats on every page.
Make vertical lines.	Border lines must be the height of a paragraph because a border-based line is a paragraph format. To make vertical lines between snaking columns, turn on the Line Between check box in the Columns dailog box.	Easy to make a line of any height. Lines can be anywhere on the page, and you can customize them more fully.
Make horizontal lines.	Border lines go above or below paragraphs. To underline a blank that someone will write	Lines can be in any location.

What you can do	Borders	Drawing toolbar
	on later, set a tab with a line leader. To underline text, highlight the text and then apply Underline through the Fonts dialog box or the Formatting toolbar. You can also press ⌘-U.	
Add lines that run along gridlines in a table.	Easy.	Possible, but not nearly as easy as using the borders and shading method.
Add boxing or lines to a style.	Easy.	Not possible.

You can apply borders from the Paragraph Borders and Shading dialog box or from the Borders toolbar. To bring up the dialog box, choose Borders and Shading from the Format menu. Common methods for bringing up the toolbar include clicking the Borders button on the far right of the Formatting toolbar and choosing Borders from the Toolbar shortcut menu.

Figure 8.10 shows the Borders toolbar. To make your Borders toolbar look like the one in this figure, make the toolbar buttons run horizontally across the screen, not vertically. See Chapter 3 for tips about positioning toolbars.

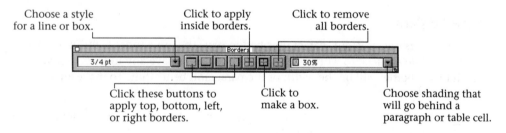

Figure 8.10 Use the Borders toolbar to make lines and boxes that work as paragraph formats or that run along gridlines in a table.

Making horizontal lines between paragraphs

You can set up three different types of horizontal borders (see Figure 8.11).

♦ An inside border goes between paragraphs that are both formatted to have an inside border.

◆ A top border sits above a group of paragraphs that are all formatted to have a top border (or above one paragraph that is formatted to have a top border).

◆ A bottom border goes below a group of paragraphs that are all formatted to have a bottom border (or below just one paragraph that is formatted to have a bottom border).

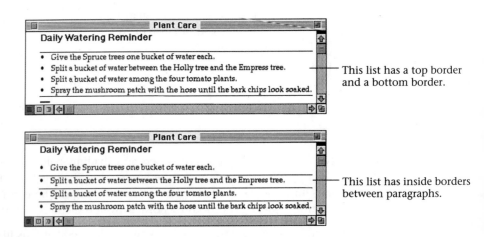

Figure 8.11 Top, bottom, and inside borders behave differently.

Inside borders

In earlier versions of Word, paragraphs had to have the same indents for inside borders (also called middle borders) to work out. In Word 6, you can have any indents that you want, but each inside border will be the width of the paragraph beneath it. To make an inside border, follow these steps:

1. Highlight the paragraphs that you want to border. You must highlight at least a portion of each paragraph.

2. Display the Borders toolbar (as explained a page or so earlier).

2. On the Borders toolbar, first choose a border style (such as 3/4 pt) and then click the Inside Border button.

3. To apply additional formatting (such as a color) to the border, choose Borders and Shading from the Format menu and select the Borders card. You should see two triangles pointing into the space between two *greeked* paragraphs—filler text that is holding the place for real text—and a border separating the paragraphs. The triangles indicate that the inside border line is selected (see Figure 8.12).

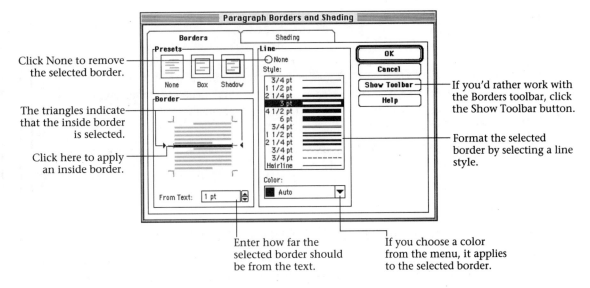

Click None to remove the selected border.

The triangles indicate that the inside border is selected.

Click here to apply an inside border.

If you'd rather work with the Borders toolbar, click the Show Toolbar button.

Format the selected border by selecting a line style.

Enter how far the selected border should be from the text.

If you choose a color from the menu, it applies to the selected border.

Figure 8.12   Click between the greeked paragraphs to apply an inside border.

4. Because the inside border is selected, you can select formats, and they will apply to the inside border.

5. Click the OK button after you finish setting up the border.

If you later want to change the style of the border, first select the paragraphs that the border goes with. Second, choose a new style from the pop-up menu on the Borders toolbar, and finally, click the Inside Borders button. If you need to change the formatting in a more complicated way, you have to select the paragraphs and re-open the Borders and Shading dialog box.

Top and bottom borders

Making a top or bottom border works much like making an inside border. Select the paragraph or paragraphs in question and then choose a border style from the pop-up menu on the Border toolbar. After choosing a style, click the appropriate button on the Borders toolbar. You can also use the Borders and Shading dialog box to apply or customize top and bottom borders.

Top and bottom borders stretch between a paragraph's left and right indents. If you border an empty paragraph, you can adjust its indents without changing the width of any text-filled paragraphs.

> ## Border Wisdom
>
> A top or bottom border applies to a group of paragraphs formatted to have such a border. Watch out for inadvertently applying a top or bottom border to more paragraphs than you originally intended because it can cause problems if you try to make more borders in the document. Remember, if you are typing in a paragraph that has border formatting and you press Return to make a new paragraph, the border formatting continues to the new paragraph.
>
> Just because a border is above the top or bottom of a paragraph does not make the border a top or bottom border. It could be an inside border.

Making vertical lines next to paragraphs

To border the side of a paragraph, use a vertical border. Creating vertical borders works much like creating horizontal borders. First, select the paragraph (or paragraphs) that you want to border. Second, choose a style from the menu on the Borders toolbar. Finally, click the Left or Right Border button on the Borders toolbar. You can also use the Borders and Shading dialog box to set up a vertical border.

To apply a vertical border in the Borders and Shading dialog box, click to the left or right of the greeked text (see Figure 8.13). After you apply the border, triangles appear and point at the border. The triangles indicate that the border is selected; if you select any of the border formats in the dialog box, the formats apply to the selected border.

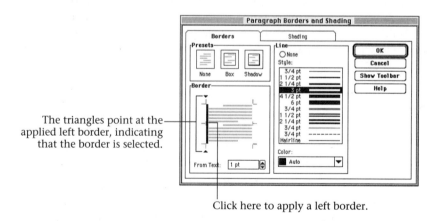

The triangles point at the applied left border, indicating that the border is selected.

Click here to apply a left border.

Figure 8.13   Click to the left of the greeked text to apply a left border.

Boxing paragraph edges

To put a box around a paragraph or a group of paragraphs, follow these steps:

1. Highlight the paragraph or paragraphs that you want to box.

2. If you have the Borders toolbar showing, choose a border style from the pop-up menu (such as 3/4 pt) and click the Outside Border button. To color the box or add a shadow, choose Borders and Shading from the Format menu and select the Borders card (see Figure 8.14).

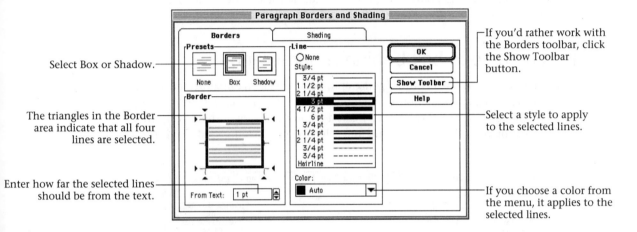

Select Box or Shadow.

The triangles in the Border area indicate that all four lines are selected.

Enter how far the selected lines should be from the text.

If you'd rather work with the Borders toolbar, click the Show Toolbar button.

Select a style to apply to the selected lines.

If you choose a color from the menu, it applies to the selected lines.

Figure 8.14   Select a box type from the Presets area and then format the box.

3. In the Presets area at the upper left, select Box or Shadow. A box appears around the greeked text in the Border area. Triangles point to the four lines that make up the box, indicating that all four lines are selected.

4. Because all four lines are selected, you can change their formatting by selecting any of the different formats offered.

5. Click the OK button after you finish formatting the box.

Caution: When boxing a group of paragraphs, each paragraph in the group must have the same margins and indents. If they don't, you may end up with more than one box or with three-sided boxes.

Removing vertical and horizontal borders

To remove all borders from a paragraph, select the bordered paragraph and then click the No Border button on the Borders toolbar. If you don't want to use the toolbar, choose Borders and Shading from the Format menu. Word displays the Paragraph Borders and Shading dialog box. Select the Borders card and click None at the upper left in the Presets area. Finally, click the OK button.

To remove some, but not all borders from a selected paragraph, display the Borders card in the Paragraph Borders and Shading dialog box. Select the border that you want to remove (so that the selection triangles point to the border) and then select the None radio button in the Line area. Click the OK button after you finish.

Putting a solid box behind a paragraph

To make a colored box behind a paragraph, you apply a Shading format. To shade a paragraph, select the paragraph and choose a shading option from the Borders toolbar. If you don't want to use the toolbar, or if you want to make a colored box, apply shading by choosing Borders and Shading from the Format menu and selecting the Shading card (see Figure 8.15).

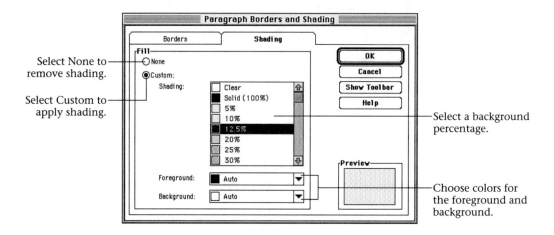

Figure 8.15   Select a shading percentage and the colors to use for the foreground and background.

In the Shading card, select the Custom option and then select a foreground percentage. If necessary, change the colors used in the foreground and background. After you finish, click the OK button.

To remove shading from a selected paragraph, go back to the Shading card, select the None option at the upper left, and click the OK button.

Bordering and shading tables

When you apply borders and shading to tables, you can apply the formatting to any or all of the following:

◆ A paragraph within a table cell

◆ An entire table cell

◆ An entire table

Figure 8.16 shows how a table looks when formatted in different ways with a box border.

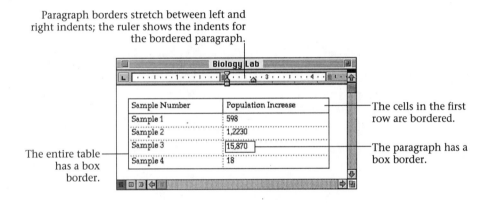

Figure 8.16   Format only a paragraph, only a table cell, or only a table to achieve different effects.

The basic steps for applying borders and shading to table cells are almost exactly the same as those for applying borders and shading to paragraphs, so flip back a few pages to find the steps. When you apply a border or shading within a table, it's important to highlight only the part of the table that you want to format. To display end-of-cell markers so that the selecting process is easier, click the Show/Hide button on the Standard toolbar or turn on all non-printing characters in the View card of the Options dialog box.

◆ To format only a paragraph, select the entire paragraph, but do not select the entire cell. Do not select the end-of-cell marker.

◆ To format only a cell, select the entire cell, including the end-of-cell marker. You can also select a group of cells and format them as a group.

◆ To format the entire table, highlight the entire table (to highlight a table, press Option and double-click the table).

217

To apply complex bordering to a table, select the table and then choose Table AutoFormat from the Table menu. If you aren't sure how to select inside a table, look for help in Chapter 7.

This concludes the information about Word that explains how to format documents, so consider yourself over a big hurdle if you've absorbed the details offered in the past several chapters. The next chapter explains how to personalize Word, an extremely worthwhile way to spend a rainy Friday afternoon.

Chapter 9

Customizing Word

The information in this chapter explains how to personalize Word by using the Customize dialog box and by creating shortcuts for yourself with macros. Because many of Word's command assignments are essentially from Mars, it's well worth your time to use the Customize dialog box or to create macros to set up shortcuts for commands that you use often. You can also customize the way that you change the font, apply styles, run macros, and insert AutoText entries. Specifically, here's what's covered:

- ◆ Setting up custom keyboard shortcuts
- ◆ Personalizing the menus
- ◆ Customizing the toolbars
- ◆ Recording a macro
- ◆ Deleting a macro
- ◆ Sharing a macro

Customizing Keyboard Shortcuts

Custom keyboard shortcuts are a fantastic way to speed up the way you work with Word. A little thought and creativity go a long way in setting up keyboard shortcuts, and the more shortcuts that you set up, the more likely you'll be to use them to your advantage. If you think that you may have trouble remembering your shortcuts, remember that the shortcuts also show on menus. You can add commands to menus and use the menus as quick references.

To create a printout of all currently assigned keyboard shortcuts, go to the File menu and choose Print. From the Print pop-up menu at the left, choose Key Assignments and then click the Print button.

 Caution: If you make more than a few customizing changes, be sure to back up the template that stores the changes. If you want to back up the Normal template, you can find it in Word's Templates folder.

Adding a keyboard shortcut

Word has a special trick for assigning a keyboard shortcut to any command on a drop-down menu. First, press ⌘-Option-+ (the plus sign on the numeric keypad). Second, with the pointer that looks like the ⌘ symbol, choose the menu item. Word switches to the Keyboard card in the Customize dialog box, where you can type the shortcut and click the Assign button.

In previous versions of Word, the ⌘-Option-= (equal sign) trick also enabled you to add keyboard shortcuts to many items in dialog boxes; unfortunately Microsoft removed this capability from Word 6.

To assign a keyboard shortcut to any command, use the Customize dialog box. Here are the steps:

1. From the Tools menu, choose Customize. In the Customize dialog box, select the Keyboard card (see Figure 9.1).

2. Select a category from the Categories list and then select a specific item to assign a keyboard shortcut to. If you are assigning a shortcut to a style, note that the style doesn't appear in the Styles list unless you have used the style to format text in your document.

3. If the command has a colon as its last character (such as the Color command in the Format category), select a more refined version of the command from the menu that appears at the lower right.

4. At the lower right, choose the template in which you want to store the shortcut.

5. Click in the Press New Shortcut Key text box.

6. Type the shortcut that you want to use. The shortcut should begin with Shift, Command, Option, or Control, and it must include Command, Option, or Control. For example, Control-S and Control-Shift-S work as keyboard shortcuts, but Shift-S does not. If the shortcut is already in use by a different command, Word displays the command beneath the text box.

7. Click the Assign button.

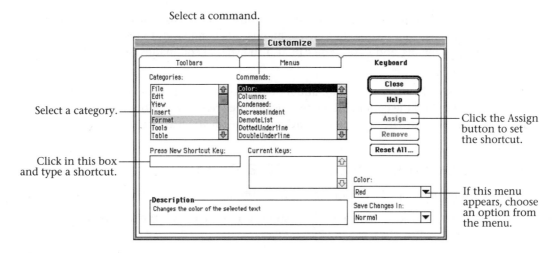

Figure 9.1   Use the Keyboard card to set up custom keyboard shortcuts.

Doubling Up Your Shortcut

You can set up double keyboard shortcuts by typing the shortcuts one after another in the Press New Shortcut Key text box. For example, if you use the keyboard to change the font, you can start every keyboard shortcut for changing the font with Control-F and then double the shortcut by adding the first character in the font's name. So the shortcut for Helvetica would be Control-F,H and the shortcut for Bookman would be Control-F,B.

To enter the Helvetica shortcut in the Press New Shortcut Key text box or to use it for real, press Control-F, release all keys on the keyboard, and finally press H. The second part of the shortcut can be just a character or it can be Shift and a character.

221

Removing a keyboard shortcut

To remove a keyboard shortcut from a particular command, you can, of course, just assign the shortcut to some other command. But if that process doesn't work, select the command from the Commands list in the Keyboard card and then click the Remove button. To go back to Word's defaults for every keyboard shortcut (on the Keyboard card), click the Reset All button.

Personalizing Drop-Down Menus

Drop-down menus drop down from the menu bar, and you can customize the menus in many ways. You can make your own menus, delete menus, add commands to menus, remove commands from menus, and so on. You can also add special commands, such as fonts and AutoText entries.

If you don't know the name of a command, but you do know its keyboard shortcut, use the Keyboard card to find the command name. Click in the Press New Shortcut Key text box and then type the shortcut. The command name appears below the text box.

Adding a command or option to a menu

To add a command or option to a menu, try these steps:

1. From the Tools menu, choose Customize and then select the Menus card (see Figure 9.2).

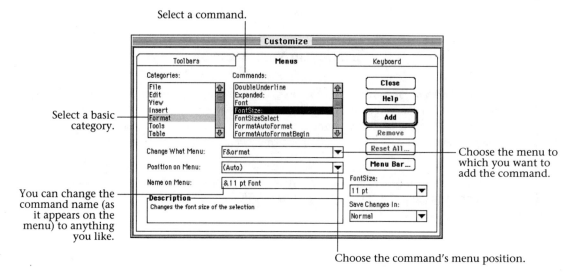

Select a command.

Select a basic category.

You can change the command name (as it appears on the menu) to anything you like.

Choose the menu to which you want to add the command.

Choose the command's menu position.

Figure 9.2   You can add a command, macro, font, style, or AutoText entry to a menu.

2. Select a category from the Categories list and then select the option that you want to add to a menu.

3. If the command has a colon as its final character (such as the FontSize command in the Format category), choose a more specific command from the menu that appears at the lower right.

4. At the lower right, choose the template where you want to store the menu change.

5. Choose the menu. The menus ending with (No Document) are versions of the File and Help menus that display only when no document windows are open. The menus ending with (Shortcut) are the shortcut menus that appear when you Control-click something. The ampersands (&) have nothing to do with adding commands to menus. They indicate which key gets underlined if you press ⌘-Tab in order to access the menus via the keyboard.

6. Choose a menu position. Auto means that Word puts the command in the location that Word thinks is best.

7. Click the Add (or Add Below) button.

Removing a command or option from a menu

If a menu seems too cluttered with commands that you don't use, or if you add commands to a menu and then decide that you don't want them any more, you can remove them with a keyboard shortcut or in the Customize dialog box.

The keyboard shortcut

To remove an item from a menu, press ⌘-Option-Hyphen. The pointer turns into a fat minus sign. With the minus sign pointer, choose the menu item that you want to remove. If you decide that you don't want to remove anything, press ⌘-Period to get rid of the minus sign pointer.

The Customize dialog box

If you happen to be in the Customize dialog box, follow these steps to remove menu items:

1. Switch to the Menus card (see Figure 9.3).

2. Choose the menu that you want to change.

3. Choose the menu item that you want to remove.

4. Click the Remove button.

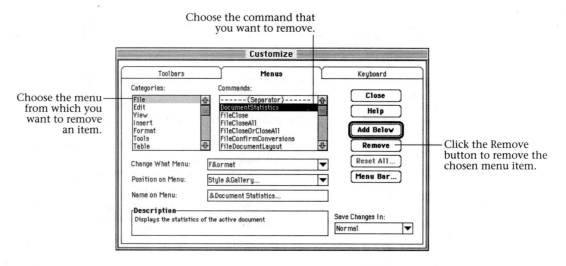

Figure 9.3 Use the Menus card to remove an item from a menu.

Adding, renaming, or removing a menu

In trying to win the award for the most flexible word processor ever, Word's designers added the capability for adding, renaming, and removing menus. Use this capability with a wee bit of caution—and practical jokers please be prepared to fix the menus that you customize. In any event, to add, rename, or remove a menu, switch to the Menus card, click the Menu Bar button, and then do the following:

◆ To make a new menu, type its name in the Name on Menu Bar box. The menu will appear to the right of the existing menu that you choose from the Position on Menu Bar list. Finally, click the Add After button. If you select the Help menu, Word adds the menu to the right of the Window menu.

◆ To rename a menu, select the menu that you want to rename and then type a name for it. Click the Rename button.

◆ To remove a menu, select it from the list of menus and then click Remove. You cannot remove the Help menu. The Help menu is the question mark in a bubble near the right edge of the menu bar.

Changes made to the menus don't take effect until you close the Menu Bar and Customize dialog boxes.

To change the complete menu setup back to the default, click the Reset All button in the Menus card of the Customize dialog box.

Customizing Toolbars

If you have a 16-inch screen, you may not care a lot about customizing your toolbars, but people on PowerBooks and smaller screens probably have room for only one or two toolbars at a time, so it is important that the toolbars contain useful buttons. For example, a PowerBook user can take the most useful buttons from the Formatting and Standard toolbars to make one especially useful toolbar. Of course, different people have different ideas about what constitutes a useful toolbar, but Figure 9.4 shows one possibility.

Figure 9.4   You can easily create a custom toolbar.

Word doesn't come with a Font menu on the menu bar, but you can add one with the help of a special (and easy!) macro. From the File menu, choose Open. In the Open dialog box, switch to the Macros folder and then open a document called 5.1 Upgrade. Follow the directions in the document to view the 5.1 Upgrade toolbar and then click the Add Font menu button.

Making a new toolbar

To make a new toolbar, press Option while you drag a button off an existing toolbar, or follow these steps:

1. From the View menu, choose Toolbars. Word opens the Toolbars dialog box.

2. In the Toolbars dialog box, click the New button. The New Toolbar dialog box appears (see Figure 9.5).

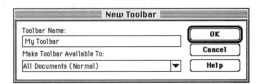

Figure 9.5   Type a name for the new toolbar.

3. Enter a name for the new toolbar.

4. Choose the template that you want the toolbar to go with. (Choose Normal to make the toolbar available in all documents.)

5. Click the OK button. The Customize dialog box opens with the Toolbars card showing.

6. You can drag any button to the new toolbar, either from the dialog box or by dragging the button from another toolbar. As long as you keep the Customize dialog box open, you can just drag the button, but if you close the Customize dialog box, you must ⌘-drag buttons. To find out more about dragging buttons from the dialog box, read the next set of steps.

Moving buttons

To move buttons within a toolbar or from one toolbar to another, press ⌘ and drag the buttons about. To copy a button instead of moving it, press Option while you drag it. To move buttons that are not on a toolbar or to make a button for a style, font, macro, or AutoText entry, follow these steps:

1. Choose Customize from the Tools menu and select the Toolbars card.

2. Select a category. For example, to make a button for a style, select the Styles category. Or to make a button that adds the numbers in a table row or column, select the Table category (see Figure 9.6).

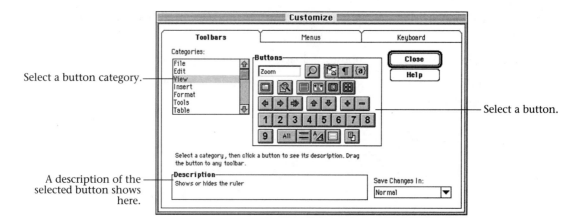

Figure 9.6   Select the button that you want to move.

3. Select the button or command that you want to move or to make a button for.

4. Drag the button or command to the location of your choice on a toolbar.

5. If the command (such as a style) doesn't already have an associated button, Word opens the Custom Button dialog box (see Figure 9.7).

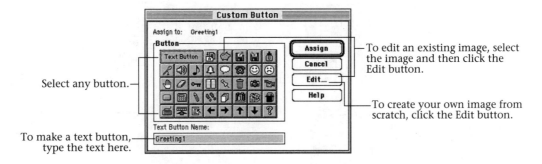

Figure 9.7   Select a graphic button or type a label for a text button.

6. Select a button or click the Edit button:

   ◆ To make a text button, enter a name for the button and click the Assign button.

   ◆ To use one of the predrawn buttons, select the button and click the Assign button.

   ◆ To change one of the predrawn buttons, select the button and click the Edit button.

   ◆ To create your own button from scratch, don't select any predrawn buttons. Click the Edit button. (To deselect any selected predrawn button, click the Text Button button.)

7. If you clicked the Assign button, you should see the button on the toolbar, and you can skip the rest of these steps. If you clicked the Edit button, a box appears onscreen where you can edit the toolbar picture (see Figure 9.8).

   ◆ To change the button, click a color that you want to use. Then click on boxes in the Picture area. The boxes should take on the color that you clicked. You can click on blank or colored boxes.

   ◆ To erase boxes, turn the pointer into an erasing tool by clicking the Erase box. You can also click the Clear button to delete everything in the picture and start again.

   ◆ The arrow buttons in the Move area enable you to move the entire image in a particular direction. If an arrow is dim, you can't move the image in that direction.

8. After you finish changing the picture, click the OK button.

Select a color to draw in that color.

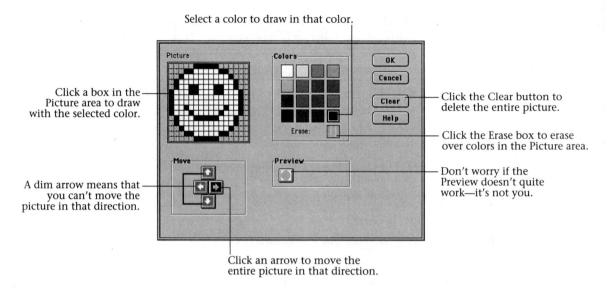

Click a box in the
Picture area to draw
with the selected color.

Click the Clear button to
delete the entire picture.

Click the Erase box to erase
over colors in the Picture area.

A dim arrow means that
you can't move the
picture in that direction.

Don't worry if the
Preview doesn't quite
work—it's not you.

Click an arrow to move the
entire picture in that direction.

Figure 9.8   Click in the Picture area to change the button picture.

Modifying buttons

To change the appearance of an existing button, you must have the button and the Toolbars card in the Customize dialog box showing. With both of them showing, Control-click the button that you want to change to get a special shortcut menu (see Figure 9.9). What to do next depends on what you want to do:

◆ To change the button's image to one that you create, choose Edit Button Image. Read the preceding section to find out how to edit the button's picture.

◆ To change the button's image to a different premade picture, select the Choose Button Image command. Word responds by displaying the Custom Button dialog box. Select a button and then click the Assign button.

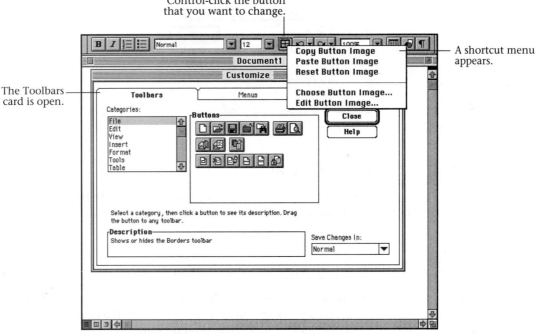

Control-click the button
that you want to change.

A shortcut menu
appears.

The Toolbars
card is open.

Figure 9.9 Control-click the button that you want to change.

Removing a button

To remove a button from a toolbar, press ⌘ while dragging the button over a document
window. If you have the Toolbars card on the Customize dialog box open, you need not
press ⌘—just drag the button off the toolbar.

> **Caution:** If you delete a custom button, you can't get it back. To keep the
> button around, move it to a custom toolbar or a toolbar that you use
> infrequently.

Renaming a custom toolbar

To rename a custom toolbar, open the Organizer dialog box. To get to this dialog box, choose
Templates from the File menu and then click the Organizer button. In the Organizer dialog
box, select the Toolbars card and then select the custom toolbar from the list on the left. Click
the Rename button. A third dialog box, the Rename dialog box, appears (see Figure 9.10). Type
a new name for the toolbar and click the OK button. Click the Close button to exit the
Organizer dialog box.

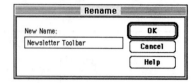

Figure 9.10 Type a new name for the custom toolbar.

Removing a custom toolbar

To remove a custom toolbar, go to the View menu and choose Toolbars. In the resulting Toolbars dialog box, select the toolbar that you want to delete and then click the Delete button.

Returning a built-in toolbar to its default setup

To return a built-in toolbar to its standard button arrangement, go to the View menu and choose Toolbars. The Toolbars dialog box should appear onscreen. In the dialog box, select the toolbar that you want to reset and then click the Reset button.

Word brings up the Reset Toolbar dialog box, asking for which template you want to make the change. To make the change apply in all documents, select All Documents (Normal). Click the OK button to exit the dialog box.

What's a Macro?

Macros are commands that you create yourself, and they make using Word more efficient by combining a sequence of commands into one.

A few examples of when to use macros include the following:

◆ If you frequently receive documents from other people, and you use the Replace dialog box to search for and fix common errors, you can chain together a series of Replace operations in a macro instead. If you then assign the macro to a toolbar button, you can just click the button and go have an espresso while Word does the work.

◆ If you frequently show and hide toolbars, you can make macros that do the showing and hiding and assign a keyboard shortcut to them. For example, you can make Control-F show the Formatting toolbar and Control-Shift-F hide it.

◆ If you have a favorite custom border that you create over and over in different documents, use a macro instead. You can assign the macro a keyboard shortcut (such as Control-B) and then press Control-B to apply the border.

How Word Thinks About Macros

From Word's point of view, a macro is a *script,* a series of programming commands that tells Word what to do. For example, the script for adding a thick, blue border to the top of a selection looks like this in Word:

```
Sub MAIN
FormatBordersAndShading
.ApplyTo = 0,
.Shadow = 0,
.TopBorder = 6,
.LeftBorder = 0,
.BottomBorder = 0,
.RightBorder = 0,
.HorizBorder = 0,
.VertBorder = 0,
.TopColor = 2,
.LeftColor = 0,
.BottomColor = 0,
.RightColor = 0,
.HorizColor = 0,
.VertColor = 0,
.FromText = "6 pt",
.Shading = 0,
.Foreground = 0,
.Background = 0,
.Tab = "0",
.FineShading = -1
End Sub
```

You can make this script by telling Word to record it while you open the Borders dialog box and select options for the border (it's easy, and you find out how to do this later in the chapter). You can give the script a name (such as BigBorder) and stick it on a menu, give it a keyboard shortcut, or put it on a toolbar button. After you make a macro, the macro acts just like any other command.

Although most people will never go further with macros than recording simple ones, you can go much, much further. You don't have to record a macro; instead, you can type it by hand (or you can partially record a macro and partially type it). If you type macros, you can use programming constructs, such as loops, and you can even create your own dialog boxes.

Recording a Macro

To record a macro, you must first tell Word that you have begun recording and then do whatever task you want Word to mimic later.

A particularly useful set of macros that you can record would be a set that automates turning on and off fractional widths. Text onscreen tends to look a little blurry with fractional widths turned on, but printed text tends to look especially well spaced when printed with fractional widths on. (If you are curious, look in Chapter 10 to find out more about fractional widths.)

Use the following steps as a general example of how recording a macro works and as a specific example for making a macro to turn on fractional widths. (These steps assume that you currently have fractional widths turned off; to check, look on the Print card in the Options dialog box from the Tools menu.)

1. From the Tools menu, choose Macro. The Macro dialog box appears. Or as a shortcut to begin recording a macro, double-click REC on the status bar (double-click REC again to stop recording).

2. Click the Record button. Word displays the Record Macro dialog box (see Figure 9.11).

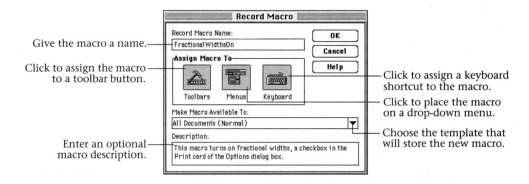

Figure 9.11   Type a name for the macro and select whether you want to run it by using a toolbar button, a drop-down menu, or a keyboard shortcut.

3. Type a name for the macro. In this case, call it "FractionalWidthsOn."

4. Select the template that will store the macro. To make the macro available in all documents, select All Documents (Normal).

5. Although it's not necessary, you can type a short description of the macro in the Description box. Press Shift-Enter to move to a new line in the Description box.

6. Click the appropriate button to assign the macro to a toolbar, menu, or keyboard shortcut. Word switches you into the Customize dialog box. Follow the directions in the Customize dialog box to set up the toolbar button, menu option, or keyboard shortcut. Click the Close button after you finish.

7. Word displays a two-button toolbar called the Macro Record Toolbar (see Figure 9.12). Word is watching you and recording your every action.

To temporarily stop recording a macro, click the Pause button on the Macro Record toolbar. Click the button again to resume recording. To select text while recording, use the keyboard.

Click the Stop button to stop recording a macro.   Click the Pause button to pause recording a macro.

Figure 9.12   Use the Macro Record toolbar to pause and stop macro recording.

8. Go to the Tools menu and choose Options. When the Options dialog box opens, click the General tab.

9. Turn on the Fractional Widths check box.

10. Click the OK button.

11. On the Macro Record toolbar, click the Stop button.

Turn off fractional widths and try running the macro. Text onscreen should look fuzzier with fractional widths on; the Helvetica font shows this problem especially well. Of course, you can also make a macro to turn off fractional widths.

If you open the Macro dialog box again, you see the new macro in the list of macros. If you select the new macro and click the Edit button, you can see the WordBasic script that Word wrote for you.

Deleting a Macro

If you have a macro that doesn't work or that you never use, you can delete it. Macros get stored in individual documents or in templates, so if you just don't want a macro in a document, delete it from the document. If you want the macro out of a template so that it doesn't show up again in future documents, you must delete it from the template. Here are some steps to try:

1. To delete a macro from a document, open the document in question and then go to the Tools menu and choose Macro.

2. In the resulting Macro dialog box, select the macro that you want to remove and then click the Delete button.

3. When Word checks to be sure that you want to delete the macro, click the Yes button. The macro disappears from your document, but it is most likely still stored in a template.

4. If you don't want to remove the macro from the template, click the Close button. You are finished! If you want to remove your macro from a template, however, stay in the Macro dialog box and click the Organizer button.

5. The Organizer dialog box has two menus labeled Macros Available In. It doesn't matter which menu you use, but do use one of them to choose the template that holds your macro.

6. After you choose a template, Word lists the macros in that template. (Look in the list above the Macros Available In menu.) Select the macro that you want to delete and then click the Delete button.

7. When Word asks whether you really want to delete the macro, click the Yes button.

8. Finally, click the Close button to exit the Organizer dialog box. You have removed the macro from the template, and it won't show up again in new documents based on that template.

Sharing a Macro

To share a macro with a friend or co-worker, use the Organizer dialog box to move the macro to a special template. You can move the template to your friend's machine and then show your friend how to use the Organizer dialog box to move the macro to her Normal template.

Making a template

If you don't already have a template to use for transferring the macro, follow these steps to make a template:

1. From the File menu, choose New. The New dialog box appears.

2. In the New area (at the right), select Template.

3. Click the OK button, and a new template opens.

Moving the macro

To move the macro to the transfer template, try these steps:

1. Choose Macro from the Tools menu.

2. Click the Organizer button. The Organizer dialog box appears, with the Macros card in front (see Figure 9.13).

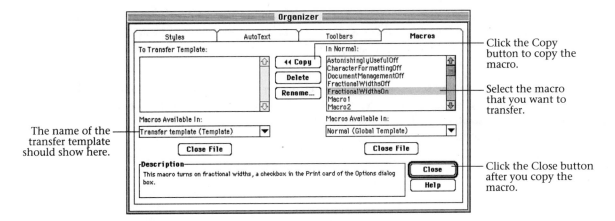

Figure 9.13   Copy the macro to the transfer template.

3. Make one of the lists show the template that currently contains the macro that you want to share. If you saved the macro in the Normal template, you may see the macro on one of the lists, but if not, click the Close File button and then the Open File button. A dialog box appears where you can open the template containing the macro.

4. After you have the template containing the macro showing in one list, make the other list display the transfer template. If the transfer template isn't showing, click the Close File button and then click the Open File button. From the resulting Open File dialog box, open the transfer template.

5. Select the macro.

6. Click the Copy button.

7. At the lower right, click the Close button.

8. If Word displays an alert message asking whether you want to save the changes to the transfer template, click the Yes button (see Figure 9.14).

Figure 9.14   Click the Yes button to save the macro in the transfer template.

Now that the macro is in the transfer template, you can transfer the template to a different Macintosh and then use the Organizer dialog box to move the macro to the Normal template on that machine. You can also attach the transfer template so that it is available only some of the time.

I hope that you have tried your hand at setting up a few personalizations and macros so that you have a good idea of how flexible Word can be. Now let's completely change the subject for the next chapter, which explains how to create form letters and mailing labels and how to merge documents.

Chapter 10

Creating Form Letters for Mail Merges

If you need to make form letters or send a mass mailing with mass-produced envelopes or labels, don't even think about doing it all by hand. After you figure out how to use mail merge, you can save hours and hours of time. Then you can send 200 of your favorite friends and family members that glorious holiday letter that they all look forward to receiving every December—and you can even personalize it! As you can guess, the information here explains the following:

◆ Making form letters
◆ Creating mass-mailing envelopes
◆ Creating labels for a mass-mailing

How to Set Up Form Letters

A mail merge enables you to make form letters and personalize each letter for its recipient. For example, you can make those annoying letters that start out saying, "Dear Ms. Woosterberry: Take our word for it—you cannot afford to miss this offer for a free vacation to Hawaii. Please give us a call and have your credit card number handy." (Of course, I don't suggest that you create such a form letter—I'm just pointing out that you have the technology.)

When you make form letters, you set up two documents: the main document and the data document. The main document has the form letter text that everyone receives. To indicate where the custom information goes in each form letter, you insert a special kind of field, called a MergeField, which acts as a placeholder. If you have field codes showing, the MergeFields appear, as shown in Figure 10.1.

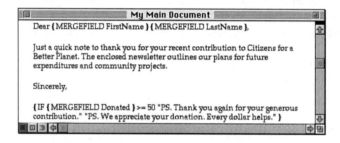

Figure 10.1   MergeFields in the main document act as placeholders for custom information.

The second document, the data document or data source, contains the specific information that customizes each form letter. The data document has specific organizational rules, which usually result in the data being arranged in a table of columns and rows (see Figure 10.2). After you complete the main and data documents, you merge the two documents together to create form letters.

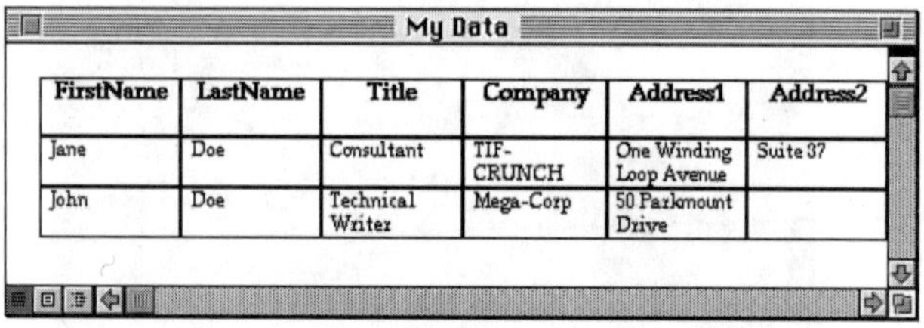

FirstName	LastName	Title	Company	Address1	Address2
Jane	Doe	Consultant	TIF-CRUNCH	One Winding Loop Avenue	Suite 3?
John	Doe	Technical Writer	Mega-Corp	50 Parkmount Drive	

Figure 10.2   The data document usually is organized in a table with structured rows and columns.

If you have already typed information into the computer and you want to use it for a merge, you probably can. Here are a few common situations where you can use an existing document as a data document:

- ◆ Data documents created in Word 6 and originally used for a different merge
- ◆ Tables originally created for a different purpose
- ◆ Data documents and tables from other versions of Word, including Word 4 and 5 for Macintosh and Word 2 and 6 for Windows
- ◆ Excel 3, 4, and 5 documents (Although you can use the Excel worksheet directly, depending on how well the converter works in a real-life situation, you may want to save the Excel worksheet as a tab-delimited text file and use the text file instead.)
- ◆ Tab-delimited and comma-delimited text files

Tab-Delimited Text Files

A tab-delimited text file consists of many bits of information. The information bits are separated by specific nonprinting characters so that the computer can easily work with them.

In a tab-delimited file, each paragraph contains a group of related information (such as a person's name and address). Within each paragraph, tabs separate specific bits of information (such as the person's name, street address, city, state, and zip code). Most, if not all, databases can export information as a tab-delimited text file.

In all cases, the first row or paragraph in a data document must contain category names, such as FirstName, LastName, Title, and Company. In a tab-delimited text file, the first paragraph must contain the category names (separated from each other by tabs). Similarly, in an Excel spreadsheet or Word table, the category names must fill the first row, as shown in Figure 10.2.

You can also look at and work with the data document through a special data viewer, called the Data Form, which helps you enter and find information (see Figure 10.3).

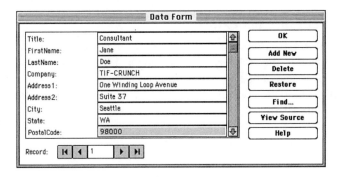

Figure 10.3 The Data Form simplifies entering and locating information in the data document.

Starting the main document

The first step involves establishing the main document—the document that holds generic text for each form letter. Launch Word and open the document that you want to use. You can open an old document or start a new document. You don't have to complete the text of the document now, but it may help to save the document with an appropriate name, such as My Main Document or Main Letter.

Go to the Tools menu and choose Mail Merge. Word responds by displaying the Mail Merge Helper, a window that walks you though the process of pulling together a merge. Drop down the Create button menu and select Form Letters. A dialog box appears, asking which document you want to use. Because your main document is open, click the Active Window button (see Figure 10.4).

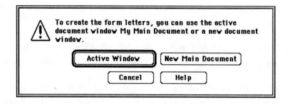

To create the form letters, you can use the active document window My Main Document or a new document window.

[Active Window]   [New Main Document]

[Cancel]   [Help]

Figure 10.4   Indicate that the active window document will be the main document.

After you click the Active Window button, the type of merge (Form Letters) and the name of the main document appear beneath the Create button menu in the Mail Merge Helper. Keep the Mail Merge Helper open while you move on to the next section.

Starting the data document

Now that you have the main document established, you need to set up the data document.

The data document already exists

If you have the information typed into the computer in a format that Word can use (see the bulleted points earlier in the chapter), select Open Data Source from the Get Data button menu. An Open dialog box appears, where you can open the document. After you click the Open button, Word presents you with a message, inquiring if you want to edit the main document (see Figure 10.5).

Figure 10.5   This message appears after you open the data document.

If you need to change data in the data document before you merge, click the Cancel button and skip ahead to the section called "Finishing the data document." Alternatively, if the data document is completely ready, click the Edit Main Document button and continue with "Finalizing the main document."

The data document does not exist

If you haven't started the data document, choose Create Data Source from the Get Data button menu. The Create Data Source dialog box appears, and in this dialog box, you can indicate the categories of information, called *field names,* that you plan to use to personalize the form letter (see Figure 10.6).

> **Caution:** A field usually refers to a code that tells Word to do something special. For example, Word fills in the name of the document in a FileName field. In a data document, however, a field name is for information that you fill in. For example, you may have a field name, called "address," to fill in the individual address fields for each person who will receive the letter. In contrast, a field in a main document has a code and a result, just like any other regular field.

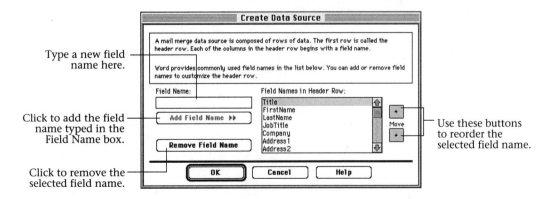

Figure 10.6   The Create Data Source dialog box automates setting up a data document.

The dialog box lists common field names, but you can customize the list so that it matches what you want to do:

◆ To delete a field name, select the name from the list and click the Remove Field Name button.

◆ To add a field name, type the name in the Field Name text box and then click the Add Field Name button. Field names cannot contain spaces.

◆ The listed fields appear in the order that you will fill them in later. You can move a field up or down by selecting it and then clicking the up- or down arrow.

> **Caution:** Make sure that your fields are specific enough for what you plan to do. For example, you may need to keep salutations, first names, and last names separate for sorting purposes (so that you can sort based on the last name) or so that you use the correct greeting. (You may want Dear Ms. Tasha Kat or Dear Ms. Kat or Dear Tasha.)

After you finish customizing, click the OK button. The Save dialog box appears, and your next move is to save the data document. Choose an appropriate folder, type a name for the file, and click the Save button. In response to your saving the data document, a dialog box appears, inquiring whether you want to work in the data document or the main document. You can click either button, but to continue with the flow of this chapter, click the Edit Data Source button.

Finishing the data document

If you followed the procedure outlined in "Starting the data document," you should have the Data Form window showing (see Figure 10.7).

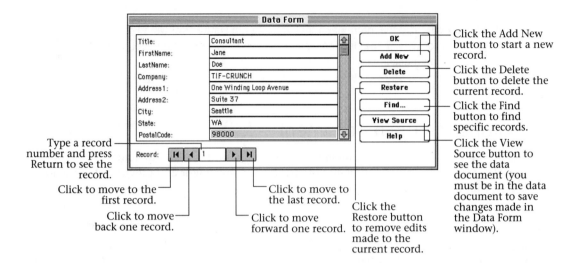

Figure 10.7 The Data Form window provides a form-like way to look at the data document.

The Data Form window provides a special way of looking at the data document. The form has blanks for one record's worth of information—a *record* is all the information for one recipient of the form letter. If you need to look at the data document or enter information into the data document, you can do so right in the Data Form window. Here are a few pointers:

◆ To move between fields, press Tab (or click in the field to which you want to move).

◆ To open a blank record, click the Add New button. If the insertion point is in the last field, press Return to open a blank record.

◆ To delete the currently showing record, click the Delete button.

◆ To reset the currently showing record to the way it was, click the Restore button.

◆ To locate a record based on its contents, click the Find button.

◆ To add more fields or edit the data document in its table-based format, click the View Source button. See Chapter 7 for more details about editing in tables.

◆ To move to a different record, use the controls in the Record area at the lower left. You can jump to the preceding, next, first, or last record. Or type a specific record number into the number box and press Return.

◆ To save the data that you enter, click the View Source button. The data document appears. Go to the File menu and choose Save. To return to the Data Form dialog box, use the Window menu to switch back to the main document. Click the Edit Data Source button (it's on the right side of the Mail Merge toolbar).

Caution: Save the information that you enter in Data Form! Data Form is a way of viewing the data document, and you save the information by saving the data document.

Finalizing the main document

Before you merge, the main document must be ready. In the main document, you should see the Mail Merge toolbar, which helps you prepare the document and preview what the form letters will look like (see Figure 10.8).

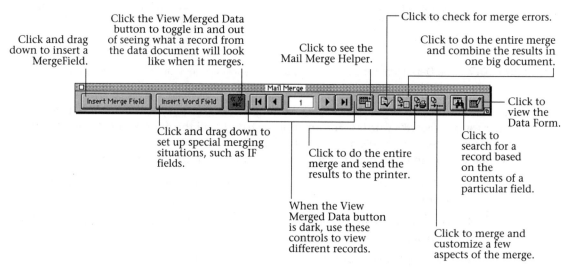

Click and drag down to insert a MergeField.

Click the View Merged Data button to toggle in and out of seeing what a record from the data document will look like when it merges.

Click to see the Mail Merge Helper.

Click to check for merge errors.

Click to do the entire merge and combine the results in one big document.

Click and drag down to set up special merging situations, such as IF fields.

Click to do the entire merge and send the results to the printer.

When the View Merged Data button is dark, use these controls to view different records.

Click to search for a record based on the contents of a particular field.

Click to view the Data Form.

Click to merge and customize a few aspects of the merge.

Figure 10.8   The Mail Merge toolbar has buttons for setting up a main document and merging.

Type the text that every copy of the form letter will have, but when you reach a place where the form letter should have personalized information, insert a MergeField. To insert a MergeField, make sure that the insertion point is located where you want the field to go. Then go up to the Mail Merge toolbar, click the Insert Merge Field button, and choose the appropriate field name.

After you choose a field name, it appears in your document as a MergeField, although its exact appearance changes depending on whether field codes are showing (see Figure 10.9). If you don't have field codes showing, the fields may disappear, or they may appear surrounded by special characters called *chevrons* (chevrons look like « and »).

Although you could type merge chevrons by hand in previous versions of Word, you cannot type them by hand in Word 6.

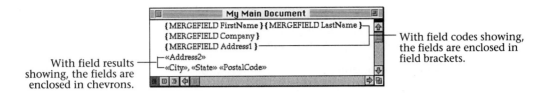

With field results showing, the fields are enclosed in chevrons.

With field codes showing, the fields are enclosed in field brackets.

Figure 10.9 MergeFields look different when they are inserted, depending on whether you have field codes showing.

To customize text that appears in a letter, use an IF field. For example, a charitable organization may want to add a special note of thanks to people donating over a certain amount of money. To insert an IF field, follow these steps:

1. Position the insertion point where you want the customization to begin.

2. On the Mail Merge toolbar, click the Insert Word Field button and choose IF... THEN... ELSE. The Insert Word Field: IF dialog box appears (see Figure 10.10).

Set up a condition.

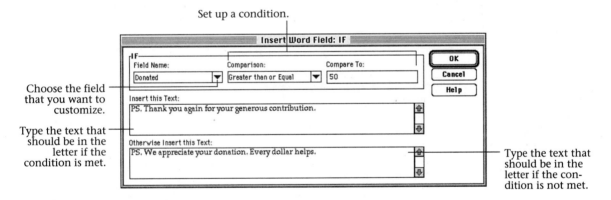

Choose the field that you want to customize.

Type the text that should be in the letter if the condition is met.

Type the text that should be in the letter if the condition is not met.

Figure 10.10 You can personalize form letters based on the contents of a particular field.

3. From the Field Name menu, select the field that will trigger the customization.

4. Select a comparison from the Comparison menu. For example, to customize the letter based on how much money the recipient donated, you can select the Field Name "Donated" and then choose Greater than or Equal from the Comparison menu. If you pick the Is Blank or Is Not Blank options from the Comparison menu, don't enter anything in the Compare To box.

5. If necessary, type a number or letter in the Compare To text box.

6. Enter the appropriate text into the Insert this Text box and the Otherwise Insert this Text box. For example, Figure 10.10 shows that people will receive different messages, depending on how much money they donated.

7. Click the OK button.

Word inserts the IF field in the document, but you may not see it if you are showing field results.

Limiting who gets the form letter

If you want to use only certain data document records for a particular form letter, use a technique called *filtering* to block some records from merging. To filter records, set up "rules" for Word to follow. Here are the steps:

1. Open the Mail Merge Helper by clicking the Mail Merge Helper button or by choosing Mail Merge Helper from the Tools menu.

2. In the Mail Merge Helper window, click the Query Options button and select the Filter Records card (see Figure 10.11).

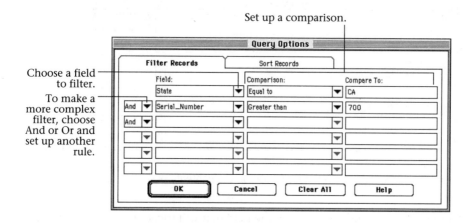

Figure 10.11 You can set up rules that limit which records end up in the merge.

3. In the Field column, from the top menu, choose the field name that will trigger which records get used in the merge.

4. In the Comparison column, from the top menu, choose a comparison. For example, if you want to send letters only to people who live in California, you can set the Field menu to State and the Comparison menu to Equal to. Or to send letters

only to people who own products with serial numbers greater than 700, set the Field menu to SerialNumber and the Comparison menu to Greater than.

5. In the Compare To column, type the text or number that you want to use as a comparison. If you want to send a letter only to people in California, you can type **CA** to set a rule telling Word to include records where the State field is equal to CA.

6. If you need to get fancy with filtering, you can set more than one rule. Use the And and Or options in the far left column to combine rules. For example, you can merge all records for people who live in California *and* have a product with a serial number greater than 700.

7. Click the OK button after you finish setting rules.

Sorting Records

You can sort records through the Mail Merge Helper. To sort records, click the Query Options button and select the Sort Records card. In the Sort records card, you can sort records based on the contents of up to three fields. For example, to sort items based on the last name and then by state, choose the last name field from the Sort By menu and choose the state field from the Then By menu.

Previewing the form letter

Previewing the form letter is not strictly necessary, but it can be a good way to find problems before you waste a lot of time and paper.

To preview a letter, click the View Merged Data button (the button that shows chevrons and *ABC*). With the button activated, you can view and print merged form letters. On the Mail Merge toolbar, just right of the View Merged Data button, you'll find the controls for seeing form letters personalized onscreen. In using the controls, note the following:

◆ To see the preceding or next record, click the corresponding left- or right-pointing triangle (the Previous Record button or Next Record button).

◆ To see a specific record, type the record's number in the Go to Record box and press Return.

◆ To see the first or last record, click the corresponding triangle that points to a line (the First Record button or Last Record button).

◆ To print the form letter showing onscreen, go to the File menu and choose Print. Print the document just as you would print any other document.

◆ To switch back into the mode where you saw either chevrons or field codes, click the View Merged Data button again.

Merging and printing form letters

After you set up the main and data documents, it's time to run the merge and to make form letters.

Make sure that you are in the main document and then click the Mail Merge Helper button on the Mail Merge toolbar. The Mail Merge Helper dialog box appears, and you should see the main document listed in the Main Document area and the data document listed in the Data Source area (see Figure 10.12). If the main document's name doesn't show under the Create button menu, refer back to "Starting the main document," earlier in the chapter. If your data document doesn't show under the Get Data button menu, refer back to "Starting the data document."

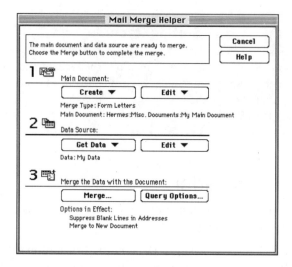

Figure 10.12   If Mail Merge Helper displays the names of the main and data documents, and if you have completed the documents, you are ready to merge.

In the Mail Merge Helper, follow these steps to complete the merge and to create form letters:

1. Click the Merge button. The Merge dialog box appears onscreen (see Figure 10.13).

2. From the Merge To pop-up menu, choose Printer.

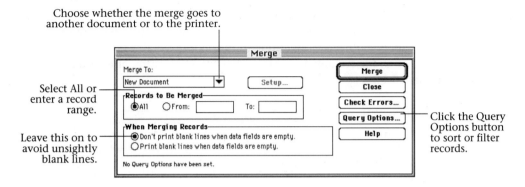

Figure 10.13   The Merge dialog box offers a few final controls for creating form letters.

3. If you don't want to merge all the records, set the starting and ending number for a range of records. For example, to merge the first 20 records only, enter **1** in the From box and **20** in the To box.

4. Generally speaking, keep the Don't Print Blank Lines When Data Fields Are Empty radio button switched on. With this option on, you eliminate blank lines that may otherwise appear in a mailing address.

5. Click the Merge button. Word responds by opening the Print dialog box.

6. Click the Print button.

How to Set Up Labels

To merge to labels, you tell Word which type of labels to use, and Word sets up a main document that looks like a page worth of labels and contains all the correct fields. To merge to labels, follow these steps:

1. In a new document, choose Mail Merge from the Tools menu.

2. In the Mail Merge Helper dialog box, click the Create button menu and choose Mailing Labels. Word responds by asking where you want to create the main document.

3. Click the Active Window button.

4. Back in the Mail Merge Helper dialog box, use the Get Data button menu to set the data document. "Starting the data document" explains exactly how to handle this step. When you finish, reopen the Mail Merge Helper dialog box.

5. In the Mail Merge Helper dialog box, click the Setup button. Word displays the Label Options dialog box, where you can indicate exactly what sort of labels to merge to. If you need more information about this dialog box, go to Chapter 11 and look in the section about labels. Click the OK button after you finish (see Figure 10.14).

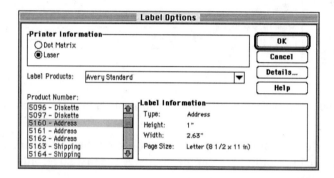

Figure 10.14   Choose a label sheet.

6. Word displays the Create Labels dialog box (see Figure 10.15). Choose fields from the Insert Merge Field button menu to add them to the label. Be sure to put each field in an appropriate location and (if necessary) to add your own spaces and text. After you finish setting up the label, click the OK button.

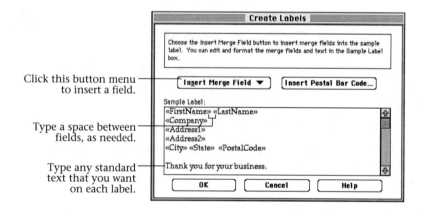

Figure 10.15   Use the Create Labels dialog box to set up what each label should look like.

7. Word returns to the Mail Merge Helper dialog box, which should look like the box in Figure 10.16. If you want to limit which records in the data document turn into

labels, click the Query Options button. To find out more, see "Limiting who gets the form letter" earlier in this chapter.

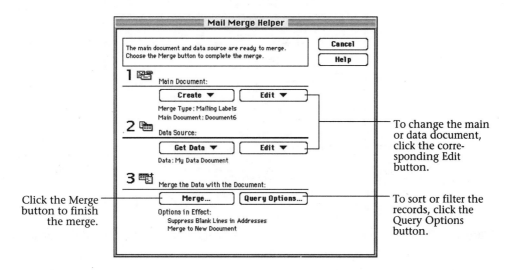

Figure 10.16   This Mail Merge Helper dialog box is completely ready to merge data onto labels.

8. In the Mail Merge Helper dialog box, click the Merge button. Word opens the Merge dialog box.

9. In the Merge dialog box, choose where you want the merge to go, tell Word to merge all records or to merge a range, and turn on the Don't Print Blank Lines When Data Fields Are Empty radio button. After you finish, click the Merge button.

If you have trouble with these steps, review the more detailed steps for creating a form letter—the basics of creating a form letter also apply to making labels.

How to Merge to Envelopes

Merging to envelopes works almost exactly like merging to labels (as explained in the preceding section). The difference is that you choose Envelopes from the Create button menu, and the Setup button lets you choose an envelope type and set it up. If you need help with the dialog boxes for choosing the envelope type, consult the envelope section in Chapter 11. After you finish setting up a merge to envelopes, the Mail Merge Helper dialog box should look like the one shown in Figure 10.17.

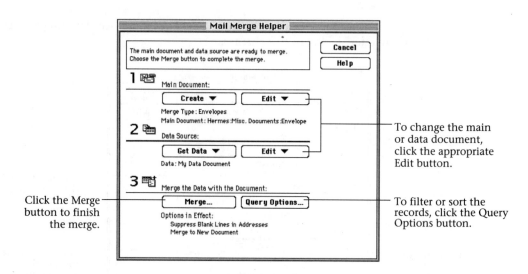

To change the main
or data document,
click the appropriate
Edit button.

Click the Merge
button to finish
the merge.

To filter or sort the
records, click the Query
Options button.

Figure 10.17   This Mail Merge Helper dialog box is completely ready to merge data onto labels.

This chapter covers merging—the process of taking many instances of specific information
(such as addresses) and using each instance to customize a generic item (such as a form letter
or envelope). In the final Word chapter, you learn about printing all kinds of documents.

Chapter 11

Printing

To find out how to print a simple document, read the first few pages of this chapter. To discover many juicy details about printing features, plunge in and read the entire chapter. (This section of the book does not cover features and capabilities offered by QuickDraw GX, optional software that comes with System 7.5 or later.) The information here enables you to check these items off your need-to-know list:

◆ Using Print Preview

◆ Printing an entire document

◆ Understanding fractional widths

◆ Printing parts of a document

◆ Printing with a reduction

◆ Printing to disk (instead of to the printer)

◆ Printing PostScript code

◆ Taking advantage of background printing

◆ Printing an envelope

◆ Printing to a sheet of labels

◆ Solving problems related to printing too close to the edge of a page

Previewing a Printout

Print Preview shows how Word plans to print a document. To switch into Print Preview, choose Print Preview from the File menu, click the Print Preview button on the Standard toolbar, or press ⌘-Option-I. After Print Preview opens, it always displays the page containing the insertion point, although it may display other pages, as well.

Figure 11.1 shows Print Preview displaying four pages. You can change the number of pages showing by dragging down from the Multiple Pages button on the Print Preview toolbar.

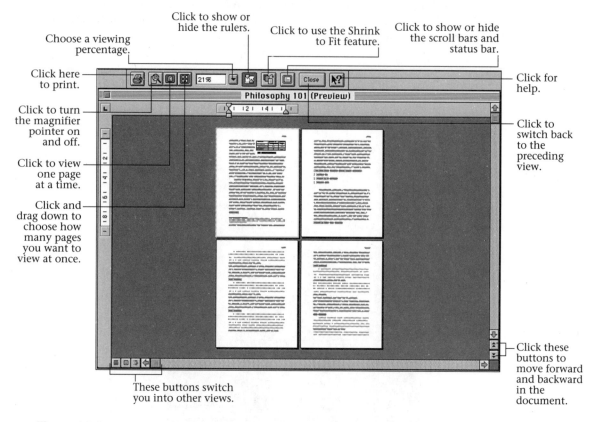

Figure 11.1   Print Preview offers an assortment of controls.

While in Print Preview, you can edit text and use many of the regular commands offered in Word's menus, although the point of Print Preview is to see if the printout is going to look right and to adjust the document if it needs adjusting.

For example, if the last page of the document has only a few lines of text, click the Shrink to Fit button. Word tries to shrink the document so that the last few lines don't end awkwardly at the top of an extra page.

Printing a Document

To print a document, you must open the Print dialog box. To open the dialog box, click the Print button on the Print Preview or the Standard toolbar, choose Print from the File menu, or press ⌘-P.

To print, Word works with software called the *printer driver*, which helps your Mac send information to your printer. (Different printers use different printer drivers.) At the top of the Print dialog box, you should see the name and version of the printer driver (see Figure 11.2).

The printer driver name.

The printer driver version.

This check box shows whether the document has more than one orientation.

Word added these extra options.

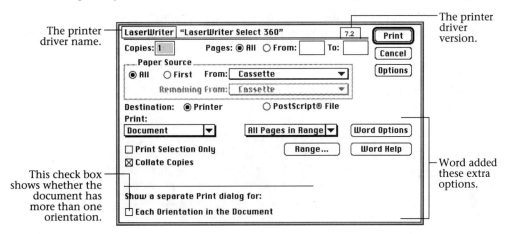

Figure 11.2   The Print dialog box is the control center for printing.

The appearance of the Print dialog box depends partly on Word and partly on the printer driver, so don't worry if your dialog box doesn't match those shown in this book. To print a document from the Print dialog box, enter how many copies you want in the Copies box and click the Print button. Keep the following tips in mind to print successfully:

◆ If you print more than one copy to a PostScript printer, use the Collate Copies check box to indicate whether you want the documents collated or not. QuickDraw printers always collate copies.

◆ To print on the front and back of each page (if your printer does not have a duplexing feature), first print the odd pages and then print the even pages (it takes a little experimenting to figure out exactly how to do this with any given printer). Choose Odd Pages or Even Pages from the pop-up menu above the Range button.

Using fractional widths

By default, fractional widths is off in new documents. The printout will look better if you turn it on because turning on fractional widths causes the printer to take advantage of its higher resolution (usually 300 or 600 dots per inch) for a better look. Unfortunately, with fractional widths on, the document may look fuzzy or have overlapping characters onscreen. This happens because the monitor can only display text at about 72 dots per inch.

If you keep fractional widths off, the printer imitates the lower resolution monitor and does not do the best job it could possibly do. If you use the Print card in the Options dialog box from the Tools menu to turn on fractional widths, the printer optimizes character shapes and widths. The monitor can't display the document exactly as it will print with fractional widths on, and the display tends to look fuzzy with characters slightly overlapping. Some fonts don't look particularly different, but Helvetica changes fairly distinctly.

To turn fractional widths on by default, open up the Normal template (you should find it in Word's Templates folder). With the Normal template open as the active document, go to the Tools menu, choose Options, and select the Print card. Turn on the Fractional Widths check box and click the OK button. Save and close the Normal template.

If you find yourself frequently switching fractional widths on and off, set up macros that turn them on and off. Chapter 9 gives the exact steps for setting up one of these macros.

Substituting Fonts

With fractional widths on, Word blocks a Page Setup dialog box option called Font Substitution (or sometimes, Substitute Fonts). If your printer has built-in fonts (any PostScript printer has built-in fonts), when you print with font substitution on, the printer prints Times instead of New York, Helvetica instead of Geneva, and Courier instead of Monaco.

Printing parts of a document

The Print dialog box offers many different options for printing only part of a document. In some cases, you have to position your insertion point in a particular spot or select particular text before you open the dialog box. In other cases, it helps to know exactly which pages you want to print. If you have trouble relating what you see onscreen to which pages you want to print, remember that the left side of the status bar displays the section and page containing the insertion point. In any event, here's a list of options for printing only part of a document:

◆ To print only the page containing the insertion point, click the Range button and then select Current Page. Click the OK button to return to the Print dialog box and then click the Print button.

◆ To print a selection of text, select the text and then open the Print dialog box. Turn on the Print Selection Only check box and click the Print button.

◆ To print a range of pages from a document that has continuous page numbering throughout the document, type the beginning and ending page numbers in the From and To boxes.

◆ To print a range of pages from a document that has noncontinuous page numbers, click the Range button. Enter the range by specifying the section and page number. For example, if the document has two sections, and each section restarts numbering at page one, to print the first section and the first two pages of the second section, enter **s1p1-s2p2** (see Figure 11.3).

Use a hyphen to indicate a range.

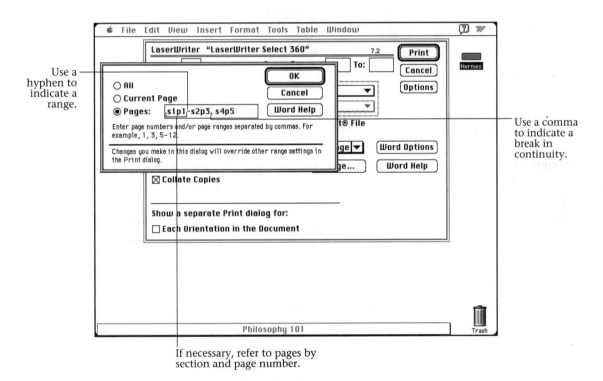

Use a comma to indicate a break in continuity.

If necessary, refer to pages by section and page number.

Figure 11.3   Use the Range dialog box to set a page range.

◆ To print a noncontiguous set of pages, click the Range button. In the Range dialog box, type the page numbers for the pages that you want to print. Specify a break in continuity with a comma. For example, to print page one and then pages six through ten, enter **1,6-10**.

Printing a reduced (or scaled) document

When Word reduces a document, it shrinks the margins, graphics, and text to the percentage that you indicate. Because of the extra space between margins and the reduced text and graphics size, more information fits on a page than it could without the reduction. Onscreen, the indents spread farther apart to accommodate more text per line.

To set up a reduction, go to the File menu and choose Page Setup. The reduction controls differ depending on your printer, so look for a pop-up menu, a box where you can type a reduction, or some other device (see Figure 11.4 for one example).

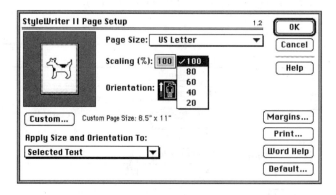

Figure 11.4   The StyleWriter II version 1.2 printer driver lets you choose or enter reductions.

How to print to disk—making PostScript and EPS files

When you print with a PostScript printer driver, the driver converts the document into a series of PostScript programming commands and sends the commands to the printer. If you don't want to print right away, you can tell the driver to send those PostScript commands to a file.

You can then take the file to a typesetter who can print the file at a high resolution, or you can take it to a computer that is not running Word 6 but is attached to a PostScript laser printer. To print the file, you must use a program that can print PostScript code. Apple's LaserWriter Utility (it comes with Apple's printers) works well.

To print to disk, in the Print dialog box for a PostScript printer, set the Destination to PostScript or to Disk (different printer drivers offer different possibilities). After you change the destination, the Print button changes into a Save button. Click the Save button. After you click the Save button, a dialog box appears asking you to save the file.

If you use version 8 or later of a printer driver, the Save dialog box should offer options for saving as PostScript text or as an EPS file. When you save as EPS, the first page of the document saves as an EPS file. To make a PostScript file, choose a PostScript text option.

If you use LaserWriter, PSPrinter, or LaserJet 8.0 or newer, turn on Balloon Help in the dialog box for saving the PostScript file. The Balloon Help has a lot of useful information.

EPS Files

EPS stands for Encapsulated PostScript. An EPS file has two parts: an image that shows onscreen and the underlying PostScript code. The code doesn't show onscreen, but when the image prints, the code tells a PostScript printer what to do. If you print an EPS file to a QuickDraw printer, only the screen image prints because the printer doesn't understand PostScript. The QuickDraw printout probably won't look all that amazing.

You can open EPS files in Word and see the picture onscreen, but you cannot edit an EPS file in Word.

Printing PostScript code

If you have a bit of PostScript code that you want to add to a Word document, and if you want a PostScript printer to interpret the code and print the coded image, you must place the code in a Print field. Here are the steps:

1. From the Insert menu, choose Field. Word opens the Field dialog box.

2. From the Categories list, select All.

3. In the Field Names list, select Print.

4. Turn off the check box for Preserve Formatting During Updates.

5. Click the Options button. The Field Options dialog box appears (see Figure 11.5).

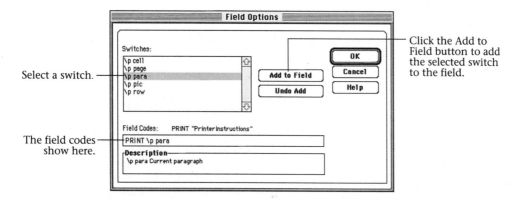

Figure 11.5 Set up the Print field so that it can hold PostScript instructions.

6. From the list of switches, select the switch that makes the most sense for your PostScript code. If you know much about PostScript code, note that the switch dictates the location of the origin (0,0). If you don't know much about PostScript code or aren't sure which switch to select, try \p page or \p para. \p page typically works for PostScript code that is based on a page, such as a box border or a watermark. \p para typically goes with code that applies to the paragraph containing the Print field.

7. Click the Add to Field button. Word adds the switch with the correct syntax to the field.

8. Click the OK button. Word closes the Field Options dialog box and puts you back in the Field dialog box.

9. In the Field dialog box, click the OK button.

10. The result of the Print field is nothing, so you must show field codes to see the field. Edit the field so that it looks like this: {PRINT \p para "code"}. In place of code, paste in your own PostScript code. The code should be enclosed in quotes (see Figure 11.6).

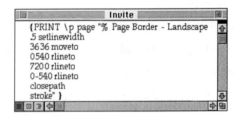

Figure 11.6   This Print field is properly set up with PostScript code for boxing a landscape page with a border.

To find technical information about the Print field and PostScript, click the Help button in the Field Options dialog box.

Using Background Printing

Use background printing to queue up more than one document to print at a time or to use your computer while you print. For most people, a program called Print Monitor handles background printing. You'll find Print Monitor in the Extensions folder inside the System Folder. Double-click the Print Monitor icon to launch Print Monitor. If you go to the File menu and choose Preferences, you get a Preferences dialog box where you can configure Print Monitor.

To turn background printing on or off, follow these steps:

1. From the Apple menu, select Chooser. The Chooser appears (see Figure 11.7).

2. In the Chooser, on the left side, click the icon representing your printer driver. After you click, options for turning background printing on or off appear at the lower right.

3. Select a background printing option.

4. Close the Chooser by clicking in the close box at the upper left or pressing ⌘-W.

Wait 30 seconds or so after you click the Print button and then choose Print Monitor from the Applications menu. Print Monitor shows how the printing is going. If you leave the Print Monitor window as the active window, the printing goes faster.

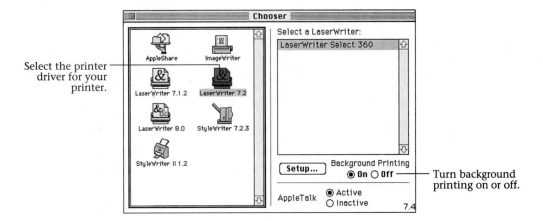

Select the printer driver for your printer.

Turn background printing on or off.

Figure 11.7   To see the background printing radio buttons, you must select the printer driver.

Printing an Envelope

If all goes well, printing an envelope works like a charm. Here are the steps to try:

1. If the delivery address is already typed in the document, highlight the address.

2. Choose Envelopes and Labels from the Tools menu. Select the Envelopes card. The Envelopes card has boxes for typing the delivery and mailing addresses as well as the extremely important Feed button at the lower right (see Figure 11.8).

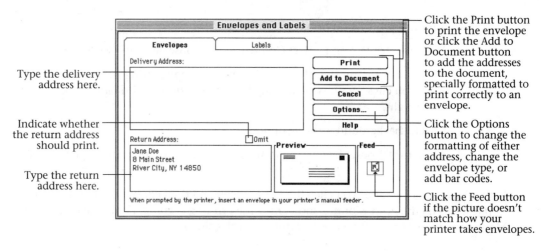

Type the delivery address here.

Indicate whether the return address should print.

Type the return address here.

Click the Print button to print the envelope or click the Add to Document button to add the addresses to the document, specially formatted to print correctly to an envelope.

Click the Options button to change the formatting of either address, change the envelope type, or add bar codes.

Click the Feed button if the picture doesn't match how your printer takes envelopes.

Figure 11.8 Set up the appearance and feeding method for the envelope.

3. Make any needed changes to the delivery and return addresses. If you have a default return address set and don't want to use it, turn on the Omit check box. Word figures out the default return address by looking at the User Info card in the Options dialog box from the Tools menu.

4. Click the Options button to open the Envelope Options dialog box. Select the Envelope Options card.

5. Choose an envelope size. If none of the sizes is right, choose Custom Size and enter your own dimensions.

6. Use the Delivery and Return Address areas to customize the formatting and position of each address. For best results, try the Auto positions first.

7. Select the Printing Options tab.

8. In the Printing Options card, indicate how the printer expects you to insert the envelope and then click the OK button. Word returns to the Envelopes and Labels dialog box.

9. To add the envelope to a separate section at the top of the document and print it later with the document, click Add to Document. Or to print the envelope, click the Print button.

Caution: If you add the envelope to the top of a document, when you print the document, you may want to turn on the Each Orientation in the Document check box in the Print dialog box. If you do, Word prints the envelope from the selected paper source (such as the manual feed tray). After printing the envelope, Word brings up the Print dialog box again so that you can choose a different source (such as the paper cassette).

10. If you changed the return address, Word asks whether you want to save it as the default return address. Click Yes if you want to save it, No if you don't.

11. If you clicked the Print button in step 9, the Print dialog box appears. If necessary, indicate that you are printing from the manual feed tray or an envelope feeder. Click the Print button.

What to do if an envelope prints wrong

Word has a poor track record with printing envelopes correctly, so if you are certain that you selected the correct envelope setting for your printer, consider the following possibilities if the envelope doesn't print correctly:

◆ If the addresses printed upside down, rotate the envelope 180 degrees on the paper tray and try again. This problem often occurs with printers designed for Windows and Macintosh users because the graphic on the printer that shows how to print envelopes is incorrect for the Macintosh.

◆ If the addresses printed far from where they should have (or if they didn't print on the envelope at all), try a few different envelope positions in the Printing Options card. Word's logic about envelope positions may have no relationship to your logic.

◆ Use the Envelope Options dialog box to tweak the exact location of the delivery and return addresses. A little experimentation here may go a long way.

Printing on Labels

Word has a card in the Envelopes and Labels dialog box that helps enormously with printing to labels. Using the card, you can print a page of identical labels or print just one label. You can also set up a page specially formatted for typing up a page of nonidentical labels.

Setting up a label sheet

To open the card, choose Envelopes and Labels from the Tools menu and select the Labels card (see Figure 11.9).

If you are printing only one address, type the address here or turn on the Use Return Address check box.

Indicate whether you want one label or a page of labels.

Click the Print button to print or click the New Document button to create a document containing a table formatted to match the selected labels.

Click the Options button or click the sample label to specify which labels you plan to use.

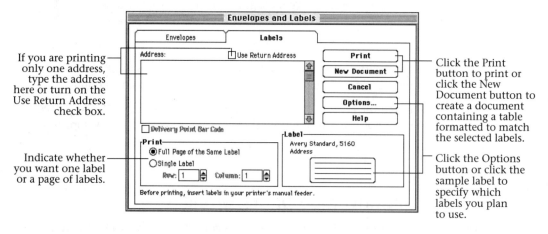

Figure 11.9   The Labels card helps you print out to a sheet of labels.

In the Labels card, the first step is to select the type of labels that you plan to use. The lower-right corner shows the currently selected label, and you can click the Options button (or click on the label) to open the Label Options dialog box (see Figure 11.10).

Select a type of printer. Select Laser if you print to any laser printer or to an inkjet printer.

Select the labels that you plan to use.

Click the Details button in the unlikely event that you need to further customize the label setup.

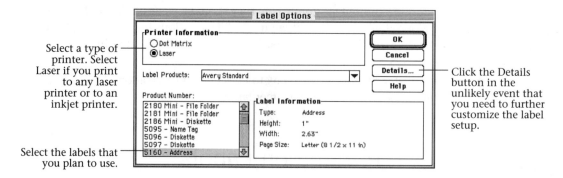

Figure 11.10   Select the label sheet closest to what you plan to use.

In the Label Options dialog box, select your printer type and label brand. Then select the actual label type from the Product Number list. (If nothing in the Product Number list matches your labels, select a close match and click the Details button. Use the resulting dialog box to further customize the setup.) After selecting the proper label options, click the OK button.

Printing just one label

To print just one label on a sheet, follow these steps:

1. Type the label information in the Address box. To format text in the Address box, use keyboard shortcuts or Control-click on highlighted text to bring up a shortcut menu. You can access the Font and Paragraph dialog boxes from the menu.

   To print the default return address instead, turn on Use Return Address. The default return address comes from the information on the User Info card in the Options dialog box.

2. Select the Single Label radio button and enter the row and column of the label that you want to use. In general, print to the bottom free row so that you can feed the label sheet through the printer again. If you print to the top row and then peel the label off, the sheet is likely to jam if you feed it into the printer again.

3. Click the Print button.

Printing a page of identical labels

To print a page of labels, try these steps:

1. Type the information for one label in the Address box.

2. Select the Full Page of the Same Label radio button.

3. Click the Print button.

Making a page of different labels

If you don't want the same address on each label, you must bring the label layout into a regular Word document and then type the individual addresses. Here are the steps:

1. If you want any text to repeat in each label, such as *To:* or a zip code, type the text in the Address box.

2. Select Full Page of the Same Label.

3. Click the New Document button. Word creates a new document and puts a table in the document. The rows and columns in the table match the rows and columns on the label sheet.

4. Type the text for each label. To move from one label to the next, press Tab. If you fill one page and want to create another page of labels, click in the lower-right table cell and press Tab.

5. After you finish filling in each label, print the document just as you would print any other document.

Caution: If you plan to create many unique labels, consider using a mail merge to place the information on the labels. If you merge the information, you can use it again to make form letters, envelopes, and so on.

Printing Close to the Edge

A problem with life is that if you get too close to the edge of anything, you fall off. In the case of printing, it's not so much that you fall off, but if you try to print too close to the edge, the text that's over the limit fails to print. For letter-sized paper, you may find that you can't print closer to the edge than .5 inches, and for legal-sized paper, you often can't print closer than .9 inches. Each printer has its own limitation, so consult your printer manual or run some tests to discover your printer's limits.

Word tries to alert you if it anticipates a problem with text cutting off around the edges, but the alert doesn't always work. Here are a few tips:

◆ To get the maximum printing area, go to the File menu and choose Page Setup. In the Page Setup dialog box, click the Options button. In the resulting dialog box, turn on the Larger Print Area check box. Click the OK button and then click the OK button again to return to the document. (If you don't have an Options button in Page Setup, you can't take advantage of this suggestion.)

◆ Adjust your margins. Click in or highlight the appropriate sections and then choose Document Layout from the File menu. Select the Margins card, change the margins, and click the OK button.

◆ If a header or footer is cutting off, move it farther from the edge. To move a header or footer, click in the correct section and then choose Document Layout from the File menu. Select the Margins card, adjust the appropriate From Edge setting, and click the OK button.

◆ If a page number cuts off, adjust the position of the header or footer containing the number. If the page number is completely missing, make sure that it is in the expected header or footer. For example, you may have the page number set to not print on the first page of a document (or section).

◆ If a table row hangs down into the bottom margin and then cuts off, click in the row and choose Cell Height and Width from the Table menu. On the Row card, turn on the Allow Row to Break Across Page check box.

◆ Increase the margins so that the text does appear on the printed page and then set up a reduction (try a 90 percent reduction, which reduces the document by 10 percent). Flip back a few pages to find out how.

Now that you know all about printing, you are ready to amaze your friends and co-workers with the astonishing depth of your knowledge.

If you read a reasonable portion of all the chapters on Word, you are now officially started with Word 6 and are probably an expert at using more than a few of the features. Congratulations!

Part III
Excel 5

Excel shows what Microsoft can do when it gets everything right. Although Excel 5 is big, and not exactly a speed demon compared to smaller products, all the new features in this application are justified in a business setting as true "power user" tools. Although the first release of Excel 5 had an assortment of bugs, the version that shipped with Office 4.2.1 was stable and trouble free.

The graphics are better; macros are better (you can actually read the macros created in the English-syntax-like Visual Basic); and the Excel workbook is a great information-handling device. The Pivot Table function and analysis tools put Excel in a class by itself as software for organizing and understanding a business or for just tinkering with home budgets. Part III covers all these aspects of Excel 5, and on top of all this, you will also find real-world examples of how to set up and interpret all sorts of data for predicting the future and analyzing trends. Excel 5 is software you can enjoy rather than merely survive.

Chapter 12

Getting Started with Excel

It helps to think of a spreadsheet as just a piece of paper. This piece of paper has two magical qualities. First, you can write and erase numbers over and over again without wrecking the paper. Second, when you write an arithmetic problem on this paper, you can make it solve itself.

Excel 5 is loaded with features that no one dreamed about back in the days of VisiCalc, the first spreadsheet program, but you can start working with Excel right away by using only a smaller feature set at first and mastering more features later. In this chapter, you start using Excel so that you can get real-world results today. You'll find these topics covered:

◆ How to enter and edit data

◆ A quick tour of the Excel toolbar

◆ How to format text and number entries

◆ Using formulas for basic arithmetic

◆ Navigating in a worksheet

◆ Using multiple sheets in an Excel workbook

◆ How to print worksheet results

A First Look

Excel 5 is the biggest, most feature-packed spreadsheet any software company has produced. Paradoxically, it's also the easiest to use because the features have been arranged in layers. At one level, you can learn a handful of commands and solve all sorts of real-world problems. At successively higher levels, you can make flashy business graphics, do statistics and engineering studies, and design elaborate what-if investigations.

The good news is that you and I can get working in this fabulous new version of Excel in a matter of minutes. This section of the book is going to be a complete reference, but the features of Excel are going to be described in order of usefulness, at increasing levels of detail as the chapters progress. I have seen an Excel book for Windows PCs, for example, in which the delicate subject of adding numbers is first broached on page 223! That's not the approach here—I want you in fifth gear on your second lap around the track.

Look at the screen in Figure 12.1. It presents a fairly bewildering array of little tool buttons in two rows at the top. In the upper right-hand corner there are two odd little icons (the light bulb and the question mark in Figure 12.2) that you won't need right now, but which will become old friends in a few days. The light bulb is a new feature in Excel 5 that gives you context-dependent tips. The question mark, when double-clicked, calls up Excel's gigantic help machinery, the equivalent of three medium-sized books.

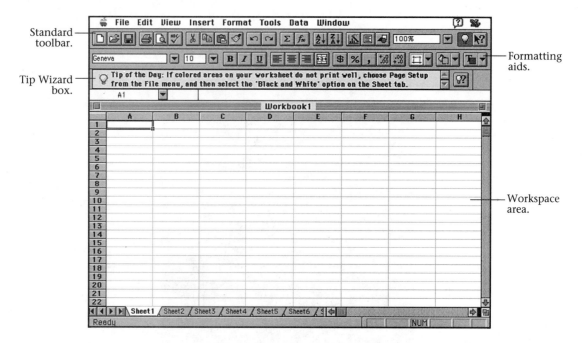

Figure 12.1   Excel 5 opening screen.

Tip Wizard button.  Help button.

Figure 12.2 Two new little friends.

What else does Excel give you when you double-click the Microsoft Excel icon? There's a grid of little rectangles where the actual work takes place, a set of labels for rows (numbers) and columns (letters) along the sides, and the large collection of buttons that correspond to individual menu commands (that is, everything you do with buttons you can do by pulling down a menu). At the bottom of the screen you see tabs (looking like file folder tabs) called Sheet 1, Sheet 2, and so forth up to Sheet 16. What you're looking at in Sheet 1 is the top sheet of a whole set linked together in a *workbook*. For big problems, Excel workbooks are great, but for a quick introduction on small problems, they're just a complication, so you'll work only in this top sheet now.

Entering numbers and text

If you move the mouse around now (see Sheet 1 of the workbook Untitled1, which Excel 5 presents on startup), you see that the mouse cursor turns into an arrow when it's over the little buttons and at the edges of the worksheet, and into a little Swiss-flag-type cross when it's out over the grid.

To get started, move the cross to cell B3 (that's column B, row 3) and click the mouse. Notice that the *name box* at the upper left shows your choice of active cell. Clicking the cell *selects* it. That gets you into the cell so that you can start entering some data.

Besides the mouse, you can also use the arrow keys to move around in the worksheet. Another navigation method is to type a cell name in the name box in the upper left-hand corner and then press Enter. And under the Edit menu, there's a Go To command that does the same thing.

Just to have a bit of practice at Excel, try this opening sequence:

◆ Type **Monthly Expense Report** into the cell B3. If you make a typing mistake, you can correct it by using the arrow keys and Delete or by picking your way between characters with the mouse. Note that you can do the editing in the cell itself or in the area, called the *formula bar*, where you see your typing reflected. After you're done typing, either press Enter (or press Return), move out of the cell by using an arrow key, or move the mouse cursor away to another cell and click.

♦ The words that you typed extend past the edge of the cell B3 box. To make the cell big enough for the words, click in cell B3 and then move the cursor up to the edge of the right-hand side of the box containing the letter B at the top of the column. The cursor changes to a little vertical bar. Hold down the mouse button and move the mouse to the right—this expands the column width. Move the column boundary until you have enough space for your words.

♦ As long as you're at it, you may as well make the words into a proper heading. Click in cell B3 again to select it and then click on the button with a capital B in the Formatting toolbar. That helps highlight the words. Then find the font size scrolling list on the toolbar and set this cell to 14 points (see Figure 12.3). You see that you now need to adjust the cell width again.

Quick buttons for bold, italic, and underline.

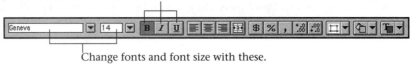

Change fonts and font size with these.

Figure 12.3 Quick formatting from the toolbar.

♦ Type in the categories of expenses in the cells shown in column A and adjust the size of the cell (see Figure 12.4).

♦ Now enter the numbers, as shown in Figure 12.4. Nothing to it—just click the first number-entry cell, type in the number, and press the Down Arrow key to get to the next cell. Press Enter after the last entry.

♦ Just to make this look professional, click the first number cell, hold down the mouse button, and drag down to select the set of number cells. Then click on the dollar-sign button. Presto, the cells are formatted as money.

What do you do now? You save your work, that's what you do. Pull down the File menu, pick Save As, and name the worksheet (something like 01.expenses). As a rule of thumb, save your work every time you have typed something that you don't want to type again, which means *save your work constantly.*

Caution: Excel 5 is a big application with lots of complicated interactions with System 7.5, and you should anticipate that it may just freeze on you from time to time, especially if you don't have lots of extra memory to spare. Rather than face the agony of rebuilding a large model after a crash, start remembering to press ⌘-S as a nervous habit. If you're just looking at the screen and thinking about what to do next, press ⌘-S.

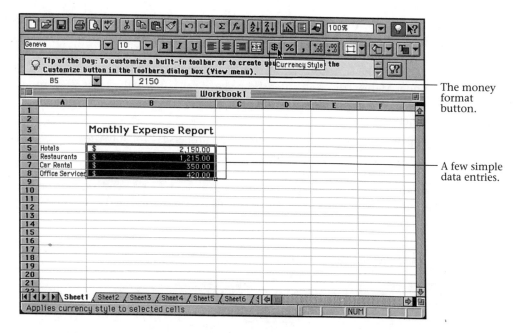

Figure 12.4   Setting up some information.

Like all other Microsoft products, Excel has an Undo function under the Edit menu. If Undo doesn't do what you want (sometimes things get truly messed up), you may need to press the Escape key and start over in a cell. There's also an Undo button on the Standard toolbar—it's the little backward-curling arrow. (Redo is the forward arrow to the right of Undo.)

A first formula

So far, of course, you haven't done anything that couldn't be done in a word processor. You've just been typing into cells as if they were tiny pages. In fact, most of the same formatting tricks now apply in all Microsoft products—Excel uses the same little buttons as Microsoft Word 6 and Microsoft PowerPoint 4.

But the point of a spreadsheet is to set up some calculations underneath the numbers. So now it's time to do a little calculation, namely adding up the numbers in the expenses column.

Type **Total** into cell A10 so that you have a label. Then click on cell B10 to select it. There are three ways to put a formula in this cell in order to get a total for expenses:

◆ You can type in the expression **=B5+B6+B7+B8**. This just tells Excel to add the numbers in those cells. By the way, when you type a formula like this into a cell, don't bother using uppercase. Excel sees b7 as B7 in a formula.

275

◆ You can use the function SUM. One way is to type the expression **=SUM(B5:B8)** directly into the cell. The notation B5:B8 means to add that whole range of cells. You can also enter the SUM function from the Function Wizard (see Figure 12.5). Just click the Function Wizard button, select the function SUM (usually hiding under Math&Trig), and enter the range of cells. It actually takes a few more key strokes this way, but in the long run, it saves you work because you can't mistype function names.

◆ Finally, because adding up columns of numbers is probably the most common use of Excel, there's a special AutoSum function (see Figure 12.5). Select the cell below the bottom of the column and click the AutoSum function; then click the top number cell, hold down the mouse button, and drag down to select the other numbers, which will fill in automatically. Press Enter to have the actual total appear in cell B10.

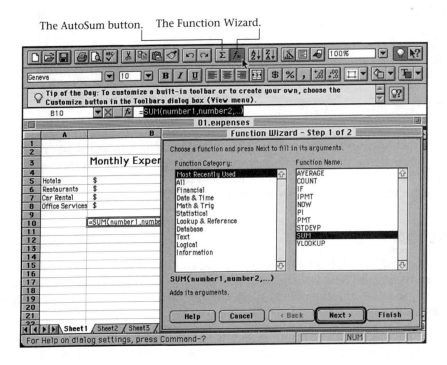

Figure 12.5 Quick clicks for formulas.

More about formulas

Now Excel 5 has dozens and dozens of functions, as you may have noticed in the Function Wizard dialog box. Some of them are used all the time (the four main arithmetic functions +, -, *, / and SUM), and some of them are notably less popular (hyperbolic trigonometric functions, for example). As a quick reference, I have set up Figure 12.6 for the four basics. Don't worry about the other functions now—there will be plenty of advanced material in the later chapters.

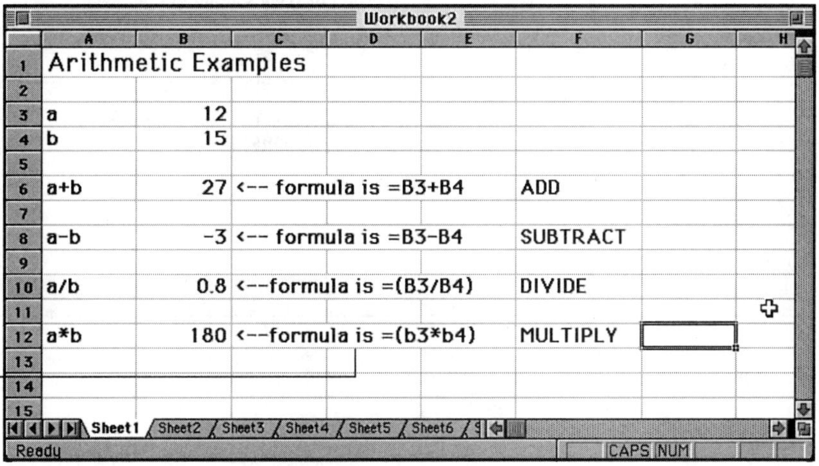

Cell arithmetic examples.

Figure 12.6 Basic Excel functions.

It's time to discuss a bit of spreadsheet jargon. When you use a cell location like B4 in a formula, that's called a *cell reference*. In particular, this one is called a *relative* cell reference. A relative cell reference means that you can copy the formula, paste it into another location, and the cell reference will move along with it (see Figure 12.7). If you don't want the cell reference to move, you have to make an *absolute* reference. For historical reasons (the earliest spreadsheets used this notation, so you're stuck with it), the way you indicate an absolute reference is with dollar signs, such as $B$4. If you name a cell that way in a formula, the formula always takes the contents of that cell, wherever you move the formula.

If you want to define a set of constants in a worksheet, you usually want to use absolute cell references. If, for example, you have a list of sales entries for a store and you want to multiply all the entries by a number for sales tax, your best bet is to enter the sales tax number in a cell somewhere near the top of the worksheet and then use an absolute cell reference when you refer to sales tax in formulas.

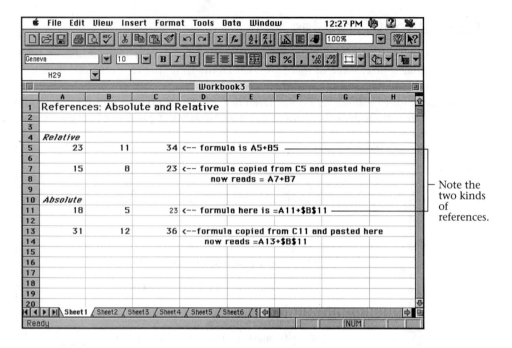

Figure 12.7   Absolute and relative cell references.

A Budget Example

Here's a slightly more ambitious example. It just uses the same commands already covered, but it uses them over and over. Just to keep your spirits up as you leaf through the thousand pages of the Excel manual, you should remind yourself that you could have a perfectly plausible career as a spreadsheet hotshot if you knew about ten percent of the features in Excel 5. As proof of this, consider that Lotus 1-2-3 version 1A—the program that made spreadsheets a permanent fixture of the American business landscape—had only about ten percent of the features now present in Excel, and plenty of people made careers out of Lotus. If you can enter numbers and use formulas, you have the essence of the whole show. Beyond that, most of the work you do in Excel is "beautification" with formatting and charting effects.

Step-by-step business

Figure 12.8 shows a sample budget that is typical of the day-to-day use of Excel. Sometimes you're going to use Excel for fancy presentation effects, but Microsoft studies show that humble little tables like this one are actually about 90 percent of Excel use. To make a table like the one in Figure 12.8, follow these steps:

1. Select the whole set of rows 1 through 16 by dragging the mouse across the gray
    row-number buttons at the left-hand edge of the workspace. Selecting whole
    batches of rows or columns is much quicker than formatting individual cells.

2. With the area selected, pick New York for a font, 12 points for the font size, and
    bold for a format. Then make the title and column headings 14 points for the font
    size.

3. Notice the date reference in the formula bar. Type in **Sept. 94,** and Excel will
    interpret the date as 9/1/94.

4. Enter the budget numbers and use AutoSum to make the total and grand total for
    this somewhat expensive organization.

5. Select the whole central area with numbers and click the money format button.

6. Just for fun, select the Grand total text cell and the total cell next to it and pick the
    solid border by clicking the Borders button.

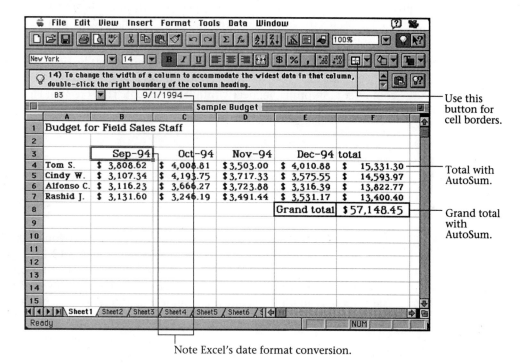

Note Excel's date format conversion.

Figure 12.8   A formatted budget.

What do you do with a document like this? Well, for starters, the individual expense numbers were concocted in reference to the original expense worksheet. As a manager, you may want to plug in the consequences of parking the field staff at cheaper hotels when they're not meeting clients and, for that matter, having lunch at Burger King when they're on the road. The point of a spreadsheet is that you can prepare a whole folio of expense options like this to study. Later, in Chapter 14, I'll show you how to make a sheet like this in which each entry is the summary cell of its own little worksheet. This way you can do an infinite amount of tinkering to meet budget goals or to decide how much revenue you'll need.

Getting into print

Sooner or later, by trying out different numbers, you'll have a budget that you want to present. Typically, that means that you need to print your work (unless you work for a company that has a Macintosh-based overhead projector). When you print in Excel, there are a few things to consider.

The fifth button from the left in the Standard toolbar (the one at the top) shows a little page with a magnifying glass. It's the button for Print Preview. You may be familiar with Print Preview from Microsoft Word, but please be aware that it's absolutely critical in Excel.

In Word, you can usually make a good guess about the printed output because a word processor is designed to represent sheets of paper in a standard page setup. In Excel, the "sheet of paper" in the computer is, in principle, nearly infinite in extent. The screen in Figure 12.8 turns into the two Print Preview pages shown in Figures 12.9 and 12.10.

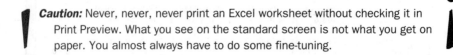

> **Caution:** Never, never, never print an Excel worksheet without checking it in Print Preview. What you see on the standard screen is not what you get on paper. You almost always have to do some fine-tuning.

What kind of fine-tuning? In this case, you have a couple of choices. After you click the Setup button at the top of the Print Preview display, you see the screen in Figure 12.11. You can scale the output until it fits on a single page. At 80 percent of normal size, it fits, but it prints on a page that's mostly white space (see Figure 12.12). A better choice, because this worksheet is wider than it is tall, is simply to print in Landscape mode (Figure 12.13), which is a better fit with the world of 8 1/2 × 11-inch paper.

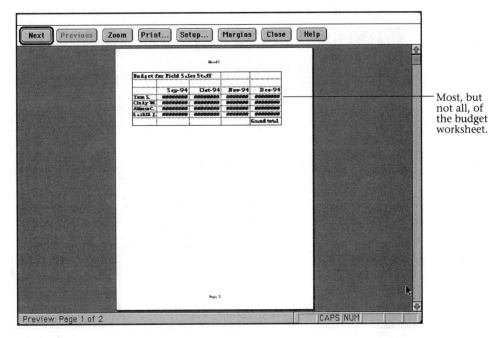

Most, but
not all, of
the budget
worksheet.

Figure 12.9   The budget sheet, page 1.

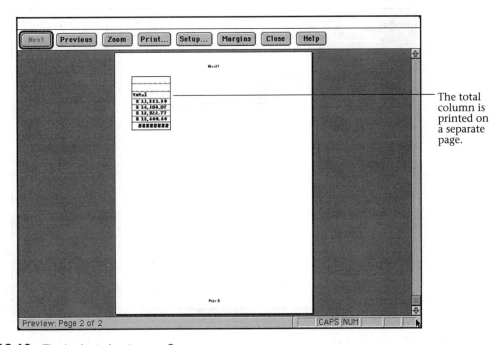

The total
column is
printed on
a separate
page.

Figure 12.10   The budget sheet, page 2.

281

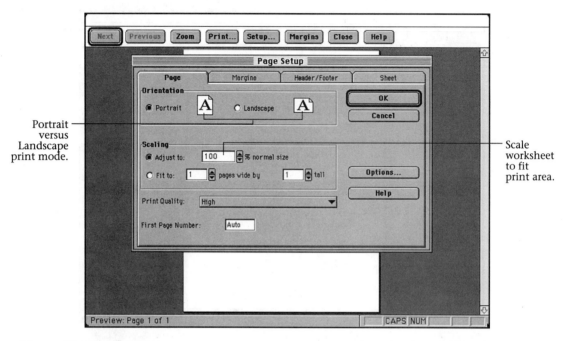

Portrait versus Landscape print mode.

Scale worksheet to fit print area.

Figure 12.11 Page Setup in Print Preview.

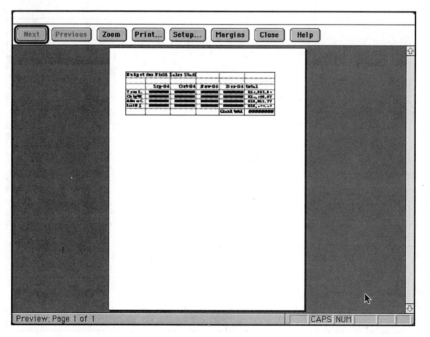

Figure 12.12 Scaling to fit.

Sheet at 100
percent
scale, but
sideways.

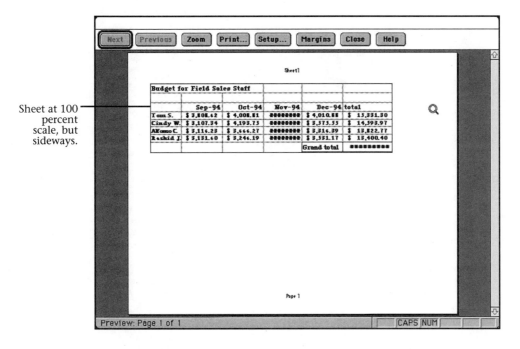

Figure 12.13   A better print format (Landscape).

This chapter is a beginner's guide to the most useful Excel operations. Each subsequent chapter will provide more depth on every topic covered here. Nonetheless, if you know only how to enter data, formulas, and get printed output, you can still use Excel 5 effectively at work. The next chapter tells you how to format your worksheets.

Chapter 13

Formatting Your Worksheets

Excel 5 has seriously overhauled Excel formatting capabilities. In part, this overhaul was caused by Microsoft's desire to make formatting techniques the same across all Microsoft applications and because some new features were long overdue. This chapter shows you the various formatting options and how to use them faster with simple tricks. If you're in a hurry, it's one of the most important chapters of the book. This chapter includes the following topics:

- ◆ Formatting with the Standard toolbar
- ◆ Formatting with the Options dialog box from the View Menu
- ◆ Using the Format Cells dialog box
- ◆ Adjusting column width and row width and wrapping text
- ◆ Using styles and the Paste Special command
- ◆ Adding artwork with the Drawing toolbar
- ◆ Filling standard sets of labels automatically
- ◆ Naming cells and ranges
- ◆ Learning rapid navigation tips
- ◆ Using Format Painter
- ◆ Using the keyboard for practically everything
- ◆ Learning rapid navigation tips, fill-handle tricks, and date and time tips

Formatting with the Standard Toolbar

Excel gives you the facilities for making tables of data look any way you want. You can make wretched little high-density, small-point size tables with tons of hard-to-read data—hey, sometimes you may *want* the data to be hard to read. You can also make data presentations so lovely that you could use them in advertising.

All sorts of possibilities lurk under the Excel 5 format menu. However, the most useful formatting commands are right on top of your Excel worksheet. As part of its duties as a good corporate citizen and as-yet-unconvicted software monopolist, Excel has done two interesting tests on its own products. First, it has established a usability lab in which it monitors patterns of use with its software. Second, it has sent out special versions of programs that record which keystrokes typical users employ to do common tasks. Armed with this information, Microsoft selects the contents of its wizards (the interactive tip system) and the toolbars. Those little buttons didn't volunteer to appear on the toolbar—they were drafted!

Column and row size

Before you format any number or text, you need to have someplace to put it, so it's time to discuss changing the sizes of the little cells in the worksheet. Figure 13.1 shows a single word ("this") in a single cell. Type the word in the cell at the default font size and then select 24 from the font size scrolling list. In Excel 5, the row height adjusts automatically when you do this. If you copy this cell and paste it somewhere else, that row adjusts itself, too.

Can you reformat columns in the same way? Going back to this cell and typing in some more words (see Figure 13.2), you can see that the column doesn't readjust. But there's another option for column width—under the Format menu, the Column choice gives you AutoFit Selection as another option (see Figure 13.3). It works like a charm. The only catch is that it applies only to a single selection. If you want this function to work all the time, drag-select across all the columns you're likely to use and then select AutoFit.

For every task that you want to accomplish in Excel, there are about a half dozen ways to do it. You can take each column in your worksheet, one at a time, and format each column by choosing Column and Width under the Format menu and then specifying the number of characters. That's the hard way. Or you can perform a width adjustment by clicking the head of each column and then adjusting the width with the little bar cursor that you see when you move the pointer cursor to the edge of the column.

That's easier, and it's sort of fun and interactive. But you bought this book to get some advice, so here it is: the easiest way to format column widths is to type your entries into the spreadsheet without paying any attention to widths. Then select the whole set of columns that you're using and format the widths all at once by using AutoFit. That's one grand drag-select with the mouse and a single command versus dozens of little adjustments in the other techniques. Unless there's a compelling reason (you need to see more of your worksheet onscreen at once, for example), AutoFit for columns is the fastest and easiest way to get proper column-width adjustment.

Change font size here.

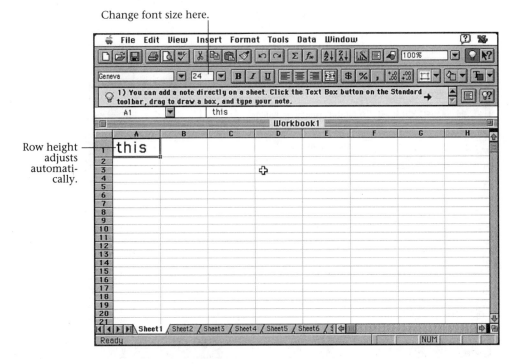

Row height
adjusts
automati-
cally.

Figure 13.1 Text size formatting.

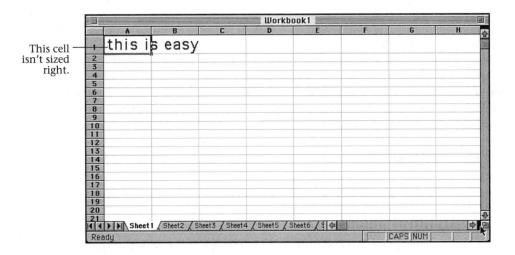

This cell
isn't sized
right.

Figure 13.2 Big text exceeds the column width.

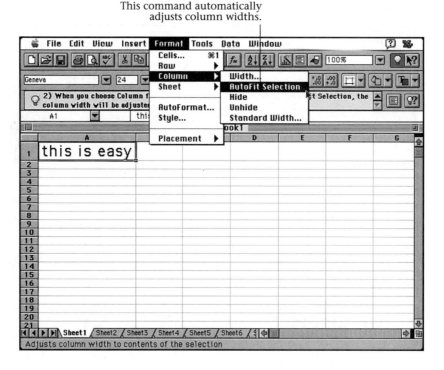

Figure 13.3 AutoFit solves all problems.

One rather annoying aspect of the implementation of AutoFit is that it doesn't remember that columns were AutoFitted. Suppose that you have used AutoFit to adjust your columns, and every column is as aesthetically perfect as the columns of the Parthenon—which, as you may know, actually have a subtle curvature to make them appear straight. If you then edit a cell and increase the font size, for example, the row height changes, but the text now slops over disgracefully into the next cell. You have to select AutoFit again to restore calm and order to your work. If you've changed fonts all over the place, you may find that selecting all the row headings in your worksheet and then choosing the AutoFit under Row in Format command will save you some valuable space.

Fonts and sizes

Rows adjust their own row heights automatically, and for columns there's an AutoFit option. That suggests that changing fonts and font sizes in Excel 5 is going to be pretty simple.

It is. If you have the TipWizard turned on (click the lightbulb button if the TipWizard isn't displayed), move the cursor to the left-hand side of the Formatting toolbar. The last two elements are not only the toolbar scroll boxes for fonts and font size, but with the TipWizard turned on, they actually announce themselves as such. "Land sakes, child," as my grand-mother used to say, "if they were dogs, they'd jump up and bite you" (see Figure 13.4).

Selecting sizes.

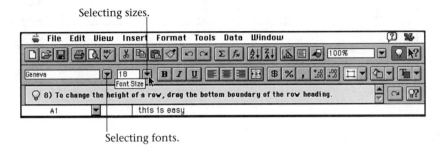

Selecting fonts.

Figure 13.4   Toolbar font formatting.

These two elements are by far the fastest way to make font changes in a worksheet because they don't require you to find what you want in a multilevel menu. And although you may not realize it, you have already absorbed a huge assortment of rules for font usage in a worksheet. All your life, you have seen layouts of tables of numbers in newspapers, magazines, and books, and even if you haven't recognized the rules, your opinion of what looks good and what doesn't is governed by those rules.

Alignment

Four more buttons on the Formatting toolbar (see Figure 13.5) control positioning of text and numbers inside cells. The commands do exactly what their appearance suggests: align contents to the left, center contents, align contents to the right, and center contents across a set of columns. Figure 13.6 shows four cells to which the buttons have been applied in sequence.

Figure 13.5   Toolbar alignment formatting.

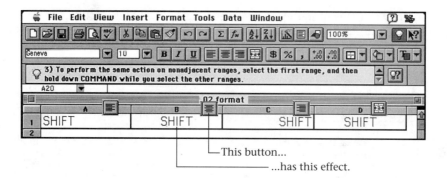

Figure 13.6   Text alignment in cells.

Numbers

Fast number formatting with the toolbar uses five buttons toward the right side. You can't miss 'em—they're the set that starts with the dollar sign and ends with little zeros.

◆ After you select a cell and click the dollar-sign button, the selected cell is formatted as currency (starts with a dollar sign, no comma, rounded to two decimal places).

◆ If you do the same with the percent button, your number is formatted as a simple rounded-off percent: 0.613 becomes 61%.

◆ The comma button lets you introduce commas into numbers to mark off thousands.

◆ The buttons with little arrows and zeros modify the number of places displayed. If you click the button with the right-pointing direction arrow, the decimal point in your number heads for the right edge of the cell; the left-pointing arrow button sends the decimal point in the opposite direction.

A little design

Later in this chapter, I show you all the glorious formats available in Excel through the AutoFormat command, but you should get a little feeling for worksheet aesthetics on your own before you start taking Microsoft's word for it. In general, here are some considerations for worksheet design:

◆ Indicate levels of heading importance with font size, but don't use a large range of sizes. A difference of two between the largest and smallest text in a worksheet looks good.

◆ You're accustomed to seeing headlines in sans-serif fonts and text with serifs. If it's good enough for magazines and newspapers, it's good enough for you (see Figure 13.7). Put headlines and big text in sans-serif and small text in serif fonts.

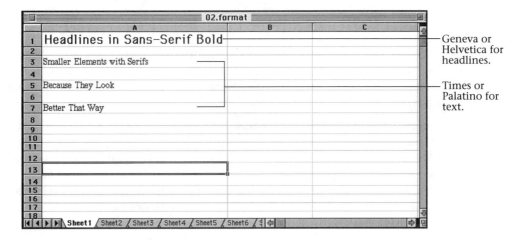

Figure 13.7 Standard headline conventions.

◆ A well-designed worksheet looks even better in print with the gridlines turned off (see Figure 13.8).

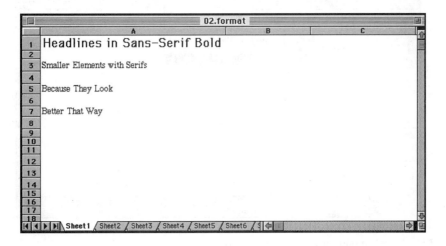

Figure 13.8 Hiding the gridlines.

◆ Use drawing elements sparingly.

◆ One or two range borders are plenty on a single page.

Options, the Hidden Formatter

I just suggested that you look at your worksheet with the gridlines turned off. But I didn't tell you how to do it. That's because I want to highlight one of the major pieces of weirdness in Excel 5: the absolute junkyard of commands stashed under the Tools menu in the Options dialog box.

For example, you may assume that the way you format or view the whole worksheet can be found in the commands under the Format or View menus. Wrong—it doesn't work that way in the Microsoft world—and they're the ones in charge. If you pull down the Format menu and choose Sheet, you find that your formatting option basically consists of *hiding* your work. Instead, after you choose Options from the Tools menu (see Figure 13.9), you get the Mother Of All Tabbed Dialog Boxes—Excel Control Central (see Figure 13.10).

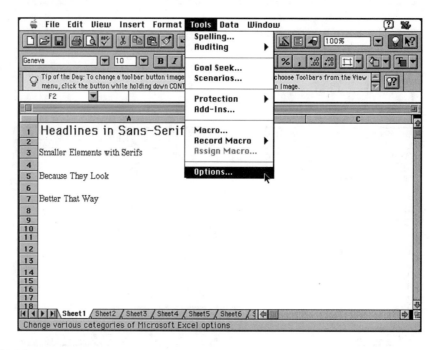

Figure 13.9   The all-important Options command.

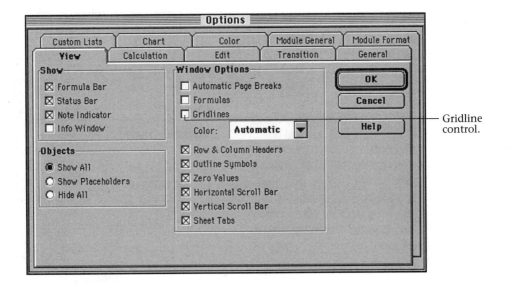

Figure 13.10 The View tab in the Options dialog box.

In this giant grab bag of leftover formats, there are really three tabs that concern formats. The View tab, shown in Figure 13.10, controls most aspects of screen appearance, including gridlines, page breaks, and the regions (sheet tabs, scroll bars) at the edges of the worksheet. The Color tab (see Figure 13.11) controls the default colors for charts and text.

The General tab enables you to set the number of sheets in a workbook and to set the default font and size (see Figure 13.12). If you like to work in 12-point Times Roman instead of 10-point Geneva (and you make better-looking worksheets if you do), you can make the default changes here and have it done with once and for all.

Finally, I should point out that almost everything I have to write about in this chapter depends on the Edit options being set to the standard defaults shown in Figure 13.13. For example, editing directly in cells (instead of editing only in the formula bar) depends on the check box for cell editing being checked as shown.

As a shortcut, if you know that you will always be working with money calculations rather than as a rocket scientist, you can set the check box in the Edit tab for two decimal places. It doesn't affect the accuracy of calculations, and it means that you don't have to keep setting the decimal places in your worksheets.

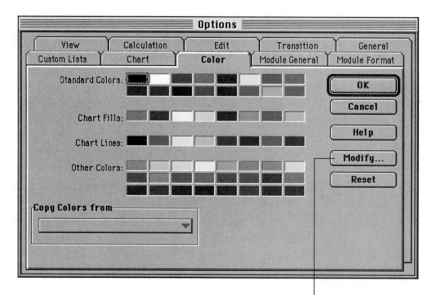

Pressing Modify gets you
to a custom color palette.

Figure 13.11 A gray view of the color tab.

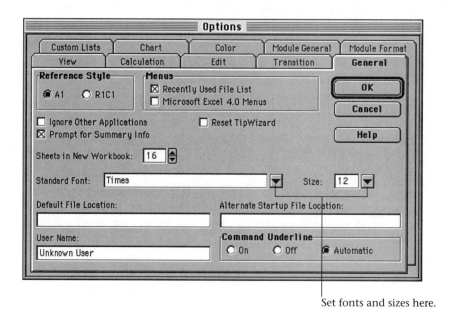

Set fonts and sizes here.

Figure 13.12 The General tab in the Options dialog box.

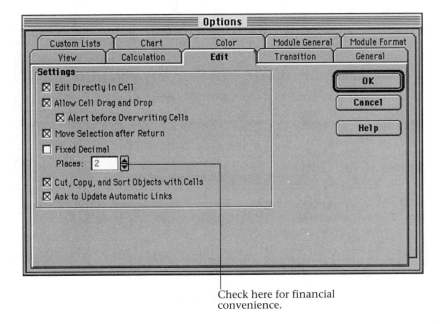

Check here for financial
convenience.

Figure 13.13   The Edit tab in the Options dialog box.

Cell Formatting

Excel 5 has taken the approach that all really complex functions should be directed from a
tabbed dialog box, and formatting is no exception. If you need more formatting than what is
available from the Formatting toolbar, use the Format Cells command. Either find Cells under
the Format menu, or press ⌘-1 (when using a PowerBook, it's often easier to use a key command instead of the delicate little trackball).

Number

Let's look at the tabs in the Format Cells dialog box one at a time. The Number tab contains
interesting information about number formatting (see Figure 13.14).

At first, this collection of formats can seem somewhat bewildering because of the odd format
notation left over from earlier spreadsheets. Here's an illustration of what happens to the
number 1234.567 under different formats:

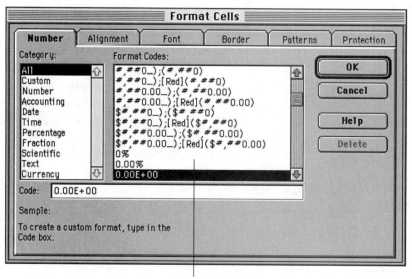

Define your own
number formats here.

Figure 13.14   The whole range of number formats.

Format	Effect	Comments
0	1235	Rounds off to integer
0.00	1234.57	Rounds to hundredth
#,##0	1,235	Rounds, adds comma
#,##0.00	1,234.57	Rounds to hundredth, with comma
#,##0_)	1,235	Negatives in parentheses
#,##0.00_)	1,234.57	Negatives in parentheses

For each of these formats, there's also a version with a dollar sign. By the way, if you look in the notorious Options dialog box from the Tools menu, the Module General tabs lets you change dollar signs to English pounds (£), if necessary.

Here are a few more useful observations about number formats:

◆ The Custom format contains a variety of fixed decimal point formats, often of doubtful utility. If you have data for which the custom format 0.000000% is appropriate, I'd like to know what it is. Write me at Hayden Books!

◆ The Accounting format is just like the general number formats except that negative numbers appear in parentheses. This is generally a better choice than putting negative number in red because sooner or later most financial data is printed in black and white anyway.

◆ The Date format uses *mmm* to indicate three-letter abbreviations of the names of months. This is somewhat confusing because the Microsoft convention for minutes in the Time format is *mm*.

◆ The Percentage format repeats most of the percentage formats that also appear under Custom. In practice, it's faster to define percentages from the Formatting toolbar and move the decimal point with the decimal button.

◆ Fractions are a problem. If you type **1/4** in a cell, Excel thinks you mean January 4, and it helpfully adds the current year. You can't go back and reformat the cell with this dialog box either. To enter a fraction, either enter it as **0 1/4** in the first place or format the blank cells where the fractions will go by using the Number dialog box and Fractions from the scrolling list. Then enter the fractions in the pre-formatted range of cells.

Alignment

Using the buttons in the toolbar, you can slosh text to the right, to the left, or pin it in the middle of a cell. In the Alignment tab of the Format Cells dialog box (see Figure 13.15), you can do a miniature page layout inside cells. Here are a few key points:

◆ In the Orientation area, you have choices for making text run up and down rather than sideways. It's tricky to find an appropriate use for this capability—a long title, for example, really displaces cells when it's printed vertically.

◆ The toolbar formatting buttons for alignment control right-to-left movement of text. Here you have Vertical options for when you want to move text around in a large box to keep it close to relevant numbers in adjacent cells.

◆ The Justify choice, in either the Horizontal or Vertical areas, means that text is fitted inside the cell—it's a sort of automatic word wrap.

◆ The Wrap Text check box gives you a cell that behaves much like a page in a word processor. If you type a long piece of text into a cell and format it for word wrap, after you enter the text, you should double-click on the bottom of the row heading to fit the cell's vertical size to display all the text (see Figure 13.16). If you adjust the cell's width, you have to readjust the height.

The way to use space efficiently in a worksheet is to use Wrap Text for every title longer than a few words. A long title imposes a whole column of white space on your worksheet and makes it difficult to keep important data on a single page.

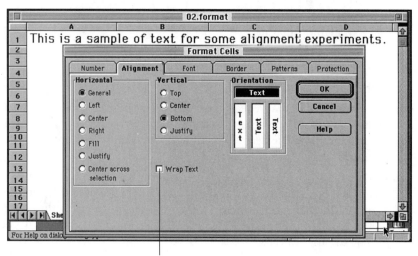

Wrap Text is the most useful option here.

Figure 13.15   Alignment formats.

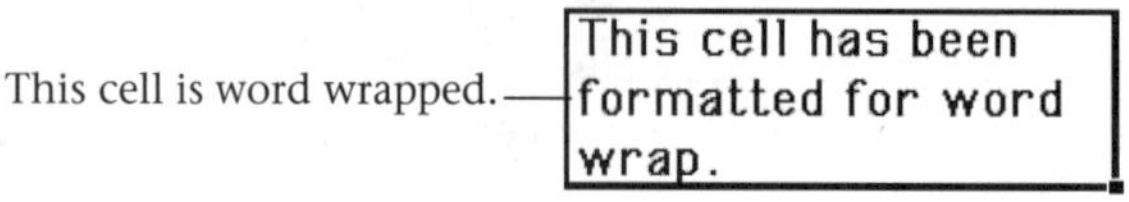

This cell is word wrapped. ——
| This cell has been formatted for word wrap. |

Figure 13.16   Word wrapping in action.

Font

Font formatting is one of the functions best represented on the Formatting toolbar. As a result, you probably won't find yourself very often in the Font card of the Format Cells dialog box (see Figure 13.17). Here are some practical uses for these options:

◆ In Excel 5, you can apply many styles to individual words and characters inside a cell (see Figure 13.18). Double-click inside the cell to get an insertion-point cursor (vertical bar) in the cell, or edit the cell contents in the formula bar.

◆ You can use the Font tab to change text color, although my usual whining caveats about color and printing still apply.

◆ Shadow and outline text are seldom seen in annual reports or accounting documents, but you can find them here.

◆ If you use subscript and superscript often, as in scientific work, you may want to make a little library of formatted cells somewhere in your worksheet so that you can copy these formats and then apply them with the Paste Special command.

◆ In the underline options, the single- and double-accounting underlines look cooler than the standard underlines.

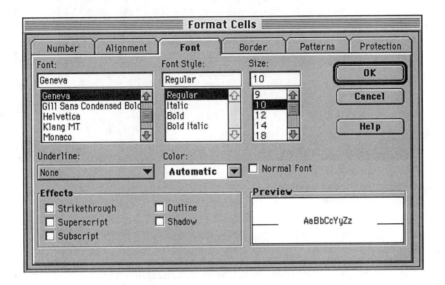

Figure 13.17 The options available in the Font card.

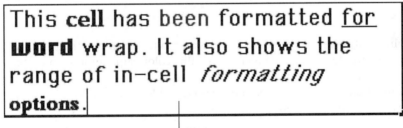

Different font, styles, and
color in one example.

Figure 13.18 Every character in a cell can be formatted separately.

Four border styles in one cell.

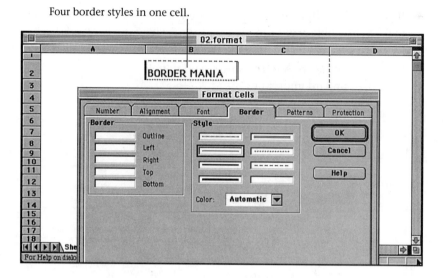

Figure 13.19   Options for cell borders.

Borders

There's really not much to the border business except that the level of control in the Border tab of the Format Cells dialog box enables you to construct some ludicrous special effects (see Figure 13.19). You can specify a different border style and color for each side of a cell.

Patterns

In my opinion, if there were a Federal law passed against the use of the Patterns tab (see Figure 13.20), no one would suffer very much. Generally, colors superimposed on black-and-white cells just make the numbers harder to read and create difficulties in printing. Patterns are a bit more useful. You can pick a light pattern to set off a block of cells (see Figure 13.21), and this kind of pattern even prints correctly.

Protection

Using the Protection command under the Tools menu, you can protect individual worksheets or a whole workbook. Using the Protection tab in the Format Cells dialog box enables you to hide and lock cells (see Figure 13.22) in protected worksheets. But here's the confusing part: you can protect a worksheet without selecting a password, meaning that anyone can open the sheet. To do this doesn't really offer protection, but it does let you use the hide and lock options.

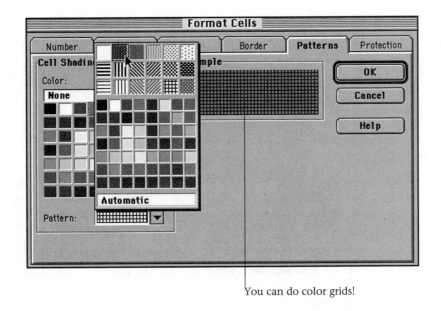

You can do color grids!

Figure 13.20   The Patterns tab, where you can choose a background pattern for your cells.

Create zones around the main data blocks.

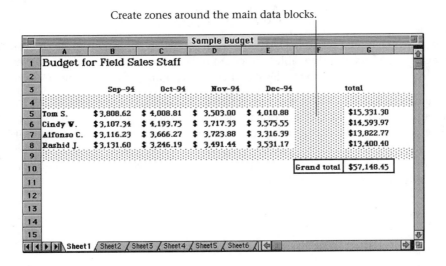

Figure 13.21   A backgound pattern frames the cells.

301

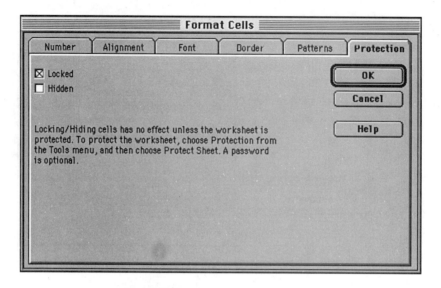

Figure 13.22   Locking and hiding cells.

AutoFormat

Earlier in this chapter, I remarked that all of us have lots of conditioning about table aesthetics from years and years of seeing tables presented in books, magazines, and newspapers. You could, in principle, reconstruct tables like these by working with the Format Cells dialog box.

But table formatting is a wheel that's been reinvented dozens of times before, and your own contributions to this effort are not exactly necessary. Microsoft has built in a gallery of common, reasonably good-looking table formats and has stashed them under the AutoFormat command in the Format menu. The table in Figure 13.21 is a good starting point for displaying some of the formats. I selected the range A1 to G7 in Figure 13.23 and then applied a variety of formats to display in Figure 13.24.

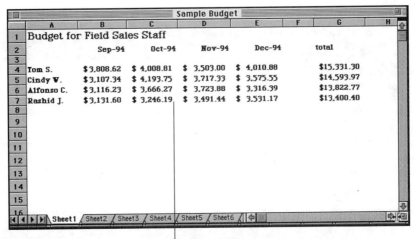

The range for formatting is A1 to G7.

Figure 13.23   A simple table.

	Sample Budget					
	A	B	C	D	E	F	G
1			Budget for Field Sales Staff				
2		Sep-94	Oct-94	Nov-94	Dec-94		total
3							
4	Tom S.	$3,808.62	$4,008.81	$3,503.00	$4,010.88		$15,331.30
5	Cindy W.	$3,107.34	$4,193.75	$3,717.33	$3,575.55		$14,593.97
6	Alfonso C.	$3,116.23	$3,666.27	$3,723.88	$3,316.39		$13,822.77
7	Rashid J.	$3,131.60	$3,246.19	$3,491.4⊞	$3,531.17		$13,400.40

Figure 13.24a   Simple.

	Sample Budget					
	A	B	C	D	E	F	G
1			Budget for Field Sales Staff				
2		Sep-94	Oct-94	Nov-94	Dec-94		total
3							
4	Tom S.	$3,808.62	$4,008.81	$3,503.00	$4,010.88		$15,331.30
5	Cindy W.	$3,107.34	$4,193.75	$3,717.33	$3,575.55		$14,593.97
6	Alfonso C.	$3,116.23	$3,666.27	$3,723.88	$3,316.39		$13,822.77
7	Rashid J.	$3,131.60	$3,246.19	$3,491.44	$3,531.17		$13,400.40
8							
9							

Figure 13.24b   Classic 1.

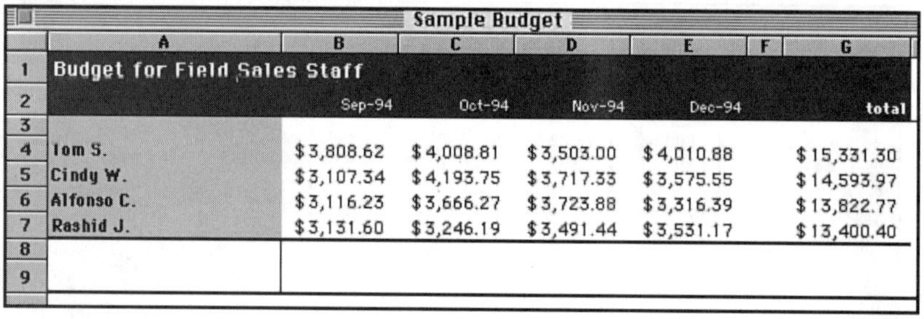

Sample Budget

	A	B	C	D	E	F	G
1	Budget for Field Sales Staff						
2		Sep-94	Oct-94	Nov-94	Dec-94		total
3							
4	Tom S.	$3,808.62	$4,008.81	$3,503.00	$4,010.88		$15,331.30
5	Cindy W.	$3,107.34	$4,193.75	$3,717.33	$3,575.55		$14,593.97
6	Alfonso C.	$3,116.23	$3,666.27	$3,723.88	$3,316.39		$13,822.77
7	Rashid J.	$3,131.60	$3,246.19	$3,491.44	$3,531.17		$13,400.40
8							
9							

Figure 13.24c Classic 2.

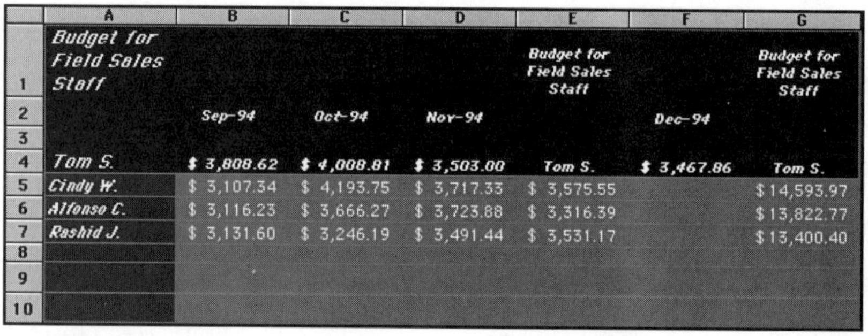

	A	B	C	D	E	F	G
1	*Budget for Field Sales Staff*				*Budget for Field Sales Staff*		*Budget for Field Sales Staff*
2		*Sep-94*	*Oct-94*	*Nov-94*		*Dec-94*	
3							
4	*Tom S.*	$ 3,808.62	$ 4,008.81	$ 3,503.00	*Tom S.*	$ 3,467.86	*Tom S.*
5	*Cindy W.*	$ 3,107.34	$ 4,193.75	$ 3,717.33	$ 3,575.55		$14,593.97
6	*Alfonso C.*	$ 3,116.23	$ 3,666.27	$ 3,723.88	$ 3,316.39		$13,822.77
7	*Rashid J.*	$ 3,131.60	$ 3,246.19	$ 3,491.44	$ 3,531.17		$13,400.40
8							
9							
10							

Figure 13.24d Colorful 1.

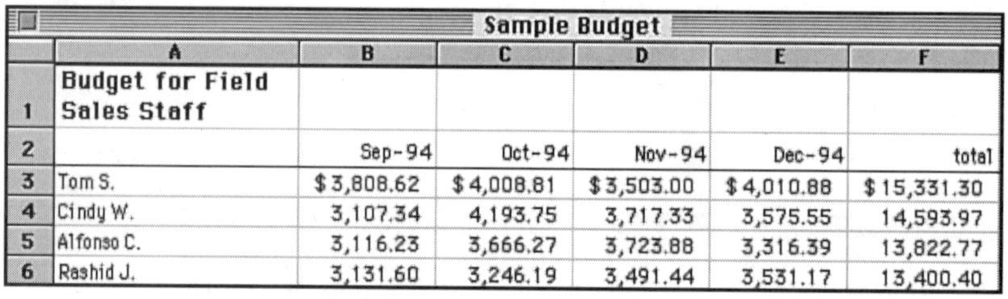

Sample Budget

	A	B	C	D	E	F
1	Budget for Field Sales Staff					
2		Sep-94	Oct-94	Nov-94	Dec-94	total
3	Tom S.	$3,808.62	$4,008.81	$3,503.00	$4,010.88	$15,331.30
4	Cindy W.	3,107.34	4,193.75	3,717.33	3,575.55	14,593.97
5	Alfonso C.	3,116.23	3,666.27	3,723.88	3,316.39	13,822.77
6	Rashid J.	3,131.60	3,246.19	3,491.44	3,531.17	13,400.40

Figure 13.24e Accounting 1.

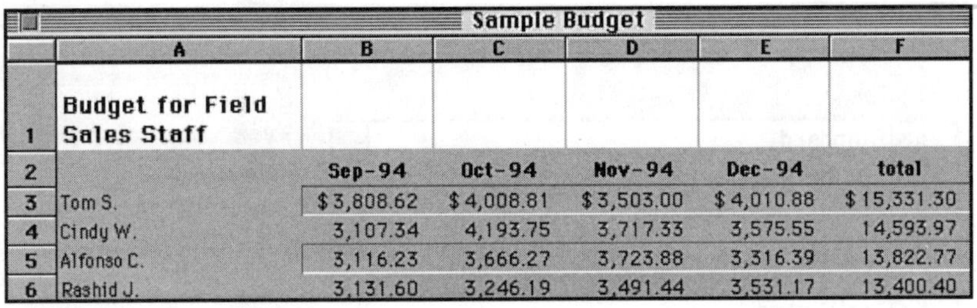

Sample Budget					
A	**B**	**C**	**D**	**E**	**F**
Budget for Field Sales Staff 1					
2	Sep-94	Oct-94	Nov-94	Dec-94	total
3 Tom S.	$3,808.62	$4,008.81	$3,503.00	$4,010.88	$15,331.30
4 Cindy W.	3,107.34	4,193.75	3,717.33	3,575.55	14,593.97
5 Alfonso C.	3,116.23	3,666.27	3,723.88	3,316.39	13,822.77
6 Rashid J.	3,131.60	3,246.19	3,491.44	3,531.17	13,400.40

Figure 13.24f   3D Effects 2.

There are a total of 17 AutoFormats for tables. You can apply an AutoFormat, modify it, and then save the format so that you can apply it with the Copy/Paste Special sequence. Some formats introduce lots of space into a table by employing wide columns—these formats call for an inspection in Print Preview before printing because they probably need to be printed in Landscape (sideways) mode. In general, though, a little Print Preview inspection is the only precaution that applies to AutoFormat.

If you want a spreadsheet that looks really professional, but you have only 90 seconds to devote to formatting, just use AutoFormat. Microsoft has done an excellent job of selecting useful formats here.

Drawing Tools

Often the simplest way to highlight some feature of a worksheet is to use Excel's built-in drawing tools. If you want to pick out a particular element, formatting a whole table with AutoFormat isn't much help—you're better off using a pointer or color coding a region.

If you don't have the Drawing toolbar showing onscreen, you can select it in the Toolbars dialog box from the View menu (see Figure 13.25). The Drawing toolbar provides a complete set of drawing tools (see Figure 13.26), including tools for grouping and ungrouping Draw objects. In real-life spreadsheet practice, the most useful elements from this toolbar are the arrow pointer and the filled-shape options (see Figure 13.27). While in principle there may be worksheet applications for the squiggle-draw tool and for placing different types of shaded blocks on a sheet, I've never seen Drawing elements make a big difference in a business presentation to venture capitalists.

Now you know about formatting cells with Excel. Let's look at how you can format them quickly!

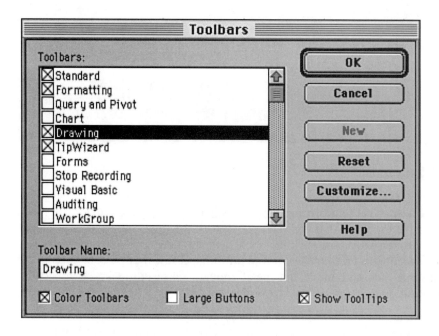

Figure 13.25   Under the View menu, you can check the Drawing option to make the Drawing toolbar appear.

	A	B	C	D	E	F	G
1	Budget for Field Sales Staff						
2		Sep-94	Oct-94	Nov-94	Dec-94	total	
3	Tom S.	$3,808.62	$4,008.81	$3,503.00	$4,010.88	$15,331.30	
4	Cindy W.	3,107.34	4,193.75	3,717.33	3,575.55	14,593.97	
5	Alfonso C.	3,116.23	3,666.27	3,723.88	3,316.39	13,822.77	
6	Rashid J.	3,131.60	3,246.19	3,491.44	3,531.17	13,400.40	
7							
8							
9							
10							
11							
12							
13							
14							

Sheet12 / Sheet13 / Sheet14 / Sheet15 / Sheet16

Figure 13.26   The Drawing toolbar as it appears in a worksheet.

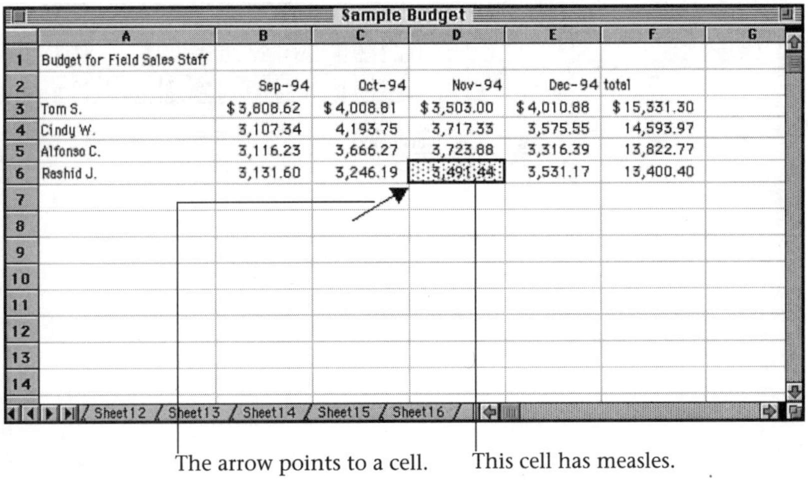

	A	B	C	D	E	F	G
	Sample Budget						
1	Budget for Field Sales Staff						
2		Sep-94	Oct-94	Nov-94	Dec-94	total	
3	Tom S.	$3,808.62	$4,008.81	$3,503.00	$4,010.88	$15,331.30	
4	Cindy W.	3,107.34	4,193.75	3,717.33	3,575.55	14,593.97	
5	Alfonso C.	3,116.23	3,666.27	3,723.88	3,316.39	13,822.77	
6	Rashid J.	3,131.60	3,246.19	3,491.44	3,531.17	13,400.40	
7							
8							
9							
10							
11							
12							
13							
14							

Sheet12 / Sheet13 / Sheet14 / Sheet15 / Sheet16 /

The arrow points to a cell.   This cell has measles.

Figure 13.27   Highlighting cells with the Drawing tools.

Filling In Cell Ranges

There's an easier way of doing all this formatting, right? Yes, there is. It's almost a defining characteristic of Excel that there are six different ways to do any common task. You can use it as an all-keyboard program, or you can use it as totally mouse-centric. You can go through the menus, or you can use toolbar buttons for most tasks. There are loads of hidden keyboard shortcuts for common tasks, and there are some simple ways to organize your work and your worksheets to make things go faster.

After you've been using Excel 5 for some time, you'll probably settle down to using a fairly small repertoire of shortcuts, mainly because it's impossible to remember them all.

> **Caution:** Using an early version of Excel 5 for the Power Macintosh, I found that all the tricks in this chapter work correctly, but in some cases, they are actually slower than simply using commands from the menus. It's not clear why this is true, and it's not clear if it will be true in later, more optimized Power versions of Excel 5. But for now, the suggestions in the rest of this chapter are for convenience rather than speed.

Suppose that you are facing the blank worksheet in Figure 13.28. You made it to this worksheet by starting up Excel—either by double-clicking on the Excel icon or by selecting New from the File menu. Now it's time to make something happen, and the goal here is to make it happen with a minimum of typing.

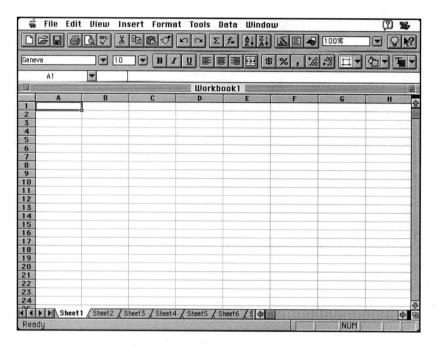

Figure 13.28   A clean slate.

Excel 5 has considerable, but quirky, intelligence built into it for filling ranges. Here are just a few examples:

◆ The simplest action for filling a range of cells is to repeat its contents. To do this, you can select a cell, choose Copy from the Edit menu, select another group of cells, and choose Paste from the Edit menu. However, there is an easier way. Every time you select a cell in Excel 5, the cell displays a *fill handle* in the lower right-hand corner. If you select a cell with data in it (see Figure 13.29) and then point to the handle, the fill handle turns into a plus sign. Click the mouse button, hold it down, and drag down, sideways, or diagonally to copy the contents to as many cells as you like (see Figure 13.30). This action loads the cells faster than the Copy/Paste routine, and as a technique in Excel, it's called *AutoFill*.

◆ Another way to fill a whole cell range with the same contents is to select the range by dragging the mouse across it, type the contents, hold down the Control key, and then press Return.

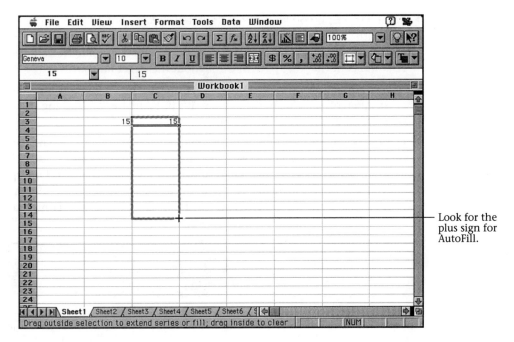

Figure 13.29 Selecting a cell to repeat.

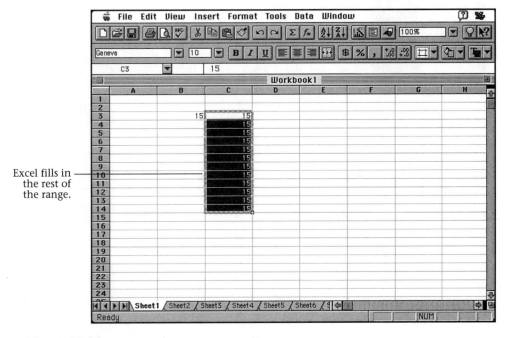

Figure 13.30 AutoFilling the same values.

◆ What happens if you have two cells with different contents? In Figure 13.31, the cells with 1 and 2 typed in are selected, and then the fill handle for the selection is dragged down. As you can see, Excel tries to figure out a pattern from the selected cells and continues the pattern throughout the larger range.

◆ In Figure 13.32, I'm having a little fun with Excel by seeing how accurately it can guess different patterns in data. Again, it's just a matter of dragging the fill handle over the range that you want to fill.

◆ Excel figures out your abbreviations. If you type Mon and Tue in your first two cells, Excel continues with Wed and Thur; typing Monday and Tuesday in the "starter" cells gives you Wednesday and Thursday. Note that Excel interprets many kinds of numbers as dates. In this case, I actually typed 1/94 and 2/94 in the starter cells for one of the date ranges and Excel translated them into month names.

After you select the cells that contain 1 and 2, Excel fills in the rest of the range.

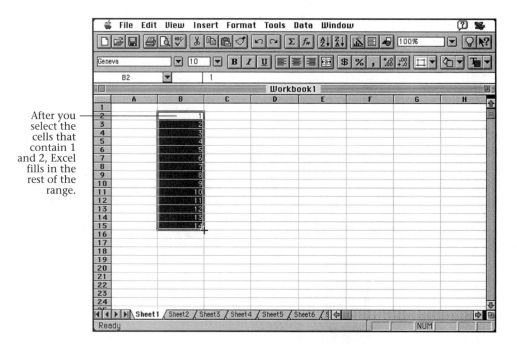

Figure 13.31   Excel figures out a fill pattern.

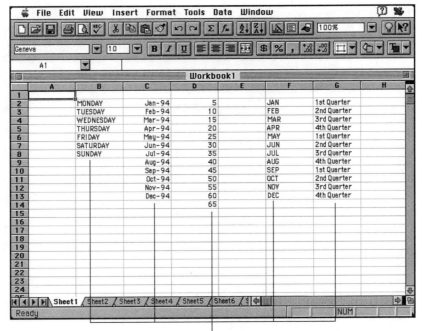

Five variations on AutoFill.

Figure 13.32   Excel figures out AutoFilling for dates, days, and numbers.

Custom Filling

If you hold down the Control key while you drag the plus sign cursor through a range, the pop-up menu in Figure 13.33 appears. This menu gives you many options, including the Series option, which gives you almost complete control over the arithmetic series that fill in the range with the first cell as a starting value. It can figure out that you want 1, 3, 5, 7 and so on as a series or 5, 10, 15 and so on, or nearly any other series. (If you used algebra class in high school to take naps after lunch, you should know that the teacher was discussing number series much of the time that you were asleep.)

Unless Excel is consistently misguessing your intentions, or unless you need something fancy—a logarithmic or exponential series fill, for example—using this pop-up menu and the Series option takes more keystrokes than taking two starter cells and AutoFilling them by using the cross-drag method.

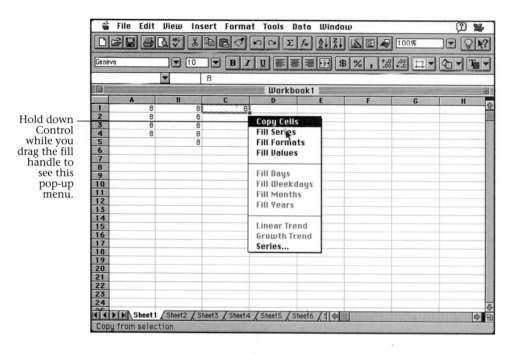

Hold down
Control
while you
drag the fill
handle to
see this
pop-up
menu.

Figure 13.33 The pop-up menu for filling contents into cell ranges.

Internally, Excel is really handling two different kinds of objects in AutoFill. It has number lists, upon which it performs small computations—that's how it can figure out that the next number in a range will probably be 3 if the first numbers are 1 and 2. And it has text lists, with the most common lists (days and months and so forth) preloaded.

As it happens, Excel stands ready to deal with *any* text list as an AutoFill subject. In Figure 13.34, I have entered a series of expense categories that journalists typically track for tax deductions (when I recently started keeping decent records, I found that I was spending nearly 20 percent of my disposable income on books!). From the Options choice under the Tools menu, I have selected the Custom Lists tab (the tabs look like the little "ears" on manila file folders), where you can see the short list of AutoFill text lists that Excel has preloaded. To get my own list included, all I do is click the Import button, and my entries now have the same status as the days of the week (see Figure 13.35).

To use this slick option, just type the first word ("Books") of the list into a cell, select it, and drag the plus sign cursor. If I type an uppercase starter word, Excel adjusts the remainder of the list to be uppercase, too. The point of all these shenanigans is that if you have a job that lasts for at least a month, you're likely to make up multiple worksheets with the same row and border labels. Rather than lock this information into whole worksheet templates, you can store these labels in Custom Lists for efficiency.

This selected list will become an AutoFill option.

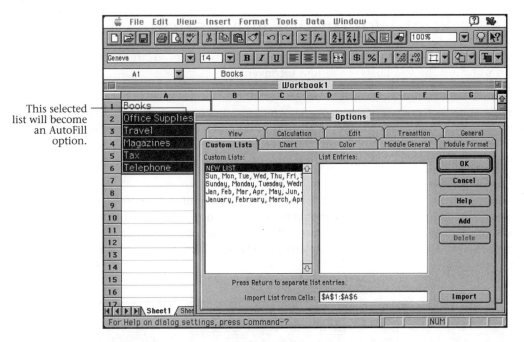

Figure 13.34 The Custom Lists tab in the Options dialog box from the Tools menu.

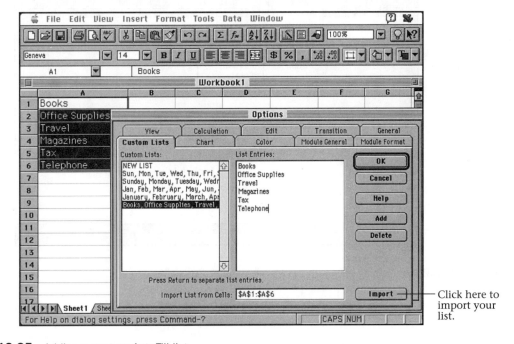

Click here to import your list.

Figure 13.35 Adding a custom AutoFill list.

Fast Worksheet Navigation

You now have before you a vast ocean of cells, a sea of little rectangles so large that scrolling around by using just the scroll bars is a serious inconvenience.

The first worthwhile navigation trick is to assign names to cells that you visit frequently. The fact is, most worksheets consist of different rectangular patches of numbers with a few labels along the edges. You can, of course, keep track of the "action areas" in your worksheet—use the Go To command under the Edit menu to zip to the place in which you're headed. But it's much easier to name a cell in the upper-right corner of each important rectangle in your worksheet.

Here's what you do. Just type a label in a cell (see Figure 13.36), pull down the Insert menu to the Name choice, and pick Define. You see that the cell name now appears to the left of the formula bar area (near the top of the worksheet). When you click the little triangle next to the cell name, you get a scrolling list of the cell names (see Figure 13.37) that have been defined for that worksheet.

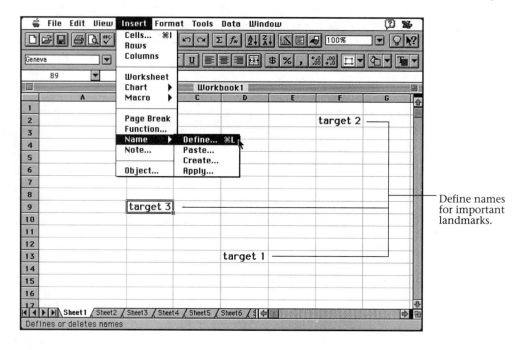

Define names for important landmarks.

Figure 13.36 Naming cells with the Insert menu.

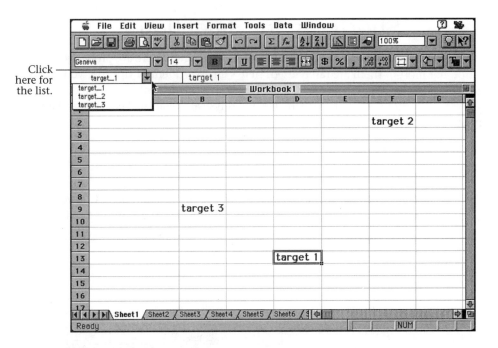

Click here for the list.

Figure 13.37   The list of named cells.

Why Name a Cell?

Now there are plenty of navigation tricks that you can learn in Excel. For example, ⌘–Down Arrow takes you to the bottom of a worksheet—16,384 lonely cells away from the familiar top-left corner at cell A1. Similarly, ⌘–Right Arrow takes you to the extreme right-hand column of the standard worksheet, column IV. But cruising over great distances at high speed is actually fairly irrelevant for most work. What you really want to do is get to Expenses or Budget or July Sales right away, and the way to do that is with cell names.

Excel 5 keeps track of cell names through your whole workbook, not just a single worksheet. You can head out to Sheet 3, define a few names, do some work, and click back to Sheet 1 with just one selection from the cell name list.

You can also name ranges, whether columns or rows or rectangles, and when you go to that name, the whole range is located and highlighted. Personally, I prefer to use single cells as navigation signposts because if I make some inadvertent slip—like hitting the Spacebar or the Delete key—I haven't removed any actual data. In principle, if I noticed what I did, I could always select Undo, but in practice, this often doesn't work.

Shortcuts for Selection

This section is a little collection of shortcuts for selecting ranges. There are probably 40 possible tips, but most of them are rarely used. Here's an assortment of tips that you are likely to use. Some of these keyboard methods, by the way, have the helpful effect of reducing your dependence on mouse/menu methods, which some physical therapists believe are a large component of common stress injuries.

◆ To select a whole row, select any cell in the row and press Shift-Spacebar. You can also click on the row number, which is found on the left-hand edge of the worksheet.

◆ To select a whole column, select any cell in the column and press Control-Spacebar. You can also click on the letter (or letters) of the column heading.

◆ By selecting a row with Shift-Spacebar and then pressing Control-Spacebar, the whole worksheet is selected (see Figure 13.38).

◆ After you have an area selected, you can erase the contents (but not the formatting) by pressing ⌘-B.

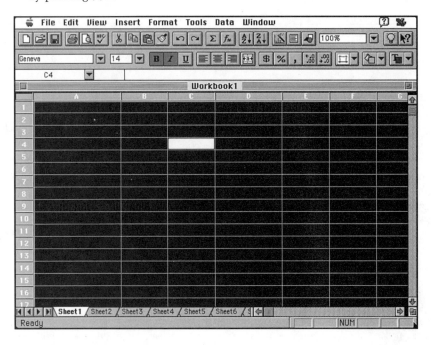

Figure 13.38   Selecting the entire document.

Style Tips

There are really two kinds of tips for rapid formatting that make practical sense: using Format Painter and using defined Styles.

Format Painter is represented by the little paintbrush button found under the word *Format* on the menu bar. Here's what you do:

1. First format a range of cells to your satisfaction.

2. Select the range by using the mouse.

3. Click on the Format Painter button.

4. The cursor now turns into a plus sign with a paintbrush (see Figure 13.39). You can drag-select a new range of cells with this special cursor, and it will transfer all the formatting attributes of the original range to the new range.

Because workbooks have a whole folio of worksheets, you may want to reserve one worksheet to be a repository of fancy formats for transferring to other worksheets.

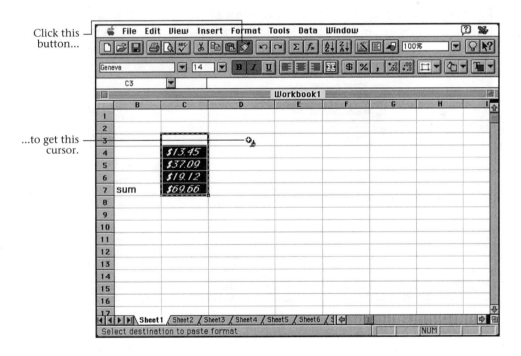

Figure 13.39 Format Painter's special cursor.

Another way to do special formats for ranges of cells is to name your own styles and apply them. If you've spent more than five minutes or so developing a complicated format (or a fancy format for a table), you owe it to yourself to save it (so that you can use it again).

In the software business, there's an ongoing debate about reinventing the wheel, called "The quest for software component reusability," which just means that you shouldn't have to do the same coding over and over again. When you format, you're really writing a little program, so when you save your formatting instructions, you're doing something programmers wish they could do at Microsoft and Apple on bigger projects. Congratulations!

Simply format cells the way you want them and find the Style command under the Format menu. In the Style Name box, invent a name for this style (see Figure 13.40) and click the Add button. Whenever you want to use this combination of formats (a particular font, size, color, number format, or font style), you can apply it by selecting it from the standard Style list in the Style dialog box. Just remember to give your style a name that's self-explanatory because you may find yourself scrolling through the style list weeks later wondering what it was!

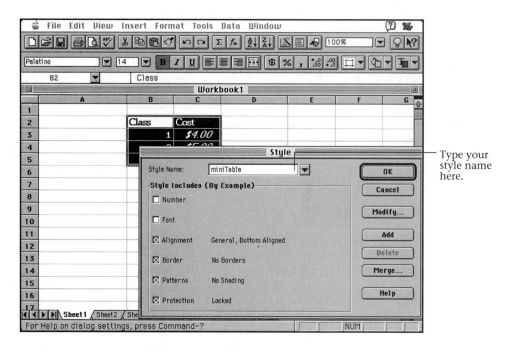

Figure 13.40 A user-defined Excel style.

318

Useful Keyboard Hints

There are hundreds of strange little keyboard combinations buried in Excel 5. Of these, a handful are worth remembering. Table 3.1 lists the important combinations. You may want to photocopy this table and keep it near your Mac for Excel work.

Table 3.1
Keyboard Operations

Key combination	Result
⌘-Home	Move to cell A1
⌘-A	Select all cells
Control-Shift-$	Format as $0.00
⌘-Option-0	Apply border to selection
⌘-PageUp	Move to preceding sheet
⌘-PageDown	Move to next sheet
⌘-L	Display Define Cell Name
⌘-Shift-S	Display Save As dialog box
⌘-Z	Undo
⌘-T	Repeat last action

Speed

Most of the time, you'll want all the formatting help you can get when setting up a worksheet. The Toolbars dialog box, reached from the View menu, shows the profusion of toolbars that you can use as onscreen guides (see Figure 13.41). You can ask for larger buttons (see Figure 13.42); you can ask to see ToolTips (little balloon-style explanations of the buttons); and you can apply both of these options to any toolbars that you care to leave on your worksheet.

After you have a worksheet formatted to your satisfaction, and you find yourself working exclusively with numbers, it's time to go back to the Toolbars dialog box and *hide everything* by turning off the check boxes (see Figure 13.43). A worksheet with all the auxiliary gunk hidden runs much faster. The same is true of graphics, a subject which will arise shortly. If you leave lots of color graphs lying around your worksheet, you take a gruesome performance hit every time you do a recalculation.

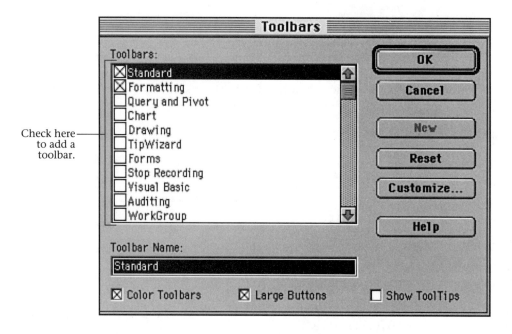

Check here to add a toolbar.

Figure 13.41   The nearly unimaginable profusion of toolbars.

This is not a small consideration. Excel 5 has plenty of cool features, but in many cases they have been added at the expense of speed. If you have a worksheet formatted to your satisfaction, and you are working mostly with the numbers in it, go ahead and hide all the formatting stuff. You can always call it back by using the View menu.

This chapter shows you several ways to format the plain, quick-and-dirty worksheets of Chapter 12 and how to do this with a minimum number of keystrokes or mouse movements. In the next chapter, you learn how to organize your worksheets into workbooks.

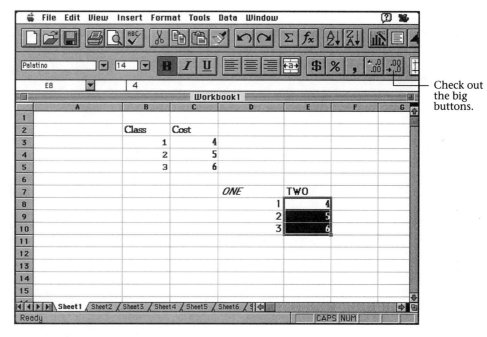

Figure 13.42 Big buttons are easier to see.

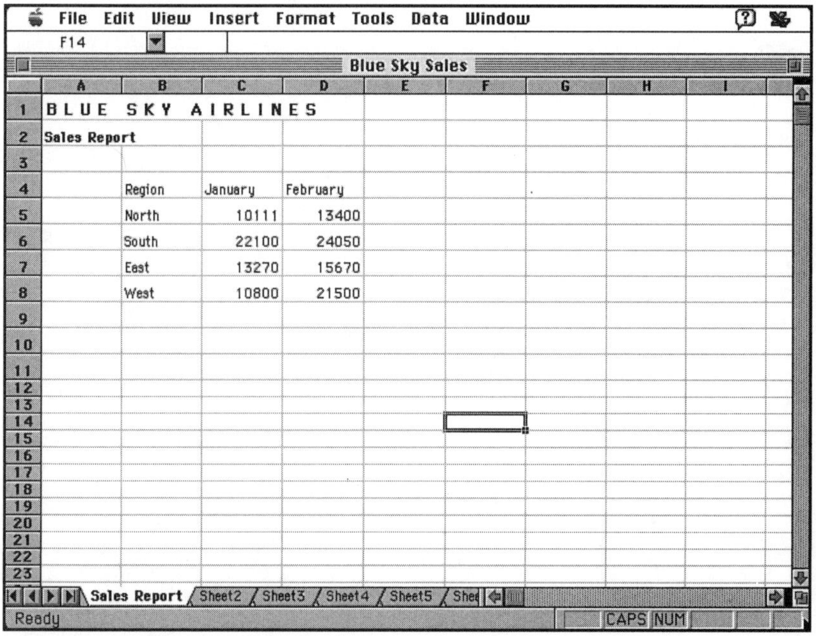

Figure 13.43 Suppressing the toolbars.

Chapter 14

Organizing Your Workbooks

A big problem in day-to-day worksheet use is keeping track of all the worksheets generated for different purposes. Excel 5 goes a long way toward solving this problem (you still have to think up filenames yourself!) with its new multisheet workbooks. Now when you open a single workbook file, you open the whole series of related worksheets that you have stashed together. Because a workbook is a collection of worksheets, Excel 5 has 3-D worksheet capabilities that enable you to perform operations on ranges of cells through whole collections of cells. This chapter includes the following information:

- ◆ Making useful summary information
- ◆ Using Find File for reviewing
- ◆ Copying and moving worksheets
- ◆ Using text blocks for documentation
- ◆ Working with cell notes
- ◆ Linking between worksheets
- ◆ Linking across workbooks
- ◆ Protecting worksheets

Summaries

Excel 5 is a big program, and this chapter shows some of what it's doing with all that memory it hogs. One example is the Find File operation, which is now truly powerful but has the complexity of a full search program that would take 200K to code as a stand-alone program. Because all this interesting stuff is built into Excel 5, and you can't unload any of it to get a smaller, faster program, you may as well enjoy the luxury touches.

In the old days, a filename was the only information you could use to identify a file (actually, in the oldest old days, the filename had to be eight letters or less!). But Microsoft designed the new Excel to meet the growing needs of corporate America—in fact, today you can literally run a modest Wall Street brokerage with Excel 5 on a Macintosh 840AV (with an array of hard drives).

With Excel 5, your worksheet files can have more identification lines than your own passport. Consider the little worksheet in Figure 14.1. All it contains is a little table of numbers and a few words. After formulating a little bit of work like this, the odds that I would remember its exact name a few months later are approximately zilch to 3000. Working with Excel day after day, you're likely to have dozens of files, and you'll probably start to have trouble finding your earlier work.

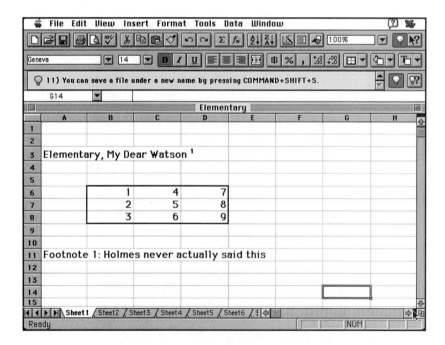

Figure 14.1   A basic worksheet.

That's why Microsoft added a form to Excel that records all sorts of information about your workbook file (see Figure 14.2). When you start a new workbook and save it for the first time, Microsoft shows you the Summary Info dialog box. Each field in this dialog box (Title, Subject, Author, Keywords, and Comments) is searchable by Excel's built-in file searching functions. If you put a little thought into the Keywords and Subject fields in particular, you'll find it relatively easy to retrieve files—even after you've forgotten what the files are named. Note that you can also call up this dialog box (from the Edit menu) as Summary Info any time you choose.

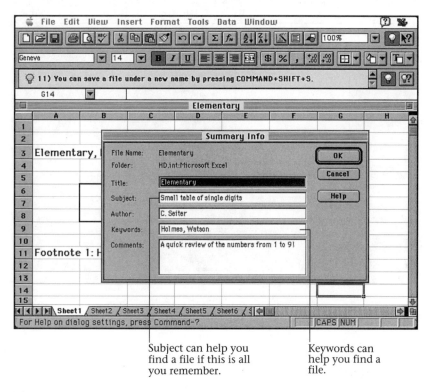

Subject can help you find a file if this is all you remember.

Keywords can help you find a file.

Figure 14.2 The Summary Information dialog box is your friend.

To make the search more efficient, put different kinds of information into each Summary Info field. That is, if you have a workbook called 1995 Budget, don't just put *budget* into the Keywords and Subject fields; instead, think of some other information to identify the workbook (expenses? tax? payroll?).

Find File

Having written a nice description of your workbook, you can practically forget about it and rely on Microsoft to retrieve it for you. You can do this from anywhere in Excel. Pick the Find File command from the File menu (see Figure 14.3).

Three different file views.

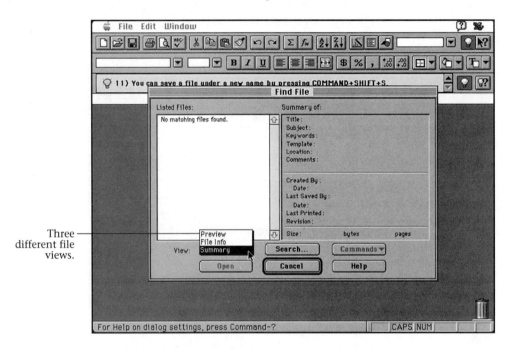

Figure 14.3   The beginning of Find File fun.

First-level searching

How do you actually find something? The simplest level depends on the Search button, which will get you to a dialog box (see Figure 14.4) that expects you to know the name of the file that you want. Note that this dialog box has a built-in provision for saving search results to a list. If you search, for example, for the word *budget* in the File Name text box, the program finds *all* your files with *budget* in the filename. This can actually be useful because Excel can keep the search results available in the Saved Searches pull-down menu. Eventually, if you have used some discretion in your choice of filenames, you'll develop a library of related files that can be found rapidly by using this dialog box.

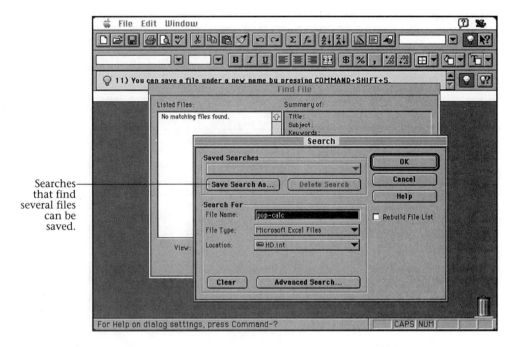

Searches that find several files can be saved.

Figure 14.4   This is the first search level in Excel's Find File system.

Advanced searches

After you click on the Advanced Search button in the Search dialog box, you can retrieve files based on Keywords and Subject (see Figure 14.5). You can speed up the search by narrowing down the search space. If you know your file is hiding on a particular hard drive, you can specify that drive in the Location tab of the Advanced Search dialog box. Then Excel doesn't waste your time churning through the wrong drive. I don't know why, but I've had better luck searching for Keywords (you can use multiple keywords if you separate them with commas); the search process just seems to go faster.

The Advanced Search dialog box has a little beehive of options in its three tabs. If you want to search for text in a workbook, there are options (Special, Use Pattern Matching) that allow you to be stunningly, delightfully vague and still produce useful search results (see Figure 14.6). You can, for example, search all workbooks for one that *doesn't* contain the letter *Z*.

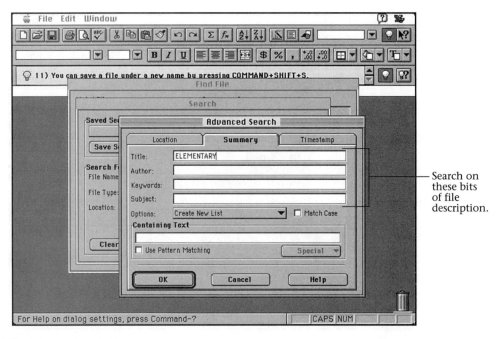

Search on
these bits
of file
description.

Figure 14.5 Advanced searching.

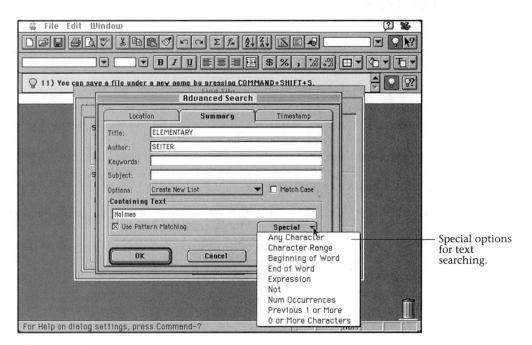

Special options
for text
searching.

Figure 14.6 Advanced Search options.

Reviewing search results

After Excel finds a file that meets your criteria (just type the criteria in the Summary tab of the Advanced Search dialog box and click the OK button), you have a number of ways to look at it as well as a number of file processing options. Figure 14.7 shows the Preview view of my humble little file. Preview is, of course, helpful for making sure that the search procedure actually found the file that you want.

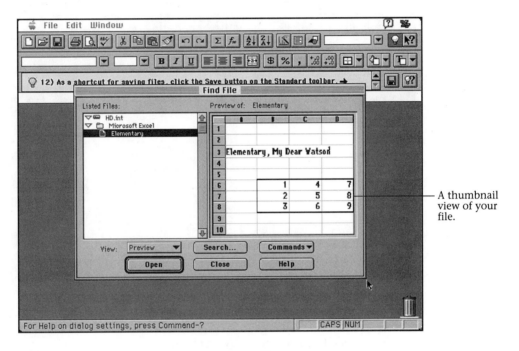

A thumbnail view of your file.

Figure 14.7   The Preview view of a search results in Find File.

Figure 14.8 shows another view of the search results, this time a listing of the information in the Summary dialog box. It's another way to make sure that a search on a few words found the file that you want. Figure 14.9 shows the simplest view option, the File Info view, which is useful mostly for scanning multiple files.

An Old-Fashioned Idea That Works!

Okay, I know that you're not always going to want to use this technique in the heat of worksheet creation, but here's a good way to keep track of your work. When you fill out a Summary dialog box, capture the screen with the Summary information (use ⌘-Shift-3). Then

continues

open this file (called Screen 0 or a higher number on your hard drive) by using the System TeachText utility and print it. Take a standard three-hole punch to the printed copy and keep it in a binder. The ring-binder technology may seem old-fashioned, but it enables you to keep track of keywords for when your memory finally goes completely to, um, ruin.

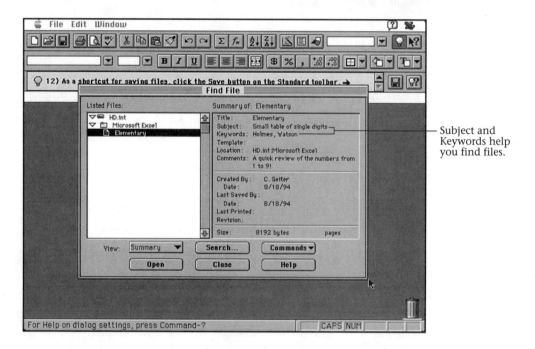

Subject and Keywords help you find files.

Figure 14.8   Summary view lets you check subject and keywords.

More file tricks

After you find a set of files in Find File, use the Commands button (see Figure 14.10) to see a few more interesting options. At the simplest level, you can open the file in Read Only mode, which may be necessary if the little Preview view doesn't show you enough to recognize the workbook. (Actually, the Preview is a corner of the first worksheet in a workbook, so unless you put something distinctive there, you may *need* to use Read Only.) You can also delete a workbook that you find in Find File.

The other Commands choices are a bit fancier. You can copy from this dialog box (see Figure 14.10). The Copy command calls up a slightly different dialog box (see Figure 14.11).

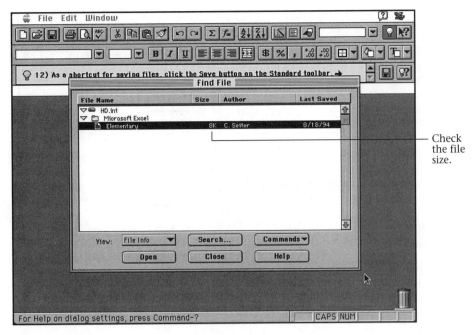

Check
the file
size.

Figure 14.9 The File Info view.

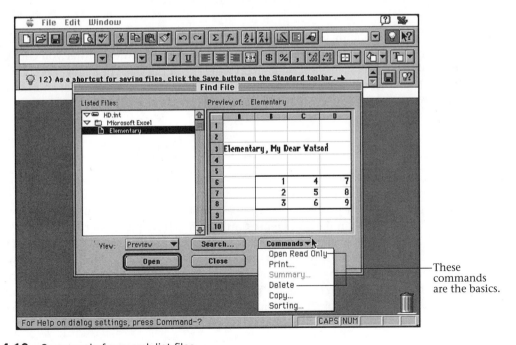

These
commands
are the basics.

Figure 14.10 Commands for search-list files.

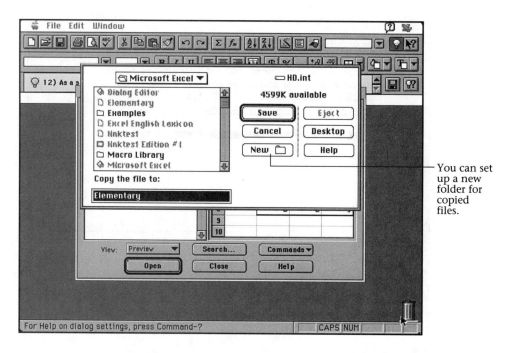

You can set
up a new
folder for
copied
files.

Figure 14.11   Copying files from the Find File system.

If you search on a fairly vague criterion and find a long list of files, you can also sort them in a specific order (Excel lists them in the order in which it finds them). After you choose Sort from the main Find File dialog box, you are presented with the Options dialog box shown in Figure 14.12. Note that you can see the folders where the workbooks are located, another guide to identifying the actual file you are trying to find.

Moving and Copying

Now that you know how to find any file that you ever made, you need to know only a bit about copying and moving worksheets to make your file-management life complete. Microsoft, in its ceaseless efforts to anticipate your every need, has put a special option called Move or Copy Sheet in the Edit menu. Can't get much simpler than that, can you? When you select this option, the whole worksheet that's currently active is ready for shipping (see Figure 14.13). Either check the tiny box for creating a copy or transfer (Move) the whole worksheet (the equivalent of cutting and pasting the worksheet) into another workbook. At this point, please note that you don't have the full standard range of Macintosh file options open (you can only access workbooks in the folder you're currently using), but you can ask to create a new untitled workbook for a destination of the Copy or Move operation.

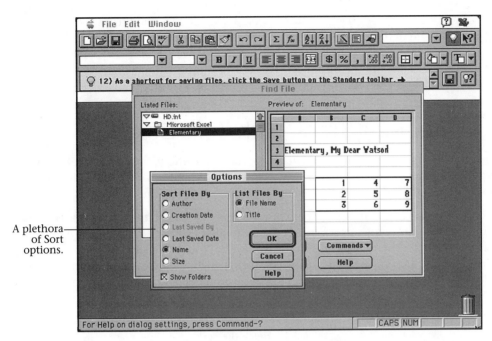

Figure 14.12 Make sense of Find File lists with the Sort options.

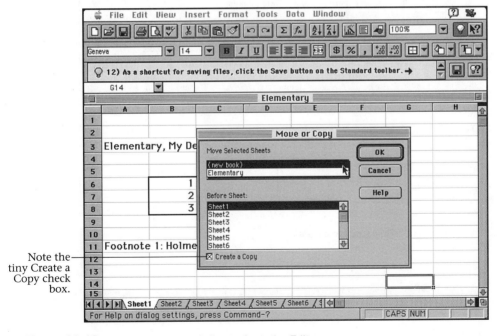

Figure 14.13 Move or copy worksheets from the Edit menu.

After you move or copy a worksheet to another workbook, you may want to give it a name with a bit of content (all these sheets labeled Sheet 1, Sheet 2, and so on get confusing). Just position the mouse cursor over the tab at the bottom of the sheet, double-click, and you get a dialog box that lets you name the worksheet. This is a vast informational improvement over the names that Excel provides for you at the end of a copy operation.

Keeping Track with Text Boxes

Sorry to keep harping on the theme of the frailty of human memory, but I think that every advantage in documentation or retrieval by keyword will redound to your credit later. In Chapter 16 in the auditing section, you see me preaching on this theme again.

Text boxes (see Figure 14.14) are a great help in worksheet documentation problems. The Text Box button is second from the right on the Standard toolbar (it's the little rectangle with lines in it). Click this button and drag a zone on the worksheet. You see a plain box with an insertion point (blinking line) cursor. Type in any comments you like—explain your formulas, tell the world what you are trying to accomplish in your worksheet, and include some hints for its use.

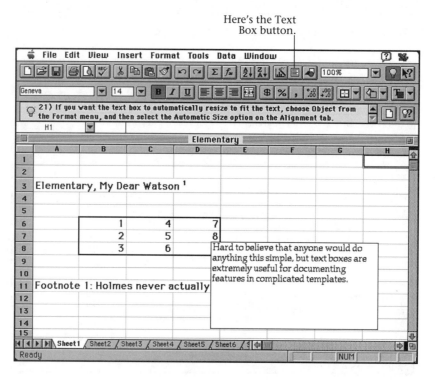

Figure 14.14 The text box is a great worksheet documentation aid.

A text box is an object, so when you pull down the Format menu to modify the tiny, hard-to-read Geneva text (which is the Excel default), you see Object as the first command. The Format Object dialog box has a collection of tabs for all purposes. I formatted the text box in Figure 14.14 by using the Font tab to produce the lovely New York 14-point text. Other formatting option choices include Properties and Protection (see Figures 4.15 and 4.16). The Properties tab deals mostly with positioning, while the Protection tab keeps others from modifying your text notes. Unless you select a text box and hide it, it floats eternally in a tranquil plane over your worksheet, always ready to be consulted. If you like, you can also select and print a text box separately.

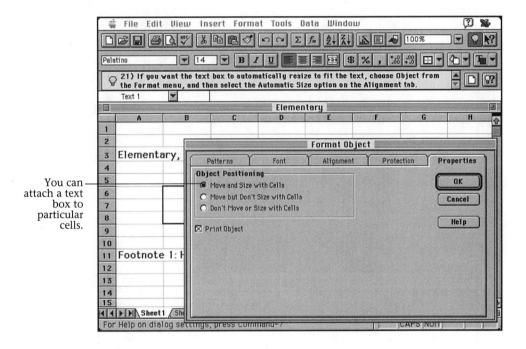

Figure 14.15 Formatting text boxes with the Properties tab.

Cell Notes

As an additional documentation aid, you can attach cell notes that also explain what you had in mind when you tucked a formula into a given cell. Unlike text boxes, which are invoked from the toolbar, you simply add a note by using the Insert menu's Note command after you select a cell (see Figure 14.17).

335

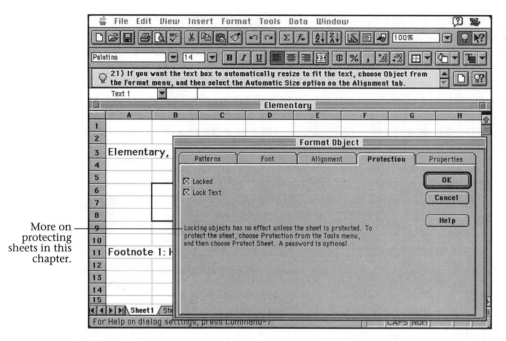

More on
protecting
sheets in this
chapter.

Figure 14.16 Formatting text boxes with the Protection tab.

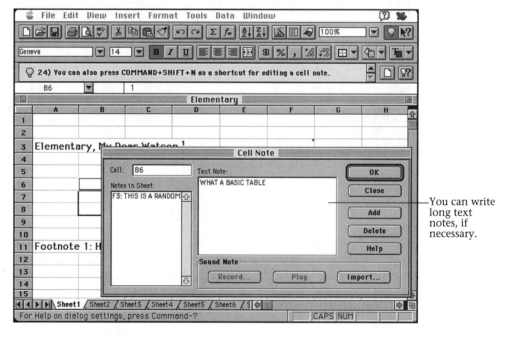

You can write
long text
notes, if
necessary.

Figure 14.17 The Cell Note dialog box.

Also, unlike text boxes, these cell notes aren't in your face all the time—you must tell Excel that you want to see the note's contents. Excel let's you know that there's a note in a cell because it displays a miniature dot in the corner of the cell (it's red on a color monitor). The simplest way to review the contents of cell notes is to display the Auditing toolbar (choose Toolbars from the View menu and click the Auditing check box), select the cell with the note, and click the Information (*i* in a circle) button (see Figure 14.18). You then get a view of the cell note's contents (see Figure 14.19), and you can close the window to hide the contents again.

In my opinion, every time you write an Excel formula that isn't painfully obvious, you should tag the cell with a little note. Excel 5 files have plenty of overhead anyway (this little file in the figures with a mere nine numbers and a few words takes more than 8K), so you may as well Get With The System and load your worksheets with documentation. Hey, lightning could strike you tomorrow, and your poor co-workers would have to puzzle out your worksheets from scratch if you don't leave a few notes. Be a pal.

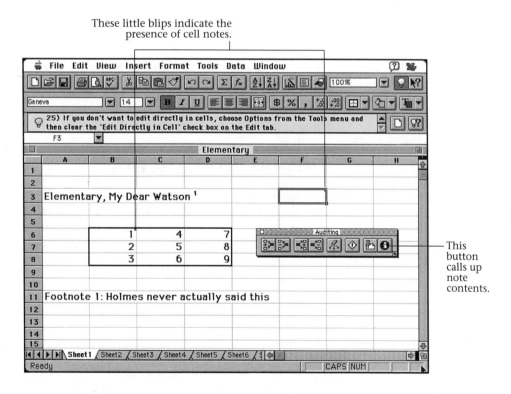

Figure 14.18 The Auditing toolbar keeps you in contact with cell notes.

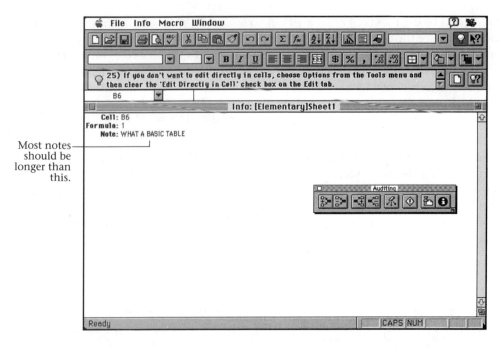

Most notes should be longer than this.

Figure 14.19   A cell note window.

Linking Worksheets

In one view of the Excel workbook, it's just a collection of independent sheets, just like sheets in a notebook. But there's a big difference between worksheets and sheets of paper: Excel sheets can be linked, which means that information from one sheet can be connected to another sheet. The information is "live," in that a change on the original sheet automatically produces changes in the linked sheet.

There are two ways to link data: linking between sheets in the same workbook and linking between sheets in different workbooks. For many purposes, the simplest way to form a link is to use the Paste Special dialog box (see Figure 14.20). This dialog box includes a Paste Link button that directs the Paste operation to maintain live links to the data in the originating worksheet.

Linking with Paste Special is a sort of tutorial in linking technology. Figure 14.21 shows the linking formula that places the little table in Sheet 1 of the Elementary workbook into Sheet 2 of the same workbook. Look at the expression in the formula bar:

= {Sheet1!$B$6:$D$8}

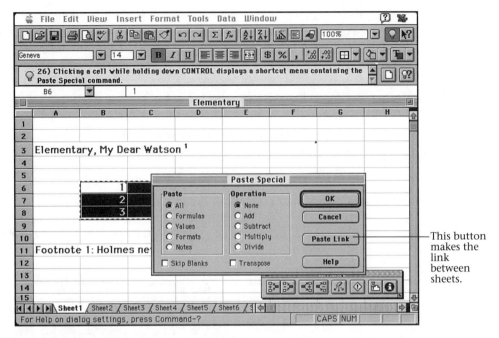

Figure 14.20   Paste Special is the simplest linking tool.

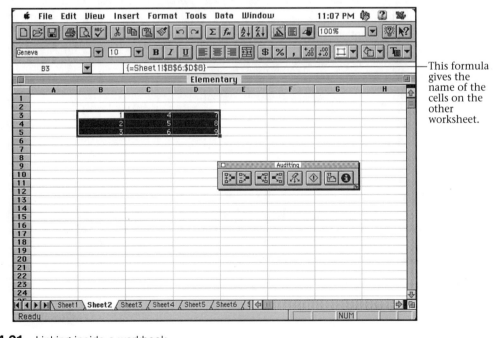

Figure 14.21   Linking inside a workbook.

This says that the range planted into Sheet 2 originates in Sheet 1 (note the ! sign) in a rectangle of cells with its upper left-hand corner in B6 on Sheet 1 and lower right-hand corner in D8. If I had put formulas into this range on Sheet 1, the Paste Link command wouldn't have worked because this trick is for linking data, and Excel gets confused if you're trying to link a range full of formulas. If you like, within a workbook you can write formulas (on other worksheets) that access data in a reference sheet. You just need to use the cell addresses of the sheet within the workbook—that is, Sheet5! $(cells) or whatever sheet is appropriate.

Now look at Figure 14.22. Here I have made another workbook, Copy2 of Elementary. Paste-linking the table of numbers into this new workbook shows the following formula:

{=[Elementary]Sheet1!$B$6:$D$8}

This formula tells you that you can make up a formula that draws on any cells in any Excel worksheet. The format requires only that you specify the workbook name in square brackets—[Elementary]—the sheet name followed by an exclamation point, and the cells in absolute reference notation (the $ signs).

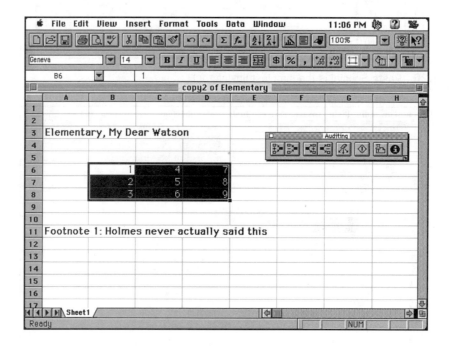

Figure 14.22   Linking between workbooks.

Locking It Up: Protection

One last bit of workbook management concerns protection. The Tools menu has a Protection option (see Figure 14.23) that lets you lock individual sheets or a whole workbook.

When you decide to protect your workbook (perhaps you will be distributing it on a network, for example, and you don't want other users tinkering with your numbers), you should usually use a password (see Figure 14.24) that you faithfully inscribe in your Excel *User's Guide* (so that you can find it again). The other place from which protection can be invoked is the Options button in the Save As dialog box from the File menu. The Options button brings up the Save Options dialog box shown in Figure 14.25. If you give a password to the Write Reservation field, other users are able to overwrite your worksheet, but they cannot save their changes under the original worksheet name. This is actually very useful if you want to distribute a template for calculations. Users can plug in their own numbers and then save their work under their own workbook names, leaving your original template model unchanged.

This chapter discusses handling worksheets and workbooks. The next chapter gives you all sorts of helpful information about incorporating charts into your worksheets.

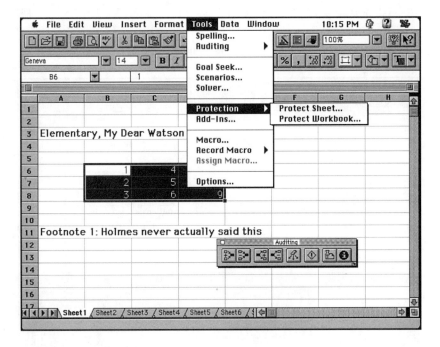

Figure 14.23 Two protection options.

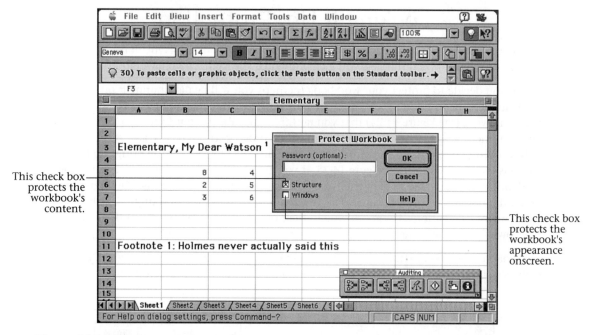

This check box protects the workbook's content.

This check box protects the workbook's appearance onscreen.

Figure 14.24   Password protection from the Tools menu.

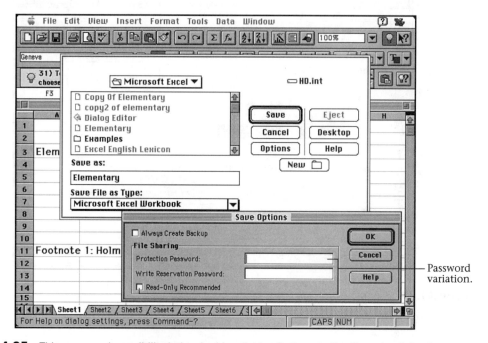

Password variation.

Figure 14.25   This password possibility is invoked by clicking Options in the Save As dialog box.

Chapter 15

Charting Your Way Through Excel

The problem with tables of numbers, even superbly formatted and appropriately highlighted tables of numbers, is that they all have a strong family similarity. If you have a story that can be summarized in a picture, most audiences prefer to see the picture rather than the numerical tables. So this chapter explains how to get numbers into chart pictures and to format these numbers by using the vast assortment of charts built into Excel. It also explains how to use charts to change the appearance of data reality without actually cheating—in other words, how to cash in on the secrets of using charts. The topics in this chapter include the following:

- ◆ Stepping through the ChartWizard
- ◆ Bar charts for business
- ◆ How to display data in pie charts
- ◆ Doughnut—the alternative display pastry
- ◆ Line charts—the choice for clarity
- ◆ Saving chart formats
- ◆ When to use fancier chart types
- ◆ How to use the quick menu for charts
- ◆ How to hide or bury problems with charts
- ◆ How to lie with a pie
- ◆ 3-D chart tips

Off to See the Wizard

In previous versions of Excel, you often spent considerable amounts of time puzzling over your charting choices. Excel 5, in contrast, has the most highly evolved version of ChartWizard, an online baby-sitter that requires only that you be able to point to the style of chart that you want. It's actually fairly entertaining to use ChartWizard, but it does impose a certain way of doing things. You and ChartWizard will, however, get along just fine after I explain a simple repertoire of reformatting tricks.

First, I'll set up some data, and then I'll get down to the business of charting. Here are the first steps:

◆ Set up a table by entering data and by putting appropriate labels along the columns and rows (see Figure 15.1). You can add labels on your charts later, but the Excel charting system anticipates that rows and columns will be labeled, so you save yourself trouble by labeling in your table.

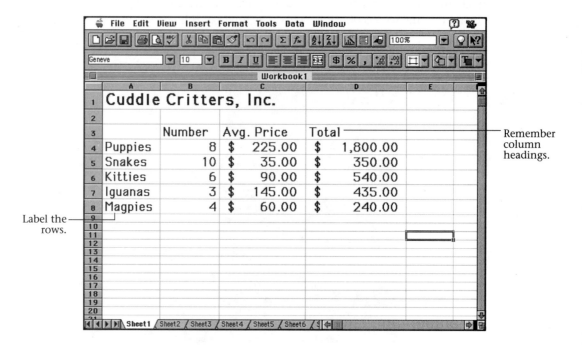

Figure 15.1 Tables should have labels.

◆ Select a range of cells containing the data that you want to chart (see Figure 15.2). If the data isn't in a connected block (a *contiguous* block, as they say downtown), you can drag-select the first data range (for example, the part containing labels) and then hold down the ⌘ key and drag-select the second range, which can exist anywhere on your worksheet.

◆ To get a chart, just click the ChartWizard icon (see Figure 15.3). Now when you move the cursor back into the worksheet area, you have the magical chart creation cursor. Find a place where you would like to put your chart, click the mouse, and drag out a chart area.

◆ That doesn't produce a chart just yet because Excel doesn't have enough information. Instead of a chart, you get the first panel of the ChartWizard sequence (see Figure 15.4).

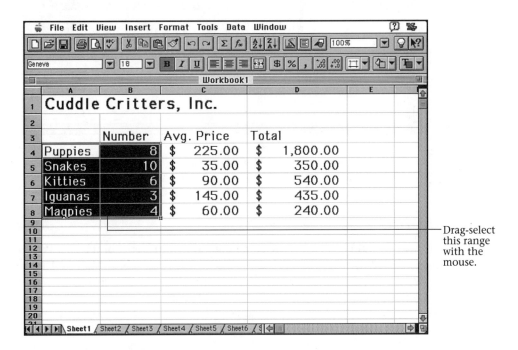

Figure 15.2   Selecting a range to chart.

Figure 15.3   The Chart Wizard icon.

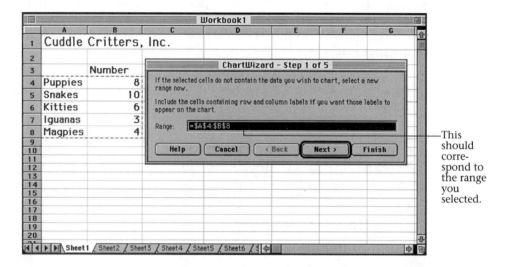

Figure 15.4   The first Wizard step asks for the data range.

Wizard options

If everything is working correctly, the data range shown in Step 1 of the ChartWizard is the data range selected with the mouse. If it isn't, or if you've changed your mind about which data you want to chart, you can enter a different range in this dialog box. To make a split (noncontiguous) range in a dialog box, enter a first range (for example, $A$3:$A$8), followed by a comma, followed by the next data range. Recall that the dollar signs mean absolute cell reference, which means that after you fire up the ChartWizard, it regards all the locations for the data you've entered as fixed for the duration of the charting events.

So far, this hasn't been too exciting. But when you press the Next button in this Wizard, you finally see some charting choices (see Figure 15.5) rendered in the Microsoft Imperial colors of mauve, lavender, and pale yellow (the gray-scale representation here doesn't do them justice). Several of the charts are old standbys that are probably familiar to you just from reading newspapers: pie, bar, line, and column charts appear every day in explanations of budgets, exchange rates, and unemployment. Their 3-D equivalents are also available in this selection, although their use requires some special consideration.

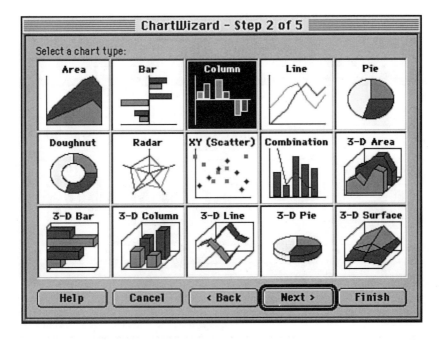

Figure 15.5   The Excel 5 chart gallery.

Some other charts are fairly self-explanatory: XY scatter charts are really the same as line charts without the lines connecting the data points, and combination charts just overlay two kinds of chart types. Area charts are a way of stacking line charts to emphasize totals rather than individual lines. 3-D surface charts are actually a sort of smoothed combination of a 3-D line and a 3-D column.

The unusual charts in Excel 5 are radar and doughnut charts. Japan has a long tradition of designing its own data graphics, so these are two examples that are used more in Japan than in the United States. A radar chart is used to display the composition of several aggregate substances in the same chart, and a doughnut chart basically lets you present multiple pie charts on top of each other (the second and third pies appear in the doughnut hole).

And more options

After you pick a chart type, you get to pick among variations on the chart. Some of these types (see Figure 15.6) are just appearance variations that look slightly better in print, while others are designed to reflect changes in trends rather than in absolute numbers. Let's pick the plainest-vanilla chart in the pack, press Next, and get to the next step in the Wizard sequence (see Figure 15.7).

Some standard column charts.

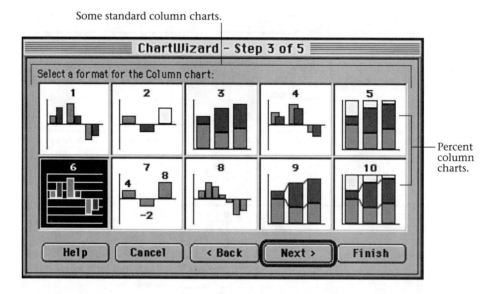

Figure 15.6   Ten varieties of column charts.

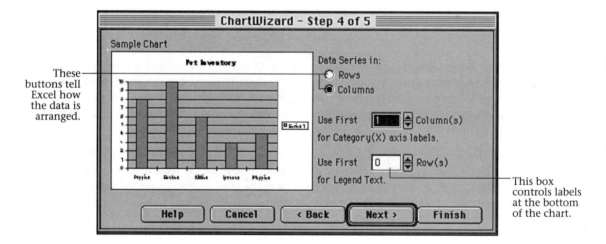

These buttons tell Excel how the data is arranged.

This box controls labels at the bottom of the chart.

Figure 15.7   Your chart preview.

In Step 4, you finally tell Excel how the data in your worksheet relates to the chart. You specify whether the data for charting is in rows or columns (remember, you can specify whole rectangular blocks, and Excel doesn't know the orientation in the blocks until you specify it). Using the first little scrolling box, you can tell Excel to pick up the data in the first column and use it as the label set along the x-axis.

Remember, the x-axis is horizontal, and the y-axis is vertical. For historical reasons, Excel calls x the category axis and y the value axis. Almost no one else follows this nomenclature. In real math, x is called the abscissa and y is the ordinate.

Although it doesn't apply to this particular chart and data set, you can use the next scrolling box to identify the *data legend* (a legend is the name of the data series).

Now when you click Next, you get a chance to do relabeling of the x- and y-axes if you want (see Figure 15.8). Also, there's an opportunity to give the chart an overall title. Having done this, you need only to click the Finish button to get a lovely chart, as in Figure 15.9. I could have thought of an imaginative name for this data series for the legend (Critter quantities? Pet population?) but I've left it as a pedestrian Series1.

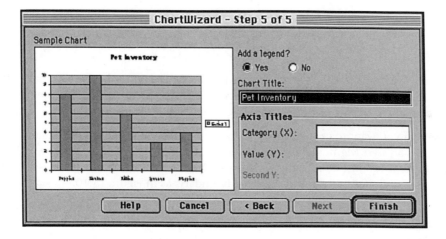

Figure 15.8   Add a title in this step.

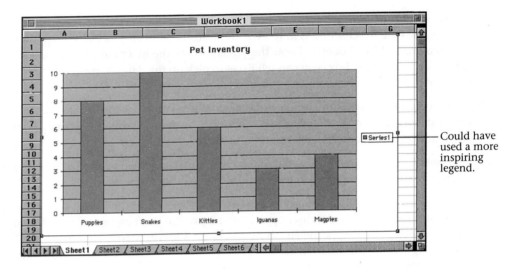

Could have used a more inspiring legend.

Figure 15.9 Classic column chart.

Chart Variety

Now that the ChartWizard has given you your chart, you might ask how you make little changes. Excel 5 has built in all sorts of delicate controls that you access, for the most part, simply by double-clicking on the chart element that you want to change.

Suppose that you want to change the typeface of the labels along the x-axis because in early childhood, you were frightened by a headline in 24-point Geneva and have been allergic to that font ever since. Just double-click inside the chart to activate chart editing—you know it's activated because the chart shows a hatched boundary, as in Figure 15.10.

Now double-click directly on the x- (horizontal) axis. Excel responds by showing you one of its new tabbed dialog boxes, a compact way of presenting you with nearly a hundred formatting choices. One of the tabs is for font changes, so you can select it and change the font to the less traumatic Times (see Figure 15.11). All newer Microsoft programs also provide you with a little Preview box so that you can see the effect of your formatting changes before you apply them. Figure 15.12 shows the formatting changes incorporated into the original chart.

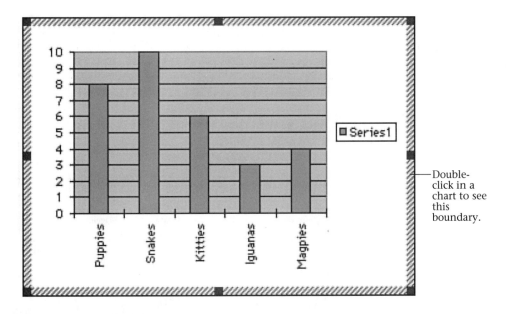

Double-click in a chart to see this boundary.

Figure 15.10   A chart ready to edit.

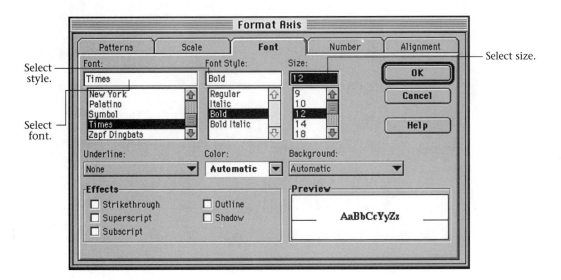

Select style.

Select font.

Select size.

Figure 15.11   Axis formatting.

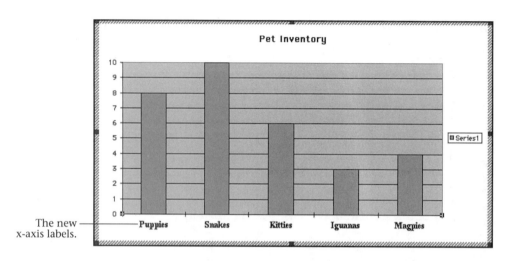

The new x-axis labels.

Figure 15.12   Times instead of Geneva on the x-axis.

Formatting: Not Just How, but Why

If you want to show your charts to other people in a presentation, you need to become intensely familiar with the Format Axis dialog box. The reason is that Excel 5's default settings are very good at making attractive screen displays but are less appropriate for making slides or printed output. If you take the default settings for axis labeling (9-point Geneva) and make slides from the output, your audience will be squinting at the screen. Microsoft itself implicitly acknowledges this situation in PowerPoint, its presentation graphics program, which has an entirely different set of charting default settings from Excel.

Similarly, for printed output that looks good in a report, you have to collect your own gallery of charts on paper from printed sources for comparison. Just take a plain manila folder, label it "Charts," and clip out charts that you find particularly striking. After you've collected a few, you'll notice that the axis labels are generally much larger than the default labels in Excel. Another thing you'll find is that the most impressive charts tend to contain fewer numbers of elements. And because most publications don't do full-color charts, they have to rely on cross-hatching and methods other than color to differentiate bars, columns, and pie segments.

Switching chart types

Besides tinkering with axes and fonts and labels, you may find that you want to change the chart type after you've set it up. Either you can go back through the sequence of ChartWizard steps again, or you can double-click the chart to activate it and find Chart Type under the Format menu (see Figure 15.13).

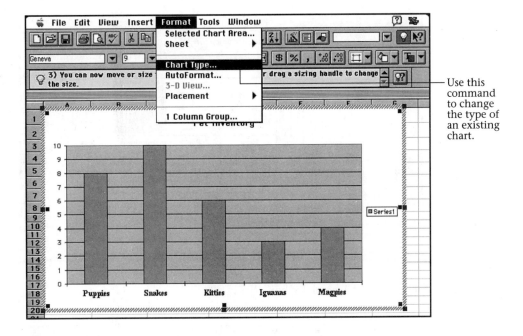

Figure 15.13   Switching chart types.

This command takes you to a dialog box that looks somewhat like Step 2 of the ChartWizard sequence (see Figure 15.14), except that the 2-D and 3-D chart types have been separated, and you can switch between them by using a radio button. For an illustration of changing chart types, I picked a pie chart (see Figure 15.15) as the next chart type.

If you remember charting with ChartWizard a few pages back, you know that after you select a basic chart type, you are given a choice of variations. That's true here in the reformatting business, too. After you double-click in the modified chart, you select AutoFormat from the Format menu. You then see a set of choices (different choices for each chart type) that look like those in Figure 15.16.

Pie charts can be confusing—the first pie chart in the dialog box requires you to look up pie segments in a legend box. Although the most informative pie type here is actually type 7, which lists the segments and their percentages right on the pie, it's a little cluttered for a pie with more than four data elements (see Figure 15.17). Nonetheless, it's the top choice if you are printing your charts on a black-and-white printer because all the shading distinctions on the color Mac screen disappear when you print. At least with type 7, someone looking at your chart can tell exactly what's going on, even if the pie segments are forced by the printer to be nearly identical grays. In the interest of simplicity, you can also select the legend and then select Clear from the Edit menu because all the information is now included in the main chart element.

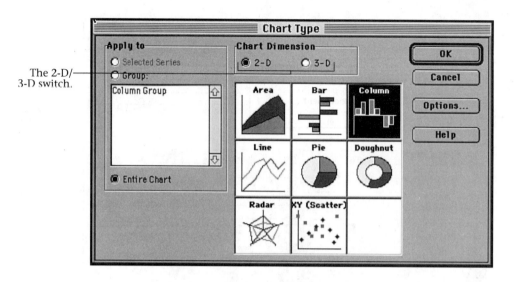

The 2-D/
3-D switch.

Figure 15.14   The Chart Type dialog box.

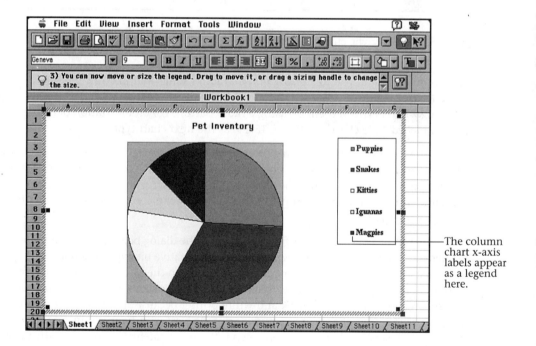

The column
chart x-axis
labels appear
as a legend
here.

Figure 15.15   An excess of snakes.

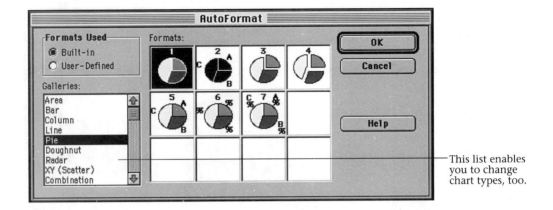

Figure 15.16   AutoFormats for pies.

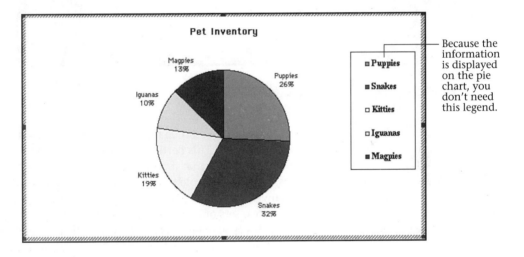

Figure 15.17   A name and number for each segment.

Before you print a set of charts to a black-and-white printer, take a look at them by using Print Preview. In Print Preview, the Setup button leads you to a tabbed dialog box, and on the Chart tab is a check box (see Figure 15.18) called Print in Black and White. If you check this, you will see which grays Excel will be selecting for color chart areas.

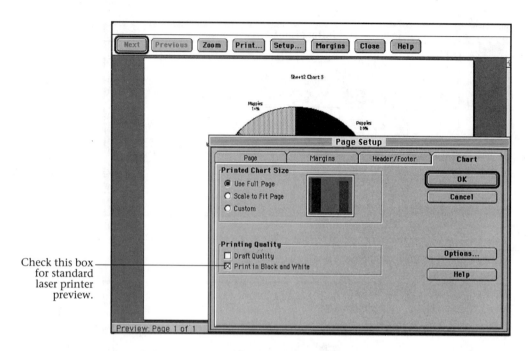

Check this box
for standard
laser printer
preview.

Figure 15.18   Print Preview in black and white.

Finally, grouping charts according to pastry, I would be remiss in my obligations if I didn't
show you a doughnut chart (see Figure 15.19). This particular chart (made by double-clicking
the pie chart, selecting AutoFormat from the Format menu, and picking Doughnut from the
scrolling list) is quite obviously just a pie with a hole in it. The fancier type of doughnut
incorporates more than one data range so that you get rings within rings (see Figure 15.20). If
you have small sets of shifts between two sets of data (for example, market share for products
changing by a few percent per year), this type of chart is fairly useful. The problem is that
Excel doesn't do a very good job of displaying and labeling these charts, so you get an unfamiliar, slightly confusing, poorly drawn chart. You may want to stick to the basics. These same
comments also apply to radar charts, in which Excel has similar labeling problems.

Using line charts

Although all the chart types are grouped together by the ChartWizard in a grand tableau of
opportunities, the chart types have distinctly different applications. For showing data that
represents quantities measured at a particular time, pies and bars and columns are fine. For
scientific data, the most common chart is the XY scatter plot.

For numbers that are changing in time, the line chart is usually the clearest representation. Referring to the ridiculous pet store example of Figure 15.1, suppose that I need to follow the course of the pet inventory over several months. Figure 15.21 shows a typical table of monthly stocks of critters over four months—it's the kind of data that occurs over and over in more serious business examples.

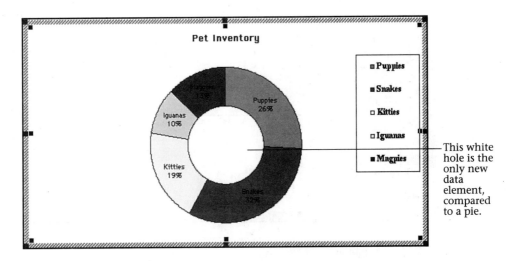

This white hole is the only new data element, compared to a pie.

Figure 15.19   Unfrosted, old-fashioned doughnut.

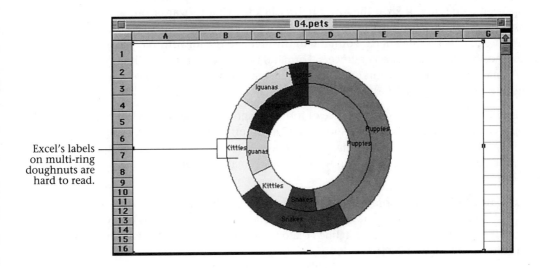

Excel's labels on multi-ring doughnuts are hard to read.

Figure 15.20   Double doughnut fun.

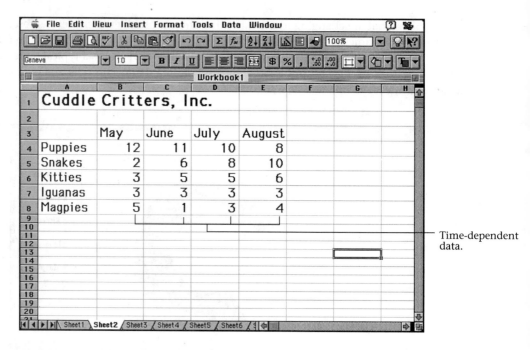

Time-dependent data.

Figure 15.21   An inventory example.

To follow the ups and downs of the critters, select the whole rectangular range from cell A3 in the upper-left corner to cell E8 at the lower right. Click the ChartWizard icon, select the Line chart in Step 2, and pick format 4 in Step 3 (see Figure 15.22). Note that Excel offers some fairly exotic formats for line charts. Format 6 in this figure has a logarithmic y-axis scale; this is useful mostly for scientists and engineers. Format 8 is a stock market style high/low/close chart; format 7 plots ranges within categories; and format 9 is a statistical plot that often appears in quality control studies.

The line chart that results from this choice of format is shown in Figure 15.23. It's reasonably clear on a color Mac screen, but it has some problems in other contexts, such as slides or a printed report. First, the lines in the chart are too thin. Second, the legend box is too small. Finally, if the chart is printed, all the lines will be black, making them quite difficult to distinguish.

So once again, it's time to do some reformatting work—fixing these problems one at a time. As always, to reformat a chart element, give it a double-click with the mouse. When you double-click on a line in this chart, you get a tabbed dialog box that lets you tinker with individual chart elements (see Figure 15.24).

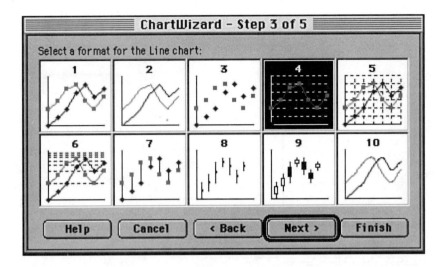

Figure 15.22 ChartWizard's line chart options.

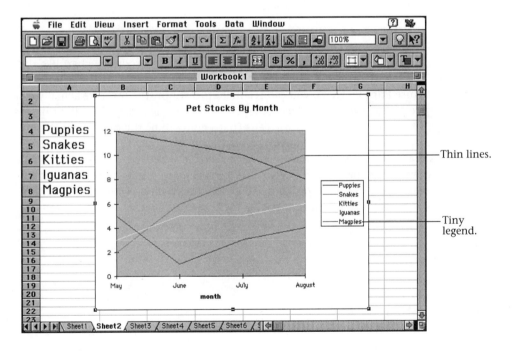

Figure 15.23 A standard Excel 5 line chart.

359

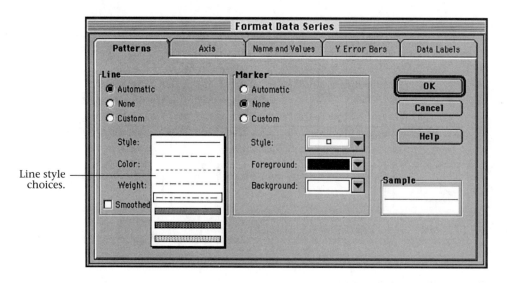

Line style
choices.

Figure 15.24   Changing chart appearance with Format Data Series.

On the Patterns tab, there's a style option that lets you pick different dotted and dashed lines for your line chart, and it also lets you select color and line thickness. After careful consideration of an appropriate line style for each animal, you can produce a chart like the one in Figure 15.25, formatting the lines one at a time. Checking the work to see if it will print properly (use Print Preview), you can see that at least now the lines are actually distinguishable (see Figure 15.26), even in the legend. Please note that the chart, as it will print, is subtly different from the one you see onscreen. That's going to be the case, typically, and it's the main reason I keep insisting that you preview every chart before you print it. The big difference is that a chart is scaled to a given size onscreen, while Excel sizes documents to fit the page on which it is printed (if you're printing the chart on its own page). Essentially, the screen version has been cropped and scaled (by you), but Excel is working with its own internal version that fits best to the available paper.

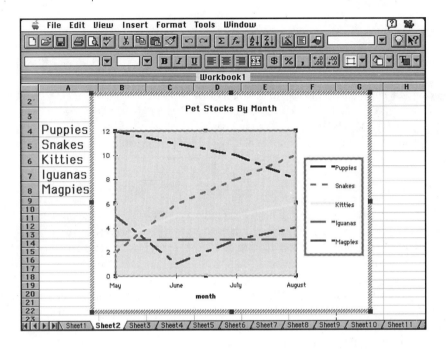

Figure 15.25   Dots and dashes.

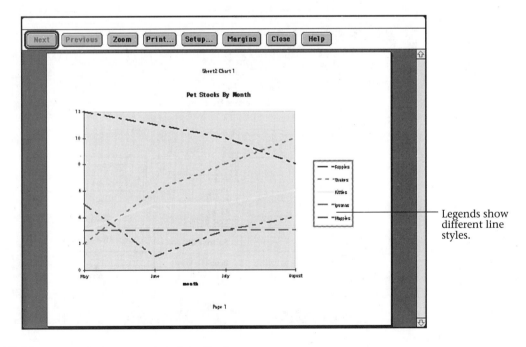

Legends show
different line
styles.

Figure 15.26   Check your chart work in Print Preview.

Oops! Cahrt Speling!

I think I've probably seen more misspelled words in charts than anywhere else. To a certain extent, it's like a sign painter's problem—when you're putting up 3-foot-high letters, you tend to concentrate more on the letters than the order. If you get absorbed in formatting lines, you don't notice that *Sales* has become *Slaes*. Chart misspellings are great fun at meetings, too. You put up a slide, everyone starts to inspect it, a slight chuckle ripples through the audience, and then some helpful character asks you, "Do you really mean 'bunsiness' or should that be 'business'?"

Fortunately, under the Tools menu, Excel 5 has a Spelling Checker, which goes into your legends and titles and axis labels and spell checks them for you. As you accumulate entries in your own dictionary (it's just like the Spelling Checker in Microsoft Word), this process will speed up considerably. And then you don't have to worry about misspelling your own company's name in a chart in your annual report (I've seen this happen—twice).

As a convenience, so that you don't spend your whole life pulling down menus, Excel 5 has a feature for accessing formatting options quickly. Hold down the ⌘ key and click in your chart. Up pops a little menu (see Figure 15.27) with the most frequently used editing commands. You'll end up using this trick a lot, I promise you.

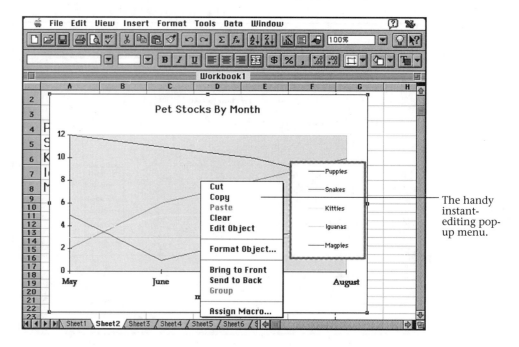

The handy instant-editing pop-up menu.

Figure 15.27   Hold down the ⌘ key and click in the chart to get this pop-up menu.

Saving Formats

Now you may expect that doing all this reformatting can be fairly time-consuming. It is. Double-click on a line, pick a line dot style, go back to the chart, pick another line, pick another dot style . . . you probably wouldn't want to do this all afternoon for a set of 40 charts.

Here's what you do. Format a single chart just the way that you want it. When you have all the elements arranged and adjusted to your satisfaction, double-click the chart. Then select AutoFormat from the Format menu, and instead of picking a canned format, select the button for User Defined in the Formats Used section of the AutoFormat dialog box (see Figure 15.28). You get the User-Defined AutoFormat dialog box. Click the button for Add because you will be adding your own format. Excel 5 asks you for a format name and a description (the description is just for your own benefit so that you can remember later what you did).

Click User-Defined to save your chart formatting in an AutoFormat.

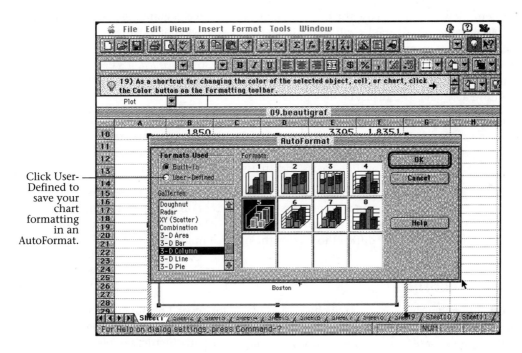

Figure 15.28   The AutoFormat dialog box.

The next time you format a chart, you have all your formatting details available with a single command under the AutoFormat selections. Because most business monthly reports tend to be reporting on the same things, for example, there will be the same number of data elements and the same preferred type of display. Some users find that in their first month or so with Excel, they can set up a repertoire of chart formats, store them in AutoFormat, and just apply these over and over, never again toiling away in the depths of the tabbed dialog boxes.

If you have a group of charts under development at the same time, you can also format one, select it, and pick Copy from the Edit menu. Then use the Edit menu's Paste Special Formats option to apply the formatting to the other charts.

So far, this chapter has covered the basic use of Excel's ChartWizard for the quick creation and formatting of simple charts. Now you're ready to see how you can use charts to make your data more meaningful.

Line Chart Secrets

Sometimes your data is not all that you want it to be. Perhaps you represent the worst-performing sales region in your company, and you have to give a presentation with graphs this Friday. You may need help.

I'm going to show you how to use the tricks available in the Excel 5 graphing system to make yourself look better. These graphs will all be different pictorial ways of looking at the same numbers. There are many subtle effects based on the facts of vision. From the anonymous artists who did perspective wall paintings in Pompeii to Picasso's *Guernica,* it's been the hallmark of professionalism to employ these facts in a representation. When you put the best face on miserable data, you're just being a professional.

If you open up a scientific journal, you see lots of plain line charts. In a science article, the whole idea is to display a collection of data in such a way that the chart accurately reflects the data. In a reputable business journal (my favorites for charting examples are *The Economist* and *Business Week*), however, you see line charts and an assortment of bar charts.

And then, as you proceed down the editorial food chain to journals with more axes to grind, you start to see more pie charts and pictographs (little stacks of oil barrels and such). By the time you get to *USA Today*, most traditional chart types have been replaced with colorful equivalents that make it fairly difficult to extract the original numbers.

Truth in charting

The most comprehensive discussion of charting available for general reading is probably Edward Tufte's great work *The Visual Display of Quantitative Information* (Graphics Press, 1983). Dr. Tufte, a professor of several subjects at Yale, explains not only the tricks of perspective and areas in different kinds of charts, but he also explains the elements of superior charting. Basically, Dr. Tufte wants to increase your charting and graphing sophistication.

Unfortunately, almost none of Dr. Tufte's extremely valuable advice was used in producing the charting functions of spreadsheet programs. Spreadsheets have, in fact, brought about a whole new Bronze Age of crappy graphics. Most programs have a difficult time making charts that are as aesthetically pleasing and representationally accurate as those in the works of Victorian sociologists. Sad but true.

So Dr. Tufte wants to show you how to make charts that accurately and faithfully mirror your data. That's okay for him—he has tenure at Yale and his own publishing company. You, on the other hand, may find yourself some day in a darkened conference room presenting dismal fourth-quarter sales numbers to your grumpy supervisors, and you will need to make things look reasonable. That's what the rest of this chapter is all about—I'm going to stand high-quality graphing advice on its ear to show you how to make declines look mild and slight increases look gigantic. Don't tell anyone you saw it here, but in a pinch, it easily justifies the price of this book.

The basic principle in all the cases here is fairly simple. The type of standard optical illusion shown in Figure 15.29 contains the essence of the tricks. After you have a diagram with a few slanted lines and after you have a chart with some 3-D perspective, your ability to judge elements quantitatively by eye just about disappears. You and I are simply going to play on that theme a bit.

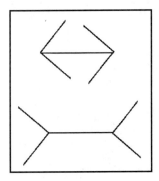

Figure 15.29   Which center line is longer?

Using line charts

Figure 15.30 shows a very simple Excel worksheet containing some sales data and a plot of the data using the line chart option with a partial grid (gridlines running in one direction instead of both).

There are a few key points you should understand about line charts:

◆ A line chart is the easiest path back from a chart to the underlying numbers. In other words, it's the easiest to read.

◆ Gridlines make it easy to extract quantitative data.

◆ "Honest" line chart axes start with zero.

Step back a minute and consider the story in the data. For this example, sales in the Atlanta area are booming. Sales in Boston aren't terrible, but they're down a bit, and things seem to have peaked in Miami. Situations like this occur all the time. As the great statistician W. Edwards Deming patiently explained to a whole generation of U. S. business leaders who simply didn't "get it," there's a certain random component to sales and market data. Sales can be up in some areas and down in others, even with every member of a company's staff working equally hard. It works that way just because a given company is only a tiny fragment of the whole economy, which follows its own rules. That's why this graphing example isn't just an example, it's *the* example for the American business office.

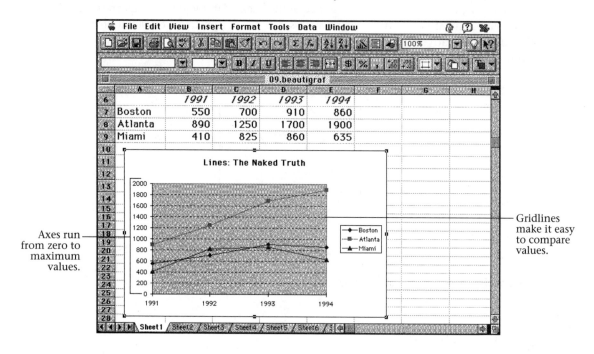

Axes run from zero to maximum values.

Gridlines make it easy to compare values.

Figure 15.30   When the facts are on your side, try an honest line chart.

You can draw those sales conclusions fairly quickly from the data in a table, but you can see them even faster in the chart. Now suppose that the data is to be presented at a meeting, and the Atlanta area sales rep is in charge of the presentation. What else can you do with this line chart?

Well, there are two simple and effective ways to modify this chart. The first and simplest method is to change line colors. After you double-click on a line in the chart, one of the first options you see is the option for changing line colors. If you have a story to tell, put your story in red (or choose a thicker line) and leave the rest of the data in drab little thin lines. The quantitative story is the same, but the impact has changed.

The second, and slightly more fraudulent, way to emphasize data in a line chart is to modify the axes. If you have a line that slants up, you can make it look like it's headed up even faster by shrinking the chart along the x-axis (x is horizontal, and y is vertical). Just click on the right-hand chart border and drag it to the left—it's the same data, but the visual slope looks greater. This principle is used constantly in financial pages of newspapers, where (partly because of space limitations in columns) all sorts of gentle changes in company earnings are made to appear either as runaway increases or near collapse.

Changing the y-axis scale is a more serious dodge. Double-click anywhere in a line chart to activate it. The Format menu gives you an Axis option, and it has a tabbed dialog box for Scale (see Figure 15.31) that you can use to set arbitrary starting and ending points on your chart axes. For this example, I'm going to reset the low end of the scale to 400 units instead of the standard zero. This action makes the rise of sales in Atlanta look much more dramatic and makes sales in the other cities look correspondingly more miserable (see Figure 15.32). By changing the axis, I have effectively changed the representation to highlight *differences* between cities rather than the fairly large quantity of sales they have in common.

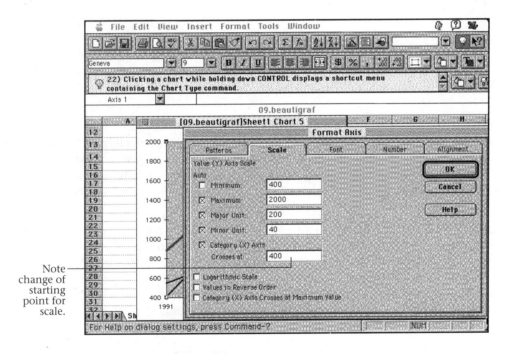

Note change of starting point for scale.

Figure 15.31   Changing an axis scale for emphasis.

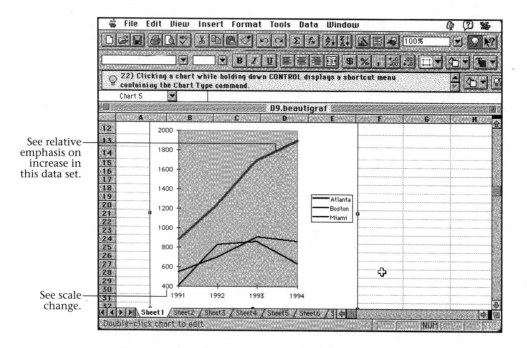

See relative
emphasis on
increase in
this data set.

See scale
change.

Figure 15.32   Atlanta takes off!

This change of axis trick is behind most of the misleading charts that you see in newspapers and elsewhere. It's used to make relatively tiny changes in an index seem gigantic. Suppose that you are comparing students' scores on a test and the values are 96 percent, 97 percent, 97.2 percent, and 98.5 percent. If you plot these on a scale from 0 to 100, they look nearly identical, as they should. If you reset the y-axis to run from 95 to 100, then 96 percent looks, quite unfairly, like a disaster compared to 98.5 percent.

The old district attorney in my county had a 91 percent conviction rate in criminal cases, and the new district attorney got 92.5 percent. This difference resulted in campaign literature in which the y-axis scale for conviction ran from 90 percent to 95 percent. The trivial increase in conviction rate (not a real increase, actually, just a random fluctuation) looked like a gigantic improvement. So whenever you see a business chart in a publication, make sure that you look at the y-axis scale carefully to see if something strange is happening.

Area Chart Secrets

If you were a sales rep for one of the other cities in this imaginary organization, the comparative numbers for Atlanta would be pretty discouraging. But because you're becoming an Excel 5 charting expert, there's no need to worry—just pick a chart that distorts the data in a favorable way.

Standard area

Because the chart types are listed in alphabetical order, the area chart is the first in the ChartWizard chart lineup (see Figure 15.33). For our data selected in the original worksheet order (Boston first, Miami last), selecting the default area chart gives us the chart in Figure 15.34.

Here's what's happening. In an area chart, the quantities in the line chart are piled on top of each other. That means that if the first data series is a rapidly increasing set of numbers, the other series are plotted with the equivalent of a slanted x-axis. Instead of all data points on a line being measured from zero, the top border of each area segment in the chart is computed from the *sum* of data points of the sections below it. It looks like a line in a line chart, but it isn't measured from zero, so it's very different. In Figure 15.34, the top of the Miami area section doesn't have much to do with Miami but is, instead, just the sum of sales for all cities for each year.

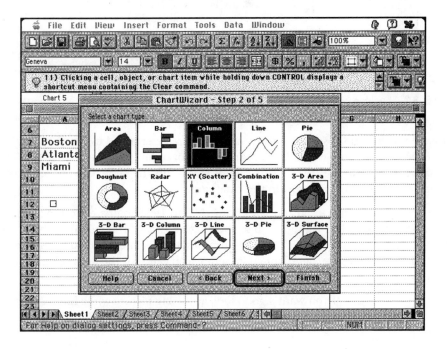

Figure 15.33   Area chart: the Wizard's first option.

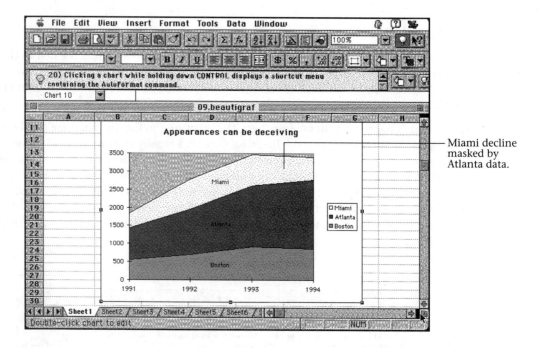

Miami decline masked by Atlanta data.

Figure 15.34   Looking better in smaller markets.

If you are the Boston sales rep in this scenario and are determined to hide last year's down-turn, a good way to do it would be to change the plot order (just interchange the Boston and Atlanta rows). Look at the area chart in Figure 15.35—it's the same data replotted with the Atlanta data series as the first row in the data range.

Can you spot the change in Boston sales from 1993 to 1994 compared to the change in the original line chart back in Figure 15.30 or even Figure 15.34? If so, you must have exceptional powers of discrimination. For all practical purposes, the decline is buried in the general upward slope provided by the Atlanta data series. You can spot the decline only with a superior ability to discriminate small changes in angles.

Just keep in mind that if you want a good look at the big picture while hiding details, area charts are just fine. If you want to bring out details in a data set, use line charts instead.

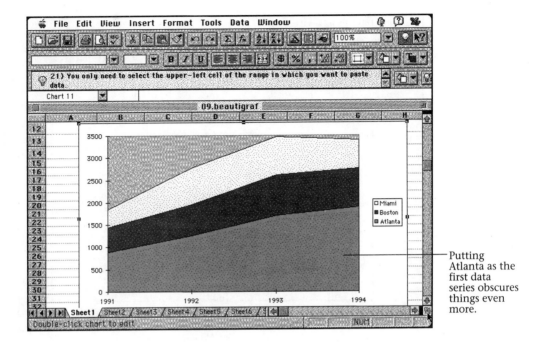

Figure 15.35   Boston data concealed by Atlanta.

Area percent charts

Area percent charts, another area chart option in the ChartWizard, have perfectly legitimate uses. If you want to show the changing contribution of different sales areas to the total sales, for example, an area percent chart is perfect. The area percent chart for our example takes data from several cities (sales data for different years) and scales the data to show the percent contribution of each city for each year (see Figure 15.36). In the process, the actual sales numbers disappear into the total.

That's a valid use. You can also use area percent charts to conceal changes in sales over a series of points in time. Because a percent chart scales the relative contributions (in this example, from cities) rather than showing absolute size, this kind of chart makes it harder to see real changes over time.

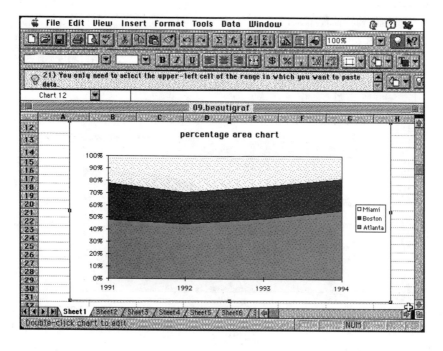

Figure 15.36   Real data disguised by an area percent chart.

Pies for Obscurity

Area charts are a good way to show *relative* relationships but a bad way to show absolute numbers. It must be admitted, however, that someone could still take a ruler to the chart in Figure 15.36 and reconstruct the actual data. If you really want to cover your tracks, use a pie chart (which is just a specialized type of area chart) to represent data that's changing in time.

In Figure 15.37, I picked the data for 1991 and 1994 and plotted it as two separate pie charts (just select the data as you normally would and find the pies in the ChartWizard menu). These two pie charts do a pretty good job of obscuring the actual sales history while purporting to show important changes in sales between the two years.

Even this representation, however, shows more than you may want to show. While your visual system has a hard time seeing the difference in the angle of the Miami pie slice, it can easily see the difference between the Atlanta segments in the two examples. Note that pie charts also give you the option of labeling the segments with percent labels, but putting in percentages would be giving the viewer a way to undo your concealment.

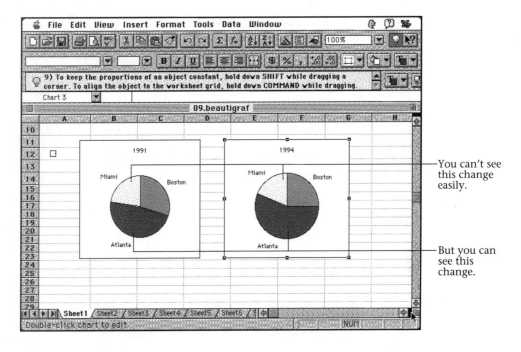

Figure 15.37   A rampant abuse of pie charts.

If your pie charts are revealing too much, try a 3-D chart, the best place to hide information. A good general rule of chart perversion is the following: if you still have something to hide in your 2-D charts, get yourself another dimension. Look at the 3-D pie chart in Figure 15.38. It's still possible to see that Atlanta has grown at the expense of the other two cities, but the 3-D presentation flattens out the pie-segment angle.

If you can gauge these angles correctly by eye, you're ready to do celestial navigation with only a pair of crossed sticks. These two charts make it appear that not much has really happened over the three years; in fact, the whole business has changed seriously.

One more pie trick should be mentioned here because I've seen it in several presentations. (I do a certain amount of venture capital consulting every year, so I've seen every way known to man to fudge numbers in a chart—these kids play for keeps). Between 1991 and 1994, total sales in this example are up by 84 percent. So in comparing the two years, why not expand the 1994 chart in size by that same 84 percent? Do this by dragging the little handles on the sides of the charts (click the chart so that the handles appear).

Because the pie size reflects total sales and because the relative contributions of the cities to sales are obscured in a 3-D pie, it looks like sales in Boston and Miami are exploding right along with Atlanta (see Figure 15.39). If you were the Miami rep, would you rather see this 3-D chart or the line chart back in Figure 15.32?

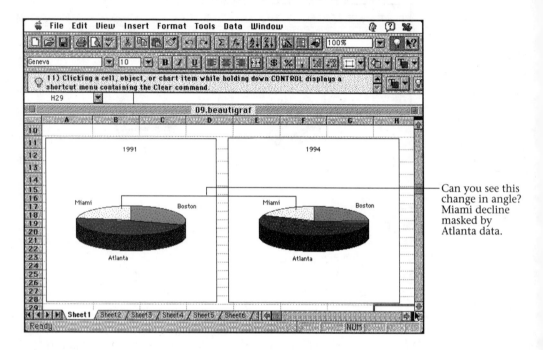

Can you see this change in angle? Miami decline masked by Atlanta data.

Figure 15.38   3-D: one more dimension where you can hide information.

And yet, these representations come from the same set of data. It happens that the designers of charting programs agonize over the chart types they include with their products because they know perfectly well how they can be used. For years, Computer Associates' Cricket Graph declined to offer 3-D charts, knowing that they were often misused—purposely or by accident.

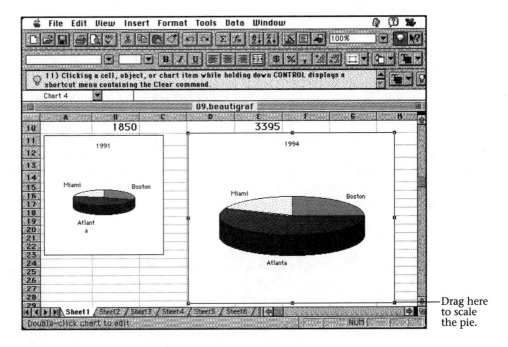

Figure 15.39   Scaling pies to match total sales.

3-D Charts: Innovation or Prestidigitation?

The fact that 3-D pie charts obscure some already foggy details in 2-D pie charts is just a preview of the magnificent effects you can produce with 3-D charts. A complaint about previous Excel programs was that they had a limited array of charts and no 3-D charts, but that's all history with the new Excel 5. Although there are certainly ways to make accurate and dramatic presentations by using 3-D charts, one of the main effects of 3-D charting is the introduction of perspective-scaling effects, which make it hard to reconstruct the original data from a chart view.

Columns

In a standard 2-D column chart, you always have a way to translate individual points along the column into accurate numbers. In a 3-D column chart, you could, in principle, perform the same conversion. The problem is that you have to guess the height of a column, and the column is displayed against a background that's been adjusted for fake 3-D perspective, making the guess tougher.

As always, in this chart deception minicourse, I propose never to give a sucker an even break. In practical terms, this means that you make quantitative estimates more difficult. Do this by picking type 5 when you reach Step 3 of the ChartWizard dialog box. The type 5 option gives you a chart in which grids have been suppressed (see Figure 15.40) so that people viewing the chart don't even have an on-chart scale for comparison.

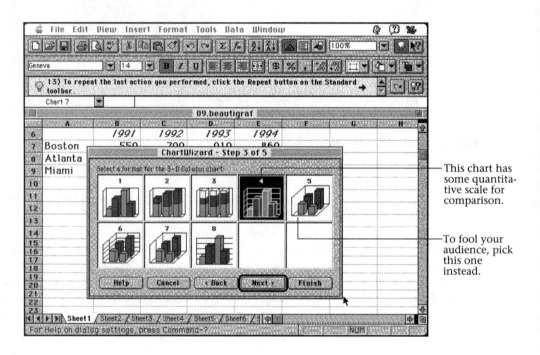

Figure 15.40   The gallery of 3-D columns.

I've selected the data again and followed the ChartWizard steps to produce 3-D columns, which means

◆ Selecting the data range

◆ Clicking Chart Wizard

◆ Picking a 3-D chart type (in this case, columns)

◆ Typing in a label in Step 4 of the ChartWizard

◆ Pressing Finish

A first plot of the data with standard settings shows one of the possible 3-D problems—you can't even see some of the data because it's blocked by other columns (see Figure 15.41). Clearly, this chart has to be rotated, and the perspective has to be changed to get all the data points, however distorted, into view. Under the Format menu, the choice to Format 3-D View gives you a way to change several aspects of the view at the same time (see Figure 15.42).

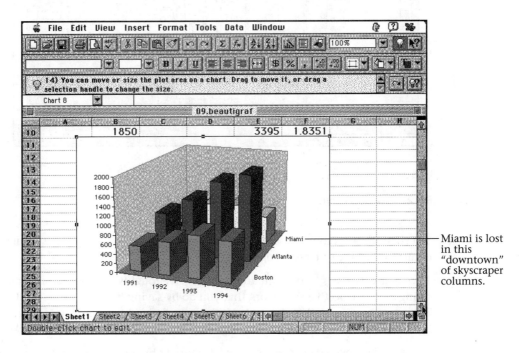

Figure 15.41   Note that this 3-D view hides some data.

A little tinkering (rotating the view with the controls in the Format 3-D View dialog box) produces the view shown in Figure 15.43. This view makes the data for Boston look okay, the data for Atlanta look great, and the data for Miami look relatively miserable. If you rotate the chart so that you're looking at the columns dead sideways instead of from a bird's-eye perspective, it becomes almost impossible to detect changes measured from the early years.

377

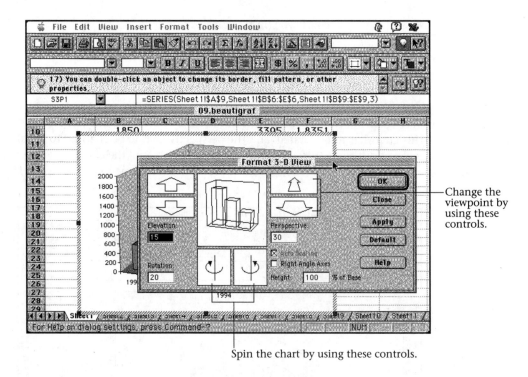

Change the
viewpoint by
using these
controls.

Spin the chart by using these controls.

Figure 15.42   3-D View control lets you pick the perspective.

Every 3-D chart deserves some experimentation with rotation and perspective, either to bring
out the truth or to conceal features of the data.

If you have many data sets to present, and they all have roughly the same story, you can store
any rotating- and perspective-shift work that you do by saving it as a custom AutoFormat (see
"Saving Formats," earlier in this chapter). After you've defined your own AutoFormat, you can
apply it to data any time you like—it's the equivalent of a style sheet in Microsoft Word.

Figure 15.44 shows how data is made somewhat murkier by "advanced" 3-D charts. This
is a 3-D line chart (this type is called a 3-D ribbon chart by everyone in the world except
Microsoft) of the original data set. Do you think it's easier to see accurately what's going on
in this chart or in the simple 2-D line charts?

Viewing
from the top
suppresses
some
differences.

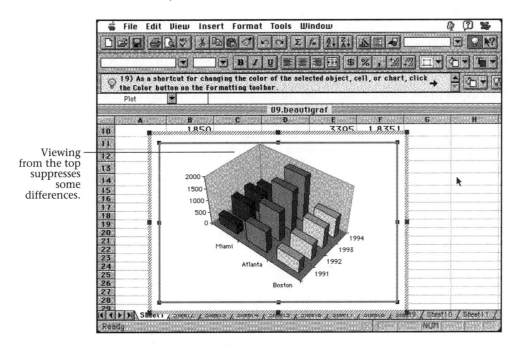

Figure 15.43   One 3-D view out of many.

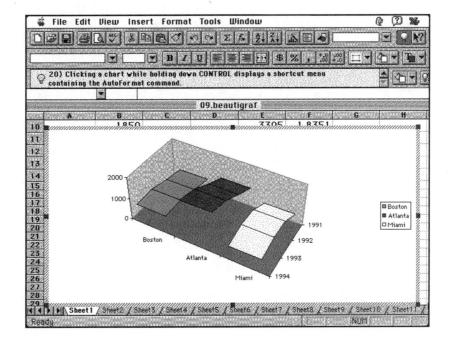

Figure 15.44   Data in an "advanced" 3-D chart.

Of course it's easier in the 2-D case. But for reasons that aren't clear, business presentations always look more impressive if there is more 3-D charting. If you pick a viewpoint on the right-hand side of this chart frame and look straight across, you can see Atlanta standing out from the other two towns. But because the years on the chart are running back to front in this view, it still isn't clear to the casual observer that Atlanta has taken over the market and that the other two cities are in decline.

This chapter covers the basic use of Excel's ChartWizard for quick creation of simple charts, and it also explains how to use some charting features to paint a visual picture that modifies the impact of the underlying numerical data. The next chapter deals with Excel's functions.

Chapter 16

Understanding Functions

You can perform virtually any numerical math calculation in an Excel worksheet by using only the four basic functions (add, subtract, multiply, and divide). Of course, because thousands of clever people before you have faced the same set of calculation tasks, all these sets of steps have already been coded into little bits of mathematical machinery called functions. In this chapter, you learn the basics of the main functions, some practical applications for more advanced functions, and how to set up your worksheet so that finding errors in the way you have entered data is easier to do. This chapter contains the following points:

◆ Using Function Wizard

◆ Experimenting with COUNT, AVG, MAX, and MIN operations

◆ Understanding function arguments

◆ Using RAND, IF, and NOW

◆ Using PMT, the payment function

◆ Figuring interest and principal payments for real-world consumer loans and mortgages

◆ Replacing cell locations with names

◆ Using the Auditing toolbar

◆ Tracing your errors

Getting Friendly with Functions

I'll tell you a little bit about functions, just in case you didn't absorb everything the teachers were trying to tell you in high school math.

Most functions in high school were presented to you in the form

$$y = f(x)$$

A typical function would be

$$y = f(x) = x^2$$

This is a rule that describes a curve called a parabola, and you get the plot of the curve by picking different values for x, squaring them, and then plotting the points (x = 3, y = 9 and x = 4, y = 16, and so forth).

While Excel includes basic functions from high school math, a function in Excel can be much more powerful than high school functions because an Excel function is really a little computer program in its own right. To use a function, you tell the function program what numbers (or text or logical values) to use as program input, and the function grinds away and produces a result. The function is really like a little numerical machine or a specially programmed key on a fancy calculator. The reason these machines are important in Excel is that they do all the work needed for even the most complex calculations—someone else has set them up for you, and all you have to do is use them.

A first function: COUNT

Consider the worksheet in Figure 16.1. I have put a border around the cells C1 to C10—that's where the data goes for this little experiment. The worksheet also contains a label identifying the experiment and labels indicating where the number average and the number count go.

Notice that in Figure 16.2, some numbers have been put into the ten available spaces from C1 to C10. How would you calculate the average of the four numbers shown? You can just add them up by using the Sum function and divide by four. But this isn't a very general solution. If you put five numbers in the boxed area, you'd have to add them and then divide by five. That's not wonderful—if you have to change the basis of the calculation every time you change a number in the space, you might as well use a calculator.

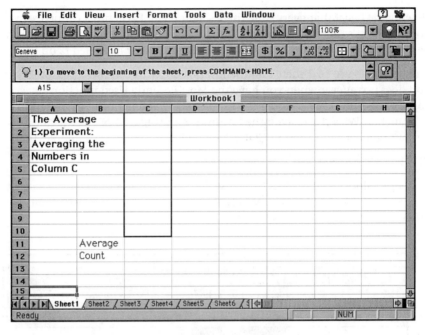

Figure 16.1   Making a function experiment.

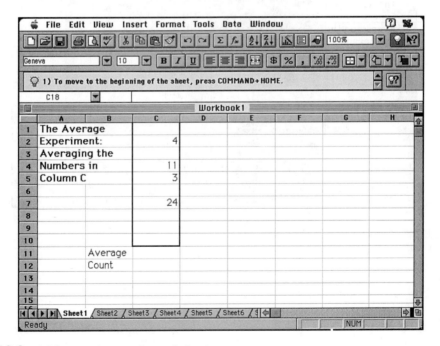

Figure 16.2   Adding numbers to the worksheet.

So following the belief that every time there's a problem, Excel has a canned answer in its function library, it's time to look in the function list for a function that counts how many numbers have been entered in a range. Click the button that is labeled *fx* on the toolbar.

Sure enough, in Figure 16.3 there's a function called COUNT in the Function Name list. If the function does not appear when you have the Most Recently Used function category highlighted, you can find COUNT under the list of Statistical functions. After you click COUNT in the list, Function Wizard gives you the lowdown on using COUNT (see Figure 16.4). Briefly, you can put numbers directly into COUNT if you like and find, for example, that

COUNT(1, 5, 9, 2.3) = 4

This is a fairly idiotic use of COUNT because you type four numbers in as *arguments* (one of the inputs of a function) and Excel tells you that you typed in four numbers. Well, "Duh!!!" as my niece says.

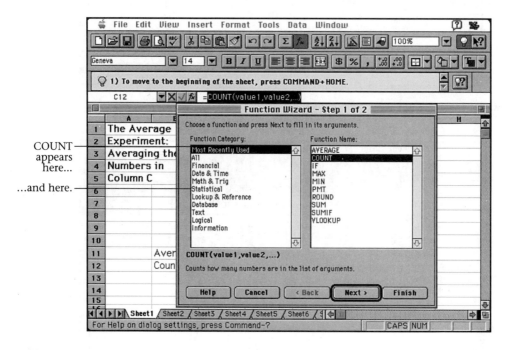

Figure 16.3   All the functions you could want.

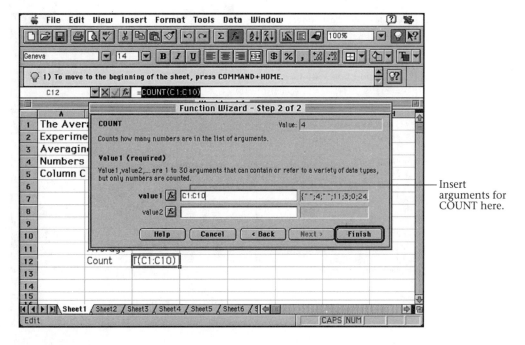

Figure 16.4   Function Wizard explains COUNT.

A better use of COUNT is this: enter the range C1:C10 (remember the : for specifying a range) as the only argument of the function COUNT. This tells COUNT to look in the range and see how many numbers it finds. Note that zero is a number, so it registers with COUNT, while a blank space isn't counted. Look at Figure 16.5, and you see COUNT churning away at its somewhat boring little task. If you think about what's involved in making Excel count numbers just by using arithmetic functions, you can really appreciate COUNT. It can be done, but it involves some extreme cleverness.

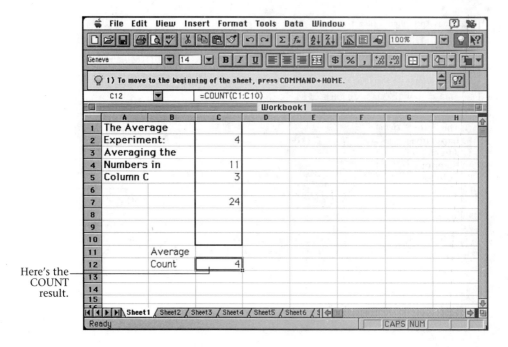

Here's the COUNT result.

Figure 16.5 Using COUNT to check the numbers.

AVERAGE

Having automated the counting procedure, it's clear that there must also be a way to automate forming an average of the numbers. As a first pass at this, you can try using the combination of the functions SUM and COUNT, as shown in Figure 16.6. Add the numbers by using SUM and divide the total by COUNT.

Even this pitiful effort, however, is more work than you should have to do personally to take an average. After all, you shelled out real money for this giant product, and you have a right to expect that Excel 5 has everything you could want. After you click the Function Wizard button to see what's available, AVERAGE appears under Statistical functions and usually under Most Recently Used (see Figure 16.7).

The AVERAGE function is more sophisticated than COUNT because it not only adds a collection of numbers, but it also counts them and then performs the division. There is, therefore, some justification for using AVERAGE in a mode in which you type in numbers directly as arguments (see Figure 16.8) rather than specifying a range. Usually, though, you'll be AVERAGing numbers already entered in a worksheet cell range.

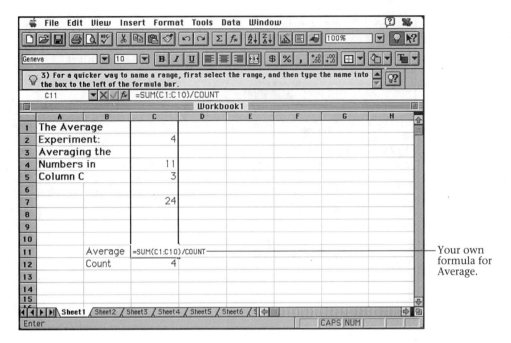

Figure 16.6   SUM divided by COUNT.

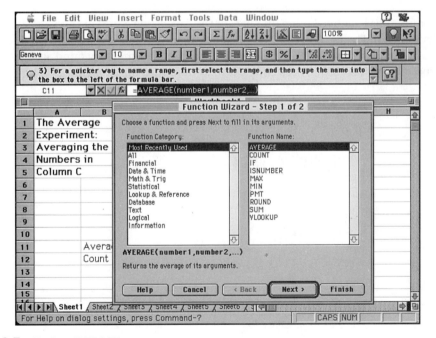

Figure 16.7   Finding AVERAGE.

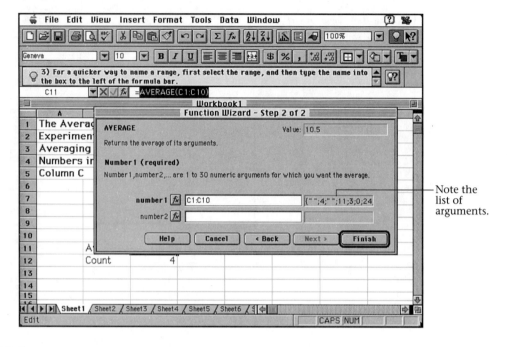

Figure 16.8 The AVERAGE dialog box.

Just for fun, I have entered more numbers in the "averaging zone" of this worksheet with the results shown in Figure 16.9. COUNT, of course, reports whole numbers, so there's not much choice of number format; AVERAGE simply makes up its own merry mind about format unless you specifically override it by selecting a format from the Format menu.

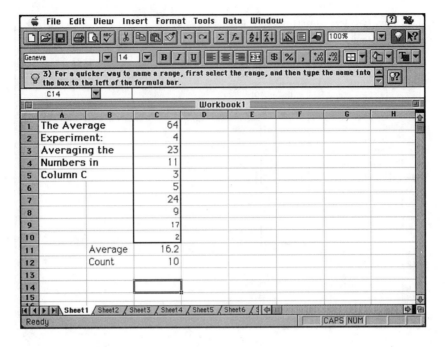

Figure 16.9 Filling in ten numbers for averaging.

More Function Fun: MAX, MIN, and RAND

There are a few more functions that you may want to meet, partly because they are useful in assessing business situations. Like COUNT and AVERAGE, the first two of these functions usually have a cell range as arguments.

MAX picks out the biggest number in its argument range, and you can find it, like the earlier functions, in the Statistical function category. MIN, on the other hand, picks out the smallest number in the range. (You can also type in a set of numbers directly to be the function arguments, although there's not much point in this.) Figure 16.10 shows MAX and MIN working together on a simple example.

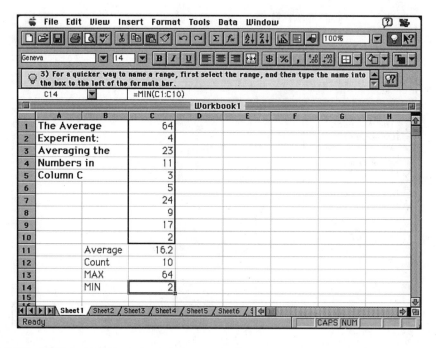

Figure 16.10   MAX and MIN look through the numbers.

Using these two functions may not seem to be a particularly dramatic use of functions, but if you have a situation in which you're tracking a number with a random component (such as month-to-month or week-to-week sales), AVERAGE, MAX, and MIN are actually better functions for characterizing the number than some other statistical functions that may appear more sophisticated. Because MAX works like COUNT, you can tell for yourself just by looking at the worksheet whether your calculations are working properly. You may not always be able to tell whether you're getting the right results from the statistical function for standard deviation, but you can tell whether MAX is doing what you want just by looking at the numbers.

Some functions don't actually require that you specify function arguments yourself. RAND, the random number generator in Excel 5, is an example of a function that doesn't need any sort of inputs as arguments. When RAND is placed in a worksheet cell, it puts a random number between 0 and 1 into the cell. For Figure 16.11, I have copied column C and pasted it into column F, put =10*RAND() into cell F1, and then copied this cell from F1 and pasted it into cells F2 through F10.

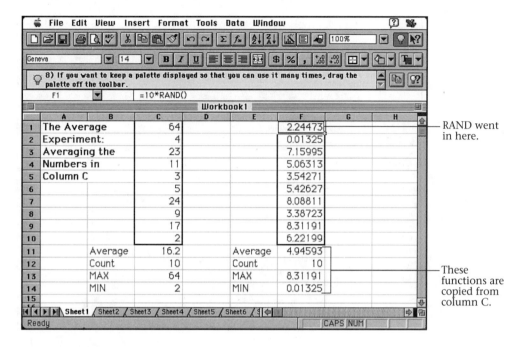

Figure 16.11   AVERAGE and other functions are applied to random numbers.

Because RAND gives you random numbers between 0 and 1, the average for this function over lots of samples should be one-half. Because I've multiplied RAND by 10, the averages should be ten times one-half, which is 5. If you look at the figure, you will see that the average is 4.94593, pretty close to 5 by anyone's standards. RAND, by the way, is a sort of self-operating function—every time you open a worksheet that has RAND in it, the random function generates a new set of numbers.

Higher Functions

If you click the Function Wizard button and begin scrolling around in the lists, you are likely to find all sorts of functions, many of them quite unfamiliar unless you took a variety of math courses in college. For example, if you took physics or statistics, you are likely to know a number of applications for the function SUMSQ, the sum of the squares of the numbers in a selected cell range (see Figure 16.12). This function won't, however, mean much to you if you were an English literature or even a business major. The list in the figure shows other functions (hyperbolic tangent, sum of products of elements of two vectors—try to guess which ones they are!) that you may not recognize as old friends unless you have some technical background, but you may take all this as reassurance that when you have to calculate something, Excel 5 has the function you need.

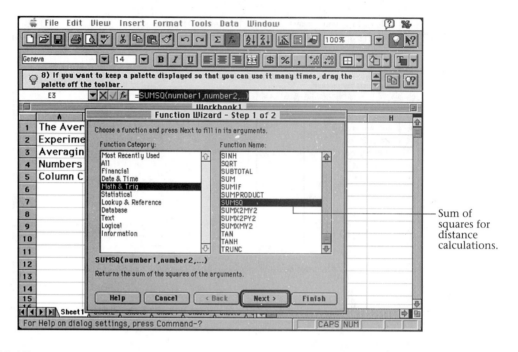

Figure 16.12   A long list of math functions.

Almost Programming: The IF Function

Figure 16.13 shows a setup to demonstrate an especially powerful function in Excel, the IF function. IF can select choices for a calculation based on input (that is, argument) conditions. The case under investigation mimics a real-life business case. In Massachusetts, there's no sales tax on clothing purchases below a certain price per item, but there is a sales tax on clothes that are perceived by the state legislature to be luxuries. The worksheet here is a bizarre hybrid of California and Massachusetts practice, incorporating California's ferocious 8 percent sales tax with a $200 luxury cutoff. In other words, I'm looking for a way to charge 8 percent sales tax in this worksheet on purchases of items that cost more than $200.

Because there is a sales tax charge if the purchase is more than $200, it makes sense to look at the function IF, found under the Logical function category. This function—unlike RAND, which is perfectly capable of looking after itself—needs three well-designed arguments to produce any results (see Figure 16.14).

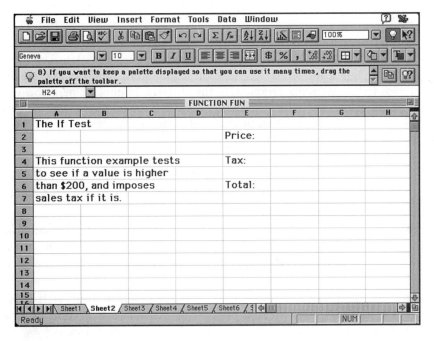

Figure 16.13   Sales tax and IF.

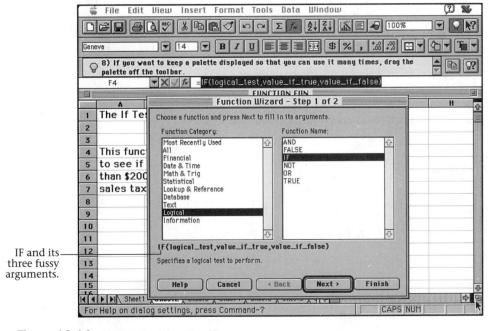

IF and its three fussy arguments.

Figure 16.14   Theological function IF.

Here's how you use IF:

◆ The first argument, "logical_test," is supposed to be an expression that will return either TRUE or FALSE as a value. The little underscore mark (_) connecting the words *logical* and *test* is necessary for programming purposes to make the whole expression seem like one word to the program. In our case here, the test is F2>199.99. That means the answer is TRUE if the number in cell F2 is 200 or more and FALSE if it's less than this value. That will decide which of the two values the function will plug into its cell.

Besides entering the IF test directly in this cell, you can write your test in some other cell and put the cell reference (by name or cell number) into this part of the argument. If you're going to change the test often, it's less work to modify the test outside of the actual function definition.

◆ The next argument, "value_if_true," is the expression that you want evaluated if the condition is true. In this case, the expression to evaluate is about 8 percent sales tax, so the expression is 0.08 times the contents of cell F2 if F2 is larger than 199.99 (see Figure 16.15).

◆ The last argument, "value_if_false," is pretty simple in this case. If the value in F2 is less than 200, there isn't any sales tax, so the value is 0. In other cases, you can put some sort of formula as this argument, but here it's not necessary.

What happens when you fire up all this complexity? Let's find out. In Figure 16.16, I try the number 125 in cell F2. The function returns zero for the sales tax, indicated by a little dash (–) instead of a the number 0 in the cell. With the number 248 in cell F2, the function decides that the value of the test is TRUE and calculates the 8 percent sales tax (see Figure 16.17).

It's possible by connecting IF statements to develop ways of looking up the right calculation for all sorts of complicated cases—you can have the result of one IF function appear in the logical test of a second or third IF function. Another way to deal with complicated cases is to use lookup tables, which will make a modest debut in Chapter 19.

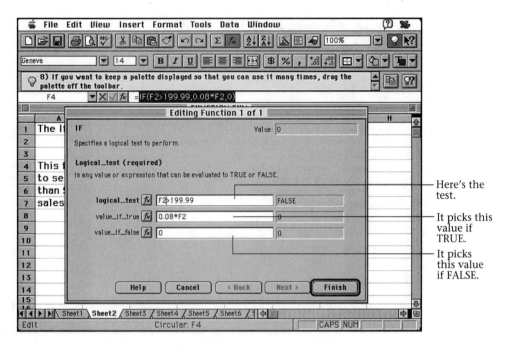

Figure 16.15 The internal machinery of IF.

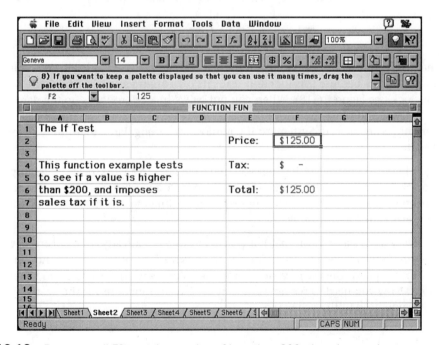

Figure 16.16 Because cell F2 contains a value of less than 200, there is no sales tax.

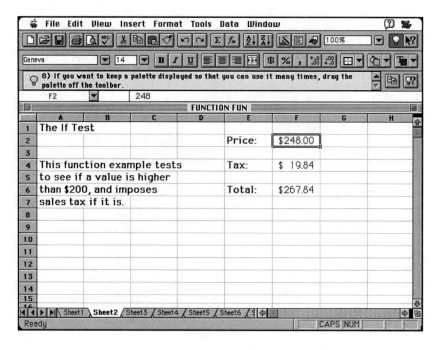

Figure 16.17   Because F2 contains a value that is greater than 199.99, you are charged sales tax.

The NOW Function

Another useful function is NOW. Like RAND, NOW can take care of itself—you don't have to specify arguments because this function reads its own arguments taken from the Macintosh System clock (see Figure 16.18). When you put NOW in a cell, it looks up the date and time from your Mac and plugs them into the cell (see Figure 16.19). It looks up, of course, whatever these numbers are on your System, so if you have the wrong date, it faithfully reports the wrong date.

It's a good idea to invoke NOW when you make changes to a worksheet, preferably with some notation that documents the changes. When you have a worksheet that can be accessed by other people on a network, this minimal effort at documentation and version identification will save everyone lots of trouble.

Almost every fancy calculation that has practical value has already been encapsulated in a function that's available in Excel 5. The Function Wizard helps you fill in function arguments (inputs) and explains the use of various functions. But there are functions, and there are functions. Now you need to see how you can use Excel's functions for the everyday calculations that you need in the real world.

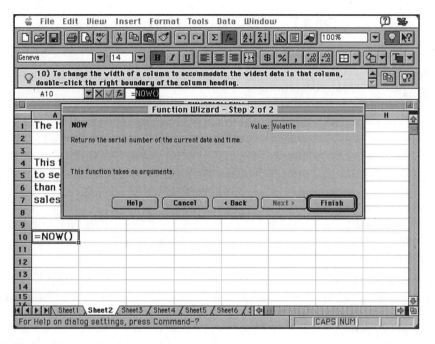

Figure 16.18   NOW...no arguments, okay?

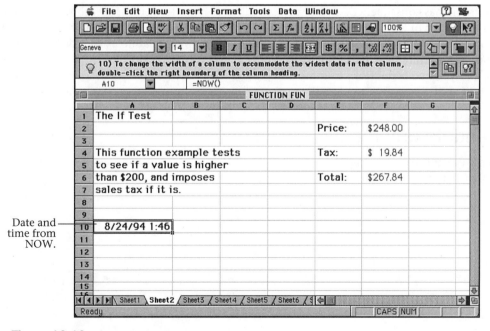

Date and
time from ——
NOW.

Figure 16.19   Putting NOW in a cell.

PMT, the Starting Point

It was once remarked by a famous person with a bad reputation as an economic predator that compound interest is the Eighth Wonder Of The World. In the United States—in which time-payment plans for nearly everything are a way of life—compound interest is nearly the dominant feature of society. The country as a whole is busy paying off the largest debt in the history of the planet (with interest on the debt ticking away, compounding, making an eventual pay-down completely implausible.) And individual families are typically enmeshed in monthly payments for everything from their houses to the smallest purchases.

You may think that it should be easy to do a payment calculation directly. After all, in the typical situation, you sign up to make monthly payments on a certain sum. Can't you just apply the interest rate per month to the balance and then add this to some fraction of the balance? Well, briefly, no—it doesn't work that way. The standard payment scheme is organized so that the first payments are always biased toward interest, and the later payments apply more to the balance.

The principle is that you always owe as much money as possible, consistent with eventually getting the loan paid back. On credit cards, for example, the minimum monthly payment pays off your purchases incredibly slowly. The fact is, if you have a department store credit card that charges 20 percent interest, the department store is in no hurry to see the balance paid off as long as you keep up payments—the store probably doesn't have any other investments that pay as good a return as you do.

This scenario has consequences, and as a result, I'll be doing some fervent preaching at various points in the rest of this chapter. You can probably survive by using dotted borders rather than solid borders around cells, and it won't ruin your life if you pick Palatino as your default font. But the game of time payments in modern America produces a well-defined set of winners and losers, and you had better learn its quite unforgiving rules. This part of the chapter is hard-core important stuff.

PMT and its arguments

The only difficult part of using PMT is getting used to its arguments and the convention for entering interest values. Take a look at Figure 16.20.

The payment function, PMT, appears in the middle of Excel's generous Financial function category. It takes the following five arguments:

◆ The first argument, "rate," is the interest rate per period for the loan. If you have an 8 percent car loan with monthly payments, the number you enter here isn't 8 or even .08 (.08 means 8%). The correct number to enter in this case would be .08 divided by 12. That's the interest rate per period because the period is a month. In the next few figures, I'm going to put in incorrect values for the arguments on purpose so that I can highlight this issue with figure callouts (see Figure 16.21).

If you're doing monthly payments, enter the interest rate by specifying it as =8%/12 (or whatever rate other than 8% you need). This gives Excel the correct number, and it gives you a format that makes it obvious when you select the cell.

◆ The next argument, "nper," is a little more straightforward because it stands for the number of periods for the loan payback. For example, it's 5 × 12 = 60 for a 5-year car loan, or 30 × 12 = 360 for a 30-year mortgage.

◆ The third argument, "pv," stands for principal value. It's the amount you're borrowing now (see Figure 16.22). In PMT terminology, the situation is upside down from consumer finance—Excel is really figuring out how much you should pay each month to have a certain total. Note in this figure that entering the wrong interest value gives you a monthly payment bigger than the principal value. This can happen with certain unsavory sports bets to underworld characters, but as yet, it's still a daydream for consumer credit companies.

◆ The fourth argument, "fv," stands for future value and is the total of all your payments and interest on the payments. Because you're paying off a loan, however, the future value of your payments is zero. You don't have to enter a zero here because if you just don't give a future value, Excel assumes it's zero. This assumption forces this function to be payments on a loan rather than an annuity (a type of investment).

◆ The last argument, "type," can be either 0 or 1. If payments are due at the end of a period, enter 0 (the usual case, so that if you don't enter anything, it's assumed to be 0). In some payment plans, it states explicitly that payments are due at the beginning of a period, so you put in 1 as an argument.

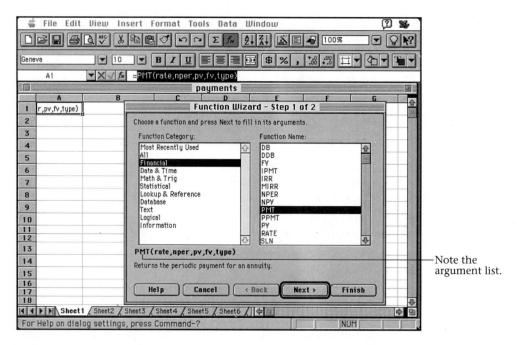

Figure 16.20 PMT, the main payment function.

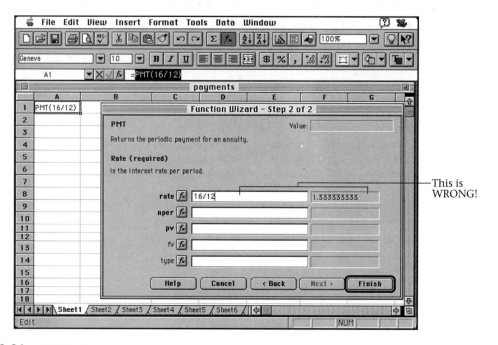

Figure 16.21 Filling in the rate.

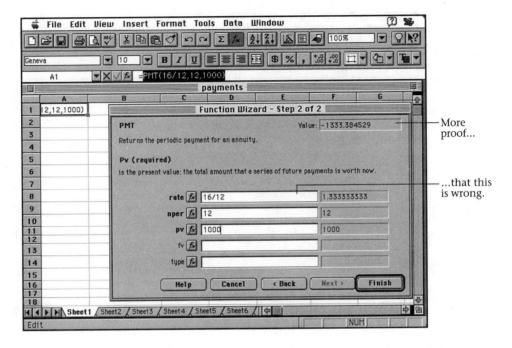

Figure 16.22 Nper and pv, the other loan arguments.

PMT at work

In Figure 16.23, Excel 5 gives you the monthly payments for a loan of $1,000 at 16 percent annual interest. The standard format for results from PMT is that numbers are reported in red and in parentheses for negative values (meaning that each payment is a negative in your checking account).

That's the payment per month—$90.73. In Figure 16.24, I've popped open another cell in which I multiply the monthly payment by 12 to get the total.

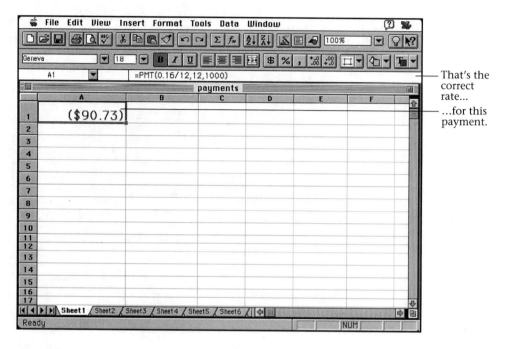

That's the correct rate...

...for this payment.

Figure 16.23 PMT results for a one-year loan.

Payment total.

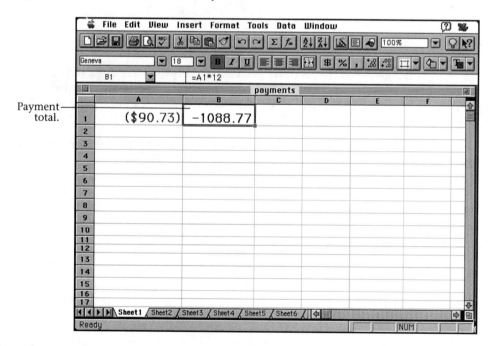

Figure 16.24 Total payments and effective rate.

Other payment aspects

Astute readers may inquire, "Hey, what's going on here?" At an interest rate of 16 percent, you may think that a one-year $1,000 loan would call for $160 worth of interest rather than the $88.77 shown here (again, Excel reports the total as negative because you pay it). But keep in mind that the principal on the loan is being paid down continuously, so for most of the duration of the loan, you don't owe the whole $1,000 and would be paying interest on the smaller balance.

Also notice that the total amount paid back seems about right. The loan was short term (one year), the amount was $1,000, and the amount paid back was $1,088.77. Generally, if you enter an argument such as interest incorrectly, you get a result that's way out of line.

The effective interest rate is a more subtle matter (see Figure 16.25). The annual rate quoted was 16 percent. For the purposes of a loan calculation, this rate is divided by 12 into a monthly rate. If this rate were left to compound every month, with no payments, the total on the loan would be

Total = $1000 x (1+16%/12) x (1+16%/12) . . . (12 times)

That total would be $117.20. The effective interest rate, called the A.P.R. (annualized percentage rate) in consumer-loan jargon, is thus 17.2 percent. It's just one of the little wrinkles of life in the United States that the law allows lenders to put the annual rate in big print but insists that the A.P.R.—for all practical purposes the real rate—be put in fine print (and/or buried) somewhere in the ad. Car leasing ads are an especially rich source of calculational amusement in this regard.

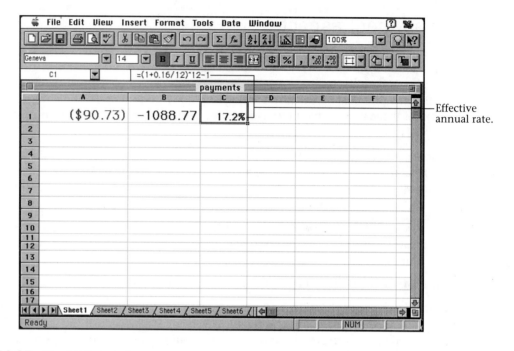

Figure 16.25   The A.P.R. in action.

Real-Life Payments

To give you some practice in using PMT, I'll run a few examples drawn from everyday loan situations. After you see how easy it is to plug in the arguments, you'll be old friends with PMT in no time.

Financing a computer

Because you've bought this Office book for the Mac, you are presumably familiar with Apple's pricing policies and perhaps its financial plans. North America has millions of people faithfully making payments to Apple credit every month, often with tears in their eyes. The tears arise because it's easy to find yourself paying off a $2,400 balance on a computer with a current street price of $800—Apple's policy of introducing new models at a furious clip and then dumping prices on the old models has often left the Macintosh faithful holding the bag, so to speak. I got hundreds of pieces of hate mail when the Mac IIvx appeared because I gave it a glowing review in *Macworld,* and then Apple dumped the price about five weeks later. For the record, I got sandbagged right along with the readers because Apple isn't particularly forth-coming to the press (people who work for Mac magazines have to buy their Macs in stores just like everyone else).

So check out the example in Figure 16.26. This is your basic IIvx story, by the numbers. It includes $3,000 for the system (with a nice monitor and a printer), Apple's stiff consumer interest rate of 20 percent per year, and a three-year payment schedule. Notice that because of the fairly high interest rate, the $3,000 turns into more than $4,000 in payments over three years.

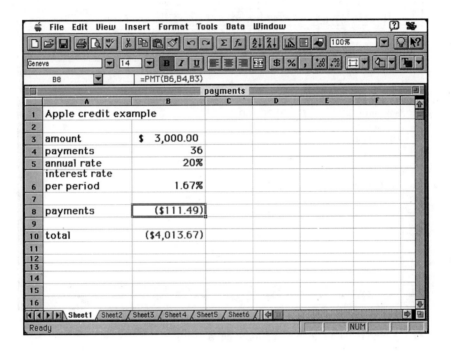

Figure 16.26   Consumer credit from Apple.

Financing a house

Home-loan calculation proceeds along the same lines, except that there's a ton of money involved, instead of a mere sack, and the long-term nature of home financing produces special sensitivity to interest rates. Although I live in California, where the current price of an aban-doned dog kennel with roof problems is half a million dollars, I've modestly chosen a mort-gage case with numbers more in line with Kansas City.

The shocker here is the payment total over the years (see Figure 16.27). Looking at it briefly from the bank's point of view, the bank is giving you $130,000 that it could instead be investing elsewhere. If it invested the money at 6 percent or so, it could expect that money to double in about 15 years. It needs that kind of investment performance from its investment in you. In this case, please note that if you can find an interest rate of 7.9 percent instead of 8 percent, the lower rate saves you about $3,000 over the loan term. That's because 30 years is a long time for loan interest to be compounding.

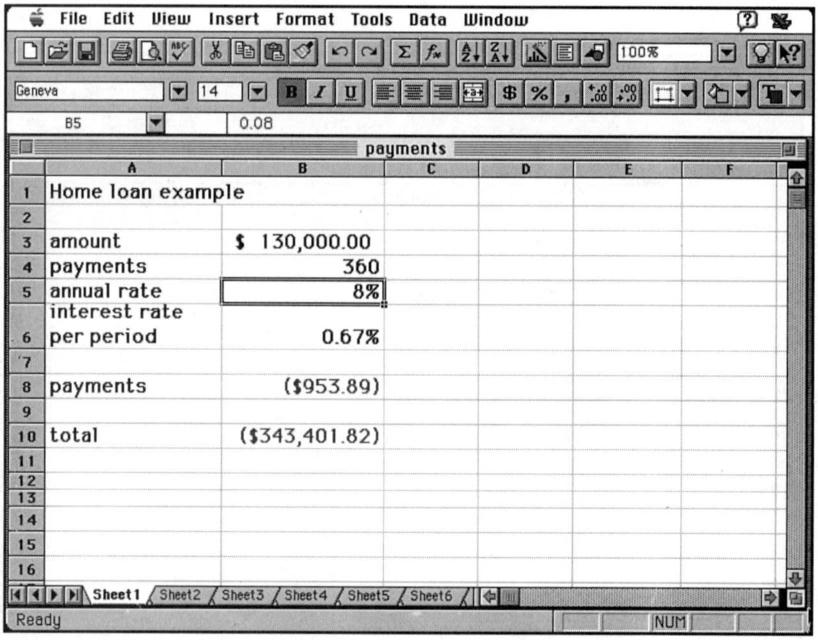

Figure 16.27   A nice mid-American home loan, circa 1985.

Very few people in America in the 1990s can expect to make it to the last payment on a 30-year mortgage. Thus it's a subject of considerable curiosity to determine how much of a loan has actually been paid back after a certain number of years. Excel 5 has some built-in functions to answer this question (see Figure 16.28): PPMT gives you payments on principal, and IPMT gives the interest amount in payments. These functions use the same function arguments as PMT, except that you need to specify which payment you want split into interest/principal.

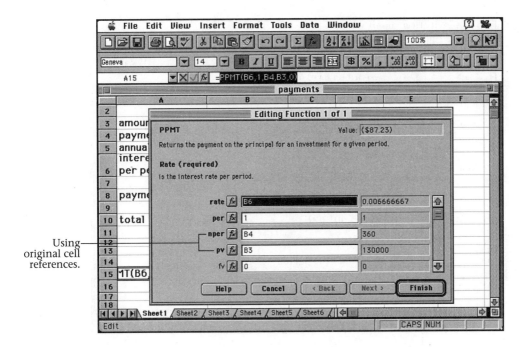

Figure 16.28 Use PPMT to determine how much you've already paid on your principal.

What you see in Figure 16.29 is that at the beginning of a 30-year loan, most of your payments are going to go to interest service. By the time you're making the last payment on a mortgage, you're paying off nearly pure principal, but at the beginning, that's not the case. If you buy a house, shell out nearly $1,000 a month for two years, and then sell it, you find that the $20,000 you have paid on the loan has made a dent of only about $2,000 in the loan principal.

That last little observation isn't particularly encouraging, unless you're a stable citizen who wants to settle down, buy a house at age 32, make payments for 30 years, retire, and get buried in the basement by your grieving but equity-rich descendants. Using PMT, you can find ways around this.

Figure 16.30 shows the same amount financed for 15 rather than 30 years. Changing the time scale of the loan by a factor of 2 doesn't double the payments—it increases them by about 30 percent. And look at the loan total for payments. If you can find another $290 a month, in this example, you can save $120,000 in total payments (not to mention that you own the house after 15 years, when you're still spry enough to water-ski or break your collarbone on a dirt bike).

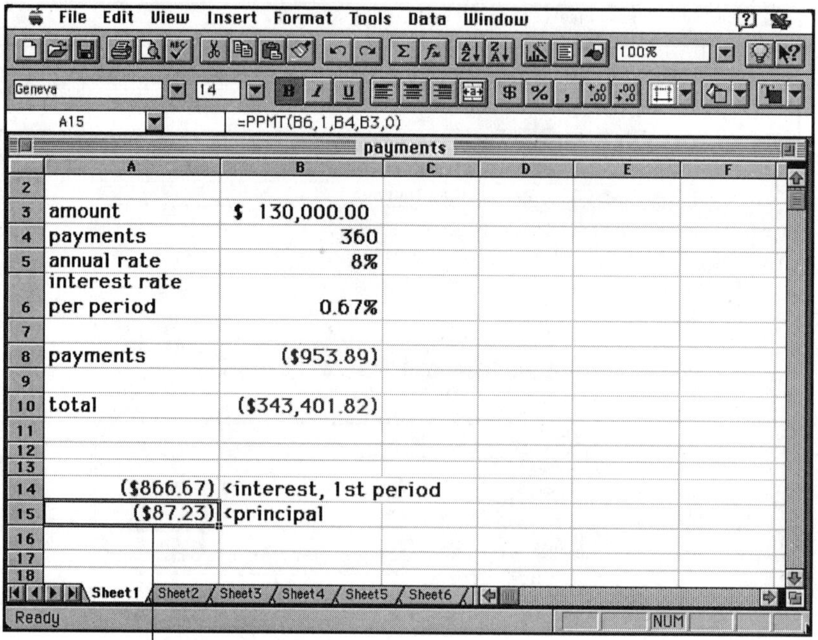

The shocking truth.

Figure 16.29   Home loan: the impact of 30 years.

Notice, comparing Figures 16.29 and 16.30, that the difference between the monthly payments in the two examples is the difference in the amount paid on principal. If you go for the shorter-term mortgage, you get back all the "extra" part of the monthly payments (that's the extra compared to the 30-year standard) if you sell the house after a few years. Also, practically all home loans these days have a provision for sending in extra principal payments along with your standard monthly payment. This opportunity works out nicely if you don't feel that you can commit to a regular higher payment schedule. The main point is that you should do everything possible to avoid owing large sums of money for 30 years with interest compounding in the background.

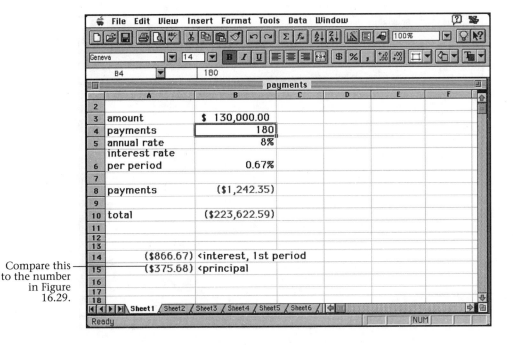

Compare this to the number in Figure 16.29.

Figure 16.30   The same mortgage in 15 years.

More on Financial Functions

Microsoft has seen fit to include a stunning array of financial functions, from special functions for comparing T-Bill yields to standard bonds through depreciation, to different internal-rate-of-return functions. (This is probably because Microsoft employees themselves need these functions. Hundreds of them became veritable plutocrats when the company made a public stock offering.)

To pick your way through the list, just click the Help button in the Function Wizard. The gigantic machinery (the Help system in Excel is bigger than the sum total of Mac software from the Mac's first two years) of Microsoft Help grinds into place. For financial functions, there's really a point to seeking out Help (see Figure 16.31) because it provides detailed examples for using all the functions. Click the Financial Functions topic in the Help window and just scroll through the list, looking for functions that you may need (see Figure 16.32). If Microsoft thought to include functions for converting decimal dollars back and forth from fractions (useful for stock market prices like 13 1/8), you can expect that nearly every useful business function has been put on the list.

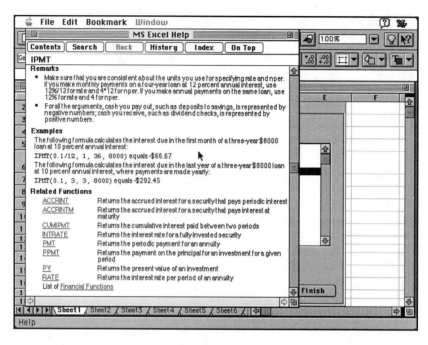

Figure 16.31 Help for these functions includes real examples.

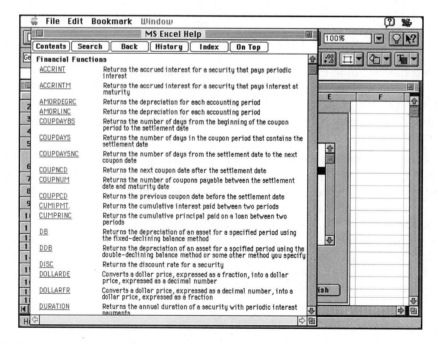

Figure 16.32 The Financial Functions Help list.

Now that you have a familiarity with functions and how to use them for practical day-by-day living, it's time to see how you can set up some protection for all the formulas and functions that you have created. In case something is wrong in your worksheets, you want to be able to find and correct the problem easily. The rest of the chapter tells you how to protect your worksheets.

What's in a Cell Name?

In the old days, a cell in a worksheet was called something like R5C3, standing for row 5 column 3, or C5, standing for exactly the same location.

Now just think about creating a nice big worksheet, perhaps a hundred rows by a hundred columns, full of financial functions that depend on the results of previous calculations. You take it and show it to a co-worker, who comes back the next day to state that the computed cash flows don't match up with the actual receipts and invoices for the time period in question. Uh-oh. Now what?

If the formulas have arguments in terms of AB83 and so forth (see Figure 16.33), you have your work cut out for the next couple of days. If, on the other hand, you used Excel's cell name function (see Figure 16.34), you have the advantage that your formulas will be readable.

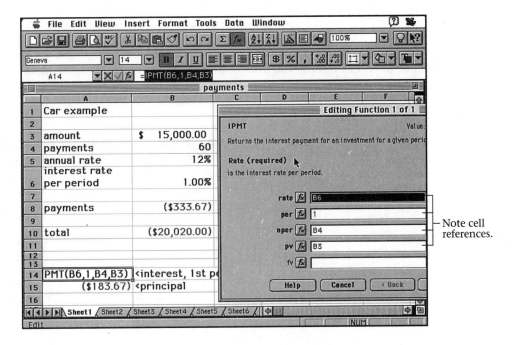

Figure 16.33 Plain old cell references.

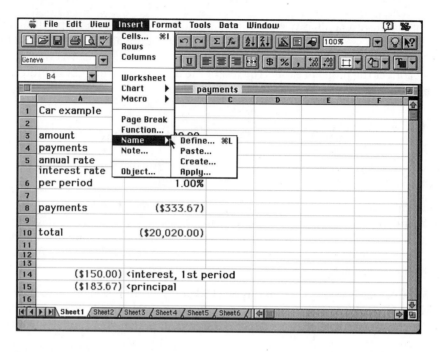

Figure 16.34   Defining cell names.

There are many different ways to implement a cell name plan. I'll show you my way, which I think makes for faster auditing, and Microsoft's way, which makes for more thorough documentation. After you see these examples, you'll probably be inclined to make up a cell name convention of your own. Your choice just depends on the naming style that you are most likely to use and remember.

I like to name cells for the argument names that they take in functions (see Figure 16.35). That is, if a financial function takes a rate argument, I find the cell that has the number for rate and name it "rate." Dazzlingly original, eh? The big advantage of this naming convention is that when you highlight a cell with a function in it and then click the Function Wizard button, you can look at the list of arguments and tell right away if the correct cells have been assigned (see Figure 16.36).

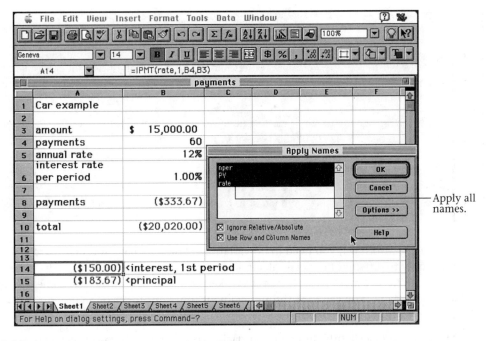

Figure 16.35   Create cell names and then apply them.

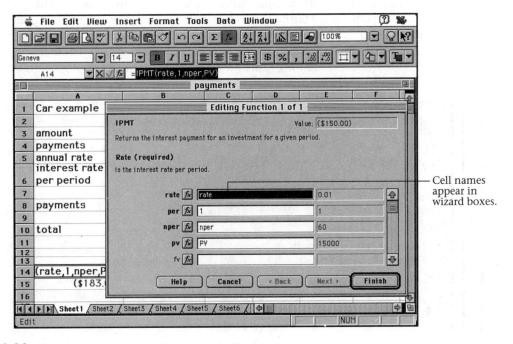

Figure 16.36   Matching cell names with argument names.

What's in the Name *Audit*?

It's really too bad that such a useful function as auditing has such a repellent name. Personally, I associate the word *audit* either with taking classes for no credit or with scrounging up mountains of receipts for presentation to the IRS. From pointless to painful, audit covers it all.

However, worksheet auditing—setting up a worksheet so that you can easily find errors and navigate around it—is absolutely necessary if you're going to be using Excel as more than a simple desktop calculator. Auditing helps you decide how to document your own work, and if done correctly, lets you read other people's worksheets. After you start making worksheets in which results of some functions are used as arguments for other functions, your choices are to use proper auditing methods or to create a hopeless uninterpretable mess.

With a big worksheet, you need to do variations. You may have several different interest rates that apply to different financial calculations. In this case, you can name cells "rate-loan1" and "rate-loan2." The main point is that if you keep the first part of the cell name the same as the argument name, you can look through all your functions for error arguments just by reviewing them with the Function Wizard.

Microsoft takes a slightly different approach to cell names. Microsoft prefers to spell out whole words (see Figure 16.37), such as "Total_payments." When you do names with multiple words like this, it's preferable to use an underscore character (_) rather than a blank space between the words. This underscore business is a convention both of the programming language C and Microsoft's operating system Windows. Although the Macintosh itself can support blanks in names of files and folders—this is an unprecedented innovation in computers, even at this advanced stage of the computing game—it is best to keep with a naming tradition that can be exchanged with other programs.

Cell Naming

The cell naming convention is just a way to make a worksheet readable. It's a notorious problem in programming that a program you wrote even a few days ago becomes very hard to understand unless you document every line by writing little explanations to yourself about what you were trying to do. And reading someone else's program is like deciphering Etruscan. (As a piece of cultural background, you should know that archaeologists have Etruscan dice from 700 B.C. with the words for one through six on the sides, and they still can't be sure what the numbers are.)

When you set up a worksheet, you're writing a program whether you know it or not. If you're working on your own, it will save you time to do decent documentation; if you're working inside a company, doing a good job of documenting your work will keep co-workers from cursing your name for eternity. So name those cells, okay? And attach a note to a cell every time you do something even moderately tricky.

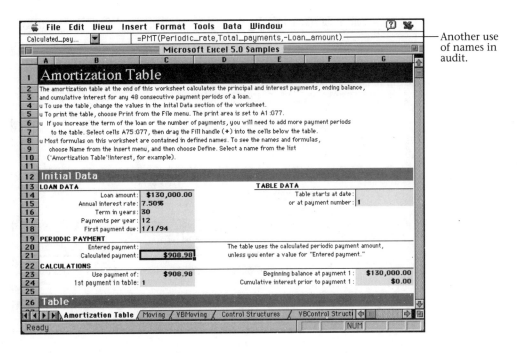

Figure 16.37   A Microsoft-style cell name.

The Auditing Toolbar

Figure 16.38 shows Excel 5's Auditing toolbar, which you can put onscreen by checking its box in the Toolbars dialog box from the View menu. In this example, I've checked the Large Buttons option in the dialog box so that the toolbar is big enough for you to see the contents easily in a standard figure, and I have also turned off the Standard and Formatting toolbars.

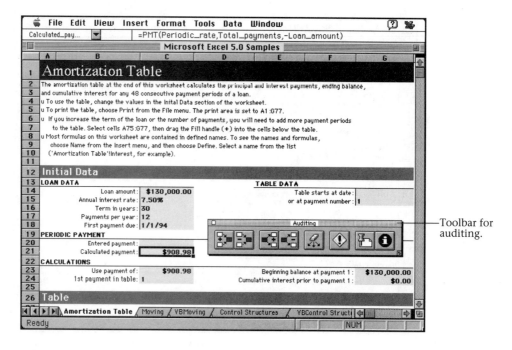

Figure 16.38 The large button version of the Auditing toolbar.

Arrows to everywhere

As you will see, most of the buttons on the Auditing toolbar feature arrows. Excel keeps track of connections between cells, and when you want to see the connections, you can click these buttons. You can also call down Auditing options from the Tools menu, but frankly, the toolbar is faster and more fun.

Here's the simplest possible application, or cell reference tracing, based on a worksheet supplied by Microsoft as a sample. I've selected the cell with a calculated payment and clicked the first button on the toolbar, which is the Trace Precedents button (see Figure 16.39). *Precedents* are the cells that send values to the cell that you've selected. In some cases, a precedent can be just a cell that's used in an arithmetic calculation to give the answer in a selected cell, or a precedent can be a cell containing a function argument.

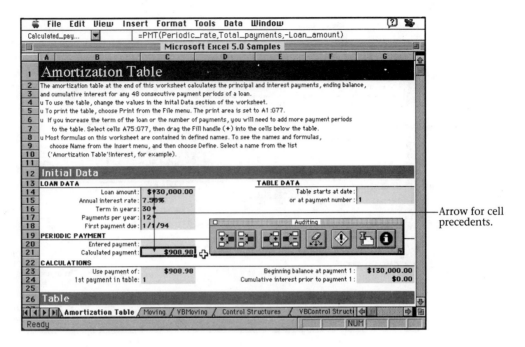

Figure 16.39   Tracing the arguments of a PMT function.

Notice that the arrow to this cell has a bunch of little bumps on the arrow line. Every bump indicates a cell precedent. It probably would have been clearer if Microsoft had chosen to use sets of arrows of different colors, but as things stand now, you just have to look for the bumps.

There are two ways to remove the arrows, which start cluttering up the screen after a while. The second button from the left on the Auditing toolbar removes the precedent arrows to a particular selected cell. The fifth button from the left is supposed to indicate an eraser, and it removes all arrows on the worksheet.

If you're a cell, then you're either an independent cell, a precedent cell, or a dependent cell. When you select a cell and click the Trace Dependents button, the arrows show you all the cells that use the information in the cell that you selected (see Figure 16.40). This is a pretty powerful trick—when you find that your numbers have gone unaccountably strange, start clicking cells near the top of your worksheet and begin tracing dependents. It's usually the fastest way to find which number was entered incorrectly, on purpose or not.

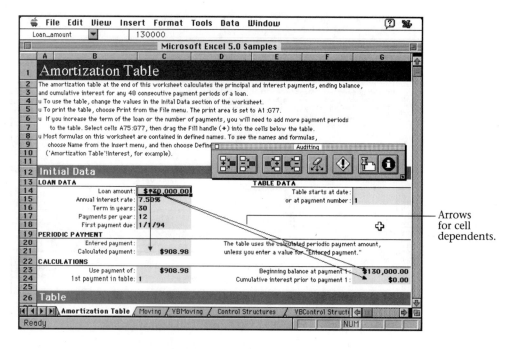

Figure 16.40 Tracing cells that depend on a selected cell.

Adding and checking information

The Auditing toolbar has two more useful buttons. One is simply the Note button (second from the right) for attaching cell notes. A big argument for leaving the Auditing toolbar onscreen all the time is that it encourages you to use notes. Having this button present means that you're just a single click away from practicing a good habit. Hey, how often does that happen?

The last button on the right, the little *i* button, gets you the Show Info Window, as shown in Figure 16.41. Show Info gives you the note's contents, the formula in the cell, and the cell name (if the cell has an assigned name). If you have the trace arrows turned on, and you are looking at the contents of the Info window at the same time, you have about all the information that Excel can give you. As a rule of thumb, if you see a whole collection of arrows when you trace dependents (see Figure 16.42), it means that you ought to take a deep breath and fill out a cell note.

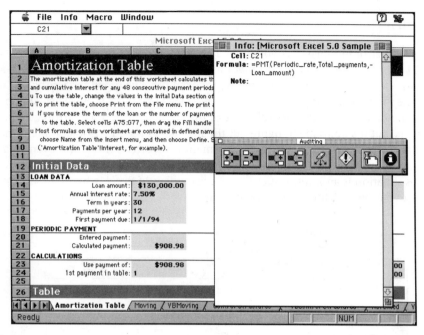

Figure 16.41   Click the *i* button for the Info window.

More cell dependent tracing.

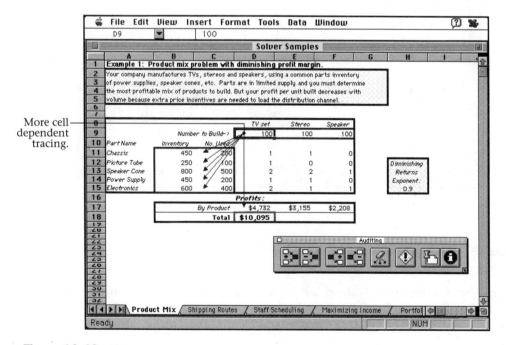

Figure 16.42   This situation calls for a note.

Error alert!

If you get an error message after you enter a formula, the Auditing toolbar is ready to help you, sort of. I say *sort of* because the information isn't really going to provide you with a detailed diagnostic (see Figure 16.43). In this figure, for example, I've typed the wrong cell name for one of the function arguments and clicked the Trace Error button. But Excel doesn't actually give me a message, such as *wrong cell name* or the equivalent. It draws arrows to the cell precedents, but it's up to me to figure out the mistake in the function argument that has been entered incorrectly. In fact, because the argument is incorrect, there isn't even an arrow to a cell. I have to inspect the arguments one by one to see which of them is missing an arrow. Still, this situation is an improvement on the early days of Excel, when you were obliged to construct your own auditing strategies by yourself.

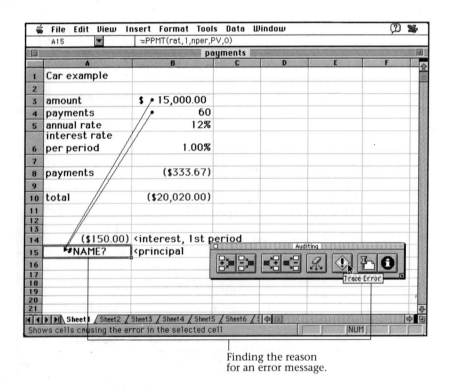

Finding the reason
for an error message.

Figure 16.43   The Auditing toolbar's Trace Error button in action.

Because it has so many useful features and because *you should use it,* the Auditing toolbar has a special place in Toolbar Land. It's the only toolbar that you can call up with its own command, instead of using the Toolbars dialog box. Under the Tools menu, choose the Auditing command, which, in turn, displays several choices, including Show Auditing Toolbar (see Figure 16.44). In honor of this special status, here's some advice so significant that I made it into a caution.

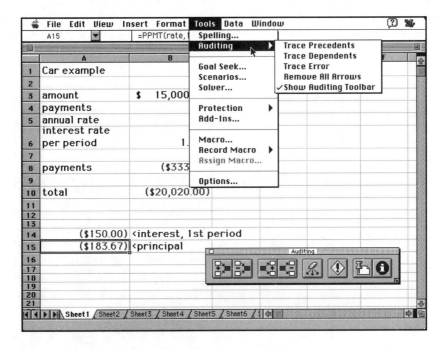

Figure 16.44   The Show Auditing Toolbar command in the main Auditing menu.

> **!** **Caution:** As you use Excel, you will discover many occasions when you are glad that you attached a cell note to a cell so that you can see later what you were trying to do when you set up a worksheet. On the other hand, there will never be an occasion when you regret adding a cell note. Cell notes don't take up much space, they're convenient, and they're more efficient than scattering text boxes all throughout a worksheet. Think of cell notes as a trail of crumbs, and you're either Hansel or Gretel trying to get home.

Looking at Formulas

Buried down in the Tools menu, under Options, on the View tab, is a little check box that's also useful when you're trying to interpret a worksheet. The Formulas check box, in the Window Options area (see Figure 16.45), makes the cells in your worksheet display formulas instead of results (see Figure 16.46). Among other things, you can use this display to check whether you've done your homework in assigning helpful and consistent cell names.

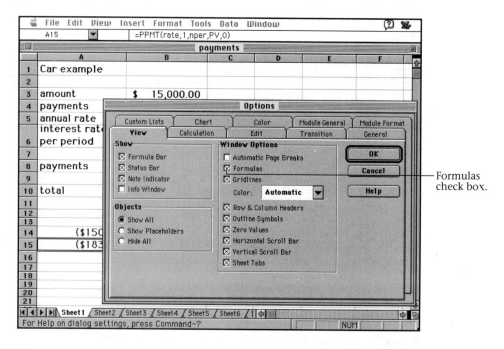

Figure 16.45   Using the View tab for auditing.

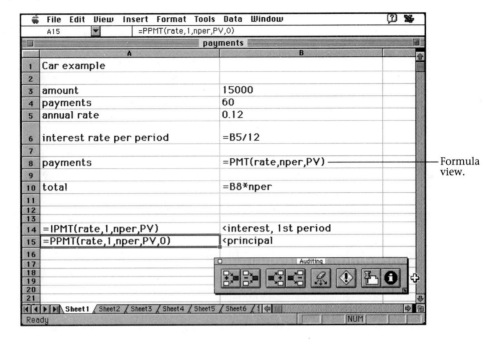

Figure 16.46   Worksheet showing formulas, not results.

In the rest of the Excel section of the book, I discuss features and expect that you'll use them because they're necessary. The auditing features are also necessary, but they tend to be underused for the same reason that bills get paid late and motor oil doesn't get changed every 3,000 miles. The simplest way to remind yourself to document your work is to keep the Auditing toolbar open as your standard worksheet default display. If you document your worksheets only out of guilt, the toolbar will at least be a little nagging grandmotherly reminder to put some cell notes in place.

Whew! You have just covered *lots* of information in this chapter. You have learned about functions and how to enter them in your worksheets. You have looked at how to figure out interest and principal payments by using special functions. And you have learned how to label your functions so that you can find errors if you have made some in your worksheets.

If you want to take a break, I don't blame you. But come back soon so that you can explore databases in all their wonderful forms in Excel.

Chapter 17

Manipulating Databases

The Excel 5 features for database management are among the strongest arguments for upgrading. Unless you're running the billing system for General Motors' network of suppliers, an Excel 5 database has enough power to do the job. A great variety of tasks that used to call for a stand-alone database can now be accomplished effectively in Excel. As you'll see, quick manipulation even of large databases is possible with just the training you get in this chapter. You're going to learn about the following points:

- ◆ The Form View of list data
- ◆ Searching with a form
- ◆ Filtering and AutoFiltering databases
- ◆ The Advanced Filter system
- ◆ Automatic totals and subtotals

Important Terms

Databases are surrounded with a certain mystique. People who have no problem with word processors or spreadsheets can suddenly feel a surge of terror at the mention of the word *database*. For this reason, there are thousands of "database consultants" who work with businesses to set up databases. Have you ever heard of a word processing consultant?

I'm going to make this simple. There are only two key concepts that you need to understand about Excel databases: *record* and *field.*

Your name and address make up a typical database record. If you add your phone number, it's in *your* record. If you add your favorite color and everything you bought from Sears last year, this information still gets entered in *your* record. A database is just a collection of these records.

In the records I'm describing, however, your first name is an example of a field. Your phone number is another field. All the catalog numbers of your stuff from Sears are other fields. Just as a database is a collection of records, a record is a collections of fields.

Excel versus Other Databases

The reason databases are thought of as confusing is that most serious commercial databases are *relational* databases, which include their own programming language. The database in Excel is a simple list, although if you want, you can do some fairly fancy programming with Excel macros (see Chapter 18).

The big difference is a matter of design. Back in the late 1970s and early 1980s, computer memory was a terribly scarce resource. Database designers decided that it was a waste of memory to have lots of redundant fields and records, so they designed relational databases as a way around this shortage of memory. In a relational database, instead of keeping all the information in one big list, the database consists of many little databases that are linked. For example, a relational database may use social security numbers as a link. It may have a name and address list and then a separate list of your Sears purchases, all linked by a social security number field in each list. The database can be expanded to include any other sort of information (credit card data, finance history) in separate lists, again linked by social security number. When you look up a particular item in a relational database, the program uses the link information to find what you need. Each piece of information is stored in only one place, and a well-designed program can use all sorts of memory management tricks to speed up searching.

The catch in this arrangement is that relational databases are harder to set up and harder to modify. If you take the brute-force approach of keeping absolutely everything in a simple list (this is called a flat-file database, as opposed to a relational one), the database is simple to set up and child's play to modify. In principle, this flat-file approach lacks some of the possible speed tricks of relational databases and results in bigger files, but memory is now cheap and Macs get faster every year, so it's not much of a problem in practice. The database in Excel isn't as fast as, say, Panorama or FileMaker Pro, but it's refreshingly straightforward.

Setting Up

All you have to do to set up a database in Excel 5 is to pick a set of fields and enter them into the first row of a new workbook (see Figure 17.1). And—here's some good news—you don't even have to get the fields correct the first time. You can change the field order and add or delete fields any time you like by using standard spreadsheet methods.

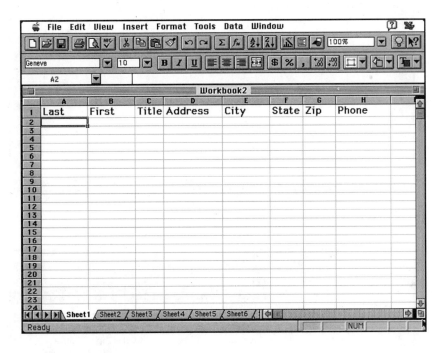

Figure 17.1 Defining an Excel database record.

When you fill in data under this first row, Excel 5 understands that this worksheet is a database (see Figure 17.2). In earlier versions of Excel, you had to define a range of cells as a database by using a command from the Data menu. Excel 5 has enough built-in intelligence to spot a database. In Excel's internal terminology, this data structure is usually just called a *list*, probably because Microsoft sells the much grander product FoxBase Pro for heavy-duty database work.

Filling in some sample fictitious data (note the required-by-law nonfunctional 555 phone numbers), I have constructed a small but usable example database (see Figure 17.3). There really is a Bob Bughunter at Microsoft, but he's too busy to answer his mail or the phone. (Microsoft claims to have put nearly a million man-hours into debugging Windows 4.0 and six months in beta-testing Excel 5.) Okay, I made that up about Bob.

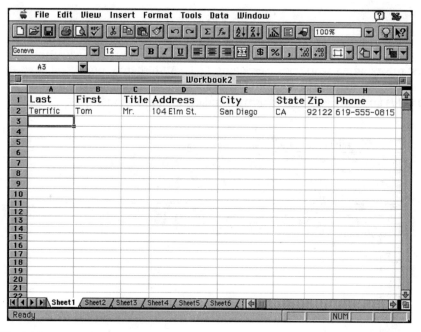

Figure 17.2 Adding to the list.

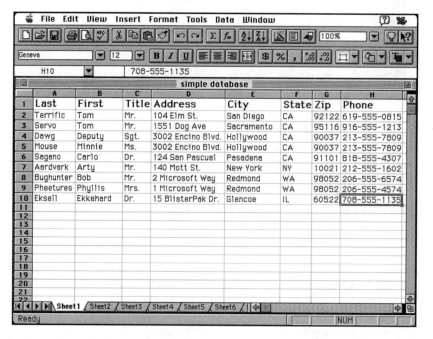

Figure 17.3 A small sample Excel database.

Using a Form View

After you construct a bigger list than this pitiful little thing, you may find it easier to look at your work with a Form view. After you pick the Form command from the Data menu (see Figure 17.4), you get a window with a view of one record at a time (you need to have at least one cell selected inside the database range for this technique to work). This screen shows the first record because I haven't given any other instructions. You can step through the records one at a time by clicking the Find Next button, or you can do something a little more ambitious by clicking the Criteria button (see Figure 17.5).

To look for a record with an address in New York, type NY as the entry for State in this window and click the Find Next button. This action produces the screen shown in Figure 17.6.

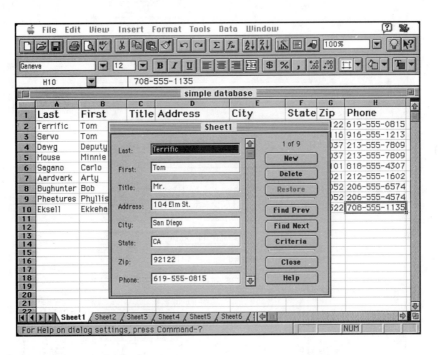

Figure 17.4   Form view of a single record.

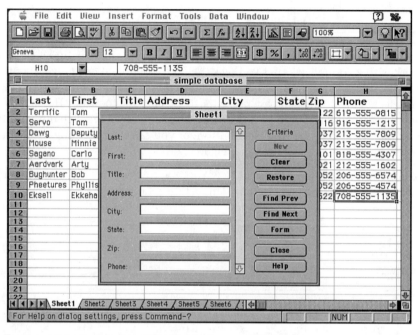

Figure 17.5 Using Criteria to find individual records.

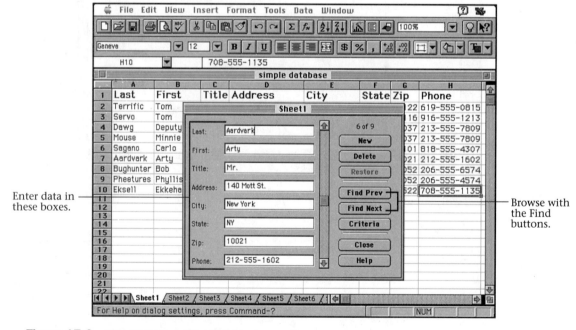

Enter data in these boxes.

Browse with the Find buttons.

Figure 17.6 Using Criteria to find individual records.

Here are a few points to keep in mind when you search with the Form window:

◆ Sometimes when you click Find Next, Excel beeps at you. This may just mean that the record you're trying to find is *ahead* of the current record in the list. In that case, you may have to re-enter the Criteria dialog box and choose Find Previous. If you get beeped again, there may not be a record that corresponds to your search criteria.

◆ The search may find multiple records. To see the records, step through them with the Find Next button.

◆ If you find a record and start to make a change in it, you can change your mind and retrieve the original field contents by clicking the Restore button. This doesn't work if you make a change and press Enter or Return—in that case the change is accepted by the database.

Sorting

Under the Data menu is Sort, another useful option (see Figure 17.7). The Sort dialog box is self-explanatory, but it's worth thinking about Sort as an alternative to searching. In the preceding example, I was searching for records with different State fields. Another way to do this—a faster way, for that matter—is simply to sort the whole list on the State field. You simply select the whole list, choose Sort, watch Excel rearrange the original list, and then look through the records grouped by state.

For further efficiency, you could have Excel perform several sorts at the same time. If you pick Sort By State and also choose Then By Zip, you will have a list in which the entries in the State field are internally organized by the Zip field.

For optimal use of Sorting, it helps to have some way to get a list back to its original order. You can create a new column (select the first column and press Cmd-I), name it Index, and fill in this column with the numbers 1, 2, 3, and so on just by typing 1 and 2 as the first two column entries and then dragging the cross cursor (the trick from Chapter 13). You can sort to your heart's content and then get back to the original order by sorting on Index.

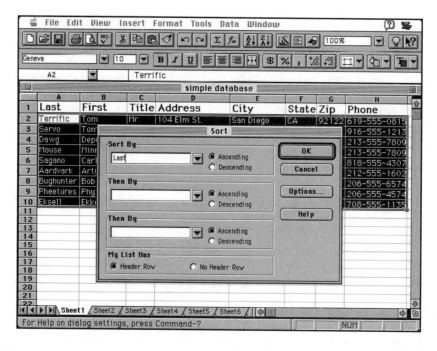

Figure 17.7   The Sort dialog box with many options.

List Filtering

Searching by using a Form view really works best if you expect to turn up only a few related records. If your search criteria will eventually find 50 records out of 2,000, it's a pretty tedious business to click through them all with the Find Next button. For big search jobs, try filtering instead. Under the Data menu (see Figure 17.8), there are two snappy new Filter choices: AutoFilter and Advanced Filter.

AutoFilter

If you pick AutoFilter, a world of convenience awaits you. As shown in Figure 17.9, Excel attaches little scrolling-list arrows to every field in your first row (the row that defines the fields). You may need to rearrange some column widths because Excel puts the arrows right over the column headings.

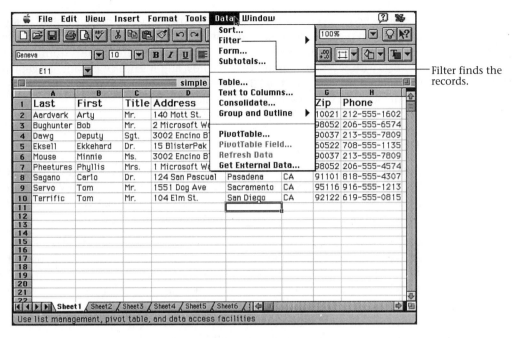

Figure 17.8   Filter is an effective alternative to searching in Form.

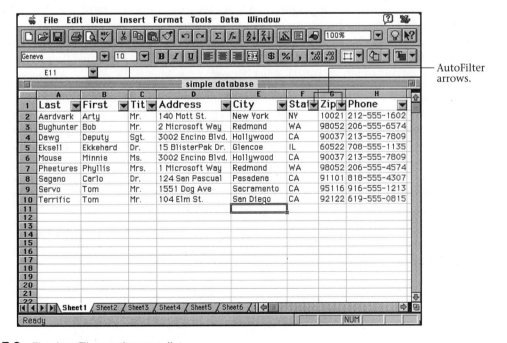

Figure 17.9   The AutoFilter option on a list.

But the list attached to each arrow has plenty of power because it's a list of all possible choices for filtering. If you pick CA from the State list (see Figure 17.10), Excel gives you a list containing only the California entries (see Figure 17.11). This procedure is also stunningly fast—I've tried it on lists with several thousand data records, and it's nearly instant. To get back to the original unfiltered list, just pick the Filter command again and you see that Show All is now an active option. Choose Show All to get the whole list back.

Advanced Filter

You may want to find all kinds of specific information in a large list. I say *large* here because AutoFilter can find anything you want, at warp speed, from several thousand records or more. If you filter on two or three fields, it can certainly get the data that you want onto the 20 records or so that can be displayed easily onscreen.

For bigger jobs, you may prefer the Advanced Filter option. To use Advanced Filter, you have to set up a separate range with field names and the criteria that you want to use for filtering. In Figure 17.12, I have picked Zip as one field and Title as another, although you can include as many fields as you like. The Zip criterion is >90000, meaning that I want to find records with a Zip greater than 90000, and the Title criterion is entered as ="Mr." Please note that Excel displays this field as "Mr." in the cell onscreen, but the equal sign and quotation marks are necessary to make the filter pick out the right text selections.

After you have your criteria properly set up in a range, you can invoke the Advanced Filter option. Advanced Filter (see Figure 17.13) asks you for the range of the list, the range of the criteria, and a range where it should put the resulting filtered list. This last option is actually pretty convenient because it means that you can keep the original list intact in its original location while the filtered list is given its own range. You can keep tinkering with criteria without having to restore the basic list between experiments.

The results of this filtering operation appear in Figure 17.14. It's not clear why this option is called Advanced Filter, except that it's not very clearly explained in either the Help system or the Excel manual, so perhaps it's intended for advanced users only. As a bit of design philosophy, you may consider making smaller lists where some presorting is built into the organization. For example, given that Excel keeps all this data in workbooks with multiple worksheets, you may want to associate single worksheets with individual states if you have thousands and thousands of records. At first glance this may seem cumbersome, but it's an improvement over scrolling through huge lists on a single worksheet.

Advanced Filter is a sophisticated type of search facility, but you may find that separating data into different worksheets according to common criteria and searching with AutoFilter is faster and more flexible in practice.

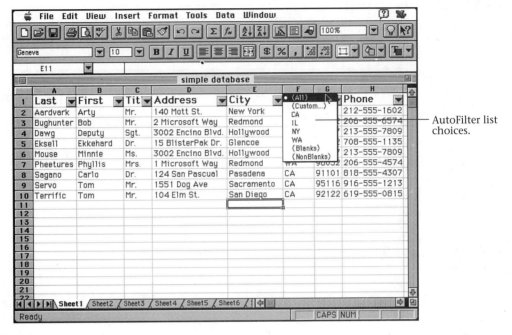

AutoFilter list choices.

Figure 17.10 Fast, easy AutoFiltering.

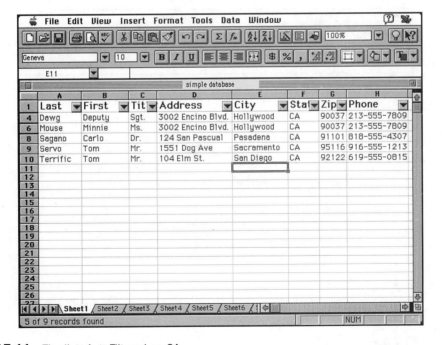

Figure 17.11 The list, AutoFiltered on CA.

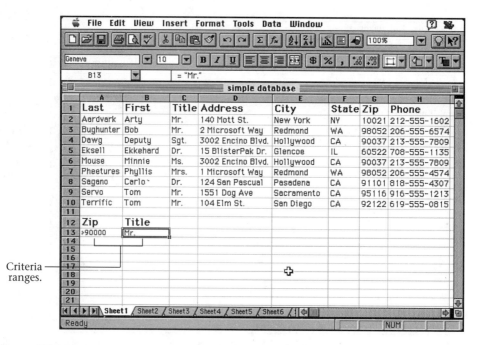

Figure 17.12   Getting ready to use the Advanced Filter option.

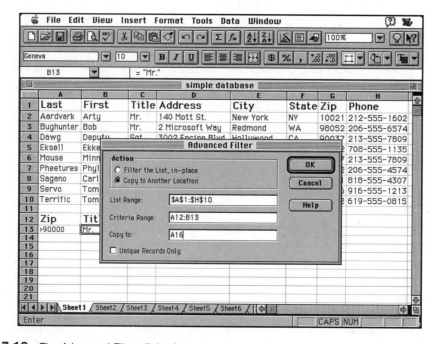

Figure 17.13   The Advanced Filter dialog box.

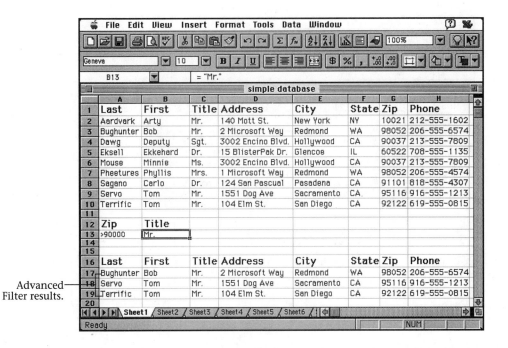

Figure 17.14   Results go into their own range.

Subtotals

If you have a relatively well-organized list, there's a command called Subtotals in the Data menu that can do wonderful things for you. The Subtotal dialog box (see Figure 17.15) is mostly useful, of course, if you have some numerical data, so I have added a field called Orders to our little list and filled in some sales numbers.

First you should sort your data list on the field you want for the Subtotals command. If you want a list subtotaled according to state, sort on State (see Figure 17.16) because Subtotals notices each change as it reads down the list. Although Subtotals typically uses SUM as the function of interest, you can also select a variety of statistical functions. Subtotals can pick out maximum or minimum values from a subgroup in the list, for example.

On a sorted list, Subtotals not only delivers subtotals and grand totals (see Figure 17.17), but it imposes outline structure on the original worksheet. Because Excel 5 has a worksheets-within-workbook structure, you may want to copy a result of this kind to its own worksheet. (After the subtotal operation, the new structure is imposed on the original worksheet—a more severe modification than sorting or filtering.) If you find outline structure objectionable, go to the Group and Outline command under the Data menu and pick Clear Outline to get rid of all the organizational spaghetti at the left of your worksheet.

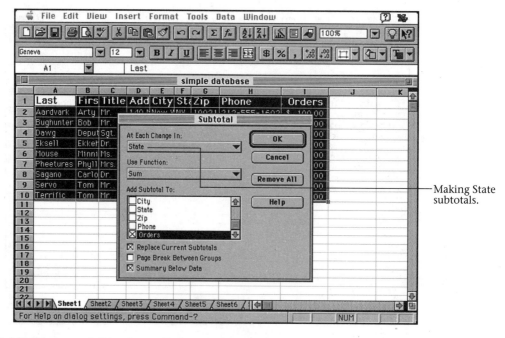

Making State
subtotals.

Figure 17.15 Many possibilities in the Subtotal dialog box.

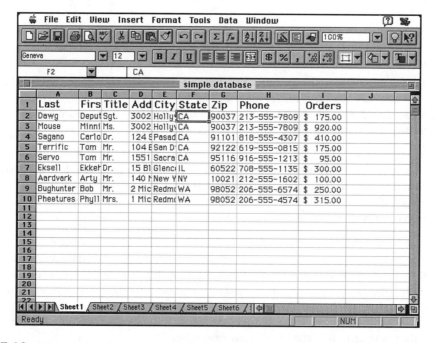

Figure 17.16 Sort your list first and then use the Subtotals command.

For producing a compact report, however, the outline format is the greatest advance since 6-point Helvetica. After you click the little 2 button in the outline column, the worksheet collapses to the bare subtotal presentation in Figure 17.18. "Just the facts, Ma'am," as Sgt. Joe Friday used to say. If you're trying to make sense of large amounts of business data, the automatic provision of an outline with each subtotal screen will start to look like one of Excel 5's best features.

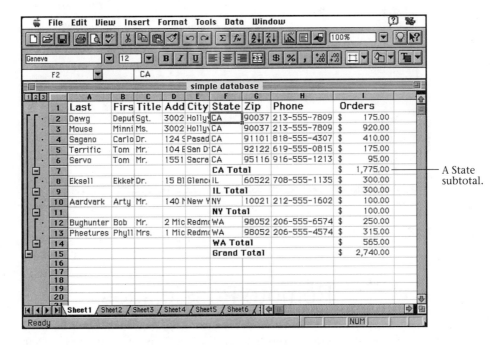

Figure 17.17   A Subtotals report with an automatic grand total.

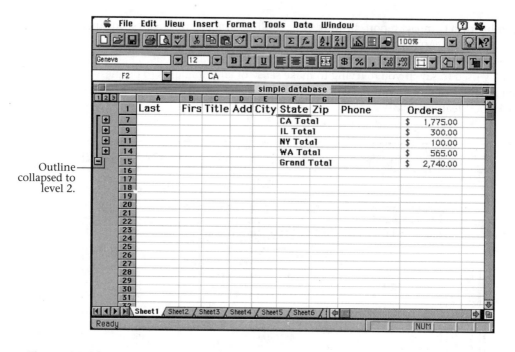

Figure 17.18   A short but sweet Subtotals report.

Remote Possibilities

Excel 5 has a large assortment of facilities for getting data from a remote database into a worksheet. In the Add-Ins dialog box, you can find options for using Apple's Data Access Language for connecting to remote database servers (Data Access Macro) and for Microsoft Query.

Most Data Access Language (DAL)-capable applications give you a specific Excel add-in to add to your menu—in general you don't have to puzzle out DAL connections if you're working in an office that has a DAL server program. Microsoft Query is ready to handle queries to remote databases that use Paradox, dBASE, Microsoft Access, and FoxPro. Only the last of these has a Macintosh version. Generally, if you're supposed to be downloading data into your own worksheet from a dBASE or Paradox database, it means that you're working in a company where it's someone else's responsibility to tell you how to do it. That's why I don't cover remote data access here—your network administrator is supposed to streamline this function for you.

The data management features of Excel 5 are one of the biggest areas of improvement over earlier versions. Unless you're handling hundreds of thousands of records—in which case you may need a real relational database—Excel's flexibility makes it a first choice for database work. In the next chapter, you learn how to customize Excel by creating your own macros and toolbars.

Chapter 18

Customizing
Excel

Excel 5 offers you customization opportunities beyond any other spreadsheet ever developed. If you diligently apply yourself to manufacturing your own toolbars, buttons, and macros, you can produce your personal version of Excel. The drawback to extensive customization, of course, is that you eventually have a piece of software that's difficult, if not impossible, for other people to use.

You'll look at the customization tricks that are the most practical, easiest to remember, and most likely to save you some time. The key points of worksheet cake decoration are as follows:

◆ Recording, naming and playing macros

◆ Using the Visual Basic toolbar

◆ Adding macros to Excel menus

◆ Changing macros in Edit mode

◆ Changing and creating toolbars to meet your own needs

◆ Customizing Help with Bookmarks

◆ Making custom buttons

◆ Assigning macros to a button

◆ Knowing when *not* to customize

Using Macros to Speed Up Your Work

Excel has always offered a macro system that lets you record keystrokes and play them back later. In Excel 5, Microsoft has taken macros to the gym and fed them steroids for a year. Even as you read this, platoons of diligent nerds—buzzed to the eyebrows on Jolt Cola—are writing Excel Visual Basic macro libraries for every conceivable business application.

The old macros produced long strings of funny little commands and were difficult to use for high-end chores. The new macros record your keystrokes and translate them into Visual Basic, a powerful application language that's as good at real programming as it is at taking notes on your work. While it's possible to write long programs in Visual Basic, you can get lots of use out of Visual Basic macros with no programming at all. After you get accustomed to macros, you'll wonder how you ever got along without them.

Excel's early advantage over other spreadsheets in the Mac market was based largely on its macro system, and Excel 5 widens this advantage (actually, there are no competitors left— Claris and Lotus having dropped out of the race).

When you start Excel, you may be surprised to see that the File menu gives you the option of recording a macro or opening an existing macro file (see Figure 18.1). That's because Excel macros, besides working inside worksheets, can direct all sorts of file management operations (for example, you can use them to open particular sets of files and groups of files at startup). For now, let's concentrate on using macros inside worksheets (and workbooks).

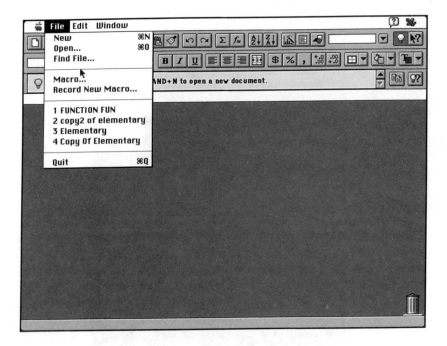

Figure 18.1   Macros with no worksheets?

444

Getting started

In a way, you've already seen some of the mechanics of macros back in Chapter 13. When you define a Custom AutoFill, you are setting up automatic playback of some text into cells. Macros let you do this and more.

Let's step through a simple example:

◆ The Macro options are hiding under the Tools menu. To record a macro, choose Record Macro, which produces its own submenu, and then select the Record New Macro command (see Figure 18.2).

◆ Excel gives you a dialog box asking you to name the macro (see Figure 18.3). Pick a name you're likely to remember! There are some restrictions on names: you can't use hyphens, for example, but you can use underscores for multiple words, as in MY_MERRY_MACRO.

◆ After you press OK in the dialog box, you're returned to the worksheet. Excel gives you a Stop button to click after you've recorded your macro. As you can see in Figure 18.4, I've recorded a shameless plug for The Don Crabb Macintosh Library (a high-quality series from Hayden Books).

◆ After you click the Stop button, all your typing is saved in the macro that you have named. If you now call down the Macro command from the Tools menu, you see your own macro as an option to run or to edit (see Figure 18.5).

More macro action

Basically, the preceding section just established that you can set the macro system to record your keystrokes and save them under a macro name for playback later. Of course, there are many other uses for macros besides this passive recording example. For instance, probably the most useful application is to use a macro to save yourself from retyping the same stuff over and over.

Although I used the first macro in this chapter to record a text-typing example, you can record anything. Macros can hold formulas, formatting information, statistical analysis and graphing, and drawings. Anything you can do in a worksheet that you think you may need to do again, you can save in a macro.

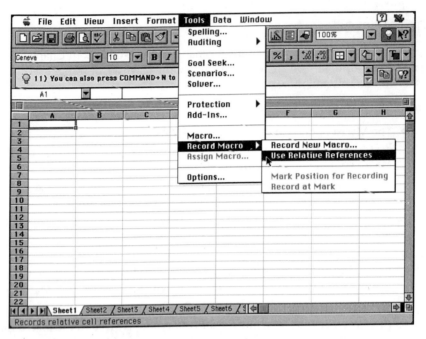

Figure 18.2 Find Record New Macro in the Tools menu.

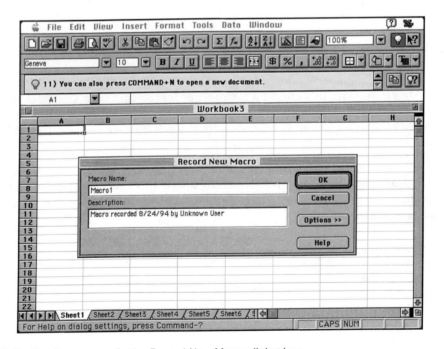

Figure 18.3 Naming a macro in the Record New Macro dialog box.

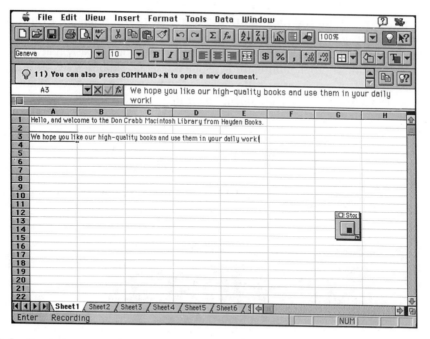

Figure 18.4 Excel gives you a Stop button to finish recording your macro.

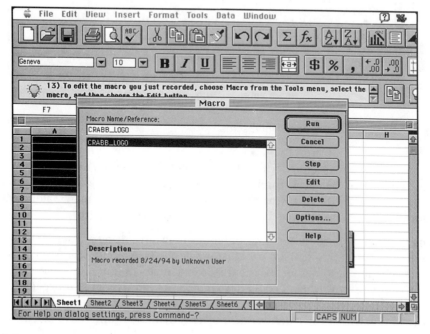

Figure 18.5 A named macro in the Macro dialog box.

Because macros are useful and important, they merit their own toolbar. It's called the Visual Basic toolbar (see Figure 18.6), and you can find it as an option to check under the Toolbars command in the View menu. The toolbar contains buttons for the basic macro operations and also buttons for fancier programming (browse objects, set breakpoints, step-through procedures) that you may not need at first. If you learn just to use the buttons for Run, Stop, and Record, you can automate all sorts of operations and look like a genius at work.

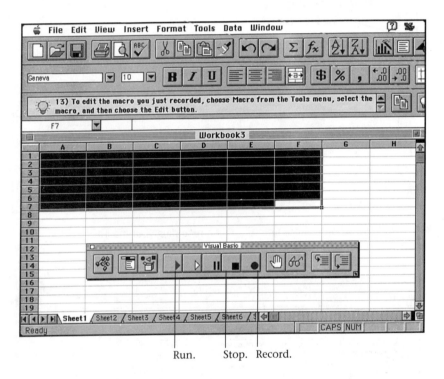

Run.   Stop.   Record.

Figure 18.6 The Visual Basic toolbar for macros.

The macros themselves are stored with your workbook, and you can open them for editing as one of the options in the Macro command in the Tools menu. After you open the text macro for editing, you can see the text clearly printed out inside quotation marks, along with other statements that tell you where the text should be placed (see Figure 18.7).

I'm going to try something a little more ambitious than advertising a series of books. I'll click the Record button on the Visual Basic toolbar, name the macro Half_year (see Figure 18.8), and then type in column headings for the months from January to June, along with the numbers from 1 through 12 as row labels. I could have put border formats or other decorations on the worksheet, too, but I wasn't feeling ambitious. Keep your own macros simple because it's easier to break tasks into two or three independent macros than to rework longer macros.

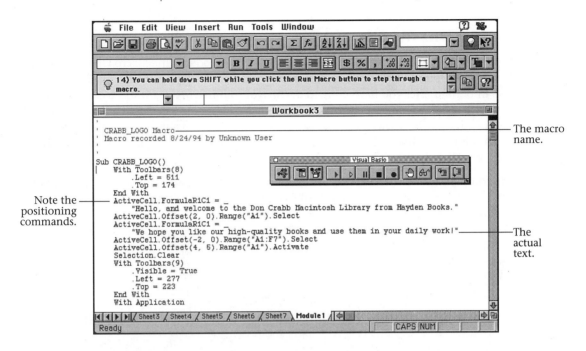

Figure 18.7 The editing window for the Don Crabb text macro.

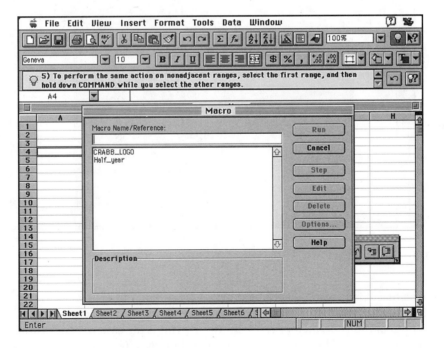

Figure 18.8 Adding another macro to the list.

Macros on the menu

The Macro dialog box has a button called Options, which produces the Macro Options dialog box. The Macro Options dialog box enables you to attach a description to the macro, which becomes important after you have more than three or four macros in a worksheet. Notice in Figure 18.9 that the default description produced by Excel has me listed as "Unknown User." I can't be sure, but I believe this is because Microsoft plans to build a monument to me personally, as The Unknown User, near its corporate offices, to compensate for my sufferings with early beta versions of Excel 5.

The important parts of Figure 18.9 are the check boxes for Menu Item and Keyboard Shortcut. Frankly, I think keyboard shortcuts are hard to remember, and a fairly large fraction of Option-⌘ key shortcuts have already been taken. So I usually attach my new macros to the Tools menu, where they appear as menu items. Notice also that you can type some advice to yourself into the Status Bar Text text box, and advanced users can make up Help system entries for their own macros.

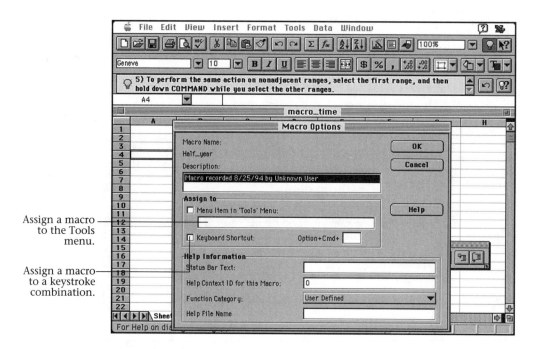

Assign a macro to the Tools menu.

Assign a macro to a keystroke combination.

Figure 18.9   Macro options let you build your macros into Excel commands.

Assigning a macro is as easy as checking the correct box and filling in a macro name (see Figure 18.10). After you follow these steps, you see your macro appear as a custom command at the bottom of the Tools menu (see Figure 18.11). This is the easiest menu customization that you're likely to find in any piece of software yet produced.

450

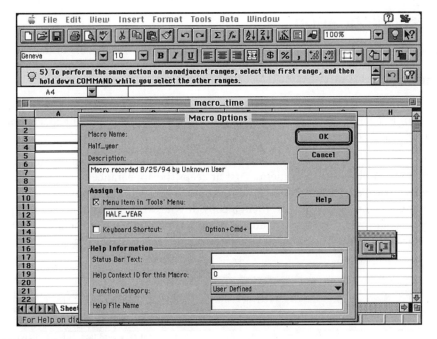

Figure 18.10 Filling in menu data.

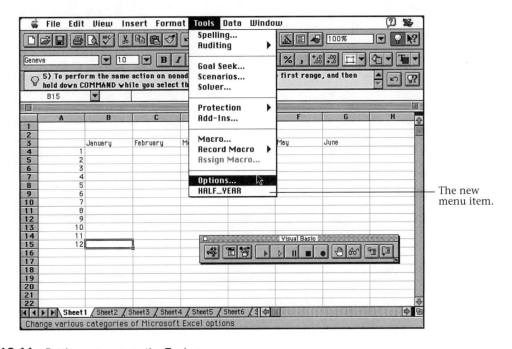

Figure 18.11 Putting a macro on the Tools menu.

Macro sophistication

But wait, that's not all! Suppose that you don't want to park your macros under the Tools menu. That's just fine with Excel 5, which is willing to put your macros on the same footing as all the commands the whiz kids at Microsoft have labored on for years.

If you click the second button from the left on the Visual Basic toolbar, you're handed to the Menu Editor (see Figure 18.12). In the Menu Editor, it's possible to put the macro command anywhere on any existing menu or in the Menu bar itself.

There are, however, two strong arguments in favor of accepting Excel's standard placement of menu macros under the Tools menu. First, it keeps the appearance of your worksheet in conformance with the Excel manuals, and for that matter, with this book. Therefore, other users don't get confused if you send them a copy of your work. Second, if you start packing the menus with your own macro commands, you can start losing track of them. At least if they always appear under the Tools menu, you know exactly where to find them.

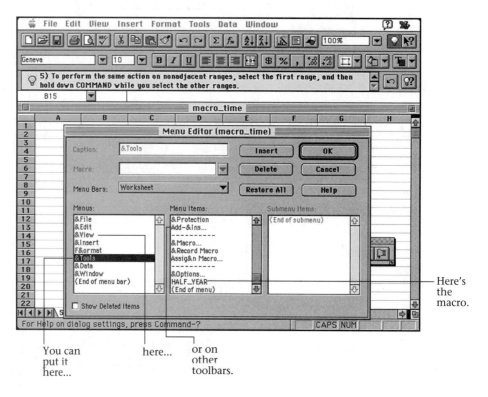

You can   here...   or on
put it   other
here...   toolbars.

Here's
the
macro.

Figure 18.12   The Menu Editor, available with a click on the Visual Basic toolbar.

So far, the two macros in these examples were fixed to absolute locations. That means that when I started typing the hymn to Don Crabb in cell A1, the macro system thought it should type the text into cell A1 every time the macro was run. If you want the text to start filling in from any cell that you have selected, you need to choose the Use Relative References option for the Record Macro command in the Tools menu (see Figure 18.13). When you run a relative-reference macro, it looks for the currently active cell in the worksheet and starts running the macro from that point.

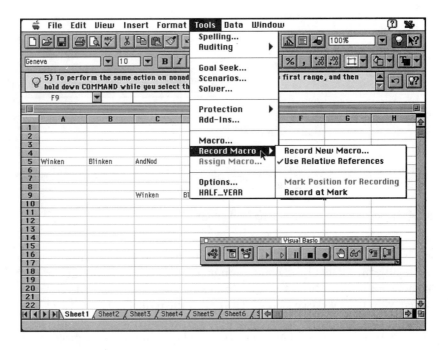

Figure 18.13   Relative references for macros.

Having checked Use Relative References, I then wrote a macro to put the words *Winken, Blinken,* and *AndNod* into three cells next to each other, and I named the macro WINKEN. I then called up Macro from the Tools menu, selected WINKEN from the list of macros, and chose Edit. In Figure 18.14, you can see that one of the first steps in the macro is to select the currently active cell in the worksheet as the starting point for the macro. Another point to observe about this macro is that it's called Module 1 (look at the bottom of the figure). This name indicates where the macros are stored in the workbook. If you look above the words *WINKEN Macro,* you can see the last commands from our old friend Half_year.

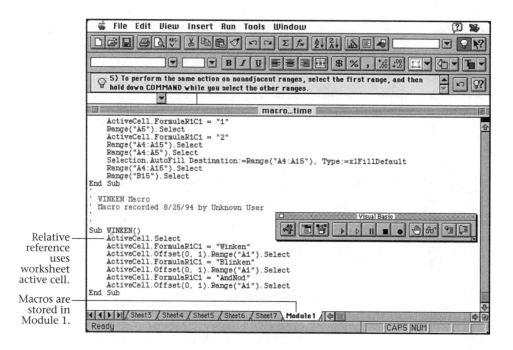

The figure contains the following:

```
  File  Edit  View  Insert  Run  Tools  Window                    ? ✂

5) To perform the same action on nonadjacent ranges, select the first range, and then
hold down COMMAND while you select the other ranges.

                              macro_time
        ActiveCell.FormulaR1C1 = "1"
        Range("A5").Select
        ActiveCell.FormulaR1C1 = "2"
        Range("A4:A15").Select
        Range("A4:A5").Select
        Selection.AutoFill Destination:=Range("A4:A15"), Type:=xlFillDefault
        Range("A4:A15").Select
        Range("B15").Select
End Sub
'
'  WINKEN Macro
'  Macro recorded 8/25/94 by Unknown User
'                                              Visual Basic
'
Sub WINKEN()
        ActiveCell.Select
        ActiveCell.FormulaR1C1 = "Winken"
        ActiveCell.Offset(0, 1).Range("A1").Select
        ActiveCell.FormulaR1C1 = "Blinken"
        ActiveCell.Offset(0, 1).Range("A1").Select
        ActiveCell.FormulaR1C1 = "AndNod"
        ActiveCell.Offset(0, 1).Range("A1").Select
End Sub

Sheet3  Sheet4  Sheet5  Sheet6  Sheet7  Module1
Ready                                              CAPS NUM
```

Relative reference uses worksheet active cell.

Macros are stored in Module 1.

Figure 18.14   Module 1 is a macro editing worksheet.

Module 1 is a text document, and you can edit it by using normal Macintosh methods. Because the little bits of text inside quotation marks are just Macintosh document text, you can edit these bits directly. Just as a whimsical experiment, I've replaced *Winken* with *STINKEN* and *AndNod* with *And...Nod* (see Figure 18.15), with the results in Figure 18.16. This is unlikely to be your first choice of a macro, but I want you to note that if you type in a long macro and misspell some words, you don't have to go back and type in the whole project again. You can fix individual words and commands in this editing window. If I were feeling *really* frisky, I could change the numbers in ActiveCell.Offset and move the other words all over the worksheet.

Macros are not the only way to customize your Excel program. The next section of this chapter deals with other ways to change Excel to meet your needs.

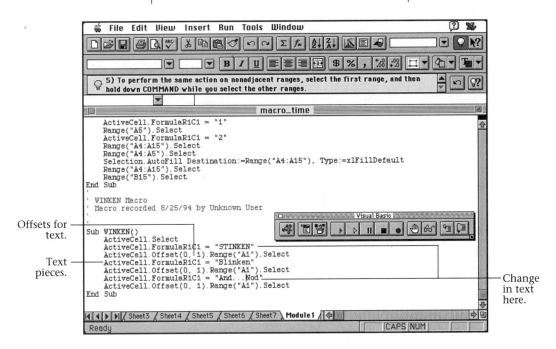

Offsets for text.

Text pieces.

Change in text here.

Figure 18.15 Editing cells in a macro.

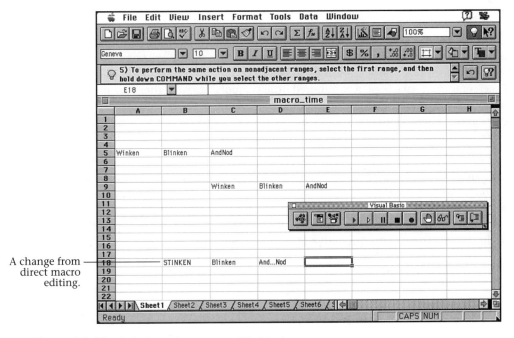

A change from direct macro editing.

Figure 18.16 Relative reference, modified text macro.

Toolbar-O-Rama

Microsoft Excel has lots of toolbars. Just in case you can't find all of them in the ludicrous complexity of Figure 18.17—there are even too many to fit in the Toolbars dialog box without scrolling (see Figure 18.18)—the toolbars include the following:

- Standard
- Formatting
- Query and Pivot
- Chart
- Drawing
- TipWizard
- Forms
- Stop Recording
- Visual Basic
- Auditing
- Workgroup
- Microsoft
- Full Screen

I'm not listing these because I like to type, but rather to make a point. It's possible in Excel to customize a huge assortment of toolbars and buttons. You should ask yourself carefully just how much customization you want to do before you set out on this task. As it stands, using Excel 5 means mastering a few hundred little symbols. Some of them are pretty self-explanatory, as in the underline button denoted by _U_. Some of them are quite cryptic—my own favorites for obscurity are the symbol for Microsoft Project on the Microsoft toolbar and the eraser with three little arrows on the Auditing toolbar.

The point is, you could get a fourth-grade-level reading knowledge of Japanese with the amount of effort you have to put into mastery of the standard Excel buttons, much less new buttons you make up yourself. There's an argument to be made for using a few standard toolbars and then using the menus and commands for operations that you don't do everyday. If you see the name of a command on a menu, for example, you can look it up in the manual or the Help system. You can do this with a button, too, but you have to identify it first.

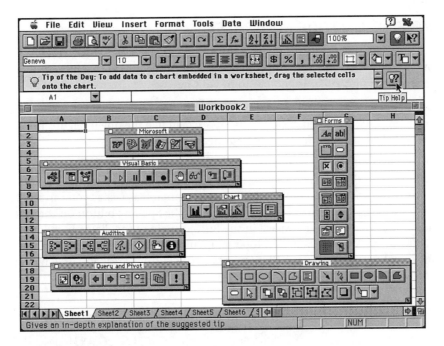

Figure 18.17   Nearly all the toolbars.

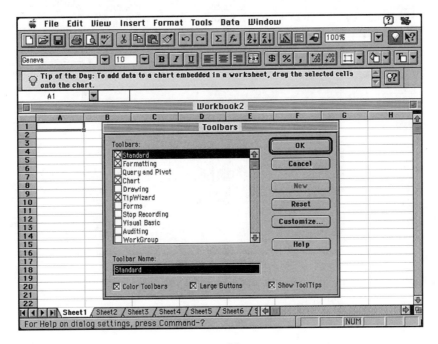

Figure 18.18   The Toolbars list, before you start adding your own.

Customizing existing toolbars

All this being said, there are advantages to making toolbars look the way you want them to look for your own convenience. You can get rid of buttons that you don't use often or move buttons around from toolbar to toolbar to fit your needs.

If you look closely at Figure 18.18, you notice an inviting button called Customize in the Toolbars dialog box. After you click it, you see a screen like the one in Figure 18.19. Using this window, you can customize toolbars to your heart's content.

You can pull off buttons that you don't use often from an existing toolbar. For example, the Spelling button on the Standard toolbar is not particularly useful because Spelling is the first option under the Tools menu (you can reach the command as fast as you can reach the button). So with the Customize window open, click the Spelling button on the Standard toolbar and drag it into the gray space in the Buttons field of the dialog box. If you need the Spelling button back on the Standard toolbar, highlight the Utility category in the Customize window, click the Spelling button that appears in the Buttons area, and drag it back to the Standard toolbar in whatever position you want it to be in.

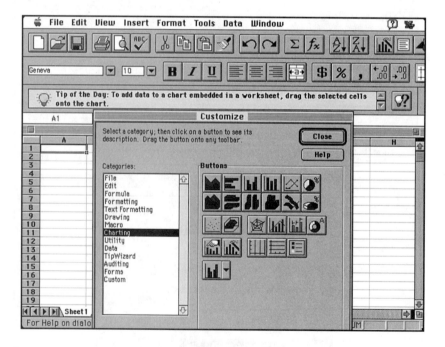

Figure 18.19   The Customize window from the Toolbars command.

You can also put your favorite buttons on the existing toolbars. In Figure 18.20, I have dragged my own favorite—the XY (Scatter) Chart AutoFormat button from the Charting category in the Customize window—out to the Formatting toolbar.

Note that the distribution of buttons in the Categories list of the Customize window is often odd. You sometimes have to hunt for unfamiliar buttons—the double underline in Figure 18.21, for example—in several categories before you find them, while you can find familiar buttons—the Function Wizard, for example—in several places (in the Formula, Macro, and Utility categories).

Also, if you have one of the floating toolbars onscreen (*floating* means a toolbar other than the Standard and Formatting toolbars), you can drag buttons to it from any of the button palettes. Figure 18.22 shows the Chart toolbar, loaded with extra buttons on an impish whim.

Here's the new button.

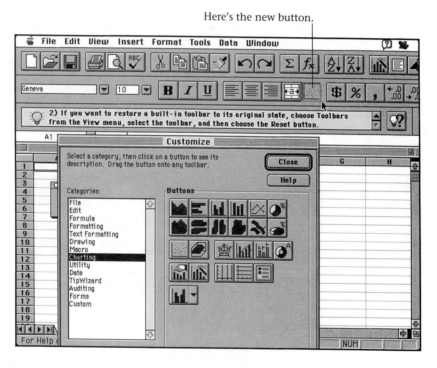

Figure 18.20   Adding a button to the Formatting toolbar.

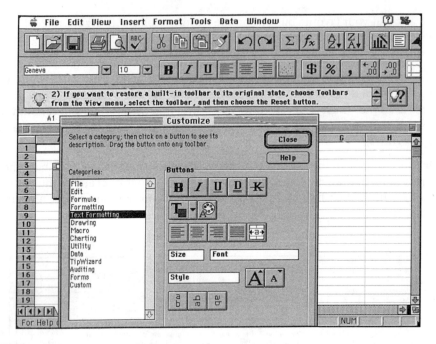

Figure 18.21 Discovering unusual buttons.

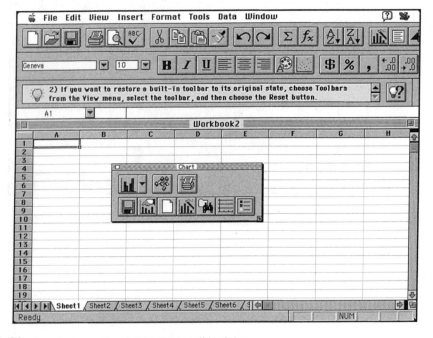

Figure 18.22 Loading up a floating toolbar until it sinks.

Creating your own toolbar

If customizing an existing toolbar does not meet your needs, you can create your own toolbars. All you have to do is click a button and drag it out into free space somewhere on the worksheet. Excel automatically assigns the name Toolbar 1 to the first toolbar you produce this way and then numbers any others you create, as well. As with other floating toolbars, you can keep adding as many buttons as you like (see Figure 18.23).

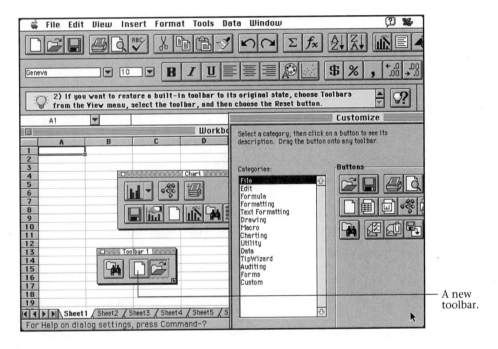

A new toolbar.

Figure 18.23   Dragging buttons onto the worksheet to create a new toolbar.

Here's a toolbar strategy for you, based on Microsoft's own design. Microsoft supposedly designed all its toolbars by tracking the way people used the product in testing labs. It didn't, however, have the opportunity to track the way *you* work. But you can do this yourself. Keep a log of the buttons you actually use for about a week (just keep a file card taped next to your computer). Then make up a custom floating toolbar with your own favorite buttons—Excel arranges them in a nice two-row format if you collect enough of them. And make sure that you save the workbook with this custom toolbar! No point going to all this trouble and then losing your work in a System crash.

Then for your own custom version of a worksheet, just close the Standard and Formatting toolbars and use your own. There are several reasons for using your own toolbar:

◆ Your toolbar is probably simpler than Microsoft's and faster to display.

◆ By putting all your customization on your own toolbar, you leave the rest of your copy of Excel intact as standard Excel so that other people can work with it and you can still recognize your worksheet when you look in the manual.

◆ You can create numerous toolbars for special purposes (math, charting and drawing, common formats), again without messing up the toolbars Microsoft has prepared.

Customizing Help

The next customizing trick worth learning is the use of bookmarks in Help.

The Microsoft Help system is nothing if not generous. It goes on for megabytes and megabytes, providing information on the nearly uncountable number of features in Excel 5—if you don't mind starting with an explanation of the error message #DIV/0! every time or scrolling through the topics index at a fairly leisurely pace.

My bet is that you will want help on a relatively small number of topics on a regular basis and that you will have mastered the information that the $ button on the Formatting toolbar means "format as money" sometime around 8:15 A.M. on your first day with Excel. For the topics you need, place bookmarks to cut down your search time.

Here's what you do. Get into the Help system by double-clicking the Help button. You get a new top-level menu bar that contains a menu item called Bookmark. First, by using the Search button, select the topic that you want to be able to access quickly. After you get the topic explanation onscreen, choose the Define command under the Bookmark menu (see Figure 18.24). When the Define Bookmark dialog box opens (see Figure 18.25), it assumes that you're defining a bookmark for the Help topic that you located with Search. (You can change the entry here if you like, but it's easier to locate the topic first—you don't necessarily know the exact name of the topic to enter here, and Excel wants the exact name.)

The next time you call up the Help system, you can proceed directly to the Bookmark menu and find the topic that you have marked as one of the choices (see Figure 18.26). The name of the selection is generated automatically. Note that the original name, "Changing general Microsoft Excel settings," is now listed as "Changing settings," and it's assigned its own keyboard shortcut.

That's pretty slick. For example, suppose that you are working on financial calculations most of the time. You can set up the Help system to call up Help files for PMT as ⌘-1, IRR as ⌘-2, and so forth. Then if you get fired from your job as an analyst and decide to design Grateful Dead T-shirts for a living, you can delete all these entries and set up new Help bookmarks for databases (of customers) and drawing tools.

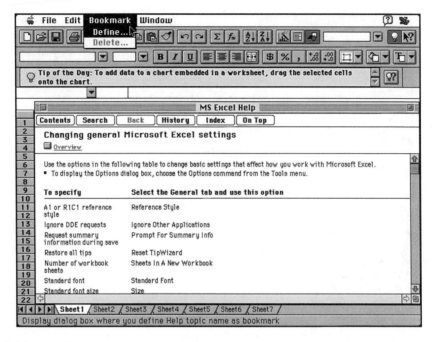

Figure 18.24   Setting up bookmarks in the Help system.

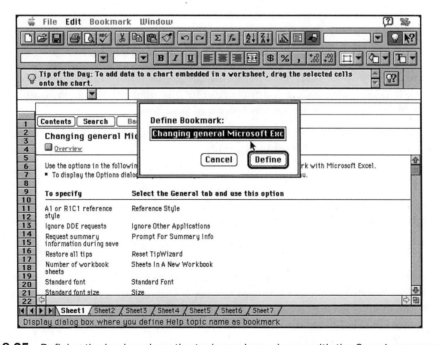

Figure 18.25   Defining the bookmark on the topic you have chosen with the Search command.

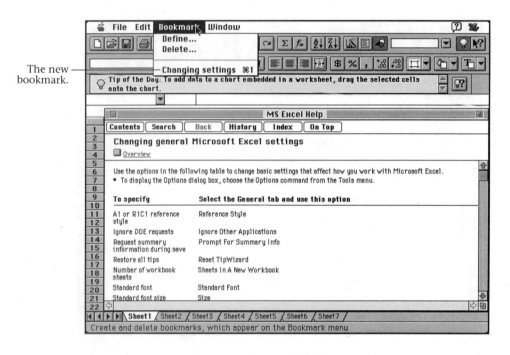

The new bookmark.

Figure 18.26 Adding bookmarks to speed up Help services.

Creating Buttons for Macros

The last truly worthwhile customization technique involves putting macro access right on your worksheet. You can make a custom button for any macro that you write and attach it to one of the existing toolbars or to a new toolbar of your own.

This, by the way, is a significantly more dramatic and sophisticated type of customization than anything I discussed earlier. Rather than simply rearranging access to Excel's canned commands, you're really writing your own version of spreadsheet tools.

Let's take this one step at a time. First, open a worksheet where you have saved some macros. In Figure 18.27, I have pulled up a set of macros with the Macro command from the Tools menu and dragged a few buttons out to a custom toolbar.

Next, pick a button that you want to customize. The reason that you're going to customize a button for your macro is that there will be no other way to remember it otherwise. You can attach your macro to an existing button, but then you have a weird situation in which you have changed the definition of a standard button. If you do this ten times, I promise you that you will lose track of everything and start muttering to yourself constantly. As your co-workers notice your strange behavior and disheveled appearance, your supervisor suggests a counseling program, and . . . you can see where this is leading, okay?

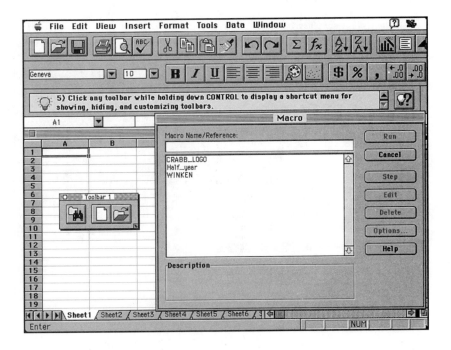

Figure 18.27   Macros and buttons, a great combination.

So, suitably motivated to customize buttons, pick a button on your own toolbar, hold down Control, and then click the mouse right on the toolbar button. You get a pop-up menu with a short set of choices (see Figure 18.28). You want to choose Edit Button Image.

The Button Editor screen lets you define a new button pixel by pixel. Actually, this has loads of entertainment value—you can make happy face buttons, pictures of your dog, cute little logos . . . anything! In this case (see Figure 18.29), I have chosen a noble armorial crest reflecting the existence of Don Crabb (remember him?).

Finally, after you have your own button (finish clicking the pixels and then click the OK button), you can assign a macro. Press Control-click on the new button and find the Assign Macro command (see Figure 18.30). When you select this command, Excel gives you your choice of macros (see Figure 18.31). Pick the one that you want and press the OK button. Now you have a button that runs the macro any time you click it. After I click the D/C button on my own little toolbar, the macro prints the Don Crabb blurb right into my worksheet (see Figure 18.32).

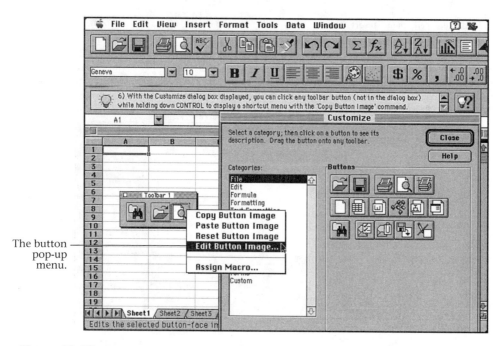

Figure 18.28 Making your own buttons for macros.

The button pop-up menu.

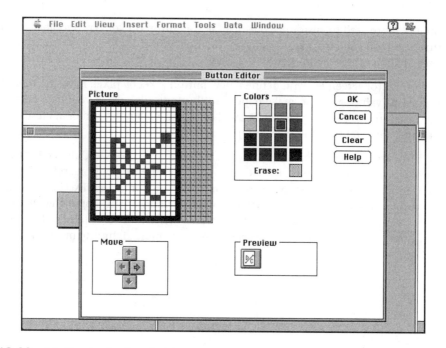

Figure 18.29 A button for the Don Crabb macro.

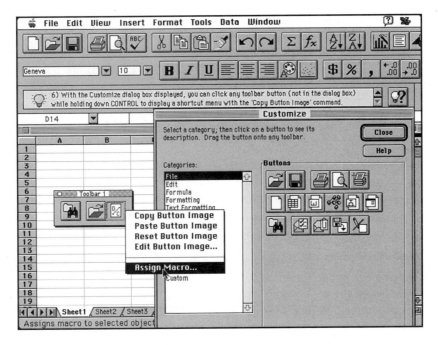

Figure 18.30 Assign Macro from the pop-up menu.

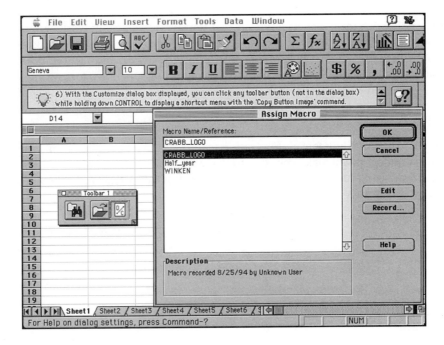

Figure 18.31 Selecting the macro for your new button.

467

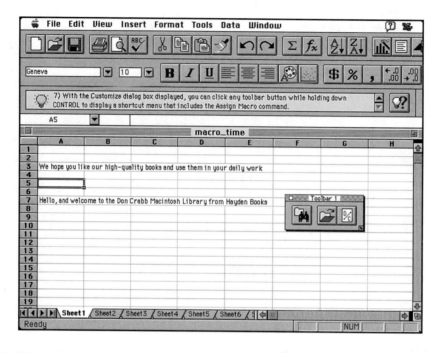

Figure 18.32   One little click on a button, and all this text pours out.

This is a vision of a really practical type of customization. It's a bit of work, but you can make your own toolbar with six or seven custom buttons to run some of these chunks of boilerplate text that you use frequently. It's not any more effort to have an array of four or five custom toolbars like this to handle a big array of tasks (combining functions, formatting, and other chores). And then you can edit these macros directly to modify the contents! That, dear reader, is the customization big leagues. Thanks to these new features in Excel, it's not very hard to do this, either.

Excel has dozens of admirable customization features. In practice, a fairly small number of customization tricks will make your day-to-day work easier, while really extensive customization may well just confuse you. Think this stuff is futuristic? Wait till you see what awaits you in Chapter 19.

Chapter 19

Predicting
the Future

Excel delights in making forecasts to analyze data, and it has at least six different ways to do forecasts. Excel has more computational machinery for producing forecasts than any other product ever released into the general software consumer market.

So . . . you're going to take a tour of the forecasting methods built into Excel. Included in the tour are actual applications of several forecasting techniques, the times when you *shouldn't* try forecasting, and a look at analysis tools in detail. These are the main points:

◆ Understanding how to correlate sample data

◆ Using the Trendline command as a chart option

◆ Understanding the forecast numbers

◆ Sampling forecasting functions

◆ Looking at a business test case for good and bad forecasting opportunities

◆ Looking at a real-life case of what-if analysis

◆ Using one-input tables and interpreting the results

◆ Using two-input tables and interpreting the results

◆ Using Scenario Manager, Goal Seek, and Solver

Trends from Good Numbers

Forecasting software is a tool. A mulching power mower is a tool, also, and you can use it to mulch your foot if you're not careful. You can, similarly, use forecasting software to convince yourself that your own common sense is wrong and, in the process, ruin your business and rain down shame upon your head.

In the old days of the data processing trade, the saying was, "Garbage in, garbage out." The equivalent expression, in Sumerian, was probably inscribed on clay tablets around 3000 B.C., as the first accountant found out that a mistaken head count of cattle could produce notable grief.

Let's get down to cases. Figure 19.1 shows part of a data set on cars—I've just picked out two columns that I think may have some connection. The first column shows the weight in thousands of pounds for a particular car, and the second column shows the horsepower for that car.

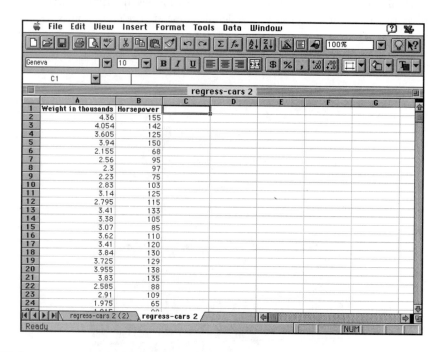

Figure 19.1   Weight versus horsepower for cars.

Correlation

Now right away you're in the middle of a decision-making process. Out of the 40 columns of data in the original table, I picked these two because there's a good underlying reason to think that there may be some sort of trend. No manufacturer is going to sell a 4,000-pound car with a 35 horsepower engine. And no matter what the hyperactive youth of this great nation may want, there aren't going to be 1,200-pound cars with 900 horsepower engines, at least not on the street. (That would be, like, whoa! *Totally Awesome!* Excuse me.)

What I'm getting at is that there's a reason to expect heavier cars to have more powerful engines. It makes sense that there would be some *correlation,* as they say in statistics classes, between weight and horsepower. There's probably also a correlation between length and weight because, in technical terms, cars are made out of *stuff*—so longer cars are going to weigh more. If you think about it a bit, you see that you can think of other likely correlations. Weight versus miles per gallon is a probable example of a negative correlation (more weight sinks your MPG), as is MPG versus horsepower.

By the way, as a bonus for reading this far in the book, I may as well give you some practical information. The data in Figure 19.1 is taken from a table on car safety prepared by the American Statistical Association. The most important correlation in the table is the correlation between vehicle weight and crash survival. In crashes, the heavier vehicle always "wins," showing serious crash survival advantages from a few hundred pounds! Once again, you can make a physical argument that there should be some correlation (consider a bicycle versus a freight train as a limiting case), and sure enough, there is.

Graphing and trendlines

If two columns of data have a perfect, 100 percent correlation, you can plot the data in the two columns as pairs of points and get a lovely straight line. That is, if there's a rigorous underlying rule connecting the data in the two columns, it means that you can just compute the points in column B from the data in column A. For most real-world data, however, you get correlations of less than 100 percent, ranging all the way down to 0 percent correlation (meaning that there's no underlying connection between the two data sets).

Let's look at a plot of the data in Figure 19.1. Using a scatter plot, the preferred chart type for investigating correlations, we get the chart in Figure 19.2. The points are more like a stretched-out cloud than a straight line, but there's clearly a correlation because the points are clustered along a line.

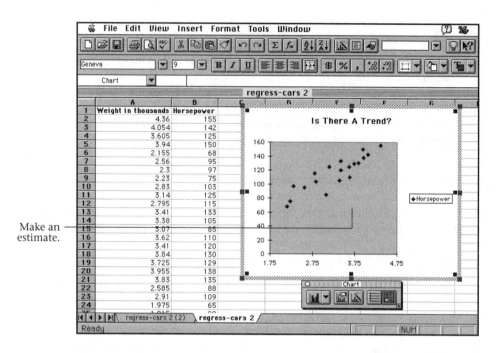

Make an
estimate.

Figure 19.2   Looking for correlation.

Again, thinking about the data, there are some reasons you can expect these points not to lie along a perfectly straight line:

- ◆ The cars in the data points are from several different countries, and different countries have different standards in acceleration. German cars, for example, would probably plot as a separate little group.

- ◆ Some manufacturers inside the United States just sell different categories of cars, from family sedans to so-called sports cars (the only true sports car made in the United States is the Jeep, according to Grand Prix champion Stirling Moss).

- ◆ Automatic-transmission cars also form a different group from manual 5-speed cars.

In each of these cases, there's an underlying reason why some cars don't have exactly the same horsepower/weight relationship as others. Nonetheless, you can tell that there's *some* relationship, so it's time to call up Excel's trend analysis system, as follows:

1. Select the data points in the chart simply by clicking them (see Figure 19.3).

2. Find the Trendline command under the Insert menu (see Figure 19.4), which produces the Trendline dialog box.

3. In the Type tab, pick the Linear trend, the simplest trend, which tries a linear fit. This means that Excel will compute the straight line that makes the best fit to the data (see Figure 19.5).

4. From the Options tab, pick some points to forecast, if you like (see Figure 19.6). *Forecast* means that Excel looks at the formula it has generated (the calculated straight line) and computes some new predicted points.

5. Just to make this official, check the two check boxes that display both the equation and the R-squared value on the chart (Figure 19.7).

6. After you click OK, you get a lovely trendline right through your points on the chart (see Figure 19.8).

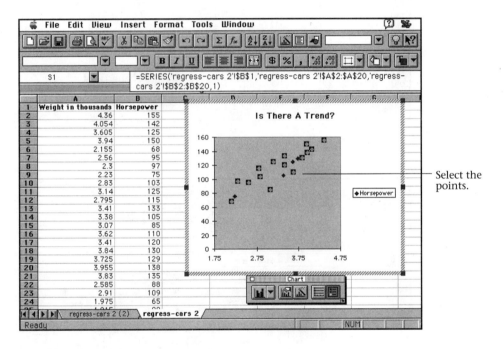

Figure 19.3 Picking trendline points.

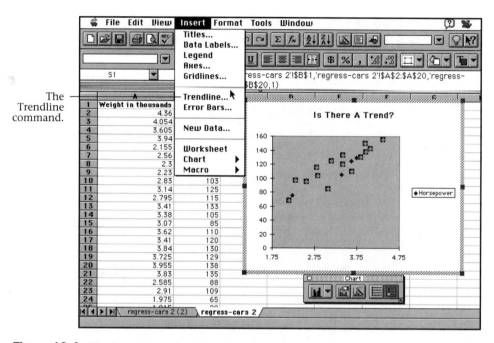

Figure 19.4   The Insert menu has the simplest trend-seeking function.

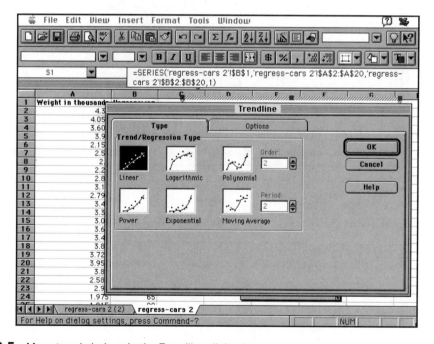

Figure 19.5   Many trend choices in the Trendline dialog box.

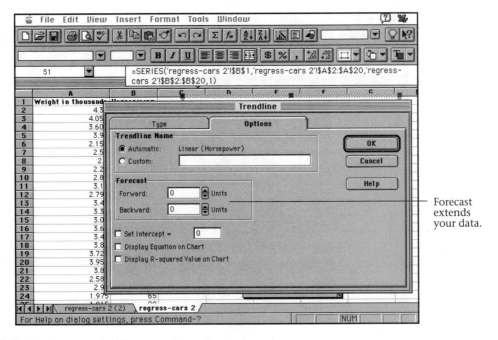

Figure 19.6   The Forecast function goes forward or backward.

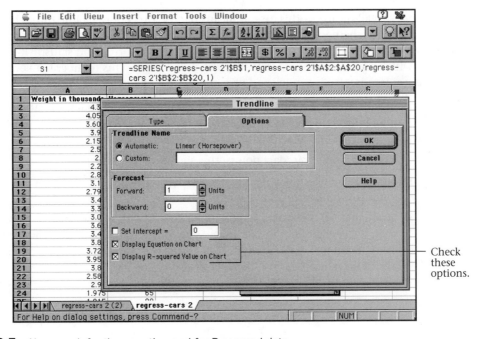

Figure 19.7   Always ask for the equation and for R-squared data.

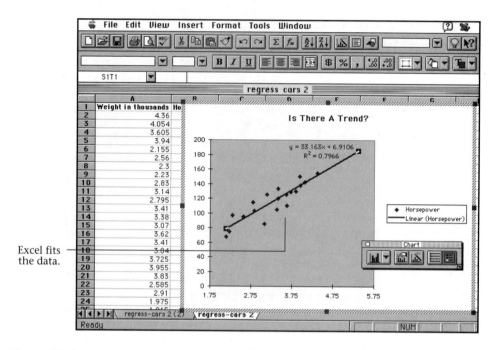

Figure 19.8   Excel 5 draws your trendline right on the chart.

What does this all mean? In this case, it means plenty. Excel draws a line through any points that you give it, whether there's a correlation that's meaningful or not. Looking at the trendline output on the chart in Figure 19.8, note that the correlation statistic R-squared is 0.7966, which you can round up to 0.80 without distortion. This number is a key indicator in finding real trends. Here's a quick and very approximate guide:

◆ R-squared = 1.0. Congratulations! You have discovered a law of nature. Your scatter plot points are perfectly correlated.

◆ R-squared = 0.8. This is still a very strong correlation. If you suspected some connection in your data points, this statistic confirms it.

◆ R-squared = 0.5 or less. Things are getting considerably cloudier. A forecast based on this sort of correlation is not reliable.

◆ R-squared = 0. Your data should look like buckshot blasted against the chart. In fact, it's very rare to see data so perfectly uncorrelated that this statistic is actually zero. If you just draw points on a chart, taking your best shot at making the distribution random, you're likely to get a value like 0.12.

As a last bit of demonstration, consider the chart in Figure 19.9. Here I've gone back to the Trendline dialog box and picked the Polynomial trend rather than the Linear trend. That means that Excel can try to find a function with some curvature instead of a straight line and then evaluate the fit to this curve. The result, as it happens, is a faintly better fit to the data, with an R-squared statistic of 0.7974. Because this more complicated trend function is only a marginally better fit to the data, the straight line is a better practical model.

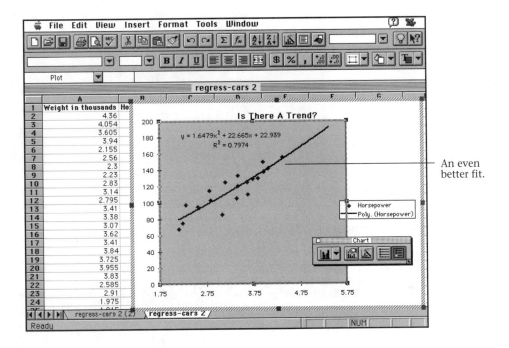

An even better fit.

Figure 19.9   A polynomial fit of the weight/horsepower data.

Other Trend Functions

Excel offers a luxurious profusion of ways to do approximately the same kind of forecast. The function TREND (Function Wizard keeps it with the statistical functions) is one example. TREND (see Figure 19.10) asks for two data series in cell ranges, computes a straight line by taking the data in pairs, and returns a straight-line set of values. In this case you would take the cell range of horsepowers as the set of "known_y's" in the TREND dialog box, the range of weights as the set of "known_x's," and set up another range for the computed "new_x's." Probably the best way to see the results of a TREND is to compare a plot of the original data with a plot of the "new_x's" (see Figure 19.11).

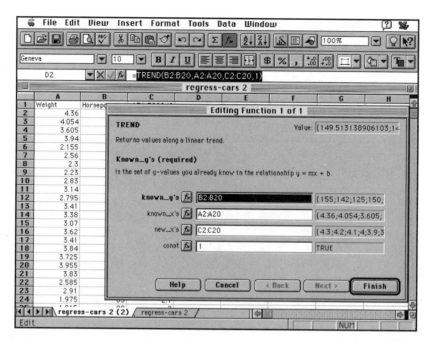

Figure 19.10 Using the Excel TREND function.

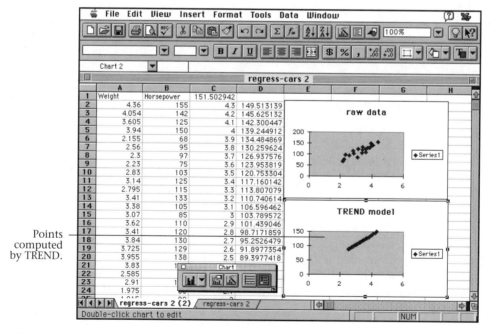

Figure 19.11 Comparing original points with TREND points.

You may have noticed that this function is a bit more trouble to use than the Trendline command, but it does give you back actual points in your worksheet. If you have a statistical background, you can use these points for further calculation. A related function is FORECAST (see Figure 19.12), which takes the set of x and y points and computes a single new x. Yet another function is LINEST, for linear estimation, which returns the correlation statistics, but not the new computed data points (see Figure 19.13). All these individual pieces of the Trendline package are more useful for people programming templates than for individual users just looking for a little data analysis.

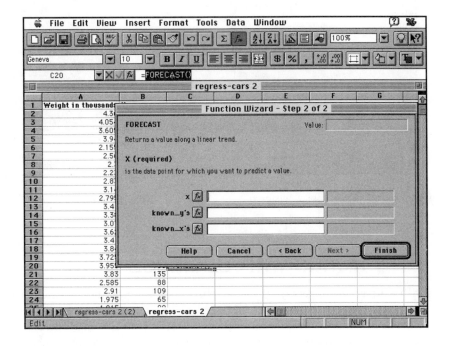

Figure 19.12 FORECAST for single forecast data points.

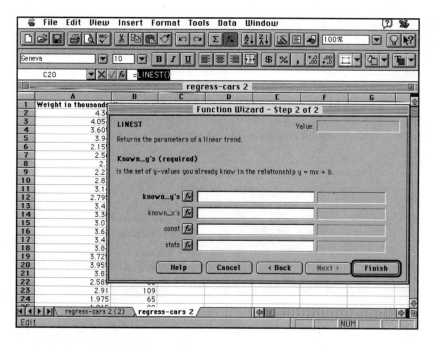

Figure 19.13 Yet another function, LINEST.

Trends with Business Data

Readers with a literary bent, keenly attuned to the supreme importance of parallelism in narrative structure, have probably observed that the first section in this chapter is called "Trends with Good Numbers," while this section is called "Trends with Business Data." This was deliberate, and is of course meant to suggest that data on physical quantities is often a more productive field for trend analysis than, for example, sales data. This, of course, is tragic because predicting sales is a matter of desperate interest, if not actual hysteria.

I would like to present a real-world business data set with some features modified so that the last representatives of the company that pursued the criminally idiotic course of betting the company's future on a trend analysis of sales data don't recognize themselves here and sue me (or, heaven forfend, Hayden Books). Let me just state, for the record, that the real case was worse than the one I present here.

Sales data

Scaled for credibility, the sales of Company X for its fabulous talking toy bear are shown in Figure 19.14. As presented, the story is an unqualified success. Sales keep going up, year after year. The big questions are how many people should the company hire, what production facilities will be needed, what sort of distribution is best, and *how do we cash in big time while we've got a winner??!!* Take a look at the data as charted in Figure 19.15. If you had been the marketing manager of this company, you wouldn't have gotten one night's sleep any time in December because you would've been so busy.

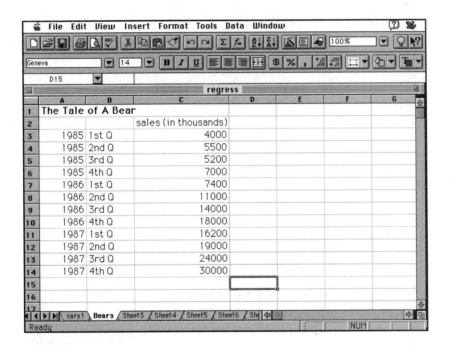

Figure 19.14   Sales data from a roaring success.

What actually happened in this case is that the company performed a trend analysis (see Figure 19.16) and believed the worksheet when it said that there was nowhere to go but up. It hired people like crazy, expanded production—and blew out in one of the most spectacular meltdowns in recent American corporate history. It happened that the appetite of the toy-consuming public could be saturated after all, and the products of this firm are now quite surely rotting in closets nationwide, right next to a motley assortment of Cabbage Patch Kids.

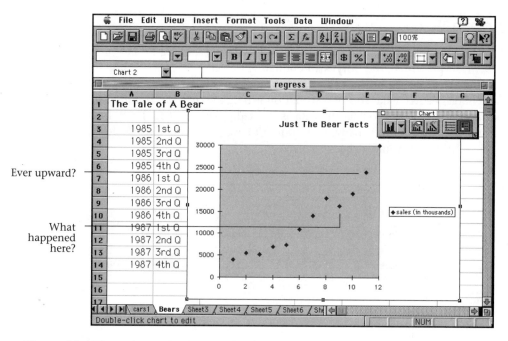

Figure 19.15 A plot of the skyrocketing bear sales.

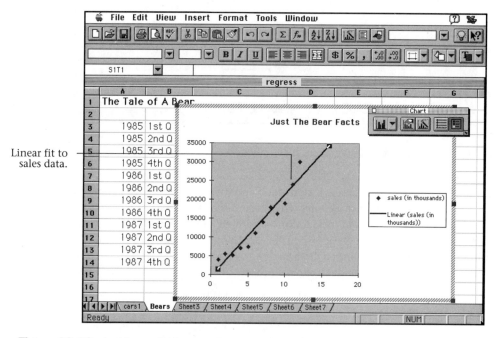

Figure 19.16 Is this a valid forecast?

Sales data forecasts

I now would like you to perform the following "visualization exercise," as they say in different psychological practices. You're speaking at the front of a conference room, and you're showing a slide of a nice straight trendline through a set of sales data. Suddenly, the lights come on, the door to the room comes crashing through in splinters, and Arnold Schwarzenegger, in full camo battle dress, strides to the front of the room and pins you against a blackboard. "I tot I tole you nevah to analise Zales Datuh dis vay!!" he screams in your face.

The principle is this: there is no *underlying reason* for a correlation between your sales data and calendar dates *per se*. There could, on a more positive note, be a correlation between

◆ Sales and advertising volume. You could try to correlate sales with ThousandsOfPeople reached in an ad campaign.

◆ Sales and number of retail outlets. When you correlate these two, you get to see if sales per outlet have started to drop.

◆ Sales and population. If you own the only dry-cleaning shop in a growing town, you could project your per-capita numbers. If you own the Water Company, this is a scientific-quality correlation.

◆ Sales and number of salespeople. When sales per salesperson start to drop, it's a telltale sign of a problem developing.

◆ Sales and your competitor's estimated sales. You can use this information to see if you're actually falling behind, even as your sales increase.

Even in the hazy world of sales data, some correlations are better than others. In the business case of the toy bears, there were two problems that no one seemed to notice. First, by the second year of operation, there was a distinct post-Christmas slump—this caused unmanageable cash flow problems during an even bigger post-Christmas slump in the third year. Second, sales were going up, but sales-per-outlet were leveling off or headed down, a sure sign that someone's "genius status" is soon to be revoked.

There are plenty of valid applications of trend analysis in business data. If you can formulate a solid, fundamental reason, based on the details of a business, of why sales should correlate with some other business variable, Excel can help you quantitate the trend. But Excel has no problem whatsoever in finding a trend in a mirage.

Rule One of trend analysis: First think through a strong argument for expecting one set of business numbers to be connected to another. *Then* see if Excel confirms your argument.

Consider, as a last irony, that an *exponential* increase in sales (see Figure 19.17) is an even better fit to the reported data of toy sales than a straight line. A careful study of this projection says that by the year 1997, every dollar in circulation on the globe would be spent on talking stuffed toy bears. It should come as no surprise to you that this isn't what happened because you had at least enough money left over to buy this book. Sophisticated mathematics is no substitute for understanding the real dynamics of a business. If you need to justify a massive salary increase for yourself based on a trend projection, please be my guest, but you should be aware of the difference between a valid analysis and sleight of hand.

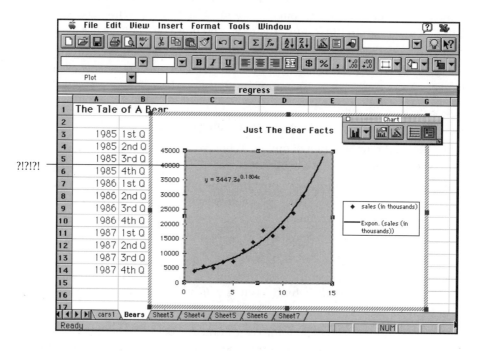

Figure 19.17 An exponential trendline fit to the bear facts.

Excel 5 has put forward the best trend analysis facilities ever incorporated in a worksheet. The people at Microsoft did a wonderful job, and incorporating trendlines into charting was a truly insightful move. Nonetheless, it behooves you to understand that trend analysis doesn't tell you anything if you don't have some understanding of the dynamics underlying your data. Excel can draw lines through your data points, but *you* have to decide whether the lines mean anything.

What-If Analysis: A Fish Story

In the previous chapters, I write about entering numbers, graphing them, and doing some calculations. Realistically, you could do most of this work on a calculator and make your own charts on graph paper.

Now I want to do something fancier, something that will actually put some of Excel 5's power to work. The idea here is to do this task simply enough so that you actually have some confidence in Excel's automated what-if methods. I know from teaching Excel classes that users often see a demonstration, nod agreeably all the way through, and then go back to doing everything by hand because there was some detail of the analysis that seemed a little hazy. After you understand how to use what-if techniques in Excel, you'll want to put them to work.

You already know how to analyze some basic situations by replacing a value in an Excel formula with different values one at a time. For example, you can poke around in a home-loan formula, trying out different amounts for the principal value to see what the resulting payments will be. The analysis tools in Excel 5 essentially let you do this same kind of investigation, but they provide a way to check out batches of test values rather than doing numbers one at a time.

The whole subject of what-if analysis is easier to explain with a concrete example. And by this, I don't mean one of those little case studies involving "widgets" or Product A versus Product B. If I may be allowed a bit of editorial fulmination, it's probably one of the greatest handicaps of American business that large chunks of it are managed by people who spent years getting their M.B.A.s by calculating widget examples.

Widgets never have defective parts or packaging, and there's no way to make a better widget by improving quality control or assembly, so in the widget trade, all business maneuvers consist of financial juggling and reducing overhead by laying off employees. During the 1970s and 1980s, American auto executives with advanced quantitative training thought they could sell cars with defective paint jobs and oil-leaking engines by managing inventories and credit financing plans better. The consequences of this approach to business school training have been pretty clear.

So, forget widgets . . . let's talk fish. I'm going to make a little model of a fishing business in Fort Bragg, CA, on the Mendocino County coast. It's a delightful community, except for the harsh economics of the fishing business. It's also the community that you see in most movies or TV programs about New England (better weather for shooting).

Figure 19.18 shows the elements of the model. Remember, the easiest way to get multiline cell entries like those in row 3 and row 6 is to select the whole row, choose Cell from the Format menu, and select the Wrap Text option from the Alignment tab. Here are the fishy facts behind the model:

◆ There are no salmon here, sorry to say. They're just about gone, like the increasingly elusive cod fish on the East Coast.

◆ Squid were bait 20 years ago. Then they were relabeled *calamari* and became Purina Yuppie Chow all over California.

◆ Rock cod is just a good old standard fish that is fortunately still abundant.

◆ Of course you can't eat sea urchins. You eat sea urchin eggs, called *uni* in sushi bars. It's a sort of an orangish paste that tastes just like you'd expect something from a spiny beach hazard to taste. You'll like the salmon and broiled eel in a sushi bar right away; *uni*, however, is an acquired taste. *Uni* from California goes mostly to the high-priced markets of Japan.

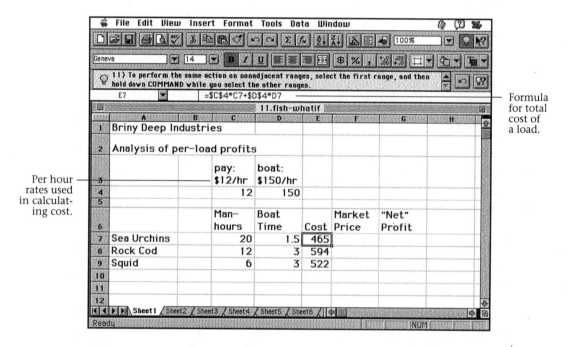

Figure 19.18   Labor and equipment costs for fishing.

The model here is a crude approximation of two facts of life: urchins are picked off the ocean floor by divers, while squid are simply netted from a boat. Figure 19.19 shows a little imaginary analysis of the profits for a single small load of each delectable seafood product. Profit in this model is just cost (labor plus boat time) subtracted from the market price. This game, by the way, is being played very seriously in the market I'm modeling here because fishing operations struggle to exist in a tough market and an increasingly empty ocean.

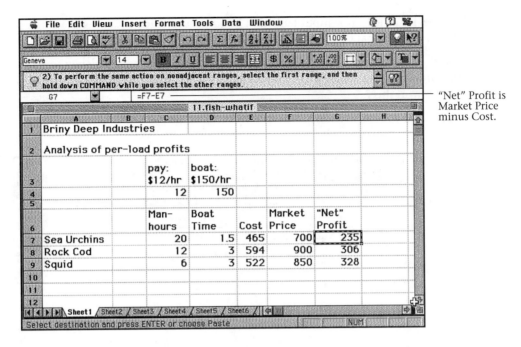

Figure 19.19 Profits from the sea.

Automating Replacement

There are many elements in this model that can be changed, and the changes will affect profits. Prices of seafood items can change, of course—*uni* prices, for example, are headed through the roof as the dollar sinks below 100 yen to the buck. I'm going to concentrate on changing production costs, instead, mainly to illustrate the way that Excel can change inputs to elaborate functions.

The cost factors are the per-hour labor rate, pegged at $12 per hour in the simple model, and at a rate of $150 per hour for fishing boat time (this is a composite of depreciation, abysmal per-hour fuel usage, and other costs). The formula in the Cost cells (column E) is simply

Cost = Man-hours * pay + BoatTime * BoatPerHourRate

I want to examine first what happens if the numbers for boat time change—this happens often as a direct consequence of changes in fuel prices.

You could just swap one number after another into cell D4 of this worksheet, but for more than two or three swaps, this gets to be tedious. There must be a better way, and there is. Excel has a device called a one-input table that handles automated swapping of values, producing a table of outputs that corresponds to the different conditions you want to test.

Now the one-input table is useful, but it's a fussy little item, requiring you to do everything perfectly. You must follow these instructions exactly, or you'll create an unsightly blob of grid on your worksheet.

Here's what you do, as shown in Figure 19.20.

This cell is the corner of the data-table rectangle.

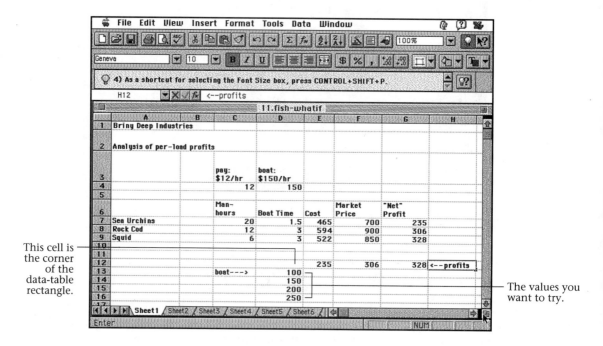

The values you want to try.

Figure 19.20 Setting up a one-input table.

1. Find a clean rectangular area to place the table. One cell (leave it blank) will be the upper-left corner that anchors the table.

2. Underneath the anchor cell (ahoy, mates), you can list the different values that you want to try in the model. Those are the boat-time numbers from 100 to 250 in Figure 19.20.

3. Then across the top, next to the anchor cell, type in the "result cells" that you want to inspect. Here I made the connection between profits and boat time by putting =G7 into E12, =G8 into F12, and =G9 into G12.

4. Unless you have the world's greatest memory, I suggest putting little text labels at the sides of the table. That's what the boat→ and ←profits tags are doing there.

5. Now use the mouse to select the area for the table (see Figure 19.21). Pull down the Data menu and choose Table. You see a dialog box that asks for some inputs.

6. In my table, I'm changing the data in a column to be variations on the input in cell D4, so I click the Column Input Cell box and click D4, and that cell is entered as a Column Input Cell.

7. Click OK. Presto! Excel gives you a whole set of profit data.

On a practical basis, the one-input data table becomes more useful if you have a longer list of possible inputs.

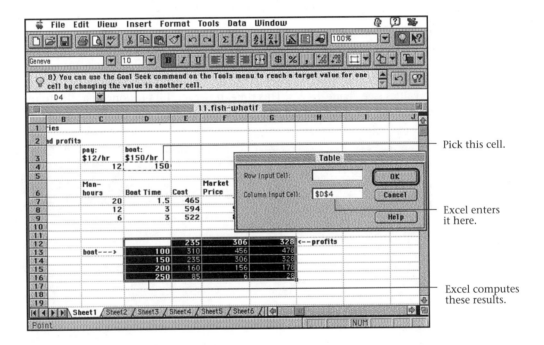

Figure 19.21   Excel tries a list of input values in your model.

Don't try to edit cells in the data table. They're protected, so you can't do it. It's possible to get caught in a shocking mess where your only hope is to press Escape, clear the whole table, and start over again.

So what do you see in the table? The first thing you see is that if the boat costs double, it's not worth getting up in the morning and heading out to sea. If boat costs drop a lot, it's time to go squid fishing. It would be pretty simple to estimate a per-load cost that makes it worthwhile to go fishing and thus turn this example into a break-even case study.

This sort of analysis happens all the time in other businesses. There are always trade-offs between production costs, materials costs, shipping costs, the contribution of different items to overhead, and so forth. Here I just modeled a little operation with two kinds of costs and three products. The real value of automating data substitution with a one-input table appears when you have more complications, such as six cost factors and nine products. If you try to solve that kind of problem by one-item-at-a-time substitution, it's pretty tedious. If you try to solve it in your head, the odds are you'll get it wrong.

More Automation

As long as I'm putting Excel to work, I might as well get a little more out of it. There's a variation on this last operation, called a two-input table, that lets me change two inputs at once while generating a table of outputs corresponding to a single quantity. Again, I'm going to pick a clean rectangular area, take the cell in the upper-left corner as an anchor, and start filling in values (see Figure 19.22). This time, however, I'll pick one quantity to monitor and give the table two kinds of inputs.

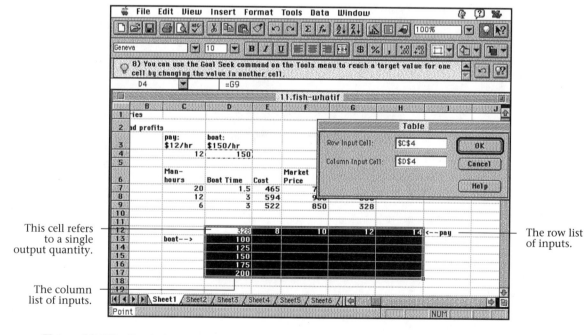

Figure 19.22 Excel tries two lists of input values in the model.

Here are the steps for a two-input table:

1. Input a set of pay levels in a row across the top of the rectangle.

2. List the boat-time data in a column, as before.

3. In the anchor cell, put =G9, corresponding to squid-catch profits. (*Oooh!* Isn't this better than widgets? Gives ya something to picture in your mind.)

4. Select Table from the Data menu.

5. The dialog box now needs both a row ("pay" in C4) and a column ("boat" in D4) entry.

6. When you click OK in the Table dialog box, you get the informative vista displayed in Figure 19.23.

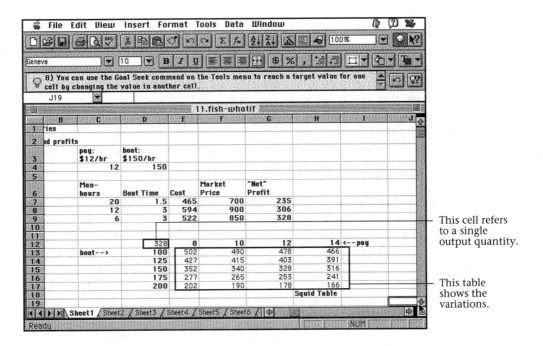

Figure 19.23 This two-input table is a definitive analysis of the squid market.

The little table shown in the figure is the quantitative expression that labor costs are not the big problem with squid. If a good local area gets fished out so that the boat trip doubles (going to the next area), there won't be much calamari with ginger-lime dip in the finer establishments on shore. What's actually happened in West Coast fishing reality, just so you know, is that sea urchin market prices are currently going berserk. At the most recent projections (using the TREND function discussed earlier in this chapter), the last sea urchin will sell for 200 million yen at an auction in the Tokyo Central Fish Market in the year 2017. I'm partially kidding.

When do you use a two-way table versus a one-way table? In my humble opinion, *most* business situations actually call for a two-way table, and the one-way table is just a simple explanatory device used in books like this to introduce the subject. The all-time killer table shows Sales along one side of the table, Payroll along the other side, with Profit as the quantity being investigated. That's pretty much the table all America wants to see at business meetings. If growing businesses used this kind of table consistently and used realistic estimates of sales rather than something computed by regression, they could avoid the ghastly destructive cycle in which they hire people and then lay them off three months later. It's an ironic problem that fast growth is statistically as dangerous to businesses as gentle decline.

Scenario Manager

Personally, I like using two-way tables for analysis, but I use another Excel feature, Scenario Manager, for presentations. The problem with tables is that they typically present more information than people can conveniently absorb from a slide in a 40-minute fast-talking pitch. It's easier to encapsulate a few high points in Scenario Manager and then display a few cases. This doesn't matter much in the fish trade, where reality catches you sooner or later, but in financial realms, a good pitch usually *is* the product. Frankly, if your argument is shaky, but your job depends on the presentation, Excel's Scenario Manager is your best computer friend (along with the short course in graphing tricks in Chapter 15).

After that build-up, I should probably show you how to use this feature. For our piscatory computational interlude, it goes something like this:

1. After you choose Scenarios under the Tools menu, the Scenario Manager pops up. Old Excel hands, please note that Scenario Manager is now part of the show, not an add-in.

2. Click Add to bring up the Add Scenario dialog box, name a Scenario, and click on the input cells that will change in the model (see Figure 19.24).

3. I'm going to define a good case and a bad case, so I click Add again, getting the screen shown in Figure 19.25.

4. To enter the data for the scenario, click on the scenario and then enter the data for the case directly in the worksheet.

5. Good fishing means cheap labor and cheap boats, bad fishing means expensive help and expensive equipment. After I enter the data (see Figure 19.26), Scenario Manager remembers it.

6. I can add more Scenarios to this worksheet any time I like.

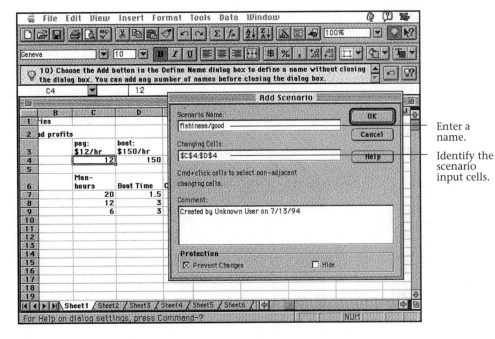

Figure 19.24 Pick a scenario name and the input cells that you want to change.

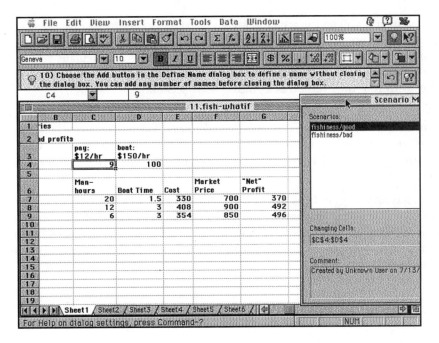

Figure 19.25 The Scenario Manager records several sets of inputs.

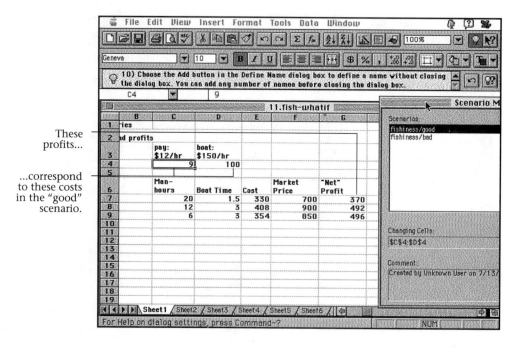

These profits...

...correspond to these costs in the "good" scenario.

Figure 19.26   The low-cost fishing scenario.

For a presentation, call up the Scenario Manager, park it somewhere at the side of your worksheet (so it's not in the way of the numbers), and click on the scenarios one at a time. Because the numbers change faster than anyone in the room can calculate, you have a real "dazzle" advantage if you whip through a high case and a low case and then present the audience with your own version of a "most likely" scenario.

For a Scenario Manager presentation, I also recommend putting a chart of the key result quantity on the worksheet (see Figure 19.27). Not only does it draw attention away from the raw numbers, but it also gives you a chance to use all the tricks I discussed in Chapter 15. The chart changes automatically every time you click on a different scenario in the Scenario Manager window.

Please understand that neither I, nor Hayden Books, nor Macmillan, nor Simon & Schuster, nor our corporate parent Viacom would advocate fraud of any kind. I'm talking about designing a presentation for a circumstance in which "your glass can be seen as half empty or half full." In Scenario Manager, you can pick the state that you want to present and also show what a full glass would look like.

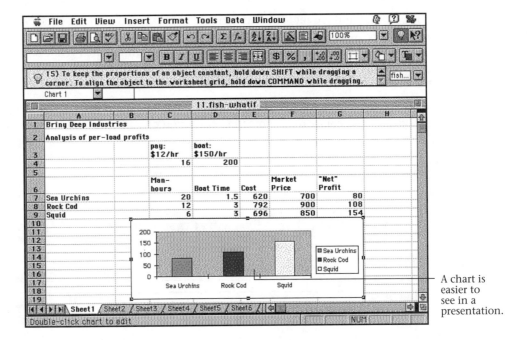

Figure 19.27   Charts beat tables, for truth or fiction.

Looking Back with Goal Seek

Now for your own investigation, there's another handy tool to employ. It's called Goal Seek, and you can find it in the Tools menu (above Scenario).

Using Goal Seek in the fishing example, I tell Excel how much profit I want, and it tells me the conditions that will yield that much profit. In other words, I pick an output that I want, and Goal Seek juggles input values until the output is right.

It's easy to use, and here's how you do it:

1. Click the output cell for your experiment. I'm picking sea urchin profits in G7, just to go for the gusto.

2. Select Goal Seek from the Tools menu. When the Goal Seek dialog box opens, you see that it has put your selected cell in the Set Cell text box.

3. Put a goal value in the To Value text box and click on the variable input cell, in this case the labor-cost cell in C4 (see Figure 19.28). Click OK.

4. Goal Seek grinds a bit. After it's finished, the Goal Seek Status dialog box and the numbers in the worksheet have changed (see Figure 19.29).

What did this command tell me? Well, at current boat costs and market prices for urchins, I'd have to find a diver who would work for $2.50 an hour if I want to make $500-per-load profits. That's not going to happen. If I want to make more money, things are even less promising. To make $610 a load on urchins, I have to find divers who will pay *me* $3.00 an hour to have them muck around in the freezing cold and dark water. That's highly unlikely.

Nonetheless, Goal Seek is a worthwhile day-to-day business tool. If you have, for example, a realistic model of your company's transaction costs, you can use it to find the minimum order you should process. You can use it to decide whether you should switch jobs, comparing salaries before and after and the costs of switching. And it's very effective in loan payment computations, solving for either loan amounts or target payments.

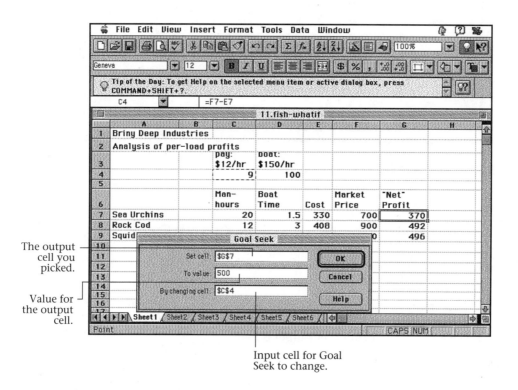

The output cell you picked.

Value for the output cell.

Input cell for Goal Seek to change.

Figure 19.28   Seeking profit goals in Excel.

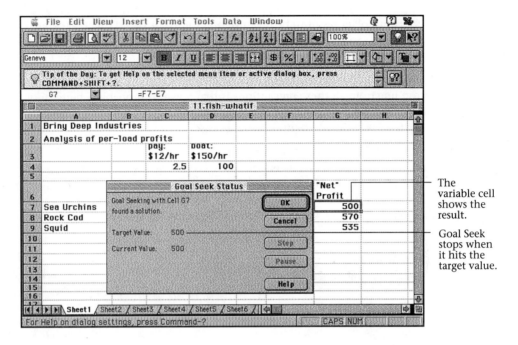

Figure 19.29   Below minimum wage in cell C4!!

Looking Everywhere with Solver

Goal Seek essentially runs through a set of input values and then reports the result to you when it has reached the desired outcome. It's fast and very useful—even for complicated models—because it's a one-dimensional optimization, changing only one number at a time.

What happens if you want to pick a goal—profit, for example—and find the particular combination of inputs that will get you to that goal? Use an add-in called Solver (Microsoft buys the Solver code from a third party—that's why it's still an add-in). In some cases, Solver is very useful, but it has drawbacks that you should understand. Microsoft, realizing that Solver is not for everyone, doesn't include it in the standard installation. You have to select the complete installation during setup, or you have to go back into the setup procedure and add it. Here are some Solver considerations:

◆ Multidimensional goal-seeking is a slow process. It's hundreds of times slower than one-dimensional seeking, not just two or three times slower.

◆ Solver can decide that it has met your goal, when, in fact, it has stopped in some weird area of input-variable space. Although it's okay for simple kinds of relationships between input and output, for complex relationships it can get "stuck."

◆ For a Solver result to be meaningful, it must be based on an accurate business model. Solver is happy to give you nonsense results if you don't know how to specify correct ranges of input values.

The bottom line from all these precautions is that Solver is probably a better tool for engineering problems (adjusting three ingredients in a mix) than for business problems. Nonetheless, here's how it works in the two-input fisheries case.

After you select Solver from the Tools menu, you see the screen in Figure 19.30. This dialog box wants you to specify a target cell and the cells that you want the program to vary. In this case, I specify squid profits in G9. I also want this quantity maximized, so I click the Max radio button (Solver can solve for a minimum or a specific value, also). In the By Changing Cells text box, I have specified C4 (pay rate) and D4 (per-hour rate for the boat).

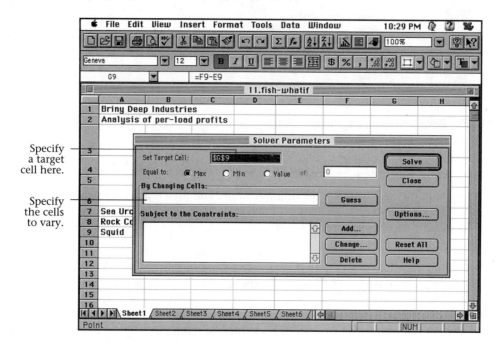

Figure 19.30   Starting up Solver.

Be aware that Solver will try values in the changing cells, so you have to specify constraints (that is, limits) to keep the values realistic. Click the Add button in the Solver Parameters dialog box to bring up the Add Constraint dialog box in Figure 19.31. Constraints are usually inequalities, giving a range of possible values for Solver to use. For this example, I decided to let the pay rate run from $8 to $18 and the per-hour rate for the boat run from $85 to $200, giving the values in Figure 19.32.

Scrolling list of choices for in-equalities.

Figure 19.31 Constraints are usually inequalities.

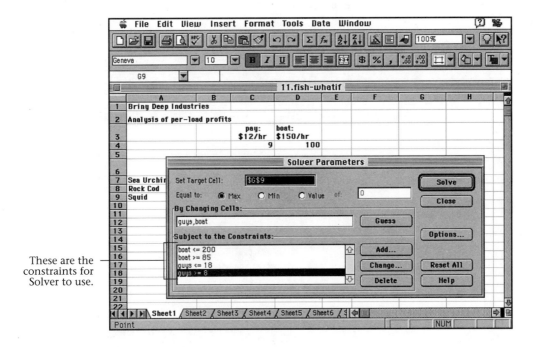

These are the constraints for Solver to use.

Figure 19.32 Solver with constraints loaded.

Just before the model is run (by clicking the Solve button), you may be saying, "Hey, Mr. Excel-Author, sir, this example is idiotic. If this model works, Solver is going to jam right away to the lowest pay rate and lowest boat charges because it's calculating maximum *profit,* and the only way to survive here is to lower costs." You're right. I congratulate you for noticing this. That's what's going to happen. The model is so simple that you can predict the outcome. I did this on purpose. If I had made a model with several quadratic or cubic equations, with complex constraints, Solver would still find an answer, but it would be much tougher to tell whether the answer was right. In general, you're better off starting with a simple, even unrealistic model, and then adding more details, tracking the changes in results as the model evolves.

If you build a fancy model for Solver (fancy in this context means that the target cell has a complicated formula), you may want to tinker with Solver Options (see Figure 19.33). Unless you are using advanced math functions in the target formula, the default settings for Estimates, Derivatives, and Search are fine, but you may want to speed up Solver by reducing the number of iterations and reducing the precision.

Reduce
iterations
and
precision
for a speed
improve-
ment.

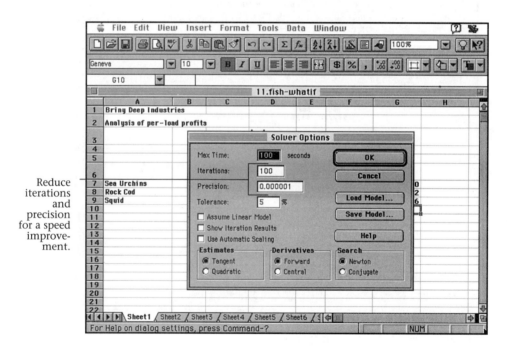

Figure 19.33   Solver Options.

When Solver is finished, it reports with a little dialog box (see Figure 19.34) that lets you accept the new values into your worksheet or revert to the original values. Solver adds a new worksheet with its computed results (the Answer Report in Figure 19.35) to the front of the tabbed stack of sheets in your workbook. As you develop a series of increasingly realistic models, you can save all the report sheets to see which features of the models are most important.

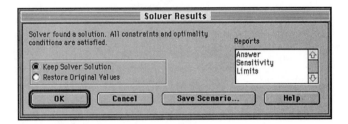

Figure 19.34   Solver tells you when it's finished.

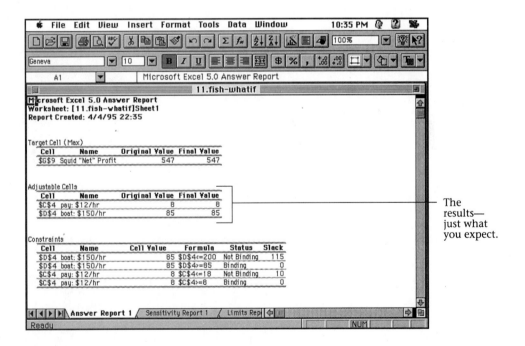

Figure 19.35   A Solver Answer Report.

Trend analysis and what-if analysis can be wonderful tools *if you understand your data* and which direction you want your data to take you in the business world. Now that you have explored the world of future possibilities, let's get back on dry land in the last chapter of the Excel section so that you can learn how to analyze all the data that you have at your disposal *now*.

Chapter 20

Analyzing Data

If you have piles and piles of business data—and most well-run operations do—someday you'll need to make sense of it all. The defining problem of the modern computer-oriented business environment is not a lack of information, but the presence of so much information that you can't begin to find what you need, much less interpret it. You need to identify the main *trends* in your business, and by trend I don't mean a bunch of points that you can fit to a straight line. I mean a significant shift, a warning signal, a sign that something is happening that's not business as usual. To help you make sense of all that data, this chapter explores category analysis and statistical analysis and shows you how to use Excel to define some trends in this data. The chapter includes the following information:

◆ Entering multidimensional data

◆ Pivot table design tips

◆ Turning data into pivot tables

◆ Pivoting for analysis

◆ Hiding details

◆ Special pivot functions

◆ Simple descriptive statistics

◆ Single factor analysis of variance

◆ Correlation analysis

◆ Plotting histograms with options

◆ Basic regression

◆ Regression diagnostics

◆ Using t-tests

The Pivot Story

Pivot tables, the central worksheet feature of category analysis, enable you to define many different ways to look at the same data in a table. You have to do some exploration yourself, but what you'll find is that after a bit of experimentation, you'll be manipulating pivot tables like a champ. Category analysis is a bit abstract as a topic, so I'll discuss it in terms of a concrete (well, a stuffed-animal) example.

Microsoft could tell that pivot tables were important because several other firms were doing a lively business marketing pivot table add-ins and accessories. Microsoft religiously adheres to the Godzilla versus Bambi Principle of Marketing, based on the short cartoon of the same name. According to the principle, Godzilla waits until Bambi emerges from the forest, and then stomps on Bambi and eats him. Microsoft typically lets small firms test the waters for new spreadsheet features and then adds the features to Excel a year or two later. That's one of the reasons Excel keeps growing, and the list of third-party vendors for Excel keeps shrinking.

In the case of pivot tables, building pivots into Excel itself has a certain compelling logic: people will be more likely to use pivots, which are really valuable, and people will come to appreciate the convenience of having the data and the feature in the same application.

Multidimensional?

What's the meaning of multidimensional data, given that all this data is entered into a standard two-dimensional worksheet? It's easier to understand this concept in an example than by defining terms.

Here's your example. You've been appointed as the American sales manager of the Australian firm, Marsupial Madness. The original sales manager, a native Australian based in San Francisco, was so humiliated by the box office and critical failure of *Lightning Jack,* Paul "Crocodile Dundee" Hogan's 1994 film, that he couldn't face his friends in San Francisco anymore and moved back to Alice Springs. He insisted on an unlisted phone number.

In the humble office on Market Street, behind a stack of cases of Foster's lager and stuffed animals in various states of disrepair, you find a Quadra 610 that has the Excel 5 worksheet in Figure 20.1.

Let's look at this closely. You have a single year, two halves in the year, three products, three product types,[1] and finally the sales data. In modeling lingo, product type can be considered a category and also one dimension of the sales data. The number 150, fourth down in the sales data column, could be characterized as

sales = 150 (1994, 2nd, Kurt Koala, Plush)

[1] Disclaimer: Please note that "real-fur" in the product type category refers to products made with the fur of rabbits that have died of extreme old age in natural bunny habitats, surrounded by family and friends after long and productive rabbit lives. No animals were injured during the production of this book, despite the fact that Roger the cat persistently walked across my Mac keyboard at crucial moments.

In other words, the number 150 is an individual data item whose location in the "space" of all the data is given by the "address" (1994, 2nd, Kurt Koala, Plush). Because the address has multiple elements, it's a piece of multidimensional data.

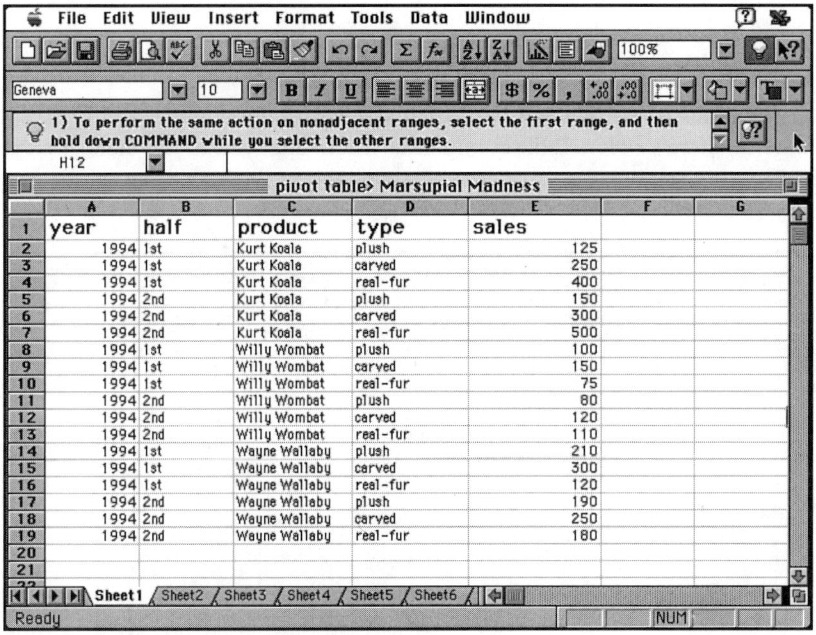

File Edit View Insert Format Tools Data Window

Geneva ... 10

1) To perform the same action on nonadjacent ranges, select the first range, and then hold down COMMAND while you select the other ranges.

H12

pivot table> Marsupial Madness

	A	B	C	D	E	F	G
1	year	half	product	type	sales		
2	1994	1st	Kurt Koala	plush	125		
3	1994	1st	Kurt Koala	carved	250		
4	1994	1st	Kurt Koala	real-fur	400		
5	1994	2nd	Kurt Koala	plush	150		
6	1994	2nd	Kurt Koala	carved	300		
7	1994	2nd	Kurt Koala	real-fur	500		
8	1994	1st	Willy Wombat	plush	100		
9	1994	1st	Willy Wombat	carved	150		
10	1994	1st	Willy Wombat	real-fur	75		
11	1994	2nd	Willy Wombat	plush	80		
12	1994	2nd	Willy Wombat	carved	120		
13	1994	2nd	Willy Wombat	real-fur	110		
14	1994	1st	Wayne Wallaby	plush	210		
15	1994	1st	Wayne Wallaby	carved	300		
16	1994	1st	Wayne Wallaby	real-fur	120		
17	1994	2nd	Wayne Wallaby	plush	190		
18	1994	2nd	Wayne Wallaby	carved	250		
19	1994	2nd	Wayne Wallaby	real-fur	180		
20							
21							

Sheet1 / Sheet2 / Sheet3 / Sheet4 / Sheet5 / Sheet6 /

Ready   NUM

Figure 20.1   Many dimensions from two?

Categories

And because the elements of the address are categories, you have a data table with multiple categories. In pivot table analysis, you make a new table with some categories along the top edge and some categories along the left side. This way you can make a table, for example, that compares different product types for different years, different products by type, or any combination of categories.

The idea here is to find (by switching the "what-by-what" in the table) categories that highlight the biggest influences on the data in the table. In other kinds of data, you may find out that sales region is a more important factor in sales than product differentiation or that all regions are having a bad quarter together or that one product alone is doing well and the rest are withering across time and region. Actually, there's a whole technique called factor analysis in statistics that performs this sort of study semi-automatically, but the pivot table approach has the advantage of requiring no math or statistics background at all.

Let's Pivot

Unto every complex task, Microsoft hath created a wizard. Pivot tables are no exception. Under the Data menu, there's a PivotTable command, which takes you to the dialog box shown in Figure 20.2.

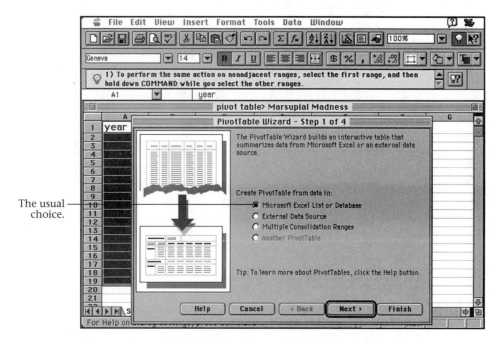

Figure 20.2   PivotTable Wizard, Step 1.

Notice that there are a few choices in this wizard step that I'm not going to pursue. If you like, you can explore Multiple Consolidation Ranges on your own. This choice enables you to use data stored in several worksheets, as long as the categories in all the worksheets are the same.

If you choose External Data Source, Excel makes pivot tables from data stored elsewhere. The only problem with this choice is that Excel's automatic connections all lead to PC-side databases. If the data resides in a FoxPro or Microsoft Access or standard dBASE database, you can import it automatically into an Excel pivot table. In a mixed-platform office, these databases are often found, but they don't have much presence on the Macintosh side. Believe it or not, if you want to find out how to use PC-based external data sources, your best bet is to read the Excel manual because it was written from a Windows point of view with only modest concessions to the existence of the Macintosh.

Setting up the table

So you're just going to take data from a standard worksheet instead of an exotic, remote source (see Figure 20.3). There's enough intelligence built into Excel 5 to interpret categorical data—all you have to do is arrange the data as shown in Figure 20.1.

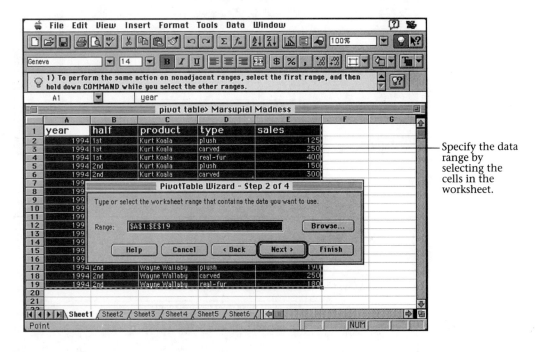

Specify the data range by selecting the cells in the worksheet.

Figure 20.3   Picking data for a pivot table.

After these simple preliminaries, the PivotTable Wizard shows your choices for column categories, row categories, and data (see Figure 20.4). If you have a big table that you want to divide into separate pages, there's a page category, as well.

To formulate the table, you just click and drag the little category boxes to their positions. Dragging "sales" to the DATA zone makes Excel pop up the element "Sum of sales" (see Figure 20.5) because Excel is not just going to partition the data but provide subtotals and totals, as well. Besides sums, you can make different kinds of data analysis by double-clicking the buttons for data elements (product, type, and so forth), which gives you other statistical options (see Figure 20.6), such as Max and Min.

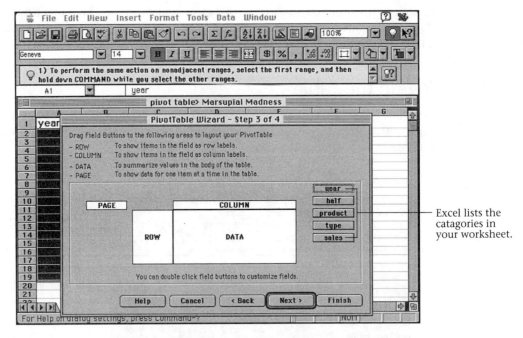

Excel lists the
catagories in
your worksheet.

Figure 20.4   Picking the categories for pivoting.

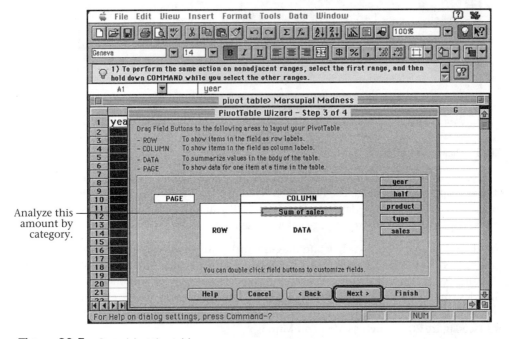

Analyze this
amount by
category.

Figure 20.5   Organizing the table.

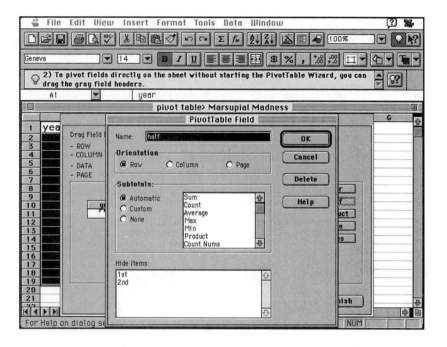

Figure 20.6   Other types of pivot statistics.

I'm going to use "year" as a page identifier and analyze products by type in my first setup (see Figure 20.7). It's easy to change row and column categories later—that's the whole point of this feature—so that you can change your mind later and do some exploring. After you have the categories assigned to your satisfaction (you don't have to assign everything because partial tables are perfectly okay), you can click the Next button, leading you to the last wizard step (see Figure 20.8). You may as well click all the option check boxes, too, so that you can see right away all the wonderful pivoting things Excel wants to do for you.

Analysis at last

After this furious bout of wizard-stepping, let's finally see what the wizard has produced (see Figure 20.9). Excel has generated and formatted and subtotaled this magnificent analysis of the Australian marsupial toy business. You should know that any little block in gray in this figure can be selected with the mouse and moved (from side to top or top to side) to generate a new table with new totals and subtotals.

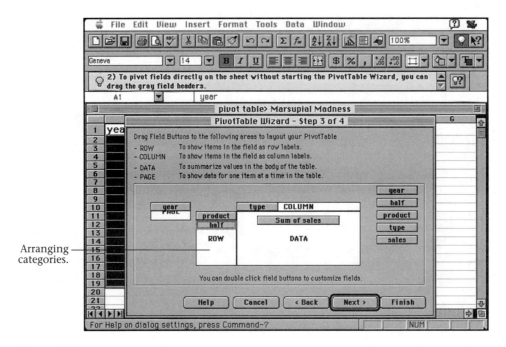

Arranging categories.

Figure 20.7 Deciding what-by-what in the table.

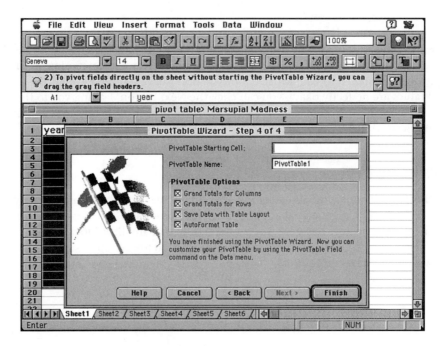

Figure 20.8 Check all the boxes! Information is free!

Just for excitement, I have popped up the Query and Pivot toolbar by checking it on the Toolbars dialog box from the View menu. The first button gets you back into PivotTable Wizard; the next button gives you an options dialog box if you have selected a data element; the arrow buttons group and ungroup categories; and the next two buttons hide details and show details (the pivot table is really a sort of outline, after all). The button with little sheets lets you view different pages, and the exclamation point button refreshes data—if you make changes in the original plain table, click here to get the new data entered into the pivot table.

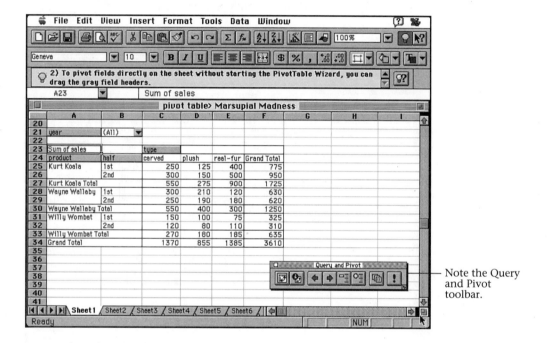

Note the Query and Pivot toolbar.

Figure 20.9 Finally, a pivot table.

But you might reasonably inquire, "What's been accomplished here?" Let's take a look:

◆ The bottom line shows clearly that the plush versions of these critters aren't moving very well, at least not compared to the bunny fur and carved (from a nonendangered, nonrainforest tree with a funny name) versions.

◆ Second half sales are down compared to first half, except for that standout marsupial Kurt Koala.

◆ If you combine these pieces of information, you would conclude that a fur version of Kurt could be this year's hot ticket. A look at the fur, second half, and Kurt numbers shows this to be the case.

◆ The wombats ain't working.

All these bits of information are present in the original big data table, but it would be hard work to isolate them. The point of a pivot table is that it lets you spot significant data easily.

Back on the last step of the PivotTable Wizard, I selected the check box for AutoFormat, which has produced this smallish table. Figure 20.10 shows some modest efforts at reformatting the results by hand so that the numbers are easier to see in a report. Also note that Excel has put the table underneath the original data. That's what it does unless you advise otherwise on the last wizard step. Because the data exists in a multisheet workbook, you may want to park your individual pivot tables on different worksheets for clarity.

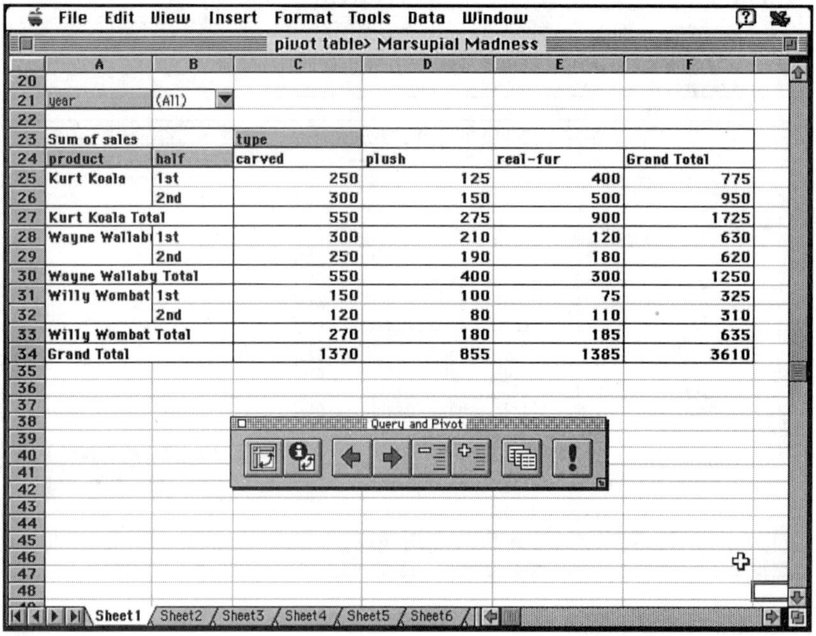

	A	B	C	D	E	F
21	year	(All)				
22						
23	Sum of sales		type			
24	product	half	carved	plush	real-fur	Grand Total
25	Kurt Koala	1st	250	125	400	775
26		2nd	300	150	500	950
27	Kurt Koala Total		550	275	900	1725
28	Wayne Wallab	1st	300	210	120	630
29		2nd	250	190	180	620
30	Wayne Wallaby Total		550	400	300	1250
31	Willy Wombat	1st	150	100	75	325
32		2nd	120	80	110	310
33	Willy Wombat Total		270	180	185	635
34	Grand Total		1370	855	1385	3610

Figure 20.10 A bigger picture with bolder numbers.

Variations on a pivot theme

What happens if you select categories and switch them around? Figure 20.11 shows the result of "pivoting" the product and type categories. Down in the extreme lower-right corner, you still see the same Grand Total, but in this view of things, there's a slightly different emphasis. In this view, you can see that there's not a huge difference between the first and second halves in 1994. But that's because the koalas have been carrying this whole show on their narrow furry shoulders. The koalas, bless their eucalyptus-munching little selves, account for the entire improvement in sales from the first half to the second. (A friend of mine who works for the San Diego Zoo once told me that working with koalas means being subjected to an endless gentle drizzle from above that smells like cough syrup.) This document clearly indicates a public slowly drifting away from interest in wallabies and wombats. Is the letter *W* falling out of fashion, or are these animals just not cute enough? That will be your decision to make for Marsupial Madness, but at least you have the data.

Switching categories.

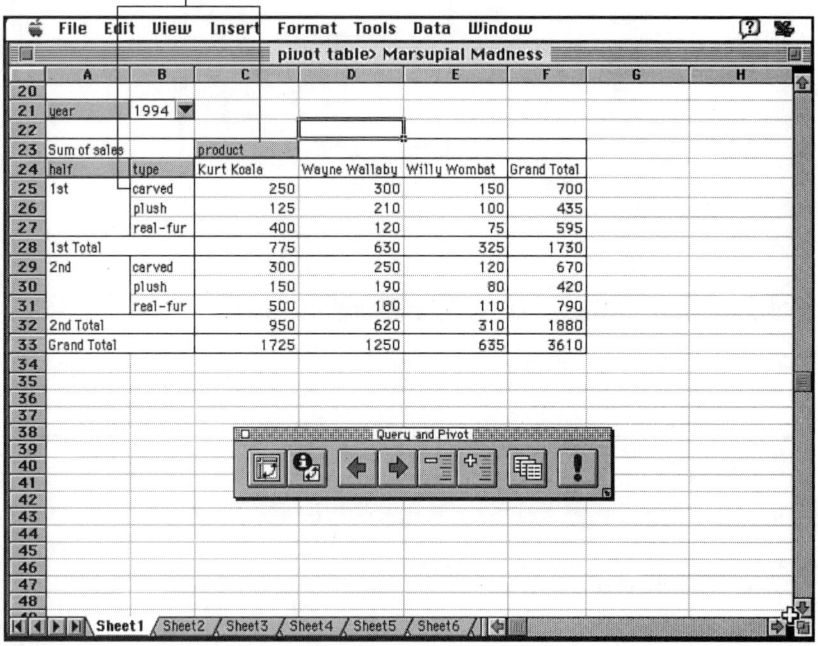

Figure 20.11   Making the table pivot.

If you are uncomfortable with dragging categories, or if you want to do a fancier analysis (such as changing the statistics from simple totals to something else), just double-click any data element in a gray box (see Figure 20.12), and you can switch the element from a row to a column label and pick a subtotal type.

You can also change the time base of the table by dragging the element "half" up to the PAGE area where "year" is posted. Clicking on "half" then pops up choices for seeing either first half data, second half data, or the whole year—still a small table, but one in which data has been summed for the whole year (see Figure 20.13).

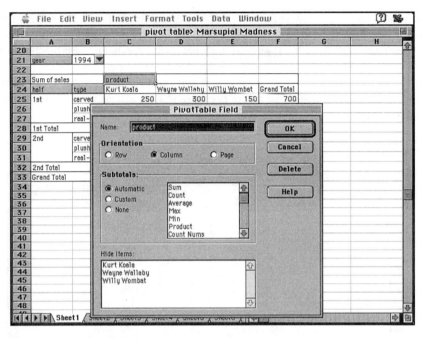

Figure 20.12   Double-click to change pivots on the fly.

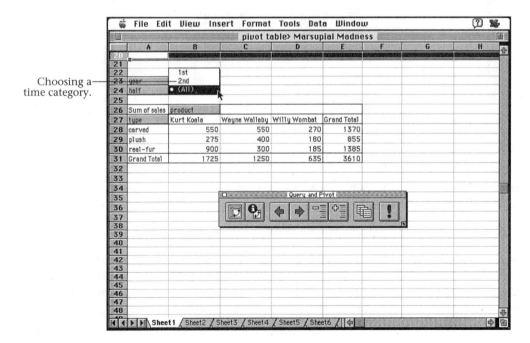

Choosing a—
time category.

Figure 20.13   A time-condensed pivot table.

Yet there's no reason to stop here. Let's pull the category half around to the top of the table and put type and product on the left side of it. We get the table shown in Figure 20.14, which displays the critters stacked right on top of each other, so a direct product-to-product situation is emphasized. Once again, two principles stand out: koalas rule, and the furrier the better. Perhaps the conclusion from this pivoting is that the next product should be a stuffed koala so furry that you can barely make out its little black nose. This is just the kind of information that you're supposed to derive from category-based analysis—it's supposed to lead you to *conclusions* rather than mere numbers.

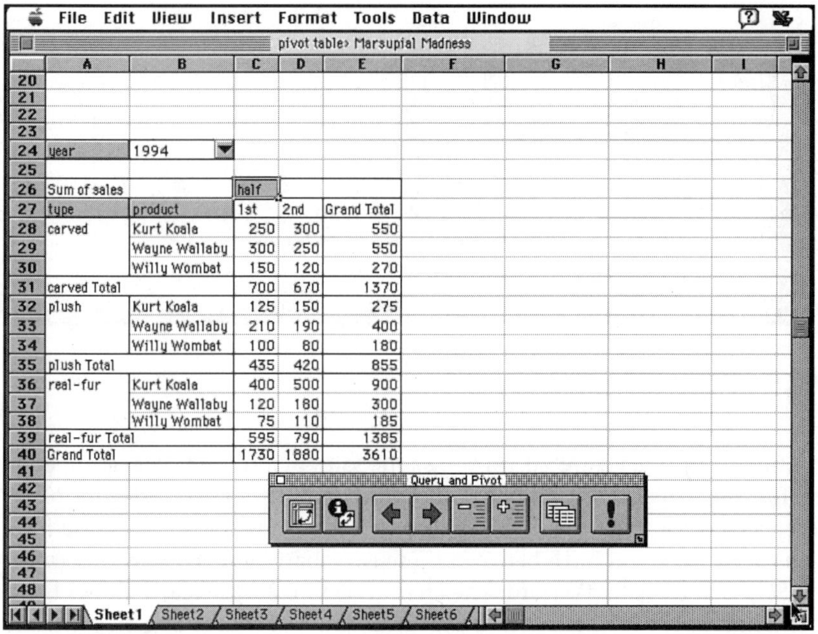

year	1994			
Sum of sales		half		
type	product	1st	2nd	Grand Total
carved	Kurt Koala	250	300	550
	Wayne Wallaby	300	250	550
	Willy Wombat	150	120	270
carved Total		700	670	1370
plush	Kurt Koala	125	150	275
	Wayne Wallaby	210	190	400
	Willy Wombat	100	80	180
plush Total		435	420	855
real-fur	Kurt Koala	400	500	900
	Wayne Wallaby	120	180	300
	Willy Wombat	75	110	185
real-fur Total		595	790	1385
Grand Total		1730	1880	3610

Figure 20.14 A table with other categories arranged against time.

Pictures from pivots

Pivot tables make it easy to see what's really going on in your data. At least, they make it as easy as it's going to be in a plain table full of numbers. For more impact, you have to turn to charts. In Figure 20.15, I was interested in product types, so I selected the three Total ranges on product type across the first and second halves of 1994. (Remember, hold down the ⌘ key to select ranges that aren't contiguous.)

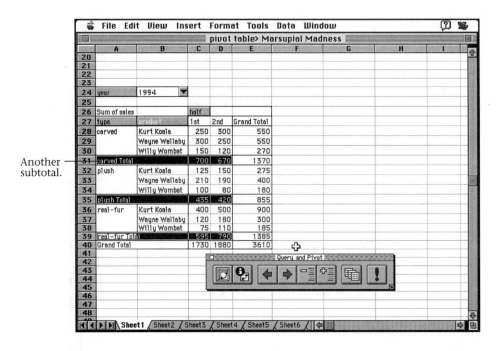

Another ─── subtotal.

Figure 20.15   Selecting ranges to chart.

The resulting chart (see Figure 20.16) shows the sales by product type, grouped into two batches (for first half and second half). Another grouping, shown in Figure 20.17, isolates each product type and contrasts the first and second halves of the year. After you have selected the data, you toggle back and forth between these two chart views by selecting category (x axis) labels in Step 2 of the ChartWizard. The chart in Figure 20.17 clearly shows the fur boom in the second half of 1994, which means that an additional source of geriatric rabbits looks like a winning resource for Marsupial Madness.

Pivot tables are a Real Big Deal. They're easy to set up, easy to use, and encourage you to explore your data until the actual meaning of the data becomes apparent. By allowing arrangement of data by different categories (Sales by State, Brand by Region, New Customers by Year), pivot tables enable you to find a way to highlight the connection among different categories and your actual data. These tables are the most important fundamentally new business tool in Excel 5.

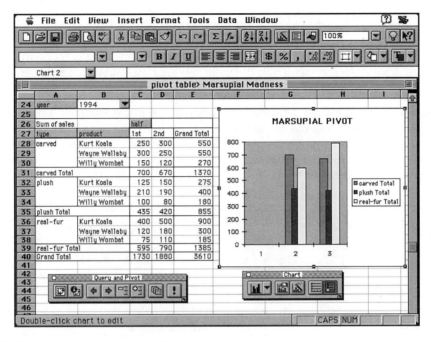

Figure 20.16   First half and second half results.

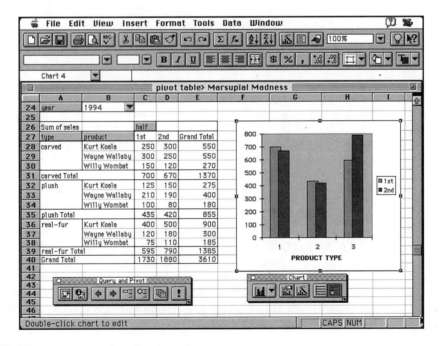

Figure 20.17   Three sets of product bars, by type.

517

Simple Descriptive Stats

The analysis tools, in many cases, appear to duplicate functions already found in the Trendline dialog box from the Insert menu. But the tools here are classic tabulated statistics, and they offer insights that aren't always clear from simpler graphical methods.

A basic starting point in analysis is the application of descriptive statistics. Let's start with a simple set of numbers—our old friend the car data set from Chapter 19 (see Figure 20.18). Because I review statistics programs several times a year, I have about 500 textbook sample data sets on my hard drive, but I think it's actually more educational to show different tests applied to the same data set than to introduce lots of variety into the numbers.

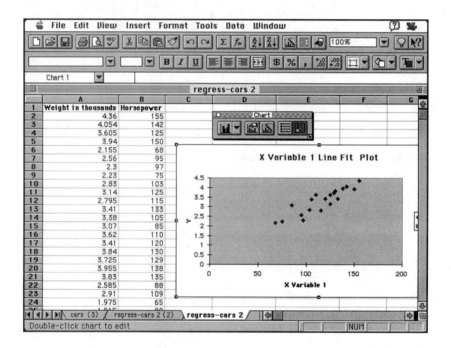

Figure 20.18   Weight versus horsepower, yet again!

In my version of Excel, Data Analysis (see Figure 20.19) appears under the Tools menu because I've picked it out as a permanent addition by using the Add-Ins manager. If you selected a minimal installation when you first installed Excel, you have to go back to your setup disks and add the Add-Ins by following the steps for modifying an existing installation. You then need to pick Add-Ins from the Tools menu and select the Data Analysis option. (Because the setup routines just transfer the Add-In material from the installation disks to your hard drive, you still have to build Data Analysis into Excel by specifically adding it with the Add-Ins Manager.)

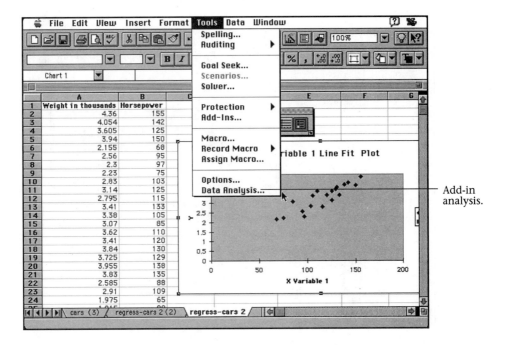

Figure 20.19   My own customized Tools menu has Data Analysis at the bottom.

When you select Data Analysis, you are greeted with a dialog box that contains most of the tests used in a basic one-year statistics course (see Figure 20.20). Here we sail into uncharted waters with Excel—if you never had a statistics course, this section of the program contains more unfamiliar elements. There's not much problem figuring out bold text formatting, number formats, or even macros, but this isn't the right place for your first exposure to two-factor ANOVA. So I'm going to stick to explaining the functions here in terms of a procedure you already know: fitting a straight line through a cloud of data points.

Just for fun, let's choose Descriptive Statistics from the Analysis Tools scrolling list in the Data Analysis dialog box (see Figure 20.21) and see what we get. Usually, this operation applies to a single column or row, although Excel can handle multiple data sets. I'm going to specify that the output table should appear on the same worksheet, although you can direct it to another worksheet in the same workbook or to another workbook altogether. This dialog box is typical in asking whether the data is labeled in the First Row—it is, and labeling rows and keeping data in columns make your Data Analysis life in Excel easier. Also, I've checked the Summary Statistics check box because summaries are a key part of descriptive statistics.

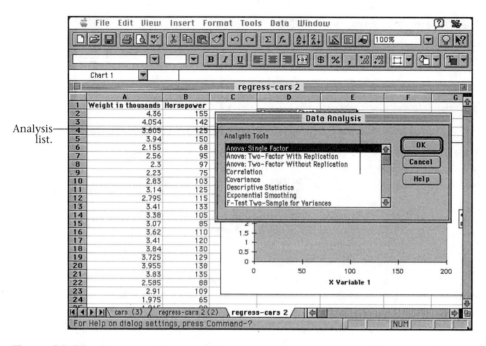

Figure 20.20   Statistics 101A in a scrolling list.

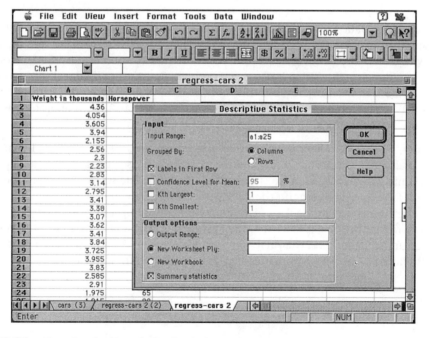

Figure 20.21   Choosing the Descriptive Statistics options.

In Figure 20.22, I put the most important calculated results in bold just to make them stand out a bit because Excel delivers a plain table. The *mean* is the numerical average, which for the cars in cells A2 to A25 turns out to be 3,149.75 pounds. The *standard deviation* (a measure of the width of the distribution of numbers), calculated to a precision that is not supported by the data (we have four-digit weights, so this ten-digit number is inappropriate overkill), is about 718 pounds. This means that two-thirds of the cars in this sample are within 3,150 pounds, plus or minus 720 pounds in weight (rounding off the numbers a bit).

Finally, the lightest car in the range is reported as 1,915 pounds, the heaviest is 4,360, and (you could figure this yourself) the range between these two figures is 2,445 pounds. The name *descriptive statistics* means just what it says—it characterizes the distribution of the numbers in your data set, but it doesn't do much beyond this.

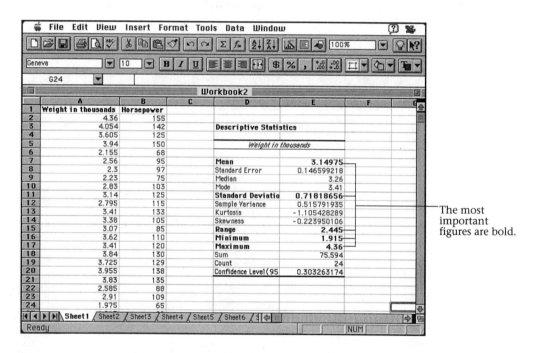

The most important figures are bold.

Figure 20.22 Descriptive Statistics output.

Sometimes it helps to think about the numbers in a spreadsheet because the spreadsheet can carry out arithmetic to meaningless precision. This example deals with cars and their weight. If you throw a six-pack of Diet Coke into the trunk of the car, the weight changes by a couple of pounds. If you sit in it, it changes more than that! The car data probably needs to be correct only to the nearest hundred pounds. What's the appropriate level of accuracy of the figures for horsepower, if you don't know whether the spark plugs are new?

ANOVA and Correlation

In ANOVA—analysis of variance—you begin to look for statistical connections, not just description (see Figure 20.23). ANOVA, from the Data Analysis list, is one statistical procedure for finding out how much variation in one data set (car weight) can account for variation in another (horsepower). The idea here is to determine whether the two columns of data are *independent*, meaning that the numbers in one column can vary all over the map without a corresponding variation in the other column.

The other possibility is that the data in column B (horsepower, for example) is *dependent* on the data in column A (weight, for example). For most situations, there should be a parameter that describes how dependent or not the two data columns are, ranging from zero (no connection at all) to 1 (you can predict the number in one column exactly if you know the number in the other column).

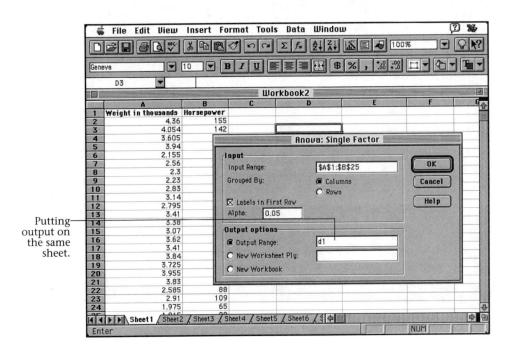

Putting output on the same sheet.

Figure 20.23 Calling up analysis of variance.

The output from the ANOVA routine concentrates on a number called the F ratio (see Figure 20.24). F measures whether (in our terms) the variation of the numbers inside a column is greater than the variation across two columns. The crude interpretation of ANOVA results is that big F numbers mean there's a significant connection between the two columns. For the data here, this analysis reports a critical value for F of 4.05 and a computed value of 421.95.

That means there's a virtual certainty (421.95 is huge compared to 4.05) that weight and horsepower are connected. Although this example isn't too overwhelming, it's often worth running this test just to make sure that you have a connection worth pursuing. If you don't find an F much bigger than the critical value ("Fcrit" in this table), there's no connection worth pursuing.

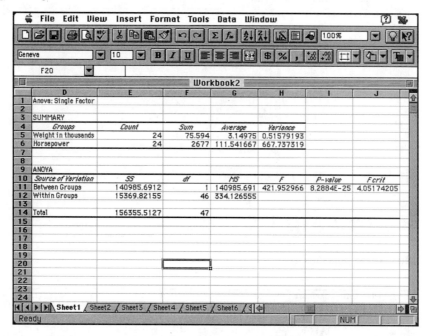

Figure 20.24 ANOVA results—keep your eye on the Fs.

ANOVA doesn't, however, give us a nice zero-to-one index of the connection between the data columns. For that, try Correlation (see Figure 20.25) from the Data Analysis list. Correlation gives you a little table with only three entries. It shows that the weight/weight correlation and the horsepower/horsepower correlation coefficients are 1 because, let's face it, they're the same columns of numbers (see Figure 20.26). The interesting number is 0.91909076, the correlation coefficient between the weight data and the horsepower data. The ANOVA results promise that these numbers are connected, and the Correlation analysis gives this convenient index.

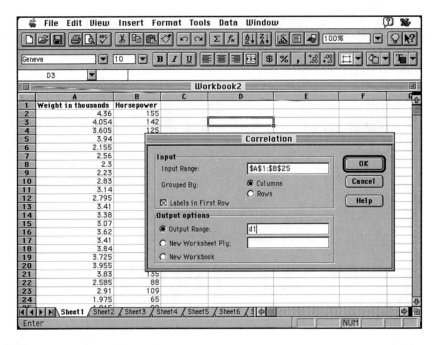

Figure 20.25   The simple dialog box for Correlation.

Correlation — coefficient.

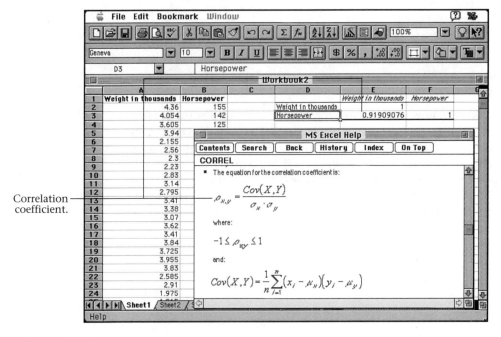

Figure 20.26   The number is 0.91909076; the definition is the formula.

The reason these topics are presented in this peculiar order is that when you use statistics on your data, it's a good idea to use a test for a valid statistical connection before you call up the index of "connectedness." The literature on statistics is full of tricky examples that give a respectable correlation coefficient but have some subtle problems that are revealed either by charting or ANOVA.

More Description—Histograms

Revisiting the area of descriptive statistics and moving down the list of possible Data Analysis options, Histogram (see Figure 20.27) is an attractive choice. There's quite a bit of intelligence built into Histogram, which groups the data into bins for analysis (see Figure 20.28). Right in the middle, you can see a bin centered on the weight value 3,137.5—compare this to the mean weight of 3,150 in the standard statistics. Basically, a histogram of this type gives you a quick and dirty visual descriptive statistics summary. In descriptive statistics, you saw that the standard deviation was 720 pounds, and I said that two-thirds of all the data entries would be found in the range [mean plus/minus standard deviation]. Here, graphically, you have a central bin (the third out of five) centered at 3,140 (I'm rounding again), within 1 percent of the real arithmetic mean; and the next two bins, together with the central bin, represent 71 percent of the whole distribution, not very far from the 67 percent of the standard deviation statistics.

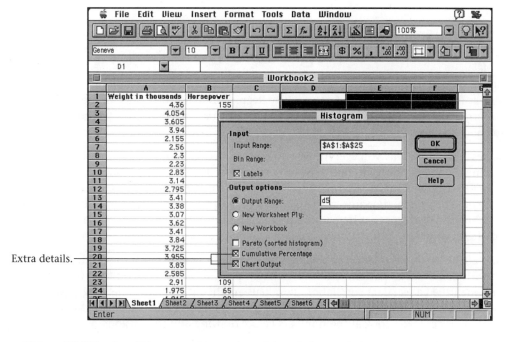

Extra details.

Figure 20.27   Specifying a graphic version of descriptive statistics.

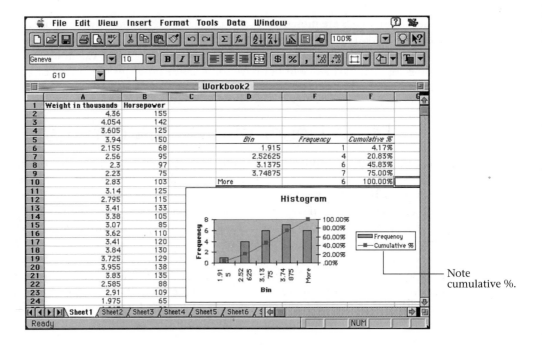

Figure 20.28   Histogram's graphic output.

Regression

Having revisited descriptive statistics, let's take a backward glance at correlations and such, available as Regression under Data Analysis. The Regression dialog box calls for most of the same information (see Figure 20.29) as the others in this area, except it gives you the opportunity to choose a check box called Residuals.

The Regression output tells you everything you ever wanted to know, and more (see Figure 20.30). One of the first things to notice is the correlation coefficient, here called "Multiple R," at 0.91909076 (proving the accuracy of Excel statistics). The value in the output table for "R Square" would be exactly the same as the quantity called "r-squared" in the trendline analysis back in Chapter 19, except that here I have picked a slightly larger chunk of car data (24 cases instead of 20), which has pushed the number a tiny bit closer to 1.

In Figure 20.30, the interpretation of residuals goes something like this: if the residuals bounce around with no particular pattern, and the number for "Multiple R" is larger than 0.75 or so, you have identified a real data correlation. Residuals are the tip-off that something strange may be happening—if the first half of the set is negative numbers and the second half is positive, you better take a look at the numbers before drawing any conclusions.

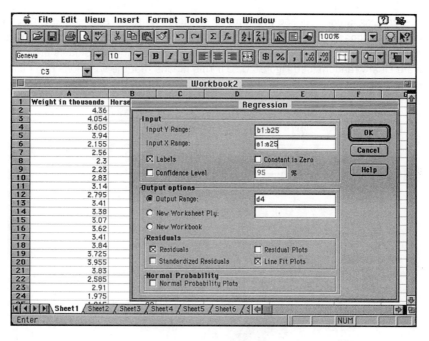

Figure 20.29 Check those Regression residuals, the custodians of truth.

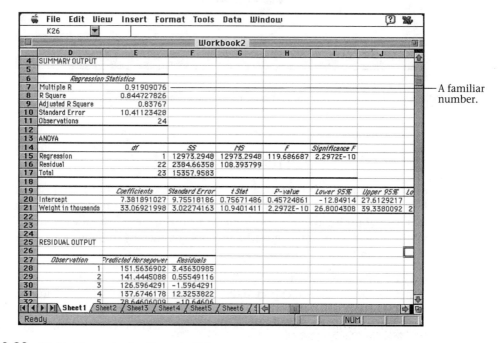

Figure 20.30 Regression output, with embellishments.

In this case, everything is fine because you can plot predicted numbers against the original data (this is why you should have chosen the Line Fit Plots check box in the Regression dialog box in Figure 20.29). The differences between the real and predicted numbers (that's what the residuals are—the differences) are clearly random (see Figure 20.31). This means that the variations don't conceal any sort of systematic pattern other than the one line computed here.

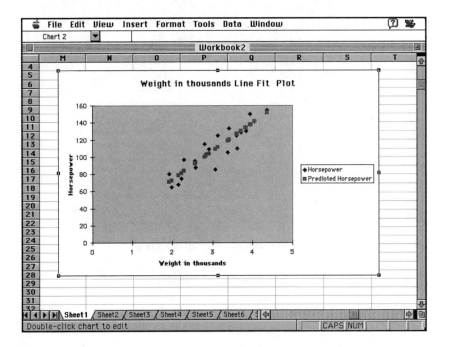

Figure 20.31   Comparing the point spreads: predicted versus actual.

One Last Test: t

Near the bottom of the list of Data Analysis tests is an assortment of t-tests. Just so that you know, these are usually called "Student's t" tests, a name that has nothing to do with students. *Student* was the publishing name of a very clever fellow named Gossett, who worked for Guinness (the brewery) in Dublin and who was obliged thereby to publish statistical papers under a pseudonym.

The Paired Two Sample for Means test gives output (see Figure 20.32) that includes some numbers that are not entirely unexpected. If you take the square root of the number for "Variance" in the table, you get the same standard deviation that we have seen earlier. The correlation coefficient of earlier figures appears here as "Pearson Correlation," with the same numerical value. All this may seem to be belaboring a point, but the general theme here is that in looking for statistical connections between two columns of data, slight variations on the same analyses appear again and again, producing the same parameters.

File Edit View Insert Format Tools Data Window

	B	C	D	E	F	G	H
1							
2							
3	Horsepower		t-Test: Paired Two Sample for Means				
4	155						
5	142			Weight in thousands	Horsepower		
6	125		Mean	3.14975	111.541667		
7	150		Variance	0.515791935	667.737319		
8	68		Observations	24	24		
9	95		Pearson Correlation	0.91909076			
10	97		Hypothesized Mean Difference	0			
11	75		df	23			
12	103		t Stat	-21.08677361			
13	125		P(T<=t) one-tail	7.60574E-17			
14	115		t Critical one-tail	1.713870006			
15	133		P(T<=t) two-tail	1.52115E-16			
16	105		t Critical two-tail	2.068654794			
17	85						
18	110						
19	120						
20	130						
21	129						
22	138						
23	135						
24	88						
25	109						
26	65						
27	80						
28	80						
29	71						

Another old friend.

Figure 20.32 A specific t-test as another approach to correlation.

There are engineering functions built into Excel, but you would be better advised to use another package (Mathematica, Matlab, MathCad) for Fourier transforms and such. The statistics functions available as a Data Analysis add-in, however, are competitive with a low-end, stand-alone program.

Well, there you have it. Excel in a nutshell. I hope you have picked up some tips about how to enter data, format data, graph data, correlate data, predict data, and analyze data. Data-ed out? I hope not—because as you delve even deeper into Excel, you'll discover more of its secrets and become an Excel junkie for sure.

Part IV
PowerPoint 4

by Barrie Sosinsky

A few short years ago, PowerPoint was a distinct also-ran compared to such Mac heavyweights as Aldus Persuasion. PowerPoint 4, however, is making itself felt as the new presentation software leader. It includes a huge assortment of already formatted presentations and a variety of ways to get existing information from Word and Excel into a visually compelling slide show. If you need to make a professional-looking presentation in a hurry (unfortu-nately, that's a typical situation), PowerPoint is your best software friend.

In a way, PowerPoint is the part of Office that you use to show yourself to the world. Nothing looks worse these days than a boring black-and-white text presentation. Nothing helps a career more than an impressive presentation that uses color and graphics to make a point! It's worth master-ing PowerPoint (and it's easy!) for the sheer oomph it gives your ideas when you present them to colleagues. In Part IV, you will learn how to create an outline for your presenta-tion and how to turn it into a visually exciting slide show. You will also learn how to survive the "butterflies" of getting in front of a group of people.

Chapter 21

Getting Started with PowerPoint

This chapter gives you an overview of what PowerPoint does, explains some of the program's features and advantages, and introduces you to the PowerPoint process by taking you through the steps for creating a sample presentation. This chapter also provides examples of how you can use PowerPoint as a valuable communication tool.

By the end of this chapter, you should be able to create a simple presentation and have a basic grasp of the following information:

- ◆ Understanding how presentation programs work
- ◆ Setting up a new presentation and adding slides
- ◆ Navigating your work areas and views
- ◆ Writing outlines and working with outline tools
- ◆ Using Pick a Look Wizard, templates, and AutoLayouts to create a personal look for your slides
- ◆ Inserting and sizing graphs and graphics
- ◆ Using the Slide Show and Slide Sorter views to see your presentation

What Is a Presentation Program?

PowerPoint is a comprehensive presentation package that features a sophisticated Help system, powerful graphic tools, an OLE (object linking and embedding) that allows full integration with Microsoft Word and Excel, text-editing tools, full graphing and charting capabilities, animated transitional and text-building effects, customizable toolbars, and a player that allows you to run presentations on workstations that don't have PowerPoint. PowerPoint is easy for the novice but is not limiting to the expert.

Keep in mind, however, that PowerPoint 4 weighs in at an elephantine 33MB when fully installed. And OLE currently runs at the speedy pace of a herd of slugs stampeding through a field of molasses. Don't even try to run Microsoft Office or PowerPoint with less than 8MB of RAM.

Although PowerPoint may lag behind some other presentation programs in its animation and multimedia support capabilities, industry publications and users alike praise the new PowerPoint for its impressive ease of use and solid features.

Such presentation programs as PowerPoint assist you in giving presentations that are accompanied by visual elements. The programs are designed primarily for creating slides and transparencies for overhead projectors. Most people begin to work on their presentations by outlining their ideas on paper before sitting down at the computer.

The process of planning a presentation involves many components. First you should keep in mind the purpose of your presentation, how much time you have, and who your audience is. Then you should think about what points you want to convey to the audience and organize the points in a concise, logical progression. Taking these factors into account, you write a script that is designed to come across effectively in a frame-by-frame format. You then decide how you want to display the presentation, and you create an overall look that integrates visual elements with text. Finally, you plan how to set up the presentation.

PowerPoint goes a long way toward making the planning process easier. With PowerPoint, you can easily create outlines, format text into slides, add visual graphics, and rehearse and time your presentation.

PowerPoint assists you with developing presentations in the following ways:

◆ **Helps organize outlines into slides:** PowerPoint automatically assigns one slide per main topic and gives you tools for assigning levels to your text. You then flesh out the outline with main topics, subheads, and bulleted lists and enter the text within the presentation package.

◆ **Makes it easy to create an appropriate look for your slides:** PowerPoint offers an array of templates, automatic layouts, and graphics for creating a vibrant look. The program also comes with powerful graphic tools for adding and editing visual elements.

◆ **Allows flexibility:** PowerPoint allows flexibility so that you can easily make changes and edits, print out supporting materials, and choose an appropriate output device.

◆ **Helps you time your presentation:** PowerPoint has a rehearsal feature so that you can actually time your presentation on a slide-by-slide basis. This feature helps you control the amount of time spent on each slide and ensures that you have sufficient time to get your points across.

Compared to other presentation programs, PowerPoint is the best choice for novice presenters because it is the easiest to learn and the most comprehensive of the presentation programs.

Getting Around the PowerPoint Screen

Before you get started, it is important to get an overview of the PowerPoint process. After you understand how PowerPoint works in general, you will have a launching point from which to explore topics that are relevant to the types of presentations that you want to create. PowerPoint is easy to learn if you know how to find your way around the PowerPoint screen, how to use the menus, and how to work in the different views. For those who learn better by doing, you can now go through the basic steps of creating a sample slide show.

Using PowerPoint's menus and navigational tools

You can activate PowerPoint's commands through the drop-down menus at the top of your screen or by clicking toolbar buttons. The various toolbars are located at the top and to the left of your screen, depending on which toolbars you currently have displayed. If the ToolTips option is activated, the name of each tool appears onscreen when you pass the cursor over the button. You can choose which toolbars to display and whether to display ToolTips by accessing the Toolbars command on the View menu.

PowerPoint has many navigational options. You can use your scroll bars to move up, down, and across each slide. The Next/Previous Slide buttons for moving from slide to slide are located on the vertical scroll bar on the right. The adjustable Zoom Control is located to the right of the Standard toolbar. By clicking the button with the downward-pointing arrow, next to the percentage indicator, you can adjust the viewing percentage.

Using PowerPoint's View tools

When developing your presentation, you will spend most of your time working with either text or visual elements. Therefore, PowerPoint gives you five ways to view your work: individual slides, a running slide show, an outline, a storyboard, and speaker's notes. You can access these views by selecting the buttons on the lower-left corner of your screen. Figure 21.1 shows the View buttons.

Slide Sorter View.

Outline View.   Notes Pages View.

Slide View.——— 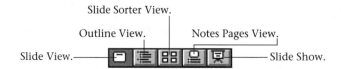 ——— Slide Show.

Figure 21.1   The View buttons.

The two views you will use the most for creating your presentation are the Slide view and the Outline view. The Slide view lets you see how each slide appears and allows you to manipulate text and graphics. The left side of your screen features the Drawing toolbar for changing the appearance of text, drawing shapes and boxes, and rotating text and visual elements. You can also access the Slide view from the View menu or by using the ⌘-Option-N key combination.

The Outline view enables you to see and work on your presentation as a text outline without the visual elements. In Outline view, the left side of your screen now features an Outlining toolbar for assigning levels to lines of text, changing the order in which text appears, and collapsing or expanding the outline. When you work with text in the Outline view, your screen will look similar to the example in Figure 21.2. You can also access the Outline view from the View menu or by using the ⌘-Option-O key combination.

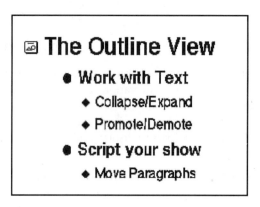

Figure 21.2   Text in the Outline view.

Setting Up a Presentation

To start up PowerPoint, either double-click the PowerPoint application icon or select PowerPoint through the Microsoft Office drop-down menu button, which appears in the upper-right corner of your desktop.

A Tip of the Day appears, which gives you helpful hints. Every time you start up PowerPoint, a daily tip appears onscreen and gives you interesting hints for working with PowerPoint.

To create a PowerPoint slide show from within the application, choose the New command from the File menu or use the ⌘-N key combination. In the first dialog box that appears, PowerPoint gives you the following options for setting up a presentation (see Chapter 22 for more information):

- ◆ **AutoContent Wizard:** This option helps you set up an outline for your presentation by prompting you for information.

- ◆ **Pick a Look Wizard:** This option helps you select a template and prompts you on details that you may not have thought of, such as the printing parameters for your handouts.

- ◆ **Templates:** This option enables you to create a certain look for your slides by selecting from PowerPoint's large collection of templates.

- ◆ **Blank Presentation:** This option literally leaves you in the Slide view with a blank title slide—an intimidating sight. Although you will choose this option for the purpose of creating a sample presentation in this chapter, a beginner usually does not start with this option.

- ◆ **Current Presentation Format:** This option works only if you are already working on a presentation, and you want to begin a new one.

- ◆ **Open an Existing Presentation:** This option appears instead of the Current Presentation Format option if no other presentations are open but you have some other files saved.

Creating a Slide Show

This sample presentation takes you through the basic process of creating your own slide show, which will help introduce you to PowerPoint's features and capabilities while giving you a basic idea of how PowerPoint works.

To set up a slide show, do the following:

1. Activate the New Presentation menu by launching the PowerPoint application, by selecting New from the File menu (if you are already in PowerPoint), or by using the ⌘-N key combination.

2. Open a new presentation by selecting the Blank Presentation option and clicking OK. The AutoLayout menu appears.

3. Select the title slide layout in the upper-left corner by double-clicking it. A blank slide with two text boxes appears (see Figure 21.3).

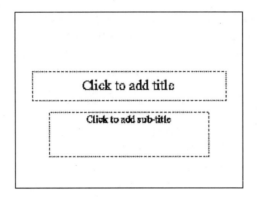

Figure 21.3 A blank title slide with text boxes.

4. Select the Text tool by clicking its button. The Text tool is identified with a letter *A* and is located on the Drawing toolbar to the left of the screen.

5. Enter the title of the slide by placing the cursor in the upper text box and typing **Presentations with PowerPoint**.

6. Enter your name in the text box located underneath the title box. Figure 21.4 shows the title slide with text entered.

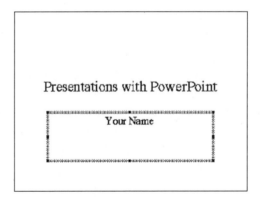

Figure 21.4 Title slide with text entered.

Congratulations! You have just launched your first PowerPoint presentation. You will return to this sample presentation throughout this chapter. In the following exercises, you learn how to add new slides by writing an outline. But first you need to learn more about how to add new slides and how to work in Outline view.

Adding new slides

You can add new slides to your presentation in several ways. You can use the Outline feature because every time you create an outline title, PowerPoint starts a new slide. You can also click the Insert New Slide button on the Standard toolbar, click the New Slide shortcut button on the lower-right corner of the screen, select New Slide from the Insert menu, or use the ⌘-Shift-M keyboard combination.

Working in Outline view

The easiest way to make sure that you have enough slides for what you want to say is to work in the Outline view. To switch to the Outline view, choose the Outline command from the View menu, click the Outline View button in the lower-left corner of your screen, or press ⌘-Option-O. Every time you enter a new main topic, PowerPoint automatically adds a slide. The Outline view also provides you with tools. For now, the most important tools are located on the right side of the Formatting toolbar, the one below the Standard toolbar at the top of your screen. Figure 21.5 shows the Promote, Demote, and Bullet On/Off buttons.

Promote (Indent less) button.

Bullet On/Off button. 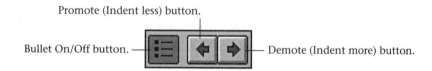 Demote (Indent more) button.

Figure 21.5 The Promote, Demote, and Bullet On/Off buttons.

You will use these three Outline tools in the following ways:

◆ **The Promote tool:** It moves a line of text one tab to the left so that the text takes on a higher level in the outline. By using the Promote tool, you can make a regular heading become a slide title or a subheading become a regular heading.

◆ **The Demote tool:** It moves a line of text one tab to the right so that the text takes on a lower level in the outline. By using the Demote tool, you can turn a slide title into a heading or a heading into a subheading. You can also demote by pressing the Tab key.

◆ **The Bullet On/Off tool:** PowerPoint automatically bullets headings and subheadings. You can omit bullets on lines by selecting the lines and clicking the button. Bullets can be added in the same way.

Starting an Outline

Now you can create an outline for your presentation by using the Outline view. The Outline view automatically creates bulleted lists and makes it easy for you to fit text into slides.

To start an outline, do the following:

1. Switch from the Slide view to the Outline view by clicking the Outline View button in the lower-left corner of your screen, by selecting the Outline command on the View menu, or by using the ⌘-Option-O keyboard combination.

2. To create a new slide, place the cursor after your name on slide 1, press the Return key, and click the Promote button once. Now your cursor is on slide 2. Slide numbers are indicated by small numbers to the left of the slide titles.

3. Type in the following main topic on slide 2 and then press Return: **Write an Outline**. Notice that you are now on slide 3.

4. Type the words **Organize your ideas**. This sentence is now the main topic for slide 3.

5. To demote slide 3's main topic and make it a subhead of slide 2, click the Demote tool or use the Option-Shift–Right Arrow key combination. Then press the Return key. Now the words "Organize your ideas" appear as a heading for slide 2.

6. Add to your bulleted list of subheads by typing the following and then pressing Return: **This is a bulleted head**. Notice that pressing the Return key again automatically places your cursor at the same heading level as the text above it.

Now you have some idea of how entering text in the Outline view works. Using the Return key automatically places text on the same outline level as the line above it. In the next exercise, you'll get more practice in using the Outline tools to adjust the levels in your outline.

Using the Outline Tools

To adjust levels for lines of text, you can use the Promote and Demote tools. The Promote tool moves lines up one level, and the Demote tool moves lines down one level.

This exercise reviews how these tools can help you organize your outline. After you get a feel for how these tools work, you can easily set up and make adjustments to your outline.

To adjust the levels of your outline and to experiment with bullets, do the following:

1. Type **This is a subheading** and make it a subheading by clicking the Demote button, pressing the Tab key, or using the Option-Shift–Right Arrow key combination. Press Return.

2. Type **Use the outline tools** and promote it by clicking the Promote button or by using the Option-Shift–Left Arrow key combination. Press Return.

3. To demonstrate how you can turn your bullets on and off, type **Bullets**, click the Demote button, and press Return. Then type **No bullets**, click the Bullet On/Off button while your cursor is still on this line, and press Return. Notice that the line that says "Bullets" has a bullet next to it, but the line that you just typed does not.

4. To reactivate your bullets for the next line, press the Return key and click the Bullet On/Off button. The next line again has a bullet next to it.

5. Promote the line that you now have your cursor on by clicking the Promote button and then typing the word **Promote**. Notice that the word "Promote" appears as a heading rather than a subheading, unlike the line above it. Press Return.

6. Create a demoted subheading by pressing the Return key and clicking the Demote tool or by pressing the Tab key. Then type the word **Demote**. Your outline should look like the one shown in Figure 21.6.

You have used the Promote, Demote, and Bullet On/Off tools to organize the text on slide 2. The next exercise lets you practice what you have learned in the previous tutorials by creating two more slides without a step-by-step approach. Go for it!

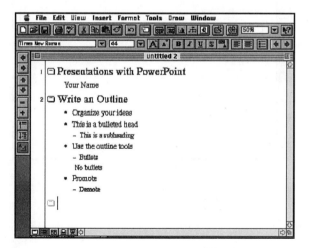

Figure 21.6   The slide 2 outline.

Adding More Slides

To complete the look for your slide show, create two more slides. Remember to use the Demote and Promote tools when necessary. Good luck.

For slide 3, type the following information into the designated categories:

Title:	**Create a Look**
First Header:	**Use Slide view**
Subhead:	**35mm slides**
Subhead:	**Color overheads**
Subhead:	**B&W overheads**
Second Header:	**AutoLayouts**
Subhead:	**Clip Art Gallery**
Subhead:	**Graphs & Charts**

Your outline for slide 3 should now look like the one in Figure 21.7.

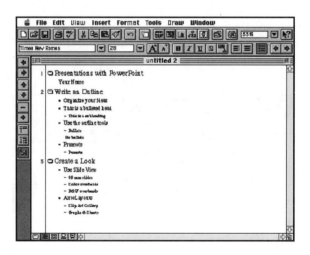

Figure 21.7   The sample presentation outline with slide 3.

For slide 4, type the following information into the designated categories:

Title:	**Illustrate Points**
First Header:	**Clip Art**

Second Header: **Graphs/Charts**

Third Header: **Tiff, EPS, Pict**

Figure 21.8 shows what your outline for slide 4 should look like.

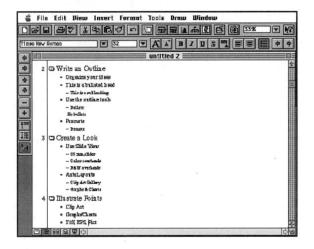

Figure 21.8   The sample presentation outline with slide 4.

Now that you have finished your first outline, you are ready to give your slide show an exciting look, so keep your outline onscreen. The next section gives you a sampling of what you can do to spice up your slides.

Adding Visual Elements to Your Presentation

PowerPoint offers many easy-to-use but powerful graphic tools that enable you to develop polished presentations that create visual impact. You can add, manipulate, and create visual elements in the Slide view. PowerPoint lets you set up your slides with an assortment of templates. You can then work on individual slides by using the AutoLayout feature. PowerPoint includes drawing and text tools, full graphing and charting functions, and a vast Clip Art Gallery (see Chapter 24 for more information).

PowerPoint's graphic features can be summarized as follows:

◆ **Templates:** Templates help you create an overall look for your presentation. Because templates exist for the purpose of cohesiveness, you can use only one template per presentation.

◆ **AutoLayouts:** AutoLayouts arrange elements on your slide for a professional, balanced look in a predesigned format.

543

◆ **Clip Art Gallery:** PowerPoint includes an extensive Clip Art Gallery that is conveniently organized by category.

◆ **Graphs:** PowerPoint has a fully functional graphing program that enables you to enter data and choose graph types.

◆ **Charts:** PowerPoint also has a charting function that makes creating organizational charts easy. The chart helps you assign hierarchical levels and add or delete boxes, while automatically moving the other boxes over proportionally to accommodate your changes.

Picking a Look for Your Slides

Now you're ready to add a template, AutoLayouts, and visual elements to your presentation. In your outline, switch from the Outline view to the Slide view by clicking the Slide View button.

To pick a look for your presentation, do the following:

1. To select a template for your slides, first choose the Presentation Template command from the Format menu or click the Template shortcut button. A finder dialog box appears. Three template categories are located in the PowerPoint template folder. The three template folders contain templates for the following media: black-and-white transparent overheads, color transparent overheads, and 35mm slides.

2. Open the 35mm slide folder by double-clicking it and scroll down the File Name box to highlight the SPARKLES.PPT template. You can see a preview of how the template looks in a box on the left side of the dialog box. Click the Apply button. Your slides now have a blue background look with a starburst to the left of the title of each slide.

3. Go to slide 3 so that you can add an illustration to it. Click the Layout shortcut button or choose the Slide Layout command from the Format menu. The Slide Layout dialog box appears with nine sample slide layouts with placeholders for arranging text, clip art, graphs, and charts. Notice that the placeholders contain larger versions of the toolbar buttons for adding clip art, graphs, and charts.

4. Select the layout in the lower-left corner (the layout with the picture of a face on it). Then click Apply or double-click the sample layout. Your slide now conforms to the layout and has a placeholder for clip art (see Figure 21.9).

5. To access the Clip Art Gallery, double-click the clip art placeholder on slide 3. The Clip Art Gallery dialog box now appears.

6. First choose the Academic category from the list of choices at the top of the dialog box and then click the mug with the pencils that is previewed in one of the boxes below the categories. The categories make it easy for you to find appropriate clip art, and the clip art previews enable you to select the clip art while viewing it.

Figure 21.9   A clip art placeholder.

7. Click OK. The selected clip art automatically appears in the placeholder on your slide. Congratulations! You have just created a snazzy layout in no time flat.

8. To add a graph to slide 4, move to the slide by pressing the Page Down key twice and click the Insert Graph button on the Standard toolbar. A graph placeholder automatically appears on your slide. Unlike the AutoLayout placeholder, however, the graph placeholder is not automatically sized to fit in with the text already placed on the slide.

9. To select your graph (or any other object), click it with the pointer from the floating tool palette to the left of your screen. You will notice that when a PowerPoint object is selected, a box appears around it. Now you can do the following to resize or move your graph:

    ◆   To resize your graph proportionally, hold down the Option key, click any corner of the selection box, and drag it diagonally inward to reduce it or diagonally outward to enlarge it. In this case, you want to move the graph away from the text and toward the right.

    ◆   To move your graph, click anywhere in the middle of the object, hold down your mouse key, and drag the graph to where you want to place it.

10. To save your presentation, select Save from the File menu or use the ⌘-S key combination. Type the filename **DEMO1** in the dialog box, save it as a PowerPoint presentation, and then select OK.

See how easy creating a presentation can be? PowerPoint helps you learn while you create your presentations so that you can get up and running fast while you increase your level of PowerPoint presentation expertise.

Viewing Your Slide Show

You can view PowerPoint presentations right on the computer screen by using the Slide Show view. The Slide Show feature turns your computer workstation into a presentation display device. You can also rehearse and preview your presentations.

To view your slide show, do the following:

1. Press the Page Up key to return to slide 1 in your sample presentation. Your presentation begins running from whatever slide you have selected.

2. Select the Slide Show view by clicking the Slide Show View button at the lower-left corner of your screen or by choosing the Slide Show command from the View menu. Your title slide now fills the entire screen.

3. To advance to the next slide, click your pointer anywhere onscreen.

4. When your presentation is finished, PowerPoint returns you to the view you were previously working on.

Now you have an idea of what a PowerPoint presentation looks like when being shown. Displaying slide shows on your computer screen is the best way to use PowerPoint's full range of options.

To see all your slides at once, which gives you an immediate overview of your entire presentation, click the Slide Sorter View button. Your slides appear onscreen in the order you created them. Hopefully, your slides look like the ones in Figure 21.10.

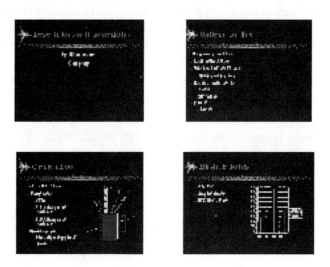

Figure 21.10   A presentation in the Slide Sorter view.

This chapter is designed to give you an overview of the PowerPoint process. After reading this chapter, you should have an idea of what to look for and how PowerPoint's features can help you create presentations of your own. Chapter 22 goes into more detail about setting up your presentations.

Chapter 22

Learning the Basics

In this chapter, you get to know the basics of PowerPoint 4 by navigating the screen and getting an overview of the menus and toolbars. Because PowerPoint is a Microsoft application, the main screen, menus, and buttons should look familiar to you. You should still take the time to glance over this section, however, because PowerPoint 4 has many unique, exciting features that you may not recognize or know how to access. This chapter tells you about the following:

◆ Creating, opening, closing, saving, and printing presentations

◆ Moving around the screen with scroll bars, arrow keys, next/previous arrows, and adjustment boxes

◆ Using the menu commands

◆ Learning about the toolbars

◆ Customizing toolbars

◆ Using Slide, Outline, Slide Sorter, Notes Pages, and Slide Show views

◆ Getting help

Choosing a Presentation Option

You can access the New Presentation dialog box by creating a new presentation from within PowerPoint or by launching the application, in which case the dialog box automatically appears.

To create a new presentation, activate the New command from the File menu or click the first button on the Standard toolbar (the one that looks like a dog-eared page). This action brings up the New Presentation dialog box, which contains the following options for creating your presentation (see Figure 22.1):

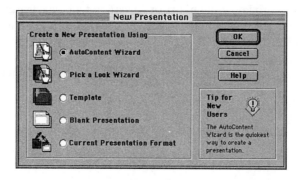

Figure 22.1   The New Presentation dialog box.

◆ **AutoContent Wizard:** AutoContent Wizard prompts you for information about your presentation. It enables you to choose from an assortment of commonly used outline topics and then places you in the Outline view so that you can fill in the precreated outline with your own information. You can follow the instructions in the AutoContent windows, which automatically appear, to finish your presentation (see Figure 22.2). The AutoContent Wizard feature is extremely useful in helping the novice get started.

◆ **Pick a Look Wizard:** The Pick a Look Wizard offers you a choice in format selection, type of output, printing options and more. Like the AutoContent Wizard, the Pick a Look Wizard places windows onscreen to help you (see Figure 22.3). The Pick a Look Wizard is not as helpful as the AutoContent Wizard in getting you started on your presentation, however, because most professionals begin the presentation process by composing an outline.

◆ **Templates:** This option enables you to create a consistent look for your presentation by offering you over 150 templates to choose from. A template gives you a background design, color scheme, and basic layout to make creating presentations easier for beginners.

Figure 22.2   An AutoContent Wizard window.

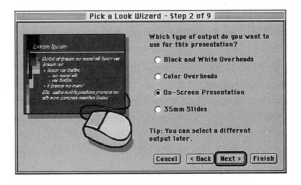

Figure 22.3   A Pick a Look Wizard window.

◆ **Blank Presentation:** As you gain more experience with PowerPoint, you may wish to experiment with a blank slate. The Blank Presentation option lets you develop your presentation slide by slide. After you choose the Blank Presentation option, a New Slide dialog box appears, where you can choose from nine different AutoLayouts. The AutoLayout feature helps you make design decisions by offering slide layouts that effectively integrate graphics and text.

◆ **Current Presentation Format:** This PowerPoint option becomes useful when you want to create a group of presentations that are similar. By selecting the Current Presentation Format from the New Presentation dialog box, you can duplicate a recently designed presentation layout.

PowerPoint offers many options for creating new presentations. As you become more proficient, you will discover which method works best for you.

Working with Existing Documents

PowerPoint lets you open, close, and save documents the same way you do with other Microsoft Office applications. Uniform commands help you work faster because you don't have to relearn commands for different applications. PowerPoint enables you to copy formats from previously created slide shows, which gives you an integrated set of presentations, and enables you to save presentations under different names. This feature permits you to change an existing presentation without eliminating the original. The following list explains the options for working with existing presentations:

◆ **Opening a presentation:** To open an existing presentation, select one of the following options: choose the Open command from the File menu; click the second button—the one that looks like an open folder—on the Standard toolbar; use the ⌘-O key combination. In the Open dialog box, double-click the filename of the presentation that you want to open. You now have the presentation onscreen.

To narrow down your search for presentations, you can keep non-PowerPoint documents from appearing in the window. At the bottom of the Open dialog box, select Presentations from the List Files of Type pop-up menu.

◆ **Closing a presentation:** To close a PowerPoint presentation without exiting the application, select the Close command from the File menu or use the ⌘-W key combination. To close your presentation and simultaneously exit the application, choose the Quit command from the File menu or use the ⌘-Q key combination. PowerPoint automatically asks whether you want to save the changes that you have made to your presentation.

◆ **Saving a file:** To save a slide show that you're working on, select the Save command from the File menu or click the third button from the left (the one that looks like a computer disk) on the Standard toolbar. Or you can use the ⌘-S key combination. Any changes you made are then saved to disk.

To save a separate copy of your document under a different name, select the Save As command from the File menu. When the Save As dialog box appears, enter the new document name.

Formatting and Outputting Your PowerPoint Presentation

PowerPoint offers many options for printing and presenting your slide show. With PowerPoint, you have the flexibility to output your presentation in virtually any format, including 35mm slides, video, transparent overheads, and onscreen demonstrations. PowerPoint also has automatic settings for printing out transparent overheads, slides, audience handouts, and speaker's notes (see Chapter 26 for more information).

Setting up your slides

To set up your slides, use PowerPoint's templates, which are already correctly proportioned for the type of slides you want, or choose Slide Setup from the File menu (see Figure 22.4). The Slide Setup dialog box appears and offers options for setting or changing the parameters of your slides, including onscreen shows, 35mm slides, letter paper, or A4 paper (used for transparent overheads). You can also customize the size of your slides by using the Width, Height, and Orientation options.

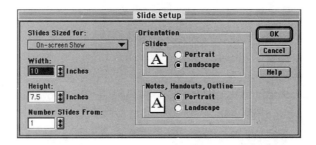

Figure 22.4   The Slide Setup dialog box.

In addition to the default On-screen Show setting, PowerPoint enables you to choose the 35mm Slides setting—which has an aspect ratio of 3:2. You can also design your slides to be used as transparent overheads by choosing the A4 Paper setting. Transparent overheads have an aspect ratio of 5:4 or 4:5, depending on whether the presentation is horizontally or vertically oriented. Notice the subtle size difference in the two slides, as shown in Figure 22.5.

The term *aspect ratio* refers to the height and width proportions required for displaying a presentation in a given medium. After setting up your slides, make sure that your frames are proportioned correctly for your output device. (For more information on aspect ratios, see Chapter 26.)

Setting up your pages

Just as the Slide Setup command enables you to set parameters for how the presentation is displayed, the Page Setup command enables you to decide how you want your presentation to appear after it is printed out. To format printed pages, select the Page Setup command from the File menu.

A dialog box appears (see Figure 22.6) and prompts you to select the paper size, number of frames per page (up to four), percentage of reduction or enlargement, and orientation. You can also choose various visual effects and printer options by clicking the Options button.

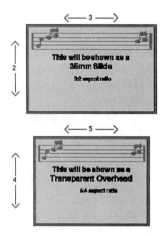

Figure 22.5 The 35mm slide template compared to the transparent overhead template.

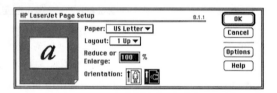

Figure 22.6 The Page Setup dialog box.

Printing with PowerPoint

PowerPoint makes it easy for you to print transparent overheads and other materials directly from your printer. To print, select the Print command from the File menu, click the button that looks like a printer on the Standard toolbar, or use the ⌘-P key combination.

When the Print dialog box appears onscreen (see Figure 22.7), you can choose from several options to print in the Print What menu box. The options include slides, notes pages, handouts, and outlines. (For more information on printing, see Chapter 26.)

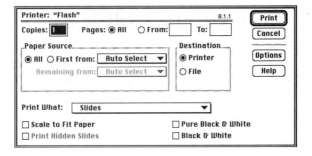

Figure 22.7   The Print dialog box.

The following list describes PowerPoint's printing options:

◆ **Slides:** This option lets you print out your presentation at one frame per page. You can also print transparent overheads directly from your printer, but make sure that the transparencies you use are compatible with your printer. Otherwise, they may get overheated or smudged.

◆ **Notes pages:** This option gives you a print of your slide on the top half of the page accompanied by your speaker's notes on the bottom half of the page. This option makes it easier for you to keep your presentation organized.

◆ **Handouts:** You can enhance your presentation by giving handouts to your audience. Handouts enable audience members to take notes so that it is easier for the people to retain the information that you are discussing. Handouts can be printed at two, three, or six slides to a page.

◆ **Outlines:** By choosing the Outline option, you can print a text-only version of your presentation in outline form. This option helps you make presentation changes and corrections before you actually make the presentation.

PowerPoint's many printing options give you more flexibility in planning your presentations. The ability to easily create an integrated set of materials to support your presentation also gives you an additional edge.

Navigating Your Screen

PowerPoint makes it easy for you to find your way around the screen. For the most part, the menus, toolbars, scroll bars, and general work area look similar to other standard applications you have already worked with (see Figure 22.11). In this section, you learn how to navigate your screen easily.

When you create a new document in PowerPoint with any option but the AutoContent Wizard, the screen defaults to the Slide view when you are ready to start entering information in your slides. (If you start your new document with the AutoContent Wizard, your screen defaults to the Outline view instead.) The Slide view contains the main working area for composing each frame of your presentation.

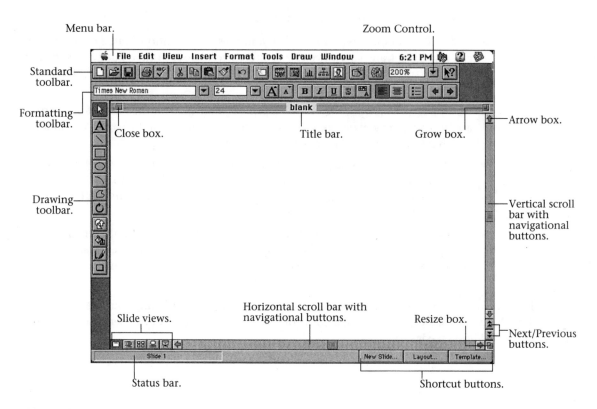

Figure 22.8   A blank PowerPoint screen.

◆ **Zoom:** You can view slides at different percentages of their original size by activating the Zoom Control. The Zoom Control on the Standard toolbar displays a percentage number and has a down-arrow button on its right. Clicking the arrow accesses a drop-down menu with percentages ranging from 25 to 400 percent. To zoom in on a specific object, select the object *before* activating the Zoom feature.

◆ **Scrolling down and across:** Scroll bars enable you to move your view up, down, or across the screen. The vertical scroll bar is on your far right, and the horizontal scroll bar is at the bottom of the screen, just above the status bar and shortcut buttons.

◆ **Arrow boxes:** Use the arrow boxes to scroll incrementally. The arrow boxes are located at the extreme ends of your scroll bars. Find the arrow pointing in the direction you want to move and either click it or hold it down with your mouse.

◆ **Scroll bars:** To move around in your document more quickly, use the horizontal and vertical scroll bars. Each scroll bar has a navigational button whose position indicates your position in relation to the entire document. You can click the navigational button and drag it in the direction you want to view, or you can click any place on the scroll bars to move incrementally.

◆ **Next/Previous buttons:** These buttons are located at the bottom of the vertical scroll bar. They look like the keys you would find on your VCR and are activated when you click them. The button with two triangles pointing up brings you to the preceding slide. The button with two triangles pointing down brings you to the next slide.

◆ **Resize box:** To adjust the size of your PowerPoint work area, click and drag on the resize box. Adjusting the size of the screen can be useful when you are working in multiple applications and you want to keep your presentation open or if you need to view two presentations simultaneously. The resize box is located at the lower right of your document window, where the vertical and horizontal scroll bars intersect.

◆ **Grow box:** To restore your work area's window to its preceding size, click the grow box, located at the top of your vertical scroll bar. It looks like a small square inside a large square.

◆ **Close box:** To close the presentation you are working on, click the close box. It is located on the left side of your title bar and looks like a little square.

Viewer control is highly important when you are working with a graphically oriented program, such as PowerPoint. By using PowerPoint's navigational tools, you can view your presentation from all necessary angles. For example, you can go to the preceding slide by pressing the Page Up key; you can go to the next slide by pressing the Page Down key.

Deciphering the status areas

Status areas are onscreen areas that provide information about where you are in your presentation. Unlike menus, which provide dialog boxes for you to choose options, you cannot interact with status areas. PowerPoint has two status areas: title bar and status bar.

PowerPoint's title bar is located just above the working area of your slide. The title bar tells you the name of the document you are working on or informs you if it is untitled. When you double-click the title bar, the screen behaves as if you clicked the grow box. In other words, if the screen has ever been another size, double-clicking the title bar returns the screen to that preceding size.

Your status bar is located on the lower-left corner of the screen. If you look closely, you will notice that messages appear while you're working. These messages tell you what you are doing and advise you what to do next.

Use your status areas to get information about your document and to learn more about PowerPoint.

Using rulers, guides, and the grid

Rulers, guides, and grids help you maintain uniformity throughout the presentations that you create. PowerPoint's ruler enables you to measure objects and distances, and the guides and grid help you align objects on your slides.

- ◆ **Rulers:** To measure an object, select the Ruler command on the View menu. Rulers appear at the top and left sides of the screen, as they do in Figure 22.9.

- ◆ **Guides:** PowerPoint provides you with guides—one vertical and one horizontal— that function as straight edges against which you can align objects. Objects moved near a guide automatically snap to the guide. To turn your guides on and off, use the Guides command in the View menu as a toggle switch. To move a guide, select it with your pointer and drag it.

- ◆ **Grid:** When you try to move an object and notice that it doesn't quite go where you want it to, you have experienced PowerPoint's grid. The grid consists of evenly spaced, invisible lines that crisscross the slide. Unless you turn off the Snap to Grid command in the Draw menu, objects align themselves to the lines on the grid. You temporarily can override PowerPoint's Snap to Grid default by holding down the ⌘ key while dragging the object that you are moving or sizing.

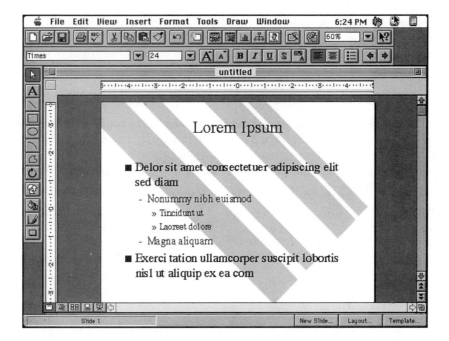

Figure 22.9   A PowerPoint slide with rulers.

Activating PowerPoint's Commands

PowerPoint offers you the choice of activating its features by using the menu bar, by using key combinations, or by clicking the buttons distributed along the various toolbars. The main menu and the Standard and Formatting toolbars are located at the top of the screen, where you can find them easily. PowerPoint also displays the Drawing toolbar, located on the left side of your working area; and shortcut buttons, located at the bottom of your screen.

Using the menu bar

The menu bar at the very top of your screen has all of PowerPoint's functions organized into categories. Each menu item contains a drop-down menu. Some items in the drop-down menu indicate a single command. Others require further input entries with a dialog box to complete a process; these commands are marked with an ellipses (...).

Although the menu bar makes it simpler for the beginner to find and activate commands, pulling down all these menus is time-consuming. You can activate PowerPoint's commands more easily by getting to know your toolbar buttons and your key combinations.

PowerPoint makes it easy for you to learn your toolbar and key combinations. After you pass your cursor over the toolbar buttons, ToolTips pop up and tell you what the name of the tool is. After you pull down your menus, key combinations appear to the right of the commands.

Using the Standard and Formatting toolbars

The people who designed PowerPoint know that you use some commands more frequently. To save you the inconvenience of dropping down your menus or remembering keyboard commands, they created a Standard toolbar (the one right below the menu bar). The buttons on the toolbars represent commonly performed functions, such as printing, inserting objects and saving. You can activate them with a simple click.

The lower row of tools at the top of the screen is the Formatting toolbar, which includes all sorts of tools for text formatting. With this toolbar, you can indicate which font and point size you want for your text. Simply drop down the menus with the arrow buttons and scroll through the available options.

Using other toolbars

In addition to the Standard and Formatting toolbars, PowerPoint features several other toolbars for drawing shapes, displaying Microsoft information, providing outlining services, and more. The Drawing toolbar is usually displayed to the left of the screen, although you can move it to whatever location you find the most convenient by clicking the toolbar and dragging it with your mouse. To display the toolbars, access the Toolbars command on the View menu and put a check mark by all the toolbars that you want displayed onscreen. Here is a list of the other toolbars that you will use most often:

◆ **Drawing toolbar:** When you work in Slide view, this toolbar displays graphic tools for composing individual elements in each slide. Options include moving and rotating objects, selecting or adding text, activating fills and lines, and drawing shapes (see Figure 22.10).

◆ **Draw+ toolbar:** The Draw+ toolbar gives you more specialized tools for modifying your visual elements.

◆ **Outlining toolbar:** When you work in Outline view, this toolbar takes the place of the Drawing toolbar that is present in Slide view. The Outlining toolbar displays text tools for editing and moving text and for adjusting priorities and headings in your outline. This toolbar offers a fuller range of options for outlining than the Formatting toolbar at the top of the screen (see Chapter 23 for more information).

Figure 22.10 The Drawing toolbar in Slide view.

PowerPoint gives you all the tools that you need for creating professional presentations and arranges the toolbars in a way that saves screen real estate.

Customizing your toolbars

As you get more familiar with PowerPoint, you may find that you use some tools more than others. You can hide the tools that you don't use or add more command buttons by customizing your toolbar. Customizing can help you make the most of your screen space and PowerPoint work area.

♦ **To hide tool buttons:** Choose Customize from the Tools menu. A dialog box with a list of command categories and a tool button storage area appears, as shown in Figure 22.11. To remove a button from a toolbar, first display the toolbar onscreen; then click the button that you no longer want on the toolbar and drag it to the gray storage area of the dialog box.

◆ **To add tool buttons:** The tool button storage area has buttons for additional functions, such as the Find File button in the File category. To add a button to a toolbar, display the toolbar onscreen, find the button that you want from the various categories, and drag the button from the storage area to the toolbar in the position that you want it to be in.

◆ **Moving toolbars:** PowerPoint's toolbars are actually floating palettes, which means that you can move them wherever you want onscreen. Just click your pointer on any part of the toolbar that doesn't involve selecting a particular tool and drag the toolbar to another location onscreen.

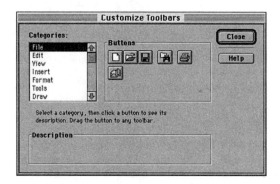

Figure 22.11   The Customize Toolbars dialog box.

If you move a toolbar from the top or side of your screen into the work area, it changes proportionally from a long rectangle into a square. Also notice that all the buttons on your toolbar move proportionally in response to your hiding or adding tools.

You can also drag toolbar buttons to a new position on a toolbar or to a different toolbar by holding down the ⌘ key while you drag the button to a new location. To copy toolbar icons, use the ⌘-Option key combination.

Selecting Views

The View menu controls what you see onscreen. Through this menu, you can work on presentations in the Slide, Outline, Slide Sorter, Notes Pages, and Slide Show views. Views can be accessed by selecting them through the View menu or by clicking the View icons on the lower-left side of the screen, just above the status bar.

PowerPoint's views are listed and briefly described as follows:

◆ **Slide view:** The Slide view is your main working area. This view enables you to work with text, graphics, and special effects on individual slides. Unless you use the AutoContent Wizard, PowerPoint defaults to this view.

◆ **Outline view:** The Outline view looks like a screen for a word processing document and helps you work with text. In Outline view, you can edit, move, and prioritize items in your outline.

◆ **Slide Sorter view:** The Slide Sorter view enables you to see your presentation in storyboard form. You can change the order of slides by selecting a slide and dragging it to its new place. You can also set and adjust special effects by using the Transition command from the Tools menu. Small slide icons with little arrows appear below each slide that has a transition effect. If you click these icons, you can view the transition effects in the storyboard. (For more information on transitions, see Chapter 25.) You can search through your slide show for all slides referring to a particular topic in the Slide Sorter view. Simply choose the Find command from the Edit menu and write in the desired topic name.

◆ **Notes Pages view:** Notes Pages view enables you to develop your presentation beyond the outline that appears on the slide. Simply jot down what you want to say in the space below your slide. These notes do not appear on the slides during your presentation, but you can print them out as supporting materials for your own notes during the presentation.

◆ **Slide Show view:** The Slide Show view enables you to rehearse and show your presentation right on your computer screen. You can either set the slide show to run automatically, or you can change slides manually by clicking the pointer on any part of the screen.

In this view, you can highlight your points with PowerPoint's Electronic Chalk feature. Simply click the pencil button in the lower-right corner of your screen (see Figure 22.12). The pointer turns into a pencil that draws lines onscreen to help you emphasize points. To deactivate, click the button again. The pencil markings disappear automatically when you finish your presentation. Keep one thing in mind as you use this feature: you need a steady hand!

Figure 22.12   The Electronic Chalk button.

PowerPoint views enable you to work on your slide show in all phases of the presentation process. This ensures continuity as you move fluidly from stage to stage in the creation of your presentation.

Getting Help

You can get up and running quickly because PowerPoint's user-friendly interface makes it easy to learn as you go along. The highly sophisticated Help system offers assistance at all levels so that you can maximize your productivity. Although there are many ways to get help in PowerPoint, you can access the main Help features through the Help menu. The Help button appears as a question mark on the right side of the Standard toolbar.

PowerPoint's array of Help menu options include the following:

◆ **Balloon Help:** This feature shows a "balloon" with explanations while your pointer is positioned on a particular feature. PowerPoint is integrated with Balloon Help, a standard System 7.5 feature. You can choose to show or hide balloons. After you pass your pointer over PowerPoint's menu and tools, balloons appear to explain what each tool does.

◆ **Contents:** This feature searches for help from a topics list. The Contents command brings up a screen that allows you to access Help via the following broad categories: Using PowerPoint (step-by-step instructions), Reference Information (updates and tips), and Technical Support (see Figure 22.13). To select a category, click the accompanying icon on the left or click the green text on the right. To select topics within the category, double-click one of the categories.

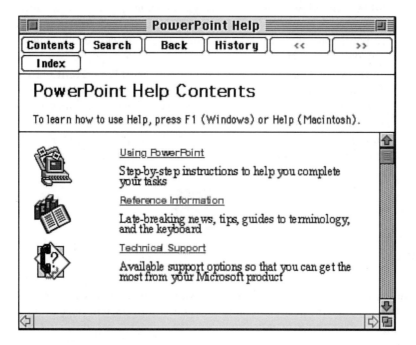

Figure 22.13   The Help Contents screen.

◆ **Search:** This feature allows you to search for help by topic. The initial screen has a dialog box and a list of topics (see Figure 22.14). To access a topic, type in the word or select it from the list. After you have made a topic selection, click the Show Topics button and select one of the topics shown. Click the Go To button on the lower-right side of the box.

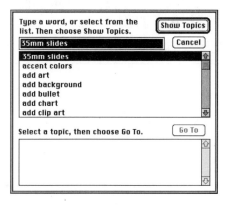

Figure 22.14   The Search Help screen.

◆ **Index:** This feature searches for help by an index (see Figure 22.15). Index displays a keyboard so that you can search for your topic by clicking, or tabbing to, the first letter of the topic. Topics appear in alphabetic order with subheadings grouped beneath them. To access your topic or subheading, just click it.

◆ **Quick Preview:** This feature gives you an overview of PowerPoint's capabilities and features. Quick Preview is a self-running, sample presentation that runs through automatically after you first install PowerPoint. This preview is quite helpful for your initial introduction to PowerPoint and can be accessed later for reviewing from the Help menu.

◆ **Tip of the Day:** This feature appears on your startup screen with handy hints for maximizing PowerPoint's potential. To view the Tip of the Day from within the application, select it from the Help menu. You can disable the Tip of the Day feature so that it does not appear every time you open PowerPoint by turning off the check box in the Tip of the Day dialog box. You can also view Tip of the Day topics by clicking the More Tips button.

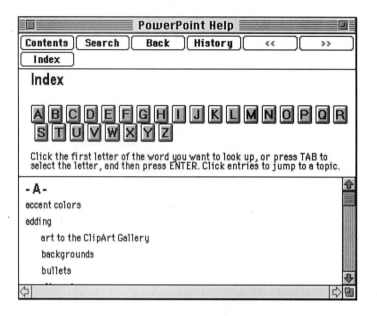

Figure 22.15 The Index Help screen.

◆ **Cue Cards:** Cue Cards function as step-by-step guides that assist you in putting together your presentation. Activate them through the Help menu or by working with wizards. The Cue Cards stay onscreen while you work, ask what you want to do next, and offer a checklist of topics to choose from. Simply follow the Cue Cards' instructions as you learn PowerPoint. To end your Cue Card session, click the little box on the upper-left corner of the Cue Card window.

◆ **Technical Support:** This feature provides contact information for the following areas of technical support: electronic services, standard support, priority support, text telephone, and training and consultation. Standard PowerPoint support for Mac users is available at no charge Monday through Friday, between 6:00 A.M. and 6:00 P.M. Pacific time, by calling (206) 635-7145. In case of emergencies, you can call priority support 24 hours a day, 7 days a week, at (900) 555-2000 for $2.00 per minute (U.S.). Or you can call (800) 936-5700 and bill the call to your VISA, MasterCard, or American Express card.

PowerPoint's built-in Help features make it easier for you to find out how to perform difficult tasks without having to leave your desk.

PowerPoint also supports you with helpful add-ons that guide you while you use the program. These are not specifically listed in the Help menu. Additional Help features include the following:

◆ **ToolTips:** This feature identifies each toolbar button with small balloons as you pass the pointer over the button. You can disable this feature in the Toolbars dialog box from the View menu. Don't confuse ToolTips with System 7.5 Balloon Help, which offers larger balloons with more detailed information.

◆ **Help button:** Use the Help button on the Standard toolbar (the one with a question mark) when you have a question about a specific task or tool function. Simply click the button once and then select the object that you have a question about. A full discussion of the object-in-question appears onscreen.

◆ **Status bar:** This feature briefly tells you how to use a tool after you select it. The status bar is located at the bottom of the screen with the status text on the left side of the bar.

These additional Help features increase your productivity by teaching you about PowerPoint while you are working.

It's easier to learn something new when you know what to look for and how to get help. After reading this chapter, you should be able to find your way around PowerPoint without too much difficulty. The next chapter tells you how to work with text and the Outline feature.

Chapter 23

Setting Up an Outline

PowerPoint is designed to help you integrate text and graphics with appealing layouts to present your message effectively. Many people regard text and visual elements to be entirely separate entities: words provide information; whereas, illustrations are meant to be looked at. This dichotomy does not exist in the world of presentations, where both elements must convey information and create visual impact simultaneously.

Despite PowerPoint's strong editing features, it is primarily a graphics program designed to structure text in outline form. This should be kept in mind when working with text. This chapter covers the following topics:

- ◆ Working in Outline view
- ◆ Using the Outlining toolbar
- ◆ Launching a presentation with AutoContent Wizard
- ◆ Adding, selecting, and editing text
- ◆ Formatting text in Slide view
- ◆ Bulleting text

Working in Outline View

PowerPoint's Outline view helps you write your script. A slide icon appears to the left of each title to indicate a new frame in your presentation. The titles appear in bold print, and the other paragraphs appear in outline form beneath. When you're working on a lengthy presentation, the Outline view gives you an overview of the entire presentation and lets you quickly rearrange the order of text and slides. The Outline format makes it easier to focus on the main points in your presentation.

The Outline view displays only text entered as part of your outline. Graphic elements and text entered directly on slides do not appear after you switch to the Outline view, although they still exist in your presentation. (For more information on graphic elements, see Chapter 24.)

The Outlining toolbar

The Outline view comes with its own Outlining toolbar, located on the left side of your screen (see Figure 23.1). These tools are provided to help you assign levels to paragraphs, move slides and paragraphs back and forth, and keep your script organized.

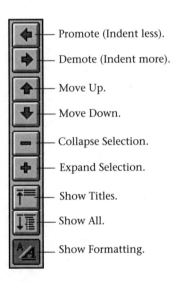

Promote (Indent less).

Demote (Indent more).

Move Up.

Move Down.

Collapse Selection.

Expand Selection.

Show Titles.

Show All.

Show Formatting.

Figure 23.1   The Outlining toolbar.

The function of the Outlining tools is listed as follows:

   ◆ **Promote/Demote:** These top two buttons promote and demote outline levels. To demote text (indent the text more), select the text and then click on the second button or press the Tab key. To promote text (indent the text less), select the text and then click on the first button or press Shift-Tab.

◆ **Move text blocks:** The up- and down arrows enable you to move blocks of text forward and backward within your presentation. Select the text and then click the tool that indicates the direction you want the text to move. The up arrow moves text backward and the down arrow moves text forward.

◆ **Collapse selected slides:** Select the slide(s) that you want collapsed by placing the cursor anywhere in the slide's text. Click the Collapse Selection button, the one that looks like a minus sign. Collapsing a slide means to display only the main point of the slide, usually the title.

◆ **Expand selected slides:** Select the slide(s) that you want expanded and then click the Expand Selection button, the one that looks like a plus sign. Expanding a slide redisplays all the levels on the slide.

◆ **Collapse entire outline:** To display only the titles of the entire outline, click the Show Titles button. A screen of collapsed slides looks like the one shown in Figure 23.2. This feature comes in handy when your outline is too long to view onscreen all at once. When you are ready, you can expand the outline again.

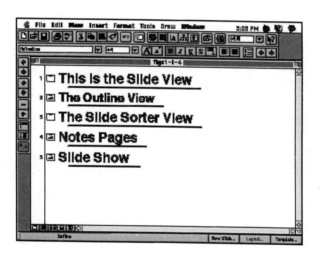

Figure 23.2 Collapsed slides.

◆ **Expand entire outline:** To display titles and all body text for all the slides in your outline, click the Show All button. An expanded slide looks like the one shown in Figure 23.3.

571

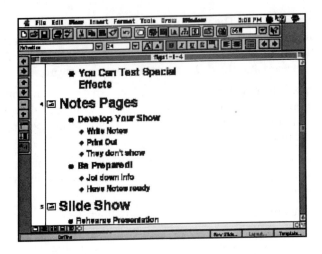

Figure 23.3   An expanded slide.

◆ **Show/Hide Formatting:** The last button, with the *A*'s on it, enables you to decide whether you want to see the text formatting or not. Viewing the text formatting lets you see which lines appear at a larger or smaller point size and what fonts and styles you have used.

PowerPoint's Outlining toolbar helps make formatting text for slides easy.

Launching Presentations with AutoContent Wizard

PowerPoint's AutoContent Wizard helps you with the hardest part of developing a presentation—getting started with an outline. The AutoContent Wizard takes you through a series of steps that prompt you on how to set up your outline. When you are finished, AutoContent Wizard leaves you in the Outline view with a PowerPoint Cue Card that prompts you on what to do next.

To activate AutoContent Wizard, select it through the New Presentation dialog box (see Chapter 22). To demonstrate the usefulness of AutoContent Wizard, try your hand at a sample presentation. If you follow along, you can get the feel for the ease of using the AutoContent Wizard to create outlines.

The scenario: launching a coffee café

You and your partners have run restaurants and clubs successfully in your city for the past 20 years. You have noticed a recent trend towards coffee cafés, and you know of people who have launched and run them with success in other cities. You and your partners decide to start up Café Olé. You have everything you need: a strong management team, steady patrons at your other establishments, and a good relationship in the community where you want to open your new café.

Selling your idea

Now you need to persuade someone to provide venture capital. CoffeeCo, a multimillion dollar international conglomerate, seems like a good target. After all, it is a related business, and you have been buying coffee for your restaurants through its distributor for years. Also, a member of its board seems interested in starting up a coffee café as a test marketing tool to soften CoffeeCo's corporate image.

Setting up the presentation

Now you have your first opportunity to pitch your ideas through a professional presentation. You need to consider the overall purpose of your presentation (selling your idea), the points you want to make (why CoffeeCo would find it advantageous to back you), who your audience is, and what tone you should adopt. You also want to use PowerPoint to put your best foot forward. The AutoContent Wizard assists you in the initial phase of writing your script.

To launch a presentation with AutoContent Wizard, follow these steps:

1. Create a new presentation by selecting the New command on the File menu, clicking the New button on the Standard toolbar, or using the ⌘-N key combination. A New Presentation dialog box appears, as shown in Figure 23.4.

Figure 23.4   The New Presentation dialog box.

2. Select AutoContent Wizard from the options offered and click the OK button. The first of four AutoContent Wizard windows appears, as shown in Figure 23.5.

Figure 23.5   The first AutoContent Wizard window.

3. Click the Next button to move on to Step 2, which produces a window like the one in Figure 23.6.

Caution: Don't click the Finish button until you have completed all four steps. AutoContent Wizard needs to finish these steps in order to help launch your presentation.

Figure 23.6   Step 2 of AutoContent Wizard.

4. Create your title slide by filling in the information as shown in Figure 23.7. The text entered in the Other Information text box will not be part of the outline. This information is visible in the Slide view, but you do not see it in Outline view.

Figure 23.7   Filling in the information for the title slide.

5. Click the Next button to get to the third window. Select the second option, Selling a Product, Service or Idea, to set up a skeleton outline (see Figure 23.8). On the left side of the dialog box, AutoContent Wizard displays a preview of your outline.

Figure 23.8   The third AutoContent Wizard window.

6. Let the AutoContent Wizard assemble your presentation by following the instructions in the last window (see Figure 23.9). Click the Finish button.

Figure 23.9   The last AutoContent Wizard window.

AutoContent Wizard ends your session by assuming that you want to develop your outline first, so it places you in the Outline view. A skeleton outline for selling a service or idea appears onscreen, along with a PowerPoint Cue Card. If the Cue Card does not appear, you can access PowerPoint Cue Cards through the Help menu.

The Cue Card asks you what you want to do next and simplifies your search for help by listing a range of options, as shown in Figure 23.10. After you click one of the buttons to tell Cue Cards what you want to learn, the Cue Card pops a dialog box onscreen with instructions.

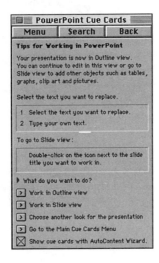

Figure 23.10   A Cue Card.

Filling in your outline

The AutoContent Wizard has provided you with everything you need to write your outline. By loosely following the skeleton outline, you can develop your own outline fairly quickly. Type the following information into the designated onscreen categories:

Objective:

Launch A Coffee Café
- ★ **Raise capital**
- ★ **Set up downtown**
- ★ **Start hiring**
- ★ **Start advertising**
- ★ **Create an atmosphere**

Customer Requirements:

The Time is Right
- ★ **Coffee craze taking off**
- ★ **Coffee consumption up 50% since 1985**
- ★ **Alcohol consumption down 30%**
  - – **Soundbites Corp.'s profits doubled last year**
  - – **Liberty Café's profits tripled over the past five years**

Meeting the Needs:

Enjoy the Experience
- ★ **Cozy, café setting**
- ★ **Coffee, drinks & snacks**
- ★ **Take a break**
- ★ **Relax with friends**
- ★ **Evening entertainment**

Cost Analysis:

The Bottom Line
- ★ **Will pay within year**
- ★ **Distribute your products**
- ★ **Test market your products**

Our Strengths:

Café Olé's Strengths
- ★ **A strong management team**
  - – **12 years restaurant experience**
  - – **Access to employee market**
- ★ **Proven successes**
  - – **Club Grunge, 1990–present**
  - – **The Macrobiotic Café, 1973–1980**
  - – **Yup's Bar & Grill, 1981–1989**
- ★ **We work hard for you!**

Key Benefits:	**See a Little Go a Long Way!**
	★ **Return on investment**
	★ **Soften your corporate image**
	★ **Capture youth market**
	★ **Forge ties with the community**
Next Steps:	**Join Our Team**
	★ **Work with us!**
	★ **An initial investment of $400,000 from CoffeeCo**
	★ **Advertising & promotional expenses**

Now save your outline as DEMO2. You will return to it, learn how to create a different look, and add graphics in Chapter 24.

Creating an outline is an important first step in the presentation process. You now know how to use the AutoContent Wizard to launch your presentation and how to use text-outlining tools to give your presentation a well-organized foundation.

Working with Text in the Slide View

PowerPoint offers many of the same text editing and formatting features that you find in Microsoft Word and other word processing programs. In the Slide view, you can adjust fonts and point sizes, cut and paste, change styles and colors, add bullets, choose bullet styles, and even use the Spelling Checker on your text. The Drawing toolbar appears to the left of the screen to offer text formatting options.

Typing text on slides

With PowerPoint, you can add text to slides either as part of your outline or as separate text blocks. Text added as separate text blocks, such as captions for graphs or illustrations, shows up on the slides but does not appear in the Outline view.

◆ **To enter text on slides:** To enter text while you are working in Slide view, click the Text tool (the one with the letter *A*) on the Drawing toolbar to the left of your screen. Your pointer changes into a cursor. Insert the cursor in one of the text placeholders and begin typing.

◆ **To create a text box:** To create your own text box, hold down the mouse key and drag the cursor across the screen diagonally until the box is the desired size.

◆ **Typing text within shapes:** You can fit text into PowerPoint's AutoShapes. To do this, draw a shape, select the Text tool, and start typing. Your text is now automatically centered within the object, as shown in Figure 23.11. (For more information on drawing AutoShapes, see Chapter 24.)

Figure 23.11 Text in an AutoShape.

◆ **Setting the text anchor point:** The text's anchor point determines how text fits into a shape and what the direction is for text growth. To set the anchor point, select the Text Anchor command from the Format menu. A dialog box appears. Make sure that the Adjust Object Size to Fit Text check box is turned off. This prevents text from running off the edges.

◆ **Adding captions:** Select the Text tool, click the area where you want to type the caption, and begin typing. Notice that as you continue typing, the text box automatically expands horizontally.

◆ **Wrapping text:** If you want your text to wrap automatically within a particular width, size your text box before typing. To size a text box that constrains text to a particular width, select the Text tool, click at the point where you want your text to begin, and then drag your cursor diagonally to where you want the text box to end. This technique is useful for creating captions and for other situations where text is centered beneath objects. Figure 23.12 shows a text box ready for a caption.

Figure 23.12 A text box sized for entering text.

◆ **Adding borders to text:** PowerPoint automatically formats text into a text box. You can add a border by clicking the Line On/Off button (the one with the paint brush).

Selecting and editing text

Selecting and editing text in PowerPoint is done the same way as you would with any Mac- or Windows-based word processing program. To select and edit text, you highlight the block of text that you want to change and then type the new text.

The basic editing commands are listed as follows:

- ◆ **To select all elements onscreen:** Choose the Select All command from the Edit menu or use the key combination ⌘-A.

  You can select a word by double-clicking it. You can select a sentence by holding down the Option key and clicking the sentence. You can select an entire paragraph by triple-clicking any word in the paragraph.

  PowerPoint defaults to select an entire word as you drag across it. To select text one letter at a time, choose Options from the Tools menu. Clear the Automatic Word Selection check box.

- ◆ **To cut text:** Choose the Cut command from the Edit menu, click the Cut button (the one that looks like a scissors) on the Standard toolbar, or use the key combination ⌘-X.

- ◆ **To copy text:** Choose the Copy command from the Edit menu, click the Copy button (the one that looks like two pieces of paper) on the Standard toolbar, or use the key combination ⌘-C.

- ◆ **To paste text from the Clipboard:** Choose the Paste command from the Edit menu, click the Copy button (the one that looks like a clipboard) on the Standard toolbar, or use the key combination ⌘-V.

- ◆ **To Undo actions:** Choose the Undo command from the Edit menu, click the Undo button (the one that looks like a curved arrow pointing backward) on the Standard toolbar, or use the key combination ⌘-Z.

Using the Clipboard

As in most Macintosh applications, PowerPoint's Clipboard enables you to select and place objects on the Clipboard through the Cut and Copy commands and then paste them into other places in your slide show. In addition, PowerPoint shares its Clipboard with other Microsoft Office applications.

If you have already created an outline in Microsoft Word, you can copy it, open your PowerPoint presentation, and paste your text into the Outline view. In this way, you can easily reformat your slides. You can also do the same with graphs from Excel. In PowerPoint, these documents remain fully editable.

Formatting text

You can add visual excitement to your words with PowerPoint's variety of text effects. With PowerPoint, you can change fonts, increase or decrease point size, and change the colors of letters; you can add bold, underline, italics and shadows to text (see Figure 23.13); you can align paragraphs to the left, center, or right; and you can use bullets.

In the Format menu, you have access to the Alignment and Font commands. You can align text through the Alignment submenu, and you can set and change type specifications through the Font dialog box, as shown in Figure 23.14.

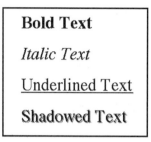

Figure 23.13   Text style examples.

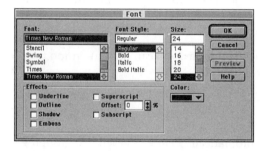

Figure 23.14   The Font dialog box.

Text formatting commands and tools are listed as follows:

◆ **To bold text:** Select the Bold option in the Font dialog box from the Format menu, click the Bold button (the one that looks like a *B*) on the Formatting toolbar, or use the key combination ⌘-B.

◆ **To italicize text:** Select the Italic option in the Font dialog box from the Format menu, click the Italic button (the one that looks like an *I*) on the Formatting toolbar, or use the key combination ⌘-I.

◆ **To underline text:** Select the Underline option in the Font the dialog box from the Format menu, click the Underline button (the one that looks like an underlined *U*) from the Formatting toolbar, or use the key combination ⌘-U.

◆ **To emboss text:** Select the Emboss option in the Font dialog box from the Format menu to add an elegant look to your presentation.

- ◆ **To return to plain text:** Select the Plain Text option in the Font dialog box from the Format menu or use the key combination ⌘-Shift-Z.

- ◆ **To enlarge text:** Select a point size in the Font dialog box from the Format menu, click the Font Size down-arrow button on the Formatting toolbar, or increase your type size incrementally with the key combination ⌘-Shift-Period.

- ◆ **To reduce text:** Select a point size in the Font dialog box from the Format menu, click the Font Size down-arrow button on the Formatting toolbar, or decrease your type size incrementally with the key combination ⌘-Shift-Comma.

- ◆ **To left-align text:** Select the Left option in the Alignment submenu from the Format menu, click the Left Alignment button on the Formatting toolbar, or use the key combination ⌘-L.

- ◆ **To right-align text:** Select the Right option in the Alignment submenu from the Format menu or use the key combination ⌘-R.

- ◆ **To center text:** Select the Center option in the Alignment submenu from the Format menu, click the Center Alignment button on the Formatting toolbar, or use the key combination ⌘-E.

By using your text formatting options, you can draw attention to specific points or create a whole new look for your slide show.

Using bullets

Notice that PowerPoint automatically delineates each text grouping or paragraph with bullets. Professional presenters generally use bulleted lists because they add visual impact, draw attention to each point, and add subtle accents to your presentations.

You can rearrange bullets on your slides by clicking the bullet and dragging it where you want the bullet to appear.

You can change the way your bullets look or remove them entirely. If you don't want bullets before every paragraph, simply click the Bullet On/Off button (the one that has three dots and three lines) on the Formatting toolbar. To replace the bullets, click this button again—it functions as a toggle switch.

If you want to customize your bullets, choose Bullet from the Format menu. The Bullet dialog box offers a full palette of different looks, as shown in Figure 23.15.

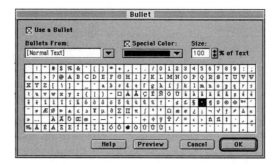

Figure 23.15   The Bullet dialog box.

Effective presentations begin with good outlines. PowerPoint offers an array of tools and features for creating outlines and working with text. The next chapter shows you how to enhance your presentations by adding graphic elements.

Chapter 24

Working with
Graphics

PowerPoint provides a variety of powerful graphic tools right at your fingertips. This versatile program also has an extensive Clip Art Gallery, fully functional graphing and charting abilities, a palette of drawing tools, adjustable color schemes, and support for inserting visual elements created in other applications. In this chapter, you will learn the basics of creating your own original look for your presentations. The topics covered in this chapter include

◆ Creating presentations
  with Pick a Look Wizard

◆ Selecting templates

◆ Using AutoLayouts

◆ Changing color schemes

◆ Utilizing Slide Master

◆ Drawing with AutoShapes

◆ Adjusting objects

◆ Choosing clip art

◆ Making graphs

◆ Building organizational
  charts

Designing a Presentation with Pick a Look Wizard

By using PowerPoint's ready-made graphic elements, the novice can produce slides with a polished look; a more experienced presenter has the flexibility to experiment with customized slide designs.

PowerPoint's Pick a Look Wizard works the same way as the AutoContent Wizard. You can activate Pick a Look Wizard by choosing it in the New Presentation dialog box, by clicking the Pick a Look Wizard button (the one that looks like a magic wand) on the Standard toolbar, or by selecting it from the Format menu. Pick a Look Wizard takes you through a set of prompts for setting up the appearance of your slides and for printing supporting materials, such as handouts, outlines, and speaker's notes.

Alas, this option is not as useful as the AutoContent Wizard, although Pick a Look Wizard does narrow down your choice of templates, thereby making the selection process less overwhelming.

Now it's time to expand the presentation that you began in Chapter 23. You have decided that you want to present a slick, professional look to your potential backers at CoffeeCo, so you decide to see what Pick a Look Wizard can do. Pick a Look Wizard can be activated at any time while developing your presentation.

To use Pick a Look Wizard, follow these steps:

1. Open DEMO2 and go into the Slide view. Notice that the slides are blank except for your outline.

2. Activate the Pick a Look Wizard by clicking the Pick a Look Wizard button or by going through the Format menu. The first Pick a Look Wizard window appears, as shown in Figure 24.1.

3. Click the Next button. The second window appears (see Figure 24.2). The Pick a Look Wizard prompts you to make your first selection. Select 35mm Slides as your presentation format choice.

4. Click the Next button and, in the third window, select the template with the blue diagonal line. After you select a template, a preview appears in the window, as shown in Figure 24.3.

5. After you click the Next button, the fourth window appears. Activate all the check boxes. You have just asked PowerPoint to print your presentation with slides, speaker's notes, audience handouts, and outline pages when you are ready to print.

Figure 24.1   The first Pick a Look Wizard window.

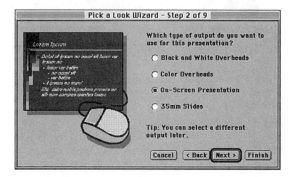

Figure 24.2   The second Pick a Look Wizard window, where you pick a presentation format.

Figure 24.3   The third Pick a Look Wizard window, where you choose a template.

6. Click the Next button. In the next three windows—Slide Options, Notes Options, and Handout Options—you have the option of adding a name, the date, and a page number to any of the four printing categories. For this exercise, you can leave these boxes blank. You can activate Pick a Look Wizard at any time if you change your mind about a page number or a date.

7. You should now be in the last window, Step 9 (see Figure 24.4). Click the Finish button so that Pick a Look Wizard can assemble your presentation.

Figure 24.4   The final Pick a Look Wizard window.

Congratulations! Your title slide should now look like the one shown in Figure 24.5.

Figure 24.5   The title slide, made with the Pick a Look Wizard.

Selecting a Template

Using PowerPoint's extensive collection of templates provides the easiest way to create a uniformly designed look. PowerPoint has over 100 templates in a choice of three formats: 35mm slide show/screen display, color transparent overheads, and black-and-white transparent overheads. The same basic design options are offered within each category, but the templates are adjusted to accommodate the output resolution and size ratio. For instance, the black-and-white overhead templates use shades of gray rather than different colors for contrast.

These templates were created with visual impact in mind. The backgrounds, text, bullets, and colors used in PowerPoint graphs automatically use your template settings. The color schemes provided in the templates have already been proven successful in terms of audience readability and design attractiveness.

After looking at your slides, you decide that you want a more festive look to show how much fun people will have at Café Olé! The original template design of your presentation can easily be changed by choosing the Template command.

To select a new template, do the following:

1. Access PowerPoint's Template command either by choosing the Presentation Template command from the Format menu or by clicking the Template shortcut button at the lower-right of your screen on the status bar. The Presentation Templates dialog box appears, as shown in Figure 24.6.

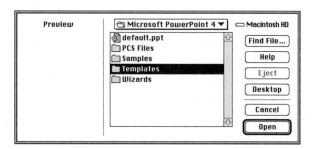

Figure 24.6   The Presentation Templates dialog box.

2. Select the Templates folder located in the PowerPoint 4 folder. Next, open the On Screen & 35mm Slides folder—found in the Templates folder, as shown in Figure 24.7.

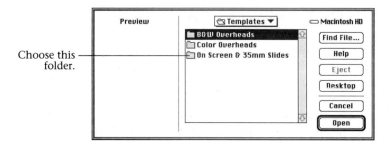

Figure 24.7   The Templates folder.

3. Highlight the template called Confetti (CONFETIS.PPT). After you highlight a template, you get a preview of it to the left of the dialog box, as shown in Figure 24.8.

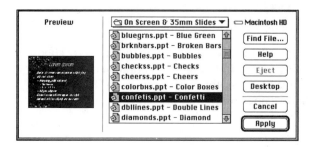

Figure 24.8   The Confetti template in the Preview window of the Templates dialog box.

4. Select the Confetti template by clicking the Apply button in the dialog box.

If you view your slides, notice that the template has done more than set up a background for you. You now have a basic layout, consistent color scheme, and type and bullet styles for your text.

Creating AutoLayouts

Unless you are an experienced graphic designer or slide show producer, figuring out how to arrange text and visual elements on the slides can be difficult. PowerPoint's AutoLayouts let you spend more time making your point and less time figuring out where to put things.

You can use AutoLayouts by selecting the Slide Layout command from the Format menu or by clicking the Layout shortcut button on the status bar. This menu also appears automatically after you add a new slide. Selecting a layout affects only the particular slide you are working on, not the entire presentation. PowerPoint offers nine different possible layouts for your slides, as shown in Figure 24.9.

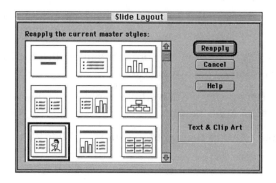

Figure 24.9   PowerPoint's AutoLayouts.

PowerPoint's AutoLayout options include layouts for the following:

◆ Text with clip art

◆ Text with graphs

◆ Text with charts

◆ Text slides with no visual elements

These predesigned slides position text and visual elements so that they complement each other and fit together well on the slide. To select an AutoLayout from the dialog box, click the layout that you want to use.

Placeholders automatically reserve space on the slide for text and visual elements. Placeholders show you where text and graphics will appear and help you make design decisions based on simple logic. For instance, if the slide you're working on has more than two or three lines of text, and you want to add a graph, you wouldn't choose the layout featuring the larger, horizontally oriented graph.

> **Caution:** Selecting an AutoLayout with two columns of text will result in frustration. Although PowerPoint will create a second column placeholder for more text, the text on your slide does not automatically format into two columns. You can, however, cut and paste text into the second column placeholder or enter text manually.

Designing Your Slides

You and your Café Olé partners basically like the way your presentation looks, but it still lacks oomph. You would like slide 2, "Launch A Coffee Cafe," to include a visual element that conveys the nature of your endeavor. You decide to use the AutoLayout command to help you accomplish this goal.

To use the AutoLayout command to lay out a slide with extra room for clip art, follow these steps:

1. Choose Slide Layout from the Format menu or click the Layout shortcut button. The Slide Layout dialog box appears.

2. Select the layout with the clip art placeholder (the one with the man's head) and then select the Apply button.

3. AutoLayout transfers the layout to your slide. Slide 2 should now look like Figure 24.10.

Figure 24.10   A clip art placeholder added to the slide.

Congratulations, you have just set up a slide layout that leaves space for inserting clip art. You will learn how to select and insert clip art in the placeholder later in this chapter.

Now you will create a slide layout that includes a placeholder for a graph by following these steps:

1. Go to slide 4, "Enjoy the Experience," by pressing the Page Down key.

2. Select Layout with the shortcut button on the status bar or through the Format menu.

3. After the Slide Layout dialog box appears, click on the vertical graph AutoLayout (the second one in the second row) to select it and then click Apply. Slide 4 should now look like Figure 24.11.

Figure 24.11   Slide 4 with a graph placeholder.

Changing Your Color Schemes

Color schemes consist of sets of eight colors that make up the text color, background color, and fill colors. You can change the color scheme by selecting the Slide Color Scheme command from the Format menu. The Slide Color Scheme dialog box appears and shows you how colors are applied (see Figure 24.12).

Figure 24.12   The Slide Color Scheme dialog box.

Caution: Changing color schemes is not recommended for the design novice. PowerPoint's built-in color schemes are combinations in accordance with established design principles for legibility and visual impact. However, as you grow more experienced in the design of slides, you may want to experiment with customizing your presentations.

Some guidelines for changing color schemes are as follows:

◆ Although you cannot change templates in mid-presentation, PowerPoint does let you alter the color schemes from slide to slide. You can alter the color in Slide view from within the individual slide that you want to change. Colors for graphs and clip art, however, must be changed individually.

◆ For those of you with access to a color printer, you can also apply separate color schemes to your handouts and notes pages. Simply select Handouts Master or Notes Master from the Master Command on the View menu. Changing these color schemes does not alter your presentation.

◆ As mentioned in the templates section earlier in the chapter, templates come with their own color schemes. You can change one or several of the color defaults through the Slide Color Scheme dialog box from the Format menu.

In the Color Schemes dialog box, you can assign colors to specific categories of objects that appear on slides. PowerPoint's color schemes are programmed to ensure that the colors of text, background items, bullets, and filled and lined objects do not clash with each other while ensuring sufficient contrast for legibility.

Color schemes assign colors to the following elements:

◆ **Background color**: Background color applies to the color of the slide as it appears before any elements are added to it.

◆ **Shadows color:** Shadows color is applied when you shadow an object. This color is generally a shade darker than the Fills color.

◆ **Fills color:** Fills color is applied when you fill an object. Fills color is designed to contrast with the slide's background, lines, and text colors. When you create graphs, the predominant colors used in the graph default to the Fills color.

◆ **Accent color:** PowerPoint gives you three options for Accent color. These options are used for secondary features and additional colors on graphs.

◆ **Title Text color:** Title Text color is used for slide titles and is designed to contrast with the Background color.

◆ **Text & Lines color:** Text & Lines color is used for text, lines, and borders on slides and is designed to contrast with the Background color.

By creating or modifying color schemes, you can customize presentations for a variety of purposes, such as adjusting a template when you like the overall design but not the colors, using colors that complement your company's logo, or changing the color schemes on a single slide so that the information presented in that frame stands out.

You can apply separate color schemes to individual slides or groups of slides. To apply separate color schemes to slides, select them either in the Slide view or in the Slide Sorter view and then select the Slide Color Scheme command in the Format menu. To select multiple slides in the Slide Sorter view, hold down the Shift key and click the desired slides with your pointer.

To create and change your slide color scheme, do the following:

1. Select the Slide Color Scheme command from the Format menu.

2. After the Slide Color Scheme dialog box appears, click the Choose Scheme button.

3. Adjust your color scheme after the Choose Scheme dialog box appears, as shown in Figure 24.13.

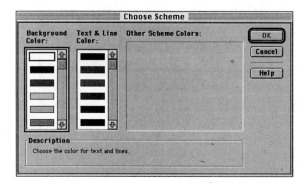

Figure 24.13   The Choose Scheme dialog box.

4. Click the OK button. After you return to your slide, you can see that your color scheme changes have been made.

Your customized color scheme is based on the colors that you choose in the Background Color and Text & Line Color areas of the Choose Scheme dialog box. The preview boxes in the dialog box show you how your other colors will appear.

Changing individual colors in a color scheme

You can change individual colors within your color schemes. This option is useful in situations where you like the overall color scheme, but you need to customize a single color element in your presentation.

To change the color of an individual element in your color scheme, do the following:

1. Select the element(s) that you want changed and then choose the Slide Color Scheme command from the Format menu.

2. After the Choose Scheme dialog box appears, select the color element that you want to change in the Change Scheme Colors area and click the Change Color button.

3. After the appropriate color palette dialog box appears, as shown in Figure 24.14, click the desired color.

4. After your new color appears in the preview area, click the OK button. When you return to your slide, the new color appears on the element(s) that you selected.

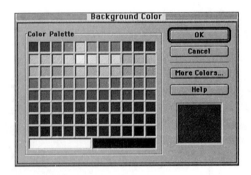

Figure 24.14   The color palette dialog box for the Background Color option.

Copying color schemes to other slides

PowerPoint also lets you copy color schemes from one slide to another. To pick up and apply a color scheme to another slide, do the following:

1. Go into the Slide Sorter view by selecting the Slide Sorter command from the View menu or by clicking the Slide Sorter View button on the lower-left corner of the status bar.

2. Select the slide with the color scheme you want to copy.

3. Click the Format Painter button (the paint brush) on the Standard toolbar.

4. Select the slide or drag a marquee around multiple slides to which you want to apply the color scheme.

5. The color scheme now appears on the selected slides.

If you want to undo your color scheme change, select the Undo command from the Edit menu or use the ⌘-Z key combination.

Using Slide Master

Slide Master lets you include any information, text attributes, and visual elements that you want to appear on each slide of your presentation, such as a company logo, a date, and a slide number. Slide Master is accessed by choosing the Master command from the View menu. The Slide Master inserts placeholders for text, with sample text for formatting within the place-holders (see Figure 24.15). The text shown in the placeholders does not appear on the actual presentation slides. To make text appear on the slides, create a new text box with the text tool and enter the text. You can use the Slide Master to set fonts, point sizes, and bullets for slide titles and supporting text. You can also change the color schemes for all your slides at once.

Figure 24.15   The Slide Master view.

To edit the format of all your slides, simply select the text shown in the placeholders as you normally would and make any adjustments to the font, color, or type size, as described in Chapter 23.

> **Caution:** All changes that you make in Slide Master view will apply to the text attributes on all your slides.

Adding background items to your slides

You can use Slide Master to add a decorative border to your slides; insert the date, time, or slide numbers; or place your company logo in the slides. Inserting graphics from other applications is discussed later in this chapter. Background items can be removed from individual slides as you work on your presentation.

The following list contains useful information that you can easily apply to your slides with the Slide Master (do not type the final period):

◆ **Date:** To make today's date automatically appear on every slide, select the Date option from the Insert menu or type the characters //.

◆ **Time:** To make the time of your presentation appear on every slide, select the Time option from the Insert menu or type the characters ...

◆ **Page Number:** To make the Page number automatically appear on every slide, select the Page command from the Insert menu or type the characters ##.

While working in Slide view, the Slide Master characters for date, time, and page (slide number) appear as you typed them (//, .. , ##). These characters appear as the current date, time, and slide number only while you are in Slide Show view.

Slide Master helps you maintain consistency in your presentation without having to apply the information to each slide manually.

Using Slide Master in your presentation

In your sample presentation, let's suppose that you want to insert the company name and slide number on each slide for easy reference. In order for this information to remain unobtrusive and not interfere with your individual slide layouts, you can place this information in smaller type at the lower right of your slides. To add this information to your presentation, do the following:

1. Return to your DEMO2 presentation and select the Slide Master command from the Master command on the View menu. Your screen should look like the one in Figure 24.15.

2. Create a text box in the lower-right border of the Slide Master, as shown in Figure 24.16. To create this text box, click the Text tool (the one with the *A*) on the Drawing toolbar at the left of your screen. Then click the lower-right corner of your slide, hold down the mouse button, and drag diagonally left and upward to the right border of the slide so that the text box is approximately $1/2$-inch high.

3. Type the words **Café Olé**, followed by a comma.

4. Hold down the Shift and Option keys while entering the letter **P**, or type ##. Shift-Option-P is the command for automatic slide numbering.

Figure 24.16   Inserting a text box into the Slide Master.

> 5. Highlight the text and change the font size to 18 points by clicking the Font Size down-pointing arrow on the Formatting toolbar and scrolling down to select 18-point type.

When you run through your presentation in the Slide Show view (the only view that automatically inserts the actual slide numbers), each slide displays the name of your company and the slide number (see Figure 24.17).

To return to Slide view after you have made the changes that you want with the Slide Master, choose the Slides command from the View menu or click on the Slide View button at the lower-left corner of the status bar.

Figure 24.17   A slide displayed in Slide Show view, displaying slide identification added by Slide Master.

Adding Visual Elements with the Drawing Toolbar

PowerPoint acts like most other graphic packages regarding images and text. You can resize, rotate, and move images; adjust the colors, draw, shade, and color shapes; add shadows and borders; and group and ungroup objects. You can do all these things with the tools on the Drawing toolbar on the left side of your screen (see Figure 24.18).

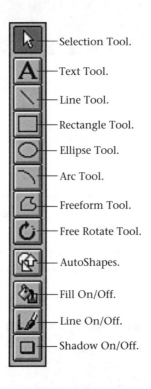

Selection Tool.
Text Tool.
Line Tool.
Rectangle Tool.
Ellipse Tool.
Arc Tool.
Freeform Tool.
Free Rotate Tool.
AutoShapes.
Fill On/Off.
Line On/Off.
Shadow On/Off.

Figure 24.18   The Drawing toolbar.

Here's an explanation of the Drawing toolbar's tools:

◆ **Selection tool:** Use the Selection tool to select and edit text and to move and resize objects that you have added to your slides. To edit text, click the text that you want to change and watch as a selection box appears around the text. Now you can edit as you normally would. To remove the box, click anywhere in the slide outside of the box. To move the text block, click on the selection box, hold down the mouse button, and drag the box to where you want it to go.

To move an object that you have added to a slide, select a point anywhere in the middle of the object, hold down your mouse button, and drag the object to the location where you want to place it.

To move an object in small increments, select the object and press the arrow key that points in the direction that you want to move your object. For smaller increments, you can turn off the Snap to Grid default temporarily by holding down the Option key while using the arrow key.

To resize an object, click it. A selection box appears. Click your pointer on a resize handle on the selection box and drag the handle toward the center to reduce the object and away from the center to enlarge the object. The resize handles look like little squares that appear on the selection box. To keep the original proportions of an object you are resizing, press the Shift key while dragging a corner resize handle.

Another way to reduce or enlarge an object proportionally is to select the object and then choose the Scale command from the Draw menu. When the Scale dialog box appears, enter the percentage by which you would like the object to be reduced or enlarged.

◆ **Text tool:** Use the Text tool to add text to slides. To add text, click the Text Tool button, create a text box, and begin typing. (For more information on how to create a text box, see "Adding background items to your slides," earlier in the chapter.)

◆ **Line tool:** Use the Line tool to create straight and diagonal lines on your slides. To draw a line, click the Line Tool button, click the place where you want your starting point to be, hold down your mouse button, and drag the tool to where you want your end point to be.

◆ **Rectangle tool:** Use the Rectangle tool to draw rectangles and squares. This tool is useful for creating borders for your slides.

To draw a rectangle, click the Rectangle Tool button, click where you want your starting point to be, hold down the mouse button, and drag the tool diagonally to where you want your end point to be. To draw a square, perform the same procedure while holding down the Shift key. To draw the object from the center outward, hold down the Option key while you drag the tool.

◆ **Ellipse tool:** Use the Ellipse tool to draw ovals and circles. To draw an oval, click the Ellipse Tool button, click where you want your starting point to be, hold down the mouse button, and drag the tool diagonally to where you want your end point to be. To draw a circle, perform the same procedure while holding down the Shift key. To draw the object from the center outward, hold down the Option key while you drag the tool.

◆ **Arc tool:** To draw an arc, click the Arc Tool button, click where you want your starting point to be, hold down your mouse button, and drag the tool diagonally to where you want your end point to be. To draw a quarter circle, hold down the Shift key while drawing an arc.

◆ **Freeform tool:** To draw abstract and freeform shapes, click the Freeform Tool button, click at your starting point, hold down the mouse button, and draw your shape as if you were drawing on paper, as shown in Figure 24.19.

Figure 24.19 A freeform shape.

◆ **Free Rotate tool:** Use the Free Rotate tool to tilt objects and text blocks. To rotate an object, select the object that you want to rotate, click the Free Rotate Tool button, and drag a handle in the direction you want to tilt the object, as shown in Figure 24.20. If you have attached text to your shape, it tilts along with it.

To automatically flip an object or text box 90 degrees to the left, right, up, or down, select the object and choose the Rotate/Flip command from the Draw menu.

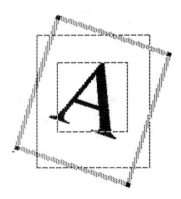

Figure 24.20 Using the Free Rotate tool to tilt an object.

◆ **AutoShapes tool:** After you click the AutoShapes tool, a pop-up menu appears with a selection of commonly used shapes, including arrows and starbursts. Use AutoShapes to add visual impact to your slides. To draw an AutoShape, select the desired shape from the pop-up menu and add it to your slide by clicking at your starting point, holding down your mouse button, and dragging the tool diagonally to your end point.

You can change any AutoShape into another AutoShape by selecting the shape and then selecting the Change AutoShape command on the Draw menu.

◆ **Fill On/Off tool:** Use the Fill On/Off tool to add or remove fills from objects. (For adjusting fills and lines, see the next section in this chapter, "Adjusting lines and fills.") To fill an object with a color, select the object and then click the Fill On/Off button. To remove a fill, select the object and then click the Fill On/Off button.

◆ **Line On/Off tool:** Use the Line On/Off tool to add or remove borders from objects. To add a border to an object, select the object and then click the Line On/Off button. To remove a border from an object, select the object and then click the Line On/Off button.

◆ **Shadow On/Off tool:** Use the Shadow On/Off tool to add or remove shadows from objects. To add a shadow to an object, select the object and then click the Shadow On/Off button. To remove a shadow from an object, select the object and then click the Shadow On/Off button.

After you learn how to use PowerPoint's graphic tools, you can create graphic objects to emphasize your points and add interest to your presentations.

Caution: Use drawn lines, borders, and shapes sparingly. Too many objects can clutter up your slides and distract from the information that you want to convey.

Adjusting lines and fills

PowerPoint automatically sets line and fill attributes. To change the color of your fill or the style of your lines, select the object and then choose the Colors and Lines command from the Format menu. The Colors and Lines dialog box appears (see Figure 24.21).

Each slide color scheme consists of eight colors. PowerPoint displays these colors after you click the Fill or Line arrow in the Colors and Lines dialog box. If you want a color other than the default color for your selected object, select a new color from the palette.

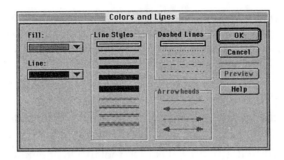

Figure 24.21 The Colors and Lines dialog box.

For increased graphic functions at your fingertips, you can display the Drawing+ toolbar (see Figure 24.22) by selecting it in the Toolbars dialog box from the View menu.

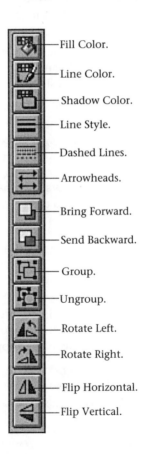

— Fill Color.
— Line Color.
— Shadow Color.
— Line Style.
— Dashed Lines.
— Arrowheads.
— Bring Forward.
— Send Backward.
— Group.
— Ungroup.
— Rotate Left.
— Rotate Right.
— Flip Horizontal.
— Flip Vertical.

Figure 24.22 The Drawing+ toolbar.

Stacking objects

Stacking objects, also referred to as layering objects, gives you more flexibility in creating your layouts by enabling you to bring an object to the front, send it to the back, or place it one layer forward or back. Stacking is useful in cases where you want to hide objects or where you want to partially cover one object with another one.

To move an object backward or forward, select the object and then choose one of the following commands from the Draw menu.

◆ **Bring to Front:** Brings an object to the front layer.

◆ **Send to Back:** Sends an object to the back layer.

◆ **Bring Forward:** Brings an object forward one level.

◆ **Send Backward:** Sends an object back one level.

Figure 24.23 shows how an object moves one level forward after activating the Send Forward command.

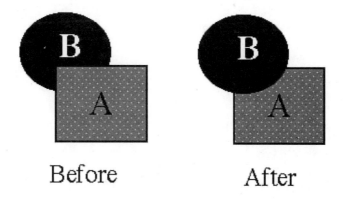

Before   After

Figure 24.23   Activating the Send Forward command.

Grouping and ungrouping objects

The Group command from the Draw menu enables you to select two or more objects and group them so that they can be sized and moved as one unit. This is convenient in instances where you use several elements to compose a single image or when two or more visual elements are designed to appear together.

To group two or more objects, do the following:

1. Select the objects either by holding down the Shift key and clicking each object or by drawing a selection box around them by dragging your pointer diagonally across them as if you were drawing a square to enclose them, as shown in Figure 24.24.

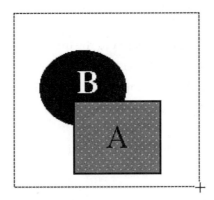

Figure 24.24   Drawing a selection box to group objects.

2. Choose the Group command from the Draw menu or use the ⌘-Shift-G key combination.

To ungroup objects, select the group and choose the Ungroup command from the Draw menu or use the ⌘-Shift-H key combination.

Inserting Illustrations from the Clip Art Gallery

PowerPoint's Clip Art Gallery contains an array of images organized by commonly used categories so that you can visually enhance your presentations. You can access the Clip Art Gallery through the Insert menu, by clicking the Insert Clip Art button on the Standard toolbar, or by creating a clip art AutoLayout.

The Clip Art Gallery features a dialog box with a scroll-down menu for selecting a category and previews of the images. To select an image, double-click the previewed clip art item that you want to add to your slide.

As you already know, using AutoLayouts makes inserting visual elements easy. Go to slide 2 in DEMO2, the one to which you applied the clip art AutoLayout earlier in this chapter (refer to Figure 24.10).

You finally get to add an actual graphic to this placeholder by following these steps:

1. Double-click the clip art placeholder in the slide. The Clip Art Gallery dialog box appears.

2. Scroll down the list of categories and select the Home Items category. A preview of the clip art within this category appears in the area below. You can scroll down with the downward-pointing arrow to see more.

3. Select the square that contains the coffee cup and then click the Apply button. Slide 2 now has a picture of a coffee cup, which automatically fits within the placeholder. This feature means never having to worry about the image over-running the text. Your slide should now look like Figure 24.25.

Figure 24.25   Slide 2 after adding clip art through an AutoLayout.

> **Caution:** To add clip art by using the Insert Clip Art button on the Standard toolbar, follow the same procedure as you would for inserting clip art with an AutoLayout. When you use the button, however, it does not automatically size the placeholder to fit the text on your slide.

Creating and Editing Graphs

PowerPoint's extensive graphing abilities include 14 types of charts and a data sheet so that you can create and edit graphs without leaving PowerPoint. You can also save your graph as a separate file to insert in other presentations that you create. As part of the Microsoft Office suite, PowerPoint also supports graphs created in Excel.

You can do the following things with graphs:

◆ **To insert a PowerPoint graph:** You can create a graph by selecting it through the Object command on the Insert menu. In the Insert Object dialog box, select Microsoft Graph 5.0 in the Object Type menu (you may have to scroll down the list to find it). After you click OK, a graph and datasheet appear on the slide, as shown in Figure 24.26. You can also insert a graph by clicking the Insert Graph button on the Standard toolbar or by choosing the graph AutoLayout.

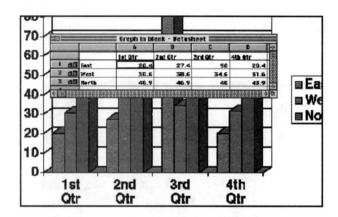

Figure 24.26 A graph and data sheet.

◆ **To enter data:** After your graph appears, select the Datasheet window and enter your data as you would with an Excel graph. When you are in the Graph mode, a special menu and toolbar appear.

◆ **To edit your graph:** To edit a graph that you have already created, double-click it. The graphing menu and toolbar appear. You can now begin making changes to your graph.

◆ **Changing graph types:** How you want your graph to appear depends on the type of data that you are presenting. To change your graph type, use the AutoFormat command on the Format menu or click the downward-pointing arrow next to the Chart Type button on the special toolbar. A drop-down toolbar appears, as shown in Figure 24.27. Select your new graph type by clicking the button representing the graph type that you want.

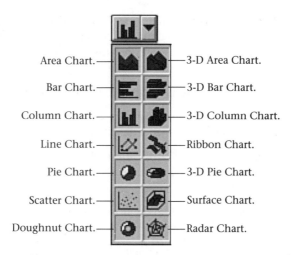

Area Chart.————————————————3-D Area Chart.
Bar Chart.————————————————3-D Bar Chart.
Column Chart.————————————————3-D Column Chart.
Line Chart.————————————————Ribbon Chart.
Pie Chart.————————————————3-D Pie Chart.
Scatter Chart.————————————————Surface Chart.
Doughnut Chart.————————————————Radar Chart.

Figure 24.27   The Chart Type drop-down toolbar.

Changing your graph's color scheme

You can change the colors on your graph by first selecting the element that you want changed and then clicking the downward-pointing arrow next to the Color button on the toolbar. You can also ungroup the graph and use the Colors and Lines dialog box accessed through the Format menu. (For more information on color schemes, see the section on "Changing Your Color Schemes" earlier in this chapter.)

Entering equations

PowerPoint's graphing function also includes an Equation Editor for entering mathematical symbols, fractions, subscripts, and more. To insert an equation, choose Object from the Insert menu. In the Insert Object dialog box, select Equation from the Object Type list. If you enter equations often, you may want to add the Insert Equation button to your toolbar. (For more information on customizing your toolbars, see Chapter 22.)

Adding a graph to your presentation

Nothing conveys credibility better than using numbers and graphs. You want to impress CoffeeCo by showing them that fewer people are drinking alcohol in bars, and more people are sipping coffee in cafés like yours. You also want to show your potential backers that similar endeavors have proven successful.

In slide 3 of DEMO2, you have written that since 1985, coffee consumption has gone up 50 percent, alcohol consumption has gone down 30 percent, and two other similar coffee cafés have increased their profits. There is no room on this slide for a graph, but it still makes sense to reinforce this information with a graph on slide 4.

1. Go to slide 4, the one that is holding the graph placeholder (refer to Figure 24.11).

2. To enter your own data into the graph, double-click the placeholder. The graph appears in the placeholder with a datasheet for you to fill in (refer to Figure 24.26).

3. Replace "East" with **Coffee Drinking**; replace "West" with **Alcohol Drinking**; and replace "North" with **Café $**. These cells represent what becomes the graph's color key.

4. Replace "1st Qtr" with **1985** in column A and replace "2nd Qtr" with **1995** in column B. These cells represent your time line on the horizontal axis of the graph.

5. To deactivate columns C and D, select them and click the Cut button on the toolbar or use the ⌘-X key combination.

6. Enter the following information:

   In cell A1, enter **20%**.

   In cell A2, enter **40%**.

   In cell A3, enter **10% profits**.

   In Cell B1, enter **40%**.

   In cell B2, enter **30%**.

   In cell B3, enter **30% profits**.

7. Exit the dialog box by clicking in any place on your slide. Your slide should now appear as shown in Figure 24.28.

Figure 24.28   Slide 4 with graph data entered.

Creating Organization Charts

PowerPoint makes it easy for you to create organization charts. To insert an organization chart, choose the Object command from the Insert menu. In the Insert Object dialog box, select the Microsoft Organization Chart 1.0 from the Object Type list. Or you can choose the organization chart AutoLayout or click the Insert Org Chart button on the Standard toolbar. The Organization Chart window appears, as shown in Figure 24.29.

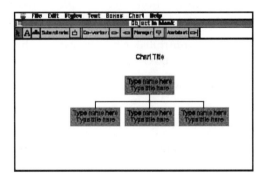

Figure 24.29   The Organization Chart window.

To build your organization chart, do the following:

◆ **To enter text:** Click inside the box in which you want to enter text, such as names and positions, and type the information. Use the Tab key to go from point to point in each box.

◆ **To add boxes and assign levels:** Click on the button of the level you want to add and then click the existing box to which you want to attach the new box. PowerPoint automatically places the box where it should go. It also automatically moves the other boxes proportionally so that the chart stays centered.

◆ **To change text and box attributes:** You can edit the size, color, and format of text and boxes by using the menu bar in this window. This menu bar gives you flexibility and allows you to create borders and change the chart's colors for added impact.

Creating Special Text Effects with WordArt

PowerPoint also includes an exciting program called WordArt. WordArt can be opened only from within OLE-supported applications. WordArt lets you bend, twist, and curve text to create special effects.

To insert WordArt, do the following:

1. Select the Object command from the Insert menu. In the Insert Object dialog box, select Microsoft WordArt 1.0 or 2.0 from the Object Type list.

2. After the Microsoft WordArt dialog box appears, as shown in Figure 24.30, enter your text in the text entry box.

3. Select the Update Preview option to view your text as it would appear on your slide.

4. Choose your text effects from the dialog box.

5. To return to your presentation, click anywhere on your PowerPoint slide.

This chapter covers how PowerPoint's graphic features work together to help you create attractive, professional-looking slides. In Chapter 25, you will learn how to add the final touches to your presentation.

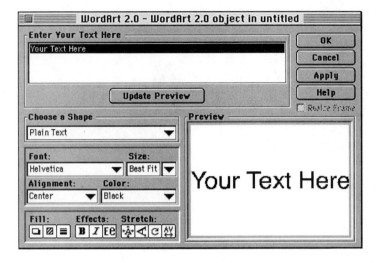

Figure 24.30   The Microsoft WordArt dialog box.

Chapter 25

Adding the
Final Touches

After you develop a presentation, it is time to review, edit, and add the final touches. PowerPoint's text editing features and transitional effects help you ensure a well-organized presentation. You can also use the Slide Sorter, Notes Pages, and Rehearse Timing features to rehearse, revise, and prepare for your talk. This chapter covers the following points:

◆ Editing text with the Speller

◆ Finding and replacing text

◆ Creating speaker's notes

◆ Adding transitional effects

◆ Arranging your slides in the Slide Sorter view

◆ Using the Rehearsal Feature to time your presentation

Using the Spelling Checker

PowerPoint is unique among graphics programs because it offers a fully functional spell-checking feature. This feature makes it easy for you to avoid potentially embarrassing spelling errors. PowerPoint's Spelling Checker works the same way it does in Microsoft Word and other word processing applications.

The Spelling Checker searches your slides for words that are not in its dictionary, informs you when it finds an unfamiliar word, and gives you the option of correcting the spelling, adding the word to your dictionary, or ignoring the word and moving on.

To check your spelling, click the Spelling button (the one with *ABC*) on the Standard toolbar or choose the Spelling command from the Tools menu. A Spelling dialog box appears, as shown in Figure 25.1.

Figure 25.1   The Spelling dialog box.

When the Spelling Checker finds a word it does not recognize, the word appears in the Not in Dictionary box. You can tell the Speller to ignore the word, add it to your dictionary, ignore all future occurrences of that word, or change the word and all future occurrences of that word.

To change a word that appears in the Not in Dictionary box, type the correct spelling in the Change To text box or scroll down the list of suggested words and highlight the correct one.

The Speller tells you when it is finished checking your presentation. Click the OK button to return to your presentation. If you want to leave the Spelling Checker before it is finished checking your presentation, click the Close button.

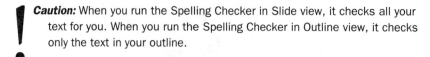

> **Caution:** When you run the Spelling Checker in Slide view, it checks all your text for you. When you run the Spelling Checker in Outline view, it checks only the text in your outline.

To quickly verify the spelling of a single word, highlight it with your cursor and either click the Spelling button or press the F7 key. You can make the Speller run faster by turning off the Always Suggest option. To turn off the Always Suggest option, choose the Options command from the Tools menu. The Spelling function is one of the many features that makes PowerPoint a flexible, comprehensive package.

Finding and Replacing Text

PowerPoint enables you to find and replace text the same way you would in Microsoft Word. The ability to locate words or quickly replace dates, company names, and other information helps you customize presentations easily and efficiently. You can activate the Find or Replace commands through the Edit menu.

Use the Find command when you are looking for a specific part of a lengthy presentation, and you remember a particular word that serves as a reference. To use the Find command, do the following:

1. Choose the Find command from the Edit menu or use the ⌘-F key combination. The Find dialog box appears.

2. In the Find What text box, type the word or group of words that you want to search for.

3. Click the Find Next button, and the Find feature searches for your text.

The Find command also lets you search for graphics, paragraph formats, and special characters within the Format and Special pop-up menus. You can choose from options, such as matching the case of words or finding complete words only.

You can repeat your last search with the Find command by pressing the ⌘-F4 key combination.

Use the Replace command when you need to replace a word or group of words that appears frequently throughout a series of slides. To use the Replace command, do the following:

1. Choose the Replace command from the Edit menu or use the ⌘-H key combination. The Replace dialog box appears, as shown in Figure 25.2.

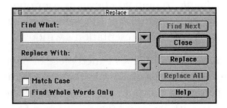

Figure 25.2 The Replace dialog box.

617

2. In the Find What text box, type in the word or group of words that you are searching for.

3. In the Replace With text box, type the word or group of words with which you want to replace the Find What text.

4. When your word is found, click the Find Next, Replace, or Replace All options.

   The Find Next button moves you to the next occurrence of the word being searched without making changes. The Replace button replaces the word and moves on to the next occurrence of the word. The Replace All button replaces all occurrences of the word being searched.

5. After the dialog box informs you that all occurrences of the word have been checked, click OK.

> **Caution:** Be very careful when you choose the Replace All button because you may make some changes that you don't really want to make. For example, if you tell the Replace command to replace all instances of *me* with *you*, the program changes *remember* to *reyoumber* in addition to making the changes that you want. To prevent this problem from occurring, select the Find Whole Words Only option and take the time to view all Replace commands individually.

You can edit a presentation while in Find or Replace modes. Simply click in the presentation window and change your text. The Find or Replace dialog box remains onscreen. To continue searching, click in the Find or Replace dialog box and select an option. The Find and Replace commands are useful when you need to find or replace recurrent words and phrases in large presentations.

Using Speaker's Notes

Speaker's notes can be invaluable to help you develop your presentation. To create speaker's notes, choose the Notes Pages command from the View menu or click the Notes Pages View button on the lower-left corner of your presentation's window.

The Notes Pages view displays as an 8 1/2 × 11-inch piece of paper, so that you can print your notes, as shown in Figure 25.3. For easy reference, there is a picture of the slide you have selected at the top of the page. The bottom of the page has room for you to type in your notes, which help jog your memory with facts and figures, prepare for questions that people may ask you, or jot down ideas that you want to remember about orchestrating your presentation.

Figure 25.3   The Notes Pages view.

You want to remind yourself of important points while making your presentation to CoffeeCo, so you want to create some speaker's notes in your sample presentation. Open the DEMO2 presentation and follow these steps:

1. Select slide 1 and go into the Notes Pages view by clicking the Notes Pages View button.

2. In the text placeholder, type the following:

   Thank you all for coming today. We greatly appreciate CoffeeCo's interest in our proposal. We look forward to the possibility of working with you and making Café Olé a success.

   In the Notes Pages view, you can adjust your text to any size that you want, but you can't change any elements on the slide.

3. To print your notes, select Print from the File menu and then select Notes Pages from the Print What pop-up menu. (For more information about printing, see Chapter 26.) Be sure to print out your notes because you will use them for an exercise later in this chapter.

To create a separate color scheme for your speaker's notes, go into the Notes Pages view and choose the Notes Color Scheme command from the Format menu. (For more information on creating color schemes, see Chapter 24.)

Arranging Slides in the Slide Sorter View

The Slide Sorter view enables you to see miniature versions of up to twelve slides at once, in the order that they appear in your presentation. You can move slides around, test transitional and text-building effects, and delete slides from the presentation. You can also add transitions and builds, hide slides, or use the Rehearse Timings button (the one with the stopwatch) on the new Slide Sorter toolbar to see how long your presentation takes. To access the Slide Sorter view, click the Slide Sorter View button in the lower-left corner of your screen.

You can use the Slide Sorter view to do the following:

♦ **Rearrange slides:** To move a slide or group of slides to a different part of your presentation, click the slide that you want to move and drag it to the place in your presentation where you want it to appear.

♦ **Delete slides:** To remove slides from your presentation, select the slide or group of slides that you want to remove and then choose the Delete Slide command from the Edit menu. You can also press the Delete key.

♦ **Hide slides:** To exclude a slide from your presentation, select the slide and then choose the Hide Slide command from the Tools menu or (in the Slide Sorter view only) click the Hide Slide button (the one with line through a slide) on the Slide Sorter toolbar.

♦ **Create text builds and transitional effects:** To create text builds and transitional effects in the Slide Sorter or Slide view, choose the Build or Transition commands from the Tools menu.

♦ **Rehearse timings:** To rehearse your presentation and time how long you spend on each slide, click the Rehearse Timings button on the Slide Sorter toolbar. You can then rehearse your presentation while PowerPoint times how long you spend on each slide.

You can double-click a slide miniature in Slide Sorter view to go directly to that slide in the Slide view.

Adding Transitional and Text-Build Effects

PowerPoint supports adding transitional and text building effects to slides. *Transitions* are animated effects that happen when one slide changes into the next. This effect creates a sense of movement during electronic slide shows. *Text builds*, also referred to as progressive disclosures, display bulleted points one at time on a slide.

Adding transitions to your slides

You can access the Transition command from the Tools menu in either Slide view or Slide Sorter view. The Transition dialog box appears, as shown in Figure 25.4, with three options: Effect, Speed, and Advance. You can view your transitions before applying them to your slides in the Transition preview box on the right of the dialog box.

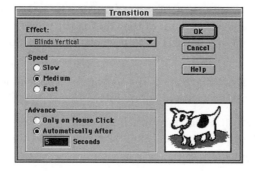

Figure 25.4   The Transition dialog box.

You have decided that your presentation on Café Olé would look more professional if you incorporated transitions. To add transitions to your slides, follow these steps:

1. Select the Slide Sorter view. The Slide Sorter view is the ideal format in which to add and test your transitions because you can see all your slides at one time, and you can select them either one at a time or all at once.

2. Select all your slides by drawing a selection box around them with your pointer, by using the ⌘-A key combination, or by clicking all of them individually while holding down the Shift key. PowerPoint also lets you apply transitions to only one pair of slides.

3. Choose the Transition command from the Tools menu.

4. Select the Blinds Vertical effect from the scroll-down list and watch what happens in the preview box. Notice that the preview box looks like vertical blinds just closed and opened on the image in the window. The preview box lets you test out your effects before applying them to your slides.

5. The Speed options enable you to select how long it takes to go from one slide to the next. Experiment with the options by clicking the radio buttons and watching the speed changes in the Preview window. Select the Slow button for your Speed option.

6. The Advance options enable you to decide whether the transition should take effect after a preset amount of time during the presentation or when you click the slide. This option enables you to pace out a self-running presentation. Select the Only on Mouse Click option.

7. Click the OK button to apply the transition to your slides. Notice the transition icons underneath each slide miniature.

8. Click the transition icons to watch the effect you have added to your slides. Notice that the transitional effect always takes place *before* the transitioned slide appears onscreen, not *after*.

! **Caution:** The insertion of too many transitional effects can cause the presentation to appear cluttered and confusing. Stick to one type of effect per presentation—or two at the most.

Transitional effects help ease the flow of your presentation from slide to slide and enable you to add interest to your slides in the form of motion. Transitional effects can also be used to signify a change in the section or topic of your presentation.

Adding text builds to slides

Text-build slides progressively add text to the slide so that each bulleted point is added to a slide in sequence. To create a text-build slide, select the slide or slides on which you want this effect and then choose the Build command from the Tools menu. The Build dialog box enables you to decide how each bulleted point will be displayed and whether you want the non-bulleted text to dim when a new bulleted point is introduced.

To create a text-build slide, do the following:

1. Select a slide or group of slides and then choose the Build command from the Tools menu. The Build dialog box appears, as shown in Figure 25.5.

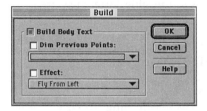

Figure 25.5   The Build dialog box.

2. Select the Build Body Text check box for a simple text build.

3. If you want each point to dim and become a different color as the next point appears, select the Dim Previous Points check box. Then select a color from the pop-up color menu.

4. For additional options, click the Effect box and browse the pop-up menu for the selection of visual effects.

Text builds help draw the audience's attention to important points and allows time for the people to absorb the presented information. Text builds can liven up even the most text-heavy slide shows and can be especially useful when summarizing sections or whole presentations.

Creating a Self-Running Slide Presentation

Because you now know that a self-running presentation has the advantage of looking as if more preparation has gone into it, you may want to make your presentation to CoffeeCo self-running. Additionally, you can gain more freedom for interaction with the audience.

To make your presentation self-running, do the following:

1. In the DEMO2 presentation, select all your slides in the Slide Sorter view, as explained in the "Adding transitions to your slides" section earlier in this chapter.

2. Choose the Transition command from the Tools menu. When the dialog box appears, it should display the transition that you selected previously in this chapter.

3. In the Advance section, click on the Automatically After radio button and enter a 5 in the Seconds text box. This option enables you to enter the number of seconds

that you want the slide to stay onscreen before going on to the next slide. You have just entered five seconds per slide. In most situations, a presenter would allow at least two or three minutes per slide.

4. Click the OK button to return to your slides. Notice that the amount of time per slide now appears in the Slide Sorter view.

Running the timed show

You are now ready to run your timed slide show. A timed slide show offers you the option of displaying your slide show as self-running. To view your self-running slide show, do the following:

1. Select slide 1 and then choose the Slide Show command from the View menu. A dialog box appears and asks what type of presentation you would like to run, as shown in Figure 25.6.

Figure 25.6 The Slide Show dialog box.

2. Select the Use Slide Timings option from the Advance area.

3. Click the Show button.

Notice that the slide show runs in accordance with your settings. Each slide remains onscreen for five seconds and then transitions into the next slide with the vertical blinds effect. After the slide show is finished, you are returned to the Slide Sorter view.

To complete your presentation smoothly, add a blank, black slide to the end of your presentation so that you can finish your speech without the use of slide graphics. If you are running an onscreen presentation, select the slide and set the Automatically After option in the Transition dialog box to 120 seconds, or two minutes.

You can alternate between a self-running series of slides and manually activated slide transitions. This allows you to create excitement with a dazzling array of graphic image slides and graph slides that fade into each other, while alternately allowing you to pause your show to interact with your audience.

Using the Rehearse Timings command

After setting your timed transitions in Slide Sorter view, you can use the Rehearse Timings command to rehearse your presentation out loud. By using this technique, you can see how long you actually need to spend on each slide and then reset the timed transitions where necessary. You can activate the Rehearse Timings command by clicking the Rehearse Timings button (the one with the stopwatch) on the Slide Sorter toolbar.

The Rehearse Timings mode looks and acts like the Slide Show view in many ways, but with one major difference. Even if you have set automatic advances, the next slide doesn't appear until you click the mouse. This action resets the amount of time each slide appears onscreen to match how long you spend discussing that slide. Also notice that a timer appears on the lower-left corner of your screen. The timer allows you to plan your presentation to the exact second.

To rehearse the timing of your presentation, do the following:

1. Use the speaker's notes that you printed earlier in this chapter.

2. Go into the Slide Sorter view, select slide 1, and click the Rehearse Timings button.

3. Start reading the short speech you typed onto the speaker's notes page of slide 1. Read the way you normally would and feel free to ad-lib or leave time to introduce Café Olé's staff. Remember, the timer is running!

4. Move to the next slide by clicking the mouse after you are finished. Ordinarily, you would repeat this procedure for the entire presentation. For now, let the other slides run for five seconds and continue clicking them until an alert box appears, as shown in Figure 25.7.

Figure 25.7 The Set Timings dialog box.

5. Click the Yes button to retain your new slide times.

After you return to the Slide Sorter view, notice that the new timings you set for each slide are indicated beneath the slides.

When using the rehearsal feature, don't spend too long on a single slide. A good pace for a presentation ranges between 50 seconds to 3 minutes per slide frame, depending on the medium and the information being presented.

Hiding Slides

PowerPoint's Hide Slide feature enables you to exclude a slide from your presentation without removing it. This feature provides you with greater flexibility during your presentations. Hidden slides help you stick to an extremely concise slide show by unhiding additional slides and allowing you to address these new topics in greater detail when a situation calls for it.

Slides can be hidden while you are in the Outline, Slide, or Slide Sorter views before a slide show, and they can be reactivated during the shows. You can hide multiple slides in the Slide Sorter and Outline views.

To hide a slide, do the following:

1. Select the slide or group of slides that you want to hide.

2. Select the Hide Slide command from the Tools menu. Or if you are in Slide Sorter view, click the Hide Slide button on the Slide Sorter toolbar.

The slide appears in Slide Sorter View as it normally would; however, the slide number is enclosed in a box with a line through it, as shown in Figure 25.8. During slide shows, the presence of a hidden slide is indicated by an icon in the lower-right corner of the slide preceding the hidden one.

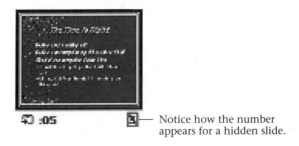

Notice how the number appears for a hidden slide.

Figure 25.8 A hidden slide.

To display a hidden slide during a slide show, do the following:

1. When you see the hidden slide icon on your slide during an electronic presentation, click the icon or type **H**.

2. To access the hidden slide from anywhere in your presentation, type the slide number and press the Return key.

Hidden slides can be revealed so that you can elaborate on information presented in the previous slides.

In this chapter, you've learned how to use PowerPoint to organize and fine-tune your presentation from start to finish. In the next chapter, you will learn more about printing and displaying your options in a presentation.

Chapter 26

Printing and
Displaying Your Presentation

PowerPoint gives you the flexibility that you need for printing your presentation. You can print supporting materials, slides and outlines, or transparent overheads. The equipment you choose for printing your presentation depends on your needs, your budget, and the equipment that is already available to you. Your options for displaying your presentation are virtually endless, including transparent overheads, self-running kiosk displays, 35mm slides, or videotape. This chapter covers the following information:

◆ Printing slides and transparencies

◆ Creating supporting materials:
  speakers notes, outlines, and
  audience handouts

◆ Learning about color printers

◆ Adding color to your presentations without a color printer

◆ Exploring presentation tips

◆ Developing presentation
  options: screen displays,
  35mm slides, overhead
  transparencies, video, and
  LCD projectors

Printing with PowerPoint

Throughout most of the PowerPoint section of this book, the importance of using PowerPoint to make an immediate impact on your audience with visually exciting slides, clearly written text, and eye-popping graphics has been emphasized. But you cannot underestimate the importance of printed materials.

Printed materials make it easier to digest and memorize information—both for you and for your audience. Handouts enable your audience to concentrate on what you are saying rather than having to take notes. Hard copies can also be filed away for easy review later because you do not need any electronic equipment to view them.

To give the "paperless office" enthusiasts in your audience something to take home with them, simply copy your presentation onto a disk and give them the PowerPoint Viewer disk. You can find the PowerPoint Viewer on the last Office installation disk. It is a separate installation and is designed to be given to people who do not have PowerPoint so that they can peruse your presentation at home on their own monitors.

Although PowerPoint was primarily created to format slides, no presentation system would be complete without the ability to create supporting materials. With PowerPoint, you can print overheads, slides, audience handouts, notes pages, and outlines.

To print a PowerPoint presentation, do the following:

1. Choose the Print command from the File menu, click the Print button on the Standard toolbar, or use the ⌘-P key combination. A dialog box appears, similar to the one shown in Figure 26.1.

Figure 26.1 A Print dialog box.

2. Select the type of document that you want to print from the Print What pop-up menu.

3. Enter the number of copies that you want in the Copies box.

4. Select the All radio button as your Slide Range option.

5. Click the Print button or press the Return key.

Details about the types of documents PowerPoint enables you to print are described as follows:

◆ **Slides:** You can print your slides on ordinary paper or as overhead transparencies—one image per page. PowerPoint automatically defaults to printing slides in the landscape format because slides are generally horizontally oriented.

When you select the Slides option from the Print dialog box, your slide automatically fits the page, as shown in Figure 26.2. You can use a Slide view print as a transparency, for proofreading, or to file away for later reference.

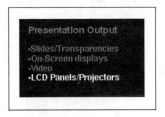

Figure 26.2   A print in the horizontal Slide view.

◆ **Slides (with builds/without builds):** This option is available only if your presentation includes text-build slides (see Chapter 25), in which bulleted points appear onscreen one at a time, with each added bullet point as a separate slide.

If you choose the Without Builds option, PowerPoint prints the last slide in the build sequence—the one that contains all the bulleted points. If you choose the With Builds option, PowerPoint prints each text-build slide as a separate slide. If you print a slide with text builds, the end product should look like the ones in Figure 26.3. Each print contains a representation of the same slide with an additional bulleted point appearing progressively on each slide.

◆ **Notes Pages:** PowerPoint prints speaker's notes for the slide numbers that you request. PowerPoint automatically defaults to printing notes pages in a portrait format. (For more on speaker's notes, see Chapter 25.)

Your onscreen speaker's notes should look like Figure 26.4. Hard to read, aren't they? They print out *much* clearer. Speaker's notes let you enter text underneath a picture of the slide that you are discussing so that you can keep additional information organized.

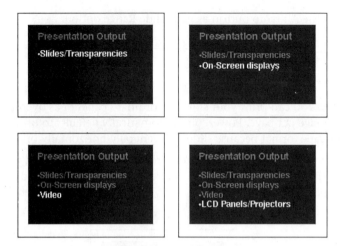

Figure 26.3   A print of a slide with text builds.

Figure 26.4   How speaker's notes look onscreen.

◆ **Handouts:** Handouts print as miniature versions of your slide presentation to help your audience remember your presentation and to let the audience easily take notes. You can print handouts at two slides per page to create the most readable images, three slides per page to leave one side of the page open for note-taking, or six slides per page to save paper (see Figure 26.5). PowerPoint's handouts options enable you to tailor supporting materials to your needs.

When printing handouts, you can use the Options button in the Print dialog box to reverse the images that you are printing out. This can be helpful with a black-and-white printer. Most slide templates use light-colored text on dark backgrounds.

Although this combination is easier to read when being displayed, printed materials are easier to read with dark-colored text on light backgrounds. (The reverse option may not be available on all printers.)

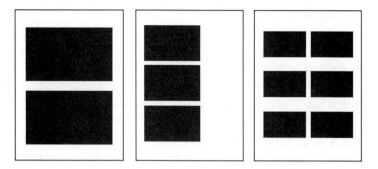

Figure 26.5   An audience handout with two, three, and six slides per page.

◆ **Outline View:** Use this option to print your outline as it appears in the Outline view. By making adjustments within the Outline view, you can collapse, expand, and format the outline's text. (For more information on working in the Outline view, see Chapter 23.) The size of the type is determined by what view scale you are working in.

The Outline view's text-only format makes it easier for you to edit your presentation's content. You can also use the printed outline as a handout, which gives your audience an idea of what information will be covered.

Using Your Print Options

In addition to types of output, PowerPoint offers various options so that you can customize your handouts to your presentation needs. The Print dialog box offers basic printing selections, but by clicking the Options button in the Print dialog box, you can bring up the Print Options dialog box, where you can choose other options for your printing process.

Selecting options in the Print dialog box

The Print dialog box appears onscreen as soon as you select the Print command. The Print dialog box lets you make basic choices regarding your handouts, such as number of copies, number of pages, and choice of material.

633

You can select the following functions through the Print dialog box:

◆ **Number of Copies and Page Range:** Indicate the number of copies that you want and then click the All button or enter the page numbers that you want to print in the page range boxes. When you select a page range from the Print dialog box, your page range must consist of consecutive pages.

◆ **Paper Source:** If your printer has multiple trays, you can change the default so that your materials print from different paper trays. This can be useful if you have one tray containing plain paper for rough drafts and one tray full of nicer paper for final versions of documents.

◆ **Print What:** This option enables you to choose among printing slides, handouts, speaker's notes, and outlines.

◆ **Print Hidden Slides:** This option enables you to print hidden slides if they exist in your presentation. PowerPoint otherwise defaults to leaving out the hidden slides. (For more information on hidden slides, see Chapter 25.)

◆ **Scale to Fit Paper:** This option enables you to size slides to fit on the paper you already have in your printer. This can be useful in cases where, for some reason, your presentation has been custom sized. PowerPoint automatically fits your printed material to the paper size specified.

◆ **Destination:** This option enables you to select a printer or a PostScript file as your print output.

◆ **Pure Black & White:** This option helps you make audience handouts and speaker's notes more readable, although the handouts look markedly less attractive. It renders all color fills to white, all text and lines to black, adds outlines and borders to all filled objects, and uses halftones for pictures.

◆ **Black & White:** This option renders quick black-and-white draft copies and turns all fills to white or black. Unbordered objects with no text are indicated with a thin, black frame.

Selecting options in the Print Options dialog box

The Print Options dialog box is accessed through the Print dialog box by selecting the Options button. The Print Options dialog box offers you further choices, as shown in Figure 26.6. Here you can enter additional information about your printer and the way your presentation prints.

The Options dialog box may prompt you for the following information (this information will vary with the type of printer you choose to print with):

◆ **Cover Page:** You can decide whether to have a cover page and whether you want it to appear before or after the document. A cover page is useful when printing materials to be used as a complete set.

◆ **Print:** PowerPoint is asking for more information about how you want your document to print. The most useful choice here is Color/Grayscale. This option enables you to print in color on a color printer or with grayscale images on a black-and-white printer.

◆ **PostScript Errors:** This option asks you whether you want PowerPoint to print a report on any PostScript errors that are present in your presentation. If you are sending your presentation to a service bureau or you are using it across Mac and PC platforms, you should run these reports. PostScript errors affect your presentation output, even when the presentation looks fine on your computer screen. Serious PostScript errors can prevent you from obtaining output from a PostScript device.

◆ **Economode/Duplex/Resolution Enhancement:** These options all let you select new settings for your printer's output. In general, however, PowerPoint defaults these settings in accordance with your Printer destination, so using these settings can prove unnecessary.

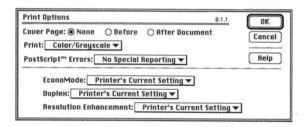

Figure 26.6 The Print Options dialog box.

Saving your presentation as a PostScript file

Destination options are also located in the Print dialog box. When you select the Printer radio button, the document is printed to the printer that is currently chosen. When you click the File radio button, PowerPoint allows you to save your presentation in a PostScript file format.

When sending a presentation to be outputted by a service bureau, it is essential that you save the presentation as a PostScript file so that the service bureau's software can read your file. To save your presentation as a PostScript file, click the File radio button in the Destination area of the Print dialog box. Then select the Options button. The dialog box shown in Figure 26.7 appears.

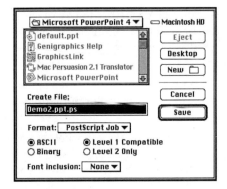

Figure 26.7 Saving a presentation as a PostScript file.

Considering a Color Printer

No matter how well designed your audience handouts or transparent overheads are, nothing grabs attention like a strategically placed splash of color. There are many ways to add color to your PowerPoint presentation materials. Color printers are becoming increasingly affordable, and many of the less expensive inkjet printers can hold their own. Despite low-end inkjet printers' reputations for bleeding images around the edges, their quality has risen markedly.

If you prepare presentations frequently, investing in a color printer can easily pay for itself. Although color printers are more expensive and print more slowly than black-and-white printers because of the increased information they must process, the prices of color printers have come down considerably in the past few years. You can purchase a decent color printer for less than $800 and one of extremely high quality for less than $10,000.

When looking for a printer, you should take a variety of factors into consideration, including the resolution, speed, volume, and paper stocks the machine can handle. You should also consider the types of images you generally use. Some printers handle text better than artwork, and some handle photographic images better than simple line art and text.

Many of these factors are determined not only by the quality of the printer but also by the implemented printing process. For example, dye sublimation printers use a continuous tone method for distributing colors. This means that prints of scanned photographs look wonderful, but line art illustrations lose their crisp detail. Make sure that you research and test printers thoroughly before buying one.

Understanding how printers work

Color printers use cyan, magenta, and yellow pigments. When mixed in different combinations, these three pigments can create a full range of colors. Printers process your materials as one color plate at a time, and they layer pigments to create various shades and mixes of colors. Consequently, color images take longer to print than black-and-white images. The printing head has to pass over the area being printed one time for each pigment used.

Most, but not all, color printers also use a black pigment. Whether your printer uses a black pigment is especially important if you frequently print large quantities of text. Because cyan, magenta and yellow are all required to create black, your printing head has to pass over the text on your page three times.

Resolution is also of prime importance. Printers represent images as the presence and absence of dots. The more dots per square inch that the printer can render, the more crisp and detailed your image is. The size, shape, and accuracy of the dots printed also determine the overall feel of your images. Processes that slightly blur dots can result in a smoother finish; processes that feature a greater accuracy of dot placement may result in a grainier finish.

When looking for a printer, you should look for an output of at least 300 dpi (dots per inch). Most offices use 300–360 dpi printers. Graphic professionals generally use 600 dpi printers. However, because color printing—especially dye sublimation printers that use continuous tone imaging—can trick the eye into perceiving a higher quality, a 300 dpi printer can be adequate for many business uses.

If you use glossy or coated paper, you can significantly increase the quality of your color prints. The clay coating keeps colors from soaking into the paper, thus losing their intensity. Glossy paper also reflects light, which makes colors appear more highly saturated.

Choosing which color printer is correct for you

Knowing the difference between laser, dye sublimation, thermal wax transfer, solid inkjet, and liquid inkjet printers can help you determine which type of printer best meets your needs. The types of color printers described in this section differ in two ways: the types of pigments used and the method of application to your paper. Different printing technologies meet some needs better than others.

The price ranges included here represent what these products generally cost. Don't get discouraged if the price range listed next to your dream printer appears to be over your budget—costs are dropping almost as fast as you're reading this. Table 26.1 shows a basic comparison of color printer types.

Table 26.1

Color Printer Types

Printer type	Price range	Strengths	Weaknesses
Laser	$9,000–$20,000	300–600 dpi resolution, photo-quality, handles line art and text well, works with most paper stocks	High maintenance, does not reproduce photos as well as dye sublimation printers
Dye sublimation	$8,000–$20,000	Continuous tone images, photo quality, ideal for pre-press	168–300 dpi resolution, doesn't handle line art and text as well as graphics
Thermal wax	$6,000–$10,000	Highly saturated colors, large array of output options, speed, colors resist fading	May get a cartoonish appearance to object fills because of the highly saturated colors
Solid inkjet	$6,000–$10,000	High-quality output for the price	Handles transparencies poorly
Liquid inkjet	$300–$1,000	Inexpensive, quality steadily increasing	Quality varies, tendency to blur

Let's look at these printers in more detail:

◆ **Laser:** Color laser printers produce vivid colors and can handle transparencies and most paper stocks. Nothing matches laser printers for fast output and high quality. However, the accompanying apparatus and four toner cartridges are expensive, requiring considerable maintenance.

QMS has recently produced the first color laser printer that costs less than $10,000. The ColorScript Laser 1000 retails for $9,999 and can handle regular photocopier bond paper rather than the more expensive laser bond paper. A recent review in *Macworld* rated the QMS 1000 poorly in terms of image quality, but it does produce documents, graphs, and presentation materials well with vivid colors.

◆ **Dye sublimation:** Dye sublimation printers produce smoothly finished, photo-graphic quality prints without the tiny dots that you see with other printers. The process of sublimation involves using transparent inks that are converted from a solid substance into gas. The pigment gets absorbed by polyester resin-coated paper. To ensure a continuous tone, dye sublimation printers generally print at a 168 dpi resolution and allow the dots to bleed slightly.

Tektronix's Phaser 480 offers speed, photo-realistic images, and high text quality. The Phaser 480 costs $14,995, but adding enough memory to print with a full-color ribbon brings the price up to $18,880. 3M's Rainbow digital color proofer is also a good choice for a dye sublimation printer. The Rainbow costs about $20,000. Both models handle tabloid-size paper and are ideal for pre-press and high-end publishing purposes.

Letter-size dye sublimation printers cost less. SuperMac's Proof Positive lists at $7,999, and Tektronix's Phaser IISDX lists for $9,995, while others in the PC market have dropped below $1,600.

◆ **Thermal wax:** Many businesses choose these printers because they combine good quality, highly saturated colors, and a fast speed. Although thermal wax printers do require a smooth surface, they otherwise accommodate most paper stocks. Thermal wax printers can also print onto a variety of materials other than paper; for example, they are used for making iron-on fabric transfers.

Thermal wax printers have print heads that press small electrical heaters against the colored ink rolls. The rolls transfer dots of wax, one color plate at a time, to a sheet of paper. Due to this process, thermal wax printers generate crisp, highly saturated colors, but they also have a tendency to impart a cartoonish appearance to objects with solid-colored fills.

Thermal wax printers offer high quality for a reasonable price. Seiko Instruments' Personal ColorPoint PSE sells for $2,999, and Tektronix offers its Phaser 200e for $2,995.

Increasing numbers of manufacturers are offering printers that combine the advantages of multiple printing technologies. Tektronix offers a thermal wax and laser printer that produces vivid colors *and* crisply rendered line art images and text. The Phaser 220i has a 600×300 dpi resolution and costs about $6,000.

◆ **Liquid inkjet:** Liquid inkjet printers are good for bold, simple graphics and color accents. Tiny nozzles squirt colors onto the paper as the printing cartridge passes back and forth over the page.

If you have ever painted in watercolors, you know that applying liquid to paper deteriorates the paper slightly, which occasionally makes the colors bleed. Yet new, quick-drying inks and recent technologies have improved the quality of liquid inkjet printers considerably. Although liquid inkjet printers perform more slowly than other types of printers, if you print only small quantities, you may not notice the difference.

Some liquid inkjet printers can produce a level of quality that is barely distinguishable from their more expensive cousins. Epson America, Inc. currently offers the Epson Stylus Color Inkjet with a resolution of 720 dpi for about $520. Hewlett-Packard also offers high-quality, low-end inkjet printers, such as the DeskWriter 560C, for about $719.

With prices coming down and the variety of printing technologies available, color printers are definitely worth the investment.

WYSIWYG and Color Printers

WYS is not necessarily WYG. Although many color monitors have come close to the WYSIWYG (What You See Is What You Get) standard, your onscreen colors may not always match in print. Your monitor displays colors that use combinations of red, green, and blue (RGB) pigments; printing processes use combinations of cyan, magenta, yellow, and black (CMYK) pigments.

If your professional needs include color precision, you should obtain a good color matching system to match the colors on your screen to the colors printed on your printer. The most commonly available color matching systems are Trumatch, Focaltone, and Pantone.

Adding Color Without a Color Printer

If a color printer remains beyond your budget, you can use your creativity to add color manually with ink, press-on type, and clip art. Or you can use transparencies or papers that already have color elements printed onto them—many companies sell these predesigned materials. Or you can have your local printer or graphic service bureau create a customized look.

The following techniques include just a smattering of ideas for adding color to transparent overheads and audience handouts without a color printer:

◆ **Design your own:** Think of this option as designing company stationery for your handouts or transparent overheads. A simple, appealing graphic—such as a logo or even a single horizontal or vertical line—printed in a striking color can jazz up those black-and-white prints. You can then have multiple copies made by a low-volume specialist printer.

◆ **Obtain specialty papers:** You can obtain predesigned papers and transparencies from vendors, such as Paper Direct, Quill, and Premier Papers. Distinctive paper stocks with exciting designs can add pizzazz to your handouts.

◆ **Use preprinted graphics judiciously:** Make sure that all preprinted graphics are positioned so that they don't get printed over. To accomplish this, you may have to adjust your overheads and commit to a specific handout form that leaves space for the existing graphic. After all, when writing a memo, you wouldn't print over your company's letterhead, right? Look at the preprinted graphic in the lower-right corner of Figure 26.8. So that you don't cover up the graphic, you have to position your slides to the left of the page.

Likewise, choose your colors appropriately: burgundy and cobalt blue create visual impact but project a reasonably conservative image. Bright, saturated colors, such as red and yellow, create a more vibrant, youthful image. Or you may choose to stick with your company's colors.

Preprinted papers are available in most office supply and stationery stores and can also be ordered from office supply catalogs.

Figure 26.8 An audience handout with a preprinted graphic.

◆ **Add color manually:** Remember coloring books? You can fill in your transparent overheads with colored permanent markers. Or you can use colored pencils on handouts so that the color doesn't bleed through the paper. You can also eliminate bullets and main titles in your presentation or leave space for graphic elements and then use colored press-on type and clip art.

Make sure that the press-on type or clip art is translucent when dealing with color overheads because opaque elements appear black. Color press-on type and clip art are available from most art supply stores. Letraset offers an extensive catalog of press-on type and clip art.

Help! I Need Color Now!

If there is no printer or graphic service bureau near you, and you are not a creative genius with your own color ideas, don't worry. With a simple phone call, ImageDirect or Genigraphics can handle your presentation needs quickly. If you need handouts for your upcoming presentation, ImageDirect specializes in fulfilling your short-run, color printing needs. And the company can have your materials delivered to you in a few days. To contact ImageDirect, call 800-A-Papers.

Genigraphics is a graphic service bureau that can convert your presentation from a disk into 35mm slides, digital color overheads, large display prints, or posters. To contact Genigraphics, call 800-638-7348. You can send your files by modem 24 hours a day and receive the printed materials overnight. The company also can deliver your materials in a cost-effective, timely manner.

continues

PowerPoint makes it convenient for you to work with Genigraphics by including a Genigraphics Driver and GraphicsLink. To install the Genigraphics Driver and GraphicsLink (if you didn't install them with the original installation), do the following:

1. Run the Microsoft Office setup program.

2. Click the Add/Remove button in the first Setup dialog box.

3. After the Maintenance Mode dialog box appears, select the Tools check box from the Components Not Yet Installed list on the left.

4. Click the Continue button.

5. After the Install Disk dialog box appears, insert the disk number that is asked for.

6. When the Installation Complete dialog box appears, click the OK button to finish the installation.

Displaying Presentations from Your Monitor

PowerPoint gives you flexibility in displaying your presentation. Your presentation output is primarily determined by your presentation setting and the equipment available to you. Important factors to consider are the lighting, the size of the room, and the number of people in your audience.

The graphics and text on your slides should be clearly visible even to those in the back row. The last row of your audience should be no farther away than eight times the height of the projection screen. The front row of your audience should be no farther away than two times the height of the projection screen, as shown in Figure 26.9.

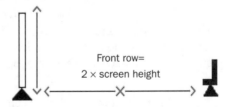

Figure 26.9   Projection screen/front row distance ratio.

You also must consider which equipment can be easily obtained. Most companies have overhead projection and slide equipment available on the premises. Increasing numbers of businesses also use televisions and VCRs on a regular basis. Overhead projection, slide equipment, televisions, and VCRs can also be inexpensively rented.

Displaying PowerPoint on a computer monitor requires nothing more than a workstation that meets PowerPoint's specifications, the PowerPoint Viewer, and a disk with your presentation on it. The PowerPoint Viewer also lets you show your presentations as read-only documents on other workstations, even if they don't have PowerPoint. This saves you from having to reload any software. The PowerPoint Viewer exists on its own disk, so you can take it anywhere.

To run a slide show on your computer monitor in the PowerPoint program, simply click the Slide Show View button or select Slide Show from the View menu. To display a self-running or repeating display, select Slide Show from the View menu and then follow the instructions in the dialog box, as shown in Figure 26.10. (For more information on self-running presentations, see Chapter 25.)

Figure 26.10   The Slide Show dialog box.

In the following list, I've explained a few of the advantages and disadvantages of running your presentations as screen displays on your monitor:

◆ **Advantages of displaying on your monitor:** This is the simplest presentation method to implement, and you can incorporate animated effects and QuickTime videos for added excitement. You also don't have to turn off the lights to ensure visibility, and familiarity with this medium enables you to build audience interactivity into your presentations.

◆ **Disadvantages of displaying on your monitor:** The text and graphics look ragged along the edges because the computer screen displays them as 72 dpi bitmapped images. Also, the size and resolution of even the most high-end computer monitor limits you to small audiences.

If your company often hosts presentations, you may want to consider investing in a larger monitor to display presentations more effectively. High-performance monitors are created especially for graphics and presentation professionals. These professional monitors offer larger screens, higher resolution, good visual quality, more adjustment controls, and (sometimes) reasonable prices.

You can obtain a decent 20-inch monitor for $1,000–$3,000. NEC offers the 21-inch MultiSync 6Fgp for just under $2,000. Radius also has a good reputation for its display monitors. Of course, larger monitors are not portable. They often weigh hundreds of pounds.

There are also many less expensive 14-inch monitors that perform well for their smaller size and cost less than $1,000. Macintosh offers its 14-inch Color Display for $599, and the Sony CPD–1400 is priced at a couple hundred dollars more. The NEC 4FGE and Nanao FlexScan F340i also fall within this price range.

For those of you who produce large-scale presentations, you may want to consider looking into *monitor banks* (sometimes called *video walls*). Monitor banks consist of a collection of monitors that are synchronized with each other for the purpose of multiple displays of a single presentation. Monitor banks are frequently found at trade shows. Although they require a costly investment, monitor banks are a highly effective medium for displaying presentations.

When looking for a color monitor, you should take the following factors into consideration:

◆ **Screen focus:** How sharp is the display of images on your screen?

◆ **Color saturation:** How well does your monitor display a wide range of colors?

◆ **Color balance:** Are colors displayed uniformly across the screen? Look out for irregularities and inconsistencies in your color display.

◆ **Convergence:** How closely do the red, green, and blue electron beams come to the same pixel on your screen? The closer these beams converge, the sharper your image is. Look for a convergence measurement of 0.45 millimeters or less.

◆ **Distortion:** Look for a monitor with minimal distortion.

◆ **Gray linearity:** How accurately does your monitor display shades of colors and grays?

◆ **Brightness**: How high can you adjust the brightness on your screen without seeing scan lines? Do not purchase a monitor that outputs less than 20 footlamberts—a unit of measurement for luminance.

◆ **Contrast:** Look for a high contrast ratio.

Footlambert, Anyone?

A footlambert is a unit of luminance equal to one candela (a unit of luminous intensity equal to 1/6th the intensity of the light emitting from a candle) per square foot or to the uniform luminance of a perfectly diffusing surface emitting or reflecting light at the rate of one lumen per square foot. Lumens measure incident light and footlamberts measure emitted or reflected light.

For optimal viewing conditions, the number of lumens per square foot should equal the number of lamberts. This ratio ensures a screen that does not absorb ambient light. Got that?

Running presentations on your computer screen can prove to be the most cost-effective display method. To run your presentation as a computer monitor display, you need the following items:

◆ A Macintosh workstation that meets minimum system requirements

◆ A large color monitor

◆ PowerPoint Viewer on disk

◆ Your presentation on disk

Displaying 35mm Slides

To convert your presentation into 35mm slides, save it onto a disk as a PostScript file by selecting the PostScript Destination option on the Print dialog box and sending the file to your local graphic services bureau. (For more information about PostScript files, refer to "Saving your presentation as a PostScript file," earlier in this chapter.) When you want to use 35mm slides, be sure that they are set up with a 3:2 aspect ratio. (For more information about aspect ratios, see Chapter 22.)

To avoid potential problems, ask the service bureau how long it takes to process slides and whether it has any slide-formatting requirements that you should be aware of. Although using a service bureau does sound expensive, prices are generally reasonable. Unless you develop enormous amounts of slides, service bureaus cost much less than purchasing your own expensive conversion equipment.

The advantages and disadvantages of 35mm slides are as follows:

◆ **35mm slide advantages:** Slide shows generally impress audiences because visually, 35mm slides display an unparalleled crispness and richness of color. You can show slides to large audiences, depending on the size of the projection screen. By planning your material well, you can even reuse many of your slides (such as a picture of the chairman of the board giving an address) for years before their colors begin to fade. Slides have the advantage of easy storage—they don't hog up disk or closet space and are easy to organize and carry around. In addition, most conference sites are equipped with slide projectors and screens, or the equipment can easily be rented.

◆ **35mm slide disadvantages:** Using 35mm slides does require advance planning and preparation. They do not allow for the sense of motion and interactivity inherent in other presentation formats. And in order to display slide shows, the room must be dark, which means that you cannot interact extensively with your audience, nor can they follow along with your presentation handouts or take notes.

Displaying slides takes considerable preparation but provides worthwhile results. To run your presentation as a 35mm slide show, you need the following items:

◆ Slide carousel and projector

◆ Slide projection screen

  For screen size, remember this rule of thumb: the distance between the last row and the screen should be no more than eight times the screen's height, and the distance between the front row and the screen should be no less than twice the height of the screen.

◆ Extra bulb

◆ Extension cords

◆ Darkened room

Displaying Transparent Overheads

To display your presentation as transparent overheads, simply use the color or black-and-white transparent overhead templates. (For more on templates, see Chapter 24.) PowerPoint automatically sets up transparencies to fit the size of standard overhead projectors, approximately $10 \times 7 \, 1/2$ inches, which reflects a 5:4 aspect ratio.

To produce transparent overheads from your printer, load your printing tray with transparent sheets, select the Print command from the File menu, and then select Slides from the Print What pop-up menu in the Print dialog box. If you want to print color overheads, but you have only a black-and-white printer, save your presentation as a PostScript file and send it to a service bureau for color printing.

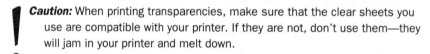

Caution: When printing transparencies, make sure that the clear sheets you use are compatible with your printer. If they are not, don't use them—they will jam in your printer and melt down.

The advantages and disadvantages of transparent overheads are as follows:

◆ **Advantages of using transparent overheads:** Transparent overhead presentations are oldies but goodies. This format has proven effective with both large and small groups. This display method allows you flexibility and enables you to interact readily with your audience. Transparent overheads are inexpensive and simple to produce. In addition, transparent overhead projection equipment is easy to obtain—most companies have this equipment on the premises.

◆ **Disadvantages of using transparent overheads:** Transparent overheads do not deliver the sense of professionalism nor the visual impact of a slide presentation.

The overhead projector and the transparencies themselves can be cumbersome to haul around. An hour-long presentation at two-minutes-per-frame's worth of transparencies can fill an entire briefcase.

Using transparent overheads as your output format is a simple, low-tech method for creating effective presentations. In situations where you can't count on the darkened room (required for 35mm slide shows), or the audience is too large for displaying your presentation on a computer monitor, transparent overheads can save the day.

A presenter often must fuss with transparent overheads to get them properly aligned and keep them properly ordered. To minimize this problem, organize them into trays—a "to be shown" tray on one side of the projector and a "has been shown" tray on the other side of the projector. This little bit of organization ensures greater fluidity in your presentation.

Transparent overheads may not be as slick as more technologically advanced presentation methods, but their advantages sometimes outweigh modern technology. To run a presentation with transparent overheads, you need the following items:

◆ Clear transparent sheets that are compatible with your printer

◆ Transparent overhead projector

◆ A screen or light-colored wall

◆ Extra bulbs

◆ Extension cord

◆ Pointer (never use your finger!)

PowerPoint on Television: Displaying with Video

Many presenters use video as a format for displaying their presentations on an ordinary television screen. You can either have a service bureau convert your slide show from disk to videotape, or you can hook your computer up to a television screen. If you choose to display in this format, however, please keep the following in mind: the aspect ratio for displaying presentations on a television screen is 4:3.

Keep the following in mind as a rule of thumb: when discussing aspect ratios and measurements, the first number always refers to the horizontal measurement.

Because of this particular aspect ratio, the television screen cuts off the edges of your frames when displaying your presentation by video. This may prove advantageous in some situations (like watching the news on TV) because it also increases the size of images; however, it can prove annoying when it cuts off part of the titles and bulleted points in your presentation.

The television screen also does not offer the higher resolution available on your computer monitor. In addition, the television displays images as alternating scan lines (rather than colored dots), which magnify the horizontal linear elements on your Macintosh screen and cause them to flicker annoyingly. This problem can be minimized by using PowerBooks for your video source, whose monitors have a liquid crystal display rather than the usual cathode ray tube display.

◆ **Advantages of presenting on video:** Video easily incorporates motion and special effects and offers the flexibility of producing interactive presentations by outputting VCR tapes from your computer. Video allows more portability than onscreen presentations because the necessary equipment is widely available, as opposed to lugging around a huge monitor. Video equipment is also cheaper to rent or buy than many of the computer-generated options.

◆ **Disadvantages of presenting on video:** The video format limits your graphic capabilities. Converting your presentation to videotape so that you can present on an ordinary television screen and then distribute copies requires a higher turn-around time. You also lose the flexibility of interacting with and customizing your presentation. Generating video presentations from your computer requires a certain amount of technical expertise to ensure that all the conversion, output elements, and colors are compatible to the video format.

> **Caution:** Do not attempt to do interactive presentations by using videotape. Stopping, starting, and pausing your videotape on a constant basis quickly damages the videotape and the VCR—and bores your audience.

Designing PowerPoint video slides

When designing your frames for video in PowerPoint, you should customize your slide setup to reflect a 4:3 aspect ratio. Your templates automatically adjust. When activated, the AutoLayout feature also takes the customized sizing into account; however, you may have to adjust the layouts that you have already created in another aspect ratio.

Use bold, sans-serif typefaces for your text; simple, high-contrast images for your graphics; and uncomplicated color schemes for your templates. (For more on graphics, see Chapter 24.) When preparing for a presentation in video format, you can use PowerPoint's templates for color transparent overheads to ensure a bold and simple design and color scheme throughout the video slide presentation.

Hooking up the television to your Mac

To generate a video presentation, you can send your presentation to a service bureau for conversion to a VCR tape. Then you can use any ordinary TV/VCR hook-up. Or you can generate interactive presentations by directly hooking up your computer to a television. To hook up your computer to a television, you need the correct jack on your TV and a computer-to-TV converter box. Converters let you connect either standard TVs and VCRs or the higher quality S-Video TVs and VCRs.

When looking for a conversion unit, there are several concerns that you need to consider. If you often present in foreign countries, make sure that your converter unit is compatible with the European television standard (PAL). Make sure that the unit you buy is compatible with your Mac—many of these converters are geared more toward PC users, and their jacks don't plug into Mac-style monitors, which means that you have to figure the price of a jack into your budget. You also need to take brightness and contrast adjustment capabilities into consideration, along with features that compensate for television's tendency to cut off— or overscan—the edges of your image.

There are many computer-to-TV converters available, and the prices range from $200–$450. The MediNet Encoder sells for a mere $159 and has adequate features. Focus Enhancement's L-TV goes for $299 with a Mac monitor jack. The L-TV offers technical support, compactness, brightness controls, compatibility with the European television standard, and a Squeeze system extension to make up for TV's overscan problem.

To convert your PowerPoint slides to a video format and show them on television, you should have the following items:

- ◆ Television with a round RCA input jack or an S-Video jack
- ◆ Conversion unit
- ◆ Jack hookup that accommodates a Mac-style monitor
- ◆ Adjustments for brightness, contrast, and overscan

Displaying with Liquid Crystal Display (LCD) Panels and Projectors

LCD products are ideal for the presenter who travels a lot. LCD panels and projectors display clear images that rival slides in quality and portability while also allowing the speaker to interact with the presentation. Many also come with sound and microphone capabilities.

Liquid crystal display devices are currently the only commercially available flat panel technology that displays full color. They reflect light rather than emit it, as the more commonly used cathode ray tube (CRT) technology in your computer monitor does. LCD technology eliminates the problems of flickering lines, which plague presenters who use electronic display methods. However, anyone who uses a PowerBook with the LCD monitor can tell you that these display devices tend to reflect images and light, which can be distracting to the viewer.

LCD products for medium-sized conference rooms with a 6- to 10-foot screen (measured diagonally) cost $3,900–$9,000. For around $1,000 more, you can buy an LCD for larger projections geared toward audiences of up to 200 people.

LCD panels and LCD projectors are compared and contrasted as follows:

♦ **LCD Panel:** An LCD panel is about the size and weight of a PowerBook, which makes it easy to carry around. To run your PowerPoint slide show, hook the panel up to the video port on your hard drive and then place the panel on an overhead projector. This setup requires a transmissive overhead projector, which illuminates your panel from below. Boxlight offers a decent LCD panel, the ProColor 1500, for just under $4,000. A recent review in *Macworld* also gave a high rating to View's Z115. The Z115 is available for $5,495.

! *Caution:* LCD panels tend to overheat, which can result in presentation disasters. To avoid overheating, use metal-halide bulbs instead of incandescent ones in the overhead projector. Also, be sure to rehearse your presentation to ensure that the LCD panel holds up for the duration.

♦ **LCD Projectors:** An LCD projector works the same way as an LCD panel; however, you don't need an overhead projector. Having one less item to worry about may be worth paying more. LCD projectors are also portable. Although they weigh more than the panels, they weigh less than the combined weight of a panel and overhead projector. The Proxima projector is easy to set up, delivers good image quality, and offers a cordless pointer system called Cyclops. The Proxima retails for $10,795.

When running your PowerPoint presentation with an LCD panel or projector, darken the room to minimize ambient light (LCD images fade even more than 35mm slides when the room isn't dark enough). Make sure that the room is well ventilated because LCD products are susceptible to overheating. Also, keep your text and graphics as close to the center of your frames as possible. LCD displays tend to dim along the edges, especially in the upper corners.

Also note that LCD panels and projectors that enable you to make your presentations without bringing your computer along, such as InFocus's Lite Show, are currently available. That sounds wonderful; however, you have to print your slide show to the appropriate printer driver and save it onto a DOS-formatted disk. Not only do the words *DOS-formatted disk* make most Mac users cringe, but you lose your ability to control and interact with your presentation. This being the case, you might as well present on video because it costs less.

The wave of the future for computerless presentations may be Sharp Electronics' QA-1500 panel, which can run presentations on Type III PCMCIA cards. Mac drivers for these cards will be widely available by the end of 1995.

To use an LCD panel or projector, you need the following items:

◆ LCD panel and transmissive overhead projector, or an LCD projector

◆ Your computer

◆ A video card and port

◆ An adapter that lets you connect with video and sound sources directly (Most LCD panels and projectors come with this kind of adapter, but some need an adapter that can cost up to $1,600.)

◆ A beaded projection screen, if possible, which displays the clearest images with LCD projectors and panels

LCD products still have a way to go before they can match the high display quality of slides. However, LCD panels and projectors combine the advantages of large screen projection and computer display interactivity. For the presenter who travels often and addresses medium to large audiences, LCD panels and projectors can prove invaluable.

Deciding Which Presentation Format to Use

Deciding which presentation format to use can be more overwhelming than creating the presentation itself. When making decisions about presentation technology, you should consider the size of your audience, where you will be giving most of your presentations, what equipment you already have available, the purpose of your presentations, and your budget.

Factors in deciding which presentation equipment to purchase include the following:

◆ **Audience size:** Remember that your presentation must be visible to people in the back of the room. If you regularly present to large audiences of 100 or more, a slide projector would be your best bet. If interactivity is a must, then consider the higher-end LCD panel or projectors that display images large enough for audiences of 200 people.

With medium-sized audiences of 50–100 people, slide and transparent overhead projectors or standard LCD panels and projectors are ideal. With small audiences, your options increase. Video and computer screen displays let you control your presentation and add special effects, and the equipment required is less expensive than LCD panels and projectors.

◆ **Audience makeup:** What audiences do you usually present to? Gatherings of colleagues or long-time clients are generally less formal. Less formal presentations don't need high levels of technology, but they should allow you and the group to interact with your presentation. Computer screen presentations and transparent overheads perform well in these situations.

If you are presenting to students or trainees, your presentation should project more authority yet allow for audience note-taking and questioning. These conditions rule out slides and LCDs, which require a dark room. With formal presentations, slides and LCDs give a professional impression. But if the presentation site does not provide accommodations for darkening the room, videos, computer monitor displays, or even transparent overheads can convey a sense of polish.

◆ **Budget:** Computer screen and transparent overheads are the least expensive ways to output PowerPoint presentations. Slides can also be produced and shown relatively inexpensively—especially because many companies and presentation sites already have the equipment available.

Investing in video output equipment costs a bit more but can pay for itself if being able to copy and distribute your presentations easily is advantageous. LCD panels and projectors require the greatest investment, but their portability makes them indispensable to the presenter who frequently travels.

◆ **Location:** Where will you be presenting your material? Computer screen displays are also ideal for trade shows—motion and special effects catch the attention of passersby. After you gain their attention, they can then peruse the presentation at their leisure, or they can allow you to show them slides as they ask questions.

Will there be light in the room? If so, LCD panels and slides are out of the question—you are better off using transparent overheads for midsized audiences or video and computer screen displays for smaller audiences. Does the location offer the facilities you need for setting up your equipment? Electrical outlets, available equipment, and other such details must be checked out as you make your presentation decisions.

◆ **On-site or off-site:** Do you generally give presentations at other companies, or do you give your presentations on-site? If your company often hosts presentations, then investing in a larger display monitor for computer-generated presentations would be worthwhile. If you travel frequently, then LCD panels and projectors with PowerBooks offer ideal presentation solutions.

When selecting presentation equipment, do your homework. Make a list of features that are important to you. Read product reviews in trade magazines and ask other presenters what they use. Ask a lot of questions and test out your equipment before you buy it. Purchase the highest quality equipment your budget allows. You will have to use this equipment frequently and in situations that are often less than ideal, so make sure that you are comfortable with the equipment.

You should now be familiar with basic presentation output. If you at least know how to print supporting materials and choose the proper venue for your presentation, you can make it through your first simple presentation. What about multimedia possibilities? The next chapter takes you one final step in exploring the possibilities that are available to you in making your presentations state of the art.

Chapter 27

Presenting with Multimedia

In addition to offering an all-in-one package for organizing, scripting, designing, and laying out slide show presentations, PowerPoint also offers multimedia capabilities. With PowerPoint, you can create added interest in your presentations by adding QuickTime videos, sound, CD-ROM clip art, and digitized photographs. In this chapter, you get an overview of how you can use PowerPoint with multimedia for presentations that will be the talk of the town. This chapter covers the following topics:

- ◆ Understanding multimedia
- ◆ Using multimedia and PowerPoint
- ◆ Purchasing hardware and peripherals
- ◆ Using QuickTime video
- ◆ Creating sound effects
- ◆ Using CD-ROM

What *Is* Multimedia?

This chapter is designed to give you a broad overview of how PowerPoint's support for multimedia can enhance your presentations. If you want to learn about using multimedia in greater detail, a good place to start is with the *Multimedia Starter Kit for Macintosh*, by Michael D. Murie, also published by Hayden Books.

Multimedia is like that old tale about the emperor's new clothes: the entire kingdom was abuzz about the emperor's wonderful new outfit, but no one—for fear of appearing unfashionable or ignorant—would admit that the emperor was parading around naked. Nowadays, *multimedia* is the emperor. Everyone keeps talking about it, and you keep seeing the word mentioned in the publications you read, but no one seems to know exactly what it means!

But don't get intimidated by a mere buzzword. *Multi,* as you know, is a prefix that means "many," and the word *media* simply refers to the materials that are used to create works or the means used for communicating these works to others. For example, Leonardo da Vinci used oil paint as his medium for creating the *Mona Lisa* (see Figure 27.1) and canvas as his medium for enabling others to view it. Today, I have used ink and paper as the media for communicating this image to you (ironic, isn't it?). Television, radio, film, and publications are referred to as "the media" because they represent the means by which images, music, art, words, and ideas are conveyed to others.

Figure 27.1   The *Mona Lisa* in ink and paper.

The art world began using the term *multimedia* as 20th century artists began creating nontraditional works that mixed materials that weren't *supposed* to be mixed together. Some confused curator or perplexed art reviewer was probably frustrated at not being able to describe a work of art simply as "the oil painting" or "the marble sculpture." And dada! The term *multimedia* was born (darn those Dada-ists). *Multimedia* is likewise used by arts writers when describing performances that mix so many elements that they cannot be pigeonholed into such set categories as a play, a dance piece, or a film.

Now you not only know what multimedia means, but you will also be creating it yourself. And your media will consist of your Macintosh, PowerPoint slides, sound effects, and QuickTime videos.

Why Use Multimedia?

PowerPoint's multimedia capabilities enable you to add sound and motion to your presentations. Nowadays, people are barraged with so much information that it is difficult to remember anything. So how do you make your audience remember your presentation? QuickTime video clips, sound effects, and exciting images help you grab your audience's attention and keep it riveted to your screen.

People will remember the information that you are communicating if you present it attractively and dynamically and if you can make your points personally relevant. A strategically placed burst of motion or sound in an otherwise still series of slides will make a lasting impression on your audience. With the proper image or sound recording devices, you can even record and add personalized footage to your presentations right on the presentation site.

You can put PowerPoint's multimedia capabilities toward the following uses:

◆ **Training:** Many corporations are beginning to use multimedia presentations for employee training purposes. The employees find that being able to learn and review information at their own pace increases memory retention. In the meantime, employers find that after the initial investment required, using multimedia presentations is cost effective.

◆ **Demonstrating ideas and processes:** Communicating complex information has always been difficult to do with words. Now, instead of using several slides to explain an involved process, you can add a QuickTime video clip that actually shows people how a process works.

◆ **Personalizing presentations:** People are always more receptive to information that directly relates to them. With the proper recording devices, you can insert QuickTime video clips containing on-site footage. For example, footage of your host's own receptionist getting swamped with phone calls can go a long way toward convincing your host to try out your company's voice mail system.

◆ **Grabbing attention:** Even if you lack recording equipment, you can use exciting sound and visual effects to grab attention. A CD-ROM drive also gives you access to a wide range of images that take up too much disk space to store ordinarily on your hard drive.

◆ **Letting people explore your presentation:** You can use multimedia effects to create convincing presentations that viewers can peruse at their leisure. This gives people opportunities to explore your product or ideas. Interactive presentations can be used for kiosk displays, or for an initial investment, they can be stored on CD-ROM discs and sent to potential clients.

◆ **Having fun:** And last but not least, your PowerPoint presentations will be more fun to create and watch when you add multimedia.

Incorporating multimedia elements in your PowerPoint presentation also gives you a cutting edge over your competitors' presentations—or at least enables you to keep up. Make no mistake. Multimedia presentations are the wave of the future and pretty soon everyone will be using them. So why not be one of the first?

What Do I Need to Run Multimedia?

Multimedia computer displays used to be the domain of highly technical professionals, including industrial modelers, engineers, and animators. Then Industrial Light and Sound made headlines for creating and animating the scenes and critters for Steven Spielberg's *Jurassic Park* while the actors filmed on blank sets. Now, all of a sudden, everyone's talking about multimedia. Are you worried that while everyone else goes whizzing down the information superhighway, you'll be left in the dust? After all, running videos and creating sound effects must be pretty complicated....

Don't worry about that. The Mac's multimedia features are easy to install and use. If you want to create extremely complex interactive displays with high-end graphics, then yes, you would need some sort of specialized training. But anybody can record, digitize, and run a simple QuickTime video in a PowerPoint presentation.

Most Macs currently on the market have the components already installed for using multimedia, or you can easily and inexpensively upgrade your computer. To play back multimedia productions, you need a machine with color capabilities, a 13-inch or larger color monitor, and 5MB of RAM or more. Creating multimedia presentations requires a greater investment. The Power PCs are currently your best bet, although the Quadra 630 is a good entry-level choice. If you plan on working with videos often, then you should at least go with the Quadra 650 or above.

To create multimedia presentations, you should look into the following:

◆ **Memory:** You need at least 8MB of RAM. Many professionals are now advising that new buyers should settle for no less than 16MB of RAM (this advice is not so outrageous considering that it takes 8MB of RAM to run Microsoft Office alone).

◆ **Hard drive:** You need at least 200MB of free disk space. We're talking *free* disk space, as in how much disk space you have left after installing your applications. You also need a hard drive that can access and transfer data fast enough to create and run multimedia.

◆ **System 6.8 or higher:** To create and run multimedia presentations, System 6.8 is adequate, but you should really upgrade to System 7.5, which offers better support for video and sound.

◆ **Video card:** Most current Macintosh models come with a video card built in. However, depending on your needs, you may need to upgrade. Mass Micro offers a 24-bit NuBus video card for less than $100, and other video cards are available

658

from various manufacturers. If you want to create QuickTime videos, you also need more video equipment and hardware.

◆ **Video memory (VRAM):** Most Macs are coming out of the factories with at least 1MB of VRAM. This lets your computer support 16-bit color (32,000 colors), which is necessary for viewing QuickTime videos. Alas, the video memory is not expandable, and if you want more VRAM, you have to get a new video card for your processor direct slot.

◆ **Color capability:** You need support for at least 16-bit color for viewing videos and 24-bit color (16 million colors!) for image processing. If you need to upgrade your color capabilities, you can purchase a new video card. Unless you frequently work with photographic images, 16-bit color should be adequate. QuickTime video runs only with 16-bit color.

◆ **13-inch or larger color monitor:** To work with digitized video or animated images, you need a reasonably sized monitor. In addition to the display monitors mentioned in Chapter 26, Nanao USA announced a new lower-cost line of display monitors slated to be distributed by the spring of 1995.

◆ **Storage:** Multimedia presentations take up a lot of disk space. Even if you compress them, they generally are too big for a normal floppy disk. SyQuest removable hard drives are popular, and they let you save files onto cartridges that hold 44MB to 270MB of information. You can purchase them through various distributors. A 270MB SyQuest drive sells for about $600. The cartridges cost between $65 and $120, depending on the amount of disk storage space.

Many people also use the Bernoulli drives. The Bernoulli 230 drive sells for about $499. The cartridges cost around $100. Although SyQuest drives are more common than Bernoulli drives, Bernoulli often offers a better price. Some people also prefer Bernoulli because the drives are all made by the original manufacturer; whereas, SyQuest allows an array of companies to make the drives and slap the SyQuest label on them.

◆ **CD-ROM drive:** CD-ROM drives store up to 600MB of information, which gives you access to large collections of information and images that are available on CD-ROM discs. Alas, CD-ROM discs are *read-only,* meaning that you can't save files onto them. Many recent Mac and Power PC models come with CD-ROM drives already built in. If not, you can have one added for less than $300.

◆ **Audio Equipment:** All Macs come with a mono speaker, which lets you play back sound. Recent models, beginning with the Mac LC and IIsi, also include digitizing hardware to enable you to record sound, although you may have to purchase a microphone.

The Quadras and Power PCs are constructed so that you can easily get inside of the hard drive and install many hardware upgrades yourself, as shown in the diagram in Figure 27.2. While building up your multimedia system, you should also consider purchasing digitized image and sound recording devices. These devices give you a greater range of options when you use sounds and images in your PowerPoint presentations.

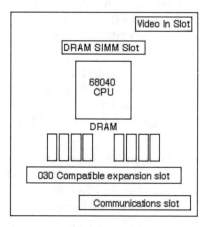

Figure 27.2   Diagram of a Quadra 630's innards.

How Does PowerPoint Fit In with Multimedia?

PowerPoint was created primarily as a slide presentation program, which limits its multimedia capabilities. However, you can design a series of frames that are shown in a particular sequence and then insert QuickTime video clips or sound clips on particular slides. Although you can build in a certain degree of control and interactivity for your presentations, PowerPoint was not intended to offer a full-fledged professional multimedia authoring environment.

Common multimedia development environments include presentation, interactive presentation, authoring, animation, three-dimensional modeling, and video editing software. Here's just a brief look at what's out there if you need more multimedia capability than PowerPoint can give you:

◆ **Presentation programs:** Presentation programs, such as PowerPoint and Persuasion, support sound and QuickTime video but are otherwise limited in their multimedia capabilities. Alas! PowerPoint on the PC does let you link different slides and presentations together, thereby allowing a degree of control and interactivity that is not yet available on the Mac. But keep on the watch for these capabilities when a new PowerPoint release comes out.

◆ **Interactive presentation programs:** Interactive presentation programs, such as Gold Disk's Astound, enable you to add buttons so that viewers can choose different paths and interact with you presentation. Interactive presentation programs also enable you to create animated charts and graphs from within the application.

◆ **Authoring programs:** Authoring programs, such as Macromedia's Director, let you develop complex interactions between your presentation and the viewer by enabling you to write scripts. Creating scripts involves using a low-level programming language that tells the program what you want it to do. Authoring programs enable you to create almost any type of production imaginable.

◆ **Animation programs:** Animation programs enable you to create objects and make them move or change shapes. Animation sequences generally involve simple drawings rather than video images, which enable them to play more easily and take up less disk space than QuickTime video clips. This makes animation a good choice for adding motion to displays. Unfortunately, unlike QuickTime, which also supports sound, synchronizing animated images and sound effects is a highly difficult process. Now some animation programs allow you to save sequences in a QuickTime video format, which enables you to import and run animation clips on PowerPoint slides.

◆ **Three-dimensional (3-D) modeling programs:** These programs are used by architects and engineers to create precise three-dimensional blue prints. Three-dimensional modeling programs make the planning process easier, and they enable viewers to anticipate potential problems. Limited animation features are also included in many 3-D modeling programs to enable users to view the model from different angles and perspectives. Most animation and 3-D modeling programs perform complex mathematical calculations, and therefore, they require computers that include a floating point unit.

◆ **Video editing programs:** QuickTime is a simple example of a video editing program. With video editing programs, you can not only digitize videos and run them on your computer, but you can cut, resequence, edit, and retouch frames, as well. Adobe Premier is an example of a popular advanced digital video editing software program.

In a way, presentation, animation, and video editing software packages work along similar lines. All these programs enable you to create and sequence images in a series of frames.

Although PowerPoint's capabilities seem limited compared to the other types of software that you just read about, don't think of it that way. Instead, look at PowerPoint as a highly useful program that is easy to learn and that lets you begin exploring multimedia. With PowerPoint, you can use QuickTime video and sound effects to jazz up your slide shows and to illustrate or emphasize particular points.

How Does a QuickTime Video Work?

QuickTime is a Macintosh program that enables you to work with digitized video sequences onscreen. It comes with your system software if you have System 6.0.7 or higher. With QuickTime, you can easily edit, manipulate, format, and save videos.

Back in the old days, you had to stop your presentation and turn on the VCR if you wanted to incorporate live footage into your presentations. Ordinary people couldn't run digitized video on their Macs because doing so required enormous amounts of memory and disk space, along with the ability to synchronize images and sounds.

Now you can easily use videos in your PowerPoint presentations. With QuickTime's compressors and timing features, along with the more powerful machines currently available to consumers, almost anyone can own a computer that enables you to play a video.

Of course, QuickTime does have its limitations. QuickTime displays videos at 16 fps (frames per second), which gives images a jerky quality. And your videos don't fill the entire screen, like your presentation does. Instead, the QuickTime window fills only a portion of your screen. Needless to say, this can be annoying when addressing large audiences. Fortunately, new technologies are changing this size limitation. Be on the lookout for new video cards that run your videos at a faster frame rate and a larger size. But for presentation purposes and sheer fun, QuickTime offers an effective medium.

Apple currently has a version of QuickTime that can run on Windows with the PCs, and Microsoft currently has its own player application called Video for Windows, which has many of QuickTime's features.

What do you need to run a QuickTime video?

Purchasing video equipment can run in the thousands of dollars, but it doesn't have to. If you plan on incorporating QuickTime videos into your PowerPoint presentations, you should take your needs into consideration. Does your company have an audiovisual department that can provide you with digitized videos? Your Macintosh probably has everything you need to run videos that have already been digitized.

To play QuickTime videos, you must have the following items:

◆ A color-capable Macintosh (such as a Macintosh II, LC, SE/30, many PowerBooks, Centris, Quadra, and Power PC models)

◆ System 6.0.7 or higher

◆ Color QuickDraw

◆ An application, such as PowerPoint, that supports QuickTime videos

Chances are that if you were able to install Microsoft Office 4.2 on your computer, you can also run QuickTime video.

If video digitizing equipment is beyond your budget and you need footage, try CD-ROM. You can order stock video clips on CD-ROM from companies like Four Palms Video, which offers an array of titles for $99.99 per CD; or the CD-ROM Warehouse, which distributes various titles starting at $99 per CD. Other companies, such as Media-Pedia offer interesting video footage ranging from $195–$495 per tape, but you still have to digitize the videos.

What do you need to create your own video?

If you must create your own videos, then you need to take more into consideration. Being able to run videos is all fine and good, but that doesn't help you jazz up your presentations unless you have relevant video footage available. After all, the main point of running videos in PowerPoint is to personalize your presentations. In order to fully reap the benefits of running QuickTime videos on your slides, you should begin recording and digitizing your own videos.

If all you need are a few good-quality video clips, and you have no ambition to be the next Fellini, then there's no need to spend large amounts of money. If you will be using video only for PowerPoint presentations, then high-end video equipment shouldn't be necessary. If, on the other hand, you need higher-quality videos so that you can use them for other purposes, then you may have to spend more.

One of the best products I have run across is QuickCam. All you need to do is purchase Connectix's QuickCam, hook it up, and start making videos. It's that simple. And it costs only $110!

The Incredible QuickCam

The QuickCam is only a little bigger than a golf ball. It captures grayscale images at 16 fps, and you can take still pictures with it, too. (Rumor has it that Connectix is working on a color QuickCam!) It comes with a cable so that you can hook it up to your printer or modem port, and it comes with utilities for grabbing frames and recording videos. You can use the QuickCam with any Mac that supports QuickTime video.

QuickCam's images are of reasonable quality, too. Your only limitations are the fixed focus lens (which you can actually adjust, but you have to take the camera apart) and the fact that QuickCam needs to be attached to your computer. Nonetheless, using QuickCam is a fun, easy, and inexpensive way to begin making digitized videos. Your QuickCam can be portable if you use it with a PowerBook (*not* a Duo)—no presenter should be without a PowerBook.

When it comes to setting up your computer for creating videos, you will spend the most money on purchasing your video source and your video digitizing board. QuickCam saves you money by capturing images and digitizing them, too.

If you need greater flexibility, color output, or a higher standard of quality than the QuickCam can provide, then you will need a video recording device, a video source, video digitizing board, sound digitizer, compatible software applications, and S-video cables. If you will be doing a lot of video work to go with your PowerPoint presentations, and you haven't purchased a computer yet, we would highly recommend the Quadra 660AV or the 840AV. Both of them offer 16-bit audio and 16-bit video capture and fast hard drive performance.

To create digital QuickTime movies from a video, you will need the following items:

- ◆ **Video source:** The video source records the initial movie. You can use a VCR or laser disc player. You can also use a camcorder as a video source. When choosing a videotape, use the Super VHS (SVHS) or Hi-8 tape formats. They offer S-video output, which is compatible with digitizing formats. If you don't already have a video source, try the Sony EV-C100 Hi-8 recording and playback deck, which costs less than $500 and offers a high level of quality.

- ◆ **Video digitizing board:** A video digitizing board is installed externally, and it converts the video signal to a digital image. Although the best digitizing boards can cost over $3,000, the MacVision Video Digitizer 4.1 offers an entry level price at $199 and captures high-quality gray-scale images. The midrange SuperMac Spigot II is a popular system that offers the ability to produce decent quality videos for $750. However, SuperSpigot II's videos do fall short of the full-resolution image quality offered by Radius's Video Vision. Many of the video digitizing boards also come with their own software for capturing and editing videos. (Keep in mind that a recording video digitizing board is not the same thing as a video card. To play only videos, you need just a video card.)

- ◆ **Sound digitizer:** If you want to record sound, you should purchase a video digitizer that includes a sound digitizer. Radius's Video Vision lets you record sound as well as video and costs $1,999. Video Vision is a complete video system with an array of features, including full-screen displays. As a less expensive choice, you may want to look into Sigma Design's MovieMovie for $349.

- ◆ **Compatible applications:** You need an application that is compatible with QuickTime and your digitizing board.

- ◆ **Cables:** If you use the wrong kind of cable, nothing will happen. You can't go wrong if you use S-video cables.

What Kind of QuickTime Videos Should You Make?

After you have everything you need to create your own QuickTime videos , your possibilities will be endless. For example, you can create stock footage that everyone in your organization can use for various purposes as well as footage that relates to a particular conference you are attending. You can even start a useful QuickTime file by saving your footage onto SyQuest cartridges, labeling them, and saving the cartridges by category.

Below are some ideas on how to incorporate QuickTime videos into your presentations:

◆ **Film the front lobby:** All employees like to feel that their office is an important place or that the conference they are attending is important. Stand in the lobby of your presentation site in the morning or during lunch while everyone is rushing around. You are guaranteed to obtain video footage that conveys a flattering sense of bustling importance. You can also show how busy your *own* company is with this type of footage.

◆ **Show people working:** You can either use footage of people working to give audiences an idea of how your organization works or show how your idea or product has helped others work more effectively.

◆ **Tell a story:** You can use before and after scenarios to demonstrate drastic improvements or to inject a sense of humor by exaggerating the "before" situation.

◆ **Evoke previous successes:** Use footage of your organization's president accepting an award, a testimonial from someone your organization has helped in the past, or a festive, cheering crowd as proof of the effectiveness of the products, services, or ideas that you are presenting.

◆ **Tie in your audience's goals with your goals:** Show footage of your host's chairman giving a talk about future goals and explain how you can help the audience meet these goals.

Eventually, you will assemble a library of stock footage that you can tailor to your presentation needs. Video cameras are easy to use, so have fun and be creative.

 Caution: Digitizing video is an easy process, but it can also be a lengthy one. Allow a full day for digitizing your video footage. You won't have to hang around and digitize all day, but your computer will.

How can you make your videos better?

A well-organized QuickTime video library with a wide assortment of videos to suit every occasion is a valuable presentation tool. You don't have to have amazing film skills or high-end equipment to create footage of a decent quality. There are plenty of video recording devices on the market that are designed so that anyone can use them. But you should plan carefully and work on your camera skills.

To ensure that you will always have just the right film footage for your PowerPoint presentation, do the following:

◆ **Purchase a SyQuest or Bernoulli drive and cartridges:** I mentioned SyQuest and Bernoulli earlier in the chapter, and I'm mentioning them again because QuickTime videos take up a lot of disk space. They don't fit on regular disks, and you can't fit many of them on your hard drive, either. To make good videos, you have to have enough storage space.

◆ **Capture more footage than you need:** Start recording before the action begins and keep recording after the activity that you want to record has ended. You can always edit out unwanted footage, but you can't add footage that doesn't exist. You should also record plenty of on-the-job scenes from different departments of your organization as well as footage from industry conferences.

◆ **Record plenty of transition clips:** Record transition clips, such as quick cuts of generic office scenes, with appropriate music or background noises. If you are ever in a situation where you need to piece different footage together, these clips will help ensure smoother transitions between one segment and the next.

◆ **Edit carefully:** Check for little problems like dropouts, frame glitches, and stutters, which can make your videos look unprofessional.

◆ **Keep your footage organized:** Your videos will be entirely useless unless you can find them when you need them. Think of the types of images that you use the most frequently, divide these images up by category, and reserve a SyQuest or Bernoulli cartridge for each category. When you digitize and edit a video segment, give it a filename that will jog your memory and save it immediately onto the appropriate cartridge.

◆ **In case of emergency, search the Internet:** If you have Internet access and you need a type of image that you can't get your hands on, try asking around. You will find many sites that offer all kinds of QuickTime footage.

> **!** **Caution:** When using shareware images, beware of possible legal liabilities pertaining to plagiarism, copyright, and unauthorized use of images. Legalities remain somewhat fuzzy on the Internet, so simply ask for permission to use the image. It is unlikely that anyone will say "no."

How do you compress a video?

When working with QuickTime videos, you will notice that QuickTime offers several options for compression. Videos must be compressed so that you can store and run them more easily. When videos are compressed, they are stored as algorithms, or numerical sequences, which tell the computer how to render the images.

QuickTime's compression options are as follows:

- **Photo JPEG:** Image sizes are reduced dramatically but maintain a high level of detail. This format is ideal for compressing photographic images.

- **Graphics:** This option can be used for compressing images from single frames but should not be used for video.

- **Animation:** Use this compressor when formatting sequences created in animation programs to be inserted on a PowerPoint slide as a QuickTime video.

- **Video:** The video option works well with digitized video and will probably be the option that you use most often.

- **Cinepak:** The Cinepak compressor works well for compressing video sequences while maintaining a high level of image quality, but it is often slow.

- **None:** This means exactly what it sounds like. When you select this option, your digitized video will not compress. This lets you access videos faster and run them at faster frame speed rates. But uncompressed files also take up more disk space.

You can experiment with different compression options to see which one works best for you.

How Do You Add a QuickTime Video to Your Presentation?

What is so wonderful about PowerPoint is that as intimidating as the words *digitized video* may sound, you can insert a QuickTime video into your presentation as easily as you can insert any other object.

To insert a QuickTime video into a presentation, do the following:

1. Choose the Insert Movie command from the Insert menu. A dialog box appears, which displays a list of available videos (see Figure 27.3) when you select the folder that has them.

2. Select the video that you want in your presentation and click the Insert button. An icon representing the video appears on your slide, as shown in Figure 27.4.

PowerPoint's default for videos is to play when you click the icon with the mouse, but you can set the video to play automatically after the slide transition. You can stop playing a video by clicking your mouse or by moving to the next slide.

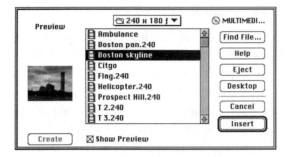

Figure 27.3   The Insert Movie dialog box.

The video icon.

Figure 27.4   An icon representing a QuickTime video.

To play a QuickTime video, do the following:

1. Click the icon representing the video you have inserted.

2. Choose Play Settings from the Tools menu. A dialog box appears, as shown in Figure 27.5.

3. In the Start Play area, select the When Click on Object option to start your video manually by clicking the icon. Select the When Transition Starts option to start your video when the transition to that slide begins. Select the When Transition Ends option to begin running the video after the specified number of seconds following the transition elapses. To activate this option, you must enter the number of seconds.

Figure 27.5   The Play Settings dialog box.

You can create self-running kiosk displays with QuickTime videos by doing the following: use the Play Settings options, run the entire show with the Rehearse Timings feature in the Slide Sorter view, and then select the Run Continuously Until Esc box in the Slide Show dialog box from the View menu.

You can also make minor changes to your QuickTime video clips by following these steps:

1. Switch to the Slide view.

2. Go to the slide with the video icon and select the video icon with your pointer.

3. Choose the Movie command from the Edit menu.

4. Select the Show Controller option.

You should now have a basic overview of working with QuickTime video clips in your PowerPoint presentations.

How Do You Add Sound Effects to Your Video?

Suddenly an ambulance siren blares and a vague feeling of fear fills the room. Everyone finally relaxes when the next slide appears and informs the audience that your hospital was able to save more lives last year thanks to the audience's generous contributions.

After focusing mostly on the visual, I must point out that sound effects can also make considerable impact on your presentations. All Macintoshes come with the ability to play and record sounds at 8 bits, so you don't have to buy all the expensive hardware required for working with video. All you have to buy is an inexpensive microphone that can be hooked into your Mac. However, 16-bit sound is optimal, so you may want to purchase a new sound card if your Mac supports it.

Macintosh also offers a compression program for sound files called Macintosh Audio Compression and Expansion (MACE) so that your sounds don't take up as much disk space. Unfortunately, the sounds sometimes lose some of their quality after being compressed and decompressed.

To obtain sound effects, you can use the beeps and sounds that you already have in your Control Panel (see Figure 27.6), record new sounds with the Object command from the Insert menu, or try one of the CD-ROM collections that is available. These collections have everything from background and crowd noises to entire songs. The CD-ROM Warehouse distributes a large selection of titles.

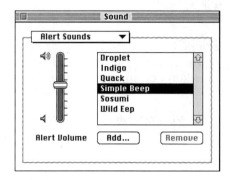

Figure 27.6   Control Panel sounds.

What Is CD-ROM?

CD-ROM technology can also help jazz up your PowerPoint presentations. You can make use of the large collections of clip art, photos, sounds, textures, and backgrounds collections available on CD-ROM. Having these collections makes it easier for you to have the appropriate image or background right at your fingertips. For an initial investment, you can also impress clients by sending them your presentation on a shiny new CD-ROM disc.

Right now, many people view CD-ROM as little more than an enormous storage space for storing clip art. Well, in a way it is, and I like it that way. CD-ROM discs look like the compact discs that you put in your stereo and play music with. They hold up to 600MB of files, an enormous amount of information. But you can't easily store anything on them because CD-ROM discs are currently read-only—which is why so many people view this medium as frivolous.

However, CD-ROM offers a new medium for communicating information that doesn't take nearly as much space as paper. Although the technology is relatively new, you can already find just about everything on CD-ROM, from samplers of different software packages to interactive games to encyclopedias and more. CD-ROMs are also wonderful for storing images because many graphic files are too large for storing more than a few on a floppy disk. And you actually can create PowerPoint presentations that take up huge amounts of hard disk space and distribute them to clients on CD-ROM discs.

But you had best make sure that it is worth the investment before producing CD-ROM presentations. Various companies, including 3M, Optical Media International, and Sony Electronic Publishing can transfer your files onto CD-ROM discs. Prices generally range around $1,500 for creating a master and $1.50 to $30.00 per CD after that, depending on the quantity.

Soon you will even be able to create and record your own CD-ROM discs. The technology is already available, except that the high-end CD recording devices ($4,000) and the low-end products are still full of glitches. In a recent *MacWeek* review, the currently available CD-ROM recording systems were unable to maintain a constant data stream, which resulted in buffer underrun errors. However, Elektroson USA offers a system called Gear for Macintosh for $995, and Incat Systems Software USA, Inc. offers the Easy CD Pro for $1,495. These systems are affordable if you are serious about distributing presentations on CD-ROM, and their afford-ability is quite an achievement. However, I recommend that you wait for further developments for a few months before making a purchase.

Many Mac and Power PC models currently come with a built-in CD-ROM drive. Most computers at least offer the ability for adding one. When purchasing a CD-ROM drive, you should make sure that the drive comes with everything you need to begin using it. To add an external drive, you should have driver software, an SCSI cable, and a power cord. You also may need a terminator. To add an internal drive, all you need is the driver software.

You don't need to buy anything too fancy if you're on a budget, but you should make sure that your drive has the following features:

- ◆ Eject button
- ◆ Emergency eject hole
- ◆ 50-pin SCSI connectors
- ◆ Push-button SCSI-ID selector
- ◆ Auxiliary outlet
- ◆ External fuse

You also may want to check and see if the drive has RCA jacks so that you can hook up an amplifier or speakers.

A recent article in *MacUser* magazine highly recommended the Chinon CDA-535, which costs $370, and the Apple CD 300e Plus, which lists at about $369. Also highly rated were the DGR Tornado, MacConnection MDS Chinon 535, and the MacProduct Magic.

This chapter discusses what's available in multimedia, and how QuickTime videos, sound effects, and CD-ROM can play a role in creating your PowerPoint presentations. Although

PowerPoint's multimedia applications are limited, it offers a user-friendly environment for experimenting and exploring multimedia's potential.

If you have worked your way through the PowerPoint chapters, you should have a basic knowledge of presentation skills and how to use PowerPoint's features. The last PowerPoint chapter will give you some tips on how to put all this information to good use by improving your presentation skills.

Chapter 28

Improving Your Presentation Skills

You have mastered PowerPoint, created a sample presentation or two, reviewed and rehearsed your talk, and gone over your slide show over and over again. You have a thorough knowledge of your subject, and you have even figured out what all those knobs and doohickeys on your newly purchased presentation equipment are actually *for*. And now it's time for the real thing. No matter how much you know, it never hurts to keep improving your presentation skills. This chapter gives you tips on improving these skills by covering the following topics:

- ◆ Developing a speaking style
- ◆ Relating to your audience
- ◆ Dealing with interruptions
- ◆ Fielding questions
- ◆ Talking your way out of trouble

Get Your Points Across

People give presentations for many purposes. But in a way, all presentations are sales, and the product you are selling is yourself. You must grab your audience's attention, earn the trust of the people as a credible information source, and convince them that your information is relevant and worthwhile.

This requires tailoring your talk to your audience's needs without straying too far from the main points of your slide show. To get your points across, you need to communicate effectively. Elements of communicating with people include being prepared, projecting confidence, developing a speaking style, and establishing a rapport with your audience.

When speaking in front of audiences, projecting confidence is half the battle. The first step in feeling good about your talk is to prepare, prepare, and prepare again. Make sure that you know your topic inside and out. Rehearse your talk with the equipment you will be using. Find out everything you can about the room in which you'll be giving your talk. Anticipate potential trouble spots and figure out how you would address them.

Also consider how you want to interact with your audience and prepare your presentation accordingly. Deliver your presentation in front of friends and colleagues and get feedback from them. If you admire a particular individual's speaking style, ask that person for pointers. You should also take body language into account when ascending the podium. After all, our first impressions of people are generally the most lasting.

Prepare, Prepare, Prepare

You can never prepare too much for an upcoming talk. Presentation environments are always fraught with numerous factors that you have little control over. Poor acoustics, lighting problems, technical difficulties, inappropriately placed electrical outlets, and even hopelessly unreceptive audiences can pose unavoidable hazards to the presenter.

Therefore, you must take charge of factors you *can* control. Spending the time required to run through your presentation thoroughly, learning your subject matter, figuring out how to use your equipment, and anticipating possible problems can pay off.

You can take the following steps to feel better prepared for your talk:

◆ **Research your topic:** Make sure that you know all angles of your topic. After all, most presentation situations require you to answer at least a few questions from the audience. And audiences can ask tough questions. The more you know, the more informed your answers will be. Researching your topic also enables you to be prepared if some unanticipated event requires you to change the entire direction of your talk. To research your talk, read related books and trade magazines, talk with colleagues who are knowledgeable about the topic at hand, and scan literature from your organization—even brochures from your competitors, if applicable.

◆ **Familiarize yourself with your equipment:** Make sure that you are thoroughly acquainted with the equipment you will be using during your talk. (For more information on presentation equipment, see Chapter 26.) Don't install any new software and hardware just before a talk—if you're not comfortable with the technical stuff, you'll be a nervous wreck. (*Macworld* and *MacWeek* magazines both feature product reviews that are helpful to Mac users.)

◆ **Rehearse:** Rehearse your presentation with the equipment you will be using, if possible. Position yourself as far away from your projection screen as the last member of your audience will be. Can you read all the text and see all the graphics without having to strain your eyes? If you can't, then you should make adjustments.

Consider the time that has been allotted to you. Can you run through your slide show without feeling rushed? Have you left sufficient time for members of the audience to ask questions? Or does the pace of your talk seem to drag at certain points?

Rehearse in front of colleagues or friends if possible. They can offer the fresh perspective that only people who haven't been looking at that darned slide show for weeks on end are capable of. Their input also helps you address potential problems before they become real problems.

PowerPoint's Rehearse Timings feature times your talk by letting you run a slide show that displays a timer in the corner of your screen (see Figure 28.1). You move forward in your presentation by clicking the pointer on the slide after you have finished discussing it. When you are finished, you can set the timings so that your slide show runs automatically. The timings for each slide are displayed underneath the slides in the Slide Sorter view. (For more on Rehearse Timings, see Chapter 25.)

Figure 28.1   PowerPoint's Rehearse Timings feature lets you time how long it takes to discuss each frame.

Adjust your pace to the medium you are using as well as the topic at hand. Although the presentation rule of thumb is two to three minutes per frame, this rule is not set in stone. Sometimes people get bored if they look at a slide that long. Spending 50 to 60 seconds per frame can be adequate for 35mm slide shows, which use little text. Transparency overhead displays, on the other hand, can take several minutes to discuss because they tend to use more text per frame and encourage a greater level of audience participation.

◆ **Scope the presentation site:** Set aside time to visit your presentation site, if possible. You need to know how many people are coming, what the distance is from your projection screen to the back of the room, where the front row of your audience will be, where you will be expected to set up your equipment, and where the electric outlets are.

If you can't bring your own equipment, make sure that the presentation site has what you need. Just to be sure, you should always arrive armed with extension cords, extra bulbs, and connecting devices. If you are displaying slides or using LCD panels or projectors, you should also bring opaque fabrics for blocking out light. (For more information on requirements for presentation display media, see Chapter 26.) Ambient light can completely ruin your presentation.

It is also safer to have extra sets of everything: disks, videotapes, notes, audience handouts, and other materials that you may need. And don't be stingy about purchasing a pointing device. You can even use a pencil if you have to, but *never* use your finger.

◆ **Anticipate potential trouble spots:** This is the time to look at your slide show with a ruthless eye and tear it apart. If something makes you feel funny about your presentation, pinpoint what that something is and correct it. If your colleagues question you about a fact that doesn't add up or the inclusion of a particular illustration, so will people in your audience—only they may not be as constructive.

While addressing potential presentation issues, consider the following: Does the equipment run the way it should? Do the graphics make an impact while project-ing an accurate image of your organization? Has all the information mentioned been fact-checked and updated? What could go wrong and what can you do to prevent or correct the problem?

After going through all these steps, if anything goes wrong, you can at least rest assured that you took all the necessary precautions.

Project Confidence with Body Language

Body language plays a great part in projecting confidence. A competent, self-assured demeanor can cover up even the most intense cases of stage fright. After all, many of the world's most famous movie and stage personalities have been afflicted with pre-performance jitters. But you would never know it by looking at them.

With everything else on your mind, body language is probably the last thing you want to think about. But first impressions do count. And if you seem relaxed, your audience will be more receptive to your message. The following simple tips can help you project far more confidence than you really feel:

◆ **Stand up straight:** Okay, so that's what your mother says. But all those fashion magazines aren't lying when they say that standing up straight makes you look ten pounds thinner and a couple of inches taller. Besides, slouching is for 13-year-old girls who feel funny about being taller than all the boys. Competent professionals with something important to say stand up straight and command respect.

◆ **Make every gesture count:** As a rule of thumb, every element in your presentation should serve to communicate information better. This rule also applies to your gestures. Some physical movement is necessary to assure your audience that you are alive. But tapping feet, excessive hand movements, and nervous pacing can distract your audience. You have made every frame count, so make every gesture count, too. For example, you can walk across the stage to make eye contact with people on that side of the room, or you can extend a pointer toward the screen to emphasize an important bulleted point.

Caution: Avoid crossing your arms. This stance alienates audiences because it makes you appear defensive.

◆ **Face your audience:** This point seems like overstating the obvious. However, you would be surprised at how many people conduct a large portion of their talks with their backs turned to the audience. Unless the room is totally dark, your audience should be able to see your face. Take this into consideration when setting up your presentation display equipment. To avoid the necessity of turning your back to the audience to run your show, consider purchasing a remote control device.

◆ **Make eye contact:** Eye contact is important. Looking into people's eyes conveys confidence and even a level of power. It also makes people feel important, as if they have been singled out for special attention. Mankind has known that for ages. The ancient Egyptians acknowledged the power of eye contact when they created human figures who stare at you even in profile (see Figure 28.2).

◆ **Dress comfortably:** Obviously, I'm not telling you to wear sweatpants. But the morning of your big presentation is not the time to experiment with a new look. Stick to tried but true, reasonably conservative clothing that looks attractive and doesn't have to be fussed with. You don't want to worry about that ripped lining edging out of your jacket sleeve or about slipping and falling in the designer shoes you're wearing.

◆ **Take deep breaths:** No, this isn't the Marlon Brando Method Acting School of Presentations. Taking deep breaths makes you feel better because it gives you more oxygen and forces you to relax your muscles. Try it; it really works. If possible, get a little exercise before dashing off to the presentation site, too.

Figure 28.2   Her eyes follow you wherever you go.

◆ **Think of good results:** After telling you to worry about *everything* in the last
section, I'm now going to tell you the opposite. There's nothing you can do at this
point, so you may as well think positive. Put yourself in a good mood. What do
you want the outcome of your talk to be? Think about how landing another sale
could get you that promotion or how it would boost your department's morale if
the big brass adopt your proposal.

If you follow this advice, you will come across as poised and confident, like the presenter
shown in Figure 28.3.

Figure 28.3   A poised and confident presenter.

Develop a Speaking Style

As you continue giving talks, you will begin to develop a distinctive speaking style. Your speaking style helps create a framework around which you will learn how to interact effectively with your audience. Your speaking style ties in closely with your writing style. To be convincing, you should develop your script in a way that is compatible with how you speak.

Developing a speaking style isn't as difficult as it sounds. You already have a speaking style, which you use every day to communicate with the people around you. Making your particular style work for you in presentation situations is a natural process that comes with time. However, you can make a concerted effort toward effective speaking by taking notes and getting feedback from others. You should also keep contributing factors in mind, such as your personality, the types of presentations you generally give, and the media you use.

Working with your personality

Your speaking style is a reflection of your personality, so work *with* it instead of fighting it. Every personality has its good and bad points in terms of giving presentations. The name of the game is to make both the good and bad points work to your advantage.

For example, if a shy person tries to project effusive friendliness and interact with the audience on a high level, he won't come across naturally. An introvert's speaking style may not be as entertaining as an extrovert's, but it can still have attractive qualities. A straightforward style, quiet competence, and the ability to listen are generally appreciated by audiences.

You should take the following factors into consideration during the process of incorporating your personality into your presentation style:

◆ **Are you extroverted or introverted?** Extroverted people have an easier time with speaking in front of other people and rolling with the punches. But they often talk too much or have difficulty sticking to the point. Introverted people find public speaking difficult, but they tend to choose their words more carefully and stay focused on the topics at hand. Extroverted people should develop a speaking style that allows interactivity and flexibility. Introverted people should do more formal presentations and have audience participation through questions at the end of the talk.

◆ **What is your energy level?** Some people have enormous amounts of energy, while others are more sedate. For those of you with high energy levels, your dynamic presence is ideal for generating excitement about products and ideas. You should keep this in mind as an angle from which to begin developing your talks. Use a forceful, animated speaking style, but don't be overbearing. If you have a more low-key personality, then you are best suited for building a sense of trust with people. Win audiences over with a relaxed, easy-going style.

◆ **How quick-witted are you?** This aspect of your personality has little to do with your native level of intelligence and more with how well you respond to someone's throwing you a curveball. Your memory plays a major part in this. The more familiar you are with your topic, the more prepared you are to handle unforeseen situations. People who are quick-witted in this way have a degree of flexibility that allows them greater spontaneity when giving their presentations.

Most of us, however, are chained to our notes. If that's the case with you, don't worry. A well-organized binder full of notes makes it look like you put considerable effort into preparing your talk. Your audience appreciates this. PowerPoint helps you create easy-to-reference speaker's notes (see Chapter 25).

Taking notes

Keep a presentation diary for a while and take notes. Make a checklist and ask yourself the following questions: What parts of your presentation did you feel good about? Why did you feel good about them? What parts did you not feel so good about? Why didn't you feel good about them?

Was the audience attentive and responsive, or did they seem to drift off? What questions did people ask? Did your presentation achieve the results you had hoped for? If you could do the presentation over again, would you do it differently? If so, how? What parts of your talk would you keep the same and why?

Notes from one presentation alone may not prove illuminating. However, a collection of notes will reveal patterns. Some phrases or gestures will consistently net the desired results; however, you may want to change your approach for other parts of your talk. Your notes can help you create better scripts and deliver them more effectively. You should also ask friends and colleagues for feedback. They may notice things that you have missed.

Modulating your voice

You shouldn't have to take elocution lessons to give your talks. However, there are basic guidelines for speaking before an audience. It's important that your voice projects clearly so that people *can* hear you and that your voice sounds pleasant enough that people *will want* to hear you.

To modulate your voice, use the following guidelines:

◆ **Use your diaphragm:** First, put your hand on your stomach and say, "Ha!" (You do this, of course, *before* standing in front of the audience!) The muscle that makes your stomach move is called your diaphragm. To project your voice more clearly without straining your vocal chords, you should use this muscle to push out your voice. This technique may seem silly at first—just wait until your co-workers hear you going around the office saying, "Ha, ha, ha!"—but it does work. Theater and singing professionals call this technique "speaking from your diaphragm."

◆ **Keep a low pitch:** By pitch, I am referring to tonal quality, not volume. High-pitched voices sound shrill and squeaky when the voice is raised or amplified; low-pitched voices sound deep and resonant. Before giving your talk, practice speaking in a lower vocal register.

◆ **Pace your speech:** All people have their own little speech glitches, such as rushing words out too fast; speaking in a monotone; filling in pauses with *like, um,* and *y'know;* and a multitude of other verbal sins. Yet what sounds like a minor problem during the ordinary course of talking to people is magnified several times over when you give a presentation. Tape record yourself and work on any negative speech patterns. Pace your talk so that you speak in a calm, steady, well-modulated manner.

◆ **Mind your Ps, Bs, and Ts:** Hard consonants that require pushing out a sharp puff of air sound like explosions when amplified by using a microphone. Practice sounding out these consonants more gently.

By using these tips, you can communicate more effectively by eliminating distracting elements from your speaking voice.

Build a Rapport with Your Audience

Audiences need to be convinced that what you have to say will somehow benefit them. It is easier to get a handle on what your audience members want to hear if you build up a rapport with them. You can do this by using humor, emphasizing things you all have in common, addressing concerns they have, and being responsive to their needs.

Listed below are some tips on building up a rapport with your audience:

◆ **Break the ice:** Begin your presentation with a joke or, in small groups, ask the people to introduce themselves. You can also begin with a short question-and-answer session and ask your audience members point blank what they are hoping to get out of your talk. This information helps you address your audience's expectations during your talk.

◆ **Encourage participation:** Even the most rigid scripts have some room for participation. For instance, if you are demonstrating how your company can save your audience members some money, let them add up the savings themselves. Give them the figures and place the answers on a separate slide that you display later, as shown in Figure 28.4. Getting people excited by involving them in financial calculations is an effective technique that is often used by sales professionals.

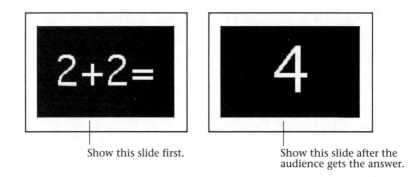

Show this slide first.

Show this slide after the
audience gets the answer.

Figure 28.4   Encouraging audience participation with slides.

◆ **Incorporate relevant material:** Even if you use the same presentation frames over and over again, you should always personalize the talking part. Research the company, organization, profession, or other group that your audience members are a part of. You can then use your research to directly relate the facts on your slides to their immediate concerns.

◆ **Arrive early:** Arrive at the presentation site early, if possible. Arriving early may give you a chance to introduce yourself and chat with some of the people you will be presenting to. Once people know who you are, they are more receptive to you. You also may find out information that can be useful in your talk.

◆ **Follow up:** Making contacts never hurts. When appropriate, a follow-up can build a rapport with the people you spoke to. For example, you can send the audience members a card that thanks them for coming and offers to provide them with more information.

After you have established a rapport with your audience, you are well on your way to having a successful presentation.

Fielding questions

Fielding questions can be fun and highly productive in terms of learning about your audience. But how do you keep this part of your presentation from becoming a free-for-all? You want to answer questions as thoroughly as possible, but you also want to make sure that as many people as possible get their turn. You also want to end your presentation on a high note and make sure that the audience retains your message.

The following tips can help you field questions more efficiently:

◆ **Set a procedure:** Before you even begin your talk, you should inform the audience members of how they should bring up questions and how you will address them.

For example, will you have a question and answer session following your talk? Or will you set aside time between sections of your presentation? You should also inform the audience of the order you will use for answering questions.

◆ **Refer people to literature:** When question-and-answer sessions yield more raised hands than allotted time, literature can be extremely useful. Whenever possible, give people a brief response, refer them to the literature, make a general announcement that others with the same question can refer to the literature, and then move on.

◆ **Stick to the point:** Don't digress and don't let questioners in the audience digress either. Briefly answer the question and tell them that you would be happy to talk more afterwards (when possible).

◆ **Admit what you don't know:** Never try to fudge knowledge that you don't have. If someone throws you a curveball, admit that you don't know the answer. You can then either ask if anyone in the audience can answer the question, or you can offer to take down the person's number, track down the answer to the question, and call him back later.

After you get the knack of fielding questions and running question-and-answer sessions, you can enjoy having these opportunities to interact with your audience.

Dealing with interruptions

Sooner or later, every speaker winds up with an audience that includes people who keep interrupting. Or sometimes the interruptions consist of factors beyond anyone's control, such as noisy construction going on outside or members of the audience getting called out for phone calls and other office emergencies. Nonetheless, interruptions disturb the flow of your presentation, make it difficult for people to concentrate on your message, and take away your control of the situation.

Sometimes there isn't much you can do. However, the following tips can help you cope with annoying interruptions:

◆ **Stay calm:** Audiences generally want to feel that the speaker is in control of the environment. If possible, stay calm, ignore the interruptions, and proceed as you normally would.

◆ **Crack a joke:** Chances are the other people in the room feel as awkward as you do. Making a joke about the interruption helps break the tension and allows you to continue your talk. For example, you could respond to the sound of a pneumatic drill by saying, "Oops, someone's Lazy-Boy went on the fritz again."

◆ **Enlist your audience's help:** The audience members want to hear what you have to say, or they wouldn't be there. People will generally help you if you ask them to. If the interruption is caused by background noise, ask if anyone has any suggestions. If the interruptions are caused by a person, however, try asking someone in the audience to "help" that person so that you can proceed as scheduled. After you acknowledge the situation, chances are fairly high that people in the audience will tell the interrupter to be quiet.

◆ **Use diversionary tactics:** If the interruptions are caused by a person in the audience, cheerfully inform the person that you will have a question-and-answer session and that she will be the first person you will call on. If the person keeps interrupting, you can use an old teacher's trick: give the interrupter some responsibility. Ask her to help with some part of your presentation, such as passing out handouts.

◆ **Reschedule:** If the interruptions persist and the situation is beyond anyone's control, tactfully inquire about whether you can reschedule your presentation. You don't have to sound angry. You can simply say, "Perhaps this isn't a good time for you folks. I would be happy to come back later."

Sometimes, none of these tactics work. But you can still handle yourself gracefully. If anything, the way you handle an uncomfortable situation will make people remember you.

The skills needed to become a good presenter are considerably different from the skills required to create good presentations. Although some people are better with audiences than others, anyone can make a solid effort. After reading this chapter, you should be on your way toward interacting with your audience effectively and developing a distinctive speaking style.

After reading the PowerPoint section of this book, I hope you have more confidence in developing your own presentations and in getting up in front of a group of people and making the presentations. Good luck in your presentation future!

Part V

Information Exchange

Information exchange includes communicating with the outside world (or at least the world outside your own Macintosh) with Microsoft Mail and sharing information between the various applications included in Microsoft Office. Microsoft Mail isn't really part of Office—you have to buy it separately—but it is included in this book because many companies use it in preference to other mail programs. Besides, all the applications in Office are Mail aware and are designed to integrate smoothly with Mail functions.

In the new world of System 7.5 and Office, many of the functions of different applications are blurring into each other. You can construct a table of numbers in Word 6, for example; and you can apply such editing functions as fonts, text styles, and hyphenation to the cells in a spreadsheet in Excel 5. But you still probably have text in Word, numbers in Excel, and presentation graphics in PowerPoint. That's why you need to be able to exchange information between the three Office partners. As you will see in Part V, some of these ways are simply better than others because Office is still a work in progress. *Surviving* data exchange is a fair way to characterize this section.

Chapter 29

Using Microsoft Mail

On the Windows side, Microsoft Mail is included with Office. Because Microsoft writes network server software used by the Windows installation, this is a pretty natural state of affairs. On the Macintosh, however, you are supposed to buy Mail server software separately from Office, with a license for a certain number of Mail client stations. Although, technically, Mail is not part of Microsoft Office for the Mac, it's popular enough that you should run through the following helpful hints and observations:

◆ Installing Mail
◆ Understanding how mail servers work
◆ Signing in
◆ Using Mail to send notes and files
◆ Avoiding crashes
◆ Managing your mailbox
◆ Dealing with returned mail

Network Matters

Microsoft Mail is different from the other programs in this book in that it is not your responsibility to install Mail and set it up, unless by chance you are your company's network administrator. The network administrator is supposed to do the following for you:

◆ Select the hardware for connecting a group of Macintoshes to the network server.

◆ Establish hardware/software *gateways,* if different networks are supposed to communicate with each other.

◆ Make sure that all the Macs are properly set up for AppleTalk (Microsoft Mail on the Mac uses AppleTalk as its customary network protocol).

◆ Assign each network user an account number, user name, and password.

◆ Install Microsoft Mail client software on each Mac.

In other words, the typical situation for Microsoft Mail users is that they simply arrive at the office, and someone else has done 95 percent of the installation and setup dirty work. That sounds fair enough! Click the Office Manager icon (see Figure 29.1) and make sure that you see Microsoft Mail as an option. If not, go see your administrator.

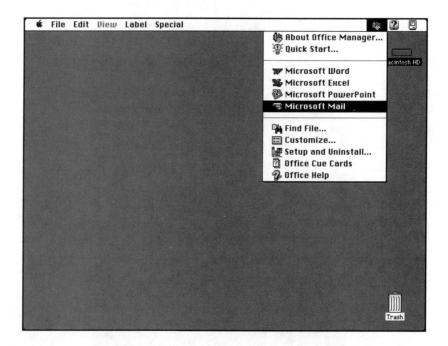

Figure 29.1   Look in the Office Manager to see whether your administrator has set you up properly.

Networks and Mail

Just so that you know what's happening—in other words, to explain why Mail works the way it does—try to think of the Mail system in terms of a traditional office paper mail scheme.

Imagine a big rectangular array of flat mailboxes, each with a user name, that can hold letters and memos and magazines and so forth. Usually you see one of these things in a hallway at a big company, and there's usually a junior employee in charge of it. You have your desk, and you have a slot in the mailbox. In this plan, you also have Bob the Mailman, who actually brings your mail to you, puts it on your desk, and collects mail from other people.

In the network world, the Mac represents your desk; a second Mac, which is being used as a network server, represents the big mailbox; and the Mail software takes the place of Bob the Mailman. When you send a message to someone in Microsoft Mail, the message gets picked up by the software and is sent as a file to the server Mac. When you check your mail, you are using the software to look on the server and see whether there are any files addressed to you.

It's all quite simple really—the only confusion is caused by the inevitable air of mystery surrounding networks, which always seem to be high-tech, wirehead things with mystery problems. The dreaded phrase, "The network is down," for example, usually means only that the server has been taken offline for a while so that someone can change the software or fix a hard drive or solve some other problem that you routinely encounter on your own Mac. When the server Mac needs to be fixed, the network administrator stops the network so that people aren't sending mail out to a disconnected server (some software isn't sophisticated enough to realize it's sending mail to a computer that's turned off!).

Your own Mail settings

To use Mail, you need to have your administrator tell you your user name—actually it's your *Mac's* user name—on the system (mary_brown? MBROWN? mbrown3?) and your password. If your are part of a network that uses more than one AppleTalk *zone,* then you need to know your zone (Sales? Marketing? Accounting?). You also need to know the network name of the Mac that is your Mail server. With any luck, the system administrator will have handed you a blurred photocopy sheet full of network jargon that contains this information.

Now select Chooser from the Apple menu. Look around in the upper left-hand box with icons of printers and so forth until you find the icon for Microsoft Mail. Click the icon to select Mail. If Chooser shows you a list of zones, then you are in a multiple-zone system, so you have to find your own zone (sounds sort of Zen, doesn't it?) and select it. Finally, in the list at the upper right of the Chooser screen, you need to select your own Mail server. Even if you are on a one-zone, one-server system, you have to make these selections. Now click the Setup button.

At this point, you are presented with two further choices: one that is quite harmless and one that is quite tricky. First, you can choose to sign into Mail automatically upon startup—the harmless choice. This option, of course, makes your startup take considerably longer, but if you want to make sure that you never miss a message, this practice is a good idea. Second, you can choose to have your password entered by the system instead of typing it in each time—the tricky choice.

> **Caution:** *Never* have your password entered automatically. First, after a week, you'll forget the password yourself. Second, this choice means that all people who sit down at your computer not only can read all your mail, but they can also send mail *as you*! If that prospect doesn't scare you, you've never had a real job.

Having selected whether you want to sign into Mail automatically and having selected the Password Must Be Typed option (trust me on this one), click the OK button to close the Chooser window.

Signing in

If you sign on to Mail automatically on startup, you see the Mail 3.1 sign-in dialog box, just as a result of turning on your Mac. If you haven't signed on automatically on startup, pick Microsoft Mail from the Apple menu or from the Office Manager menu. Enter your name and password and click OK. Like most other Mail systems, when you type your password, all you see is a set of bullets entered in the password space onscreen. These bullets keep anyone standing near you from reading your password in the interest of merry mischief.

You are now greeted with the Mail Summary window. The Summary window has the following items:

◆ A list of incoming messages. To read a message, simply select it and click the Read button at the bottom of the window.

◆ Buttons for deleting the message, printing it (thus defeating some of the purpose of email), forwarding it to another user name in the Mail system, or moving it to another folder on your hard drive.

◆ The Reply button, the most commonly used button. Click the Reply button and the response you write is automatically sent back to the person who sent you the message in the first place, with the heading Re: (original message title). Then that person answers, giving a message called Re: Re: (original message title). And so on and so on. . . .

◆ The Note icon to the left of the window. Use this icon so that you don't end up with Re: Re: Re: as the title of everything. Clicking the Note icon starts a new message from scratch.

When you click the Note icon, you get a window with a blank area for typing, an Address icon, and an Enclosure icon. Type anything you like, keeping in mind at all times the rules of email etiquette. Then click the Address icon, and you are presented with a list of names that you can reach on your network. Some fancier installations have gateways to the outside that can handle Internet addresses for people on other networks—this feature will be more common in the future, but it's not typical just yet. So, normally, you will be selecting a name of a co-worker in your company or within your own workgroup.

Email Etiquette

When you communicate through email, remember that no one can see your face or hear your voice. The tiny words on a tiny screen have to convey your thoughts accurately. Follow these simple rules to make your email experiences more successful.

◆ Tone down your messages. Because there's no way to convey tone through facial or vocal expression in email messages, everything you write seems a bit sterner. An angry message, for example, looks really murderous onscreen.

◆ Remember that CAPITAL LETTERS LOOK LIKE YOU'RE SHOUTING.

◆ Make sure that your full name and your phone number are included in the message. You may be assigned a network name, such as BradE, and the recipient has to figure out which Brad sent the message.

◆ Don't send anything in an email message that you wouldn't mind explaining at a meeting. Officially, these communications are secure, but there are reams of corporate horror stories about email messages ending up in the wrong hands.

◆ Keep to the point. People find themselves inundated with email in a busy office. If you want to tell a story about your vacation, do it at lunch.

The Enclosure icon enables you to select any file on your Mac and send it along with the note. This very important feature also turns out to be exceptionally robust (even Office 4.2.1 works with Mail 3.1, which hasn't been updated for a few years because, after all, it works!). In the Note window, you write a short message that explains the Word document. After clicking Enclosure, you select the document that you want to send from a Finder-like list and click Done. Then *with all other applications closed* except Mail, click the Send button and send your file on its way. Even on networks that have been experiencing problems, sending files with Mail *as the only application running at the time* usually works.

Alternatively, because Microsoft Mail installs itself in the menus of your other applications, you can call it from the File menu inside Word 6. After all, when you save a file to a hard drive or send it to a printer, you're just sending bytes down a wire. The same thing happens when you send a file out on the network. Should be no problem, right? Umm . . . maybe and maybe not. Using Mail from Word 6 usually allows a message to be sent properly, but sometimes Word 6 itself crashes the Mac that is doing the sending. In the worst cases, the messaging Mac that crashes in the middle of a Mail session then confuses the Mail server to the point where mailbox services are interrupted (meaning, in effect, a network crash).

> **Caution:** Although it takes a few more steps to save your files, close out of Word and run Mail separately. Taking this precaution is a more reliable way to send files.

Mailbox Management

It is not hard to work with the main Summary window that you see when you sign in to Mail. Reading messages, replying, and making up your own messages are straightforward Mac-style tasks.

When you are looking at the Summary window in Mail, you will notice that you have an item called Mail on the main menu bar at the top of the screen. This menu option gives you choices for the following tasks:

- Changing your password
- Opening your mailbox (⌘-G)
- Closing your mailbox (and signing off, too, as ⌘-Q)
- Editing the set of addresses that appears in the scrolling address list when you click the Address icon in Note mode
- Assigning personal groups
- Managing your messages in folders

The last function, managing your messages, is critical. In the next few paragraphs, you will learn how to save your messages in the appropriate places with the New Folder command (⌘-N) from the File menu. You can choose to save the messages to a new file or to an existing file with the Save Messages command.

Consider for a minute what happens when your office gets Microsoft Mail up and running. At first, you get a few messages per day, and you keep them in your Inbox. As you start to get more messages, you realize that you have to delete some of them just so that you don't lose them in the messages that you want to keep. Finally, you have so many messages that one folder isn't enough.

This, by the way, is absolutely guaranteed to happen. Studies of email use show that after people get comfortable with it, they send 20 messages a day. Someone is receiving all those messages. After a year, you will have literally thousands of messages—your Mail files will outnumber, by file count anyway, every other category of file on your hard drive.

So it's time to think about a folder structure that helps you keep important information but discard junk. What you want to do is simple. First, using the New Folder command under the File menu in the Finder, you should set up folders for your main activities and drag them into the Microsoft Mail folder. For example, you might have a folder for Meetings, Personal, Policies, and Travel. For these main-level folders, you should have somewhere between five and ten topics (there's a tradeoff here between detail and speed). Then inside these main-level folders, you can create Month folders—6/95, 7/95, and so on—by using the New Folders command again. Now you have a place to put all the messages you need to keep. It's really the equivalent of having a file cabinet where drawers correspond to main-level topics and folders in a drawer correspond to months.

Now, when you open your Mailbox folder in the Summary window, you can Shift-select a group of files on a similar topic. Then you choose the Save Messages To New File command from the Mail menu. Type in a name that describes the contents of the files. Be sure to include the date of the mail messages in the filename. For example, if your mail messages are about the Omaha meeting, and they came in the week of May 2, 1995, you can name the file "OmahaMtg-5/2/95-msgs." Click OK to create this new minifolder.

You can let these grouped messages pile up for a while, and then every few weeks, you can "file" all your little minifolders into one of the month folders inside the appropriate topic. Just drag the folders in the classic Macintosh style. This organizational technique means that you will usually be performing very efficient searches for older information. Although Find File lets you search for files by date, you're better off having files and folders with names that contain dates so that you can do the searching yourself. You can drag all the little grouped files out of your Mailbox and into a nice safe place where you can find them again in seconds. This system really works!

Grouping

One last convenient item in the Mail menu is Personal Groups. When you select this option, you are prompted to make up a group name, and you are then given a list of the names that you can reach on your network to select for membership in the group.

After you select the set of names and click the Save button, you will see that a new name has been added to your address list—the name that you assigned to the group. When you need to send out a memo to all the group's people at once, you just address it to the group. The members see it as individual mail addressed to them. Because it's no more work to assign a group than to address mail to everyone individually, it's worth setting up groups even if you use them only once or twice a week.

Returned mail

Sometimes your mail comes back with a cute little "Returned" sticker. Because addressing inside a network is done by selecting valid names from an address list, returned mail almost never happens with mail addressed to someone on your own network. But when you deal with outside mail addresses, the most common causes of returned mail are as follows:

- ◆ You type an address for someone on another server, and you have some tiny detail of the address wrong (the name is Stan_Voronych rather than StanVoronych).

- ◆ The gateway to the other network's server wasn't connected or wasn't working at the time you sent the mail.

- ◆ The server for the other network was temporarily disconnected. If your own server was down, you couldn't have sent the message in the first place, so it's "the other guy's fault."

For addressing problems, the only fix-up that always works is to call the other person on the phone to validate the exact address. With server and gateway problems, you just have to keep trying to send the mail. After the third failure, send your network administrator a copy of the message, including the address, as mail inside your own system, and let the administrator puzzle it out.

Now you know about how to create mail, send it, and store it. The next chapter tells you how to integrate all the Microsoft programs.

Chapter 30

Integrating
the Applications

The big argument for using Microsoft Office, as opposed to smaller integrated programs, is that Office gives you tight integration among big-time, competitive, full-featured, stand-alone applications. All sorts of connections are possible, but this chapter will review the most useful intra-application connections inside Office, which include the following:

◆ Excel data into Word
◆ Excel charts into PowerPoint
◆ Word items into PowerPoint

A Few Words About Linking

In principle, there are four different ways to do data exchange inside the applications of Microsoft Office. Two of them use the Macintosh's own exchange facilities that are built into the operating system. The other two use Microsoft's object linking and embedding technique (OLE). You should understand that these methods are not equivalent in terms of functionality, nor are they equivalent in their "likelihood of success."

Paste versus Paste Link

Using the Paste command is a straightforward Mac technique—you already know all about it. The Paste Link command may also be familiar to you if you have been using earlier versions of the Office applications. One big difference between the Paste and Paste Link commands is that Paste simply inserts information into a file, while Paste Link maintains the link to the originating document. The content of an item that has been inserted with the Paste Link command is updated from the originating document every time the receiving document is opened, saved, or closed.

Perhaps the biggest difference between Paste and Paste Link is that the underlying software technology for Paste Link, which is OLE2, isn't particularly well debugged for use with System 7.5, at least not through Office 4.2.1. In the mildest kind of Paste Link crash, the Word 6 document that receives the data locks up, and you have to restart your Mac by turning it off and on again. This technique is not recommended because it leaves incorrectly closed files on your hard drive. These files can, in turn, lead to all sorts of weird behavior. In the worst kind of Paste Link crash, Word 6 no longer recognizes the file type of the Word document, so you can't recover it, and Excel can't read the original Excel file any more.

Not a pretty picture—and these crashes are maddeningly unpredictable. For this reason, make sure that you send in your registration so that you get updates of all the Office applications. Word is the principle crash offender, and somewhere around version 6.2.1, Microsoft will finally be providing a more stable product. If it's any consolation, the Windows version of Word 6 has a comparable set of problems.

Embedding and Publishing

Nothing would be more thrilling in a chapter on using Office applications together than presenting a section on object embedding. An embedded object (for example, a chunk of Excel worksheet in a Word page) is a "live" document—when you click in the embedded worksheet, you're effectively back in Excel. This is what OLE is all about. After nearly four months of testing object linking, I regret to report that in Office 4.2.1, it doesn't work acceptably. Even with a minimal installation of System 7.5 and all non-Microsoft extensions turned off, crashes are sufficiently frequent that object embedding is not a good choice for day-to-day work.

The Mac System's own Publish and Subscribe, in contrast, has proved itself exceptionally robust. Probably because it's been around for a few years and is thus more or less bug-free and because Microsoft's own programming efforts don't appear to conflict with it, Publishing from one application and Subscribing in another is a reliable way to exchange data. It is better than using the Paste Link command and far better than object embedding, at least in the current state of Word 6 and its friends.

Special data exchange: Present It and Report It

One built-in Microsoft technique, however, works very nicely. Word 6 has a special PresentIt macro that sends documents into PowerPoint, and PowerPoint returns the favor with a button called Report It. I'll give you details on this slick arrangement at the end of this chapter.

Excel Data into Word

The first tip you need is this: get Word 6.0.1, the early 1995 update. The simple reason for this recommendation is that the first version of Word 6 is prone to crash when you try to establish Excel links!

Then you have a decision to make before you send data from Excel into Word:

♦ Will the Excel data be changing frequently? If so, it's worth the effort (and performance hit) that results from live data links between documents.

♦ Is the Word document supposed to be a "snapshot" of conditions at a particular time? In this case, you will just be creating confusion unless you do a one-time, one-way data transfer.

Pasting

Using the Cut, Copy, and Paste commands is still the easiest way to transfer modest amounts of data between applications. First make sure that both Excel and Word are open. You can use Office Manager—the little icon to the left of the Help button on the Finder menu—to open the applications. Then in an Excel worksheet, you can select the table of information that you want (see Figure 30.1) and choose the Copy command from the Edit menu.

Now switch to Word, open the document in which you want to insert the Excel table, and put your cursor in the proper place for the table. Choose the Paste Special command from the Edit menu. The Paste Special dialog box appears (see Figure 30.2). In this dialog box, you can choose to paste the Excel data into the Word document as regular text, paste the data as formatted text (RTF), or choose the Paste Link option to make a live link, whether you retain the formatting or not.

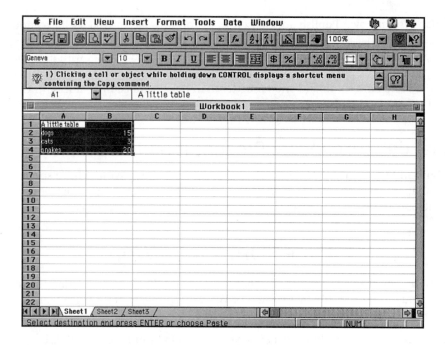

Figure 30.1 A little Excel table for export.

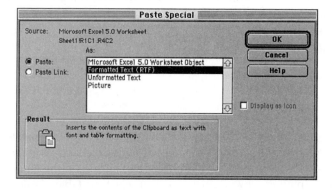

Figure 30.2 The many kinds of Paste.

An RTF paste link gives you the table shown in Figure 30.3 in your Word document. When you choose the Paste Link option rather than the Paste option, the data in the Word document changes when you change the original data in the Excel worksheet (the update occurs every time you open or save the Word document).

698

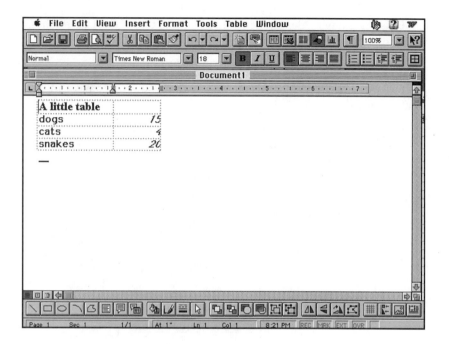

Figure 30.3   The Excel table in Word.

If you do lots of reporting, here's a tip that can save you plenty of grief. When you make a table in Excel that you propose to use in Word, use the Insert Date command to put an active date somewhere in the table. In this way, by just looking at the table in the Excel document, you can determine which version number of the table you are using because the last update is clearly indicated by the date.

Publishing

The Paste Link option works through Microsoft's own object linking and embedding (OLE) scheme. This way of transferring information duplicates the services that Apple already built into the Macintosh system long ago in its Publish and Subscribe features.

In principle, the Paste Link option and the Publish and Subscribe feature should work in almost the same way to exchange data. In practice, however, using Publish and Subscribe is significantly more stable than using either linking or embedding. Furthermore, because the rest of your Macintosh applications also use the Publish and Subscribe method of transferring information between applications, using this method in Office doesn't require any training or re-orientation. In the first few editions of Office, using OLE2 links between documents was fairly troublesome, while using the Publish and Subscribe links caused no problems at all.

Microsoft, if history is any guide, can be counted on to fix its Mac OLE2 glitches, but without any sense of urgency.

To transfer information by using Publish and Subscribe, follow these steps:

1. Select an area in your Excel spreadsheet that you want to paste into a Word document.

2. Choose Create Publisher from the Publish options on the Edit menu. A dialog box similar to the one shown in Figure 30.4 appears. Give the selection its own name in the Name of New Edition text box. This action creates a file within a file and defines your selection as a "publishable" edition of data. Click the Publish button.

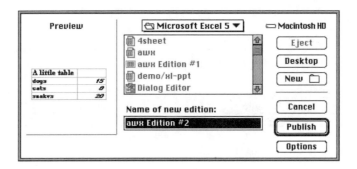

Figure 30.4   Publish, a nice safe choice.

3. Switch to Word, open the document, and place the cursor in the place that you want the Excel table to go. From the Edit menu, choose Subscribe. The dialog box similar to the one shown in Figure 30.5 appears. Highlight the name of the new file that you've created and click the Subscribe button. The text is automatically inserted into the Word file. (If you never have done Publish and Subscribe before, you may want to review this technique in the Apple Guide.)

When you make the connection between your Word and Excel documents in this way, the files are mutually updated every time they open, close, or save. In this type of linkage, you shouldn't try to edit the table that appears in Word because Excel has been defined as the data source. If you want to have editable Excel data in Word, simply perform a simple Paste function (not Paste Link).

Figure 30.5 Subscribing in Word.

Excel and PowerPoint

Because PowerPoint was originally designed as a stand-alone application, it has its own facilities for maintaining tables of data and creating charts. But the business reality is that most companies in the Office milieu use Excel as the main collection point for data because Excel has such well-defined links to external databases. So you probably have your data in Excel along with various lovingly hand-crafted and fine-tuned charts, as well.

But Excel charts are dull, while PowerPoint charts provide a nice set of attractive stock backgrounds and shadings so that your presentations look professional. It doesn't make sense to redo all this work in PowerPoint, so you need to transfer your Excel charts to PowerPoint by following these steps:

1. In your Excel worksheet, double-click the chart that you want to import into PowerPoint (see Figure 30.6). You need to see the gray cross-hatched border around the chart to know that you have activated it.

2. Open PowerPoint (if you haven't already), choose Blank Presentation, and double-click one of the AutoLayouts in the New Slide dialog box that has room for a chart. A screen like the one in Figure 30.7 appears.

3. Go back to Excel and choose Copy from the Edit menu, which copies the selected chart to the Clipboard. Now switch to PowerPoint and choose Paste Special from the Edit menu. The Paste Special dialog box appears. The dialog box has, in fact, anticipated the Excel chart import as a likely action (see Figure 30.8).

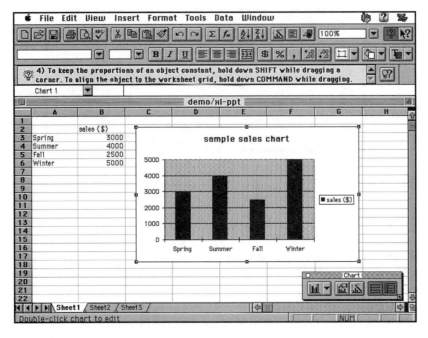

Figure 30.6   An Excel chart for export.

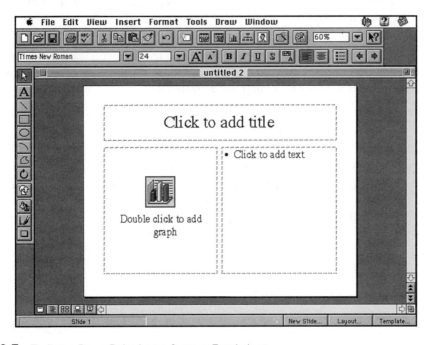

Figure 30.7   Finding a PowerPoint home for your Excel chart.

Figure 30.8   PowerPoint knows that you want to use Excel charts.

4. After clicking the OK button in the Paste Special dialog box, your chart is pasted into the PowerPoint slide as a resizable object (see Figure 30.9). You can also modify chart properties, if necessary, by using the Formatting toolbar, and you can add text and a title to the slide.

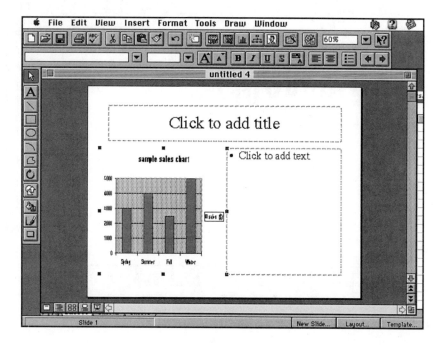

Figure 30.9   The Excel chart pasted into a PowerPoint slide.

WordArt in PowerPoint

There are several ways to use Word in connection with PowerPoint. PowerPoint can accept Word text when you use the Paste command or when you use the Paste Link command, which updates itself. If you have already written a Word report on some topic, you can cannibalize most of it to make a snappy presentation in PowerPoint. You may also have developed some zingy special effects (company logos, special headings, or titles) for your Word documents by using WordArt. Rather than create these effects again, you can place them directly in PowerPoint.

Simply follow these steps to transfer a WordArt graphic from Word to PowerPoint:

1. Open the word document that contains the WordArt graphic you want to use.

2. The WordArt appears in your Word document surrounded by the little sizing handles that accompany graphics (see Figure 30.10). Select it with a single click and choose the Copy command from the Edit menu.

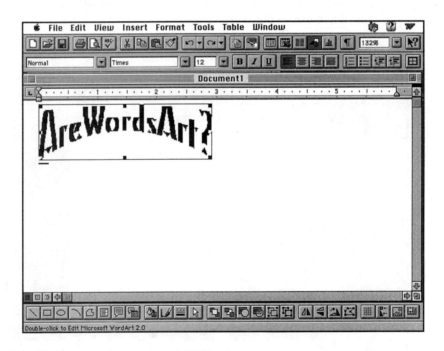

Figure 30.10   WordArt as a sizable object in a Word document.

3. Switch to PowerPoint and paste the WordArt graphic where you want it to go in a PowerPoint slide (see Figure 30.11). If you use the Paste Link command, changes will be updated in PowerPoint when you make them back in the Word document. However, Word 6 still seems to have some problems with the Paste Link command, so using the plain Paste command is probably much safer from a crash-proofing standpoint.

So far this section has concentrated on importing WordArt to PowerPoint from a Word document because it's very likely that you have done most of your WordArt experimentation in Word. By this time, you may already have a repertoire of flashy or interesting WordArt graphics in your Word documents.

But what if you have never used WordArt, and you want to insert a graphic into a PowerPoint slide? In this situation, put your cursor at the position in the slide where you want the graphic to go. Then choose the Object command from the Insert menu. From the Object Type list in the Create New tab, select a WordArt option, and in the dialog box that appears, create your own WordArt from scratch (see Figure 30.12). WordArt, like Microsoft Graph and Equation Editor, is actually an independent stand-alone "helper" application that can be called up from any application in Office.

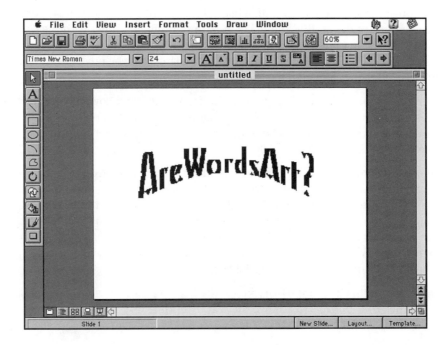

Figure 30.11 WordArt in a PowerPoint slide.

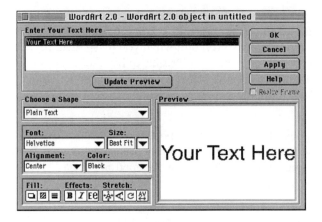

Figure 30.12   Create your own WordArt in this dialog box.

Word Outlines in PowerPoint

PowerPoint can also accept Word outlines. At the simplest level, you simply copy an outline document from Word and paste it into a blank PowerPoint slide. You can also expand the individual points of the outline and make *them* into individual slides with the Cut and Paste commands. There's a lot to be said for this ready-made approach to outlines from the standpoint of logical clarity, as opposed to picking a template from the prepared choices in PowerPoint and then making up the slides from scratch.

But Microsoft has installed a special pipeline between Word and PowerPoint, one that preserves outline structure. There are a few variations on this trick, but they all involve the PresentIt macro on the Word end of the pipeline and the Report It button on the PowerPoint end.

To make this technique work, by the way, you need to have installed the complete version of Word 6 and the complete version of PowerPoint 4. The macros that make this outline transfer possible are obscurely located in the Wizards folders, so if you do a minimum installation of either application, you won't get this feature. By the way, not only is this installation information not explained in any detail in the Microsoft documentation, but information about this kind of file transfer between applications is amazingly skimpy everywhere. Present It doesn't even appear as an item in the index of the Word manual.

First, make an outline in Word 6 by typing some headings in Outline view (see Figure 30.13) and using the arrow buttons to arrange the text by outline level.

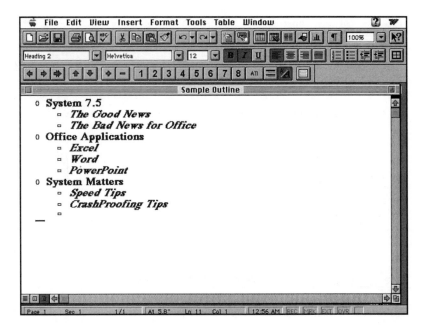

Figure 30.13 A simple Word outline for export.

Now there are two choices. In the first one, you go into the Finder and double-click the Present It icon to open a Present It window. You then cut and paste the outline into this window (see Figure 30.14) and save the file. When you switch to PowerPoint, choose the Open command from the File menu. In the Open dialog box, one of the options now available is to import an outline saved in this way. You just open the file, and the outline structure is preserved.

The second choice is to activate the PresentIt macro from the Macro command in the Tools menu (see Figure 30.15). When you run this macro with an outline document open (actually, you can do it with any sort of Word document), the macro performs the file format conversion, switches to the PowerPoint application, and opens the new outline file in PowerPoint in an untitled window (see Figure 30.16).

What if you have developed an outline in PowerPoint that you would like to transfer to a Word document for further elaboration (see Figure 30.17)? An outline in PowerPoint (remember that PowerPoint has an Outline view just like Word) can be exported to Word with a mere click of the Report It button, the button to the left of the Zoom Control on the Standard toolbar. A single click on this button fires up a PowerPoint macro that delivers the outline into Word (see Figure 30.18). If you switch to Word's Outline view, you see that the level structure of the outline has made the journey intact.

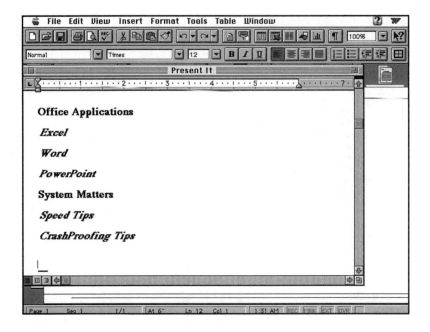

Figure 30.14   Present It as a transporter to PowerPoint.

Figure 30.15   When you run this Word macro...

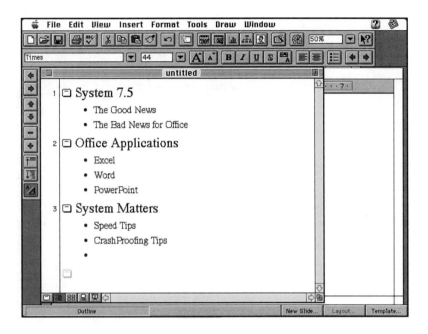

Figure 30.16   ...this window opens in PowerPoint.

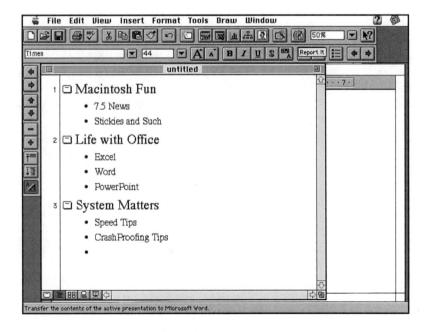

Figure 30.17   An outline in a PowerPoint slide.

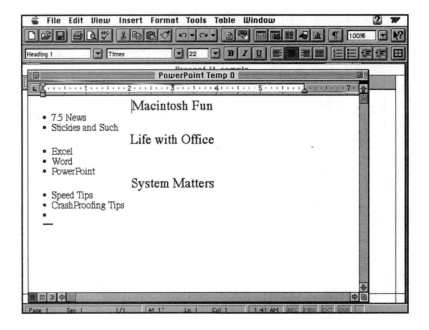

Figure 30.18   The PowerPoint outline arrives in Word.

The nice thing about Microsoft Office is that you have to make elaborate creations, such as tables, outlines, and graphics, only once in the originating document. Because the Office applications are linked together in different ways, you then can import these creations into Word, Excel, or PowerPoint with just a few steps—a much easier technique than generating your creation from scratch all over again. Take the time to experiment with these links in the Office suite. The time you invest in learning how to transfer these creations will be time saved over and over again in the future.

Part VI

Speed Tips

by Charles Seiter

Speed, the subject of Part VI, is exactly what Office doesn't have. The simplest way to understand the often poky behavior of Office applications is by thinking about the Macintosh interface itself. Every time you click the mouse somewhere onscreen, the application that is running at the time has to look through its list of possible actions. If the list of actions (corresponding to the number of features) is gigantic, this is going to take lots of time. And the Office applications are the very definition of gigantic.

So Part VI offers some tips for getting some speed back into operating the applications in Office. There are more Word tips than other kinds because Word is the worst offender—Excel is not much slower than its earlier versions, and PowerPoint 4 is actually faster than PowerPoint 3. Besides, there's nothing more annoying than waiting and waiting for Word to load when you just want to type a four-line memo. Surviving Office largely means getting Word to perform adequately, so you should implement every bit of this hard-won advice.

Word 6 Speed Tips

Get the upgrade!

If you are still using the United States version of Word 6.0, update to Word 6.0.1, the fastest version of Word for the Mac. You can get it at no cost by calling (800) 315-5081. If you don't have the United States version of Word (and you almost certainly don't if you bought Word outside of the United States), consult the introduction to the Word *User's Guide* to find the phone number of your Microsoft subsidiary and call the subsidiary.

If you run Word on a Power Macintosh, use the PowerPC-compatible version of Word. To get the PowerPC version of Word, call Microsoft at (800) 426-9400 or (206) 936-8661.

To find out more about your copy of Word, with Word launched, choose About Microsoft Word from the Apple menu. Look at the top of the About Microsoft Word dialog box to discover your Word version number. If you are running the PowerPC version of Word, the dialog box describes it as being for Power Macintosh.

When a new upgrade of Word comes out, contact Microsoft to find out what speed and performance boosts you can expect from the newer version, and don't buy anything if you don't think it will be worthwhile.

Eliminate extensions

Turning off your extensions is the standard remedy for any Macintosh problem. It is particularly recommended by Microsoft tech support people because they know that Word has a long list of incompatibilities with popular Mac extensions.

To see if you have a problem with extensions, shut off your Mac and then restart it while holding down the Shift key. You see an `Extensions Off` notice while your Mac reboots. After the Mac restarts, launch Word and see if it runs faster. If turning off the extensions didn't help speed up Word, don't worry about it. Just restart your Mac again and things will be back to normal.

If, on the other hand, turning off extensions did help get you more speed, you have to figure out which extension is slowing down Word and then figure out what to do about the problem. Usually, a minimal installation (see Chapter 2) takes care of this problem so that you don't have this headache.

Allocate more RAM for Word

If enough RAM is available, but you plan on using a lot of graphics in Word documents, give Word at least six megabytes of RAM. If enough RAM is available, and you don't anticipate using many graphics in Word documents, give Word only four megabytes of RAM.

To allocate more RAM, make sure that Word is closed, select it with a single click, and pick the Get Info command from the Finder's File menu. In the Microsoft Word Info dialog box, select the Preferred size option and reset it for a bigger allocation. Allocating more RAM is worth doing any time you will be having a long session in Word because it greatly reduces the time it takes to run Word.

Turn on your Power Mac's virtual memory

Power Macintosh users should turn on virtual memory in the Memory control panel to get more speed for running Word. Turning on virtual memory ensures that when you launch the PowerPC version of Word, only a portion of Word copies into RAM, which saves a lot of application loading time. Without virtual memory on, the entire Word application (a bit over 4MB) must copy into RAM.

To make matters even worse, the Microsoft Office "shared libraries"—which take up another megabyte or so of RAM—must load, as well. If you then launch another Microsoft program (such as Excel), the shared Microsoft Office libraries in the System folder must load again for the other program.

Double-click the Memory option in the Control Panels folder to bring up the Memory control panel. When you turn on the Virtual Memory option, you automatically get a text box where you can choose how much disk space to allocate as a substitute for RAM. Leave it set at 32MB as a good choice.

Set up a RAM disk

Another trick from the Memory control panel for getting Word to run faster is to set up a RAM disk. In a RAM disk, you allocate an area of RAM and load a program into it. Then the program loads into this RAM memory at startup and never bothers with disk access, at least for the application itself, while it runs. It's worth trying this experiment on your system.

Check your RAM to see if you have enough for a Word RAM disk by choosing About This Macintosh from the Apple menu in the Finder. Figure VI.1 shows a system that has 16MB of RAM, so there's plenty of room to give Word a 6MB partition.

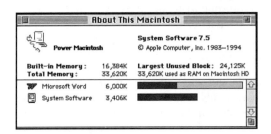

Figure VI.1   Discovering how much RAM you have to spare.

In the Memory control panel, click on the RAM Disk option and set the slider to 6MB or a bit more—it's hard to stop on 6MB exactly. The RAM Disk Size box should read about 6016K. Restart your Mac to make these changes take place. Now when your Mac starts up, you should see a RAM disk icon on the desktop. You can treat it just like a high-speed disk drive.

Click the RAM disk icon and drag Word 6 into this drive. Now when you restart, Word automatically loads into this area of RAM. There won't be any swapping of Word parts from disk into RAM while Word is running; therefore, Word should run much faster for you.

This approach obviously doesn't do much for you if you're trying to run Office on a 4MB Centris (actually, you can pretty much forget about Office altogether on really modest hardware), but if you have a shiny new Power Mac with 16MB of RAM, this approach is your best bet.

Change bitmap memory allocation

If you don't import bitmapped graphics, such as TIFF images (EPS and PICT images are not considered bitmaps), into Word documents, you may speed up Word by setting its bitmap memory allocation to 512K. To change this allocation, you need to make the change in the Advanced Settings dialog box. To make this dialog box available on a menu, choose Customize from the Tools menu and click the Menu card. From the Categories list, select Tools, and from the Commands list, select ToolsAdvancedSettings. Click the Add button and then click the Close button. The Advanced Settings command now appears on the Tools menu.

In the Advanced Settings dialog box, select Microsoft Word from the Categories list. In the Option box at the bottom of the dialog box, delete any text that may be in the box and in its place type **BitMapMemory**. In the Setting box, type **512** (see Figure VI.2). Click the Set button and then click the OK button.

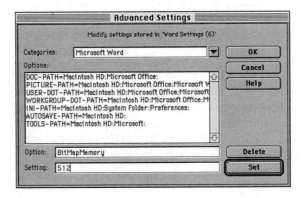

Figure VI.2   Changing the bitmap memory allocation.

Use Word for a while to see if the change makes Word run faster. If changing this setting makes Word run slower, then put the setting back to the way it was before. If you must put the bitmap memory allocation back the way it was, open the Advanced Settings dialog box, select Microsoft Word from the Categories menu, select BitMapMemory=512 from the Options list, click the Delete button, and then click the OK button.

Change cache size allocation

If you frequently use Word with documents over 64K in size (25 pages or so without graphics), you may experience a speed boost by upping Word's cache size allocation from its default 64K to a more generous 128K. To change the cache size setting, open the Advanced Settings dialog box (see "Change bitmap memory allocation"). In the Advanced Settings dialog box, select Microsoft Word from the Categories list. In the Option box at the bottom of the dialog box, delete any text that may be in the box and in its place type **Cache Size**. In the Setting box, type **128** (see Figure VI.3). Click the Set button and then click the OK button. (If your Macintosh has more than 4MB of RAM, you can experiment with setting the cache size to more than 128K.) Click the Set button and then the OK button.

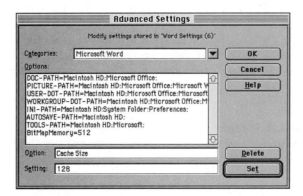

Figure VI.3 Changing the cache size allocation.

Use Word for a while to see if the change makes Word run faster. If changing this setting makes Word run slower, then put the setting back to 64K. The point here is that your other software, the amount of memory you use, and the kinds and sizes of files you use all affect Word's performance. The only way to optimize is by performing these experiments to see what happens to Word's speed. Really, you don't have much to lose—you may have to take two minutes to reset some defaults, but these two minutes can save you two minutes every time you open a file!

Increase your disk cache

Poke around in your Memory control panel and try a few Disk Cache settings. Increase the disk cache a bit and see if the change makes any difference. It may not, but some users have reported finding "magic" settings for their systems simply by experimenting with this setting.

Change your monitor settings

Let's say that you're trying to knock out a document that will be printed on a standard black-and-white printer. Looking at your monitor, you may be just as happy seeing black text on a white background, with little monochrome icons, as you would be seeing the same thing with color icons. In the Monitors control panel, every additional simplification counts. The Black & White option is faster than the 16 colors option, which is faster than the 256 colors option, which is much faster than the other color options. The speed is directly related to the amount of information sloshed out of video RAM at each screen refresh; therefore, the Black & White option is notably faster than the color options.

Rebuild the desktop

As the weeks roll by, you may notice that it takes your Mac longer to start and longer to load Word. When this happens, it's time to rebuild your desktop, which is a good activity not only for speed but also for crashproofing.

To rebuild your desktop, shut down your Mac and then restart while holding down the Option and ⌘ keys. You will get a warning box asking whether you really want to rebuild the desktop. Click the OK button. If you have a big hard drive, the rebuilding process may take a minute or two.

Excel 5 Speed Tips

Purchase a disk-utility package

If you discover that Excel is too slow for you, especially at starting up, loading files, and saving files, you should get a third-party disk-optimizing utility. Excel 5 is a big program, and its files are also larger than the older Excel 4 files, so you need all the disk speed you can get. The Speed Disk utility from the Norton Utilities package (see Figure VI.4) looks for disk *fragmentation* (files and parts of files stored all over the place on the disk instead of physically together) and moves files around to a storage configuration that allows for faster access.

Excel 5 seems to be particularly sensitive to this fragmentation problem. Even when Speed Disk promises only a slight improvement in speed, actual loading times for files speed up by nearly a factor of two. If you don't want to buy a whole disk-utility package, but you have an online account (with America Online, Prodigy, or CompuServe), you can find shareware disk optimization programs that can give you the same kind of speed increase.

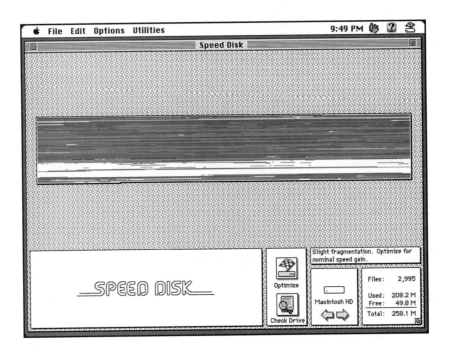

Figure VI.4 Excel 5 needs the best hard drive performance you can get.

Invest in a faster Mac

Every few years Apple increases the speed of SCSI bus data transfers (besides upgrading the central processor), so you get better hard drive performance with one of the newer, faster Macs. The disadvantage of a newer Mac is that, as of 1995, a faster Mac means a Power Mac. In principle this should be nothing but good news. It's not. Microsoft's in-house compiler technology does not seem to be getting as much speed improvement in Power Mac applications versus 680x0 as any other vendor. But the Power Mac is a great platform, and nearly every other vendor has learned to take advantage of it. Hopefully, sooner— rather than later—Microsoft will, too.

Get an accelerator

In the meantime, if you have a middle-of-the-road 68030 system from a few years ago, you actually get more cost-effective acceleration from a 68040 plug-in accelerator card than from upgrading to a whole new system. Unfortunately, the Power Mac version of Excel 5, at least in its first version, has worse problems with mystery bugs than the 680x0 version, so accelerating may be less frustrating than switching to full Power.

Turn off Balloon Help

Make sure that you have Balloon Help turned off. Balloon Help has pretty much been guaranteed to contain no useful information whatsoever, at least for users with more than one day's Mac practice. When you shut down this unnecessary function, Excel can concentrate on direct interaction with the workspace itself.

Remove unnecessary toolbars

You have the option of putting lots of toolbars onscreen (see Figure VI.5). If you're not actually using one right now, however, close it. Do not leave extra toolbars floating around because this practice seriously slows down screen updates.

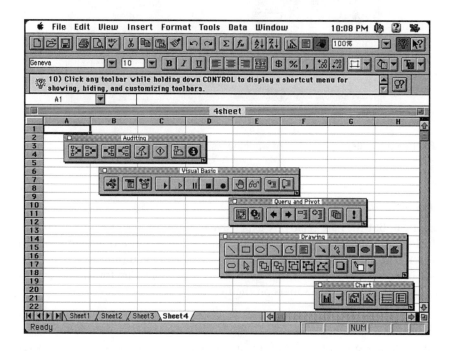

Figure VI.5 Clean up your worksheet display.

Limit the number of worksheets in your workbooks

In the Options dialog box from the Tools menu (see Figure VI.6), you can find the default number of worksheets per workbook. The default has been set by Microsoft to 16, probably on the assumption that people are using Excel to make up monthly budgets for a whole year and are producing summary sheets, as well. The reality is that you can easily add new sheets to a smaller workbook with the Move or Copy Sheet command from the Edit menu. If you set the workbook default to 3 or 4 sheets, Excel opens much faster. There's no reason to lug around a bunch of blank worksheets in every workbook.

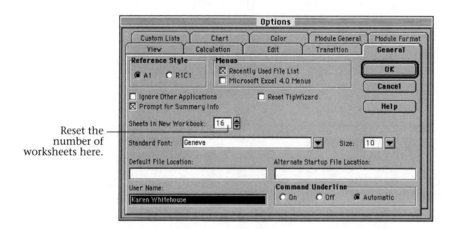

Figure VI.6 Reset the default number of worksheets per workbook.

Don't link your worksheets

Links are great, but they are relatively expensive in terms of performance. If you design individual worksheets that contain the same information as four or five linked worksheets, you get faster recalculation. Links between workbooks are even more of a performance drag than intra-workbook links. Links are a great software feature for the systems of the future, but their performance suffers on the modest systems of today.

Turn on virtual memory

Microsoft customer support says that turning on virtual memory in the Memory control panel is Tip #1 to increase the performance speed of Excel. With virtual memory on, only 3MB of code needs to be loaded at startup rather than the whole program. However, this advice needs to be explained a bit.

If you have a Power Mac with less than 24MB of RAM, you have to use virtual memory just to get Excel to run at all. If you have 24MB or more of RAM (which you should have because other important RISC applications also need lots of memory), however, and you turn off virtual memory, you pay a penalty in startup time, but the application runs faster after it's opened.

On 680×0 systems, Excel itself is smaller. You will have much better results if you just accept the Will of Mr. Gates and buy more memory (at least 12MB). Virtual memory just loads slower in 680×0 systems, so using it extensively is just about the opposite of a speed tip. On the other hand, virtual memory at least makes Excel 5 a possibility for PowerBook owners—you probably don't have a 16MB of RAM PowerBook, but you can run Excel 5 at a leisurely pace if virtual memory is active.

Appendix

Installing
Microsoft Office

The current shipping version of Microsoft Office 4.2 arrives on 29 disks—30, actually, if you include the PowerPoint Viewer. Although this is the biggest Macintosh software product, it's just a country cousin of Office for Windows, which, in its Professional Edition, includes the FoxPro database, as well. Microsoft Mail, as noted in Chapter 29, is a separate option—you buy a Mail server license and then get client software either with the license or as a separate purchase. In this chapter, you will learn about the installation options for the following:

◆ Microsoft Excel
◆ Microsoft Word
◆ Microsoft PowerPoint
◆ Microsoft Office Manager
◆ Office shared applications
◆ Office tools

Getting Going in the First Place

Microsoft Office is *big*. One reason for reviewing the options is to decide which parts of Office you need and which parts you can live without. Although, as Microsoft points out, the Office suite of today actually uses a slightly smaller percent of the hard disk space on a current high-end Mac than the analogous software of a few years ago, everyone else's software has bloated to outrageous size, too, so there's not a particularly notable *surplus* of hard drive space on the desktops of America. That is, maybe you have an extra 12MB (!) that you don't mind devoting just to PowerPoint clip art, but maybe you don't. You'll learn how to customize Office so that rather than having the all-purpose solution to every software problem found in Corporate America, you can have the nice, compact solution to *your* problems.

In Chapter 2, you learned about doing the Minimum installation. The ensuing hundreds of pages should not have changed your minds. If you are starting a new installation of Microsoft Office, try it this way first:

1. Double-click the Memory control panel in the Control Panels folder of your System folder. If you're using System 7.5, The Memory control panel should look like the one in Figure A.1. In each individual setting, click to make the setting match those in the figure. Don't second-guess on this advice—the settings are a hot tip right from Microsoft support! Set the Cache Size to 96K, turn off Modern Memory Manager, turn off Virtual Memory, and turn off RAM Disk.

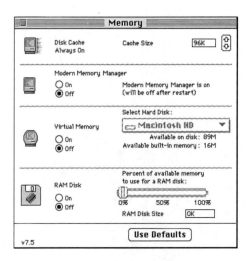

Figure A.1   Memory settings for Office installation.

2. Restart your Mac while you hold down the Shift key. This technique starts the Mac with your extensions turned off. You don't need them for the installation, and there's an excellent chance that one or more of them will conflict with Microsoft's setup procedure anyway.

3. Insert Install Disk 1. You should see the contents shown in Figure A.2.

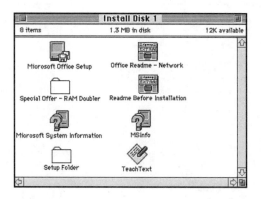

Figure A.2   Install Disk 1—what's inside.

4. Double-click the Microsoft Office Setup icon.

5. When you see the screen in Figure A.3, everything is proceeding according to plan. Click OK to get to the "serial number" screen.

Figure A.3   The second Office installation screen.

6. Write down your serial number (see Figure A.4), *right now*, on the inside page of each one of the manuals provided with your Office software. This redundancy can prove to be a great help to you later on, when you can find only one manual, and you have to call customer support.

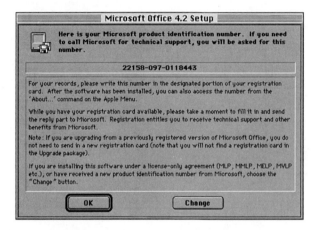

Figure A.4   Copy your serial number into several places.

7. Office starts a new folder for your software (see Figure A.5).

8. Click the Setup button to continue from the last screen. Now you have to make the big choice: the mode of installation. Choose the Minimum option (see Figure A.6)—you'll be glad you did. Anything else that you want can be added later.

9. Now all you have to do is keep track of your disks and insert them as ordered. The Minimum installation uses only about a third of all the Office disks. As you insert the disks, you are asked one or two more questions, depending on your Office version number, like the one in Figure A.7, but your job now is mostly disk-swapping.

Figure A.5 Installation creates an Office folder.

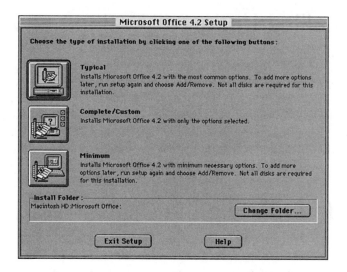

Figure A.6 The three Office choices.

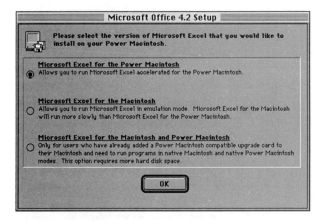

Figure A.7   In Office 4.2, the software can't yet sense the CPU type.

Installing Updated Versions of Word

Microsoft is issuing updates to Office software every few months. If you are a registered user (you *are* a registered user, aren't you?), you will be notified of these updates. If you are updating Word 6 to Word 6.0.1, you should not install only the new Word software. You should install the entire new Office set that Microsoft will send you. In the new world of Office, which depends heavily on shared libraries, all sorts of strange problems can occur if you try to stick a new application into the Office suite. All sorts of bits of code have to be changed, not just the application itself, and installing a single new application by itself doesn't make these changes.

Understanding the Official Microsoft View of Things

Microsoft—partly as a way of dealing with the absolute firestorm of criticism about Office's size and partly as a way of mitigating the shock and dismay of its first users—has published a little guide to Office installation sizes. From this information, you can see why you should pick Minimum as the installation choice:

◆ Minimum installation on a 68K Mac takes 17MB of hard drive space.

◆ Typical installation on a 68K Mac takes 30MB of hard drive space.

◆ Complete installation on a 68K Mac takes 62MB of hard drive space.

The Power Macintosh installations are somewhat larger. These statistics refer to Office 4.2, in which only Excel 5 has been coded for the Power PC RISC chip (Word and PowerPoint run in emulation mode as 68K applications). When the Power versions of the other applications ship, more disk space still will be required—RISC applications are always larger than their conventional CPU counterparts. The Power Macs require the following amount of space:

◆ Minimum installation on a Power Mac takes 24MB of hard drive space.

◆ Typical installation on a Power Mac takes 37MB of hard drive space.

◆ Complete installation on a Power Mac takes 76MB of hard drive space.

Taking a Guided Survival Tour

You now will get the details of installing Office, option by option. If you followed the advice about extensions and memory and Minimum installation, your installation should have been successful. If it wasn't, you'll have to call Microsoft Customer Support because the advice in this book is actually based on Microsoft's best guess about how to get Office installed.

It's time to look at all the Office components and see which ones you may need to add. However, the Minimum installation of Office is so feature-packed that you can easily spend six months working with it before you feel that anything may be missing.

Installing Excel

Excel 5.0a, bless its little computational heart, is the most trouble-free application in Office, and despite its size, it really doesn't have terrible speed problems. Start the installation again with Install Disk 1 and follow the steps in the preceding section up to step 8. At this point, click the button for Complete/Custom installation. The first screen you see looks like the one in Figure A.8. The main point to remember about the Custom installation is this: *if a check box has an X in it, that software is going to be installed.*

If you are just updating or changing one application, make sure that no other boxes are checked. For example, if you are making changes to your Excel installation, click in the boxes of the other applications so that the installation doesn't waste your time installing the complete software set.

When you click the little triangle next to the Microsoft Excel check box, the list expands to show you the different Excel components (see Figure A.9).

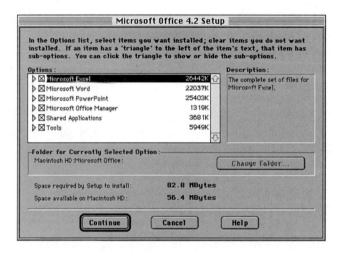

Figure A.8   A tableau of options to install.

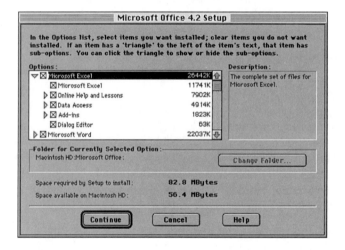

Figure A.9   Basic Excel options.

The first thing you should notice is that some options cost you a lot of space. Excel by itself (this figure shows the Power Mac installation, although most numbers are comparable for a 68K) takes almost 12MB of hard drive space, and there's nothing you can do about this. This is why the Power Mac version of Excel calls for virtual memory, even on a Mac with 16MB of RAM.

Excel Help

The full Help suite and the Data Access suite together cost about 13MB of RAM, so it's worth checking out the options (click the appropriate little triangle) to see what you get. The Help options (see Figure A.10) are interesting and ask the question, "Are you a programmer or not?" If you aren't going to do any Visual Basic programming, you don't need Visual Basic Help. Similarly, if you aren't going to try to do macros in the old Excel style, you don't need the Excel 4.0 Macros Help. Readers who are inclined to irony might note that the 4.0 Macros Help in this giant program is bigger than the application Excel 4.0 itself.

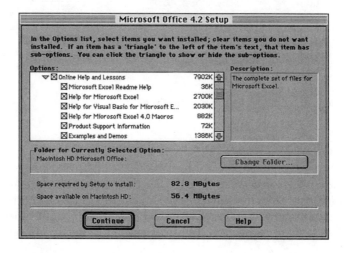

Figure A.10   Excel's Help options.

Microsoft Excel Help is worth having, especially if you want to use the built-in functions, so you should leave that box checked. The examples and demos, however, are useful mostly if you've never used Excel before and aren't particularly educational if you already know your way around.

Data Access

The Data Access options deal with whether you will be using Excel on a network and whether you will be getting data into Excel from a remote database (see Figure A.11). The database may use the query language SQL, or, alternatively, it may be a database in Microsoft's own FoxPro. But if you are using a stand-alone Mac, you don't need any of these options. And if you are using your Mac on a sophisticated data network, your system administrator will come around and *tell* you which options to use.

731

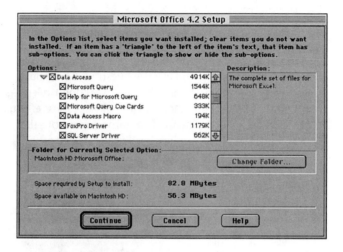

Figure A.11   Choices for getting remote data into Excel.

Add-ins

The add-in options are a sort of strange mixed bag (see Figure A.12). The Analysis ToolPak adds a separate set of statistics functions that are already present in another form anyway, so you don't really need to install this option. Excel's excellent Solver, on the other hand, is well worth adding because it does the most realistic what-if models you can construct.

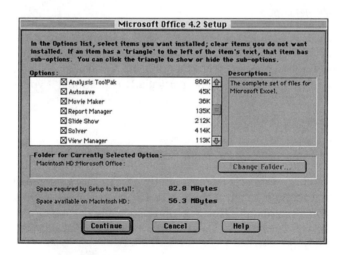

Figure A.12   Add-ins (or leftovers).

The Report Manager is a brilliant and efficient application for those who generate lots of reports. Slide Show, by contrast, is a curious feature for adding to Excel in Office because if you are generating a presentation in Office, it will probably be a series of graphs in PowerPoint. The slide shows that you can generate in PowerPoint are much classier and more colorful than those that Excel itself generates. So don't waste the space with Excel's own Slide Show option.

Installing Word

Word is a rather different installation proposition from Excel—the application itself is actually rather compact, but it offers a huge assortment of additional features (see Figure A.13).

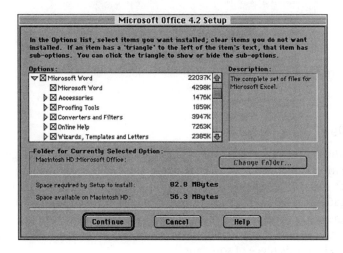

Figure A.13   Word options to install.

Accessories

Merrily clicking triangles, you can start with Accessories (see Figure A.14). If you're going to be using WordArt, you need the WordArt fonts for best effect. Voice Annotation and Movies, however, are only going to be needed if you want to make multimedia documents. In both cases, adding voice or animation to documents can turn a 5,000 character text piece into a 3MB file—too big for email—in no time at all.

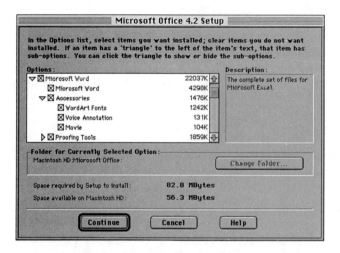

Figure A.14   Word accessories—some critical, some not.

Proofing Tools

Once again, Microsoft's capacity to amaze provides a few surprises (see Figure A.15). First, you see a Hyphenation Checker that's a bigger application than most Spelling Checkers. Unless you know that you will be writing text that is fully justified, you will not use this option, so turn it off because it takes up too much space. You also see a Grammar Checker, although neither this one nor any other one has appeared to entirely positive reviews. The day a Grammar Checker can correctly distinguish the correct use of *it's* from *its* is probably the day you should load this piece of software.

Converters and Filters

If you are going to work only in Microsoft Word 6, you don't need the converters and filters (see Figure A.16). On the other hand, if you deal with word processing files from other applications, it's worth the disk space to have the whole set of converters installed. The converters are not invoked unless you are actually doing a conversion, so there's no speed penalty, and it's a nuisance to go through the installation again just to translate the occasional file. There's also a separate utility from Microsoft to translate Word 6 files back down to Word 5.1—it's available to registered users from Microsoft's Customer Support.

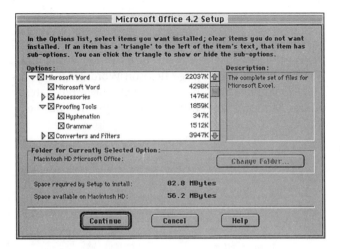

Figure A.15   Grammar and hyphenation?

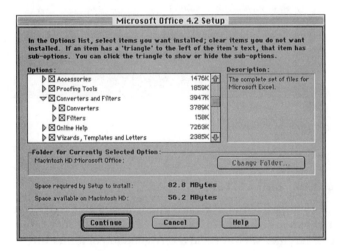

Figure A.16   Converters and filters—necessities of life.

Online Help

Unless you will be writing bits of automated text-processing in Visual Basic, you don't need that part of the Help options (see Figure A.17). The examples and demos are also not very relevant, unless this is your first time using Microsoft Word. (Actually, if your first exposure to Word is Word 6, I would like to apologize on behalf of Mr. Bill Gates. Word 6 certainly has plenty of nifty features, but sometimes it feels like a Greyhound bus negotiating a small parking lot.)

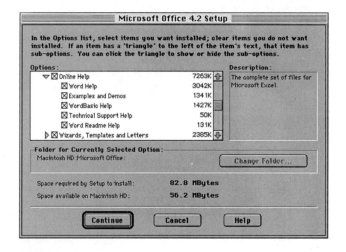

Figure A.17   Almost 8MB of Online Help.

Wizards, Templates, and Letters

Click the triangle to inspect Word's Wizards and related material (see Figure A.18). This unassuming set of options contains one of the most space-efficient choices in the Office suite—the little Letters file. Microsoft did a very good job of formatting a collection of standard letters, and the file is only 200K or so. By all means, load this material into your Word folder. Both Letters and Templates affect the speed of Word only when the files are actually accessed, so you should definitely check both options. Wizards, on the other hand, actually affect the speed at which Word runs, so if you don't need the tips that the Wizards provide, turn them off.

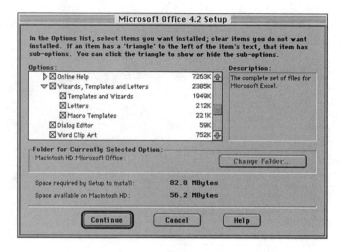

Figure A.18   Big Wizards and little details.

Installing PowerPoint

PowerPoint is the epitome of an installation dilemma—the application itself is reasonably compact, but to make it work with minimum effort on your own part, you are well advised to load all sorts of other files in the options (see Figure A.19). Basically, Microsoft has supplied PowerPoint with all sorts of ready-made components for assembling an impressive presentation, so you may as well use them.

One item at this level that deserves attention is the Genigraphics driver option. Most graphics service bureaus that make slides accept this format, so if you plan to get your PowerPoint efforts onto 35mm slides (as opposed to a computer presentation) you will probably need this option.

Accessories and Converters

If you propose to do any serious work with PowerPoint (that is, presentations in which there is actual money riding on the outcome), you should check all these options (see Figure A.20). They allow you to cannibalize the best parts of presentations from other sources, bring in text from anywhere, and assemble organizational charts in a twinkling.

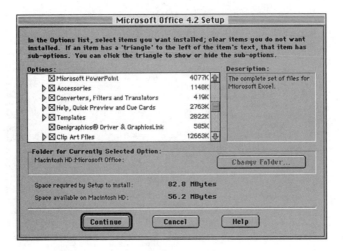

Figure A.19   The PowerPoint environment.

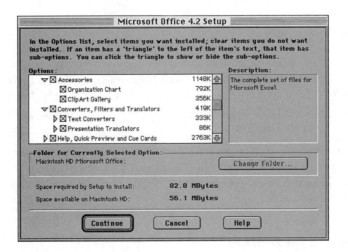

Figure A.20   Useful options for PowerPoint.

Help

Similarly, although we have been dismissing template files and even different kinds of help as a waste of disk space, the Help files for PowerPoint are a different matter (see Figure A.21). Most people do more word processing and spreadsheet work than presentations, so they are less likely to remember the details of PowerPoint from one session to the next. So load the whole shootin' match if you propose to use PowerPoint.

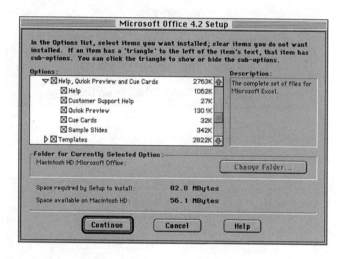

Figure A.21 PowerPoint Help is actually helpful.

Templates and Clip Art

Here we have a contrast. *All* the templates are useful (see Figure A.22), and, in fact, the listing contains one of Microsoft's rare flashes of humor. On the other hand, the gigantic files of PowerPoint Clip Art (see Figure A.23) are not only somewhat clichéd, but they also repeat some aspects of WordArt, and after this version of PowerPoint has been on the market for at least a year, they will have lost their power to impress. The templates are great, but you should probably import your own clip art.

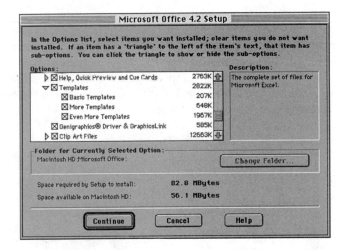

Figure A.22   Essential PowerPoint templates.

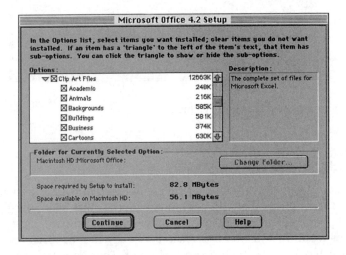

Figure A.23   Nonessential PowerPoint clip art.

Installing Microsoft Office Manager

Most of the Office Manager material (see Figure A.24) is loaded when you perform a Minimum installation. Office Manager is necessary for almost every function of the individual applications in Office. Don't worry about this option.

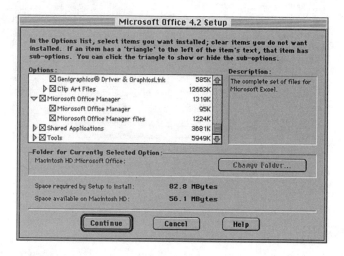

Figure A.24   Office, automatically.

Installing Shared Applications

Shared applications (see Figure A.25) can be called from any other application (Word, Excel, or PowerPoint). If you don't work with math, you probably don't need the Equation Editor. Although Graph is a gigantic application (compared to stand-alone graphing applications), you need it unless your PowerPoint presentations can import PICT graphs from elsewhere. Cue Cards are automatically loaded if you have already selected Cue Cards in other places (for example, Cue Cards in remote database access).

741

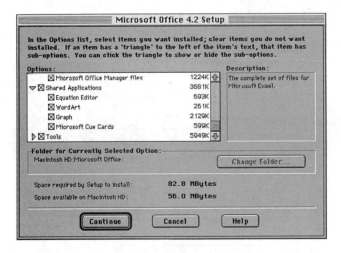

Figure A.25 Options for shared applications.

Installing Tools

Figures A.26 and A.27 show the options in the Tools menu. The inescapable fact is that you need everything you see here. Many of these items have already been loaded with a Minimum installation, but if you are doing a Custom install modification, you may as well check them all. Office is happiest, most of the time, with its own TrueType fonts, for example.

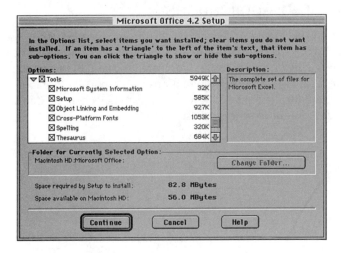

Figure A.26 Necessary tools.

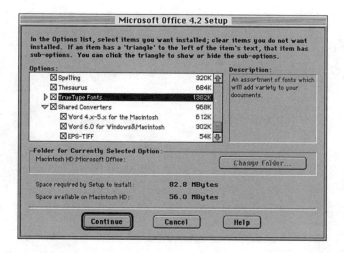

Figure A.27   Equally necessary fonts and converters.

Doing It

If you have reviewed all the Custom options and have checked all the boxes you think you will need, then you should click the Install button. As the installation grinds away, you are treated to various informative background screens (see Figure A.28) to keep you awake as you shuffle disks in and out of your Mac's floppy drive.

If you change your mind about installation components, you can go back at any time and re-install. It's relatively safe to pull components out of the application folders and the Microsoft Office folder, but it's not worth the hassle to remove any folder that says Microsoft from anywhere in the System folder. If you decide you need the space you devoted to Word Help, you can delete it from the Word 6 folder. But you can get into very strange waters if you begin tweaking the Preferences file in the System, for example. Leave well enough alone.

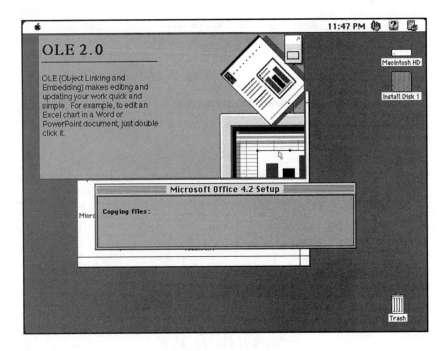

Figure A.28   Installation in progress.

Index

X–Y–Z

GET CONNECTED
to the ultimate source of computer information!

The MCP Forum on CompuServe

Go online with the world's leading computer book publisher!
Macmillan Computer Publishing offers everything
you need for computer success!

Find the books that are right for you!
A complete online catalog, plus sample
chapters and tables of contents give
you an in-depth look at all our books.
The best way to shop or browse!

Get fast answers and technical support for
MCP books and software

in discussion groups on major computer
jects

eract with our expert authors via e-mail
d conferences

ownload software from our immense
ibrary:

    ▷ Source code from books
    ▷ Demos of hot software
    ▷ The best shareware and freeware
    ▷ Graphics files

Join now and get a free CompuServe Starter Kit!

To receive your free CompuServe Introductory Membership, call **1-800-848-
8199** and ask for representative #597.

The Starter Kit includes:
➤ Personal ID number and password
➤ $15 credit on the system
➤ Subscription to *CompuServe Magazine*

Once on the CompuServe System, type:

GO MACMILLAN

for the most computer information anywhere!

MACMILLAN
COMPUTER
PUBLISHING